THE ART OF RHETORICAL CRITICISM

Edited by

JIM A. KUYPERS

Dartmouth College

PEARSON

Boston ■ New York ■ San Francisco
Mexico City ■ Montreal ■ Toronto ■ London ■ Madrid ■ Munich ■ Paris
Hong Kong ■ Singapore ■ Tokyo ■ Cape Town ■ Sydney

Executive Editor: Karon Bowers
Series Editor: Brian Wheel
Series Editorial Assistant: Jennifer Trebby
Senior Editorial-Production Administrator: Beth Houston
Editorial-Production Service: Walsh & Associates, Inc.
Marketing Manager: Mandee Eckersley
Composition and Prepress Buyer: Linda Cox
Manufacturing Buyer: JoAnne Sweeney
Cover Administrator: Kristina Mose-Libon
Electronic Composition: Publishers' Design and Production Services

For related titles and support materials, visit our online catalog at www.ablongman.com.

Between the time website information is gathered and then published, it is not unusual for some sites to have closed. Also, the transcription of URLs can result in typographical errors. The publisher would appreciate notification where these errors occur so that they may be corrected in subsequent editions.

Library of Congress Cataloging-in-Publication Data

The art of rhetorical criticism / [edited by] Jim A. Kuypers.
    p. cm.
  Includes bibliographical references and index.
  ISBN 0-205-37141-8
  1. Rhetorical criticism. I. Kuypers, Jim A.
PN4096.A78 2004
801'.95—dc22   2004051071

Printed in the United States of America

10 9 8 7 6 5 4 3 2 1   08 07 06 05 04

CONTENTS

PREFACE

The Art of Rhetorical Criticism is designed to introduce students to selected perspectives of rhetorical criticism. Well known and practiced perspectives and modes of rhetorical criticism are covered; however, some less known, yet important perspectives are also presented. For example, in addition to the perspectives usually highlighted in criticism textbooks, you will find chapters on the Rhetorical Situation, Mythic Criticism, Framing Analysis, Ideographical Criticism, and Critical Rhetoric.

Some of you might be asking, "Why use this book? Aren't there already enough good books on rhetorical criticism on the market?" Well, yes, there are numerous good books. But collectively they seem to miss the important mark of student accessibility. And it was that very concern—accessibility—that drove the creation of this book. A secondary concern of mine was with originality. The way most texts arrange material often encourages a rather formulaic approach to writing criticism. I wanted to stress the very personal nature of criticism in this book.

Those two concerns led to the creation of the book you now hold in your hand, and several features differentiate it from others already on the market. First, each chapter detailing a perspective is written by a nationally recognized scholar in that area. Thus, instead of one person writing a short synopsis of numerous perspectives, a noted expert with experience using that perspective has written the theoretical explanation.

Second, each chapter also includes a short example of criticism written by the chapter author. Usually one finds previously published works included for students to read. Since these articles were often written for the readers of a particular scholarly journal, they are not easily accessible to students. Because of this, they may actually defeat their purpose of providing useful examples of criticism for new critics to emulate. The critical essays contained herein were written with *student accessibility* in mind. Each essay provides a touchstone for students to use when crafting their own essays.

Third, each chapter contains the author's personal comments on the decisions they made when writing their essay. This allows students insight into the process of crafting a critical essay; in our case, one written by a noted expert in that area. Any writing project involves decisions about what to include or exclude, what to stress, and what to ignore. These personal comments allow students to see what questions and concerns guided the writing of the chapters they read.

Fourth, each chapter provides a "potentials and pitfalls" section that calls attention to what the particular rhetorical perspective highlights or ignores. Authors expose those aspects of the rhetorical artifact (the communication event analyzed) that their particular perspective highlights, thus stressing the artistic and insight producing aspects of the critical process. These comments shed light on how different perspectives both enable and discourage particular readings of artifacts.

Finally, authors provide an annotated recommended reading list for students who wish to study a particular perspective or mode of criticism in greater detail. Many of these lists prioritize the readings, thus helping students read in order those articles and books most helpful in beginning the process of writing criticism using a particular perspective.

With only a few special exceptions, each of the analysis chapters in this book loosely follows a pattern of theoretical discussion followed by an example essay. The example essays generally follow the D.A.E. organizational model for criticism (Description, Analysis/Interpretation, and Evaluation). Some authors did deviate from this model, but they offer an explanation for readers that explains why that deviation was desirable. Criticism is an artistic process, yet far too often this personal nature of criticism is not stressed. There are rules, but there are also instances when if followed they would stifle the critical process and produce sterile criticism.

Not all perspectives lend themselves well to the D.A.E. model. However, students will benefit from knowing a basic structure around which they can organize their own efforts at writing criticism. Moreover, students will be presented perspectives that deviate from this model and will be given reasons why this is desirable, thereby empowering them to make these decisions for themselves.

It is my hope that this book will encourage students to ask new questions about the rhetoric around them and that, in doing so, they will fulfill the critic's quest to produce both insight and understanding about the world in which we live.

I would also like to thank the reviewers for their time and input: William Denman, Marshall University; Carolyn D. Holbert, Matanuska-Susitna College; James Jasinski, University of Puget Sound; Jason Munsell, Wesleyan College; John M. Murphy, University of Georgia; Edward Schiappa, University of Minnesota; John Sloop, Vanderbilt University; John Tapia, Missouri Western State College; and Marsha Watson, University of Nebraska-Omaha.

Jim A. Kuypers
Dartmouth College
2004

CHAPTER ONE

WHAT IS RHETORIC?

JIM A. KUYPERS

ANDREW KING

We imagine some of you asking, "What? Why study rhetoric? Isn't that a tactic sneaky politicians use when they don't want to talk about the issues?" If you were thinking along these lines, you would not be wholly wrong. However, the meaning of rhetoric is considerably richer than the everyday usage of the word suggests.

Rhetoric has many meanings, some old, some new. To get at the heart of the definition let us first consider how the term rhetoric is most commonly used. When a politician calls for "action, not rhetoric," the meaning seems clear; rhetoric denotes hollow words and flashy language. It also connotes associations with deceit and tricks that mask truth and forthrightness. For example, former President Richard M. Nixon used the term rhetoric in this way in his 1969 inaugural address: "The simple things are the ones most needed today if we are to surmount what divides us and cement what unites us. To lower our voices would be a simple thing. In these difficult years, America has suffered from a fever of words; from inflated rhetoric that promises more than it can deliver; from angry rhetoric that fans discontents into hatreds; from bombastic rhetoric that postures instead of persuading." Although the type of rhetoric of which Nixon speaks is often worthy of study, it also leaves one thinking that it is certainly not the kind of language that an intelligent and civil person would willingly wish to use.

Rhetoric is also used to describe what some today would consider embellished or over-ornamental language. The perception of excess has its roots in eighteenth and nineteenth century American oratorical practice. During these centuries before radio and television, public speeches were opportunities for audiences to be informed and entertained; a certain lushness of language was exceeded, even expected. It was not at all uncommon for speeches to last several hours and for the speakers to use no notes. This "spread eagle" style of American speaking was most evident in patriotic orations. Albert Beveridge, in *The March of the Flag,* provides a common example of what we might consider embellished speech today:

1

It is a noble land the God has given us; a land that can feed and clothe the world; a land whose coastlines would enclose half the countries in Europe; a land set like a sentinel between the two imperial oceans of the globe, a greater England with a nobler destiny.

It is a mighty people that he has planted on this soil; a people sprung from the most masterful blood of history; a people perpetually revitalized by the virile, man-producing working-folk of all the earth; a people imperial by virtue of their power, by right of their institutions, by authority of their heaven-directed purposes—the propagandists and not the misers of liberty.[1]

Although the above examples are certainly forms of rhetoric, they but scratch the surface of rhetoric's rich meaning. The study of rhetoric is an invention of early Western Civilization and has its roots in the fledgling democracies of ancient Greece.

A SYNOPTICAL SKETCH OF RHETORIC

The Greeks developed the original model of rhetoric, a systematic body of knowledge about the theory and practice of public speaking in the law courts, the governing assemblies, and on ceremonial occasions. Rhetoric was codified by Aristotle in his famous treatise, *The Rhetoric,* written somewhere around 335 B.C. He defined rhetoric as the "power of discovering the means of persuasion in any given situation" a much more comprehensive and intellectually respectable meaning than today's common attributions of bombast and deception. The Sophists, wandering teachers and exiles in the ancient world, often taught rhetoric as a popular course designed to prepare ambitious youths for fame and success. The Greeks believed in the power of eloquence and delighted in hotly contested debate. On the other hand, philosophers such as Plato condemned rhetoric, finding it a serious rival to philosophy in the ancient educational system.

Later, the Roman republican government provided many opportunities for the practice of rhetoric in their popular assemblies, in provincial governing bodies, in their law courts, and in their huge civil service and military. The best known Roman orator was Marcus Tullius Cicero (106–43 B.C.) who took over the Greek ideas of rhetoric and adapted them to the needs of a far-flung world empire. From modest origins he rose to the highest office in Rome, the Consulship, and was considered by many to be the greatest lawyer, speaker, and writer of his time. Fifty-eight speeches and 900 letters have come down to us. They still read well today and stand as models of powerfully persuasive oratory, biting wit, and incredible verbal skill. Cicero argued for an ideal rhetorician, an orator–statesman who would use rhetoric as a means of serving the people. A century later, Cicero's rhetorical teaching was codified by Quintilian (35–118 A.D.), Rome's greatest teacher and codifier of rhetorical knowledge. Thus, the Greco–Roman world established a tradition of discourse that has been taught throughout Western history and continues to grow and to develop today.

Saint Augustine (354–430 A.D.) was largely responsible for early Christian uses of rhetoric, and his writings were used extensively by churchmen throughout the middle ages. Augustine reasoned that since the Devil had full access to all of the available resources of rhetoric, others ought to study it if only for their own protection. Knowledge of its great power was essential for everyone, and both "in theory and practice the Christians forever influenced the development of rhetorical thought."[2] Likewise the influence of rhetoric on the spread of Christianity should not be underestimated. During the middle ages rhetoric was at the heart of education. It was taught in the cathedral schools. It inspired the great university debates and disputations, and it set rules for the composition of sermons and royal proclamations. It even extended its domain over poetry and letter writing, and rhetorical modes of expression guided government bureaucracies.

In the Renaissance, rhetoric became even more important, recapturing the high status it had enjoyed at the time of Cicero. Renaissance leaders revered Cicero as the ideal of the practicing rhetorician, the active agent in the service of the state and the people. Jean Dietz Moss noted "a widening wave of literacy extended beyond the church and the court to include as secular public, merchants, bankers, lawyers, artisans and others of the middle class."[3] In the fifteenth and sixteenth centuries, rhetoric dominated philosophy, literature, and politics. Early in the seventeenth century, the great Italian rhetorician Giambattista Vico extended the study of rhetoric to include the study of language and the evolution of society.

During the late eighteenth century there was a vast expansion of the middle class in Britain and North America. The tremendous growth of literacy was aligned with the growth of the press and the publishing industry. Like today's internet, the printing press was a dynamo for the circulation and expansion of knowledge. As a result, rhetoric expanded beyond matters of political and legal conflict to areas of reading, criticism, and judgment. Vast fortunes were being made via the industrial revolution, and upwardly mobile and newly rich individuals were eager to assimilate the speech, the ideas, and the manners of their higher status counterparts. The three greatest rhetorical theorists of the period "Hugh Blair, Richard Whately, and George Campbell—were Christian ministers."[4] They emphasized matters of ethics and of individual accountability in rhetorical theory.

The nineteenth century was a time of huge industrial, political, and educational expansion in Europe and in the United States. Parliamentary Democracy penetrated to many points of the globe. Nineteenth-century practitioners of rhetoric cultivated the discipline as a form of individual intellectual training. They believed that knowledge of rhetoric would prepare any speaker or writer from age fifteen to age ninety to inform, to persuade, or to entertain any audience at any time on any occasion. The optimistic how-to-do-it rhetorical manuals of that day were an invitation to train in the privacy of one's own home for self-improvement and social power. One example was the young Frederick Douglass studying his rhetoric book in secret in order to prepare for a career in public life that would lift him out of both slavery and poverty. Eloquence was seen as a means of gaining entry to the corridors of power. Books provided strategies for persuading others and provided models of great speeches for readers to imitate. A pantheon of great orators and their greatest speeches was established through books such as Chauncey A. Goodrich's *Select British Eloquence* in 1852. The book contained the speeches of the greatest British orators together with critical guides for study and tips on rhetorical emulation. Collections of great American orators soon followed, and these became style models for the ambitious youth who saw the acquisition of rhetorical skill as a path to influence and wealth.

Although rhetorical treatises had been written since Ancient Egypt, academic departments did not come into being until the early twentieth century. There scholars recovered the full range of the classical tradition and greatly expanded the study of rhetoric. Criticism became the major thrust of study; theory was developed to explain the vast changes wrought by mass media, modern propaganda, and the immense social movements and revolutions of the first half of the century. In the latter half of the century and in the early twenty-first century, students of rhetoric moved far beyond the classical tradition. Traditionally scholars have focused on how gifted and influential individuals used rhetorical arts to shape their world and affect social change. More recently scholars have studied the ways in which history and culture have shaped the practice of rhetoric itself. The very conditions in which rhetoric takes place are objects of study; they include who is allowed to speak in a public place, whose speech will be taken seriously, and the range of ideas that are considered debatable at any given time. Scholars have also emphasized the role of language or symbols in the process by which social influence occurs; and they have broken down the walls between visual, verbal and acoustic messages. Rhetoric includes far more than public speaking; it embraces discourse in print, radio, television, internet, and symbolic action in many different forms and settings. Small wonder that rhetoric is now being studied across a whole spectrum of academic subjects and has become one of the central disciplines of our time.[5]

THE MEANINGS OF RHETORIC

Accordingly, at the start of the twenty-first century the study of rhetoric has expanded greatly, as have its definitions. What follows is an introduction to some of those meanings.

Rhetoric has both an informative and persuasive element. For example, you might want to persuade someone to donate money to a worthy cause; or, you might want to persuade your friends to vote for a particular candidate for public office. Both instances would use rhetoric. However, in order to effectively persuade, you must first provide information in the form of examples, statistics, stories, definitions, and the like. In short, you must use other than mere assertions as your arguments. In this sense, rhetoric involves the proper interpretation, construction, and use of supporting materials to back assertions and gain audience acceptance.

With this in mind, let us move to a working definition of rhetoric. When we use the term rhetoric in this chapter we mean: *The strategic use of communication, oral or written, to achieve specifiable goals.* There are two main ideas expressed by this definition. One involves the strategic, or intentional, nature of the language we use; the second involves knowing what goals we wish to reach through the language we use. This is an intentionally narrow definition of rhetoric, but we think using such is justified for now. Afterall, we need someplace to begin the inquiry, and it seems to us that a definition rooted in the most practical examples of intentional persuasion is a good place from which to launch our investigation.

The Strategic Nature of Rhetoric

We use symbols to communicate. These symbols essentially are something we use to represent something else. Words, spoken and written, are such symbols. Musical notes are such symbols as well. Certain gestures are symbolic representations of meaning, too. Of importance to us here is that words, spoken or written, are symbols whose meanings are more readily agreed upon than the meanings of other symbols used in communication. That is to say, a lion's share of those hearing or reading a particular word can come to some consensus concerning its meaning, whereas this does not hold true with other types of symbols. For example, the symbols used in art, architecture, dance, or clothing are all vague in their meanings; thus a communicator would have less control over their precise interpretation by a given audience. Unfortunately, the further we travel from the *intentions* of the communicator, the closer to the *inferences* of the audience we find ourselves. Since rhetoric works using symbols, the more variation in the symbolic meaning (word meaning versus architectural meaning, for example) the less precision in the communication in general.

Nonetheless, rhetoric viewed from this broader aspect should be considered. For example, in the first edition of her book on rhetorical criticism, Sonja K. Foss wrote: "*[R]hetoric* means the use of symbols to influence thought and action. Rhetoric is communication; it is simply an old term for what is now called *communication.*" In her second edition she refines that definition: "[R]hetoric means the action humans perform when they use symbols for the purpose of communicating with one another."[6] Rhetoric, for Foss, does involve action on the part of a communicator; it involves making conscious decisions about what to do. However, in part of her definition she states: "Rhetoric is not limited to written or spoken discourse. . . . [Any] message, regardless of the form it takes or the channel of communication it uses, is rhetoric. . . ." As such, she writes: "Speeches, essays, conversations, poetry, novels, stories, television programs, films, art, architecture, plays, music, dance, advertisements, furniture, public demonstrations, and dress are all forms of rhetoric."[7]

Foss presents a rather extreme definition, one that clashes with a more pragmatic conception of rhetoric. Or as Marie Hochmuth Nichols wrote: "[R]hetoric is an act of adapting discourse to an end outside of itself. It serves many ends, from promoting decision to giving pleasure. It does not include ships, guns, an alluring sun, the dance, or the Cathedral of Chartres. It does not include rolling drums or the sound of marching feet; it does not include extralinguistic symbols of peace or the clenched fist of power. It does not deny that there are other symbolic forms for altering behavior, which often accompany or reinforce it."[8] Conceptions of rhetoric similar to that given by Foss minimize the point of view that as one moves further away from the use of symbols with generally agreed upon meanings (words) to the use of symbols with imprecise meanings (furniture, dance) one finds that the *intentions* of the rhetor plays less a part in the rhetorical exchange and that the *impressions* of the receiver plays a greater role.[9] In this sense the meaning behind the rhetoric moves from the person crafting the message to the impressions of those receiving the message irrespective of the intentions of the original communicator.

This distinction was not lost on Hoyt Hopewell Hudson. In his landmark essay, "Rhetoric and Poetry," Hudson highlighted the differences between efforts aimed at rhetorical influence (rhetoric) and efforts aimed at symbolic expression (poetry). He began his comparison by citing numerous great poets in order to demonstrate the general focus of a poet: "The Poet . . . keeps his eye not on the audience or the occasion, but on his subject; his subject fills his mind and engrosses his imagination, so that he is compelled, by excess of admiration or other emotion, to tell of it; compelled, though no one heard or read his utterance."[10] In order to better discuss the differences, Hudson clearly marked where rhetoric begins and poetry ends: "For the moment, then, we shall say that poetry is for the sake of expression; the impression on others is incidental. Rhetoric is for the sake of impression; the expression is secondary—an indispensable means."[11]

This distinction is subject to exceptions, and here Hudson showed a discerning grasp of the differences between rhetoric and poetry. He provided examples of how a poet might stray into the field of rhetoric; for example, a poet envisioning a speaker attempting to persuade listeners must use rhetoric. Mark Antony in Shakespeare's *Julius Caesar* and the speeches of the Fallen Angels in the first and second books of *Paradise Lost* are two such examples. He calls this imitative rhetoric, which may be studied for its own sake. A poet may at times consider the audience (a drama, for example), but there exist differences in the conception of the audience: "The poet thinks of a more general and more vaguely defined audience than the orator. The poet may even think of all mankind of the present and future as his audience. . . ."[12] Hudson even provided a loose scale to show the relationship between the most purely poetical—personal lyric and rhapsodic poem; then idyll, pastoral poetry; then narrative poetry, romance, the epic—to the more purely rhetorical—tragedy and comedy; finally didactic poetry, satire, odes, and epigrams. Hudson also demonstrated how an orator may cross over into the field of poetry: "Though the orator's end is persuasion, it is not hard to believe that there are moments in his discourse when this end is forgotten in his delight or wonder before some image which fills his inner eye. In such moments he has his eye on the subject, not the audience."[13]

The discussion above should point clearly to the differences between the more personally *expressive* use of ambiguous symbols—words of poetry, painting, dance, architecture—and the more publicly *impressive* use of symbols with generally agreed upon meanings—words spoken and written for the sake of persuasion.

It is the latter that is the focus of this chapter and beyond. This is not to say that other forms of more ambiguous rhetoric cannot be studied, rather that we will take our first step on the firmer soil of rhetoric understood as strategic and intentional.

Rhetoric as Strategic, Goal-Oriented Communication

Coming back to the definition of rhetoric given above, we find that rhetoric is strategic because it is intentional. Communicators, who wish to control the manner in which their messages are understood, plan ahead. They think about what they are going to say and what impact their words are likely to have upon those listening to them. When they use rhetoric in this way they provide reasons for their listeners to agree with them. Just as importantly, rhetoric is intentional in the sense that it is employed only when words can make a difference. That is to say, rhetoric is *persuasive*. It seeks to influence our personal and collective behaviors through having us voluntarily agreeing with the speaker that a certain action or policy is better than another action or policy. Rhetors often think about their goals so that they are better able to plan what to say for a desired effect. Since there is no scientific certainty to human affairs, that is, we do not know for certain which policy will produce the absolute best results, rhetoric attempts to persuade listeners that one policy will *probably* be better than another. It is in this sense, then, that rhetoric is based upon probability—communicators try to convince us not that their proposed course of action is the only correct one, or that it will work with guaranteed certainty, but rather that it *probably* has a good chance of success. The trick for the person trying to persuade is to make certain that the level of probability is high enough to convince the particular audience being addressed. This is to say, that the audience will believe that a certain course of action will *probably* be better than another course of action.

Rhetoric works toward a goal. It may involve simply trying to have your audience believe a certain way, or it could work toward the enacting of one course of action or policy over another. In suggesting rhetoric is policy oriented, we mean to say that it seeks to influence how we act at either a personal or a public level. All of us use rhetoric to influence those around us. For example, think of the last time you were together with a group of friends and you were trying to decide where to go for dinner. You most likely had several competing options and had to advance your good reasons for choosing one restaurant over another. The policy option resulting in action is simple: where to go eat? At a more public level, consider President Bush's February 27, 2001 speech to the Joint Session of Congress. In it he set out several policy goals and hoped to convince the nation to stand with him as he started his work as president.

A more detailed yet common example of how rhetoric works shows that the good reasons rhetoric uses to persuade us very often incorporate the human qualities we use everyday when communicating with a goal in mind. Let us give you an example.

A friend of ours was president of her neighborhood's homeowners association for several years. At one point during her tenure as president her neighborhood saw a rash of mail thefts. The sheriff's department could do little; this was a rural setting, wooded, with little likelihood of catching whoever was stealing unless someone was willing to keep watch twenty-four hours a day. Our friend decided that the post office could be prevailed upon to install lock boxes in place of the old stand alone type mailboxes. The post office agreed, then decided to place the new boxes in a wooded area along side of the road where there was no light during the evening hours. Our friend asked that they be placed in a more central, lighted area near the road and the postal worker said, "no." Not to be swayed, our friend began her use of rhetoric.

She used common examples in her efforts: Many of those who would be getting the mail would be women, driving alone or with their children. With daylight savings time soon to end they would be driving home at night. Where the postal service wanted to place the mailboxes would necessitate the women getting out of their cars and walking away from them in order to get the mail. Our friend pointed out that all it would take was one woman being attacked and that particular postal worker would feel terrible. She also pointed out the very real possibility of the postal service being held responsible for any attacks that were facilitated by poorly placed boxes. The next day she had a phone conversation with the regional director of the postal service. By the next week the new boxes were installed in a new location so that no night driving mom would have to leave her car to collect the mail.

The persuasive effort used by our friend tells us a great deal about the nature of rhetoric. She used no extravagant arguments; rather she used everyday logic and reasoning (common sense), evoked little emotion within her listeners, and ended up getting what was best for those in her neighborhood. It was not that her arguments had no weakness or that they were scientifically reasoned out. Rather the arguments she used were constructed in order to convince the postal authorities that there was a high possibility that what she said would indeed happen. And that possibility was just high enough to persuade them to agree with her. So, this example shows how rhetoric is used everyday. Importantly, though, it also points out that rhetoric is concerned with contingent matters, too. Simply put, rhetoric addresses those problems that can be changed through the use of words. So, for example, it was only because the possibility existed of having the location for mailboxes moved that rhetoric was able to effect a change.

As the above example shows, rhetoric is goal directed. Our friend knew she wanted those mailboxes in a different location. She then thought of ways of constructing her arguments so that they would work with her particular audience; in this case, the postal workers who could change the location of the boxes. As you think about the goals communicators have in mind, it is important to remember another important aspect of rhetoric. When rhetoric is used, it is concerned with *informed opinion*. Most of us are not mathematicians trying to prove an equation or chemists following a formula. Instead we deal with human beings' thinking on uncertain matters; we deal with their opinions. Humans act based upon what appears probable to them, and not always upon what they know for certain.

When we deal with questions of what we should do in a particular situation, there is no way to demonstrate using the scientific method that a certain course of action will be the best. Although *we* might know with certainty, those with whom we communicate may feel just as certain about a different course of action. What rhetors do, then, is try to persuade their listeners that their proposed course of action has the maximum probability of succeeding. Successful rhetors attempt to narrow the choices from which their audiences can choose. These audiences may have many choices for action; rhetoric helps them to decide which course is the best to take. As Donald Cross Bryant so competently put it, rhetoric is not a body of knowledge, but a means of applying knowledge: "It does rather than is."[14]

The Moral Dimensions of Rhetoric

The foregoing example has illustrated the strategic and goal oriented nature of rhetoric. Rhetoric always presupposes the existence of an audience. A rhetorician addresses a particular audience anchored in time, space, culture, and circumstance. Intellectuals who dismiss rhetoric and wish to present unvarnished truth are often people who do not understand the power of audiences. Like Plato, they believe that clear ideas, strong evidence, and a rational plan of reform are enough. They underestimate the influence of self interest, the fear of change, and the ways in which unequal power distorts communication.

The very practice of rhetoric has an impact upon the practitioners. But persuading others is always a matter of negotiating between the flux of local conditions and the enduring principles of political judgment. The mere exercise of deliberation helps nurture audiences by strengthening the norms of fairness. Communities do not exist prior to talk. They are built over time through communal understanding, argument, negotiation, and common action. Rhetorical practice is ethical in nature because it is advisory, and this advice has consequences for which the advice giver is held accountable. It is not an ethically neutral act such as target shooting or throwing clay pots on a wheel. Participation in rhetorical discourse involves people in building citizenship and in constructing community. And the decisions they make or the ideas they embrace can ruin or enrich their lives. Thus, rhetoric is an ethically significant practice that seeks to engage audiences in sound judgment; those judgments have consequences that we can judge to be good or bad.

Finally rhetoric sustains democratic culture. Rhetoric uses accepted beliefs to produce new beliefs and in so doing builds the stock of communal wisdom. It safeguards the stable beliefs that provide communal identity yet allows the community to manage change in ways that do not rend it apart and leave its people adrift.

WHAT FUTURE FOR RHETORIC?

But despite our friend's success in the matter of the mailboxes, is there still an important future for rhetoric? Some persons worry that the places for public deliberation are becoming smaller and fewer. They remind us that beyond the scope of the town meeting and neighborhood conclave, significant issues are selected and framed by the mass media, not local citizens. These issues are debated by experts while the citizenry watches, sometimes enjoying the "illusion" of participation but often feeling like powerless spectators. Such civic voyeurism, scholars such as Jurgen Habermas argue, could undermine the legitimacy of our institutions. After all, most Americans have never discussed public education, free enterprise, the income tax, or our immigration laws, yet they are imposed upon us by the dead hand of the past. These systems were largely developed before you were born and are imposed upon you without your consent. Their direction is mostly in the hands of unaccountable public officials who enjoy lifetime tenure. Policy details are complex, often known only to special interest groups.

Since many of our problems of race, ethnicity, poverty, and aging have been placed in the hands of government and state bureaucracy, they are effectively removed from the arena of public discussion. Further, the sheer number of issues and the volume of information concerning them are mind numbing and intimidating. Matters that were once seen to be the province of ordinary citizens are now the property of specialized technical elites. We may fear that although these "intellectuals" can organize data and design complex "solutions," they may understand very little about the fears, prejudices, and aspirations of ordinary people. Denied participation in civic debate, we become less skilled in managing discourse. Increasingly, we may view ourselves as mere masses manipulated by experts, not active citizens who are in charge of their own fate.

Finally, it can be argued that ever increasing diversity and pluralism have destroyed the basic consensus that the practice of rhetoric requires. Rhetoric was born in the Greek polis, a small face to face homogenous community in which civic identity was undergirded by the premise that everyone shared a common destiny. Our society is becoming a vast congeries of warring groups characterized by unbridgeable controversies and sedimented suspicion. Thus some critics argue that rhetoric is a method that only worked in the past and that it no longer has a place in twenty-first-century life.

We argue that these criticisms predate the rise of a multicultural, technologically advanced, megastate; neither are these objections new. In one form or another they have been made for the past century. Despite numerous pronouncements about the death of rhetoric and civil culture, persuasive discourse persists. The practice of rhetoric is alive and well. Audiences and speakers are still engaged in building practical wisdom. Common dilemmas are still being attacked and resolved. Can rhetoric still be powerful, useful, and moral? Roderick Hart and Courtney Dillard still think so:

> Is deliberation still possible? Some say no, others find the question fatuous. In defense of deliberation they point to democracies in which women were given the vote by men and in which blacks were enfranchised by whites. They find wars being stopped by college students, environmental laws being passed by the children of corporation executives, and Nelson Mandela's cause assisted by a distant band of college professors. They point to an American president being driven out of office by free press, a Russian president honored for dismantling a mighty Communist machine, and an Iraqi dictator stopped in his tracks. . . .[15]

We simply cannot do without rhetoric. In fact, knowledge about the wise use of discourse has never been more necessary than it is today. Little wonder rhetorical studies is enjoying a vast revival throughout our system of higher education. The chapters that follow will give you a sense of the variety and artistry of rhetorical discourse and of the cultural and historical faces that have shaped it. As you move through each chapter, you will find that the conception of rhetoric it advances modifies or moves beyond the working definition given above. This is as it should be. Take note of *how* the conception changes. Rhetoric is nuanced, and may be understood on many different levels. Each chapter that follows underscores this idea and will present a point of view that will add rich variety to the definition given above.

SUGGESTED READINGS

Bryant, Donald Cross. "Rhetoric: Its Function and its Scope." *Quarterly Journal of Speech* 39 (1953): 401–424.

Hauser, Gerard A. *Introduction to Rhetorical Theory*, 2nd ed. (Prospect Heights, IL: Waveland Press, 2002).

Hudson, Hoyt Hopewell. "Rhetoric and Poetry." *Quarterly Journal of Speech Education* 10.2 (1924): 143–154.

Nichols, Marie Hochmuth. "Rhetoric and the Humane Tradition." in *Rhetoric: A Tradition in Transition*, eds. Lloyd F. Bitzer and Edwin Black. (Lansing: MI: Michigan State University Press, 1974), 178–191.

Smith, Craig R. *Rhetoric and Human Consciousness: A History*, 2nd ed. (Prospect Heights, IL: Waveland Press, 2003).

Wallace, Karl R. *History of Speech Education in America: Background Studies* (New York: Appleton Century-Crofts, 1954).

NOTES

1. Speech contained in Ronald F. Reid, *American Rhetorical Discourse*, 2nd ed. (Prospect Heights, IL: Waveland Press, 1995), 657.

2. James L. Golden, Goodwin F. Berquist, and William E. Coleman, *The Rhetoric of Western Thought*, 4th ed. (Dubuque, IA: Kendall/Hunt Publishing Company, 1989), 128–129.

3. Jean Dietz Moss, "Renaissance Rhetoric: An Overview," *Encyclopedia of Rhetoric* (Oxford U. Press, 2001), 681.

4. James L. Golden, Goodwin F. Berquist, and William E. Coleman, *The Rhetoric of Western Thought*, 4th ed. (Dubuque, IA: Kendall/Hunt, 1989), 129.

5. For overviews of the development of rhetorical theory see the following: Hoyt Hopewell Hudson, "The Tradition of Our Subject," *Quarterly Journal of Speech* 17.3 (1931): 320–329; Craig R. Smith, *Rhetoric and Human Consciousness: A History*, 2nd ed. (Prospect Heights, IL: Waveland Press, 2003).

6. Sonja K. Foss, "The Nature of Rhetorical Criticism," *Rhetorical Criticism: Exploration and Practice*, 2nd ed. (Prospect Heights, IL: Waveland Press 1996), 4.

7. This and the immediately preceding quote, Foss, 6.

8. Marie Hochmuth Nichols, "Rhetoric and the Humane Tradition," *Rhetoric: A Tradition in Transition*. Walter R. Fisher, ed. (Lansing: Michigan State University Press, 1974), 180.

9. As will be seen in the chapter on "The Art of Criticism," one "receiver" of the rhetoric is the critic who examines the instance of rhetorical discourse. The further removed from agreed upon meaning the symbols under consideration are, the more power the citric has over deciding what they mean (over and above what the author of the rhetorical discourse intended them to mean). This can, and sometimes does, lead to abuses by the critic. For more on this see Jim A. Kuypers, *"Doxa and a Critical Rhetoric:

Accounting for the Rhetorical Agent through Prudence," *Communication Quarterly* 44.4 (1996): 452–462.

10. Hoyt Hopewell Hudson, "Rhetoric and Poetry," *Quarterly Journal of Speech Education* 10.2 (1924): 145.

11. Hudson, "Rhetoric and Poetry," 146.

12. Hudson, "Rhetoric and Poetry," 148.

13. Hudson, "Rhetoric and Poetry," 153.

14. Donald C. Bryant, "Rhetoric: Its Function and its Scope." Quarterly Journal of Speech 39 (1953): 401–424.

15. Roderick P. Hart and Courtney L. Dillard, "Deliberative Genre," in *Encyclopedia of Rhetoric* (Oxford, UK: University of Oxford, 2001), 213.

CHAPTER TWO

THE ART OF CRITICISM

JIM A. KUYPERS

The previous chapter provided a working definition of rhetoric. The goal of this chapter is to introduce you to another concept: the art of rhetorical criticism. In short, the purpose of this chapter is to show you how you can be a critic of rhetoric, how you can engage in the critical act.

Recall the working definition of rhetoric provided in Chapter One: *the strategic use of communication, oral or written, to achieve specifiable goals.* Rhetoric is strategic in the sense that it is intentional; it is employed only when words can make a difference. That is, rhetoric is *persuasive.* It seeks to influence our personal and collective behaviors by having us voluntarily agree with the speaker that a certain action or policy is better than another option. It is contingent in that we can choose among several alternative courses of action. The speaker is ultimately trying to make one course of action seem the best: thus, our decision is contingent upon the words we hear.

There is no scientific certainty in the realm of human affairs: that is, we do not know for certain which course of action will produce the absolute best results. Therefore, rhetoric attempts to persuade listeners that one policy will *probably* be better than another. Thus, rhetoric works toward a goal—the enacting of one policy over another.

When we criticise instances of rhetoric, often called *rhetorical artifacts,* we are allowing ourselves to take a closer, critical look at these efforts to persuade and influence us. Criticism has many broad applications, but in general it is a *humanizing* activity. That is to say, it explores those qualities that make us human. As Andrews, Leff, and Terrill have written, criticism is "the systematic process of illuminating and evaluating products of human activity. [C]riticism presents and supports one possible interpretation and judgment. This interpretation, in turn, may become the basis for other interpretations and judgments."[1] For our purposes, we are interested specifically in the analysis and evaluation of rhetorical acts. We are looking at how humans strategically communicate to bring about a certain state of affairs.

T. S. Eliot is reputed to have said, "We do criticism to open the work to others." This is exactly what we are about when we perform rhetorical criticism. Why one critic performs criticism may well be different from the reasons another performs criticism, but in general we perform criticism for two broad reasons: greater understanding and increased knowledge. Simply put, we wish to enhance both our own and others' understanding of the rhetorical act; we wish to share our insights with others, and to enhance their appreciation of the rhetorical act. We also produce knowledge about human communication which in theory should help us to better govern our interactions with others. On this point Wayne Brockriede wrote, "By 'criticism' I mean the act of evaluating or analyzing experience. A person can function as critic either by passing judgment on the experience or by analyzing it for the sake of a better understanding of that experience or of some more general concept of theory about such experiences."[2]

CRITICISM AS METHOD

In its most basic form, a method may be understood as a particular manner or process for accomplishing a task. The researcher's task, both humanist and scientist, is to generate knowledge. How they go about this task, the method they use, is quite different. The use of rhetoric is an art, and as such it does not lend itself well to scientific methods of analysis. Criticism is an art as well, and as such is particularly well suited for examining rhetorical creations. Numerous critics have commented upon the Humanistic nature of the study of rhetoric. Marie Hochmuth Nichols wrote that humane studies, of which the study of rhetoric fits prominently, are "concerned with the formation of judgment and choice." They teach us that "technical efficiency is not enough, that somewhere beyond that lies an area in which answers are not formulary and methods not routine." Beyond "the area of the formula lies an area where understanding, imagination, knowledge of alternatives, and a sense of purpose operate."[3] That area is criticism.

Of course, various methods exist for studying phenomena which surround us, and these methods differ greatly in the amount of personality allowed to influence the results of the study. For example, in the sciences researchers purposefully adhere to a *strict* method (the scientific method). All researchers are to use this same basic method, and successful experiments must be replicable by others. Generally speaking, the researcher's personality, likes and dislikes, religious and political preferences are supposed to be as far removed as possible from the actual study. Even the language scientists employ to describe the results of their studies distances them from the results of those studies. For example, in scientific essays one normally finds a detached language use, with researchers forcing themselves into the background by highlighting the working of the study itself: "This study found . . ."

In sharp contrast, criticism (one of many Humanistic methods of generating knowledge) actively involves the personality of the researcher. The very choices of what to study, and how and why to study a rhetorical artifact, are heavily influenced by the personal qualities of the researcher. In the sciences, the application of the scientific method may take numerous forms, but the overall method remains the same—and the personality of the researcher is excised from the study. In the humanities, methods of research may also take many forms—criticism, ethnography, for example—but the personality of the researcher is an integral component of the study. Further personalizing criticism, we find that rhetorical critics use a variety of ways when examining a particular rhetorical artifact, with some critics even developing their own unique perspective to better examine a rhetorical artifact.[4] Even the manner in which many critics express themselves in their writing brings the personal to the fore: "I found" instead of "This study found. . . ." This distinction was not lost on Edwin Black, who eloquently wrote:

> Methods, then, admit of varying degrees of personality. And criticism, on the whole, is near the indeterminate, contingent, personal end of the methodological scale. In consequence of this placement, it is neither possible nor desirable for criticism to be fixed into a system, for critical techniques to be objectified, for critics to be interchangeable for purposes of [scientific] replication, or for rhetorical criticism to serve as the handmaiden of quasi-scientific theory. [The] idea is that critical method is too personally expressive to be systematized.[5]

In short, criticism is not a science, but an art. It is not a scientific method; it uses subjective methods of argument; it exists on its own, not in conjunction with other methods of generating knowledge (i.e., social). As Marie Hochmuth Nichols articulated so well, "It is reason and judgment, not a [computer], that makes a man a critic."[6] Put another way, insight and imagination top statistical applications when studying human action.

THREE STAGES OF THE CRITICAL ACT

Superior criticism is not mechanistic in its application. Even though an art, criticism does, however, possess certain norms that critics follow when producing criticism. After all, good critics are trying to generate knowledge and insight; they are not simply flashing their opinions about. In general, there are three stages involved in producing criticism: conceptual, communication, and counter-communication.

The Conceptual Stage

The conceptual stage takes place in the mind of the critic; it is an act of cerebration. It is a private act, and its purpose is to generate some type of insight concerning the rhetorical artifact. Since this is a very personal act—that is, not mechanistic—there is no standardized way critics go about flexing their cerebral muscles. Generally, however, insight is generated in one of two ways. The first is a type of spontaneous inception. Think of the *Eureka!* of Archimedes, or of the proverbial light bulb popping on inside your head. Critics often generate involuntary, almost instinctive reactions to rhetorical artifacts. This involves more than a simple reaction to an artifact, however, because critics are trained to observe: additionally, their training has a bearing upon what they see in an artifact. In a sense, the experienced critic has assimilated particular ways of viewing rhetoric; these modes of seeing are part and parcel of the critic's personality. Some critics may even come to see rhetorical artifacts in such a way that others recognize it as characteristic of that particular critic.

The other way a critic might generate insight is through a somewhat systematic examination of the rhetorical artifact. With this approach, the critic uses some type of guide, formal or informal, that allows for an orderly progression through the rhetorical artifact. Often these guides take the form of *perspectives* on rhetoric, which is discussed below. Often, too, the search for insight is started with a question the critic has about the workings of the world (often called a research question). Simply put, the critic starts with a question or two in mind and then examines various rhetorical artifacts looking for answers to that question. For example, the authors of Chapter Eleven, Fantasy Theme Analysis, state in their critical essay that they were guided by questions, such as, "What do we expect from our universities?" and "Why do we go to college?" With those questions in mind, they decided that Fantasy Theme Analysis would be a fruitful perspective to use when looking at different rhetorical artifacts. In this way, the authors were guided by their initial research questions in both the decision about what approach to use as well as in what to look for in the rhetorial artifacts they examined.

Whether a critic spontaneously generates an insight or systematically searches a rhetorical artifact for information, it should be the critic, not the method or perspective, that is in control of the insights and knowledge generated. As Black wrote, "The critic's procedures are, when at their best, original; they grow ad hoc from the critic's engagement with the [rhetorical] artifact."[7] Of course, not all insights generated prove sound; some ideas are never meant to move beyond mere personal musing. A minority of ideas, however, are birthed alive and well, waiting to grow. These ideas move to the next stage of the critical act: communication.

The Communication Stage

The second stage of the critical act is a quasipublic act of writing out the criticism in preparation for sharing it with others. Your reasons for writing criticism will help to determine the particular audience for whom you will write. For example, you could be writing a letter to the editor of your local paper concerning the rhetorical efforts of a politician running for office; you could be writing a term paper for your professor; or you could be writing with a specific scholarly journal in mind. This stage of the critical act encompasses the private act of writing, sharing initial ideas with trusted friends and colleagues, and ultimately sharing with a wider audience.

When sharing your criticism with others, it is not simply a matter of providing a detailed picture of your opinions. You are instead sharing *propositions* with those who will be reading your work. Propositions are only naked assertions, however, until you provide a very basic step: giving supporting evidence with which to back up those assertions. Craig R. Smith wrote that critics must hold themselves to "standards of argumentation" when writing criticism. Specifically, he suggested that "when we write criticism . . . we ought to confine ourselves to solid argumentation inclusive of valid arguments built on sufficient and high quality evidence produced from close textual readings and masterings of context."[8] In short, critics must *invite* their audiences to agree with them. This is accomplished through stating their case and then providing evidence for the audience to accept or reject.

When writing you must always keep in mind the audience that will be reading your criticism. Recall that part of the purpose of criticism is to enhance the understanding of others concerning the rhetorical artifact. On this point Black wrote: "The critic proceeds in part by translating the object of his criticism into the terms of his audience and in part by educating his audience to the terms of the object. This dual task is not an ancillary function of criticism; it is an essential part of criticism."[9] For example, consider the speeches given by presidential candidates George Bush and Al Gore on December 13, 2000. I can honestly say that both of these speeches were rhetorical "home runs" and that I liked them. So far we have only my opinion. I might go one step further, however, and make specific assertions concerning the speeches. I could say that Al Gore's speech worked well because it attempted to achieve several objectives: heal wounds, keep the door open for a presidential run in 2004, and remove a possible "sore loser" stigma. I could then say that the Bush speech worked well since it, too, attempted to achieve several objectives: reach out to Democrats: to have Bush perceived as a gracious, not arrogant, winner: and to assure the nation of the proper transfer of power.

At this point you would find yourself with additional information, but still I have only provided you with *unsupported assertions*. I have merely given you my opinion about the speeches. I move into the realm of criticism when I provide the support for these assertions of mine, when I provide you with evidence that asks you to agree with me or that makes you aware of some aspect of the speeches that you had previously overlooked (the sharing of insights). For instance, I could provide specific sentences from both speeches that I feel support my assertions. In terms of Vice President Gore's attempt to keep the door open for a 2004 presidential race, I could highlight this statement: "I do have one regret: that I didn't get the chance to stay and fight for the American people over the next four years, especially those who need burdens lifted and barriers removed, especially for those who feel their voices have not been heard. I heard you and I will not forget."[10] In terms of then-Governor Bush's attempt to reach out to partisan Democrats, I could highlight this statement: "Our nation must rise above a house divided. Americans share hopes and goals and values far more important than any political disagreements. Republicans want the best for our nation, and so do Democrats. Our votes may differ, but not our hopes."[11] From these examples I would then share my reasoning about the connection I see between the examples and my assertions.

The main point to be remembered from this is that critics are trying to argue for a certain understanding of the rhetorical transaction. In this sense they are actually using rhetoric to try to gain acceptance of their ideas. The best critics simply do not make a judgment without supplying good reasons for others to agree with them. On this point Bernard L. Brock, Robert L. Scott, and James W. Chesebro wrote, "[S]tatements of tastes and preference do not qualify as criticism. [Criticism is] an art of evaluating with knowledge and propriety. Criticism is a reason-giving activity; it not only posits a judgment, the judgment is explained, reasons are given for the judgment, and known information is marshalled to support the reasons for the judgment."[12]

The idea of rhetorical criticism being a form of argument is not new. Wayne Brockriede wrote in 1974 that useful rhetorical criticism must function as an argument to be effective criticism.[13] In his landmark essay, Brockreide advanced five interanimated characteristics of an argument:

> (1) an inferential leap from existing beliefs to the adoption of a new belief or the reinforcement of an old one; (2) a perceived rationale to justify that leap; (3) a choice among two or more competing claims; (4) a regulation of uncertainty in relation to the selected claim—since someone has made an inferential leap, certainty can be neither zero nor total; and (5) a willingness to risk a confrontation of that claim with one's peers.[14]

More significant arguments will have a greater number and strength of the above five characteristics than less significant arguments. This is to say, the five qualities of arguments given above are on a sliding scale of sorts. The fewer of the five, or in weaker form, the less the criticism is effective argument. The greater the number of the five, or in stronger form, the more likelihood the criticism is effective argument. As Brockriede wrote,

> When a critic only appreciates the rhetoric or objects to it, without reporting any reason for his like or dislike, he puts his criticism near the nonargument end of the continuum. On the other hand, when an evaluating critic states clearly the criteria he has used in arriving at his judgment, together with the philosophic or theoretic foundations on which they rest, and when he has offered some data to show that the rhetorical experience meets or fails to meet those criteria, then he has argued.[15]

The propositions and claims used by a critic are generally advanced through the use of different *perspectives* on criticism. Because a rhetorical artifact is a multidimensional, complex, and nuanced event, there exists no one best way of viewing it. Moreover, no one effort to describe or to evaluate it will yield all the knowledge that there is to know about that artifact. Academic criticism usually takes its structure from a particular perspective. Perspectives allow critics to view the rhetorical artifact from different angles. Later in this book you will be exposed to twelve different perspectives designed for generating insight and understanding about a rhetorical artifact. There are more, and some critics even blend perspectives.

Using an established perspective to produce criticism has both strengths and weaknesses. One particular strength is that adopting a perspective allows critics to see an artifact differently than if no perspective had been adopted. In a sense, the critic is allowed to see the world in a particular way. A perspective will highlight certain features of a rhetorical artifact that will not be featured by another perspective. Adopting a particular perspective will also allow you to stay focused because, when properly used, the perspective *guides* rather than dictates your analysis.

On the opposite side of the coin, adopting a particular perspective will introduce certain biases into the criticism. A perspective is partial, and it encourages critics to view the world in a certain manner. So while some aspects of a rhetorical artifact are highlighted, others are screened out. Moreover, as Lawrence Rosenfield wrote, "A critic who comes upon a critical object in a state of mind such that he has a 'set of values' handy (or, indeed, any other system of categories) does not engage in a critical encounter so much as he processes perceptual data."[16] Thus a critic who follows too closely the dictates of a particular perspective runs the risk of producing stale and lifeless criticism. In short, improperly used, a perspective would be allowed to *dictate* rather than guide what a critic does in the analysis.

The different number of perspectives available to a critic is staggering. This book presents some of the more popular, as well as a few less well known but rather interesting perspectives. As you become familiar with the different perspectives presented in this book, you will see how they differ in the type of material they allow the critic to focus on, as well as the type of material they exclude. A central question remains, however: How does one choose which perspective to use? A critic's choice will be guided by several factors. First, the critic's personal interest will play a crucial role in determining which perspective to adopt. As you study the perspectives detailed in this book, you will find that some appeal to you and others do not. This attraction or aversion is natural, so your first clue to which perspective to use should be your personal interest in using that perspective. Second, and just as important, a critic must consider the type of rhetorical artifact being examined. As already mentioned, perspectives focus a critic's attention upon certain aspects of a rhetorical artifact. A critic should take this into consideration when choosing a particular perspective to use. Of course, more experienced critics may well choose to combine perspectives, modify perspectives, or develop a completely novel perspective. As a critic, the choice is yours to make. The greater your knowledge of the nuances of different perspectives, the greater your ability to discern the intricacies of individual rhetorical texts—thus, the greater the likelihood of producing productive criticism.

Advancing your propositions through different perspectives also makes an important contribution to the development of a critical vocabulary for both you and other critics to use. You will be contributing to both the understanding of human communication and the development of rhetorical theory. In one sense, you will be accumulating knowledge for others to draw upon. Ultimately, though,

I am inclined to believe Stephen E. Lucas hit dead center when he wrote, "In the last analysis, our scholarship will be judged, not by the perspectives from which it proceeds, but by the quality of the insight it produces."[17]

The Countercommunication Stage

Once the criticism is actually performed the final stage of the critical act, counter-communication, can be entered. This is a public act, and at this stage the critic shares openly with others. For instance, your criticism could take the form of a letter to the editor. If published, it will allow others the opportunity to share your thoughts and possibly to respond. In more academic settings, you will submit your term paper and receive feedback from your professor and possibly your classmates. You could even have written your paper for a conference presentation or submission to a scholarly journal. The idea is to share your criticism with some segment of the public with the hope that it will provoke some type of feedback. The best criticism does just this.

Feedback can take many forms, as can the public exchanges about the critic's ideas. A problem critics often encounter is the charge of *de gustibus non est disputandum,* there is no disputing taste. In other words, you might hear from others that your point of view is simply subjective, and that their points of view are equally valid. However, if you paid attention to providing the good reasons mentioned above, then the exchange does not necessarily boil down to "I'm right, you're wrong," but arguing who can see better. As Brockriede wrote, "Critics who argue are more *useful* than critics who do not."[18] Along these same lines Black wrote: "The critic can only induce us, and therefore it is we, the readers of criticism, who demand the critic's compliance with certain of our expectations. We expect the critic to see things for us that we are unlikely to see for ourselves until the critic has called them to our attention."[19]

What we are about at this stage of the critical act is none other than entering into dialogue about matters of importance. The exchange and discussion of ideas is crucial to criticism. Only the best criticism provokes this. Actually, the cry of many critics might well be, "Love me, hate me, but don't ignore me." Remember that good criticism *is* an act of rhetoric.

KEY ISSUES IN CRITICISM

When you begin to write your criticism, it will be helpful to know beforehand about several issues that all critics must wrestle with at some time or another. These issues are longstanding and have various "solutions," although one also finds that different critics seem to apply different solutions to the same issue.

One important issue involves the most basic question in criticism: *what to include in your writing.* Generally speaking your essay should contain three components: a description, an analysis, and an evaluation. Every critical essay should have these components, but each essay will present them in a slightly different manner (as you will see in the critical essays included in the chapters that follow).

Description refers to both a description of the rhetorical artifact and, in more academic settings, a description of the theoretical background you intend to use in the essay. A description of the artifact is crucial if your readers are to be able to follow you. The way you describe the artifact may well be the only exposure they have to it, so you must take care in presenting as accurate a picture as possible. In more formal instances of criticism—term papers, conference presentations—description refers also to a discussion of the theory being used to perform the criticism. This allows others to learn from your examples, and it also adds to the theoretical body of knowledge.

When you describe the artifact and the method used to examine it, you will also want to relay the importance of the artifact, the study itself, or both. In short, at some point you will want to justify what you are doing. Given the countless appeals for our attention each day, readers may well ask, "Why is this important for me to know?" Although you might think what you are doing is important, not everyone else will think the same way. It is up to you to share with others the reasons why they should invest their time and energy to read what you have written.

After you share with your readers what you will be examining (the rhetorical artifact), how you will be going about that examination (rhetorical theory), and the importance of what you are doing, you move on to the actual analysis of the rhetorical artifact. This section of your essay will generally consume the most space. In this section, you share your insight and understanding of the artifact and you actively make a case for your conclusion. This leads to the final component of a criticism essay: evaluation.

Evaluation of the rhetorical artifact boils down to the judgments you make about it. Judgments may certainly be made, and appreciation or disdain expressed, but they must be made after two conditions are met: one, the fair minded description of the inner workings of the rhetorical artifact has been presented for the world to see; and two, the standards of judgments used by the critic are provided for all to see. In this way readers may themselves judge whether or not the critic imposed his ideology upon the artifact. The types of judgments made will differ depending upon the type of perspective used and also upon the critic's personality.

Another important issue facing critics is the seemingly easy decision concerning *which perspective to use in their critical endeavour.* Simply put, how will a critic go about producing criticism? As you read additional chapters in this book, you may well find that a certain perspective appeals to you. You may not be certain why it does, but you seem to gravitate toward it. The perspective seems natural for you to use. As you use it, you become increasingly familiar with its nuances and potentials. Some critics are well known for producing insightful and nuanced work using a particular perspective. For example, Bill Benoit is well known for using genre theory in his criticism; Marilyn Young's work using the situational perspective is another such example; mythic criticism and the names Rushing and Frentz are no strangers.

Perspectives are not to be used as formulas, however. Although they do suggest a particular way of viewing the world, as the critic you must direct the criticism. When critics first begin to use a perspective, they often apply it *rigidly* to the rhetorical artifact. As critics become more knowledgeable about the perspective they use they often become more *flexible* in its application, allowing for personal insight and interests to guide the criticism. In the best criticism, the personality of the critic begins to blend with the perspective used. As Michael Leff has written, "Interpretation is not a scientific endeavor. Systematic principles are useful in attempting to validate interpretations, but the actual process of interpretation depends on conjectures and insights particular to the object [rhetorical artifiact] at hand."[20]

Regardless of the perspective chosen, a critic must be cautious in its application. Perspectives are to help a critic, not direct the criticism; a successful critic's ideas blend in with those of the perspective. Perspectives are not molds to be forced upon a rhetorical artifact—mechanistic and rigid criticism. Black puts this idea, and the consequences, in proper perspective:

> Because only the critic is the instrument of criticism, the critic's relationship to other instruments will profoundly affect the value of critical inquiry. And in criticism, every instrument has to be assimilated to the critic, to have become an integral part of the critic's mode of perception. A critic who is influenced by, for example, [Burkean Dramatism] and who, in consequence of that influence, comes to see some things in a characteristically dramatistic way—that critic is still able to function in his own person as the critical instrument, and so the possibility of significant disclosure remains open to him. But the would-be critic who has not internalized the pentad, who undertakes to "use" it as a mathematician would use a formula—such a critic is certain (yes, *certain!*) to produce work that is sterile. An act of criticism conducted on mechanistic assumptions will, not surprisingly, yield mechanistic criticism.[21]

A minority of critics, myself included, take the process of assimilation one step further by blending and developing their own framework from which to proceed with criticism. This type of criticism is often called *eclectic* criticism: "Eclecticism is the selection of the best standards and principles from various systems of ideas. It requires more orderliness to be a pluralist than to apply a single theory. . . . Criticism is exciting because you must use everything you are and everything you know that is relevant."[22] From my own work, let me give you an example:

Several years ago I came across a letter written by James Dobson, president of Focus on the Family. The letter intrigued me on several levels and I wanted to study it further. As I pondered how to go about this, I discovered that no single perspective would do justice to the rich intellectual and moral cultures embedded within the letter. In the end I approached the letter combining judgmental analysis and Burkean theory (namely, semantic–moral poetic analysis, and a motivational analysis).[23] The end result was a *method* of analysis (criticism) that blended *perspectives* (judgmental analsysis and Burkean dramatism). This flexible combination allowed me to study the letter on three different levels, thereby more fully explaining the inner and outer workings of the letter better than if I had used any one perspective alone.

Yet another issue involves *how one should approach a rhetorical artifact* (what Ed Black calls rhetorical transactions). This is to say, should one begin with a theoretical orientation or should one begin with the artifact itself?[24] Black described this distinction as *etic* and *emic* orientations. One using an etic orientation "approaches a rhetorical transaction from outside of that transaction and interprets the transaction in terms of pre-existing theory." In contrast, one using an emic orientation "approaches a rhetorical transaction in what is hoped to be its own terms, without conscious expectations drawn from any sources other than the rhetorical transaction itself."[25] A pure etic or emic orientation is, of course, impossible. One should think of them on a sliding scale of more or less. The more one adopts an etic orientation, the less of an emic orientation is used: and the opposite holds true as well.

Both orientations have strengths and weaknesses. An etic orientation allows for a fuller development of rhetorical theory. The major end of criticism would be to develop and to advance rhetorical theory, thus adding to our overall knowledge concerning human communication. An emic orientation allows for a more nuanced description of the rhetorical artifact, and it also provides more room for the critic's personality and intuition to play a part in the criticism. A weakness with the etic orientation is that critics may very well find exactly what they expect to find. A weakness with the emic orientation can arise because critics may "aspire to so sympathetic an account [during the descriptive and interpretive phases of criticism] that the critic's audience will understand that object as, in some sense, *inevitable*."[26] The problem is with the "good faith" of the critic. After so sympathetic an account of the rhetorical artifact, the critic will be hard pressed to return to a more objective role during the evaluative phase of criticism.[27]

Yet another concern involves *the notion of criticism as an objective or a subjective endeavour.* It is clear that criticism is not a scientific act; the very best criticism involves the personality, insights, and imagination of a critic. Yet for all that, there are critics—I among them—who maintain that a certain degree of objectivity is necessary for honest, productive criticism. When I use the term "objective," I do not mean that critics ought to possess or are capable of possessing a scientific detachment from the object of criticism. This would surely produce a sterile criticism devoid of its lifeblood: the critic's intermingled intuition, insight, and personality. What I am suggesting is that the critic may approach the artifact under consideration with a fair and open mind. In this sense the critic sets aside personal politics or ideological "truths" and approaches the artifact with a sense of curiosity. The artifact under consideration ought not to be altered to fit the prejudgments of the critic, but be allowed to voice its inner workings to the world. The work of the critic is to make certain that this voice is intelligible to and approachable by the public.

This in no way detracts from the critic bringing to bear an individual stamp upon the criticism produced. Nor is it the antiseptic application of a method upon an unsuspecting rhetorical artifact. What it does suggest is that the critic must learn how to appreciate the inner workings of a text, even if personally the critic finds that text to be repugnant or wishes it to be other than it is. In this sense, the critic is being "objective," or disinterested, when approaching and describing a text.[28]

Although I agree heartily with Rosenfield that, "Partisan involvement may be a civic virtue, but insight derived therefrom must be continually suspect,"[29] other critics disagree with me, as you will find while reading some of the chapters that follow. For these critics, the act of criticism involves a more active attempt at persuasion in all three phases of criticism—description, analysis, and evaluation. Very often the direction of this persuasion takes its form from the political ideology of the critic. For example, Robert Ivie defined productive criticism as "a detailed and partisan critique. . . ."[30] According to Ivie, a critic "intentionally produces a strategic interpretation, or structure of meaning, that privileges selective interests. . . . in specific circumstances."[31] The purpose of criticism is made clear. Those who engage in rhetorical criticism are, or should be, advocates: "criticism, as a specific performance of general rhetorical knowledge, yields a form of scholarship that obtains social relevance by strategically reconstructing the interpretive design of civic discourse in order to diminish, bolster, or redirect its significance. [Criticism] is a form of advocacy grounded in the language of a particular rhetorical situation. . . ."[32]

Often some attempt at political fairness is made, although the result is the same, the politicization of the critical act. For example, Michael McGee wrote:

> "When interpellating 'the critic' and 'criticism,' the first thing a rhetorician should do is to identify her political orientation. Her syllabus should contain a paragraph describing the trajectory of her course. Her book should have a chapter that aligns her politics with that politics practiced in the workaday world by political parties competing for control of the State. She must be fair, describing the politics of those who disagree with her in a light that leans more toward portraiture than caricature."[33]

However, regardless of the attempt, I am inclined to agree with Rosenfield when he asserts that a difficulty with ideological criticism is that the "very notion of commitment to an ideology, no matter what its value system, implies a kind of immunity to those experiences of the world which in any way contradict the ideology."[34] In the same article as cited above, McGee stated, "That which [ideologically driven] critics do today is proactive, openly political in its acknowledgment of its bias and its agenda to produce practical theories of culture and of social relations (including political relations)," and thus appears to embrace the very action Rosenfield described above.[35]

Although summarizing a much larger conversation on this topic, the positions advanced are clear. On the one hand we have critics striving to keep personal politics and feelings from the initial stages of the criticism—most notably, during the description and analysis phases of the critical act. This position presupposes that part of the purpose of criticism is to produce knowledge that disputants can draw upon when making decisions about how to live—academic critics should not be partisan agents of social change. On the other hand we have critics allowing their politics and personal feelings to guide them during all three stages of criticism. This position presupposes that critics begin by seeing the world differently than the public they seek to persuade, and that the job of the critic is to produce partisan social change in the direction of that critic's chosing.[36] A good example of this contrast is found when looking at the chapters on framing analysis and feminist criticism.

The chapters that follow will give you a sense of the variety and artistry of rhetorical criticism. As you move through each chapter, you will find that the way in which the authors practice criticism both modifies and moves beyond the definition I give here. This is as it should be. Take note of *how* the the the authors change the nature and scope of criticism. Criticism is not a sterile endeavour, and you will find that some of the chapters resonate more strongly with you than do others. Criticism is, as is rhetoric, nuanced, and may by understood on many different levels. Each chapter that follows underscores this idea and will present a point of view that will add rich variety to the definition I have presented.

SUGGESTED READINGS

Black, Edwin, *Rhetorical Criticism: A Study in Method* (Madison, WI: University of Wisconsin Press, 1978), ix–xv, 1–9.

Brockriede, Wayne, "Rhetorical Criticism as Argument," *Quarterly Journal of Speech* 60 (April 1974): 165–174.

Kuypers, Jim A., "Must We All Be Political Activists?" *The American Communication Journal* 4.1 (2000). <http://acjournal.org/holdings/vol4/iss1/special/kuypers.htm>.

Rosenfield, Lawrence W., "The Experience of Criticism," *Quarterly Journal of Speech* 60.4 (1974): 489–496.

Sillars, Malcolm O., "Persistent Problems in Rhetorical Criticism," *Rhetoric and Communication: Studies in the University of Illinois Tradition*, Jane Blankenship and Herman G. Stelzner, Eds. (Urbana, IL: University of Illinois Press, 1976), 69–88.

NOTES

1. James Andrews, Michael C. Leff, and Robert Terrill, "The Nature of Criticism: An Overview," *Reading Rhetorical Texts: An Introduction to Criticism* (Boston: Houghton Mifflin Company, 1998), 6.

2. Wayne Brockriede, "Rhetorical Criticism as Argument," *Quarterly Journal of Speech* 60 (April 1974): 165.

3. Marie Hochmuth Nichols, *Rhetoric and Criticism*, (Baton Rouge: Louisiana State University Press, 1963), 7.

4. See "The Experiential Perspective," in Bernard L. Brock, Robert L. Scott, and James W. Chesebro, eds. *Methods of Rhetorical Criticism: A Twenti-*

eth-Century Perspective, 3rd ed. (Detroit, MI: Wayne State University Press, 1989), 85–169.

5. Edwin Black, *Rhetorical Criticism: A Study in Method* (Madison: University of Wisconsin Press, 1978), x–xi.

6. Marie Kathryn Hochmuth, "The Criticism of Rhetoric," *A History and Criticism of American Public Address*, vol. 3, Marie Kathryn Hochmuth, ed. (New York: Russell & Russell, 1954), 13.

7. Edwin Black, "On Objectivity and Politics in Criticism," *American Communication Journal* 4.1 (2000) <http://acjournal.org/holdings/vol4/iss1/special/black.htm>.

8. Craig R. Smith, "Criticism of Political Rhetoric and Disciplinary Integrity," *American Communication Journal* 4.1 (2000) <http://www.acjournal.org/holdings/vol4/iss1/special/smith.htm>

9. Black, *Rhetorical Criticism*, 6.

10. Al Gore, "Concession Speech," Campaign 2000, C-Span. <www.c-span.org/campaign 2000/gorespeech.asp>. Of course, we now know that Al Gore declined to run again for president. That does not preclude, however, that he kept that option open. If one takes into account the massive amount of speculation concerning the potential for Gore to run again, one sees that Gore actually succeeded in leaving that door open.

11. George W. Bush, "George W. Bush Speech, December 13, 2000," Campaign 2000, C-Span. <www.c-span.org/campaign2000/bushspeech.asp>.

12. Brock, Scott, and Chesebro, 13.

13. Wayne Brockriede, "Rhetorical Criticism as Argument," *Quarterly Journal of Speech* 60 (April 1974): 165–174.

14. Brockriede, 166.

15. Brockriede, 167.

16. Lawrence W. Rosenfield, "The Experience of Criticism," *Quarterly Journal of Speech* 60.4 (1974): 491.

17. Stephen E. Lucas, "Renaissance of American Public Address: Text and Context in Rhetorical Criticism," *Landmark Essays on American Public Address*, Martin J. Medhurst, ed. (Davis, CA: Hermagoras Press, 1993), 199.

18. Brockriede, 173.

19. Black, "On Objectivity."

20. Michael Leff, "Interpretation and the Art of Rhetorical Criticism," *Western Journal of Speech Communication* 44 (1980): 343–344.

21. Black, *Rhetorical Criticism*, xii.

22. Pauline Kael, *I Lost It at the Movies* (Boston: Little, Brown, 1964), 309.

23. Jim A. Kuypers, "From Science, Moral Poetics: Dr. James Dobson's Response to the Fetal Tissue Research Initiative," *Quarterly Journal of Speech* 86.2 (2000): 146–167.

24. This is not a new problem in rhetorical theory. See Michael Leff, "Interpretation and the Art of Rhetorical Criticism," *Western Journal of Speech Communication* 44 (1980): 337–349.

25. Edwin Black, "A Note on Theory and Practice in Rhetorical Criticism," *Western Journal of Speech Communication* 44 (1980): 331–332.

26. Edwin Black, "A Note on Theory and Practice in Rhetorical Criticism," *Western Journal of Speech Communication* 44 (1980): 334.

27. For a different take on the etic/emic orientation that includes a methodological suggestion for emic criticism, see W. Charles Redding, "Extrinsic and Intrinsic Criticism," *Essays on Rhetorical Criticism* Thomas R. Nilsen, ed. (New York: Random House, 1968), 98–125.

28. The preceeding two paragraphs can be found in Jim A. Kuypers, "Must We All Be Political Activists?" *The American Communication Journal* 4.1 (2000) <http://acjournal.org/holdings/vol4/iss1/index.htm>. My notion of objectivity is in some ways similar to the notion of "appreciation" put forth by Lawrence W. Rosenfield in "The Experience of Criticism," 494. In the above article, I define "objective" criticism and position it between a politically partisan criticism and detached scientific objectivity. Rosenfield defines "appreciation," and positions it between ideologically driven criticism and scientific objectivity. For Rosenfield, appreciation is "founded on an inherent love of the world, while [scientific] objectivity, the effort to establish distance on the world (for whatever laudable ends) sometimes betrays an essential distrust of the world, a fear that one will be contaminated in some manner if one is open to its unconcealment."

29. Rosenfield, "The Experience of Criticism," 492.

30. Robert L. Ivie, "A Question of Significance," Quarterly Journal of Speech 80.4 (1994).

31. Robert L. Ivie, "Productive Criticism," Quarterly Journal of Speech 81.1 (1995).

32. Robert L. Ivie, "The Social Relevance of Rhetorical Scholarship," Quarterly Journal of Speech 81.2 (1994).

33. Michael Calvin McGee, "On Objectivity and Politics in Rhetoric," *American Communication Journal* 4.3 (2001) http://acjournal.org/holdings/vol4/iss3/special/mcgee.htm.

34. Rosenfield, "The Experience of Criticism," 494.

35. McGee, "On Objectivity and Politics in Rhetoric."

36. How and why we practice rhetorical criticism is an ongoing conversation. Those seeking to better understand the changing nature of our critical practices have a wonderful resource in the following special collection of essays published in 1957, 1980, 1990, and 2001, respectively. Taken together they present a wonderful opportunity for students of rhetoric to better understand criticism's changing nature. See, "Symposium: Criticism and Public Address,"

edited by Ernest Wrage, in *Western Speech* 21 (1957). These essays were later reprinted along with five others in Thomas R. Nilsen, ed., *Essays on Rhetorical Criticism* (New York: Random House, 1968). See also, *"Special Report:* Rhetorical Criticism: The State of the Art," edited by Michael C. Leff, *Western Journal of Speech Communication* 44.4 (1980); "Special Issue on Rhetorical Criticism," edited by John Angus Campbell, *Western Journal of Speech Communication* 54.3 (1990); and *"Special Issue:* Rhetorical Criticism: The State of the Art Revisited," *Western Journal of Speech Communication* 65.3 (2001).

A critical exchange worthy of notice has been published by the *American Communication Journal:* "Criticism, Politics, and Objectivity," edited by Jim A. Kuypers 4.1 (2000) <http://www.acjournal.org/holdings/vol4/iss1/index.htm>; "Rhetoric, Politics, and Critique," edited by Mark Huglen, 4.3 (2001) <http://www.acjournal.org/holdings/vol4/iss3/index.htm>; and the final essay in the exchange, Jim A. Kuypers, "Criticism, Politics, and Objectivity: Redivivus," 5.1 (2001) <http://www.acjournal.org/holdings/vol5/iss1/special/kuypersresponse.htm>.

CHAPTER THREE

ON OBJECTIVITY AND POLITICS IN CRITICISM

EDWIN BLACK

In his invitation to participate in this colloquium, the editor wrote: "These are opinion pieces, so it is your thoughts on these matters our readers will be interested in."

It is my thoughts that readers will be interested in? What a luxury! Does it mean that I don't have to be "objective?" That I can write whatever I please, without restraint, without discipline, without discretion? Well, not quite. I still want to avoid appearing to be an ass. And so, out of concern for my reputation (subjective), I will try to present something that will make sense to an intelligent reader (objective). Which, in turn, suggests that the polarities of subjective and objective are not always antithetical. Sometimes they may be complementary.

I can certainly understand how the issue of objectivity in criticism arises. Scientific inquiries always seek to minimize the influence of the investigator by their methods of research and their requirement of replicability. This quest for objectivity has become, along with other attributes of scientific inquiry, an intellectual standard that some people apply indiscriminately. It's a mistake. Objectivity is not universally desirable.

No one, to my knowledge, has represented criticism as scientific. At most (or least?), it has been characterized as "prescientific"—a condescending representation that assumes, quite gratuitously, that human mental activity is a pyramidal hierarchy with something called "science" hovering halolike above its apex and a grotesquely conceived "criticism" buried somewhere in its nether region. The conception itself is prescientific in the historic sense in which anything medieval can be called prescientific.

If we want to know about criticism, we look to people who have practiced it, who have engaged its problems and have somehow resolved some of them in tan-

This essay originally appeared in *The American Communication Journal* 4.1 [Fall 2000]. <http://acjournal.org/holdings/vol4/iss1/special/black.htm>. Reprinted with permission from the *American Communication Journal.*

gible acts of criticism. And what accomplished critic has ever claimed that criticism should only be objective? Criticism is not supposed to be always objective. It is, of course, supposed to be always intelligent. More to the point, it is supposed to be always fair. Sometimes fairness requires objectivity, and sometimes it doesn't. Therefore, the relationship between objectivity and criticism is not constant; it is variable.

In my use of the term *criticism*, I cannot extricate it from its origin in the Greek term *krisis*, which translates into *judgment*. The critic exercises judgment. In fact, in Greek the term for *judge* and the term for *critic* were the same term. Let's play with that ambiguity a bit:

> We do not demand that a judge in a courtroom be uniformly "objective." We demand that the judge be fair. If the judge's being fair requires, at some phase of the judicial process, neutrality or detachment or distance—all, qualities associated with objectivity—then those are what we expect. On the other hand, if the judge's being fair requires, at some other phase, empathy or compassion or introspection—all, qualities associated with subjectivity—then those are what we expect. What is important is that the judge be whatever is required for being fair. Exactly the same obtains with the critic.

Sometimes, at some stages of the critical process, it is important to be as objective as it is possible to be. There are critical problems that require for their solution a puritanical self-control—a disciplined indifference to one's own proclivities and one's own local conditions. That is especially true of rhetorical criticism, which can be at its most valuable when it focuses on odious rhetors—bigots, demagogues, habitual liars—the understanding of whom may require critics to suspend their repugnance temporarily and, for a period, try to see the world with the cold neutrality of a sociopath. But such acts of objectivity are only intermittent and never an end in themselves.

Of course, the analogy between the critic and the courtroom judge can be taken only so far. A critic's being fair in criticism is not wholly the same as a judge's being fair in a courtroom. Conventional procedures of law prescribe to a considerable extent the claims and counterclaims to which a judge is obliged to attend in order to be fair. Such a prescriptive order is not available to the critic. The critic's procedures are, when at their best, original; they grow ad hoc from the critic's engagement with the artifact. And because the critic has to generate not only a judgment of the artifact, but also the procedure by which the judgment was reached—because, in short, the critic's responsibilities are legislative as well as judicial—the critic may have to be subjective more often than the judge in the court. That is because critics, unlike judges, cannot lay responsibility for their judgments on any code for which the critics themselves are not individually responsible.

The critic's subjectivity is also the consequence of the critic's having no powers of enforcement. The critic cannot compel our compliance with the critic's judgment. The critic can only induce us; and therefore it is we, the readers of criticism, who demand the critic's compliance with certain of our expectations. We expect the critic to see things for us that we are unlikely to see for ourselves until the critic has called them to our attention. That means that we expect the critic to tell us things that we do not already know. Because the critic's perceptions are supposed to be valuable and uncommon (otherwise, why would we bother to read about them?), there is much in critical activity that ought to be subjective in the sense of being individual, novel, unconforming, sometimes even shocking.

So, far from encouraging critics to be objective all the time, I hold rather that a critic can be excessively objective. Indeed, excessive objectivity is a failure that occurs with unfortunate frequency in criticism.

Impersonal criticism is, by definition, objective. Objectivity, therefore, is manifested in more than just a passive facticity. Objectivity inheres in the substitution of any a priori method for the critic's own perceptions and judgments. It follows, then, that the application in criticism of a political or ideological program that is not the critic's own invention is an exercise in objectivity. And such exercises frequently display the deformities common to excessive objectivity in criticism, which are predictability and pedantry and wearisome uniformity. That is why excessively objective criticism—criticism that is without personality—is so repressive to write and so deadly to read.

Political judgments are certainly relevant to criticism, and political presuppositions are probably unavoidable in criticism. But politicized criticism—criticism that is in the service of an ideology—is another matter. The problem has been that so much of politicized criticism is heavy-handed and closed to discovery. The impetus of politicized criticism is to exploit its subject for the ratification of itself.

In 1844, Karl Marx said, "The essential sentiment of criticism is indignation; its essential activity is denunciation." Marx's view is reflected in much of the dyspeptic criticism written by his acolytes, even those who are many levels removed from the Master: the echoes of echoes of echoes. A critical agenda that confines itself to indignant denunciation seems to me awfully constricted. Criticism has richer possibilities.

Good criticism is always a surprise. It is a surprise in the sense that you can't anticipate what a good critic will have to say about a given artifact.

I don't think that the expression of conventional opinions constitutes interesting criticism. By "conventional opinions" I mean to refer not just to the views of the Rotarian in Peoria; I mean to refer also to the pieties of any coterie whatever. The inventory of opinions that defines a political movement—no matter whether progressive or regressive, rational or psychotic, popular or insular—must become, at least to the adherents of that movement, conventional. It must in order to function as the ideological adhesion for a collective identity. Even anarchists have an orthodoxy.

Although it seems impossible for any of us to live a civic life without subscribing to some body of received doctrine, that doctrine, even if the critic conceives it vividly and believes it ardently, is not the stuff of enlightening criticism. Whatever its merits may be, it is derivative, and it intercedes between the critic and the object of criticism by effecting trite observations and stock responses in the critic.

T. S. Eliot wrote that "the readers of the Boston Evening Transcript sway in the wind, like a field of ripe corn." They're not the only ones. We all have episodes of marching in the parade or dancing in the chorus. It is gratifying sometimes to move in synchrony with others. But we just shouldn't try to be professional critics while we're in the ripe corn mode.

It seems to me reasonable to demand of any writer: Surprise me. If the writer can't deliver, the writer can be dismissed, no matter whether what is written is critical or political or fictional or anything else. Note that the demand is not, "please me;" nor is it, "comfort me." It is not a demand for conformity to any sort of bias in the reader. It is simply a demand that a writer have something to say. And repeating the pieties of an ideology is not having something to say. I think it was Truman Capote who once said of a fellow novelist's work, "That isn't writing; that's typing." The same can be said of echoic ideologues.

So that these remarks are at least the semblance of an argument instead of being simple dogma, let me try to be clear about their premise. They are predicated on a proposition having to do with the relationship between criticism and its reader. The proposition is that although criticism is generically epideictic, since it engages in praise and blame, it is not functionally epideictic. That is, I am assuming that you do not read criticism solely in order to have your own opinions confirmed, but that you read criticism in order to be brought to see something that you hadn't noticed on your own. If, on the other hand, it is personal confirmation that you want—if you want to be reassured and to have your intellectual passions licensed—you don't then sit down and read criticism. You seek an epideictic occasion—some sort of rally or ceremony where cobelievers can celebrate their articles of faith. Really good criticism is too singular to be confirmatory.

We don't want to read criticism that tells us nothing that we didn't already know. We don't want to read criticism that reiterates yet again what we have heard before.

Certainly there is nothing wrong with a critic's having political convictions. It is unavoidable. Only an idiot is without political convictions—in rare cases, maybe a holy idiot, but an idiot all the same. The very term *idiot* is from the Greek word for *nonpolitical person*. We don't want to read rhetorical criticism written by an idiot, which really means that we don't want to read rhetorical criticism that has no political dimension to it. It may be possible to write apolitical but still luminous criticism of pure music or of nonrepresentational painting, but it is hard to imagine apolitical rhetorical criticism that isn't desiccated. So, yes, rhetorical criticism is likely to have a political dimension, and it ought to.

The inhibiting complication is that although the critic's political convictions may merit respect, they are not necessarily going to be any more interesting or intelligent or original than the general run of political convictions. Just being a critic doesn't qualify one to have anything to say about politics that has not already been said—and maybe better said—many times. So, I think that unless the critic has something fresh and knowledgeable to say, the critic should just shut up about politics. If the critic does that, then the political convictions of the critic will be presuppositional. That is, the critic will observe, judge, and argue from some political convictions rather than to them. The critic's politics will be implicit rather than explicit. Even so, the contours of the critic's political convictions will be clear enough from the criticism.

In the end, there are no formulae, no prescriptions, for criticism. The methods of rhetorical criticism need to be objective to the extent that, in any given critique, they could be explicated and warranted. But it is important that critical techniques also be subjective to the extent that they are not mechanistic, not autonomous, not disengaged from the critics who use them. The best critics have so thoroughly assimilated their methods that those methods have become their characteristic modes of perception.

The only instrument of good criticism is the critic. It is not any external perspective or procedure or ideology, but only the convictions, values, and learning of the critic, only the observational and interpretive powers of the critic. That is why criticism, notwithstanding its obligation to be objective at crucial moments, is yet deeply subjective. The method of rhetorical criticism is the critic.

CHAPTER FOUR

THE SITUATIONAL PERSPECTIVE

KATHLEEN FARRELL

MARILYN J. YOUNG

In "The Rhetorical Situation" Bitzer defines that term as "a complex of persons events, objects, and relations presenting an actual or potential exigence which can be completely or partially removed if discourse introduced into the situation can so constrain human decision or action as to bring about the significant modification of the exigence."[1] Further, he writes, in "any rhetorical situation there will be at least one controlling exigence which functions as the organizing principle: it specifies the audience to be addressed and the change to be effected." The rhetorical audience, then, is that which can alleviate the exigence. Thus, as an example, when President Franklin Roosevelt addressed Congress following the Japanese attack on Pearl Harbor, he was responding to that attack as the controlling exigence. The attack would seem to require a response in kind—a declaration of war. Yet, Roosevelt was constrained by the Constitution, which grants Congress the responsibility for declarations of war. The attack, then, required Roosevelt to ask Congress to declare war on Japan; in that way, the controlling exigence—the attack—entailed the necessary audience—Congress—and the action to be taken—the declaration of war.

Yet it was not enough for Roosevelt to merely address Congress, for even with a declaration of war, Roosevelt needed the support of the American people. It is also true that the public needed to hear from the president. Thus, his speech was designed to respond to two exigencies: the need for a declaration of war and the need of the people to hear from their leader.[2]

Bitzer's ideas about the rhetorical situation are best understood when considered in relation to his notions of public knowledge, where he articulates his understanding of the role of the public in rhetorical practice. When he refers to the "public" Bitzer is not referring to the audience, although these concepts may overlap. Bitzer's construction of the public is a community of persons who share values, interests, and outlook. Publics form around specific values, ideas, policies, and proposals. Yet Bitzer recognizes that these publics are fluid, that specific publics can form, disband, and re-form in a different configuration. Further, there can be "subpublics" within a larger public, such as ethnic groups within a particular community. These persons are interdependent and possess the power to validate community truths and values. It is this group that has the power to "authorize" decisions and actions—not in any formal way as with Congress, but in the sense that some decisions become part of the public sense of truth and value.[3]

Part of the function of the public in a situation such as December 7, 1941, is to authorize the president to seek declarations of war in times of attack. In a way this is the actualization of the notion imbedded in the U.S. Constitution: "with the consent of the governed." That consent is offered formally through Congress, but it is also granted informally through the notion of public assent, a concept that is most successful when public knowledge is informed and has coalesced.

American democracy works because we believe it will, and we therefore defer to its precepts. In that sense, democracy is a process of communication: and it is the role of the public in discourse to communicate—formally and informally—its assent to the actions of our leaders. For example, at the conclusion of World War II, in the face of strong public sentiment to "bring the troops home," Roosevelt could not guarantee our allies the presence of an American occupying force in Europe; Churchill's proposal for an alliance of the "English speaking peoples" fell on deaf ears; and American women, who had been the backbone of the workforce during the war, were expected to return home and make room for returning soldiers. The public authorization for the war effort and its exigences no longer existed; decisions had to reflect that new truth.

In the case of the Japanese attack on Pearl Harbor, the situation—the exigence—was relatively clear, as was the fitting response. When things are not so clear, the development of public knowledge becomes critical; before assent can be communicated, the public must accumulate enough knowledge to

1. Agree on the situation itself.
2. Understand the options open for a fitting response.
3. Debate the costs and benefits of those options.

If these elements do not materialize, the notion of public assent cannot entail the notion of consent, but rests on ignorance.

Bitzer's ideas are grounded in the notion that all rhetoric is "situated." That is to say, rhetorical discourse derives its meaning from the situation in which it is created. Absent that situation, meaning is often lost. Think about the "great speeches" in American history; how many of them make real sense outside the time in which they were spoken? Certainly, there are speeches that may come alive while one is studying the era in which they were salient, and many "great" speeches have passages that ring though the ages. Usually, though, these are passages that can be given new life by applying them to a current situation. Nevertheless, by far the majority of speeches given in this country during all its years of existence have fallen into obscurity, not because they were not good examples of the art and craft of speechmaking, but because they no longer speak to us.[4]

Even those speeches that carry powerful impact over time derive much of that strength from the situation they address. Martin Luther King's "I Have A Dream," judged the most influential speech of the twentieth century,[5] draws its power from the situation of segregation, the march on Washington, the imagery King employs, the vigor of his delivery, and the fact that his dream has yet to be fully realized. The Gettysburg Address, also full of imagery and poetry, nonetheless is memorable at least in part because of the situation in which it was conceived: a commemoration of the deadliest battle in American history, a great civil war testing the strength of the union, and a challenge that tried the principles of equality and liberty on which that union was founded, as well as the fact that we need to continuously renew our commitment to those ideals. Lincoln's second inaugural, considered one of the best inaugural addresses ever given, is nonetheless remembered only in part, rather than in whole. Like most great addresses, those passages that one recalls are those the public has "authorized" by moving them into public knowledge.

In Bitzer's view, the situation in which rhetoric is called forth encompasses more than the context of the speech or the events that gave rise to the occasion for the speech. It includes all of the elements that influenced the moment: the events, the individuals involved, the circumstances, and the relationships among these factors. Thus, returning to Roosevelt's request for a Declaration of War, the situation would consist of Roosevelt himself and the attack on Pearl Harbor; but it would also include the Congress and the Constitution, the negotiations that had been going on between the United States and Japan, the ongoing war in Europe, the rampant isolationism of most Americans prior to the attack, and so on. In analyzing a speech using the situational perspective, the critic must take into account the totality of the situation and must consider the role played by each element.

1. List each of the elements that constitute the particular situation. Intitially, this list should be inclusive, even exhaustive; elements can be omitted later if analysis demostrates their role to be negligible.
2. Analyze each element, in terms of the role each played.
3. Determine the dominant element or exigence that will govern the response.
4. Analyze the response to determine if the exigence is modified and if the response is "fitting."

This is not an exhaustive list of steps in a method to be applied as a sort of "cookie cutter," but they provide a beginning point for analysis that focuses on the significance of the situation. As with any critical effort, it is the rhetorical artifact that will determine how the critical narrative develops. Situational analysis is seldom used as a stand alone tool to evaluate a rhetorical artifact; more typically, it enriches other analytical methods by providing a deeper understanding of context in all its dimensions. Only by understanding the full context of a rhetorical event can the critic comprehend and evaluate the artifact itself.

CRITICAL ESSAY

In the following essay, we treat situational analysis as an isolated tool and apply it to administration rhetoric following the September 11, 2001, terrorist attacks on the World Trade Center and the Pentagon. As a first step, we describe the situation facing the Bush administration in the period following the attacks. We follow the rhetoric of the President, as well as selected advisers and cabinet members, from his first address to the American people on September 11, 2001, through the State of the Union address in January 2002.[6] We have chosen this time period because the State of the Union represents exactly what its name implies—it is an accounting of the condition of the country, socially, legislatively, economically, and militarily (from the perspective of the current administration), as well as a preview of the short term future. Although this address itself becomes part of public knowledge, that knowledge should have developed sufficiently for the public to decide whether to accept or reject the President's accounting. Therefore, this annual address, required by the Constitution, seems a fitting endpoint for the rhetorical aftermath of the terrorist attacks on the United States.

Critical Essay: A Case Study of Administrative Rhetoric from a Situational Perspective

On September 11, 2001, nineteenth Islamist terrorists boarded four American flag airliners (two in Boston, one in Newark, and one scheduled to depart from Dulles Airport near Washington, D.C). At approximately 8:45 A.M., American Airlines flight 11 crashed into the North Tower of the World Trade Center in New York City; approximately twenty minutes later, United Airlines flight 175 flew into the South Tower. A short time after that, 9:43 A.M., American Airlines flight 77 from Dulles crashed into the Pentagon.[7] Only United Airlines flight 93 failed to reach a target, crashing into a field in Pennsylvania shortly after 10:00 A.M.[8] Moments before, at approximately 10:05, the South Tower of the World Trade Center collapsed, followed by the North Tower. The death toll was 2,752, including the passengers and crew of the two airliners.[9]

At the time of the attacks, President Bush was in Sarasota, Florida; he left immediately, flying first to Barksdale Air Force Base in Louisiana, then on to Offutt Air Force Base in Nebraska, before returning to Washington, DC. Secretary of State Colin Powell, in South America, returned to the United States. The President sent a plane for former Vice President Al Gore, who was in South Africa. Los Angeles International and San Francisco International, the destination airports for the hijacked planes, were evacuated and shut down. All airports were closed; inbound airliners were diverted to Canada; for the next twenty-four hours, there was no air traffic in the skies over the United States. All federal office buildings in Washington, DC were evacuated; Governor Pataki closed all state office buildings in New York City. The military and border patrol were placed on high alert; the Air Force flew "homeland defense" missions over Washington, DC. For Americans, the world had changed forever.

Because this essay is a situational analysis of the aftermath of these terrorist attacks, we elected to include the discourse of major administration spokespersons during the period under examination. In 1988, Young and Launer argued that, when studying the rhetoric of a Presidential administration, all parties in the administration should be included in the definition of the rhetoric, particularly in times of crisis, because the entire "text" often emerges over time, with segments assigned to various functionaries or surrogates.[10] Also, this extended discourse forms part of the situation itself, as the interplay between text and context becomes reflexive; each additional "text" or statement by an administration official becomes part of the situation within which subsequent remarks are made.

Thus, in this essay, we have identified the major architects of public knowledge and incorporated their rhetoric about the crisis into our definition of the "text" as well as the "situation" for this analysis. Our reading of the text reveals five important presidential surrogates on key topics: Secretary of State Colin Powell, National Security Adviser Condoleezza Rice, Secretary of Defense Donald Rumsfeld, Vice President Richard Cheney, and, of course, President George Bush. Each played a significant, though very different, role in the development of U.S. anti-terrorist rhetoric.[11]

If ever there was a rhetorical opportunity driven by the situation, this would seem to be it: a nation stunned, waiting for the leader to speak, anxious for a "fitting" response, seeking solace and retribution. In Bitzer's view, as noted above, it is the publics which constitute that nation who ultimately would authorize actions and policies as appropriate, and it is rhetorical leadership that would provide the information to create the public knowledge necessary to the authorization process. Analysis of administration discourse following 9/11 reveals that the two Secretaries, the National Security Advisor, and the Vice President acted as surrogates for President on three key topics: 1. Who is the enemy? 2. Who is our ally? 3. What is the appropriate response?

The remainder of this essay will proceed in two main sections. First, we will detail elements of the rhetorical situation; second, we will look at the Bush administration's rhetorical construction of the answers to the above three questions.

Elements of the Situation.   As in the case of Pearl Harbor, clearly the immediate situation was the terrorist attacks on the World Trade Center and the Pentagon. But initially the sense of the situation was incomplete. When the Japanese used carrier-based aircraft to bomb the U.S. fleet at Pearl Harbor, they did so in vessels that were clearly marked with the Rising Sun emblem of the Japanese empire. When the nineteen Al Qaeda terrorists commandeered flights out of U.S. airports and flew them into the Twin Towers and the Pentagon, they used U.S. flag civilian aircraft against U.S. targets. In the ensuing confusion, it was difficult to determine the source of the attacks. Thus the situation could not be immediately understood or responded to.

Consequently, much of the first part of the aftermath of the attacks was spent in trying to identify the perpetrators and to comprehend the elements of the situation:

The Attacks.   Four aircraft were hijacked. Two were flown into the World Trade Center buildings; one crashed into the Pentagon; the fourth airliner crashed into a field in Pennsylvania. It was assumed that the hijackers intended to fly this airplane into the Capitol building or the White House; it is believed that the passengers overpowered the terrorists and forced the plane down before it reached its intended destination. Approximately 2,900 persons died in the three "successful" attacks or their aftermath.

The Terrorists.   Initially officials did not know who the terrorists were or what organization they represented. Gradually, it was learned that they were operatives of Al Qaeda, a group headed by Osama bin Laden and based in Afghanistan. All had been in the United States for some time, some on student visas; some had taken flying lessons in places such as Florida.

The President.   George W. Bush had entered office with a cloud over his administration. He was an unknown quantity; no one knew how he would react. Generally, the media had portrayed him as being less decisive, and not as bright as many of his predecessors. He disdained foreign involvements and preferred to focus on his domestic agenda. This crisis was immediately seen as a test of his mettle as President.

The Bush Administration.   President Bush had made some remarkable appointments. He selected former Chairman of the Joint Chiefs of Staff Colin Powell as Secretary of State, the first African American to hold such a prominent position. And he picked Condoleezza Rice as his National Security Advisor, another first, as she is both female and black. Other appointments echoed the Cold War days of his father's administration as he chose many of the same persons to hold key posts, such as Donald Rumsfeld as Secretary of Defense.[12] This administration was generally seen as "hawkish" on foreign policy and not inclined to negotiate or appease friends or enemies. One of the first acts of the new administration was to abrogate the thirty-year-old ABM treaty with Russia.

What was not widely known was that some of the President's advisers had strong views about the role of America in a post–Cold War world in which the United States was the only superpower. Indeed, the views of these advisers did not become generally known until the United States was preparing to invade Iraq in early 2003, although these views were largely contained in the 2002 National Security Strategy prepared by the Bush Administration and released September 20, 2002. The essence of this position is that the United States should use its military to enforce peace in areas of geopolitical interest to the United States, including the Middle East. These ideas were first proposed in a report prepared by the Project for the New American Century, released in September 2000, so they pre-date the September 11th tragedy.[13] That document acknowledges its debt to a document drafted in 1992 under Richard Cheney, then Secretary of Defense; Paul Wolfowitz, who at the time was Undersecretary of Defense for policy, wrote the earlier report.[14] In the second Bush Administration, Wolfowitz is also part of the Defense Department.

The Intended Victims.   It is not entirely clear whether members of the Bush administration were intended victims, had the fourth plane made its way to Washington instead of ending its journey in a Pennsylvania field. Nevertheless, it is assumed that either members of the administration or members of Congress were the targets of that failed effort. President Bush was in Florida and took a circuitous route back to Washington, as procedures dictate in situations of national emergency. Vice President Cheney was taken to an undisclosed location out of potential harm's way.

Other intended victims were not as lucky, or as identifiable. The passengers on all four planes were obvious victims, and some became known for their heroism and bravery. The occupants of the Twin Towers were also intended victims, as were those at work in the Pentagon; yet they were targeted because of their presence not because of their positions or identity. Still, some of them became known for their bravery and heroism in the face of terrifying circumstances. In some cases, whole organizations were virtually wiped out: and many of those who were saved because they were not at work that morning, felt guilt for their fortunate circumstances.

One thing that is clear is that the number of casualties was far lower than first feared, due primarily to the timing of the attacks. On a Tuesday, the airliners were carrying a minimum number of passengers, and at 8:45 A.M., many had not made their way to their desks in the World Trade Center or the Pentagon.

In this instance, it is not enough to confine our description of "intended victims" to individuals who were involved, for clearly the ultimate "intended victim" of these attacks was the psychological well-being of the American people. It is the country's psyche that was under attack and the reaction of the populace was both a recognition of that fact and an attempt to deflect it.

Unintended Victims.   Many who lost their lives did not work in the WTC; firefighters, police, and rescue personnel, who were called to the scene, died in the line of duty and became, along with their colleagues who survived, instant heroes.

Financial Consequences.   Financial markets were shut down for several days; airlines suffered debilitating losses as all airports were shut down and then, when flights resumed, as the flying public stayed home in droves; New York City experienced losses due to the cleanup as well as a dramatic reduction in tourism. Some brokerage houses whose offices were in the World Trade Center lost most of their personnel in the collapse of the Twin Towers.

Geopolitical Implications.   Nation after nation offered condolences and pledged support. NATO invoked the clause in its charter that required all members to come to the aid of one. Even Russia, a former enemy, declared solidarity with the United

States on this issue. Some in the Middle East were shown on television celebrating the first major international terrorist attack on U.S. soil; most Middle Eastern governments, however, expressed unity with the fight against terrorism. Only Saddam Hussein's Iraq failed to send condolences.

In 1991, in what has come to be called "The First Gulf War," the United States military drove Iraqi forces out of Kuwait, a small oil-rich nation that Saddam Hussein had invaded. U.S. troops drove all the way to Baghdad, but stopped short of attempting to depose Hussein. Subsequently, in 1993, U.S. intelligence uncovered an Iraqi plan to assassinate former President George H. W. Bush during a visit to Kuwait.[15]

Domestic Implications.   America's Muslim population (arguably .75 to 1.5%, excluding black American Muslims) feared reprisals from angered "patriots," and, indeed, there were instances of violence against known Muslims and some who were merely thought to be Middle Eastern. In general, it appeared, at least at the beginning, that the September 11th attacks united most Americans, regardless of ethnic heritage. However, there was great concern about the price that would be paid in civil liberties for an all-out war on terrorism that included greater domestic security measures.

Ecological/Medical Consequences.   The cleanup presented an unprecedented challenge. Two 100+ story buildings had collapsed; the debris alone was several stories high. Untold numbers of bodies were buried, and the rescue efforts continued for many days, followed by attempts at recovery. Heart-rending tales were told about the rescue and recovery efforts, including the rescue dogs, whose paws were cut by the broken glass and who were depressed because they could not find anyone alive. The dust was pervasive, as was the smoke, and no one wanted to think too much about the composition of either.

Which element is dominant? All other elements are entailed in the attacks on the World Trade Center and the Pentagon. That is the exigence that demands a response, and that is the source of the questions: Who is our enemy? Who are our allies? What is the appropriate response?

However, the fact that one element is dominant does not necessarily vitiate the power of the remaining elements. Before a response can be crafted, the terrorists must be identified and located. The personalities and life experiences of the president and his advisers will also weigh heavily in the nature of the response. Bitzer writes of the "controlling exigence"; he does not, however, indicate that there is one and only one exigence. In the aftermath of 9/11, the controlling exigence is the attacks themselves, but the "fitting response" will be influenced by other elements as well.

Following the attacks, there was a flurry of rhetorical activity. Informed of the attack while speaking at an elementary school in Florida, the President immediately spoke to the nation; he provided additional remarks at Barksdale Air Force Base in Louisiana, where he stopped before returning to Washington. That evening, the President spoke to the nation on national television, promising that we would find and punish those responsible for the attacks.[16] On that first day—and those that followed—other administration spokespersons provided briefings, made statements, gave interviews. The day after the attacks, for example, Secretary of State Colin Powell appeared on all of the major morning news shows: *ABC News, CBS Morning News,* CNN, *Fox Morning News,* NBC's *Today Show,* and even National Public Radio. There was a total, concerted effort on the part of the administration to demonstrate command of the situation, a situation in which the central question—Who is the enemy?—remained unanswered.

Who Is the Enemy?   In his remarks on the evening of the attack, President Bush made that an open question with his promise to include those nations who harbor terrorists, "We will make no distinction between the terrorists who committed these acts and those who harbor them."[17] That vow was echoed over the next several days by each of the major players. Initially seen as a warning to whatever country was playing host to those who masterminded and carried out the attacks on the United States, it soon became clear that the statement was directed at a much wider audience.

Colin Powell was one of the first to reiterate Bush's pledge during an interview on *ABC News* on September 12, the day following the attacks:

> [W]hat we will especially do is go after those nations, those states, those organizations, that provide haven for this kind of activity. . . .we will make sure that all of our friends and allies and those who would be our friends who have anything to do with harboring this kind of activity will discover that they cannot have a friendly relationship with the United States if they continue to do so.
>
>   The reality is that there are nations, there are organizations out there, that give support to these kinds of terrorist activities. . . .And we're going to go after all of them.[18]

Also on September 12, Powell said much the same thing on the *CBS Morning News* when he noted, "And once this trail leads us to who is responsible, if there are nations that bear responsibility. . . for hosting them, then we will be doing something about that as well."[19]

Tony Snow, on *Fox Morning News,* asked Powell about specific countries that might be on a list of those offering aid and comfort to terrorists. "Iran, Iraq, Syria, Libya, Sudan, Afghanistan. Are any of those off the list?" Powell responded, "No."[20]

On NBC, Powell was still more specific in the following exchange with Tom Brokaw:

> **Secretary Powell:**   We are not only going after the perpetrators. We will go after those nations, states, and organizations who give them succor, who provide them assistance and give them a place from which they can launch their terrorist attacks.

> **Mr. Brokaw:**   But, Mr. Secretary, it is one thing to go after a headquarters of a terrorist organization or even its leader, but when you begin to attack the country that may be harboring them, that can change the political equation very quickly can't it?
>
> **Secretary Powell:**   Well it can, and we will be very cautious in how we might use our military strength. . . . But at the same time, these countries tend to put themselves at risk by harboring terrorist activity.[21]

In an on-the-record briefing the next day, September 13, Powell spoke specifically of Saddam Hussein. The questioner points out that of all the countries on the State Department's list of state sponsors of terrorism, only Iraq has failed to condemn the attacks on the World Trade Center and the Pentagon. Powell's response is telling, "I am not surprised. He is one of the leading terrorists on the face of the Earth, and I would not expect the slightest drop of the milk of human kindness to be flowing in his veins." Later in the briefing, Powell speaks of an expanded war:

> What I'm saying is that we are assembling the evidence that will tell us, in a way that the world will fully concur with us, who is responsible for this. And when we have done that, we will announce it. And at that point, we will go after that group, that network, and those who have harbored, supported and aided that network, to rip the network up. And when we're through with that network, we will continue with a global assault against terrorism in general.[22]

Others were making similar statements, effectively preparing the country for a long, drawn-out war against terrorism that might include military action against a number of governments, particularly in the Middle East. Secretary of Defense Donald Rumsfeld was among the most vocal. While Powell's focus seemed to be on U.S. interaction with those who harbor or tolerate terrorists, Rumsfeld spoke of strategy, as in this September 16 interview on *Fox News Sunday:*

> And the reality is that the best defense against terrorism is an offense. That is to say, taking the battle to the terrorist organizations and particularly to the countries across this globe that have for a period of years been tolerating, facilitating, financing, and making possible the activities of those terrorists."[23]

Later in the interview, Rumsfeld spoke of the relationship between the terrorists and the countries that harbor them and how the United States might handle that situation:

> **Snow:**   You said early on that we were going to have to use unconventional methods in waging this war. What were you talking about?
>
> **Rumsfeld:**   Yes. Well, I mean, if you do not have an army to go after, or a navy to go after, you have to go after the network. And you have to then also go after the countries that are harboring. Some of the countries that

are harboring terrorist networks do in fact have high-value targets. The do have capitals, they do have armies. They do have—

Snow: So you are saying, if some of those nations continue to harbor terrorists, we would not hesitate to strike high-value targets within those borders?

Rumsfeld: We have no choice. . . .[24]

Rumsfeld reiterated the message in a press briefing later that morning. The following morning on ABC's *Good Morning America,* he explained why the offensive strategy is necessary:

I think the important thing to keep in mind is that this is not a question of punishment or retaliation. This is a question of self-defense. The only conceivable way that the United States can be protected against terrorist acts of this type that take place inside of our country—and, I might add, potential terrorist attacks of considerably greater magnitude—is if we attack the problem of terrorism at its roots and go after the people who are doing it. That is what needs to be done.[25]

Again, on September 20, several hours prior to Bush's address to the nation, Rumsfeld repeated the self-defense argument in a news briefing at the Department of Defense. "The President has made clear, very clear, that this is a—considered a direct attack against the United States of America and our way of life. And he intends to provide for our defense by taking the effort to the people who are attacking the United States and those countries that are supporting that."[26]

As a security measure, Vice President Richard Cheney remained mostly out of sight during the period immediately following the attacks of September 11th. At the time of the attacks, he was taken to a secure location; for several weeks afterward he rarely appeared in public. On September 16, however, Cheney did appear on *Meet the Press,* where he gave a lengthy interview, reiterating many of the same themes posited by the Secretaries of State and Defense:

Vice Pres. Cheney: If you've got a nation out there now that has provided a base, training facilities, a sanctuary, as has been true, for example, in this case, probably with Afghanistan, then they have to understand, and others like them around the world have to understand, that if you provide sanctuary to terrorists, you face the full wrath of the United States of America. And that we will, in fact, aggressively go after these nations to make certain that they cease and desist from providing support for these kinds of organizations.

Mr. Russert: Full wrath. That's a very strong statement to the Afghans this morning.

Vice Pres. Cheney: It is, indeed. It is, indeed.[27]

Later in the interview, Russert asked specifically about Saddam Hussein:

> **Mr. Russert:**   If we determine that Saddam Hussein is also harboring ter-
> rorists, and there's a track record there, would we have any reluctance of
> going after Saddam Hussein?
>
> **Vice Pres. Cheney:**   No.
>
> **Mr. Russert:**   Do we have evidence that he's harboring terrorists?
>
> **Vice Pres. Cheney:**   There is—in the past, there have been some activities
> related to terrorism by Saddam Hussein.

The Vice President goes on to note that the current focus is on Al Qaeda; that
Saddam Hussein is "bottled up" as a result of U.S. policies vis-à-vis Iraq; and, that
we have no evidence linking Hussein or any Iraqis to the September 11th terrorist attacks.[28]

It is clear that the Bush Administration was beginning to focus on Osama bin
Laden as the mastermind of the attack on the United States. Administration comments and press questions make this clear. And, although Powell, Rumsfeld, and
Cheney echoed Bush's words in their warnings to those governments who were
considered state sponsors of terrorism, all three were very careful not to name any
specific countries or individuals, even when pressed by the media; all was left to a
hypothetical future.

Thus, for nine days, the public pondered the question of who was our
enemy. Then, on September 20, 2001, the President answered it in an address to
Congress and the nation.

> The evidence we have gathered all points to a collection of loosely affiliated ter-
> rorist organizations known as Al Qaeda. They are some of the murderers indicted
> for bombing American embassies in Tanzania and Kenya and responsible for
> bombing the USS Cole.
>
> This group and its leader, a person named Osama bin Laden, are linked to
> many organizations in different counties, including the Egyptian Islamic Jihad, the
> Islamic Movement of Uzbekistan.
>
> There are thousands of these terrorists in more than 60 countries.
>
> The leadership of al Qaeda has great influence in Afghanistan and supports
> the Taliban regime in controlling most of that country. In Afghanistan we see Al
> Qaeda's vision for the world. Afghanistan's people have been brutalized, many are
> starving and many have fled.
>
> [The Taliban regime] is threatening people everywhere by sponsoring and
> sheltering and supplying terrorists.[29]

The President then presented the following demands to the Taliban:

> Deliver to United States Authorities all of the leaders of Al Qaeda who hide in your
> land.
>
> Release all foreign nationals, including American citizens you have unjustly
> imprisoned. Protect foreign journalists, diplomats and aid workers in your country.
> Close immediately and permanently every terrorist training camp in Afghanistan.

And hand over every terrorist and every person and their support structure to appropriate authorities.

Give the United States full access to terrorist training camps, so we can make sure they are no longer operating.

These are not open to negotiation or discussion.

The Taliban must act and act immediately.

They will hand over the terrorists or they will share in their fate.[30]

And to the rest of the world:

[W]e will pursue nations that provide aid or safe haven to terrorism. Every nation in every region now has a decision to make: Either you are with us or you are with the terrorists.

From this day forward, any nation that continues to harbor or support terrorism will be regarded by the United States as a hostile regime. Our nation has been put on notice, we're not immune from attack. We will take defensive measures against terrorism to protect Americans.[31]

Thus, the Administration drew a line in the sand, warning governments that they would be considered enemies if they could not be regarded as allies.

On October 6, the President issued a "Final Ultimatum to the Taliban," reminding nations around the world of the choice presented on September 20: "Stand with the civilized world, or stand with the terrorists."[32] In defining the enemy, Bush begins by telling his audience who is not our enemy: "Our enemy is not the Arab world. . . . Our enemy is not Islam, a good and peace-loving faith. . . . And our enemy is not the people of any nation, even when their leaders harbor terrorists. Our enemy is the terrorists themselves, and the regimes that shelter and sustain them."[33] Bush then argues that the Taliban regime has made Afghanistan a haven for terrorists and notes that we will help rebuild that nation after we have rid it of the Taliban and the terrorists.

In the developing scenario, Afghanistan and the Taliban—and the planned military action against them—serve two purposes. At the same time that this action functions as retribution for the attacks on the United States, it also serves as an example to other state sponsors of terrorists of what is to come.

The next morning, Bush announced that we had begun strikes against al Qaeda training camps and Taliban military installations. Reminding his audience that there is "no neutral ground," and that the United States is "an enemy of those who aid terrorists," he also announced measures to strengthen domestic security.[34]

On November 10, Bush spoke even more directly to the governments of the world as he addressed the United Nations General Assembly. In this speech he reminds his audience that terrorists can strike anywhere and that all of them might become targets. He notes that the United States, in its actions against Afghanistan and in the future, is defending itself. And, for our purposes, most importantly, he reminds them that, "For every regime that sponsors terror, there is a price to be paid. And it will be paid. The allies of terror are equally guilty of murder and equally accountable to justice. The Taliban are now learning this lesson. . . ."[35]

Truly, the rhetorical situation had changed. As the president noted, in past wars the United States had never experienced hostilities on its own soil, with the exception of the attack on Pearl Harbor. September 11, 2001, changed that reality and made clear that the United States is vulnerable like any other country.

Unlike the past fifty years, there was no stable frame for viewing this conflict, for terrorists do not owe allegiance to one single government, nor are they the instrument of a nation-state. Governments generally act in predictable ways, because they have an investment in the status quo. Governments often can be swayed through inducements or threats because there is much to gain or lose. Although Afghanistan and other countries harbor and support terrorists, the groups are scattered throughout the world and often move between countries. Thus, President Bush made clear what his spokespersons had been hinting at, namely that any number of nations were potential targets of U.S. retaliation.

When the United States began military action against Afghanistan in early October 2001, over forty nations supported the attacks. Nevertheless, on September 23, 2001, Condoleezza Rice told Tony Snow on *Fox News Sunday* that the President believed he had the authority to take whatever action he felt necessary to defend the nation, regardless of whether there was international support. "There was an attack on the United States, an act of war against the United States. The United States has the right to self-defense. That is fully recognized in international law. The right to self-defense is recognized by the United Nations itself."[36] Referring to President Bush's statement on September 20 that countries are either "with [the United States] or against us," Rice reiterates, "if you sponsor terrorism, you are hostile to the United States." The notion of self-defense, posited early in the rhetorical run-up to hostilities, was essential to U.S. plans to prosecute a wider war against terrorism.

Snow did not ask Rice about any specific country, but later that same day, Wolf Blitzer of CNN did: "Is the U.S. setting its sights on Saddam Hussein and Iraq, as well as Afghanistan?"[37] In response, Rice refers to the president's September 20th speech to a joint session of Congress, "The President made it clear . . . that this is a broad campaign."[38] She continued:

> Now, there has to be an initial phase to this campaign. And the initial phase focuses on the Al Qaeda network and the country that harbors them most nearly, which is the Taliban and Afghanistan. But clearly, when you talk about rooting out terrorism broadly, you're going to look at where terrorism exists—global terrorism exists, how it's supported, who supports it, and step-by-step you're going to have to go after all of those bases for terrorism.

When Blitzer asks whether Iraq might be stage two, Rice responded:

> Stage two—first of all, let me just say, stage one has already begun. There will be some military operation undoubtedly as a part of this. The president has told the

armed forces to get ready. We will see what happens with other states that harbor terrorism. We will see what we do about other threats to American interests.[39]

The rhetorical situation surrounding U.S. relations with the Middle East had changed enough that the door was left open virtually from the moment the attacks occurred for the war on terrorism to spread more widely.

On October 15, Rice appeared on the Arab network, Al Jazeera, and identified Saddam Hussein of Iraq as an enemy of the United States. The arguments she made to the interviewer presage those that would be repeated by various administration spokespersons and by the President himself over the next several months.

> Iraq has been a problem not just for U.S. policy, but for policy in the region, as well. . . . This is a country that has threatened its neighbors, that has been harmful to its own people. And we believe that our policies toward Iraq simply are to protect the region and to protect Iraq's people and neighbors.

The interviewer asked expressly about military action and Dr. Rice responded:

> The President has made very clear that the war on terrorism is a broad war on terrorism. You can't be for terrorism in one part of the world and against it in another part of the world. We worry about Saddam Hussein. We worry about his weapons of mass destruction that he's trying to achieve.
>
> There's a reason he doesn't want U.N. inspectors—it's because he intends to acquire weapons of mass destruction. But for now, the President has said that his goal is to watch and monitor Iraq; and, certainly, the United States will act if Iraq threatens its interests.[40]

Rice becomes increasingly specific on the subject of Iraq in subsequent interviews and press briefings. For example, on November 8, 2001, in response to a question about Iraq she comments:

> [T]he President's made very clear that Iraq remains a threat to American interests, to interests in the region, and to Iraq's neighbors and its own people. That was true before September 11th, that's true now.
>
> The Iraqis have been trying to acquire weapons of mass destruction. That's the only explanation for why Saddam Hussein does not want inspectors in from the U.N. . . . There is plenty of reason to watch Iraq, there is plenty of reason to make very clear to the Iraqis that the United States does not intend to let the Iraqis threaten their own people, threaten their neighbors, or threaten our interests by acquiring weapons of mass destruction.[41]

Rice was not alone in identifying Iraq as an enemy and a potential target. Indeed, caught up in the grief and horror of the September 11th attacks, most Americans did not notice the steady question and answer, "call and response" antiphonal on Iraq. All of the major players mentioned in the beginning of this essay—Rice, Rumsfeld, Powell, and even Vice President Cheney made the same points. In fairness, it was the media who asked the specific questions about Iraq; Administration spokespersons merely responded to those questions. But the opening was provided by the repetition of Bush's warning to those nations that harbored or supported terrorists.

Thus, in the weeks and months leading up to the State of the Union Address in January 2002, the American people heard and saw the Secretary of State, the Secretary of Defense, the President's National Security Advisor, and the Vice President argue for a wider war, a longer, more drawn-out conflict than it appeared the Afghan engagement would be.

The President, too, joined in making the case for an all-out war on terrorism. In his first remarks following the attacks, Bush had promised to "hunt down those folks who committed this act"—perfectly reasonable comments and within the bounds of what is expected in situations such as this.[42] By the time he landed at Barksdale Air Force Base, the President had been told of the plane that had crashed into the Pentagon, and he amended his remarks slightly, saying, "The United States will hunt down and punish those responsible for these cowardly acts."[43] But by that evening, when he went on television to address the nation, Bush had expanded the target, saying, "We will make no distinction between the terrorists who committed these acts and those who harbor them."[44] It is this perspective on the task before us that became the mantra of administration spokespersons—including the President—over the days and months leading up to the State of the Union Address on January 29, 2002.

The 2002 State of the Union Address.   Obviously, the rhetorical situation in which a speech occurs is the accumulation of events and discourse that has preceded it and that necessitates its creation. In this instance, the State of the Union is mandated by the Constitution as a recounting of the condition of the nation at the beginning of each year.[45] Thus, the President was compelled by law and by custom to speak to the Congress and, by extension, to the American people about the state of affairs. In 2002, the dominant consideration was the terrorist attacks of September 11, 2001, and the subsequent war on terror. Not surprisingly, then, the President began by recounting the immediate state of affairs, "As we gather tonight, our nation is at war, our economy is in recession, and the civilized world faces unprecedented dangers." However, a State of the Union address is never downbeat, and Bush quickly moved to lighten the tone of the evening: "Yet the state of our Union has never been stronger." This was followed by a recounting of what we had accomplished at home and abroad in countering the effects of terrorism. The speech then segued to a discussion of the task ahead. After mentioning the action in Afghanistan, Bush reiterated the theme of the past four months—that as long as there are nations that harbor terrorists, "freedom is at risk. And America and our allies must not, and will not, allow it."[46]

At this point in the speech, Bush introduced a new note, making mention of chemical, biological, or nuclear weapons as potential threats in the hands of terrorists. Up to this point, the only real mention of chemical–biological warfare had been in terms of Saddam Hussein's known efforts to secure such weapons. This is the first time that the general possibility of weapons of mass destruction had been inserted into the discussion of the war on terrorism. "Our second goal is to prevent regimes that sponsor terror from threatening America or our friends and allies with weapons of mass destruction. Some of these regimes have been pretty quiet since September the 11th. But we know their true nature."[47] There was a sentence about North Korea, which had been much in the news as that government threatened to resume development of nuclear weapons; a sentence about Iran being a exporter of terror; and a paragraph about Iraq, its attempts to develop weapons of mass destruction, its use of poison gas against its own citizens, and its refusal to allow international inspections. "This is a regime that has something to hide from the civilized world."[48]

> States like these, and their terrorist allies, constitute an axis of evil, arming to threaten the peace of the world. By seeking weapons of mass destruction, these regimes pose a grave and growing danger. They could provide these arms to terrorists, giving them the means to match their hatred. They could attack our allies or attempt to blackmail the United States.
>
> We will work closely with our coalition to deny terrorists and their state sponsors the materials, technology, and expertise to make and deliver weapons of mass destruction. . . . And all nations should know: America will do what is necessary to ensure our nation's security.
>
> We will be deliberate, yet time is not on our side. I will not wait on events, while dangers gather. I will not stand by, as peril draws closer and closer. The United States of America will not permit the world's most dangerous regimes to threaten us with the world's most destructive weapons.
>
> We can't stop short. If we stop now—leaving terror camps intact and terror states unchecked—our sense of security would be false and temporary. History has called America and our allies to action, and it is both our responsibility and our privilege to fight freedom's fight.[49]

Most of the remainder of the speech was devoted to the ways in which the war on terrorism would be reflected in the budget that would be presented to Congress, and to Bush's plan to turn around the economy to provide the security that only a strong economy can bring. Mindful of the helplessness most Americans felt in the face of the events of the past several months, Bush also gave his domestic audience actions to take so they could help make things better. He announced the creation of the USA Freedom Corps, a volunteer effort designed to bolster homeland security, rebuild communities, and extend the promise of the Peace Corps. It is a principle of effective persuasion that the advocate must give the audience something that it is within his or her power to do. In this portion of the speech, Bush asked his audience to build on the efforts that followed the September 11th attacks and volunteer their time and expertise to accomplish these goals. Building on the unity that had developed four months earlier, he noted that common danger erases old rivalries, not only within the country itself but between the United States and nations such as Russia and China.

Finally, he brought the speech back to where it began, to the choice that lay before the United States and every other nation, reminding them of the road that lay ahead.[50] What is interesting about this passage and those that precede it is the way in which the entire speech is a culmination of the rhetoric that had been building since September 11th.

- From the first hours following the attack, the administration promised to go after those who harbored and provided succor to terrorists, though no countries were mentioned by name.
- On September 20, the President made clear that those who were not with us in this effort would be considered enemies of the United States.
- A few days later, Vice President Cheney indicated that such countries would experience the "full wrath" of the United States.
- On October 7, the President pointed out that Afghanistan was an object lesson to those who would harbor terrorists.

Meanwhile, highly visible members of the Bush Administration, including the Secretary of State, the Secretary of Defense, and the National Security Advisor, were consistently repeating the same message. And, while no specific countries were named by these spokespersons, in response to questions from the media about Syria, Iran, and Iraq, there were no denials. Thus, the naming of North Korea, Iran, and Iraq in Bush's speech represents a direct warning to those regimes that, in Bush's words, "constitute an axis of evil."[51]

Part of the rhetorical situation of a speech is what the speech itself creates for future rhetorical action. Clearly, President Bush was preparing the United States for a long and drawn-out war on terrorism, as he and his administration had been doing since 9/11. However, a close reading of the totality of administration rhetoric in the period between September 11, 2001, and January 29, 2002, reveals that the administration was preparing the public for the next stage in this battle, the doctrine of preemptive action.

Consider the arguments: The United States was brutally attacked; like any country, the United States has a right to defend itself. The United States does not need the permission of the United Nations to defend itself. Terrorists exist in more than sixty countries. They are harbored and aided by the governments of certain states, including Iraq. These governments are trying to develop weapons of mass destruction, which they could make available to the terrorists in their midst. The terrorists could use these weapons to threaten or even attack America and/or its allies. The only way to defend against terrorism is to take the war to the terrorists before they mount more attacks on U.S. soil. To the extent the terrorists are protected by states, those states have declared themselves enemies of the United States.

By blurring the distinction between the terrorists and those who support their existence, the Bush administration also succeeded in confusing the public about who was responsible for the attacks on the World Trade Center and the Pentagon, thus making it easier in the months ahead to transfer responsibility for terrorism to any number of unfriendly regimes. With the "axis of evil" announcement in the State of the Union Address, Bush identified North Korea, Iran, and Iraq as potential sites of future hostilities in the war against terrorism. Indeed, the arguments recounted above are essentially those used by President Bush in March 2003, as he announced the U.S. invasion of Iraq.[52]

PERSONAL COMMENTS ON THE ESSAY

As with any critical essay, there are a number of analytic approaches that can be taken in examining the rhetorical artifact. Indeed, it is unusual for situational analysis to be used alone: so in another context, we would probably combine it with one or more additional critical tools. One that we might have chosen is the narrative approach—what story is told by the Bush Administration about the attacks, the terrorists, and the U.S. response? How do the details of this story resonate with the American people? What does internal logic obtain, and how does it mesh with public knowledge about such events as terrorist attacks?

Another approach might have been framing. Although this method is generally used when studying the media treatment of an event such as a speech, in this instance we might have used it in connection with situational analysis to examine how the Administration framed the acts and our response to them. This analysis would be similar to using the narrative approach, so we might have combined all three.

Yet another way to look at this artifact would be through the Burkean lense, combining Kenneth Burke's notions of identification, consubstantiation, and portions of the Pentad with situational elements. This would be particularly salient, since Burke's ideas about situation undoubtedly informed Lloyd Bitzer's.

We elected to do a straight situational analysis primarily for simplicity. To incorporate other lenses would detract from the power of the situational analysis. The aftermath of the September 11, 2001, terror attacks was dominated by the situation—the exigence of the attacks—yet, in some respects the situation was constantly evolving. We were intrigued by the roles played by the presidential surrogates and felt that this would be a fruitful analysis, one that would be overlooked by other critics.

POTENTIALS AND PITFALLS

The beauty of situational analysis is that it allows the critic to account for outside forces that impact a rhetorical event in ways that other methods do not. If we recognize that all rhetoric is situated—that it is dependent for meaning on the time, place, and circumstances in which it occurs—then situational analysis allows us to view rhetoric as an organic phenomenon. We are then able to view differently those rare instances of discourse that transcend the situation and live on in national memory.

Situational analysis also allows us to examine the choices a rhetoric makes in constructing a particular discourse. Those choices are ultimately influenced by the situation in which the discourse arises—whether ceremonial or as a result of crisis. It also combines naturally with a number of other critical perspectives, allowing the critic to construct a richer, more robust analysis.

The downside of situational analysis is that it is seen by some as mechanistic. The idea of the exigence is viewed by some theorists as robbing the rhetor of invention. In Bitzer's view, the exigence calls forth rhetoric to craft a fitting response: and if the response is not deemed fitting, the response is not rhetorical. Although this is a pretty shallow view of situational analysis, it does cause some to reject its utility as a critical tool.

There is also the possibility that the critic might overlook elements that are not part of the situation but that would illuminate the rhetorical artifact, such as logical elements, rhetorical devices, or fallacies. Finally, the critic must not lose sight of the fact that the rhetor is responsible for what is said, regardless of the forces that impinge on his or her rhetorical choices.

SITUATIONAL ANALYSIS TOP PICKS

Benoit, William L. "The Genesis of Rhetorical Action," *The Southern Communication Journal,* 59:4 (Summer 1994): 342–355. In this essay the author argues that critics and theorists should overlay Kenneth Burke's notion of scene and purpose onto Bitzer's ideas of exigence and constraints. Benoit views Burke's framework as superior to Bitzer's, but notes that the language of situation has entered the critical lexicon.

Bitzer, Lloyd F. "The Rhetorical Situation," *Philosophy and Rhetoric,* 1 (1968), 1–14. This is the essay where Bitzer first explains situational analysis.

Bitzer, Lloyd F. "Rhetoric and Public Knowledge," in Don Burks (ed.) *Rhetoric, Philosophy, and Literature: An Exploration* (West Lafayette, IN: Purdue University Press, 1978), 67–94. In this essay Bitzer discusses his theory of public knowledge: how cultural truths are absorbed by groups and used to acknowledge new information and authorize action in response to rhetorical situations.

Bitzer, Lloyd F. "Functional Communication: A Situational Perspective," in Eugene E. White, (ed.), *Rhetoric in Transition: Studies in the Nature and Uses of Rhetoric* (University Park: Pennsylvania State University Press, 1980), 21–38. Bitzer responds to his critics and offers some modifications of his theory.

Bitzer, Lloyd F. "Rhetorical Public Communication," Critical Studies in Mass Communication, 4:4 (1987): 425–428. Bitzer discusses public communication, focusing on "journalists as a new and important class of rhetors."

Garrett, Mary and Xiaosui Xiao, " 'The Rhetorical Situation' Revisited," *Rhetoric Society Quarterly,* 23:2 (1993): 30–40. Garrett and Xiao seek to expand situational theory, in this case by applying it to nineteenth-century Chinese political discourse. Examining the rhetoric surrounding the Opium Wars, Garrett and Xaio suggest alterations in our understanding of the rhetorical situation.

Grant-Davie, Keith. "Rhetorical Situations and Their Constituents," *Rhetoric Review* 15 (Spring 1997): 264–279. Grant-Davie argues that the roles of rhetor and audience are dynamic and interdependent. Audience as a rhetorical concept has transcended the idea of a homogenous body of people who have stable characteristics and are assembled in the rhetor's presence.

Kuypers, Jim A., Marilyn J. Young, and Michael K. Launer, "Of Mighty Mice and Meek Men: Contextual Reconstruction of the Iranian Airbus Shootdown, *Southern Journal of Communication* 59:4 (Summer 1994): 294–306. This essay uses situational criticism to examine the rhetoric surrounding the incident in 1988 when United

States forces shot down an Iranian passenger airliner in the Persian Gulf.

Patton, John H. "Causation and Creativity in Rhetorical Situations: Distinctions and Implications," *The Quarterly Journal of Speech*, 65 (1979): 36–55. Patton notes that exigences, although necessary conditions for rhetorical discourse, are not, in themselves, sufficient conditions. Underlying this argument is the assumption that "rhetoric is essentially historical," and that it is through invention and creativity that the rhetorical situation—including exigences and constraints—is appropriately addressed, producing the "fitting response" that every rhetor seeks.

Smith, Craig R. and Scott Lybarger, "Bitzer's Model Revisited," *Communication Quarterly*, 44:2 (1996): 197–213. The authors discuss responses to Bitzer's theory and describe Bitzer's own attempts to refine it. What is most significant to Smith and Lybarger, however, is that Bitzer, in his refinements, opened the door to a more complex view of perception and situation. Smith and Lybarger test the revised model against the anti-drug speeches of President George H.W. Bush.

Young, Marilyn J. "Lloyd F. Bitzer: Rhetorical Situation, Public Knowledge, and Audience Dynamics," in *Twentieth Century Roots of Rhetorical Criticism*, Jim A. Kuypers and Andrew King, eds. (Westport, CT: Praeger, 2001), 275–301. In this essay the author reviews the criticisms of Bitzer's work and argues that most of his critics have underestimated the power of the theory of situation. Bitzer's theory gains power and becomes more complete when considered in conjunction with his ideas about public knowledge.

Young, Marilyn J. "When the Shoe is on the Other Foot: Comparative Treatments of the KAL 007 and Iran Air Shootdowns." In *Reagan and Public Discourse in America*, Barnett Pearce and Michael Weiler, eds. (Tuscaloosa: University of Alabama Press, 1992), 203–224. The author compares the media treatment given two international incidents: when Soviet forces shot down a Korean airliner in 1983 and when U.S. forces shot down an Iranian passenger airliner in 1986.

NOTES

1. Lloyd F. Bitzer, "The Rhetorical Situation," *Philosophy and Rhetoric* 1 (1968): 6. According to Miriam-Webster On-Line, "exigence" [exigency] is "that which is required in a particular situation."

2. See, Franklin Delano Roosevelt, "A Day That Will Live in Infamy," at http://www.americanrhetoric.com.

3. Lloyd F. Bitzer, "Rhetoric and Public Knowledge," in Don M. Burks, ed., *Rhetoric, Philosophy, and Literature: An Exploration* (West Lafayette, IN: Purdue University Press, 1978), 67–94.

4. The only speech that can be set outside this description is the Gettysburg Address.

5. See http://www.americanrhetoric.com.

6. We owe an enormous debt of thanks to Kathleen Farrell's research assistant, Andrea Davis, who compiled all of the data on which this analysis is based.

7. The death toll for the Pentagon is 184. This figure was taken from the story at http://www.pbs.org/newshour/terrorism/sept11/pentagon.html. This figure includes the passengers and crew of American Airlines flight 77; it does not include the hijackers.

8. All 40 passengers and crew perished in the crash. This figure is found at: http://onenews.nzoom.com/onenews_detail/0,1227,232081-1-9,00.html.

9. This is the figure as of October 29, 2003, accessed at www.cnn.com. It does not include the hijackers.

10. Marilyn J. Young and Michael K. Launer, *Flights of Fancy, Flight of Doom: KAL 007 and Soviet-American Rhetoric* (Lanham, MD: University Press of America, 1988).

11. This is not to suggest that there were not other spokespersons, for indeed there were. General press briefings did not always include one of the principals; some military figures, such as Gen. Myers, Chairman of the Joint Chiefs of Staff, gave briefings; various assistant secretaries, such as Paul Wolfowitz also spoke to the media. But it is clear that Powell, Rumsfeld, Rice, Cheney, and, of course, President Bush, took the lead. Thus, we have confined our analysis to them.

12. Condoleezza Rice had also served during the first Bush Administration, though in a lesser capacity than her current post.

13. See Jay Bookman, "Bush's Real Goal in Iraq," *Atlanta Journal & Constitution,* September 29, 2002, p. F1. Bookman points out that many of the authors of the Project's Report are currently in the Bush Administration, including Wolfowitz, who wrote the 1992 document. Donald Kagan, one of the authors of the Project document, disputes Bookman's conclusions, but does not deny the provenance of the policy. See Donald Kagan, "Reaction to 'Bush's Real Goal in Iraq'," *Atlanta Journal-Constitution,* October 6, 2002, p. F1. The Project for a New American Century can be accessed at: http://Thenewamericancentury.org. The title of the report is "Rebuilding America's Defenses."

14. See Bookman, online version, p. 3. Accessed at: http://nl.newsbank.com/nl-search/we/Archives.

15. David von Drehle and R. Jeffrey Smith, U.S. Strikes Iraq for Plot to Kill Bush, *Washington Post,* Sunday June 27, 1993, p. A01. Accessed at: http://www.washingtonpost.com/wp-srv/inatl/longterm/iraq/timeline/062793.htm.

16. George W. Bush, "Address to the Nation," September 11, 2001. Accessed at www.whitehouse.gov/news/releases/2001.

17. George W. Bush, "Address to the Nation," September 11, 2001. Accessed at www.whitehouse.gov/news/releases/2001.

18. Colin Powell, "Interview by ABC News," September 12, 2001. Accessed at www.state.gov/secretary/rm/2001.

19. Colin Powell, "Interview on CBS Morning News," September 12, 2001. Accessed at www.state.gov/secretary/rm/2001.

20. Colin Powell, "Interview on Fox Morning News with Tony Snow," September 12, 2001. Accessed at www.state.gov/secretary/rm/2001.

21. Colin Powell, "Interview on NBC's Dateline," September 12, 2001. Accessed at www.state.gov/secretary/rm/2001.

22. Colin Powell, "On-the-Record Briefing (1300 hours)," September 13, 2001. Accessed at www.state.gov/secretary/rm/2001.

23. Donald H. Rumsfeld, "Secretary Rumsfeld Interview with Fox News Sunday," September 16, 2001. Accessed at www.defenselink.mil/news/Sep2001.

24. Donald H. Rumsfeld, "Secretary Rumsfeld Interview with Fox News Sunday," September 16, 2001. Accessed at www.defenselink.mil/news/Sep2001.

25. Donald H. Rumsfeld, "Secretary Rumsfeld Interview with ABC Good Morning America," September 17, 2001. Accessed at www.defenselink.mil/news/Sep2001.

26. Donald H. Rumsfeld, "DoD News Briefing," September 20, 2001. Accessed at www.defenselink.mil/news/sep2001.

27. Richard Cheney, "The Vice President Appears on Meet the Press with Tim Russert," September 16, 2001. Accessed at www.whitehouse.gov/vicepreisdent/news-speeches.

28. Richard Cheney, "The Vice President Appears on Meet the Press with Tim Russert," September 16, 2001. Accessed at www.whitehouse.gov/vicepreisdent/news-speeches.

29. George W. Bush, "Address to Congress and the Nation," September 20, 2001. Accessed at www.Washingtonpost.com.

30. George W. Bush, September 20, 2001.

31. George W. Bush, September 20, 2001. In this speech, the President also announced the formation of the cabinet-level Office of Homeland Security and named Tom Ridge, Governor of Pennsylvania, to head it. Ridge was sworn in the day after hostilities began in Afghanistan.

32. George W. Bush, "Final Ultimatum to the Taliban," President's Radio Address, October 6, 2001.

33. George W. Bush, October 6, 2001.

34. George W. Bush, "Operation Enduring Freedom Begins: President Bush's Statement on U.S. Strikes in Afghanistan." October 7, 2001.

35. George W. Bush, "President Bush Speaks to the United Nations: Remarks by the President to United Nations General Assembly," November 10, 2001.

36. Condoleezza Rice, Fox News Sunday, September 23, 2001. Accessed at www.americanrhetoric.com.

37. In fairness, this was in reference to a *Wall Street Journal* editorial stating, "The terrorist threat won't vanish until Saddam does."

38. Condoleezza Rice, "CNN Late Edition," September 23. 2001. Accessed at www.americanrhetoric.com.

39. Condoleezza Rice, "CNN Late Edition," September 23. 2001. Accessed at www.americanrhetoric.com.

40. Condoleezza Rice, October 15, 2001; released by U.S. Department of State.

41. Condoleezza Rice, "National Security Advisor Briefs the Press." November 8, 2001. Accessed at www.whitehouse.gov/news/releases/2001.

42. George W. Bush, "Remarks by the President After Two Planes Crash into World Trade Center," September 11, 2001. Accessed at www.whitehouse.gov/news/releases/2001.

43. George W. Bush, "Remarks by the President Upon Arrival at Barksdale Air Force Base," September 11, 2001. Accessed at www.whitehouse.gov/news/releases.2001.

44. George W. Bush, "Statement by the President in His Address to the Nation," September 11, 2001. Accessed at www.whitehouse.gov/news/releases/2001.

45. Indeed, the State of the Union need not be a speech, and for the early part of U.S. history was a letter delivered to Congress. Only in the twentieth century did it become customary for the President to deliver the message in person in the form of a speech to a joint session of Congress. With the advent of television, the speech become an annual event in which the President outlined his plans for the coming year.

46. George W. Bush, "State of the Union Address," January 29, 2002. Accessed at www.whitehouse.gov/news/releases/2002.

47. George W. Bush, "State of the Union Address," January 29, 2002. Accessed at www.whitehouse.gov/news/releases/2002.

48. George W. Bush, "State of the Union Address," January 29, 2002. Accessed at www.whitehouse.gov/news/releases/2002.

49. George W. Bush, "State of the Union Address," January 29, 2002. Accessed at www.whitehouse.gov/news/releases/2002.

50. George W. Bush, "State of the Union Address," January 29, 2002. Accessed at www.whitehouse.gov/news/releases/2002.

51. George W. Bush, "State of the Union Address," January 29, 2002. Accessed at www.whitehouse.gov/news/releases/2002. Interestingly, Syria is not mentioned by Bush.

52. There is evidence to indicate that the Bush administration decided to go to war against Iraq in the late Fall of 2001, after the hostilities in Afghanistan had essentially concluded. See John B. Judis & Spencer Ackerman, "The Selling of the Iraq War," *The New Republic,* June 30, 2003. Accessed online at http://www.tnr.com/docprint.mhtml?l=20030630&s=ackermanjudis0. See also, Barton Gellman & Walter Pincus, "Depiction of Threat Outgrew Supporting Evidence," *Washington Post,* August 10, 2003, p. A01.

CHAPTER FIVE

THE "TRADITIONAL" PERSPECTIVE

FORBES I. HILL

Traditional criticism is usually taken to mean criticism guided by the theory of rhetoric handed down from antiquity.[1] Although this theory takes several different shapes and forms, they are mostly variations on a theme–that although rhetoric describes reality and does not create it, people's perceptions of the real world can be changed by persuaders who insist that their own perceptions are more accurate or, at least, more advantageous to themselves or to the public interest. The tools for changing other peoples' understanding of reality are arguments that can be analyzed by a rhetorician and are in some cases found to be effective, though spurious. Arguments are presented in language, which in most cases is believed to have more impact when it keeps perspicuity but is made attractive with artfully plotted phrasing. Normally, the arguments are marshaled in a compelling order and presented to the listeners by speakers who have mastered the art of paralinguistic features (varying volume or rate of speaking, for example) and the art of kinesics (using the body to convey meanings and emotions).

Up through the Renaissance, it was assumed that most written documents were merely reflections of oral presentations; the reader could distinctly hear the sound of the human voice behind the alphabetic characters on the page. Therefore traditional rhetoric was easily applied to writings, especially those intended for the popular audience. Recently some critics have used traditional theory to explain advertisements, propaganda, docudramas, and even novels and films, especially those with a covert propagandistic purpose. This is, of course, not a new idea. In the early 1920s, Hoyt Hopewell Hudson advocated broadening the paths of rhetorical study to include radio, pamphleteering, newspapers, radio broadcasting, and others—what he called commercial rhetoric. The importance of this was stressed in the "Field of Rhetoric": "with modern wielders of publicity to observe, and with the increasing use of a method for sending human speech broadcast, so that a speaker may address thousands where he once addressed scores, the significance of persuasive discourse is continually being enhanced." Along these same lines,

Hudson provided clues for still other venues of critical endeavor: "Editorial writing . . . the immense business of advertising and the still more immense business of propaganda,—these are occupations which modern rhetoricians may follow."[2]

Traditional Criticism

A traditional rhetorician assumes that criticism entails both explication of what went on when speakers engaged listeners or readers and evaluation of how well the speakers performed the task of changing these receivers' understanding of reality. These twin tasks, explication and evaluation, together comprise the rhetorical critique. In its simplest form it is a critique of the assumed interaction of a speaker with his audience or an author with his readers at a particular point in time. But in their more complex forms rhetorical critiques may be used to explicate and evaluate the performance of several speakers or writers engaged in a campaign or perhaps a social movement; for example, a study of the changing rhetorical arguments in the campaign for abortion reform during the twentieth century.

Aristotle, often considered the fount of traditional criticism, was no doubt thinking of the interaction of an individual with a particular audience when he set out the elements which we today use for analysis: "A discourse involves three factors: the speaker, the matter about which he speaks, and the persons to whom he is speaking."[3] If we add to this, as most rhetoricians do, the occasion on which the speech is given, it is still a simple plan for a critique. This plan may be made more inclusive by using slightly more complex terms that are near synonyms for the four factors. In place of the term *speaker,* for example, we often use *source,* by which is meant ghost writer, public relations agent, campaign committee, or advertising team.

In place of matter about which one speaks, modern writers use the term *message;* that is, whatever matter is formulated for transmission to others. In place of persons who are addressed, even Aristotle used the term audience. The audience is understood as the group of people who have similar reactions to the message. In modern cases these auditors may not even be in the same space as the person presenting the message; they may be reading the message in a book, or receiving it via radio, television or the internet.

For occasion the term *context* is now used. Traditional criticism is highly contextual; it looks at source, message, and audience as they interact within a given span of time. Not all criticism is like that; a generic critic may look at a rhetorical work as representative of certain conventions that are nearly the same through many ages. For example, if he is examining speeches of self-defense, he may look at examples from Socrates to Nixon and note that wherever possible sources will deny that the defendant ever did what he is accused of doing. If, on the other hand, denial is impossible, they will state that everybody does it, and probably add that if seen in the proper context what the defendant did is not wrong anyway.[4]

Looking at it that way decontextualizes the message: Whoever generates it, whether from the West Coast or the East, has to adopt one of these well nigh universal lines. But, in its purest form, traditional criticism is not much concerned with the universality of lines of argument. Its "point of view," Herbert Wichelns wrote, "is patently single. It is not concerned with permanence, nor yet with beauty. It is concerned with effect. It regards a speech as a communication to a specific audience, and holds its business to be the analysis and appreciation of the orator's method of imparting his ideas to his hearers."[5] Even if one expands this notion of audience to include a number of related groups of people, targets of a persuasive campaign for example, he is still dealing with *effect*—that is, analysis and appreciation of the method used by strategists planning the campaign to impart their ideas to these people over this limited period of time.

Wichelns's concern with effect follows Aristotle's statement "the audience is the end—the reason for making the discourse."[6] Aristotle believed that all natural activities are directed toward some end state: *telos* in his language; hence his philosophy is said to be teleological. He thought that the *telos* of any activity was its purpose for being and defined its essential nature. This orientation is basic to traditional criticism. Some utterances may be entirely self-expressive; crying "ouch" when one touches a hot stove, for example. Rhetorical utterances, however, are not primarily expressive; they are made holding in the forefront of the mind the impact they will have on other people they seek to impress one's ideas upon the minds of the audience. They are the product of strategic choices about how the speaker wants auditors to respond.

An account of the audience logically comes first when one is composing a critique of a rhetorical event. Nevertheless, it is in practice difficult to start a highly contextualized critique, such as the one a scholar writes, without answering the question, "When does this audience come into being and under what conditions?" Reconstructing the audience is inseparable from determining the context of a rhetorical production.

What follows is an overview of how one might begin a crticism that uses traditional criticism. We do not wish to imply that all critical efforts of this nature follow this exact pattern. The majority of traditional critiques do, however, touch upon the following areas, which for the sake of convenience we present as steps. These are: recreation of the context; recreation of the audience; description of the source of the message; the analysis of the message; and the evaluation of the discourse.

Recreating the Context of Rhetorical Events

The first step in a traditional critique is to reconstruct the context in which the speech occured. Context is often divided into two parts: the physical setting for the event or events, the so-called *mise en scene,* and the social and political context out of which the need for using rhetoric arose.

An oft-cited example in traditional criticism is Abraham Lincoln's Gettysburg Address. Why did President Lincoln go to speak at Gettysburg? One reason is that the state of Pennsylvania had planned a ceremony dedicating a cemetery right on the battlefield where many thousands had fallen. Near the field, but somewhat removed from the burial operations, a platform was erected on which sat numerous important political figures. The audience, numbering some 20,000, stood near rows of graves in the crisp November sun. Is this *mise en scene* important? Definitely so in this case. The fact that Lincoln was facing the field of battle and the graves is a controlling factor over the speech: "We are met on a great battlefield of that war; we have come to dedicate a portion of that field as a final resting place. . . ."

In a more contemporary example, President Clinton's first apology to the Nation should be considered. The setting was important enough to his purpose for the President to make specific refrence to it in his speech: "This afternoon, in this room, in this chair, I testified before the Office of Independent Counsel and the Grand Jury. . . ."[7] Often, however, the setting is not so important. If a contemporary president makes a statement from the NBC studio in a large city, a description of the scenery may actually get in the way of creating an adequate critique. The studio might be anywhere; the important question, aside from whether he's in prime time, is what was the political situation that this administration thought required a presidential speech?

Although the actual scene is often described, the social or political context must also be described. For example, Lincoln could have turned down the invitation to appear at Gettysburg. As Garry Wills noted, he was not the featured speaker; the ceremony was centered on a great oration to be delivered by another. Lincoln was in a busy period of his presidency, overwhelmed by the various duties of the office and by the cares of his family life. He chose to go to Gettysburg because of the importance of the occasion: It was the celebration of a battle where many lives had been lost. It was also an opportunity to make news in anticipation of the coming presidential campaign. But above all, it was time for him to put his spin on the significance of the war, to prepare for the postwar period of reconciliation. He dropped everything to take an exhausting train journey to the battlefield.[8] This is the political context of his speech.

For the critic, creating the political context is often a difficult task. Out of all the events in the life of the speaker and the history of the times, which are those that determine the rhetorical situation? Answering this question becomes even more difficult the further removed one's rhetorical artifact is from the present day. The critic simply cannot reproduce a complete account of an era as the jumping off place for his critique. For example, it is obviously important to President Roosevelt's War Message that the Japanese made a surprise attack on Pearl Harbor, but is it also important that Japan had an alliance with Germany, that the Japanese imperialists had been occupying territory throughout Asia for many years, that American political and business interests in Asia were compromised, that a large peace movement had prevented America's planning for war, that people were psychologically unprepared for war, and that many people were distracted by the military victories of Germany? A narrative about all these factors could overwhelm a critic's account of the War Message itself. Probably the important factors in this case have to do with how complacent Americans were and how startled they became at the unexpected attack, along with their sense that the attack was completely undeserved. These are the factors that Roosevelt assumed and developed in his message. The effect various factors have upon the message should usually be the principal criterion for their inclusion in the section of an essay that recreates context.

Constructing Audiences for Rhetorical Events

The people receiving a message are collectively known as the audience. Traditional rhetoric regards them as free agents who make largely rational choices about the matters at hand. Their choices are influenced by their emotional states, but even the most manipulative of traditional rhetoricians do not assume them to be infinitely malleable. Traditional rhetoricians divide audiences into three kinds: They are jurors in a court of law, who decide about a public or private action that took place in the past (forensic discourse): they are legislators who decide about some course of action to be taken in the future (legislative discourse): or they are spectators who come to experience a celebration or commemoration of some person or event—that is, a ceremony in the present (epideictic discourse). Aristotle, at least, emphasized the audience's function as decision makers; even the auditors at a ceremonial speech, who primarily serve as spectators at a performance, in the final analysis are judges of the expedience and inexpedience of decisions made by those who are praised or blamed.[9]

The second step in a traditional critique, then, is to decide which of these kinds of audience a speaker was asking to make a decision. Often this choice is obvious as in the case of Roosevelt's War Message, which ends: "I ask that the Congress declare that since the unprovoked and dastardly attack by Japan on Sunday, December 7, 1941, a state of war has existed between the United States and the Empire of Japan." But though it is certain that the War Message was a speech to a legislature about a course of action in the future, the same cannot be said of the Gettysburg Address. What decision did Lincoln expect his audience to make? To care about the honored dead? They already cared—cared enough to have come in most cases from far away. Even those who read his speech in the newspapers undoubtedly cared at a time when everyone had a relative who fought in the war.

Lincoln also recommended a course of action, that we "take increased devotion to the cause for which they gave their last full measure of devotion." Does this phrase's orientation to the future make the speech deliberative? After a careful examination of text and context, Gary Wills judged it to be a speech that changed people's attitude toward the war: No longer were they to be caught up in the blood and guts of the fray, or even the contentiousness that brought on the war. They were to transcend such matters, which go unmentioned in the address, to see the war as a necessary phase in the nation's progress toward a more perfect Union. If we accept this interpretation, then it is clearly a ceremonial speech. It does not aim at a decision about some imminent course of action. By praising the common sacrifice of all those who struggled in the battle of Gettysburg, it aims to change people's whole belief system from one that dwells on the strife to one that is oriented to the making of peace. Use of praise and blame to forge the auditors into an audience that agrees on common values, such as peace and progress, is what ceremonial addresses are all about.

The choice of the kind of audience at which the discourse is aimed is in this case, as well as others, not obvious. Making that choice requires careful examination of the text as well as the context. This examination is complicated when rhetorical productions are designed to change the perceptions and beliefs of more than one group of people, as is often the case in modern times. For example, President Clinton's August 17, 1998, speech of apology. This speech addresses several distinct groups, and is in response to numerous competing political and social contexts. In antiquity, one could conceive of the audience as those citizens in the popular assembly, mostly male native born speakers of a common language, but even in early modern times, speakers began to aim at an audience that read the speech as well as those who heard it. With the advent of mass media, 24-hour news coverage and the internet, the concern with audience takes on especial importance for the critic.

A famous address in 1766 by William Pitt, the elder, illustrates this situation in its simplest form. Mr. Pitt, asking for unconditional repeal of the Stamp Act, took the American position that Parliament had no right to raise a revenue in the colonies without consent of their representatives. The Americans read about his speech in their colonial newspapers where it was presented as if a new revelation; they showed their approbation by naming half a dozen towns within a few years for Pitt. The address totally failed of its object in Parliament, which passed the so-called Declaratory Act as part of the repeal. But it did not fail among the Americans who read it. Wasn't Pitt aiming at this audience of readers? He was known to desire any step that would bind the colonies to the mother country, and this may have been as much his object as to convince the legislature at home.

Back to Lincoln and Gettysburg. We can assume that Lincoln knew that many more people would read his speech than hear it. His message, which undoubtedly owed a great deal to the *mise en scene,* would not have had a chance at reinterpreting the war had it not been read by every literate American. Roosevelt's War Message, ostensibly addressed to Congress, was heard on the radio by millions; its brevity and simplicity is a clue that it was intended to be a deliberative speech aimed at a decision by the larger audience of Americans. The War Message, heard in schools and churches and public buildings throughout the country, may have been one of the last speeches where members of the media audience were in contact with each another. President Clinton's apology went out over the major news networks during prime time; its message was designed to speak to everyone who heard it. However, then as now, an address by a great public figure is heard by an audience totally fragmented—a collection of individuals. Does this make a difference? Traditional criticism seems forced to answer this question in the negative. Here is a rationalization for this position.

Any analysis of the audience is a construct. Let us say that a speaker's audience is the U.S. House of Representatives: 435 members from 50 states. That is a diverse group, and even in the age of maximum information one can hardly know empirically what the range of individual opinions is, especially since there are always some curmudgeons that defy classification. A rhetorical strategist needs to make a profile: most are not young, none are poor (Congressional salary is $154,700 per year—in the top 5% income bracket); almost all affect some kind of Judeo-Christian religious belief, almost all are either committed Democrats or Republicans; most desire to be reelected; none of them reveal the whole truth about themselves. This profile is based on a minimum of real data. It is what Aristotle would call *probability:* that is, what one would reasonably expect about people elected every two years as Representatives. Since some improbable things actually happen, we also expect that several members do not now and never will fit the profile, but we ignore them. Given the right subject, for example, war with Iraq, the Congress can be forged into something that approaches a unity; they can become a true audience. Even though bickering about Iraq is now (2004) commonplace, the House (296–133) and Senate (77–23) voted to authorize President Bush to use U.S. military force to make Iraq comply with U.N. resolutions.

Though the media audience is fragmented, can we construct it in the same way we constructed the Congress? Some considerations are obvious: If the source is the head of a large adminstration, there are some potential supporters out there, as well as some who are disposed to oppose. We have some data about them: There are polls, both formal and informal, and sometimes focus groups. The polls are often broken down demographically: Regions of the country are separated; the young are separated from those in their prime and the elderly; the wealthy from the middle class and the poor; and women from men. Aristotle provides some probable statements characterizing these groups. He states that the young are sanguine and expect life to become better for them; the elderly are more skeptical having often experienced failure. The wealthy expect to control affairs; the poor tend to expect disappointment.[10] Although Aristotle did not characterize women as distinct from men, modern pollsters do tabulate data for women and contrast that to men. Such hints about the ages and fortunes of people provide us with materials to refine polling questions and to better interpret polling data.

From polling data and Aristotle's character sketches, a critic can construct a profile of the fragmented media audience. The profile, if carefully made, will probably be nearly as accurate as one's profile of a divided Congress. The critic operating from a traditional perspective should search biographies and accounts of journalists to find out how the speaker conceived of the audience so that he can contrast the speaker's construction with potentially more accurate ones.

Describing the Source of the Message

The third step in traditional critique is to describe the source of the message. Traditional rhetoricians have historically thought about the source as a singular person—an orator skilled in the art of speaking. The roster of speakers who fulfilled that vision is almost, but not quite, congruent with the list of great statesmen. A few exceptions can be noted, Thomas Jefferson was not much of a speaker, but for his time he was an exception. Most orators wrote their own speeches, perhaps with a little editorial help. From this point of view it makes sense to ask questions, such as: What was the nature of the orator's unique personal charm? What was his education? And what were the orator's peculiar qualifications as thinker and stylist? What obstacles did the orator overcome on the road to rhetorical celebrity? Such questions are the stuff of rhetorical biography. It is still a pleasure to read a short biographical essay—one which touches the peaks of a man or a woman's speaking career. When done well, it makes the reader consider himself a close watcher of a great career.

Historical figures may still be treated this way. Imagine a retrospective of Franklin D. Roosevelt: his home schooling directed by an imperious mother, his editorship of the *Harvard Crimson*, his mediocre performance in law school, his dashing entrance into politics, his marriage to the woman who became a truly re-markable public figure in her own right, his overcoming a crippling illness to reestablish an impossible political career, his use of that remarkable voice to com-pensate for an inability to move around the platform, his discovery of radio, his adventurous spirit that explored the map of expedients and proposals as a navi-gator explores new galaxies, and yes, his confidence that bordered on arrogance making him at times a divisive figure. Such an essay can never go out of date.

As exciting as a rhetorical biography can be, though, it is only a small part of a traditional critique. Going back to antiquity one finds the personality of a speaker thrust strangely into the background. Dionysius of Halicarnassus, who left us a number of well-developed critiques, illuminates the life of the speaker in only a sentence or two. What he develops instead is the speaker's construction of a public image, his *ethopoeia;* he avoids any implication that he is constructing a true character.

In *Rhetoric,* Aristotle presents copious materials from which a discourse should be composed: lines of argument, directions for logic, systems of values, and clues as to how to bring auditors into emotional states, such as anger. When he comes to talk about the speaker, he presents only a minimum theoretical frame-work for developing *ethos.* The three sources of *ethos,* he says are good sense, good character, and good will, since people disbelieve speakers either because they think them senseless, or of such bad character that they do not give their true opinions, or they lack good will toward the auditors so that even being sensible and honest they do not say what they think. That is all that Aristotle says about the speaker.

In recent times a speaker is likely to serve as a spokesman for an organiza-tion: He is a cabinet member or public relations officer of an agency or corpora-tion. The message he delivers is not his own; even if the speaker drafted it, numerous others in the organization have edited it and revised it to the point where it has become a message put together by a committee. And the text of the message is probably given out to the newspapers before the speech is delivered. Take the July 13, 2003, comments made by National Security Advisor Condolezza Rice. She spoke to both *Fox News Sunday* and *Face the Nation.* During these talks she stated: "The president took the nation to war to depose a bloody tyrant who had defied the world for twelve years. . . ."[11] Rice was speaking for President Bush and his administration, not for herself.[12]

Under these circumstances it no longer makes sense to ask about the speaker's education, or his unique language choices. The question is, what kind of a committee of writers put together the message? What interests did they represent? For a president this often means State versus Defense, for example. How did the writers work together and interface with the spokesman? The question about *ethopoeia* is still relevant: What does the text show about how they built a favorable public image for the spokesman? How did committee and spokesman construe what would build credibility? Covering these factors are what we now mean by describing the source.

It's still relevant to ask: Did the spokesman deliver the message with conviction? With a flair? Did he or she show great energy? Was he or she serious or lighthearted? Did he or she dominate the audience and seem to reach into their hearts? Appropriate delivery is itself a source of credibility. Think of Franklin D. Roosevelt's voice when he declaimed, "The only thing we have to fear is fear itself." Think of President Bush's vocal and physical expression of great determination as he insisted that Iraq must be disarmed. These are important elements of the traditional critique.

Analyzing the Message

The fourth step in a traditional critique is the actual analysis of the message itself. Traditional rhetoric begins its consideration of the message by asking about the text—a written document that recreates what a speaker said to that audience on that particular occasion. (Traditional rhetoricians do not use the contemporary redefinitions of the concept of text, to which you will be exposed in later chapters.) If one is going to consider questions of proof or of rhetorical style, it is desirable to have an accurate account of the verbal utterance of the moment or, at least, of what the author intended a reader to read.

Often a good text is available; some independent agent has made an audio or video recording.[13] We should be alert if the recording or document is available only from the source. Texts are often edited; it is well attested that Congressmen may revise the Congressional Record at any time until the printing presses start to move. Often a speaker will be asked to write out his remarks for publication after the presentation. The text of Lincoln's remarks at Gettysburg are admittedly slightly changed from what he actually said. The importance of finding a reliable text is well exemplified by this example: The text published by the *Boston Globe* of Professor George Wald's signature utterance, *A Generation in Search of a Future*, furnished to the newspaper by the speaker does not contain the lines italicized in the quote given below:

> Nobody is the aggressor any more except those on the other side. *And this is why that, that Neanderthal among Secretaries of State—Rusk—went to such [applause]—went to*

such pains, went to such pains, stuck by his guns, because in him, uhh, stubbornness and density take the place of character, [laughter] uhh, went to such pains to insist as he still insists that in Vietnam we are repelling an aggression. And if you're repelling an aggression, anything goes.

This characterization of Dean Rusk is grotesquely unfair; he never held that if you are repelling an aggression, anything goes, and he did not resemble Neanderthal man. Professor Wald apparently had second thoughts when he edited this passage out of the version he gave the press. The independent recording put out by Cadmon Records gives what he said unedited.[14] It also shows why the unedited version is important: Wald received by far the most vociferous reaction to these statements of anything else in his speech. They resonated wildly with an audience of 1960s radicals who were united in their hatred of established authority figures such as the Secretary of State. What you know from other sources about Wald's audience is amply confirmed.

Another example details how important it is to obtain the primary document and not rely on secondary sources or press accounts. On November 8, 1997, President Clinton spoke at a fund raiser sponsored by a homosexual advocacy organization, the Human Rights Campaign. At one point in his speech he was interrupted by a member of the audience who yelled, "People with AIDS are dying." The president responded with what appears to be a spontaneous addition to his planned remarks: "People with AIDS are dying. But since I've become President we're spending ten times as much per fatality on people with AIDS as people with breast cancer or prostate cancer." If one were only to rely on reports of the press, one would never know that the president uttered these highly controversial words.

For instance, the *Los Angeles Times* wrote that as he "spoke, Clinton was interrupted twice by AIDS activists. . . . Clinton said, 'I'd have been disappointed if you hadn't been here tonight. People with AIDS are dying. But since I became president, we're spending ten times as much on AIDS research and treatment programs.' " *The New York Times* wrote that the president faced one man who "cried out, 'People with AIDS are dying!' " The crowd hushed him, but Mr. Clinton chuckled. 'I'd have been disappointed if you hadn't been here tonight,' he said. He added, 'People with AIDS are dying, but since I became President we're spending ten times as much' combatting the disease." Not one major paper reported the rest of the President's controversial sentence. The full text is only available from the White House.[15]

Historical speeches pose an even more difficult problem. The text of the Attic orations derives from copies made by the orators as examples for use in the schools of rhetoric. Naturally, the orators transmitted to the schools only the fairest texts of what they said. Speeches in the eighteenth and early nineteenth century House of Commons and House of Lords were mostly recreated by reporters who stood closely packed in the galleries where they were not supposed to make transcriptions of the proceedings. The Lincoln–Douglass debates were collated from newspaper reports by Lincoln; it is small wonder that his speeches look more finished in the received text than Douglass's. The traditional critic will often need to make a caveat about most speeches: "I don't vouch for every word of the text; I worked with the best text available."

Traditional rhetoric considers the message itself under the headings of invention, disposition, and style. By invention is meant the finding of appropriate materials for the discourse. This is usually done by checking through an inventory of stock materials—topics—looking to see whether the speaker has used all available means of persuasion, as Aristotle put it. Topical thinking is a type of systematic brainstorming using predefined categories. Although developed in ancient times, more recent applications are available. For example, John Wilson and Carroll Arnold developed sixteen topics for the contemporary student. These include the "existence or nonexistence of things"; "degree or quantity of things, forces, etc."; spatial attributes"; "attributes of time"; "motion or activity"; "form, either physical or abstract."[16] By disposition is meant the arranging of these materials in a structure as well plotted as the order of battle when skilled generals make a plan for victory. Structure can be influenced by many factors, although it is generally agreed upon that your audience, topic, and purpose play a deciding role. By style is meant the use of the right language to make the materials of exposition and argument clear and convincing. We will now consider each of these in turn.

Invention.   When a critic seeks to investigate invention, he is dealing with both artistic and inartistic proofs. Artistic proofs are the invented proofs, the ones that lie within the art. They are created by the speaker, the arguments that he uses to try to persuade the audience. They are usually, if somewhat inaccurately, grouped under the headings of logos, ethos, and pathos. Inartistic proofs are not created by the speaker, but instead exist on their own: contracts, wills, or other documents, for example.

In relation to *logos,* the critic should look to see whether the appropriate commonplace arguments, deduced from the list of topics, have been used. Logos refers in general to logic based on reason. This is not a scientific logic, but rather a rhetorical logic, one based upon probabitily rather than scientific demonstration. Technical arguments for the popular audience are to be avoided; spokesmen need to look at those based on common notions of what is probable. To prosecute a company for spreading toxic waste, one looks for the green water and brown air in the neighborhood; the prosecutor seeks out people who claim to be sick and compares them to those in comparable areas who are not sick. He points to the prevalence of cost cutting among companies who look at the bottom line and the absence of witnesses and regulators and the arrogant behavior of company executives. These are the commonplaces of environmental claims, and failure to use them should be construed as not making the most effective speech possible.

Although there are many ways to examine the logic used in a speech, one particularly important aspect to be examined is the concept of the enthymeme. The essence of the enthymeme is that some parts of the logical argument are omitted when the speaker or writer can predict that the auditors will supply them. Take this example from Richard Nixon: "The American people cannot and should not be asked to support a policy which involves the overriding issues of war and peace unless they know the truth about that policy. Tonight I would like to answer some of the questions that I know are on the minds of many of you listening to me."[17]

This is a typical example of an enthymeme that builds the speaker's credibility and that also requires the listener/reader participation in supplying a crucial missing term. Presented as a traditional syllogism this would look like this:

> *Premise:* All policies that the American people should be asked to support are policies about which they will know the truth.
> *Premise:* The policies that I reveal when I answer your questions are policies that the American people should be asked to support.
> *Conclusion:* The policies that I reveal when I answer your questions are policies about which you will know the truth.

Nixon's actual statement is making the claim that he will tell the truth about his policies. He says that people should not be asked to support them unless they will know the truth about them. Although I supplied all three parts of the syllogism, Nixon never actually explicitly claims that he is going to tell the truth. The second premise I give is actually not stated by Nixon; rather, one is tempted to supply it: and if the auditor supplies it, the very activity of completing the logical structure starts the process of the auditor assenting to the argument. As Lloyd Bitzer wrote: "Enthymemes occur only when speaker and audience jointly produce them. . . . Because they are jointly produced, enthymemes intimately unite speaker and audience and provide the strongest possible proofs. . . ."[18] That process will be completed unless the auditor checks himself and looks at it. He is more likely to yield to the process because the formal logic behind this argument is good enough, though the second premise is unsupported and probably false.

Persuasive discourse is constructed so that there are a number of *ethos* claims like this one. Ethos is basically an interpretation by the audience of qualities possessed by a speaker as the speaker delivers his or her message. Thus, by the way a speaker argues, an audience makes judgments about his or her intelligence, character, and good will. A speaker becomes unpersuasive if he has to claim directly, "I am not a crook." or "I did not have sexual relations with that woman. . . ." If he needs to state it in this bald way, he has already lost credibility. An exposition of how a speaker establishes ethos is a significant part of a traditional critique. Sometimes the discourse will contain a narrative of the discovery of the right course of action. Such a narrative shows the good sense of the spokesman and his advisors who did not make decisions off the top of their heads, but only after consideration and reflection. The way in which a speaker supports his arguments and organizes his materials can impact the assessment of his intelligence. Very often his character—moral qualities—can be assessed by how qualities such as justice, courage, generosity, and so on are exhibited in his arguments.

Finally, a speaker could also show good will by finding common ground with the readers/listeners. The speaker who comes to campus tells us, "I remember when I was a student; like so many of you I didn't have enough time in the day to do everything. I worked part time in the dining room and stole away to the quietest corner of the library every night. But hard as that was, it was worth it." Speakers also indulge in a little subtle flattery: "[Y]ou who have a university education easily recognize that group behavior differs from individual behavior." Commenting on such statements is part of a traditional critique as it relates to ethos.

The first step in dealing with *pathos* in the critique is identifying the emotional states that dominate the discourse. The speaker's words will invite us to feel a particular way. Sometimes this is obvious. In the case of Roosevelt's War Message the emotional states are anger and confidence. The anger springs from our sense of betrayal by an inferior people from whom we are entitled to receive respect. The confidence comes from our feeling of unity and our sense of righteousness. Roosevelt amplified the sneakiness of the attack and the innocent lives lost to bring people into a greater state of anger, and he represented himself as speaking for all our people who recognize the facts of Japanese aggression which are so obvious that they speak for themselves. When auditors are angry enough they minimize feelings of fear; they become ready to accept with confidence hardships and sacrifices: Hence, the above listed *pathe* are the stuff of War Messages.

Another example is seen in the 2003 commercials for the Christian Children's Fund. These commercials begin with images of poor children in truly impoverished conditions. Many of the children are shown playing in what might well be open sewege; many have flies around their eyes, and walk with distended bellies. This is quickly contrasted with images of those children helped by this charity: better clothing, healthier looking, and so forth. All this in the background reinforces the same verbal message by the speaker. Your emotional register goes from pity and perhaps guilt to hope. A critic would look for these emotional appeals and determine their effectiveness toward moving us along toward doing whatever it is the speaker wishes us to do. In the case of the Christian Children's Fund, sponsor a child.[19] In contrast, the dominant emotional state in the Gettysburg Address is less obvious, thus more difficult to find. Perhaps the calm and elevated tone of the address should give us a clue. The pathos is the opposite of anger; in Aristotle's terminology that is gentleness. Auditors feel gentle when the factors that produce anger remain unamplified to the point that they are forgotten. And we feel gentle toward those who in the future are willing to participate with us in accomplishing the great task that lies before us.

Disposition.   The critic must also ferret out dispositon, or the speech's organization as it relates to persuasion. In almost no case is a discourse arranged randomly, though occasionally a speech writer will try to make it appear random. Roosevelt's War Message, Stelzner points out, falls almost into two halves, separated by the sentence "As Commander in Chief of the Army and Navy I have directed that all measures be taken for our defense." All material prior to that sentence is in the past tense and the Japanese empire is the actor. What follows that sentence is in the present tense; the President, Congress and the people become the actors.[20] Such is the disposition of this celebrated speech.

Take Lincoln's Address at Cooper Union for another example; it divides into three parts: first, a forensic section in which the speaker refutes the belief that Congress could not constitutionally legislate as to slavery in the Federal territories; then a shorter constructive section on the idea that Republicans are the ones who perpetuate the constitutional doctrines of the Founding Fathers, it's the Southerners who have made a radical change; then the shortest section, a little deliberative speech to Republicans exhorting them to act with restraint while refusing to compromise their basic ideals. Accusation to constructive defense to exhortation (in long, shorter, and shortest sections) is the pattern for disposition in the Cooper Union Address. There ought to be some discernible rationale, as in the cases cited, for the disposition of the materials of the discourse. It is the task of the critic to figure out that rationale.

Style. Traditional criticism treats the language of the discourse as dressing for the arguments. That is not to say that critics do not think of it as essential, but it is essential in the way that clothing is for the person, for warmth and for identification or to enhance or perhaps deemphasize sexuality. In most cases, clarity is assumed as the cardinal virtue of style. This is because traditional rhetoricians thought transmission of information to be necessary to achieving the ends of rhetoric. Clarity is achieved with factors such as using common words, avoiding jargon, creating metaphors that make matters vivid, using active verbs, and avoiding more than the minimum of adjectives. The speaker on conflict who uses such locutions as "the optimum moment of contact" is probably not persuading as well as one who says "timing's important; there's a right moment for everything." That is, of course, unless the audience is composed of those predisposed to accept a specific technical vocabulary. When Thomas Paine refutes the argument that America has flourished under her former connection with Great Britain by writing, "We may as well assert that because a child has thrived upon milk that it is never to have meat," he chooses a metaphor that is both concrete and familiar.[21] Observations of this sort are the meat of traditional criticism in relation to clarity of style.

Working against this preference for the common word unmodified by numerous adjectives is the notion that style should be impressive—that statements should have a certain heft to give an idea presence. That is also a precept of traditional rhetoric; the style of public address is never colloquial, though it may be deliberately kept simple. So the speech writer is to make a certain admixture of long words and a few unusual ones; he is occasionally to look for a unique way of phrasing something even amid the clichés.

Clarity and impressiveness are also to be gained from figures of syntax: parallel structure of clauses and sentences and the devices that reinforce it. When Lincoln declaimed, "Fondly do we hope, fervently do we pray that this mighty scourge of war may speedily pass away," he created a syntactical structure that speaks seriously; it is hard, however, to sing it to a merry tune. The contrast of hope and pray (antithesis) would be entirely broken up if he had said, "Fondly do we hope and we also pray fervently." Fondly and fervently, too, must be in the same grammatical position in each clause; then the alliteration works to reinforce the structure. The rhyming of pray and away (epistrophe) is also important to the structure. Traditional rhetoric views this artistry in structuring prose as a significant part of rhetorical effectiveness.

The rhetorical critic should also check to see that the style of the discourse is appropriate to subject and audience. When Senator Douglas in the middle of a discussion of slavery states that his opponent, Lincoln, "could ruin more liquor than all the boys of the town together," he was clearly not speaking appropriately to the subject.[22] Similarly, when a professor gives a highly technical lecture to a group of ordinary people he is violating the criterion of appropriateness to the audience.

Summary.   When looking at the message, a critic will look to see whether the discourse is deliberative, forensic, or epideictic. Deliberative discourse is concerned with the future, and its auditors are asked to make judgments about future courses of action. Forensic discourse is concerned with past acts, and its auditors are asked to make judgments concerning what actually happend in the past. Epideictic discourse is set in the present, and concerns speeches of praise or blame. Its auditors are being asked to make judgments concerning how well the speaker accomplishes his goals.

Generally, a critic looks for three items in a text: invention, disposition, and style. Under invention, a critic looks to see how well the speaker created his rhetorical appeals; were all the available means of persuasion used? Both artisic—logos, ethos, and pathos—and inartisic proofs will be examined. A critic wil also look hard at the disposition or organization of a speech, to determine its impact upon persuasive effect. Finally, a critic will look at the style of the speech. How might the language choices made impact the persuasive effort?

Evaluating the Discourse

Aristotle lays down the rule that a discourse should be judged by whether it uses sound method; indeed, "it is not the function of rhetoric to persuade but to observe the available means of persuasion for situations like this one, just as in all the other arts. For example, the function of medicine is not to make healthy, but to bring the patient as far toward health as the case permits. For sometimes it is impossible to bring health, but one must give sound treatment."[23]

If he follows this rule, the critic goes through a checklist of the available lines of argument to see if any are omitted that might persuade this audience on this subject; he considers the possible ways of disposing the narrative and arguments to see if the best way has been used; he looks at the stylistic devices that clothe the arguments to see if there are others more appropriate to the situation. If everything is done, he is ready to render a judgment: this must be the best discourse— or, possibly, it falls short in the following ways. Regardless, there is a certain concern with the aesthetics involved with the speech making process: How well were the arguments constructed? Was the message well organized? And was the style used appropriate for the specific audience?

In practice, almost no critic is wholly satisfied with this kind of purely internal critique. Almost invariably critics add some kind of external measure: The legislature did not pass the bill. The jury did not convict. The voters did not elect the candidate. The president gave a speech on the economy, and the stock market rose or fell. These *effects* are the simplest indicators of success, but anyone knows that they are often misleading. Sometimes legislators have commitments that make it impossible for them to respond even to the most finely crafted speech. Some juries will nullify the law because of their sympathy for the defendant even though the presentation of the case has been artistically satisfactory.

We may look to somewhat more indirect measures as well: The legislature took up the bill next session or the one after, and without much additional debate passed it. The jury did not convict, but all the editorial writers agreed that they should have. The stock market immediately reacted like a bear to the president: but two weeks later the bull market began, and it ran a long course. Take, for example, Susan B. Anthony, who was the center of controversy throughout most of her life, but never lived to see woman's suffrage. When the suffrage amendment finally passed, she was honored as the ancestor of all suffragettes. These historical results are, perhaps, more just indications of the success or failure of a persuasive campaign than a decision made in the midst of the struggle. George Orwell's critique of the totalitarian tendencies of the modern state did not result in the overthrow of any totalitarians, but it has become a standard against which states are judged. The use of Orwellian language is almost universally taken as the sign of approaching danger.

Thus a critic using the traditional perspective will discuss the speech's internal dynamics, but also touch on its impact on its audience. Rhetoric, viewed from a traditional perspective, is used for a purpose: it is intentionally created, and this is taken into consideration when a critic offers an evaluation. A thoughtful discussion of the historical context and some speculation on the influence of the discourse forms the conclusion of a traditional critique.

CRITICAL ESSAY

Much of the writings of those who used traditional criticism assumed a general knowledge concerning the classical roots of the rhetorical theory that underpinned the criticism. The essay that follows proceeds along the same path. Instead of a fully developed review of literature this essay instead focuses upon putting into practice the steps of traditional criticism outlined above. You should be aware, however, that if you are writing for an academic audience that you most likely will need to take time to define your terms and outline your theoretical perspective. You can ask your instructor for guidance here.

When reading this essay, look for the reconstruction of context, the construction of audience, a discussion of the source (speaker), and an analysis of the message. In this last section, look in particular for a discussion of invention, disposition, and style. Finally, look for an evaluation of the rhetorical artifact.

Critical Essay: Mr. Douglass's Fifth of July

Following the Compromise of 1850 the abolitionist movement, somewhat dispirited by the failure to block the Fugitive Slave Law, renewed its efforts to publicize the evils of slavery. In Rochester, New York, which was a center of anti-slavery activity, the Rochester Ladies Anti-Slavery Society decided to mark Independence Day 1852 with their own celebration featuring an address by their neighbor, the famous abolitionist speaker Frederick Douglass. The celebration was held on July 5th since the 4th fell on a Sunday, and the custom of that era prohibited secular events on the Sabbath.

The Rochester Ladies rented Corinthian Hall, where five to six hundred people assembled, having paid 12 cents each as entry fee.[24] After the opening prayer and a reading of the Declaration of Independence, Mr. Douglass made his presentation: "What, to the Slave, is the Fourth of July?" His recitation, according to Frederick Douglass's paper, was "eloquent and admirable, eliciting much applause throughout." Before the meeting was adjourned, "A Request was . . . made that the Address be published in pamphlet form, and seven hundred copies were subscribed on the spot." It was also published in Frederick Douglass's paper on July 9 and many times subsequently. Perhaps we should now consider it an American classic. It is especially appropriate to make a critique like this using the standards of traditional rhetoric because Mr. Douglass and many in his audience were familiar with these standards.

The Audience.   In constructing Douglass's audience, let us first ask, who is to make a decision about what? Those immediately before the speaker were abolitionists, their sympathizers, and their friends. Many of them were followers of William Lloyd Garrison, with whom Douglass had recently made a rancorous break. Douglass demanded that they condemn slavery—not just in an intellectual way, but with an emotional fierceness that would keep them agitated until it was abolished. What the audience might have expected on the Fourth of July was a speech praising our ancestors, our country, and our people. In an astonishing reversal Douglass gives them a discourse of uninterrupted blame: a true epideictic speech of vituperation.

If the audience before him consisted of anti-slavery zealots, it was nevertheless not of one mind about how slavery was to be ended. A special group of auditors were strict Garrisonians, who believed that the Constitution supported slavery. Therefore, it should be wiped away: and a new Republic without the South should be established to avoid any contact with the evil of slavery. Others present took a more centrist position, and some may have been opponents of slavery only in the sense that they thought it an evil whose spread should be prevented. The auditors were united enough in their anti-slavery sentiments that Douglass could give a speech so critical of the Republic that no patriot would sit still for it. A different audience, even in the North, might have driven him from the platform.

But what of the reading public, the ones who got the speech from the papers and pamphlets? At first the address was carried only by the abolitionist papers; there Douglass could be assured of a favorable response. Soon it was published as a pamphlet, probably circulated mostly to abolitionists and those to whom they were proselytizing. The pamphlet certainly had no circulation in the South. Three years later an extract containing the most impassioned parts of the Fourth of July oration was made an appendix to Douglass's second autobiography, *My Bondage and My Freedom*. In this form it enjoyed a national circulation. A measure of acceptance by the larger audience was guaranteed by the indubitable fact: The American Revolution did not bring freedom to the slave. On the other hand, there must have been an ample number of readers irritated by the insult to our great national holiday. We can reasonably conclude that the oration aimed at energizing the friendly rather than converting the hostile.

The Spokesman.   By 1852, Frederick Douglass was well known as a speaker: He had traveled throughout the Northeast and the middle states as a fulltime agitator for the Massachusetts Anti-Slavery Society from 1841 to 1845. Born in 1817, he spent the first twenty-one years of life as a slave. Nevertheless, he learned to read and write as a child. In his autobiographies he tells the story of getting an important book, *The Columbian Orator*, used in the schools as a source of precepts exemplified by extracts from speeches and dramas. In 1838 he escaped from the plantation, making his way north to Massachusetts. He changed his name from Frederick Augustus Washington Bailey: but after publication of the first autobiography, *Narrative of the Life of Frederick Douglass, an American Slave*, his cover was blown. He could have been arrested as an escaped slave. He fled to England, where he lectured on temperance and abolition until his freedom was bought from his old master in 1847. In England, he became the most glamorous spokesman for the anti-slavery cause—the one who spoke from first hand experience and with great fervor and eloquence. On his return, "a series of enthusiastic reception meetings was held to honor him; he completely dominated the annual meeting of the American Anti-Slavery Society, held on May 11, 1847; and two weeks later his co-workers installed him into the Garrisonian establishment by electing him president of The New England Anti-Slavery Society."[25]

Douglass's first autobiography went through four editions in the year of its publication. Loren Reid explains its success on the grounds that it appeared at a time when the narrative form was becoming increasingly popular, as evidenced by the sales of novels and travelogues and by the popularity of evangelical sermons which relied more on Biblical narrative than direct argument.[26]

The sponsors of the Fourth of July celebration in 1852 knew what they were doing when they made Frederick Douglass their main speaker. He was at the height of his oratorical powers in 1852, a physically impressive figure, obviously strong and vital with a large head of hair, not yet gray, and a resonant baritone voice. He could be counted on to give a good show, as he had many times before.

It hardly needs to be said that the whole ceremony was built around that good show the orator was expected to give. In the nineteenth century, as Gary Wills has remarked, the orator at a public celebration was intended to be a virtuoso performer who presented a long speech replete with rhetorical flourishes. Anything less would disappoint the people who came to celebrate.[27] Douglass was conscious of his obligation to perform: "I have been engaged in writing a Speech," he wrote Gerritt Smith after the fact, "for the 4th July, which has taken up much of my extra time for the last two or three weeks. You will readily think that the Speech ought to be good that has required so much time."[28]

Disposition and Summary of the Speech.   Douglass's exordium is given over to a conventional expression of modesty: "He who could address this audience without a quailing sensation, has stronger nerves than I have. I do not remember ever to have appeared as a speaker before any assembly more shrinkingly, nor with greater distrust of my ability, than I do this day." In this case, as in most such expressions in eighteenth- and nineteenth-century orations, such expressions must be taken ironically. The speaker could not have failed to know that he was among the dozen most celebrated orators of his time.

Douglass organized the central section of this address on the principle of contrast between *then* and *now*. The first third of it consists of conventional praise for what happened in the past. He does what any 4th of July orator would be expected to do: celebrate the birth of the nation. This occasion is to you "what the Passover was to the emancipated people of God." It is "easy now to flippantly descant on how America was right and England wrong, but when your fathers first talked this way, they were accounted plotters of mischief, agitators and rebels, dangerous men." They petitioned the throne, but the British government kept its course, with "the blindness which seems to be the unvarying characteristic of tyrants since Pharaoh and his hosts were drowned in the Red Sea." One can view this section like a classicist, as an historical narration; or one may see it as the first part of the section that is usually called the proof (which naturally follows assertions); in either case, the reason for praising the courage of the Fathers is to prepare for a contrast with contemporary politicians, and the reference to the Passover and to Pharaoh is meant to cue us to the denunciation of slavery to come. Typically, in conventional speeches these historical narrations are used for foreshadowing.

Suddenly Douglass switches gears: He no longer speaks about then but now and announces his subject, "American Slavery." He identifies himself as a speaker for the bondman, who knows that America is false to the past, false to the present, and solemnly binds herself to be false to the future. "What have I, or those I represent, to do with your independence. . . . The sunlight that brought life and healing to you has brought stripes and death to me. This Fourth is yours not mine. You may rejoice; I must mourn. . . . I do not hesitate to declare, with all my soul, that the character and conduct of this nation never looked blacker to me than on this 4th of July!" The rest of the proof is taken up by a development of the blackness of character and conduct of the nation.

The arguments used to justify slavery are mere rationalizations, not even worthy of serious refutation. He makes outstanding use of the figure *paralepsis,* claiming not to be refuting these arguments, while in fact making a summary refutation of each.[29]

> Must I undertake to prove that the slave is a man? Of course not; it is beyond doubt: [Y]ou hold him responsible for crimes like other humans. Laws in most Southern states forbid teaching him to read. No one makes such laws about the beasts of the field. When the dogs in your streets, when the fowls of the air, when the cattle on your hills, when the fish of the sea and the reptiles that crawl shall be unable to distinguish the slave from a brute, then will I argue with you that the slave is a man!

He claims not to make the arguments that he has made. Is not man entitled to liberty? That's not a matter to be debated by Republicans, to be settled by logic and argumentation. "How should I look today, in the presence of Americans, dividing and subdividing a discourse, to show that men have a natural right to freedom?" With a magnificent *ad hominem,* Douglass concludes that he cannot argue this (though he has) because: "There is not a man beneath the canopy of heaven who does not know that slavery is wrong for him."

Is it not wrong

> to make men brutes, to rob them of their liberty, to work them without wages, to keep them ignorant of their relations to their fellow men, to beat them with sticks, to flay their flesh with the lash, to load their limbs with irons, to hunt them with dogs, to sell them at auction, to sunder their families, to knock out their teeth, to burn their flesh, to starve them into obedience and submission to their masters?

Such a system is obviously wrong; "I have better employments for my time and strength than such arguments would imply," Douglass avers, but, of course his list of these oppressions of slavery has made the strongest of arguments.

Is slavery sanctioned by God? "There is blasphemy in the thought. That which is inhuman cannot be divine! Who can reason on such a proposition? They that can, may: I cannot." But he *has* reasoned. Thus with repeated *paralepsis,* Douglass minimizes the justifications for slavery into insignificance. He concludes his refutation, "What to the American slave is your 4th of July?" A day that reveals to him, more than all other days, the gross injustice and cruelty to which he is the constant victim. The extent of the gross injustice and cruelty is now to be exemplified through several examples.

There is the internal slave trade, thought somehow to be more respectable than the African slave trade. Douglass uses his unique ethos; he claims to be have been born amid the sights and scenes of the trade. He lived in Baltimore near the market. After the auction, the flesh-mongers gathered up their victims by dozens and drove them in chains to the general depot. A ship had been chartered to convey the forlorn crew to Mobile or to New Orleans. From prison to ship they must be driven in the darkness of night due to the anti-slavery agitation, but as a child he heard the rattle of their chains and their cries.

There is the Fugitive Slave Act, through which Mason and Dixon's line has been obliterated; New York has become Virginia, and the power to hold, hunt, and sell men, women, and children remains no longer a mere state institution but is now an institution of the United States. In court two witnesses testify that this individual is the escaped slave; he may not testify on his own behalf or bring witnesses, and at the end of the proceeding he is taken in chains back to slavery. By way of amplification, this law stands alone in the annals of tyrannical legislation.

There is the attitude of the clergy who support the Fugitive Act. Using the traditional topos (topic) of inconsistency between their behavior and their pretensions, Douglass charges: "[If] the Fugitive Slave Law concerned the right to worship God according to the dictates of their own consciences, a general shout would go up from the church demanding repeal, repeal, instant repeal." But the church of our country does not esteem the law as a declaration of war against religious liberty. In supporting the law the church has made itself the bulwark of American slavery, and the shield of American slave hunters. Let us "welcome infidelity, welcome atheism, welcome anything in preference to the gospel as preached by our Divines." Douglass attacks by name a number of prominent pastors who defended the Act and concludes that the church is superlatively guilty, since the common sense of every man at all observant of the actual state of the case knows this truth: "There is no power out of the church that could sustain slavery an hour, if it were not sustained in it." What a difference between the attitude of the American church towards the anti-slavery movement and that occupied by the churches in England towards the movement in that country. There the question of emancipation is a highly religious question. It is demanded in the name of humanity and according to the law of the living God. An all-out attack on the American church is a daring move by Frederick Douglass; he made himself the enemy of the churches, for they claimed, of course, to be upholding law and order.

In an appended section that would be labeled subsidiary remarks by traditional rhetoricians, Douglass attempts to prove that slavery is not protected by the Constitution. It is not even true of the fathers, he states. It is a slander upon their memory. Read the preamble; slavery is not among its purposes. Neither slavery, slaveholding, nor slave can anywhere be found in the rest of it. The principles of liberty on which the Constitution is based are entirely hostile to the existence of slavery. "I defy the presentation of a single pro-slavery clause in it." In his peroration Douglass does find some hope. For the first time he explicitly invokes the Declaration of Independence, "the genius of American Institutions." It is at the head of the obvious tendencies of this age.

> No nation can now shut itself up from the surrounding world, and trot round in the same old path of its fathers without interference. The time was when such could be done. . . . But change has now come over the affairs of mankind. Walled cities and empires have become unfashionable. The arm of commerce has borne away the gates of the strong city. Intelligence is penetrating the darkest corners of the globe. God speed the year of jubilee the wide world over. . . ."

It is plain that from the disposition of the material in an order where one part follows another that there is a logical structure to Douglass's oration. The arguments are vividly sketched rather than developed, and the figure *paralepsis* is used to justify not giving them a full development. What is more notable is the use of the *pathe,* which are not just sketched but are amply developed.

Pathos and Ethos.   Fundamental to the effect of this speech is pity: pain at a destructive or painful evil when it comes on those who do not deserve it. We feel it when we think that we could easily suffer in the same way as the objects of our pity. Identification with the sufferer is a necessary condition of pity. The slave in this oration does not deserve to be shut out from the independence ceremony; we are celebrating independence, but he is not independent. He "is engaged in all manner of enterprises common to other men, digging gold in California, capturing the whale in the Pacific, feeding sheep and cattle on the hillside, living, moving, acting, thinking, planning living in families as husbands, wives and children, and, above all, confessing and worshipping the Christian's God, and looking hopefully for life and immortality beyond the grave. . . ." We can see ourselves in his position: What would it be like for us to be always subject to sale, instant separation from our families, perhaps never to see them again? The slave dealer socializes with the buyers; he is "ever ready to drink, to treat, and to gamble. The fate of many a slave has depended upon the turn of a single card; and many a child has been snatched from the arms of its mother by bargains arranged in a state of brutal drunkenness."

We who are free and believe in virtue and family are the very type of those who can feel the injustice of undeserved disaster, particularly as we are not so close to the disaster ourselves as to be filled with dread (which drives out pity). The black person is the type of those pitiable; he is never at ease; if he has committed no crime, it hardly matters; whether he is honest and industrious or the opposite, it does not make a slave safe. He is subject to the whim of the master; what happens to him is not tied to merit; it usually comes undeserved. No good thing occurring to a slave is ever sure for more than a minute, so good fortune is hard for him to enjoy. The listeners' pity for the slave becomes a basis for anger, the pain that is felt at an unjustified debasement of ourselves or those near to us. Anger must be directed against persons, in this case against the slave drovers, the legislators, and the clergy. The traffic of the slave merchants is today in active operation. Douglass visualizes it: "I see clouds of dust raised on the highways of the South; I see the bleeding footsteps; I hear the doleful wail of fettered humanity on the way to the slave markets, where the victims are to be sold like horses, sheep, and swine, knocked off to the highest bidder. There I see the tenderest ties ruthlessly broken, to gratify the lust, caprice and rapacity of the buyers and sellers of men." By definition those we get angry with are those who devalue their victims, as when they treat those we identify with as horses or swine. We get especially angry when the signs of victims' suffering are brought before the eyes (and ears) as when the "fettered marchers' footsteps bleed," and we hear them wail. Being separated from friends and family is pitiable as when slaves are sold far away. If the debasement is public, as at a market, the victims' suffering provokes greater anger: and the injustice of it is greater because the targets of our anger are motivated only by lust, caprice, and rapacity.

Legislators became fully complicit in this debasement of the slave with the fugitive slave act. They put the power of the United States behind the right to hold, hunt, and sell men, women, and children as slaves. They made the fugitive a bird for the sportsman's gun and made the "broad republican domain a hunting ground for men. Your lawmakers have commanded all good citizens to engage in this hellish sport." The law makes mercy to the fugitive a crime and pays judges to try them. Again, anger is justified because the legislators have debased those we now identify with, making them animals to be hunted by sportsmen and forbidding making them subject to acts of humanity and mercy. Yet these legislators have no regrets; while they enforce this law, they celebrate a tyrant-killing, king-hating, people-loving, democratic, Christian America.

The clergy, too, are targets of anger. They are indifferent to what is happening to the slaves, so they also, in effect, debase them. "If the law abridged the right to sing psalms, to partake of the sacrament, or to engage in any of the ceremonies of religion, it would be smitten by the thunder of a thousand pulpits. A general shout would go up from the church demanding repeal, repeal, repeal!" The fact that the church of our country (with fractional exceptions) does not esteem "the Fugitive Slave Law as a declaration of war against religious liberty, implies that the church regards religion simply as a form of worship, an empty ceremony, and not a vital principle, requiring active benevolence, justice, love and good will towards man. It esteems sacrifice above mercy, psalm-singing above right doing. . . ." The religious leaders consider what is happening to the slaves insignificant; in their preoccupation with the forms of religion, they belittle real humans.

Last, there is the role of shame in the address. Shame is a pain that is felt at doing bad things that bring a person into ill repute. It is obviously most felt by people who have pretensions to virtue, like you Americans, who are tyrant-killing, king-hating, people-loving Christians. You are ready to carry democracy to all the countries of the world, so long as it does not imply freedom for the slave. Even your inferiors, like the savages or the subjects of Kings and tyrants are not guilty of practices more shocking and bloody than are the people of these United States at this very hour. Those who stand outside the system, like God and the crushed and bleeding slave, cannot help but denounce this shamefulness, "in the name of humanity which is outraged, in the name of liberty which is fettered, in the name of the constitution and the Bible, which are disregarded and trampled upon." Acts of cruelty, such as supporting the slave trade are particularly shameful, taking advantage of weakness, playing the coward in the face of the slave merchant, enacting laws that protect his shameful dealing. Acts that spring from vices are also most shameful: Slavery is motivated by avarice and perpetuated by cruelty and cowardice. All this is public and well known, which makes it the more shameful. You must respond, if you are the kind of people you claim to be.

Frederick Douglass's use of the pathe is supplemented by his peculiar ethos. He lived through slavery: Who is to tell him that his view of suffering by the slaves is not accurate? This is especially true of the section on the slave market:

> To me the American slave trade is a terrible reality. When a child, my soul was often pierced with a sense of its horrors. I lived on Philpot Street, Fell's Point, Baltimore, and have watched from the wharves the slave ships in the Basin, anchored from shore, with their cargoes of human flesh, waiting for favorable winds to waft them down the Chesapeake.
>
> The flesh-mongers gather up their victims by dozens and drive them chained to the general depot in Baltimore. When a sufficient number have been collected here, a ship is chartered for the purpose of conveying the forlorn crew to Mobile or to New Orleans.
>
> In the deep darkness of midnight, I have been often aroused by the dead heavy footsteps and the piteous cries of the chained gangs that passed our door. The anguish of my boyhood heart was intense; and I was often consoled, when speaking to my mistress in the morning, to hear her say that the custom was very wicked; that she hated to hear the rattle of the chains and the heart rending cries. I was glad to find one who sympathized with me in my horror.

This kind of eye witness account, buttressed indeed by the reluctant testimony of the slave mistress herself, is hard to deny. It gains effectiveness from being the narrative of a child who naturally is terrified at seeing people like him led off in chains. The pathe, pity, shame, and anger, are fully exploited in these ways.

Douglass does not criticize the Revolution; rather, he identifies with the ideals of the founding fathers. Washington could not die until he had broken the chains of his slaves. The fathers in their admiration of liberty lost sight of all other interests. They believed in order, but not the order of tyranny. The Constitution they framed is a "Glorious Liberty Document." Douglass also picks up considerable credibility from his familiarity with the Bible. Asking him to praise the Fourth of July is like the Hebrews being asked to sing a song of Zion after having been removed to a foreign land (Psalm 137:1–6). The preachers who justify the fugitive slave law are like the scribes and Pharisees "who pay tithe of mint, anise and cumin" while ignoring the weightier matters of the law, judgment, mercy, and faith (Matthew 23:23).

Theirs is a religion for oppressors, tyrants, man-stealers and thugs, not that "pure and undefiled religion" that is from above and that is "first pure, then peaceable, easy to be entreated, full of mercy and good fruits, without partiality and without hypocrisy" (James 1:27). And in a striking *apostrophe* the American church might well be addressed in the language of the prophet Isaiah,

> Bring no more vain oblations; incense is an abomination unto me: the new moons and Sabbaths, the calling of assemblies, I cannot away with; it is iniquity, even the solemn meeting. Your new moons and your appointed feasts my soul hateth. They are a trouble to me; I am weary to bear them; and when Ye spread forth your hands I will hide mine eyes from you. Yea! When ye make many prayers, I will not

hear. Your hands are full of blood; cease to do evil; learn to do good. (Isaiah 1:13–17).

Douglass even identifies his position with the Constitution. It is the fundamental law. It is a slander on the memory of the Fathers to believe that it guarantees slavery. In his peroration Douglass identifies his views with progress: "Intelligence is penetrating the darkest corners of the globe . . . oceans no longer divide, but link nations together." All the good things of the Bible and history and those that are coming to us, he identifies with his cause when building ethos.

Rhetorical Style.   A traditional rhetorician would describe the language of this address as grand style. The emotional tone is enhanced by a fullness in the development of relatively simple themes. Here is a series of *parallel* phrases in which Douglass develops the statement that the 4th of July is a day which reveals to the slave, more than all other days, the gross injustice and cruelty to which he is the constant victim.

> To him, your celebration is a sham; your boasted liberty an unholy license; your national greatness swelling vanity; your shouts of liberty and equality hollow mockery; your prayers and hymns, your sermons and thanksgivings, with all your religious parade and solemnity are to him mere bombast, fraud, deception, impiety and hypocrisy—a thin veil to cover up crimes which would disgrace a nation's savages. There is not a nation on the earth guilty of practices more shocking and bloody than are the people of these United States at this very hour.

One can easily point to the rhetorical hyperbole of this series—could even an intelligent slave think that all the celebration is utterly false, that there is no pious feeling to the hymns and sermons nor anything but self-deception to the feeling of national pride? Could the educated black man not have known of the shocking and bloody practices of the French troops in the Napoleonic wars or the Australia of the prison ships? We understand, of course, that this flamboyance is part of the show, and although there's more than a grain of truth to it, there's also a grain of salt.

It is justified because it is told from the point of view of the slave, though certainly not in the language of the slave. There is the exploitation of *anaphora,* the repetition of the same word or phrase at the beginning of each clause, along with the hint of a rhyme in vanity, mockery, hypocrisy, and bloody—just enough there to constitute *epistrophe,* the repitition of the same phrase at the end of each clause. More than that, however, how many words does it take to say that much of the pageantry on the 4th is hypocritical, something that we all have occasionally felt at the end of an overlong ceremony? The excess of near synonymy is there to build the rhythm into a solemn march, abruptly broken by the conclusion of that last sentence with the finality of "at this very hour."

One of the characteristics of grand style is the freedom in the use of rhetorical figures of speech. These figures, such as anaphora and epistrophe, are useful in lectures and expositions, but figures of thought such as hyperbole and paralepsis are the language of feeling. Rhetorical questions are of this sort, particularly when used in a sequence that builds, like this one:

> Would you have me argue that man is entitled to liberty? That he is the rightful owner of his own body? Must I argue the wrongfulness of slavery? Is that a question for Republicans? Is it to be settled by the rules of logic and argumentation, as a matter beset with great difficulty, involving a doubtful application of the principle of justice, hard to be understood?

This sequence in particular is an example of how a series of rhetorical questions get a listener into the mindset of yea or nay saying.

Besides rhetorical questions there is the use of paralepsis as principle for structuring the section refuting the imagined justifications of slavery. By claiming not to refute these justifications, he belittles them almost out of existence. Taken all in all, the style of this speech is exciting, as befits this kind of occasion.

Evaluation.   If we take the purpose of this speech to be vituperation, bringing people into a state of wrath and fury at the institution of slavery, a greater success at using the armamentarium of traditional rhetoric could hardly be imagined. It is a real case of strategic employment of all the available means of persuasion. As an educational tool, to be sure, it falls short. The view of slavery is without depth or nuance. All that is presented is chains and beatings and moanings. It is stereotyped; it is the propagandist's eye view of the institution. But Douglass's purpose was *arousal,* not *education.* One would like to think that he could have accomplished both purposes, but that is not what he set out to do.

It seems to have been almost a total failure in convincing the Garrisonians. Though Douglass quoted Garrison favorably three times and closed with a complete rendition of one of his anti-slavery poems, they were not mollified; they continued to hold the view that the Constitution must be rewritten and the union reestablished without the South.

The many reprintings of this famous address indicate the extent to which it has intrigued readers over the years. For us it is a window onto a long lost stage dominated by men whose states of feeling are far different from ours. But it fully exploits the precepts of traditional rhetoric.

Personal Comments on the Essay

This essay could have taken forms different than that written above. For example, I decided to make the essay more of a journey through the stages of traditional criticism than a regular style academic paper. I did this because I thought it would make traditional criticism more accessible for students to read. I wanted a bit more of a conversation and less of the usual academic paper. Traditional style criticism is not lacking in sophistication, so a more accessible journey through the stages seemed better than putting up a bunch of lists for you to follow.

It is not unusual for those drawn to traditional criticism to also be drawn to history. I am very certain this shows in many of the examples I have used in this essay. This reflects my personal interests in American political history, as does my choice for a rhetorical artifact to analyze for my essay. Frederick Douglass's 5th of July oration was one of hundreds of such orations I could have chosen to study. I decided upon this one since it is the most famous and is most likely to be familiar to you; moreover, I simply like this speech. My decision to use this particular speech was also influenced by my liking for Douglass's orations in general. Other black orators—Henry Highland Garnet or Al Sharpton—could have as easily been analyzed as well. As could almost any rhetorical effort.

Potentials and Pitfalls

I am certain that you noticed that in the above examples for speakers I used a contemporary speaker. This represents both a potential and pitfall of traditional-style criticism. Far too often those teaching traditional-style criticism give the impression that it is only useful for explicating historical texts. Nothing could be further from the truth. Traditional criticism will serve you well even if you decide to look at a contemporary speaker such as President Bush, President Clinton, James Dobson, or Dr. Laura. The choice of rhetorical artifact is up to you. What differentiates traditional style criticism from the other critical perspectives to which you will be exposed has to do with the type of information that is generated.

Another potential pitfall involves formulaic criticism—also known as "cookie cutter" criticism. This is often the result if one simply uses theory as a checklist, looking for instances of each and every concept covered, and then writing it down to share. This is simply not criticism. Yes, there is some of this type of criticism written by those using a traditional perspective; it has been, afterall, practiced longer than any other perspective covered in this book. Be that as it may, it is also a common pitfall associated with numerous critical perspectives. For example, genre criticism has often come under just such a criticism. Even so, we have examples of genre criticism approaching the sublime, just as we do with traditional criticism. The possbility for formulaic criticism rests more with the critic than with the perspective used.

To avoid fomulaic criticism you need to learn as much about the perspective you intend to use as possible. A good place to start is with the Top Picks I list below. There you will find excellent examples of criticism that is reflexive, not stale.

TRADITIONAL CRITICISM TOP PICKS

Cooper, Lane. *The Rhetoric of Aristotle, an expanded translation with supplementary examples for students of composition and public speaking* (New York, London: D. Appleton and Company, 1932). The gold standard translation for this text. It went unchallenged for decades until Kennedy's book was published in 1991. Either one will work well. See George A. Kennedy, *Aristotle on Rhetoric: A Theory of Civic Discourse* (New York: Oxford University Press, 1991).

Hitchcock, Orville A. "Jonathan Edwards," *A History and Criticism of American Public Address,* William Norwood Brigance, ed. (New York: McGraw-Hill, 1943), 213–237. The essay represents a classical application of traditional criticism.

Hochmuth [Nichols], Marie Kathryn. "The Criticism of Rhetoric," *A History and Criticism of American Public Address,* Vol. 3, Marie Kathryn Hochmuth, ed. (New York: Russell & Russell, 1954). A solid definition of rhetoric as conceived during the reputed heyday of Traditional criticism. The essay complements well a functional approach to communication studies and rhetorical criticism.

Howell, Wilbur Samuel and Hoyt Hopewell Hudson, "Daniel Webster," *History and Criticism of American Public Address.,* Vol. 2. William Norwood Brigance, ed. (New York: McGraw Hill, 1943). An excellent essay that shows the possibilities of traditional criticism when it moves beyond analysis of a single speech and occasion.

Thonssen, Lester, A. Craig Baird, and Waldo W. Braden, *Speech Criticism,* 2nd ed. (New York: The Ronald Press Company, 1970). You may well find a copy of this once common text in your school's library. In it you will find detailed explanations of the concepts outlined in the chapter above.

Contemporary Essays

The following is a short selection of more contemporary essays that draw upon the traditional perspective in greater or lesser degrees. They show the dynamic possibilities for using the perspective today.

Gross, Alan G. "Renewing Aristotelian Theory: The Cold Fusion Controversy as a Test Case," *Quarterly Journal of Speech* 81 (1995): 48–62.

Henry, David. "The Rhetorical Dynamics of Mario Cuomo's 1984 Keynote Address: Situation, Speaker, Metaphor," *Southern Speech Communication Journal* 53 (1988): 105–120.

Hogan, J. Micheal, and L. Glen Williams, "Defining 'the Enemy' in Revolutionary American: From the Rehtoric of Protest to the Rhetoric of War," *Southern Communication Journal* (Summer 1996): 277–289.

Medhurst, Martin J. "Eisenhower's 'Atoms for Peace' Speech: A Case Study in the Strategic Use of Language," *Communication Monographs* 54 (1987): 204–220.

Ritter, Kurt, and David Henry, *Ronald Reagan, the Great Communicator* (Westport, CT: Greewood Press, 1992).

Zagacki, Kenneth. "Eisenhower and the Rhetoric of Postwar Korea," *Southern Communication Journal* (Spring 1995): 233–246.

NOTES

1. Traditional criticism is often called Neo-Aristotelian criticism.
2. See, Hoyt Hopewell Hudson, "De Quincy on Rhetoric and Public Speaking," *Studies in Rhetoric and Public Speaking in Honor of James Albert Winans by Pupils and Colleagues.* A. M. Drummond, ed. (New York: The Century Co., 1925), 133–152; and Hoyt Hopewell Hudson, "The Field of Rhetoric," *Quarterly Journal of Speech Education* 9.2 (1923): 167–180.
3. *Rhetoric,* I 3, 1358a 37–1358b 1.
4. See Wil A. Linkugel, R. R. Allen , and Richard L. Johannesen, Contemporary American Speeches (Belmont, CA: Wadsworth, 1965).
5. Herbert Wichelns is routinely given credit for broadening the communication discipline's rhetorical horizons to include written as well as oral discourse in his 1925 essay, "Literary Criticism of Oratory." Hoyt Hopewell Hudson is deserving of this credit, however, since in his 1921 essay, "Can We Modernize the Study of

Invention?" he implied the use of topics for "speech or argument." "The Field of Rhetoric" contains more explicit definitions. In this essay Hudson fully defined the term rhetoric, which included the study of written as well as oral discourse. Because rhetoric is the "faculty of finding, in any subject, all the available means of persuasion," the rhetorician is "a sort of diagnostician and leaves it to others to be the practitioners; the rhetorician is the strategist of persuasion, and other men execute his plans and do the fighting. In practice, however, and in any study of the subject, this distinction can hardly be maintained, since the person who determines the available means of persuasion . . . must also be, in most cases, the one to apply those means in persuasive speech and writing." See Herbert A. Wichelns, "The Literary Criticism of Oratory," *Studies in Rhetoric and Public Speaking in Honor of James Albert Winans by Pupils and Colleagues,* A. M. Drummond, ed. (New

York: The Century Co., 1925); Hoyt Hopewell Hudson, "Can We Modernize the Theory of Invention?" *Quarterly Journal of Speech Education* 7.4 (1921): 326; and Hoyt Hopewell Hudson, "The Field of Rhetoric," *Quarterly Journal of Speech Education* 9.2 (1923): 169–170.

6. (*Rhetoric,* I 3, 1358a 3–4)

7. William J. Clinton, "Address to Nation, August 17, 1998."

8. Garry Wills, *Lincoln at Gettysburg: The Words That Remade America* (New York: Touchstone Books, 1993).

9. (*Rhetoric,* II 18, 15–17)

10. (*Rhetoric,* II, 2–12)

11. Thomas Eichler, "Rice Downplays Significance of Iraqi Uranium Claim," July 13, 2003 http://www.usinfo.state.gov.

12. Some have called such utterances an "administrative text." For a fuller explanation see Jim A. Kuypers, Marilyn J. Young, and Michael K. Launer, "Of Mighty Mice and Meek Men: Contextual Reconstruction of the Shootdown of Iran Air 655," *Southern Communication Journal* 59.4 (1994): 294–306; and Jim A. Kuypers, *Presidential Crisis Rhetoric and the Press in a Post Cold War World* (Westport, CT: Praeger, 1997), esp. pp. 3–8.

13. For numerous American speeches, many of which have been copyedited against the original sound recording, see http://www.americanrhetoric.com/.

14. (Cadmon Records, TC 1264)

15. Elizabeth Shogren, "Clinton, In Historic Speech, Urges Acceptance of Gays," *Los Angeles Times* (November 9, 1997): A20; James Bennet, "Clinton Is Greeted Warmly as He Speaks to Gay Group," *The New York Times* (November 9, 1997): A30.

16. John F. Wilson and Carroll C. Arnold, *Public Speaking as a Liberal Art,* 5th ed. (Boston: Allyn and Bacon, 1983), 83–88. For an excellent and detailed discussion of topics see, Sharon Crowley and Debra Hawhee, *Ancient Rhetorics for Contemporary Students,* 2nd ed. (Boston: Allyn and Bacon, 1999), 75–102.

17. Nixon, November 3, 1969

18. Lloyd L. Bitzer, "Aristotle's Enthymeme Revisited," *Quarterly Journal of Speech,* 45 (1959): 408.

19. I wish in no way to minimize the work of the Christian Children's Fund. This is an outstanding charity. See http://www.christianchildrensfund.org/ for details.

20. Jane Blankenship and Hermann G. Stelzner, eds. *Rhetoric and Communication: Studies in the University of Illinois Tradition* (Urbana: University of Illinois Press, 1976).

21. Thomas Paine, 1776.

22. Paul M. Angle, *The American Reader, from Columbus to today* (New York: Rand McNally, 1958).

23. (*Rhetoric* I 1, 1355b, 10–16)

24. In 2002 dollars that is somewhere between $2.50 and $12.00, depending upon whose fomula one uses.

25. Gerald Fulkerson, "Exile as Emergence: Frederick Douglass in Great Britain, 1845–1847" *Quarterly Journal of Speech* 60 (February 1974): 69–82.

26. Ronald F. Reid, *American Rhetorical Discourse,* 2nd ed. (Prospect Heights, IL: Waveland Press, 1995).

27. Wills, *Lincoln at Gettysburg.*

28. Douglass to Gerritt Smith, July 7, 1852, quoted in Blassingame, 1982.

29. Paralepsis is one of over 100 rhetorical figures, stylistic devices used by speakers to acheive a certain effect. In this particular instance, a parlepsis emphasizes something either by mentioning it cursorily or by neglecting to mention it altogether.

CHAPTER SIX

GENERIC RHETORICAL CRITICISM

WILLIAM BENOIT

Human beings are inveterate classifiers: To help understand a complex and variegated world, we often make use of generalizations which are sometimes referred to as stereotypes. We can use a generalization such as "Bob's a conservative" to draw reasonable, but not certain, conclusions about Bob. If we want to know whether Bob supports private school tuition vouchers, the best way to find out the answer to this question is to ask Bob or to locate a statement by Bob about his position on vouchers. These options, however, are not always available. In the absence of better ways to answer our question, we can use Bob's political leanings to make an educated guess about his position: Because many conservatives support vouchers, Bob, who we know is a conservative, probably supports vouchers too. Knowing something (support for private school vouchers) about most members of a group (conservatives) allows us to make educated guesses about other members of that group (Bob). Similar generalizations about groups of discourse or "genres" can also be helpful.

Generic rhetorical criticism is based on the idea that observable, explicable, and predictable rhetorical commonalities occur in groups of discourses as well as in groups of people. A critic using the generic approach would first identify a distinctive group or category of discourse, a genre: for example, presidential nominating convention keynote speeches, presidential inaugural speeches, graduation commencement addresses, or eulogies. Then, the critic utilizing the generic method adopts an inductive approach, examining numerous past instances of this genre to develop a description or generalization of its characteristics. It is also important for the critic to explain *why* speeches of this kind ought to have the commonalities found in the analysis. Take presidential nominating convention keynote speeches as an extended example.[1] These speeches are designed to sound a "key" note or set a tone for the convention. The keynote is designed to celebrate the ideals of the party and the fitness of the nominee to represent the party in the general election campaign and, ultimately, to win the office of the presidency. All keynote speeches are given in a similar situation: the Republican or Democratic presidential nomination convention. The result of this process, the description of the rhetorical characteristics of a genre (keynotes, for instance), can be used in at least three important ways.

First, generic descriptions can be used as part of a rhetorical theory that describes rhetorical practices according to genre. Rhetorical theory can describe the practice of rhetoric, as well as offering prescriptions about how it ought to be conducted. Inductive generic descriptions can provide an empirical foundation for descriptive rhetorical theory. For example, we might want to describe the practice of campaign rhetoric (keynote speeches) or political rhetoric (state of the union addresses) or ceremonial rhetoric (commencement addresses, eulogies). If so, the generalizations discovered through a generic analysis could be very useful to theory building.

Second, generic descriptions can be used by practitioners, by rhetors who seek advice about how to develop a speech that falls in that genre. Those who are confronted with a need to invent a particular kind of discourse can be guided by systematic descriptions of past instances of that kind of discourse. If you need to write a eulogy, for example, it could be very useful to know what other eulogists have said in the past. A description of the practice of past eulogies could give you ideas, a starting point, and perhaps even "models" to imitate.

Third, rhetorical critics can apply what we have learned about a genre to help understand and evaluate other, as yet unexamined, instances of that genre. That is, we can compare a new instance of a genre to past practices.[2] On March 20, 2003, President Bush announced the beginning of "Operation Iraqi Freedom," the war in Iraq. We can learn something about this speech by comparing it with other presidential speeches announcing military action. We could compare the 2003 speech with one or more other, earlier speeches, but it would be more efficient to compare it with the results of a generic rhetorical criticism that describes a group of similar speeches.[3]

It should be obvious that the fundamental assumption of the genre method is that rhetorical artifacts examined by a critic to establish a genre or to develop the inductively derived generic description, will resemble in important ways other rhetorical artifacts that fall into that genre. The power of generic criticism is that, if this assumption is reasonable, critics, practitioners, and theorists can learn something about some rhetorical artifacts by examining other similar rhetorical artifacts. Rhetorical critics, schooled in the humanistic tradition, do not ordinarily make this idea explicit, but the basic argument is that the texts studied in a generic rhetorical criticism are a sample of a larger population of texts and that the results of generic rhetorical criticism can be generalized to other similar discourses.

Of course, the generalizations derived from the discourses studied to identify and define the genre must be applied cautiously to other discourses. Discourses that belong to the same class or genre and therefore have *some* similarities could be different in other important ways. For instance, Bob may be one of the few conservatives who does not favor school vouchers. Similarly, when faced with accusations of wrong doing (like shoddy or deliberately false accounting at Enron that cost employees retirement funds), many corporations deny wrongdoing. The fact that many such messages deny wrongdoing does not guarantee that all of them have, or will, do so. However, even if there are exceptions, knowing that many corporations deny wrongdoing could be useful information.

Furthermore, the generic description is inherently limited by the characteristics of the artifacts examined to develop the description. Genre criticism can only describe—and not improve on—the actual practice of discourse. This means that if rhetors who have created discourse in a genre have not yet discovered the best or most effective approach for that kind of rhetoric, the generic description cannot include the optimum approach.[4] It also means that as our culture changes through time, discourses that were effective or appropriate in the past—the discourses studied to describe the genre—may be ill-suited to understanding future discourses given in different times. The remainder of this chapter is divided into two sections. First, I provide an overview of the theory and practice of generic rhetorical criticism. Second, I provide a sample essay that highlights how one may use generic rhetorical criticism.

THE THEORY AND PRACTICE OF GENERIC RHETORICAL CRITICISM

A common thread in this literature is that genres are a class, set, or group of related discourses. For example, Walter Fisher argues that "a genre is a category" and "genres are generalizations."[5] Similarly, Jackson Harrell and Wil Linkugel explain that "At base, genre means class. A genus is a class or group of things. The decision to classify a particular group of things as a genus rests on recorded observations which indicate that one group of entities shares some important characteristic which differentiates it from all other entities."[6] This statement contains an important implicit claim: A genre, or each member of a genre, is distinct from other genres.[7] A keynote is one kind of campaign speech and these speeches are different in some ways from nominating convention acceptance addresses,[8] presidential television spots,[9] or presidential debates.[10] Because these are all forms of presidential campaign discourse, they probably share some features in common, but if they are distinct genres they must have distinguishing differences.

As Karlyn Campbell and Kathleen Jamieson observed, specific generic studies proliferated in the latter part of the 1960s: "In the late 1960s [there was] an explosion of articles describing 'genres,' 'rhetorics,' or the salient formal attributes of certain groups of rhetorical acts."[11] Some genre studies seem to adopt a *situational* base, such as examination of gallows speeches[12] or inaugural addresses.[13] Other instances of generic criticism seem to focus on *purpose*, including investigations of agitation and control,[14] redemption,[15] and polarization.[16] Still other genre studies focusing on the rhetorical characteristics of groups of *rhetors* include studies of early African American feminists,[17] radical-revolutionary speakers,[18] radical, liberal, and conservative rhetors,[19] the religious right,[20] or the radical right.[21] Finally, some genre studies focus on characteristics of the *medium* of discourse, such as analysis of political pamphlets[22] or songs.[23] There can be no question that a great deal of interesting scholarship of extremely diverse nature has been conducted under the rubric of generic rhetorical criticism. It can be difficult to explore this literature, because critics do not always label their work "generic criticism" even though we might consider it as such. In reviewing this body of literature, three areas seem to me to stand out: the relationship between situation and genre, the relationship between purpose and genre, and the relationship of genre to other elements. To each of these we now turn.

Situation and Genre

Rhetorical scholars have described recurrent forms of discourse since at least as early as Aristotle's *Rhetoric*, which identified three broad genres of rhetoric: forensic (legal), deliberative (legislative), and epideictic (ceremonial).[24] Edwin Black offered one of the earliest, if not the earliest, conceptual discussion of the assumptions of rhetorical genre:

> First, we must assume that there is a limited number of situations in which a rhetor can find himself. . . . To be sure, there may be accidental factors peculiar to a given situation; but our assumption is that there will be a limited number of ways in which rhetorical situations can be characterized, and that the recurrent characteristics of rhetorical situations will make it possible for us—if we know enough—to construct an accurate and exhaustive typology of rhetorical situations.[25]

Black assumes that the number of rhetorical situations—and therefore, the number of potential genres—is limited. This makes the task of identifying genres and locating a sufficient number of texts to study more practical than if there were an infinite number of rhetorical situations. Black continues his description:

> Second, we must assume that there is a limited number of ways in which a rhetor can and will respond rhetorically to any given situational type. Again, there may be accidents of a given response that will prove singular, but on the whole—we assume—there will be only a finite number of rhetorical strategies available to a rhetor in any given situation, and his playing his own variations on these strategies will not prevent the critic from identifying the strategies as characteristic of the situation.[26]

This assumption, that there are a limited number of potential responses, means that the texts of a genre are likely to share common features (which the critic can identify and describe). The alternate, an unlimited number of responses, could mean that every member of a genre could be completely different. Finally, Black discusses the possible uses of generic rhetorical criticism:

> Third, we must assume that the recurrence of a given situational type through history will provide the critic with information on the rhetorical responses available in that situation, and with this information the critic can better understand and evaluate any specific rhetorical discourse in which he may be interested.[27]

So, understanding past instances of a genre may provide insight into other examples of that kind of rhetorical message. Of course, the artifacts that participate in or belong to a genre will not be identical in all regards: but for generic criticism to be a useful method of criticism, the similarities must be important.

The emphasis on understanding genre as rooted in a particular situation is popular in the literature.[28] Harrell and Linkugel agree that genres are situationally based: "We think that rhetorical genres stem from organizing principles found in recurring situations that generate discourse characterized by a family of common factors."[29] Similarly, Campbell and Jamieson's often quoted definition stipulates a situational base for rhetorical genres:

> Genres are groups of discourses which share substantive, stylistic, and situational characteristics. Or, put differently, in the discourses that form a genre, similar substantive and stylistic strategies are used to encompass situations perceived as similar by the responding rhetors. A genre is a group of acts unified by a constellation of forms that recurs in each of its members. These forms, in isolation, appear in other discourses. What is distinctive about the acts in a genre is the recurrence of the forms together in constellation.[30]

The term "constellation" is especially well chosen, suggesting that the recurrent elements appear in a recognizable configuration or pattern.

Purpose and Genre.   A second thread in the literature grounds genres in the rhetor's purpose.[31] Carolyn Miller points out that "genres have been defined by similarities in strategies or forms in the discourse, by similarities in audience, by similarities in modes of thinking, by similarities in rhetorical situations." Her recommendation is that "a rhetorically sound definition of genre must be centered not on the substance or form of a discourse but on the action it is used to accomplish."[32] In my opinion, there is overlap between situational and purposive approaches to genre, but they are not entirely identical.

Certainly the rhetor's purpose and the rhetorical situation frequently coincide. For example, eulogists face a situation in which a person has died. When a person dies, the survivors will never again be able to see or talk with the deceased, a cause for sadness. A death also reminds everyone concerned in a very direct fashion that they are mortal. Hence it is appropriate for a eulogist to praise the departed, to ease the transition, and to try to help auditors deal with their grief and heightened sense of mortality. As Jamieson and Campbell explain it, "In Western culture, at least, a eulogy will acknowledge the death, transform the relationship between the living and the dead from present to past tense, ease the mourners' terror at confronting their own mortality, console them by arguing that the deceased lives on, and reknit the community."[33] Here, the situation and the rhetor's purpose are completely compatible: and it is difficult to see or draw a distinction between the situation and the rhetor's purpose.

However, I believe that it is not always the case that a rhetor's purpose is consistent with the situation. For instance, consider a eulogy for someone killed by a gunshot wound. If the eulogist felt strongly about gun control, he or she might choose to include such an appeal in the eulogy; if the eulogist did not feel strongly about gun control, he or she would likely not discuss gun control. An appeal for gun control is not a necessary part of such a eulogy. If a eulogist failed to praise the deceased, the eulogy would seem odd and incomplete if not wrong, but if a eulogist failed to include a plea for gun control, the speech would not seem incomplete. Although the particular situation may be seen to authorize such an appeal for gun control, it does not require it; rather, the rhetor's purpose (advocating gun control) would determine whether to include this idea in the eulogy.

To extend this analogy one step further, Senator Charles Percy eulogized Robert Kennedy, who was killed by a gunshot wound. As Jamieson and Campbell point out, one controversial paragraph included an appeal to end the war in Vietnam. Had the deceased been killed in that war, this reference might have been an appropriate, but not a necessary, topic. However, in this case the deceased had not been killed in Vietnam. Nothing in this eulogy's situation authorized this topic. Although a listener might happen to agree in principle with the appeal for an end to the war, such an appeal had nothing to do with the deceased or the eulogy itself. It seems an inappropriate plea for ending the Vietnam war probably detracted from the ceremony for some of the audience. More recently, a speech by Rick Kahn at Senator Paul Wellstone's memorial service pleaded "We are begging you to help us win this Senate election for Paul Wellstone." In both of these cases, the rhetor's purposes produced discourse that was in part irrelevant to if not incongruent with the immediate situation.

As a final argument for the importance of distinguishing between situation and purpose, consider any rhetorical discourse that occurs in a controversy. Those rhetors who supported and opposed prohibition spoke and wrote in essentially the same situation. Similarly, the situation confronting pro-choice and pro-life advocates is exactly the same; the situation in which the Equal Rights Amendment was debated was the same for supporters and opponents. These groups of rhetors—and it would be easy to add additional groups in this list—produced contradictory rhetorical artifacts; and the primary reason for those differences was their purpose, not differences in the situation. Of course, one could argue that opponents' perceptions of the situation are different: but Bitzer at least argues that the situation is "objective and publicly observable historic facts in the world we experience."[34] Thus, the rhetors' purpose can be a source of generic similarities in rhetorical messages: and, although purpose may overlap with situation, conceptually they are distinct concepts.

Genre: "Act" at the Intersection of Scene, Purpose, Agent, and Agency

The third thread in the literature highlights the interanimated nature of situation and purpose with three other considerations. There is no question that situation and purpose do, or should, influence the production of discourse. However, in actuality, five factors jointly influence the production of rhetorical discourse. Kenneth Burke's notion of ratios[35] helps clarify the relationships between these factors.[36] Ratios are made by combining two terms from Burke's pentad—act, scene (situation), agent (rhetor), agency, and purpose. Ratios essentially describe the influence of the first term on the second. Given that in this chapter we are discussing the production of discourse, or acts, "act" is the second term in each of these four ratios:

- Scene–Act: The situation in which a discourse is produced exerts an influence on that discourse.
- Purpose–Act: The rhetor's purpose, goal, or intent influences the discourse he or she produces.
- Agent–Act: The nature of the rhetor influences the discourse he or she produces.
- Agency–Act: The means, including the communicative medium, influences discourse.

The scene–act ratio corresponds to situationally based approaches to genre (e.g., gallows speeches,[37] inaugural addresses[38]). The purpose–act ratio relates to genre approaches based on the rhetor's purpose (e.g., polarization,[39] resignation[40]). The agent–act ratio pertains to genres focused on rhetor (e.g., radical, liberal, and conservatives[41]). Finally, the agency–act ratio corresponds to studies of kinds of discourse (e.g., pamphlets,[42] song[43]). All four of these ratios or factors can influence the production of discourse and can serve as the basis for a genre.

Situations are opportunities for discourse, which rhetors may choose to exploit to further their own purposes. This can help explain why discourse that occurs in similar situations, such as the eulogies discussed above, would share important similarities. However, some rhetors have different purposes, which can also influence the discourse they produce, even when they face similar situations. Thus, one rhetor may take the opportunity presented by a hand-gun death to plead for gun control; another rhetor with different goals and purposes would omit such pleas.

However, I believe that critics are certainly capable of identifying or creating groupings of discourse that share a common source (such as situation, purpose, rhetor) but that ordinary people have not conceptualized at any level. A little imagination can devise diverse categories that could be used to divide discourse into a variety of groupings.

Generic Description: An Inductive Approach

I want to stress that there is no single way to write a genre criticism. It is important for a rhetorical critic who wants to write a generic rhetorical criticism to read a variety of genre studies before attempting the task. Still, some observations are worth making. There are two fundamental approaches to genre criticism: generic description (inductive) and generic application (deductive).[44] Generic description examines particular instances of a potential genre in order to identify the genre and describes its common features. Generic application begins with a generalization and applies it to specific members of the genre. Generic application begins with a genre that has already been described; it applies the characteristics of that genre deductively to another instance of that genre in order to explain or to evaluate it.

When a critic suspects the existence of a genre, he or she may use generic description to examine particular instances of a possible genre for common features. There are three basic steps in this process: (1) identify the defining characteristic (e.g., the situation, purpose, or kind of rhetor that constitutes the genre); (2) carefully scrutinize examples of the possible genre to identify similarities; (3) explain the observed similarities in terms of identifying characteristics (identifying the "internal dynamic" of the genre). Each of these step is discussed below.

Identifying Defining Characteristics.   If the critic believes that he or she may have found a useful genre, he or she must identify the defining characteristic(s) of that candidate genre. For example, the defining characteristic could be the situation/scene in which the rhetorical artifacts occur (keynote speech or eulogy), the rhetor's purpose that prompts the rhetorical discourses (celebrating the party's presidential nominee or helping the bereaved confront their own mortality), salient characteristics of the rhetor/agent (Republicans or women), or the medium/agency (speech, television spot, or political debate) that shapes the artifacts. One cannot select artifacts at random to discover genres; the critic must be able to clearly define the candidate genre in order to select appropriate particular rhetorical artifacts, instances of the category, for analysis.

For example, President Bush's speech of March 20, 2003, is an example of a speech announcing a war. However, it may not be clear whether speeches about the search for Bin Laden and Al Queda are about *war*. (Perhaps the struggle against terrorism is not the same as a war against a country.) The genre critic needs to make a clear decision about which messages to include in a study. However, given a clear understanding of the defining characteristics of the candidate genre, the critic can select appropriate texts for scrutiny.

Having identified the defining characteristics of the candidate genre, the critic must acquire several instances of the discourse in question for analysis. The critic must be prepared to read, watch, and perhaps even listen to the artifacts repeatedly, closely, and carefully, in order to determine whether these texts have rhetorical commonalities and to identify those similarities. Two important questions arise in this phase of generic description: what to look for, and how many discourses to examine.

Unlike most other critical methods, such as metaphor, narrative, or fantasy theme analysis, generic rhetorical criticism helps the critic decide *which* artifacts to examine but does not prescribe *how* to analyze artifacts. The whole idea of genre criticism is that rhetorical artifacts in the past can be studied and that the results of this study will tell us about future artifacts of the same kind (or other past artifacts that were not included in the initial study). Thus, it is very important for the critic to select the appropriate artifacts to study. If the critic accidentally includes artifacts that do not really belong to the genre, the generic description will inevitably be flawed.

For example, a critic employing the generic approach could look for common metaphors in war speeches. A genre critic might look to see whether such speeches displayed similar rhetorical visions or fantasy themes, or used narrative in similar ways. Thus, the method of generic rhetorical criticism helps the critic decide which rhetorical artifacts to examine, and it tells the critic to look for commonalities. However, the generic method itself does not help the critic know what sorts of similarities to look for.

In my opinion, a critic using the generic approach should be familiar with several methods of rhetorical criticism and with rhetorical theory, generally. It is useful to know what features might be important in a genre. When the critic utilizing the generic approach is repeatedly reading the artifacts of the candidate genre, he or she may notice that certain kinds of metaphors are used frequently. Or, the critic could notice that the rhetors seem to be engaging in a certain form of identification frequently. It is possible that the artifacts tend to feature certain values. Critics using the generic approach who are generally familiar with numerous rhetorical perspectives are probably more likely to notice important rhetorical similarities than critics who are not widely read.

Generic description, as noted above, is an inductive approach. This means that it is subject to the tests of inductive argument. The most important test is whether a sufficient number of instances—in this case, enough rhetorical artifacts—have been examined.[45] There is no simple answer to this question: The number of instances a critic should examine to establish the nature of a genre depends in part upon the complexity and variety of artifacts examined. The greater the complexity of the artifacts in the possible genre, the more variety in the artifacts, the greater the number of instances that ought to be studied to have confidence in the study's conclusions. The number of artifacts needed also depends on how prominent the common rhetorical features appear in the artifacts. The more obvious and important the rhetorical similarities, the fewer artifacts may be needed to persuasively establish the genre. If few artifacts are available and they are difficult to acquire, readers may accept a critic's decision to examine fewer of them.

Identifying Similarities. Once the texts to be analyzed have been identified and located, the generic rhetorical critic must examine them carefully to identify rhetorical similarities. If the critic discovers seemingly important similarities in the texts under scrutiny, he or she should organize those commonalities and locate clear examples from the discourses that can be used to illustrate the features of the genre. For example, if I were to simply say that war speeches often include metaphors, that would not be as clear as if I gave examples of metaphors from such speeches.

It is possible that any randomly selected group of speeches will show similarities simply through the operation of coincidence. Most speeches are supposed to have introductions, main bodies, and conclusions, but that does not mean they all belong to the same genre. I suspect this may in part account for Campbell and Jamieson's statement that "a genre is composed of a constellation of recognizable forms bound together by an internal dynamic."[46] Harrell and Linkugel write about the "organizing principles found in recurring situations that generate discourse characterized by a family of common factors."[47] The point is that the common rhetorical features that are discovered through generic description must be explained by the genre's identifying feature. This way we are more likely to accept the claim that the critic has in fact identified a genre, and that—because it "really" is a genre—other instances of the group of artifacts will resemble the ones examined so far. Take, for example, a keynote speech. This type of speech is designed to encourage viewers to support the nominee; because of this, it makes perfect sense for a keynote to praise the party's nominee. Similarly, the two presidential nominees face off in the general election campaign, so it is reasonable for a keynote speaker to attack his or her nominees' opponent. Thus, the nature of the situation facing rhetors who deliver keynote addresses can explain the presence of certain rhetorical features of those addresses.[48] This raises the question of subgenres; would it be useful to distinguish between keynote speeches during a seriously contested nomination and keynote speeches to an essentially unified party?

Explaining Observed Similarities.   Because coincidental similarities are possible, it is important to explain the similarities found in the rhetorical texts. Those who base genres on rhetors' purposes must be able to link those purposes to the common features of the rhetorical artifacts in those genres. For example, the similarities found in messages of redemption (following Kenneth Burke) should be related to that purpose.[49] We should be able to explain why common features of discourse that is designed to polarize[50] issues and ideas should be expected to occur in artifacts with that purpose. Rhetors who engage in rhetoric designed to agitate or control[51] should produce messages that can be better understood through a consideration of that purpose.

Those who base genres on the nature of groups of rhetors must be able to link the common rhetorical features to the character of those rhetors. The constellation of features found in the discourse of African American feminists[52] should be explicable because they are African American feminists (their stated purpose, to counteract oppression of minority groups, might surface here as well). We ought to be able to account for similarities in messages produced by rhetors with similar political beliefs (e.g., radical, liberal, conservative) by considering those beliefs.[53] If those who belong to the religious right[54] produce similar messages, the critic using the generic approach should be able to show how their political/religious beliefs explain the existence of those similarities. We might wonder again about the possibility of subgenres: Are Republican keynotes different from Democratic ones?

Generic Application: A Deductive Approach

The process of generic application can occur only after someone has already conceptualized a genre. Most commonly, genres would be developed through generic description: inductively describing the nature of a conceptually related group of speeches. However, it is possible that one could generate a generic description theoretically, rather than through an examination of instances of that genre. Regardless of how the genre was conceptualized, generic application includes three basic steps.

First, a genre must have already been described. The critic pursuing generic application must identify the nature of the genre (keynote speeches) and then describe the salient features of that genre. What would discourses in this genre be likely to look like or to have in common? Second, an artifact that is a member of the genre is identified and shown to participate in, or belong to, the genre described in the first step. For example, one might choose to apply the genre of keynote speeches to President Ford's 2000 keynote speech. In this step, the critic refers to the defining features of the genre (in this case, situational) and demonstrates that the new artifact belongs to the genre. This is an important step, because, as Rowland correctly observes, "If a work is inappropriately placed in a given category the analysis of it inevitably will be flawed."[55]

Sometimes this will be quite simple. If "keynote speeches" is considered to be a genre, it should be sufficient to note that the artifact under consideration is identified as one. In other cases it could require an argument. If the genre is defined by the rhetors' purpose, the critic may need to provide evidence of the rhetor's likely purpose in the new artifact. If the genre is defined by situation, it is possible that the critic may need to provide a rationale for the claim that the rhetor and/or the salient audience perceived the situation as the critic suggests. It must be clear to the reader of the rhetorical criticism that it is reasonable to view the new artifact as a member of the genre.

Finally, we are ready to begin making arguments about the "new" artifact based on the claim that it is a member of the genre. Here, evidence for these arguments can be based on the description of the genre as a standard for evaluation as well as on the message itself. It is possible to draw a variety of conclusions in a generic application. For example, the critic might measure the new artifact against the standards articulated in the genre: Based on past examples, is the new artifact well or poorly conceived? Did the rhetor include the proper elements and were they developed effectively?

If the artifact shares the common features that comprise the genre, there is no problem for the critic. The "internal dynamic" explains why these features ought to occur in the kind of genre identified by the defining characteristics. Of course, if the new artifact follows the strictures of the genre but appears to have been a failure, the critic has some explaining to do.

Even more complex is when the artifact violates the expectations established during generic description. What can the critic utilizing the generic approach conclude if the artifact does not conform to the characteristics of the genre? Although there can be numerous reasons which account for deviations from the genre, there are four which deserve special attention. First, it is possible that the "new" artifact doesn't really belong in the genre. The critic should make certain that the discourse being examined in fact fits the defining characteristics of the genre. It is conceivable that the critic would decide either that the artifact doesn't really belong in the genre after all, or that the defining characteristics need to be revised.

Second, the artifact could be a generic hybrid, which means it "belongs" to two genres at once. If so, it could contain some, but not all, of the rhetorical features specified in each of the genres that contribute to the rhetorical hybrid. If so, Jamieson and Campbell's discussion of rhetorical hybrids should prove useful to the critic facing this set of circumstances.[56] If the critic has reason to believe that this discourse is not unique, that other messages may well resemble this one, the critic may propose the existence of a rhetorical hybrid.

Third, it is possible that the rhetor who created the artifact under examination made mistakes. Perhaps the rhetor did not understand the implications of the situation. Perhaps the rhetor did not examine previous artifacts or deliberately chose to ignore them. It is possible that the rhetor did not correctly analyze the audience or chose to ignore them. The critic using the generic approach, however, should make arguments about why the differences between the artifact and the common features of the genre were mistakes if that is the claim being advanced.

Fourth, it is also possible that the rhetor is experimenting and improving the genre rather than making errors. It was suggested earlier that previous rhetors may not have yet discovered the optimum discourse, and the rhetor being analyzed here may have developed an idea or ideas about how to invent a better discourse. The situation may have changed, as the difference between Greek participatory democracy and American representative democracy changed the nature of political discourse. Ironically, if the audience has developed expectations, it is possible that they will not like the changes even if a more objective analysis concludes that the changes made by the rhetor are improvements. Here again, if the rhetorical critic believes that the differences between the artifact and the common features of the genre are an improvement, the critic must explain why the changes should be considered improvements.

CRITICAL ESSAY

This section will illustrate the basic features of generic rhetorical criticism through analysis of presidential inaugural addresses. Every four years, America elects a president. The first duty of the newly elected president is to take the oath of office and give an inaugural address. I want to conduct a brief generic description of inaugurals given from 1961 through 1997.[57] Then I will use the results of that investigation to perform a generic application to George W. Bush's 2001 inaugural address. I could have included earlier inaugural addresses, but these should be sufficient to illustrate this approach. I could have included the 2001 inaugural in the sample, but omitting it allows me to also illustrate the process of generic application by applying the results of the generic description to Bush's text. My goal in the essay that follows is not so much to present a standard academic essay, but rather to demonstrate the process of both generic description and generic application.

Critical Essay: Inaugural Addresses

The critic employing the generic approach should begin by examining the litera-ture. Most rhetorical criticism of inaugural addresses focus on particular speeches, and so they are not genre studies.[58] Still, rhetorical criticism of individual inaugu-rals could be very helpful to the critic seeking to understand the genre of inaugural addresses. I was able to locate two studies of inaugural addresses as a genre.[59] Given that my analysis here is designed simply to illustrate the process of generic criticism, I will not review this work. However, in a standard academic essay, this literature should be reviewed and also drawn into the evaluation section, dis-cussing points of similarity and difference between your analysis and previous re-search on speeches in the genre.

Nature and Context of Inaugural Addresses.   Inaugural addresses are an instance of situational genre. They are speeches that are given in a particular sit-uation: the occasion in which an elected President assumes office. These speeches are also given by a particular rhetor, the President; but the situation in which in-augurals are given distinguishes this kind of speech from other presidential dis-courses, such as campaign speeches or State of the Union addresses. By definition, inaugurals are points of transition. They mark the end of a presidential campaign, one contested by the winner and the loser(s), as well as by their supporters. Just as a presidential nomination acceptance address can be expected to appeal for unity after a contested primary, it is reasonable to expect that an inaugural address ought to attempt to unify the country.

Inaugurals also mean change from the old administration to the new ad-ministration or movement from the first to the second term of a reelected presi-dent. At the same time, an inauguration signals a beginning, the start of a new administration. Because of this, inaugural addresses might be expected to discuss change and to sketch out the principles that will guide the administration. It also means that second inaugurals, initiating a president's second term in office, might offer less emphasis on change and more stress of continuity.

Generic Description: Analysis of Inaugurals from 1961–1997.   I repeatedly read transcripts of these inaugurals; when I had videotapes of these speeches, I watched them repeatedly. I looked for commonalities and, not surprisingly, I found several. Common themes in these speeches were: change, appeals for unity, identification of the enemy, values and ideals, goals, and religious references. Some similarities, such as change and appeals for unity, were expected. Others, such as identification of the enemy, were unexpected. I will illustrate each theme with excerpts from these addresses.

Acknowledgment of Change.   John F. Kennedy succinctly noted that "The world is very different now" from the time of our founding fathers. Lyndon B. Johnson noted that "Even now, a rocket moves toward Mars. It reminds us that the world will not be the same for our children, or even for ourselves in a short span of years." He also observed that "Change has brought new meaning to that old mission" of world peace. Richard M. Nixon's first inaugural acknowledged that "The spiraling pace of change allows us to contemplate, within our own lifetime, advances that once would have taken centuries." His second inaugural implied change, observing that "we stand on the threshold of a new era of peace in the world." He also noted a "shift from old policies to new." Jimmy Carter's inaugural quoted his high school teacher, Julia Coleman: "We must adjust to changing times and still hold to unchanging principles." He also observed that "This inauguration ceremony marks a new beginning." Ronald Reagan's first inaugural noted the importance of the "orderly transfer of authority" that occurs when a new president is inaugurated. His second inaugural acknowledged that "So much has changed" since George Washington was president. In 1989, George Bush declared that "a new breeze is flowing. . . . the totalitarian era is passing. . . . There is new ground to be broken and new action to be taken." Bill Clinton observed in his first inaugural that our founding fathers "knew that America, to endure, would have to change. Not change for change's sake, but change to preserve America's ideals." He also noted that "When George Washington first took the oath I have just sworn to uphold, news traveled slowly. . . . Now the sights and sounds of this ceremony are broadcast instantaneously to billions across the world." He also noted that "We have changed the guard." Clinton's second Inaugural noted that over the last century, "America became the world's mightiest industrial power." We "harness[ed] the Industrial Revolution" and now we face the "Information Age." This is important, because "as times change, so government must change." Thus, each of these inaugurals commented on past and current changes in America and the world.

Appeals for Unity.   Kennedy argued for the importance of unity: "United, there is little we cannot do in a host of cooperative ventures. Divided, there is little we can do—for we dare not meet a powerful challenge at odds and split asunder." He also suggested that we should "let both sides explore what common problems unite us instead of belaboring those problems which divide us." Johnson argued that "Our fate as a nation and our future as a people rest not only upon one citizen, but upon all citizens." Nixon, in his 1969 inaugural, noted that "we are torn by division, wanting unity." His second speech explained that "I pray for your help so that together we may be worthy of our challenge." Carter's inaugural address asked, "Let us learn together and laugh together and work together and pray together." Reagan in his 1981 speech indicated that he would unify the country by adopting their goals: "Your dreams, your hopes, your goals are going to be the dreams, the hopes, and the goals of this administration, so help me God." His second speech asked that "with heart and hand, let us stand as one today." He ended by declaring that we are "one people under God." Bush explained that "we need compromise; we have had dissension. We need harmony; we have had a chorus of discordant voices" and he declared that "We will work hand in hand." He argued that in "crucial things, unity. . . is crucial." Clinton's first inaugural asked "Congress to join with me. But no President, no Congress, no government, can undertake this mission alone. My fellow Americans, you, too must play your part in our renewal. He added, "we recognize a simple but powerful truth—we need each other." Clinton's 1997 inaugural declared that "There is work to do, work that government alone cannot do." Clearly, these inaugurals included appeals for unity.

Identification of the Enemy.   In 1961, the Communists were an obvious enemy, and one mentioned by Kennedy. However, he also called for "a struggle against the common enemies of man: tyranny, poverty, disease, and war itself." Johnson turned inward to find an enemy, talking about poverty, hunger, and illiteracy, explaining that "injustice to our people, . . . waste of our resources, was our real enemy." Nixon's first inaugural also turned inward to find an enemy: "America has suffered from a fever of words; from inflated rhetoric that promises more than it can deliver; from angry rhetoric that fans discontent into hatred; from bombastic rhetoric that postures instead of persuasion." The theme of internal enemies continued in 1977, as Carter explained that "we will still fight out wars against poverty, ignorance, and injustice—for those are the enemies against which our forces can be honorably marshaled." The enemy in Reagan's first inaugural was the economy: "We suffer from the longest and one of the worst sustained inflations in our national history. It distorts our economic decisions, penalizes thrift, and crushes the struggling young and the fixed-income elderly alike. It threatens to shatter the lives of millions of our people." Poverty and war were enemies in 1985: "Every blow we inflict against poverty will be a blow against its dark allies of oppression and war. Every victory for human freedom will be a victory for world peace." For Bush, an important enemy was drugs: "The most obvious area now [where we must rise up united and express our intolerance] is drugs." The economy returned to the forefront in Clinton's first inaugural: Our economy "is weakened by business failures, stagnant wages, increasing inequality, and deep divisions among our people." "We have drifted, and that drifting has eroded our resources, fractured our economy, and shaken our confidence." In his second inaugural, the enemy was "prejudice and contempt" that "cripple both those who hate and, of course, those who are hated." Although the enemy was sometimes external and sometimes internal, these inaugurals identified enemies.

Identification of Values and Ideals.   Peace and freedom were important values in Kennedy's inaugural. Johnson discussed three key ideals: justice, liberty, and union. Nixon's first inaugural stressed peace, freedom, justice, and mentioned "Goodness, decency, love, kindness" as well. His 1973 speech stressed peace and freedom and mentioned civility, decency, and dignity. Carter spoke of the American dream, liberty, equal opportunity, compassion, justice, peace, humility, and mercy. Reagan's 1981 inaugural talked about liberty, freedom, and hope. His second inaugural stressed freedom, dignity, and opportunity. Bush emphasized freedom and discussed moral principle, unity, diversity, generosity, kindness, and gentleness. Clinton's 1993 inaugural discussed life, liberty, the pursuit of happiness, fairness, and responsibility. In 1997, Clinton spoke of liberty, diversity, peace, freedom, and the human spirit. These inaugurals appealed to values that were likely to resonate with the American public.

Delineation of Goals.   Kennedy explained that he wanted to "assist free men and free governments in casting off the chains of poverty," to help empower the United Nations, to seek peace (including arms control agreements). Johnson, in keeping with his three ideals, wanted to improve justice, overcome "tyranny and misery," and "turn our unity of interest into a unity of purpose." Nixon's 1969 speech mentioned the "goals of full employment, better housing, excellence in education; in rebuilding our cities and improving our rural areas; in protecting our environment and enhancing the quality of life." However, he also spent a great deal of time talking about achieving peace. His second inaugural again talked about achieving peace with honor. Carter's inaugural discussed equality of opportunity, enhancing freedom abroad, eliminating nuclear weapons, providing jobs, strengthening the family, increasing respect for the law, and restoring pride in government. Reagan's first inaugural goals were to decrease inflation, create jobs, and thwart terrorism. His second speech revealed that he wanted to "permanently control government's power to tax and spend." He explained that "From new freedom [from government intervention] will spring new opportunities for growth, a more productive, fulfilled, and united people, and a stronger America." He echoed Carter's call for elimination of nuclear weapons while maintaining a strong defense. Bush observed that "There are the homeless, lost and roaming. There are the children who have nothing; no love, no normalcy. There are those who cannot free themselves of enslavement to whatever addiction—drugs, welfare, the demoralization that rules the slums. There is crime to be conquered, the rough crime of the streets. There are young women to be helped who are about to become mothers of children they can't care for and might not love." Clinton's first inaugural set as a goal "To renew America." He noted that "we must meet challenges abroad as well as at home. . . . The world economy, the world environment, the world AIDS crisis, the world arms race—they affect us all." Clinton's second inaugural suggested that we should be "teaching children to read; hiring people off welfare rolls; coming out from behind locked doors and shuttered windows to help reclaim our streets from drugs and gangs and crime." These passages show how these speeches articulated goals for the next four years as president.

Religious References.   Kennedy's speech ended by "asking His blessing and His help, but knowing that here on earth God's work must truly be our own." Johnson mentions God four times, once explaining that "But we have no promise from God that our greatness will endure. We have been allowed by Him to seek greatness with the sweat of our hands and the strength of our spirit." Nixon ended his first inaugural "sustained by our confidence in the will of God and the promise of man." His 1973 inaugural ask for citizens' "prayers that in the years ahead I may have God's help." Carter quoted from the Bible near the beginning. Reagan's first inaugural declared that "together, with God's help, we can and will resolve the problems which now confront us" (note that this passage also discusses unity). Reagan's 1985 inaugural ended with, "God bless you and may God bless America." Bush took his oath of office with the same Bible used by George Washington, and then told the audience that "My first act as President is a prayer." Clinton ended his first inaugural by declaring that "with God's help, we must answer the call."

His second inaugural closed with this appeal: "May God strengthen our hands for the good work ahead—and always, always bless our America." So, religious references occurred in these speeches.

Summary.   Examination of these inaugurals revealed features both expected and unexpected. First, these speeches openly acknowledge change and transition. Second, appeals to unity were common, as were descriptions of the goals for the next four years. There were recitations of values and ideals as well. These are reasonable features of an inaugural address. However, analysis of these texts also revealed themes that were not expected. First, these speeches tend to identify a common enemy. This makes sense, because one way to unite a group is to fight against a common enemy. Thus, this theme reinforces the unification appeals. Second, these speeches, like the majority of American political discourse, contained religious references. The only question I raise is whether this feature occurs because these discourses are inaugural addresses specifically or presidential addresses generally.

I want to acknowledge that these speeches had other features as well. For example, Carter offered a nice contrast when he noted that "We must adjust to changing times and still hold to unchanging principles." Still, in my opinion the themes identified above are the most prominent and important similarities for the genre of inaugural addresses, given the situation in which these addresses occur. I would also like to note that not every speech discussed each theme as extensively as other speeches. Furthermore, some seemed to me to do a better job at developing these themes. For example, Kennedy explained why unity was important: "United, there is little we cannot do in a host of cooperative ventures. Divided, there is little we can do." On the other hand, some inaugurals asked the audience for unity without explaining why it was so important: Nixon's second inaugural stated: "I pray for your help;" Reagan asked in his second speech, "Let us stand as one today." Furthermore, some speeches seemed to do a better job relating their goals to values and ideals that would guide implementation of those goals.

As I mentioned earlier, if this were intended as more than an illustration of the process of generic rhetorical criticism, I would at this point return to the literature on inaugurals and discuss points of similarity and difference between my findings and theirs. I would also spend more time teasing out specifics. For example, I would talk more about the common values and ideals. Still, this brief application should give readers the basic idea of how generic description is conducted.

Generic Application: George W. Bush's 2001 Inaugural Address.   The above generic description of recent inaugural addresses identified six common themes: acknowledgment of change, appeals for unity, identification of common enemy, identification of values and ideals, delineation of goals, and religious references. Using generic application, I will next examine George W. Bush's 2001 inaugural address to see whether it conforms to the common themes found above.

President Bush began by acknowledging the change: He explained that "With a simple oath we affirm old traditions and make new beginnings," acknowledging that the inauguration is a transition. He then observed that "Sometimes our differences run so deep, it seems we share a continent but not a country." Then he noted the importance of unification: "Our unity, our union, is the serious work of leaders and citizens and every generation. And this is my solemn pledge: I will work to build a single nation of justice and opportunity." The enemy Bush identified was terrorists, which seems eerily prophetic in the wake of the terrorist attack on the World Trade Center and the Pentagon about nine months later: "We will confront weapons of mass destruction so that a new century is spared new horrors. The enemies of liberty in our country should make no mistake: America remains engaged in the world." Values discussed included civility, courage, compassion, and character, opportunity ("everyone deserves a chance"), freedom, and hope. In addition to building a strong defense, his goals were to "reclaim America's schools," "reform Social Security and Medicare," and "reduce taxes to recover the momentum of our economy." Finally, Bush ended his speech by saying, "God bless you all, and God bless America." So, Bush's inaugural address conformed to the standards set by previous inaugurals.

In evaluating his speech, I would say it enacted these themes generally well. One minor weakness was that he promised unity without working very hard to give citizens a reason to unite behind him. That is, I do not think it is enough for the President to *pledge* unity, particularly after the bitterly contested election of 2000 and the fact many people believe Bush actually lost the popular vote to Gore.[60] Bush ought to have offered citizens a reason to join with him. Second, he could have easily used the common enemy of terrorism as a justification for unity. The common enemy should have served as an explicit justification for unification. Third, I would have tried to relate the values and ideals he articulated more closely to his goals. In other ways, though, his speech was acceptable.

Once again, if this were intended as a complete rhetorical criticism, I would discuss the relationship of this analysis to prior research on inaugurals. Similarly, I would spend more time discussing specifics, especially details of the historical context that existed at the time of the inaugural. However, this essay was designed to outline how generic description and application proceed.

PERSONAL COMMENTS ON THE ESSAY

I could have made other choices in examining these speeches. For example, I could have looked for the use of emotional appeals, or metaphors, or myths in inaugural addresses. However, I tried to let these texts "speak" to me, trying to see what stood out, rather than explicitly searching for particular rhetorical elements such as metaphors. I believe it is important to try to identify the "internal dynamic," explaining *why* these common features make sense for discourses written for, and presented in, these situations. Furthermore, it should be clear that my analysis reflects a scene–act perspective. The observed common rhetorical features are (I argue) a result of the nature of the situation in which these texts emerged: the newly elected president's first formal address to the country.

POTENTIALS AND PITFALLS

Generic rhetorical criticism has many advantages. First, it is well designed for attempting to understand the nature of rhetorical practice. What do speeches announcing a war, or inaugural addresses, or diatribes, or resignation speeches, look like? What features do they have in common and why should these commonalities exist? Generic description can help rhetorical theorists and practitioners alike. Furthermore, generic application can help rhetorical critics understand and evaluate new examples of speeches that belong to a given genre, once generic description has occurred.

The rhetorical critic must keep in mind that the generic method offers advice on which speeches to study, but not on precisely how to study them. As I suggested before, another critic could look at inaugural addresses (or any other genre) looking for metaphors, or myths, or fantasy themes. Any particular method of rhetorical criticism can be used to guide the critic's analysis of the speeches in a genre.

One limitation of generic analysis is that the method lumps good messages with mediocre and bad ones.[61] The inductive method of generic description suggests that the critic locate a sufficient number of examples of the potential genre. It never suggests that the critic only examine successful messages or place the best texts in one subgrouping and the failures in another. As discussed in the preceding section, it is conceivable that a rhetoric creating a keynote speech in the future could try something new, something better than any previous keynote. Unless we believe that the best possible examples of discourse in a genre have already been created, there is always room for improvement.

It can also be objected that generic rhetorical criticism ignores the nuances of individual rhetorical discourses. This criticism applies more to rhetorical criticism that focuses too heavily upon description. By its very nature inductive generic description searches for commonalities among the instances of the genre, ignoring differences between individual instances of the genre. Because the critic who is conducting generic description is attempting to discover what these texts have in common, the differences are truly irrelevant. Of course, subsequent generic application should focus on the individual nuances of the specific instance of the genre under examination. For example, keynote speeches from 1960 through 1996 attacked in 48 percent of their utterances. But Barbara Jordan's Democratic keynote in 1976 contained only a single attack (the Republican keynoter that year, Howard Baker, made sixteen attacks).[62] A critic using the deductive generic approach could argue that Jordan failed to include enough attacks on the opposing party. Understanding the particular nuances of this speech—for example, that she was the first woman to present a keynote speech at a presidential nominating convention—might shed some light on her reluctance to attack. So, although generic description must by nature ignore the nuances of individual members of the genre, generic application can and should take particulars into account.

Generic rhetorical criticism takes advantages of the fact that, although no two discourses are identical, discourses do fall into groups or genres that have important similarities. Knowing the nature of these groups, and their common rhetorical characteristics, can be useful to rhetors, theorists, and practitioners alike. Of course, critics must never lose sight of the fact that there *are* differences even between members of the same genre, and critics must realize that genres can develop over time and potentially improve over past practice. Still, intelligent use of the method of generic rhetorical criticism can provide powerful insights into the nature of rhetorical discourse.

GENERIC RHETORICAL CRITICISM TOP PICKS

Benoit, William L., Joseph R. Blaney, and P. M. Pier, "Acclaiming, Attacking, and Defending: A Functional Analysis of Nominating Convention Keynote Speeches, 1960–1996," *Political Communication* 17 (2000): 61–84. This essay takes a more explicitly content analytic approach, but it is still concerned with identifying important common features of this message form.

Campbell, Karlyn K. and Kathleen H. Jamieson, (eds.), *Form and Genre: Shaping Rhetorical Action* (Falls Church, VA: Speech Communication Association, 1978). This volume pulls together essays from a diverse array of scholars addressing the nature of genre.

Clark, Thomas D., "An Analysis of Recurrent Features in Contemporary American Radical, Liberal, and Conservative Political Discourse," *Southern Speech Communication Journal* 44 (1979): 399–422. This essay is interesting be-

cause unlike most genre studies, Clark contrasts three different (although related) groups of discourse.

Condit, Celest M., "The Function of Epideictic: The Boston Massacre Orations as Exemplar," *Communication Quarterly* 33 (1985): 298–298. Classic treatment of a genre that is often overlooked.

Jamieson, Kathleen H. and Karlyn K. Campbell, "Rhetorical Hybrids: Fusions of Generic Elements," *Quarterly Journal of Speech* 68 (1982): 146–157. Genres are not always static. This essay discusses the merging of two genres into a single new genre.

Ware, B. L. and Wil A. Linkugel, "They Spoke in Defense of Themselves: On the Feneric Criticism of *Apologia*," *Quarterly Journal of Speech* 59 (1973): 273–283. One of the earlier studies of genre and a classic treatment of the important genre of apologia.

NOTES

1. William L. Benoit, Joseph R. Blaney, and P. M. Pier, "Acclaiming, Attacking, and Defending: A Functional Analysis of Nominating Convention Keynote Speeches, 1960–1996," *Political Communication* 17 (2000): 61–84.

2. The "new" speech need not be chronologically more recent than the speeches studied in making the generic description; it only needs to be new in the sense that it was not included in the inductive, descriptive analysis.

3. For rhetorical criticism of justifications of war, see Kathleen M. German, "Invoking the Glorious War: Framing the Persian Gulf Conflict through Directive Language," *Southern Communication Journal* 60 (1995): 292–302; Robert L. Ivie, (1974). "Presidential Motives for War," *Quarterly Journal of Speech* 60 (1974): 337–345;

Mary E. Stuckey, "Remembering the Future: Rhetorical Echoes of World War II and Vietnam in George Bush's Public Speech on the Gulf War," *Communication Studies* 42 (1992): 246–256.

4. William L. Benoit, "In Defense of Generic Rhetorical Criticism: John H. Patton's "Generic Criticism: Typology at an Inflated Price," *Rhetoric Society Quarterly* 10 (1980): 128–135.

5. Walter R. Fisher, "Genre: Concepts and Applications in Rhetorical Criticism," *Western Journal of Speech Communication* 44 (1980): 291.

6. Jackson Harrell and Wil A. Linkugel, "On Rhetorical Genre: An Organizing Perspective," *Philosophy & Rhetoric* 11 (1978): 263.

7. Thomas D. Clark, "An Analysis of Recurrent Features in Contemporary American Radical,

Liberal, and Conservative Political Discourse," *Southern Speech Communication Journal* 44 (1979): 400–401.

8. William L. Benoit, William T. Wells, P. M. Pier, and Joseph R. Blaney, (1999). "Acclaiming, Attacking, and Defending in Nominating Convention Acceptance Addresses, 1960–1996," *Quarterly Journal of Speech* 85 (1999): 247–267.

9. William L. Benoit, "The Functional Approach to Presidential Television Spots: Acclaiming, Attacking, Defending 1952–2000," *Communication Studies* 52 (2001): 109–126.

10. William L. Benoit and Allison Harthcock, "Functions of the Great Debates: Acclaims, Attacks, and Defense in the 1960 Presidential Debates," *Communication Monographs* 66 (1999): 341–357.

11. Karlyn K. Campbell and Kathleen H. Jamieson, "Introduction," *Form and Genre: Shaping Rhetorical Action* (Falls Church, VA: Speech Communication Association, 1978): 15–16.

12. Bower Aly, "The Gallows Speech: A Lost Genre," *Southern Speech Journal* 34 (1969): 204–213.

13. Karlyn K. Campbell and Kathleen H. Jamieson, "Inaugurating the Presidency," *Presidential Studies Quarterly* 15 (1985): 394–411; Halford R. Ryan, "Roosevelt's Fourth Inaugural Address: A Study of Its Composition," *Quarterly Journal of Speech* 67 (1981): 157–166.

14. John W. Bowers, Donovan J. Ochs, and Richard J. Jensen, *The Rhetoric of Agitation and Control* (2nd ed.) (Prospect Heights, IL: Waveland Press, 1993).

15. A. Cheree Carlson and John E. Hocking, "Strategies of Redemption at the Vietnam Veterans' Memorial," *Western Journal of Speech Communication* 49 (1988): 14–26.

16. Andrew A. King and Floyd D. Anderson, "Nixon, Agnew, and the 'Silent Majority': A Case Study in the Rhetoric of Polarization," *Western Speech* 35 (1971): 243–255; Richard D. Raum and James S. Measell, "Wallace and His Ways: A Study of the Rhetorical Genre of Polarization," *Central States Speech Journal* 25 (1971): 28–35.

17. Karlyn K. Campbell, "Style and Content in the Rhetoric of Early Afro-American Feminists," *Quarterly Journal of Speech* 72 (1986): 434–445.

18. James Chesebro, "Rhetorical Strategies of the Radical-Revolutionary," *Today's Speech* 20 (1972): 37–48.

19. Thomas D. Clark, "An Exploration of Generic Aspects of Contemporary American Campaign Orations," *Central States Speech Journal* 30 (1979): 122–133.

20. Bernard K. Duffy, "The Anti-Humanist Rhetoric of the New Religious Right," *Southern Speech Communication Journal* 49 (1984): 339–360.

21. Dale G. Leathers, "Belief–Disbelief Systems: The Communicative Vacuum of the Radical Right," In G. P. Mohrmann, Charles J. Stewart, and Donovan J. Ochs (Eds.), *Explorations in Rhetorical Criticism* (University Park, PA: Pennsylvania State University Press, 1973), 124–137.

22. Carl R. Burgchardt, "Two Faces of American Communism: Pamphlet Rhetoric of the Third Period and the Popular Front," *Quarterly Journal of Speech* 66 (1980): 375–391.

23. David A. Carter, "The Industrial Workers of the World and the Rhetoric of Song," *Quarterly Journal of Speech* 66 (1980): 365–374.

24. Aristotle, *The Rhetoric* (trans. W. Rhys Roberts) (New York: Modern Library, 1954).

25. Ed Black, *Rhetorical Criticism: A Study in Method* (Madison: University of Madison Press, 1965, 1978), 133.

26. Black, Rhetorical Criticism, 133.

27. Black, Rhetorical Criticism, 133.

28. See Lloyd F. Bitzer, "The Rhetorical Situation," *Philosophy & Rhetoric* 1 (1968): 1–14; cf. William L. Benoit, "The Genesis of Rhetorical Action," *Southern Communication Journal* 59 (1994): 342–355.

29. Harrell and Linkugel, 263–264 (italics omitted).

30. Campbell and Jamieson, "Introduction," 20.

31. It is impossible to know with certainty any rhetor's purpose; although, situational factors and evidence from the text and rhetor can be used to make a argument about the rhetor's likely purpose. Still, I think it is difficult to deny that, for example, pro-life rhetors in general have a different purpose than pro-choice rhetors (and it would be difficult to deny that their purposes conflict).

32. Carolyn R. Miller, "Genre as Social Action," *Quarterly Journal of Speech* 70 (1984): 151.

33. Campbell and Jamieson, 147.

34. Bitzer.

35. Kenneth Burke, *Counter-Statement* (Berkeley: University of California Press, 1968; originally published in 1931); Kenneth Burke, "Dramatism," *International Encyclopedia of the Social Sciences* 7 (1968): 445–452; Kenneth Burke, *A Grammar of Motives* (Berkeley: University of California Press, 1969; originally published 1945); Kenneth Burke, "Questions and Answers about

the Pentad," *College Composition and Communication* 29 (1978): 330–335. See too, the special section of volume 1, issue 3, of the American Communication Journal. There you will find essays on each of the following topics: "motive," "sacrifice and moral hierarchy," identification," "the pentad," and the cycle of "guilt, purification, and redemption." http://acjournal.org/holdings/vol1/iss3/curtain3.html.

36. William L. Benoit, "Beyond Genre Theory: The Genesis of Rhetorical Action," *Communication Monographs* 67 (2000): 178–192.

37. Aly.

38. Campbell and Jamieson, *Inaugurating the Presidency*; Ryan.

39. King and Anderson; Raum and Measell.

40. Howard W. Martin, "A Generic Exploration: Staged Withdrawal, the Rhetoric of Resignation," *Central States Speech Journal* 27 (1976): 247–257; Gerald L. Wilson, "A Strategy of Explanation: Richard M. Nixon's August 8, 1974, Resignation Address," *Communication Quarterly* 24 (1976): 14–20.

41. Clark, *An Exploration*.

42. Burgchardt.

43. Carter.

44. Harrell and Linkugel; Robert C. Rowland, "On Generic Categorization," *Communication Theory* 1 (1991): 143.

45. David L. Vancil, *Rhetoric and Argumentation* (Boston: Allyn and Bacon, 1993); George W. Ziegelmueller and Charles A. Dause, *Argumentation: Inquiry and Advocacy* (Englewood Cliffs, NJ: Prentice-Hall, 1975).

46. Campbell and Jamieson, "Introduction," 21.

47. Harrell and Linkugel, 263–264 (italics omitted).

48. William L. Benoit and J. J. Gustainis, "An Analogic Analysis of the Keynote Addresses at the 1980 Presidential Nominating Conventions," *Speaker and Gavel* 24 (1986): 95–108.

49. Carlson and Hocking.

50. King and Anderson; Raum and Measell.

51. Bowers, Ochs, and Jensen.

52. Campbell.

53. Chesebro; Clark, *An Exploration*; Leathers.

54. Duffy.

55. Robert C. Rowland, "On Generic Categorization," Communication Theory, 1 (1991); 129.

56. Kathleen H. Jamieson and Karlyn K. Campbell, "Rhetorical Hybrids: Fusions of Generic Elements," *Quarterly Journal of Speech* 68 (1982): 146–157.

57. Keep in mind that the campaign ends in November, but the Inauguration occurs in January of the following year.

58. Ronald H. Carpenter, "In Not-So-Trivial Pursuit of Rhetorical Wedgies: An Historical Approach to Lincoln's Second Inaugural Address," *Communication Reports* 1 (1988): 20–25; Suzanne M. Daughton, "Metaphoric Transcendence: Images of the Holy War in Franklin Roosevelt's First Inaugural," *Quarterly Journal of Speech* 79 (1993): 427–446; Barbara A. Harris, "The Inaugural of Richard Milhouse Nixon: A Reply to Robert L. Scott," *Western Speech* 34 (1970): 231–234; Anthony Hillbruner, "Archetype and Signature: Nixon and the 1973 Inaugural," *Central States Speech Journal* 25 (1974): 169–181; Michael Leff, "Dimensions of Temporality in Lincoln's Second Inaugural," *Communication Reports* 1 (1988): 26–31; Stephen E. Lucas, "Genre Criticism and Historical Context: The Case of George Washington's First Inaugural Address," *Southern Speech Communication Journal* 51 (1986): 354–370; Martin J. Medhurst, "American Cosmology and the Rhetoric of Inaugural Prayer," *Central States Speech Journal* 28 (1977): 272–282; Ryan; Robert L. Scott, "Rhetoric that Postures: An Intrinsic Reading of Richard M. Nixon's Inaugural Address," *Western Speech* 34 (1970): 46–52; Vito N. Silvestri, "Background Perspectives on John F. Kennedy's Inaugural Address," *Political Communication and Persuasion* 8 (1991): 1–15; Amy R. Slagell, "Anatomy of a Masterpiece: A Close Textual Analysis of Abraham Lincoln's Second Inaugural Address," *Communication Studies* 42 (1991): 155–171; Martha Solomon, "'With Firmness in the Right': The Creation of Moral Hegemony in Lincoln's Second Inaugural," *Communication Reports* 1 (1988): 32–37; David Zarefsky, "Approaching Lincoln's Second Inaugural Address," *Communication Reports* 1 (1988): 9–13.

59. Campbell and Jamieson, Inaugurating the Presidency; Karlyn K. Campbell and Kathleen H. Jamieson, "Inaugurating the Presidency," in Herbert W. Simons and Aram A. Aghazarian (eds.), *Form, Genre, and the Study of Political Discourse* (Columbia: University of South Carolina Press, 1986), 203–225.

60. There remain over 1.5 million uncounted absentee ballots. Until they are counted, we will never know for certain who "won" the popular vote.

61. Benoit, *In Defense*.

62. Benoit, Blaney, and Pier.

CHAPTER SEVEN

CRITICISM OF METAPHOR

THOMAS R. BURKHOLDER

DAVID HENRY

On August 28, 1963, Martin Luther King, Jr., began his speech on the steps of the Lincoln Memorial in Washington, DC: "Five score years ago, a great American, in whose symbolic shadow we stand today, signed the Emancipation Proclamation. This momentous decree came as a great beacon light of hope to millions of Negro slaves, who had been seared in the flames of withering injustice. It came as a joyous daybreak to end the long night of their captivity."[1] Rhetorical scholars recognize immediately the "trope" or figure of speech present in this passage—and throughout King's speech—that contributed to making "I Have a Dream" the greatest speech of the twentieth century—metaphor.[2] The vividness and rhetorical force of King's language, the Emancipation Proclamation as a "beacon light of hope," the "searing flames of injustice," the "joyous daybreak to end the long night" of slavery, created indelible images in the minds of two generations of Americans.

Most undergraduate students probably encounter metaphor and its companion figure, simile, in introductory English composition or public speaking classes. Usually, those figures are discussed as means of embellishing the style of written compositions or speeches. For example, Stephen E. Lucas, author of perhaps the best-selling undergraduate public speaking textbook in the United States, asserts that "speakers can use imagery . . . to make their ideas come alive." Two means of generating imagery, he explains, are metaphor and simile.[3] Likewise, Patricia Hayes Andrews, James R. Andrews, and Glen Williams say that "language that is striking or impressive can create interest and contribute to understanding." Figures of speech such as metaphor and simile, they continue, "are special ways of using language to heighten the beauty of expression or the clarity of ideas."[4] And in his public speaking textbook, David Zarefsky points out that "analogy is a powerful form of reasoning: [A] comparison can help people to accommodate a new idea or new information by deciding that it is similar to what they already know or believe. Comparisons can be made vivid by using similes and metaphors."[5]

Zarefsky's comment suggests how metaphor and simile are alike: Both are comparisons of one thing to another. Technically, the difference between metaphor and simile is that similes always include either *like* or *as* while metaphors do not. Thus, saying that "lowering the drinking age to eighteen is *like* giving a stick of dynamite to a baby"[6] is a simile, while saying that "teenagers drinking *is* dynamite in the hands of babies" is a metaphor. Imagine other ways of expressing the same idea. Instead of using a metaphor or simile, one might say: "Lowering the drinking age to eighteen would be dangerous." The meaning is virtually the same, but with the metaphor or simile, the statement gains its vivid, memorable quality. Thus, regardless of whether the figure is technically a metaphor or a simile, it functions to embellish the style of a written or spoken message by making ideas vivid. In that sense, distinctions between the two figures matter little.

Despite those important stylistic or ornamental functions of metaphor and simile, critics are most interested in their *rhetorical* functions, in their capacity to influence the thoughts and actions of readers and listeners. That is especially true of metaphor, which rhetorician Kenneth Burke has called one of the four "master tropes."[7] In this chapter, we explore the rhetorical functions of metaphor. Then, we suggest how the criticism of metaphor might proceed. Finally, we illustrate criticism of metaphor through analysis of former New York Governor Mario Cuomo's famous keynote address to the 1984 Democratic National Convention.

HOW METAPHORS WORK

A metaphor consists of two terms that draw a comparison between two things, people, places, situations, events, and so forth that belong to "different classes of experience."[8] One of those two terms, usually called the *tenor* or *focus*, is *relevant to* or *continuous* with the topic under discussion. The other term, usually called the *vehicle* or *frame*, is *discontinuous* with, or of a different class of experience from, that topic.[9] When the two terms, the *tenor* or *focus* and the *vehicle* or *frame*, are brought together by a speaker or writer to form a metaphor, readers or listeners are invited to see the comparison between the two.

For example, while discussing means of coping with the pressures and stresses of contemporary life, the popular TV psychologist Dr. Phil McGraw tells his audience, "Life is a full-contact sport and there's a score up on the board."[10] The discussion is about life's problems, so the term "life" is the *tenor* or *focus* of the metaphor because it is *continuous* with the topic under discussion. The term "full-contact sport" is the *vehicle* or *frame* of the metaphor because it is *discontinuous* with that topic; in other words, it is from a different class of experience.

McGraw's metaphor serves obvious stylistic or ornamental functions. It is vivid and memorable because we usually do not think of life as a sport. But it serves potentially more powerful *rhetorical* functions as well. Listeners are invited to consider the similarities between "life" and "a full-contact sport." In doing so, their thoughts—their perceptions or understanding of life—are altered, and perhaps their everyday actions are changed. The potential for such changes in thought and action is evident when we consider an alternative metaphor. A television advertisement for a popular Italian restaurant, Macaroni Grill, says that "Life is delicious." If we follow that metaphor, the way we think about life and plan our everyday actions will be very different from "a full-contact sport."

Rhetorical Functions of Metaphor

Rhetorically, metaphors ask readers or listeners to see one thing, represented by the *tenor* or *focus*, "in terms of" another, represented by the *vehicle* or *frame*. When that happens, certain relevant and important characteristics of the *vehicle* or *frame* are "carried over" to the *tenor* or *focus*, thus providing a new understanding of that term.[11] According to rhetoricians Malcolm O. Sillars and Bruce E. Gronbeck, "metaphor, because it draws an analogy among situations that are unrelated (e.g., 'the war on drugs,' 'a marriage of convenience,' 'loan sharks'), is a way to create new thought through language use. Thus, it is central to making sense through language."[12] That sense making, however, depends upon whether readers or listeners can make the link; that is, on whether they understand what elements or characteristics of the *vehicle* or *frame* appropriately "carry over" to the *tenor* or *focus*. Critic Martha Cooper provides an additional example that explains this rhetorical function of metaphor:

> Probably the classic metaphor is, "man is a wolf." This statement encourages the audience to associate the characteristic(s) of a wolf with man. Stated more directly, the pattern is simply "man is like a wolf." The metaphor works like an enthymeme in that the audience is asked to participate by supplying the characteristics of a wolf and drawing the comparison between wolves and man. The metaphor, by suggesting an association, triggers a pattern of thinking in which comparisons are chained out.[13]

Although we cannot be certain, we imagine that the original author of that "classic" metaphor used "man" to mean all human beings. Thus, when readers or listeners make the association that Cooper explains, when they complete the enthymeme, their perception or understanding of "man," (that is, of humans) is changed.

That intended change in perception, however, occurs only when the appropriate characteristics of the *vehicle* or *frame*, "wolf," are carried over to the *tenor* or *focus*, "man." After all, wolves walk on four feet. Their bodies are covered with fur. They have tails, an acute sense of smell, long teeth, and sometimes they howl at the moon. Although possible, it is doubtful that the speaker or writer who says, "man is a wolf," intends for "man" to be seen in terms of those wolf-like characteristics. On the other hand, wolves are strong, powerful, cunning predators. They are fiercely territorial. They are dangerous to other animals and sometimes to each other. It is almost certainly wolf-like characteristics such as those that the speaker or writer intends for listeners or readers to "carry over" to humans. Thus, listeners or readers must "get it;" they must complete the enthymeme for the metaphor to have its intended effect.

Such rhetorical functions of metaphor grow from what anthropologist J. David Sapir calls "the simultaneous likeness and unlikeness of the two terms." According to Sapir, "by replacing a term continuous to a topic with one that is discontinuous or by putting the two in juxtaposition, we are compelled . . . to consider each term in relationship to the other."[14] Thus, to complete the enthymeme presented by the metaphor, "man is a wolf," listeners or readers must be aware simultaneously of how men and wolves are both alike and different. In the process of completing the enthymeme, the differences are discarded and the likenesses emphasized. Or, in Burke's words, the metaphor "brings out the thisness of that, or the thatness of this."[15] Michael Leff explains that the thought process involved "works in two stages; the juxtaposition of the two terms first causes the vehicle to assume a pattern of foreground associations, and then this pattern serves to direct our understanding of the tenor." The "mutual attraction of terms belonging to different classes," Leff writes, "causes a response that decomposes the elements associated with these terms and then recombines them into a new structure of meaning."[16] In the case of our example, "man is a wolf," when the process is complete the metaphor has performed its *rhetorical* function and listeners or readers begin to think of men in terms of the appropriate characteristics of wolves.

Cooper's assertion that metaphors function like enthymemes, arguments in which the audience participates in forming the conclusion, is especially important for rhetorical critics. If the function of metaphor depends on cooperation between the rhetor (the writer or speaker) and the audience (the readers or listeners) to produce meaning, then both must be part of the same "speech community." That is, they must at minimum share knowledge and experiences that allow the rhetor to form, and the audience to complete, the enthymeme. Ideally, in addition to knowledge and experience, they must also share beliefs, attitudes, and values that would permit the audience to complete the argument as the rhetor intends. Imagine audience members who have no knowledge whatsoever of the *vehicle* or *frame*, wolf. For them, the metaphor, "man is a wolf," would do little to alter their understanding of the *tenor* or *focus*, man. Or, imagine an audience whose beliefs, attitudes, and values related to "man" have been previously influenced by a competing metaphor, such as the Christian teaching that "man is a temple for the Holy Spirit." Even though that audience may understand the appropriate characteristics of wolves that the rhetor wishes them to carry over to man, they may be extremely reluctant to do so. As Leff explains, "metaphor draws its materials from communal knowledge, achieves its effects through the active cooperation of the auditor, and assumes its form in relation to a particular context."[17] Thus, if rhetor and audience are from different speech communities, the metaphor is likely to have little rhetorical, or even ornamental, effect.

Metaphor in Political Discourse

Sometimes the associations between the metaphoric *tenor* or *focus* and the *vehicle* or *frame* are relatively simple and straightforward, as in the examples provided thus far. But in other cases, those associations can become extremely complex and powerful, altering our understanding of significant issues and events. According to Leff, "Since metaphoric structure limits and organizes our perception of a situation, it seems to establish the ground for viewing that situation; it creates a perspective and hence defines the space in which we encounter the situation. A metaphoric meaning localizes our attention," says Leff. "It produces a frame within which we can synthesize our reactions to the ongoing flow of events in time."[18] In other words, metaphors can determine how we think about issues and the actions we take with regard to those issues. That function of metaphor is arguably most obvious and potentially most powerful in political discourse.

"Politics" and its companion subject "government" are extremely complex issues. When we think of "politics" we may think first of politicians, those individuals who seek elective government office. We may also think of the citizens whose votes determine the outcomes of elections, and of the various campaign staffers, fundraisers, consultants, and the like who play important roles in political campaigns. We may even think of the "political process" within which all of this takes place. Yet as complex as that process and the relationships between those individuals are, this is just the beginning.

We "do" politics at the local, state, national, and international levels. At least at the first three, politics involves executive, legislative, and judicial functions. Elected officials are joined in those functions by tens of thousands of public employees, staff members, researchers, aides, advisers, law enforcement officers, military personnel, diplomats, and the like. Those individuals, even more so than elected officials, are the "elites"[19] of politics—highly skilled or trained individuals often with considerable experience in dealing with myriad social, economic, legal, environmental, medical, and foreign policy issues, to name only a few. In the area of foreign policy, the complexity of "politics" is magnified by similar systems and processes in the nations with which the United States must deal.

Obviously, the details of "politics" are far too complex for any single individual to grasp fully. That fact holds significant implications for political discourse, the persuasive efforts to influence thought and action within the political system. To cope with the almost unending complexity of government, political discourse relies heavily on metaphor. Or as political scientist Seth Thompson explains, "routine political discourse consistently uses metaphors to capture an otherwise elusive reality."[20]

In one important sense, metaphors are essential simply for understanding complex political issues. Psychologist Jeffrey Scott Mio asserts that "metaphors can act as both filters that screen out much of the available information, leaving only the core ideas consistent with the metaphors, and as devices to collapse disparate information into smaller, more manageable packets."[21] That is, by drawing comparisons between complicated political issues (the *tenor* or *focus*) and more familiar, relatively simple events or ideas (the *vehicle* or *frame*), metaphors in political discourse render those complicated issues understandable. Thompson provides a typical example:

> [T]he flow of revenue to the Federal government is determined by, among other things, macroeconomic policy, international trade and capital flows, and the per-

turbations of the business cycle. The pattern of expenditures is influenced by social entitlements, continuing programs, new defense or civilian programs, and the
vagaries of disaster relief. Individuals have experience with budgets, but they are
typically simple enough affairs—income determined by one's salary and perhaps
investments, and expenditures largely determined by the necessities of survival at
the level to which one has become accustomed. In several fundamental ways the
federal budget is not just a personal or household budget writ large. But for the
typical citizen, and even for the relatively sophisticated policy maker, thinking
about the federal budget typically begins with the metaphor of a household or
business budget: *"[I]f the government were a company, it would have gone bankrupt
years ago"; "in government, just like your own home, you can't spend money you don't
have."*[22]

Thus, for both policy-making elites and for average citizens, the *tenor* or *focus*,
in this case the federal budget, becomes understandable in terms of the *vehicle* or
frame, the more familiar and considerably less complex budgets of a business or
family.

In perhaps a more important sense, metaphors in political discourse influence not only understanding but also actions—the policies enacted in response to
public issues or problems. Talking about and envisioning the issue of illegal drugs
as "a problem of addiction" or as a "symptom of social dysfunction" would lead to
policies that focus on the role of social workers, counselors, and medical personnel, whereas declaring "war" on drugs would shift the focus to law enforcement
and punishment or perhaps even to the military.[23] Historically, United States policy toward Vietnam was heavily influenced by what was called the "domino theory," the idea that if the Communists took control of South Vietnam, other
nations in the region, such as Cambodia, Laos, and Thailand, would also "fall"
under Communist control. In this case, the *tenor* or *focus* of the metaphor—the
complex political and military conditions in Southeast Asia—came to be seen in
terms of a simple, familiar *vehicle* or *frame*—a line of dominoes falling one after another when the first domino is pushed over. U.S. policy was formulated in an effort to stop that first domino, South Vietnam, from falling.[24]

So important is this rhetorical function of metaphor in political discourse that
competing political forces—candidates for office, political parties, liberals, conservatives—struggle for a sort of "metaphoric superiority." The metaphor that gains
widest acceptance, within the government, in the public at large, or both, often
determines the outcome of political contests. During the Vietnam conflict, supporters of U.S. military action in Southeast Asia, known metaphorically as
"hawks," frequently offered the domino theory to justify continued military efforts. On the other side of the issue, opponents of military action, known
metaphorically as "doves," came to label the Vietnam conflict as a "quagmire"
from which the United States should extricate itself. Neither the domino theory
nor the quagmire, of course, explained fully the extremely complex social, economic, political, and military situation that existed in Southeast Asia. Nevertheless, both elite policy makers and ordinary U.S. citizens came to see that
geographic region as either a line of dominoes waiting to fall or as a quagmire.

Eventually, the quagmire metaphor gained wider acceptance than the domino theory, and the United States withdrew its military forces from South Vietnam.

Thompson points out that metaphors function in exactly the same way in domestic politics. "As much as they would like to, policy makers are unable to control the range of metaphors available or the uses to which they are put," he explains. "Opponents and interest groups in domestic politics compete vigorously to establish the winning metaphor in policy debates and, without too much exaggeration, campaigns can be seen as struggles over metaphors." How one voted in the 1992 U.S. presidential election, for example, may have been determined by whether one saw Bill Clinton as "Slick Willy" or "The Man From Hope."[25]

Critics must also keep in mind that these potentially powerful, rhetorical functions of metaphor are not without potential risks. One of those risks is that use of metaphor may so oversimplify complex issues or problems that proposed remedies are themselves oversimplified to the point of ineffectiveness. As already noted, Mio explains that metaphors "screen out much of the available information, leaving only the core ideas." Unfortunately, the key to resolving complex political issues often lies in managing details rather than in core ideas.

Metaphors may also be a "double-edged sword" that can work both for and against the interests of rhetors who use them. Put differently, although metaphors may produce desired rhetorical effects, they can also entrap the rhetors who use them. As we explained earlier, declaring "war" on drugs leads to policies that feature intensified law enforcement efforts and perhaps even the use of U.S. military forces to interdict drug shipments and to arrest and punish drug dealers. The metaphor also has significant rhetorical power to rally public support for those efforts. Nevertheless, the United States simply cannot "win" a war on drugs in the sense of "winning" a war against another nation; that is, "drugs" can never be forced to sign an "unconditional surrender" and submit to an "army of occupation" to enforce the terms of that surrender. So, although officials who declare "war" on drugs may enjoy some short-term rhetorical success in the form of public support for their programs, and those programs may produce some dramatic results, the metaphor may also create expectations for the outcome of that "war" that are simply unattainable. Continuing frustration with the drug problem in the United States may be a result.[26]

Likewise, when Iraqi forces invaded a smaller and weaker Kuwait in 1989, U.S. President George H. W. Bush justified military rather than diplomatic action to remove Iraq from Kuwait in part by using metaphors that compared Iraqi President Saddam Hussein to Adolf Hitler. Those metaphors undoubtedly came naturally to Bush, a former World War II Navy pilot. According to Thompson,

> for a generation of American foreign policy makers who were formed by the experience of the 1930s and 1940s, *"Munich"* was the metaphor for the dire consequences of seeking to negotiate with perceived aggressors. . . . The emotional loading of the metaphor was . . . compelling—in the specific instance of the failed attempt by Britain and France to reach an accommodation with Nazi Germany at Munich, the result was the horror of World War II.[27]

The metaphor worked by carrying over characteristics of the archetypal villain, Hitler, to Hussein. Nevertheless, when Operation Desert Storm ended with Hussein still in power in Iraq, many questioned why Bush had let a "Hitler" go.[28] Once again, continuing United States frustration with Iraq may be a result.

Perhaps the greatest of those risks occurs when metaphors become "literalized"; that is, when we stop thinking of one thing *in terms of* another and begin to think of it as literally *being* the other. As rhetorician Robert L. Ivie explains, "We are in the presence of a literalized metaphor when we act upon the figurative as if it were real, not recognizing that two domains of meaning have been merged into one despite their differences."[29] Ivie's analysis of Cold War rhetoric revealed a cluster of metaphoric images that were commonly used to characterize both the United States and the Soviet Union. "Summarized briefly, these vehicles illustrate the rhetorical essentials of the logic of confrontation," he notes. "The nation's adversary is characterized as a mortal threat to freedom, a germ infecting the body politic, a plague upon the liberty of humankind, and a barbarian intent upon destroying civilization." Equally vivid were the metaphors that depicted the United States. Ivie continues: "Freedom is portrayed as weak, fragile, and feminine—as vulnerable to disease and rape. The price of freedom is necessarily high because the alternatives are reduced symbolically to enslavement and death."[30] The problem, says Ivie, was that these metaphors became literalized in a way that severely and unnecessarily limited the policies available to the United States. According to Ivie, these metaphors "evolved over four decades into powerful conventions of public discourse that diminish the political imagination, undermine the incentive to envision better alternatives, and thus reduce the scope of practical options available to leaders of both nations. . . . Yet, the stuff of which these durable motives are made is mere metaphor."[31] In other words, Cold War rhetors were also trapped by their language.

Similarly, in his analysis of Cold War rhetoric, Edwin Black suggests that the pervasiveness of the "cancer of communism" metaphor in the rhetoric of the most radical elements of the right in U.S. politics may have brought the world to the brink of nuclear war. Noting that the "cancer of communism" metaphor is "simply not present in 'liberal' or leftist discourses," Black argues that "it seems to crop up constantly among Rightists—Rightists who sometimes have little else in common besides a political position and the metaphor itself." Further, Black suggests that the "cancer of communism" metaphor may have been "literalized," to use Ivie's term, in a way that risked nuclear annihilation:

> We understand well enough that when the Rightist speaks of communism he refers to virtually all social welfare and civil rights legislation. What we understand less well is that when he refers to America, he refers to a polity already in the advanced stages of an inexorable disease whose suppurating sores are everywhere manifest and whose voice is a death rattle. . . . The patient is *in extremis.* It is in this light that risks must be calculated, and in this light the prospect of nuclear war becomes thinkable. Why not chance it, after all? What alternative is there? The patient is dying; is it not time for the ultimate surgery? What is there to lose? In such

a context, an unalarmed attitude toward the use of atomic weapons is not just reasonable; it is obvious.[32]

Ivie and Black are not alone in warning of the perils of literalizing metaphors of disease and illness. Steven Perry's analysis of the "infestation metaphor" in the rhetoric of Adolf Hitler helps to explain how significant segments of the German population of the 1930s and 1940s were persuaded to turn violently against their own Jewish brothers and sisters. Perry explains:

> Though there was unquestionably a very real current of anti-semitism in central Europe at the time of National Socialism's rise, the Jews nonetheless were not popularly perceived as enemies of the German nation. Hitler had to shape and channel popular anti-semitism; particularly, he had to explain how it was that the heretofore *scorned* Jew was actually a dangerous and foreign threat to the very foundation of the German nation. The use of infestation metaphors provided Hitler with the answer. Such metaphors were suitably de-humanizing, and, even more important, they provided a figurative explanation of the Jewish threat: The Jew was like the disease-causing microbe, the internal parasite, or the secretly-administered poison, wreaking an invisible but ultimately fatal havoc on the national body. Hence, it was not as though the Jew had somehow suddenly metamorphosed from a worthless but harmless object of scorn into a full-blown national threat. Rather, the Jew had always posed such a threat, and the German masses had only needed a savior, a Hitler, to rise and show them the real working of the insidious, invisible Jewish plague.[33]

Thus, Perry suggests, Hitler was able to persuade Germany to follow him into the holocaust.

In sum, metaphors work by drawing comparisons between two things, people, places, situations, events, and so forth. In doing so, they can embellish the style of written and oral messages alike. More important, they also have the capacity to perform powerful rhetorical functions, altering the thoughts and actions of readers and listeners. And although metaphors are potentially powerful figures of speech, their use also entails potential risk. Now, we turn to how rhetorical critics might make use of this knowledge of metaphor.

Critiquing Metaphor

We view rhetorical criticism as a primary means for creating knowledge in the humanistic study of communication. Further, we believe strongly that for criticism to fulfill that function, it must be an "organic" or inductive process. That process ends by bringing together textual, contextual, theoretical, and interpretive or evaluative elements in a finished critique. It begins, however, with a close, exhaustive reading of the rhetorical artifact (the text) under consideration, the end of which is largely descriptive at the initial stage. When that descriptive analysis is complete, the discourse is placed within its historical and cultural context and the rhetorical problems or obstacles to success faced by the rhetor must be explained.

In the third stage of the critical process, based on a thorough understanding of both text and context, critics select or invent a theoretical framework or analytical tool, such as a theory of metaphor, that both guides the completed analysis and suggests criteria or standards for interpretation and evaluation. Only when those three stages are complete can the textual, contextual, theoretical, and evaluative or interpretive elements be brought together.[34]

Thus, we believe that to talk about "metaphor criticism" as a distinct form or type of rhetorical criticism is both misleading and potentially counterproductive. Rather, we see metaphor as one of many analytical tools available to critics, a theoretical framework that can guide rhetorical analysis. Put differently, critics should "do" metaphor criticism only when careful descriptive analysis of the text in question reveals that metaphor is a significant—perhaps *the most* significant—rhetorical element in that text. To reverse that process, to start with a theory of metaphor and then apply it indiscriminately to whatever text happens to be in question, we believe, renders the entire critical process fraudulent.[35] That process, then, must begin with a thorough, close reading of the text under consideration. When that initial step reveals that metaphor is a salient rhetorical element in the text, relevant theory can become a useful analytical tool. However, critics should remember that appropriate figures must be major elements in that text before metaphoric criticism can be productive.

When metaphor is a significant element of the text, critics should determine whether a single major metaphor is developed throughout the text or whether a series of metaphors are present. If a series of metaphors are present, critics should determine whether they operate independently or whether they cohere into a single vision or image. For example, a close reading of Martin Luther King, Jr.'s famous speech, "I Have a Dream," reveals that three major, interrelated metaphors dominate the text: (1) the "promise" set forth in the Declaration of Independence "that all men would be guaranteed the unalienable rights of life, liberty, and the pursuit of happiness" (the *tenor* or *focus*) characterized metaphorically as a "check" or "promissory note to which every American was to fall heir" but that had yet to be paid in full (the *vehicle* or *frame*); (2) King's goal of a free and just society if only the check were to be cashed (*tenor* or *focus*), characterized metaphorically as his "dream" (*vehicle* or *frame*); and (3) King's vision of the "great nation" the United States could become (*tenor* or *focus*), characterized metaphorically as freedom "ringing" throughout the land (*vehicle* or *frame*).[36]

Those three major metaphors in King's speech cohere into a single vision in that they "move" chronologically from the past (the promise set forth in the Declaration of Independence), to the present (conditions of oppression for black Americans as a result of the failure of the United States to "cash the check"), and into the future (the vision of freedom ringing throughout the land). Moreover, the metaphors cohere even further in that they also move from bad (the appalling conditions faced by black Americans) to good (the free and just society King envisioned).

Critics should determine as well whether minor or secondary metaphors are present in the text and, if so, how they interact with the major metaphor or metaphors. Once again, secondary metaphors appear throughout King's "I Have a Dream" speech. Some stand alone to create vivid images in the minds of listeners. For instance, appalling social conditions (*tenor* or *frame*) are depicted metaphorically when King explains that black Americans are "still sadly crippled by the manacles of segregation and the chains of discrimination" (*vehicle* or *frame*). And economic conditions (*tenor* or *focus*) are depicted when he says that black Americans are living "on a lonely island of poverty in the midst of a vast ocean of material prosperity" (*vehicle* or *frame*). However, other secondary metaphors function to reinforce the past-present-future and bad-to-good relationship between the major metaphors. "Now is the time to lift our nation from the quicksands of racial injustice to the solid rock of brotherhood," said King. "The whirlwinds of revolt will continue to shake the foundations of our nation until the bright day of justice emerges," he continued.

When major and secondary metaphors have been identified, critics might productively ask: What elements or characteristics of the *vehicle* or *frame* does the rhetor intend for the audience to carry over to the *tenor* or *focus?* How do those elements or characteristics function to alter audience understanding of the *tenor* or *focus?* How is that altered understanding related to the *purpose* or *purposes* the rhetor wishes to achieve? How do the metaphors interact with other rhetorical strategies present in the text? And finally, how might the use of metaphor best be interpreted or evaluated?

We hope this brief description suggests at least a general direction for critiquing metaphor. Now, we turn to an example of metaphor criticism that incorporates all of the elements of a finished critique that we mentioned earlier: contextualization, a theoretical framework or analytical tool, application of that theory to illuminate the text, and evaluation or interpretation.

CRITICAL ESSAY

The text we have selected for analysis in our example of metaphor criticism is the keynote address delivered on July 16, 1984, to the Democratic National Convention in San Francisco by New York's then-Governor Mario Cuomo. Although the speech was delivered nearly twenty years ago, it is especially well suited for this example. Rhetorical scholars have named Cuomo's speech one of the greatest speeches of the twentieth century. Late in 1999, Professors Stephen Lucas of the University of Wisconsin, Madison, and Martin J. Medhurst of Texas A& M University surveyed academics in the field of speech communication and rhetorical studies, asking them to identify the century's greatest speeches. One hundred thirty-seven individuals responded to the survey, ranking speeches based on impact, rhetorical artistry, organization, style, and presentation of arguments. Mario Cuomo's keynote address to the 1984 Democratic National Convention was ranked eleventh.[37] Thus, all students of rhetoric and rhetorical criticism should be familiar with this example of rhetorical artistry and sophistication. Moreover, even a cursory reading of Cuomo's speech reveals that metaphor is a significant—perhaps *the most* significant—rhetorical element in that text. Thus, the speech is not only a model of rhetorical excellence, but its analysis also provides beginning rhetorical critics with a clear example of a text that warrants metaphor criticism.

Critical Essay: Mario Cuomo's Keynote Address to the 1984 Democratic National Convention[38]

Immediate reactions to New York Governor Mario Cuomo's keynote address to the 1984 Democratic National Convention were extremely positive. Delegates in the convention hall were lavish in their praise. "'He's reaching an emotional chord that hasn't been touched since John Kennedy,' said Lucille Maurer, a Maryland legislator from Silver Spring."[39] "It was a perfect speech," added Virginia state party chairman Alan A. Dimondstein. "He talked about the middle class. We're talking about a man who stood up and expressed the feelings of the majority of people in America."[40]

Media pundits were likewise kind in their assessment of the speech. Hedrick Smith of the *New York Times* observed that Cuomo "built a speech like a lawyer making a case,"[41] and then added: "Beforehand, [Cuomo's] aides had said the keynote was 'not a stemwinder, not a podium-pounder' but a carefully constructed indictment of the Reagan legacy. Yet with eyes welling with tears and a powerful rhythmic delivery, the Governor repeatedly roused the Democrats to foot-stomping applause and roaring partisan chants."[42] Howell Raines, also of the *New York Times*, noted the "persistent, preacherly rhythm" of Cuomo's speech.[43] Lou Cannon and Helen Dewar of the *Washington Post* observed that "the delegates . . . listened in rapt attention to the New York governor and interrupted him with applause 42 times."[44]

Interesting as those comments are, they do little to explain the rhetorical force of Cuomo's speech. That is, although those comments describe Cuomo's delivery of the speech and the positive reactions of both the delegates and the press, they do not reveal the elements within the text that had the capacity to produce those positive reactions. The rhetorical force of the speech, we believe, grew from the Governor's use of metaphor first to refute President Ronald Reagan's own metaphoric depiction of the United States as a "Shining City on a Hill," and then to depict the people of the United States as a "family" that must reject Reagan's policies and elect a Democrat as president.

The Context: Obstacles to Rhetorical Success.   Cuomo suggested the purpose of his keynote address in the third paragraph of the speech when he said that he would "deal immediately with questions that should determine this election and that we all know are vital to the American people."[45] But a simple enumeration of campaign issues was obviously not his ultimate aim. Instead, he sought to unite Democrats and other voters to elect Walter Mondale and Geraldine Ferraro president and vice president of the United States. At the end of the address he said:

And, ladies and gentlemen, on January 20, 1985 . . . we will have a new president of the United States, a Democrat born not to the blood of kings but to the blood of pioneers and immigrants.

And we will have America's first woman vice president, the child of immigrants, and she . . . will open with one magnificent stroke, a whole new frontier for the United States. Now, it will happen.

It will happen—if we make it happen; if you and I can make it happen.

In his effort to achieve that purpose, Cuomo faced significant rhetorical problems growing from the generic obstacles encountered by all keynote speakers as well as from obstacles unique to his specific situation.

Generic Obstacles.   The opening of a political party's national convention is an identifiable, regularly recurring ceremony that requires that a speech be given to fulfill expectations for the occasion. Wayne N. Thompson thus called keynote addresses "a subgenre of ceremonial speaking,"[46] making them epideictic in Aristotelian terms and suggesting that their method should be praise and blame.[47] But the purpose of keynote addresses goes beyond traditional aims of epideictic speaking. As Edwin A. Miles observed, the "keynote speech has two primary purposes: to raise the enthusiasm of the delegates to a high pitch and to rally the voters of the nation to the party's standard."[48] That is, in addition to any purely ceremonial functions, the pragmatic aim of keynote addresses is to help the party's nominee win the coming presidential election. Cuomo's purpose reveals just that aim.

The keynote address, then, is a rhetorical hybrid. It employs epideictic means—praise and blame—appropriate to the ceremonial occasion in order to achieve deliberative ends, election of the party's candidate. Thus, Miles explained that highly partisan audiences in the convention hall came to expect keynote speakers' "language . . . to be bombastic, for custom demands that he 'avoid no extravagance of speech, either in praise or blame' in glorifying the brilliant accomplishments of his own party or in lamenting the dismal failures of the opposition."[49]

Unfortunately, perhaps, for contemporary speakers, widespread television coverage of keynote addresses has been problematic. Keynoters encounter not only the partisan, immediate audience, but also a large and diverse audience watching the televised speech at home. Some members of that larger audience are equally partisan, but most vary in their conviction and many support the opposition.[50] Those dual audiences present keynote speakers with a dilemma. According to Thompson, "whereas emotional partisans of a speaker's own party expect a vigorous attack on the opposition, neutrals and members of the other political party are likely to find strong attacks irritating and offensive."[51]

Cuomo faced those obstacles generic to the keynote situation as he addressed the 1984 Democratic National Convention. But like any other keynote speaker, he also faced obstacles growing from the specific problems that developed as Democrats prepared to meet in San Francisco in mid July.

Specific Obstacles.   On the eve of Cuomo's address, Democrats were dispirited and divided. Political commentators Jack W. Germond and Jules Witcover noted that many convention delegates (and probably many other Democrats as well!) despaired of Mondale's chances of defeating Ronald Reagan in November.[52] But the delegates' spirits were buoyed significantly, Germond and Witcover reported, "when the word of Gerry Ferraro's selection [as Mondale's vice-presidential running mate] filtered out on the Wednesday night before the convention was to open." The delegates' reaction to Ferraro, according to Germond and Witcover, was "akin to pulling the living room drapes back and letting the sunshine in. . . . [W]hat shook the Democrats out of their doldrums was the evidence in Mondale's decision that he was not the storefront Indian he seemed to so many of them to be—dull, unimaginative, the cardboard New Dealer who dared to be cautious," they explained. "Choosing a woman was not the act of a cautious man; a desperate one, maybe. But even so, how much more interesting it was, and challenging, to have a prospective presidential nominee who was swinging for the fences for a change."[53]

Despite the excitement over the selection of Ferraro, opinion polls indicated that the Democratic ticket was in trouble. As Robert Strauss, former head of the Democratic National Committee, explained: "If [Mondale and Ferraro] try to win a popularity contest with Ronald Reagan, they're not going to make much headway. The people of America like Ronald Reagan too well."[54] Strauss was right. The day after Cuomo's speech, the *Los Angeles Times* reported a Gallup poll indicating that "based on in-person interviews with a national sample of registered voters . . . Reagan-Bush beats Mondale-Ferraro, 53% to 39%. When Reagan and Mondale alone are pitted against each other, Reagan's margin is 55% to 36%." Among women voters, the same poll revealed, "the contest would be a virtual toss-up, with 47% choosing Reagan-Bush compared to 45% for Mondale-Ferraro. Among men, the GOP ticket leads 59% to 34%."[55]

Whether those figures signaled distrust of Mondale, approval of Reagan's political agenda and policies, or simple affection for the amiable president, they did not look good for the Democratic candidates. Moreover, coupled with the generic obstacles faced by all keynote speakers, they constituted significant rhetorical problems for Cuomo. To overcome those problems, Cuomo relied in large part on the strategic use of metaphor.

Metaphor as Rhetorical Strategy.   Cuomo's reliance on metaphor was consistent with expectations for epideictic speaking's elevated style. Nevertheless, consideration of the nonornamental capacities of metaphor is essential for understanding its functions in Cuomo's keynote address. That metaphor serves more than embellishment or semiotic purposes has been demonstrated by scholarship in interaction theory and adapted in critical studies illustrating the significant interplay between metaphor and topical invention, wherein metaphor "frames rhetorical situations" and "topics order the elements within the frame."[56] Figures that frame situations support George Lakoff and Mark Johnson's thesis that metaphor is "primarily a matter of thought and action and only derivatively a matter of language," instrumental to the creation of reality (especially "social realities"), and advantageous to people in power who "get to impose their metaphors."[57] The power to create a new order by imposing a metaphor that "redescribes reality," Paul Ricoeur argues, is contingent on first "creating rifts in an old order."[58] Moreover, the creation of dissonance is promoted when the similarities selected for a metaphorical frame are experiential rather than objective. As Lakoff and Johnson point out, objectivists may be correct to suggest that "things in the world" constrain our conceptual systems, but that matters only if the "things" are experienced.[59] Metaphor's capacity to displace one "reality" with another by focusing on experiential themes is central to Cuomo's use of the trope.

Textual Analysis: Cuomo's Use of Metaphor.   Cuomo's ultimate objective was to promote a vision of the American people as a "family." Movement toward that goal proceeded through three phases. First, consonant with the dictates of Ricoeur's theory of metaphor, Cuomo aimed to raise doubts about the accuracy of a favored Reagan figure, that of America as a "shining city on a hill."[60] Once that perception was altered, he moved to the articulation of the American family alternative. And finally, Cuomo offered his own family's experience as an embodiment of the metaphor's accurate reflection of the American reality.

Since the creation of a new perception of reality is enhanced by an initial denigration of an old conception, Cuomo began his appeal with a revision of a favorite Reagan metaphor:

> Ten days ago, President Reagan admitted that although some people in this country seemed to be doing well nowadays, others were unhappy, even worried, about themselves, their families and their futures.
>
> The president said that he didn't understand that fear. He said, "Why, this country is a shining city on a hill."
>
> And the president is right. In many ways we *are* "a shining city on a hill."
>
> But the hard truth is that not everyone is sharing in this city's splendor and glory.
>
> A shining city is perhaps all the president sees from the portico of the White House and the veranda of his ranch, where everyone seems to be doing well.
>
> But there's another city, another part of the city, the part where some people can't pay their mortgages and most young people can't afford one, where students can't afford the education they need and middle-class parents watch the dreams they hold for their children evaporate.
>
> In this part of the city there are more poor than ever, more families in trouble, and more and more people who need help but can't find it.
>
> Even worse: There are elderly people who tremble in the basements of the houses there.
>
> And there are people who sleep in the city streets, in the gutter, where the glitter doesn't show.
>
> There are ghettos where thousands of young people, without a job or an education, give their lives away to drug dealers every day.
>
> There is despair, Mr. President, in the faces that you don't see, in the places that you don't visit in our shining city.
>
> In fact, you ought to know Mr. President, that this nation is more a "Tale of Two Cities" than it is just a "Shining City on a Hill."

The "Tale of Two Cities" metaphor was designed to "displace" Reagan's vision of reality, the "Shining City on a Hill," with a new vision. Significantly, Cuomo's contrasting metaphor did not force his listeners to see America from *either* the perspective of the Shining City *or* the perspective of its opposite—perhaps a "wasteland." Rather, America was *both* the Shining City that Reagan saw *and* a much more dismal place. Cuomo built the remainder of his anti-administration appeal on the foundation of the two-cities theme as he proceeded through a series of paired consequences he described as inevitable results of Reagan's programs. Republican policies, he argued, "divide the nation: into the lucky and the left-out, the royalty and the rabble. The Republicans are willing to treat that division as victory. They would cut this nation in half, into those temporarily better off and those worse off than before, and call it recovery." The Democrats' task, he continued, was to work for the election of a "new President of the United States." The challengers' success in 1984, Cuomo maintained, was contingent on supplanting one vision of the nation with another.

The objective, he intoned, was first to "make the American people hear our 'tale of two cities'," and then to "convince them that we don't have to settle for two cities, that we can have one city, indivisible, shining for all its people." The metaphorical framing of his theme allowed Cuomo to describe figuratively the objectionable consequences of the president's policies without alienating an increasingly patriotic electorate overwhelmingly enamored of the incumbent. At the same time, by raising doubts about the opposition's ideas, he fulfilled one of the functions of the keynote speech—blaming the opposition.

Praise of the Democratic Party, an equally important keynote function, stemmed from the subsequent introduction of the family metaphor. The trope addressed the concerns of both the immediate convention observers and the "middle America" target audience. For partisans, the figure of the family served two purposes. At one level, Cuomo's enunciation of party achievements differentiated what he termed realistic, principled Democrats from their Republican counterparts. Cuomo contended, for instance, that whereas GOP policies preclude the metaphoric "wagon train" of American progress from reaching the "frontier unless some of our old, some of our young, and some of our weak are left behind," Democrats believe that "we can make it all the way with the whole family intact." That "we have," he continued, is attested to by "wagon train after wagon train" of success, ever since Franklin Roosevelt "lifted himself from his wheelchair to lift this nation from its knees." Democrats led the way, in Cuomo's view: "To new frontiers of education, housing, peace. The whole family aboard. Constantly reaching out to extend and enlarge that family. Lifting them up into the wagon on the way. Blacks and Hispanics, and people of every ethnic group, and Native Americans—all those struggling to build their families and claim some small share of America."

The principles that underlay Cuomo's description of the party surely meshed with the personal facts influential in the target audience's thinking—family, mutual support, equality, and progress. Cuomo made explicit the link between such values and the ideals of the middle class when, late in the speech, he extended the family theme from the past and present to the future. "We can have a future that provides for all the young of the present," he asserted in a subtly worded play on the guiding family metaphor, "by marrying common sense and compassion." Success will depend, he suggested, on continued recognition of the importance of the party's "progressive principles. That they helped lift up generations to the middle class and higher: gave us a chance to work, go to college, to raise a family, to own a house, to be secure in our old age, and before that to reach heights that our own parents would not have dared dream of."

Although it is unlikely that many members of the larger public would take issue with the desirability of the middle class family ideals he described, Cuomo clearly believed that his perspective of the American "city" and "family" differed sharply from that of citizens who consistently expressed favor with President Reagan's performance. Consequently, he sought to revise the dominant perception of the country's status. Cuomo spoke of Republican policies guided by a philosophy that dictated that government "can't do everything," so it should settle for taking care of "the strong and hope that economic ambition and charity will do the rest. Make the rich richer and what falls from the table will be enough for the middle class and those trying to make it into the middle class." Left to their own survival skills in a nation governed by such a philosophy are the "retired school teacher in Duluth," the "child in Buffalo," the "disabled man in Boston," and the "hungry in Little Rock." An alternative, Cuomo maintained, was the Democratic principle of mutuality that underlay a government committed to the "good of us all, for the love of this great nation, for the American family, for the love of God."

What distinguished his pronouncement of this litany of stock political god-terms was Cuomo's personalization of them, for the ideas were not merely lines in a speech but convictions produced of a lifetime. Thus, when he moved into his peroration, Cuomo reinforced the metaphorical base of his message. In so doing, he offered his own experience as a warrant for a shift in the focus of public attention, away from a now tarnished "shining city on a hill" and toward recognition of a strong future via the "American family." The philosophy of mutuality that had moved Democrats to protect the retired, the young, the disabled, and the hungry, he claimed, "is the real story of the shining city. It's a story I didn't read in a book, or learn in a classroom. I saw it, and I lived it. Like many of you." Then, Cuomo's own family became the symbol of the American story:

> I watched a small man with thick callouses on both hands work 15 and 16 hours a day. I saw him once literally bleed from the bottoms of his feet, a man who came here uneducated, alone, unable to speak the language, who taught me all I needed to know about faith and hard work by the simple eloquence of his example. I learned about our kind of democracy from my father. And, I learned about our obligation to each other from him and from my mother. They asked only for a chance to work and to make the world better for their children and they asked to be protected in those moments when they would not be able to protect themselves. This nation and this nation's government did that for them.
>
> And that they were able to build a family and live in dignity and see one of their children go from behind their little grocery store in South Jamaica on the

other side of the tracks where he was born, to occupy the highest seat in the great-est state of the greatest nation in the only world we know, is an ineffably beauti-ful tribute to the democratic process.

With the choice of the family metaphor, Cuomo not only offered an alter-native to the dominant Reagan trope, but also provided through his own experi-ence a case for the efficacy of the alternative.

Conclusion.   Assessed for its effect, Gov. Mario Cuomo's keynote address to the 1984 Democratic National Convention merits a largely negative evaluation. His aim had been to rally support for the Democratic candidates, Walter Mondale and Geraldine Ferraro. But despite his best effort, Ronald Reagan and George H.W. Bush rolled to an impressive victory in November, carrying forty-nine states with 525 electoral votes to Mondale's 10—the largest electoral-college margin in his-tory.[61] However, given Reagan's enormous personal popularity, it is probably un-fair to expect any keynote address, no matter how brilliant, to carry the election for Mondale and Ferraro.

Judged by an aesthetic standard, however, Cuomo's speech is worthy of praise as a highly skilled effort to overcome significant rhetorical problems. Clearly, his rhetorical strategy met the situational and audience challenges posed by the keynote setting. By first raising doubts about the accuracy of Ronald Rea-gan's vision of America as a "shining city on a hill," Cuomo united his diverse lis-teners around the shared values and experiences common to both target audiences. He did so by packaging his theme of progressive pragmatism or tradi-tional Democratic principles in the metaphorical container of the family, thereby offering an appealing alternative to the president's preferred but allegedly mis-leading trope.

Convention speakers faced with similar demands thus might be well advised to give due attention to the potential of figurative language as a powerful force for framing complex issues and engaging multiple audiences. The demonstrated ca-pacity of metaphor to challenge established images and present attractive alterna-tives suggests the prospective value of such endeavors.

PERSONAL COMMENTS ON THIS ESSAY

As its rank (eleventh) among the top one hundred speeches of the twentieth cen-tury suggests, Mario Cuomo's keynote address to the 1984 Democratic National Convention provides fertile ground for rhetorical analysis. Thus, although we be-lieve our critique that focuses on Cuomo's use of metaphor yields significant in-sight into how the speech was intended to work, we also know that our metaphor analysis does not exhaust the text. Other critical approaches grounded in other rhetorical theories could have produced equally insightful analyses.

For example, a close reading of Cuomo's speech reveals the presence of an-other figure of speech that Kenneth Burke has also labeled one of the four "master tropes"—irony.[62] Interestingly, Cuomo's use of irony grows out of the metaphors he develops in the speech. More specifically, by contrasting Ronald Reagan's metaphor of the United States as a "Shining City on a Hill" with his own metaphor of the United States as a "Tale of Two Cities," Cuomo portrays Reagan as an "ironic victim" who is blind to the true condition of the country and out of touch with the needs of the people.[63] So, rather than focusing exclusively on Cuomo's use of metaphor, critics could focus on his use of irony or even on the interaction between the two.

Likewise, although we chose to examine Cuomo's speech as a single rhetorical act bounded by a relatively narrow historical context, it could also be viewed as a member of a group or class of similar rhetorical acts—the *genre* of political convention keynote addresses.[64] Taking that approach, critics might carefully describe the keynote genre, develop from that description a set of standards or criteria that might be used to evaluate individual speeches that form the genre, and then apply those criteria to Cuomo's speech.

We are not suggesting that any one of these three critical approaches—metaphor, irony, genre—is inherently superior or inferior to the others. Quite the contrary; we believe that the richness of Cuomo's speech allows for significant, insightful analysis from any of these approaches, and probably others as well. In other words, careful descriptive analysis of Cuomo's speech indicates that metaphor, irony, and genre are all three major rhetorical elements of the text. Critics might productively exploit all three, but it would be a mistake to assume that there is one—and *only* one—approach to the speech. In the case of our critique, we chose metaphor criticism because in this chapter we wanted to illustrate that approach.

POTENTIALS AND PITFALLS

Appropriately used, metaphor criticism has the potential to reveal the rhetorical functions of language—of tropes and figures of speech—frequently imagined to be primarily ornamental. Although texts rich in metaphor may be aesthetically pleasing, metaphor analysis can reveal their capacity to alter thought and action and to influence—for good or ill—the policy decisions made by individuals and even by entire nations. Our critique of Cuomo's speech is one example of such analysis. Others are included in our list of "Top Picks" below.

Earlier we suggested that critics should engage in metaphor criticism—that is, that critics should select metaphor as an analytical tool or theoretical perspective—only when close analysis reveals that metaphor is a dominant element of the text in question. Thus, we believe that the major "pitfall" of metaphor analysis would be to use that theoretical perspective when it is not warranted by the text.

For example, on July 29, 1998, U.S. Supreme Court Associate Justice Clarence Thomas, a politically conservative black American, addressed the National Bar Association (NBA), a largely liberal organization of black American lawyers. In that speech, Thomas sought to answer criticisms from many members of the NBA, as well as from the public, that his conservative judicial philosophy and many of his judicial rulings were somehow inappropriate for a black American jurist. Thomas's speech is rhetorically interesting and is especially important both socially and historically as a defense of black American conservatism. A close reading of Thomas's speech reveals that it contains many metaphors: "The hope that there would be expeditious resolutions to our myriad problems has . . . evaporated"; "the stench of racial inferiority still confounds my olfactory nerves"; "the opaque racial prism of analysis . . ."; "some who would not venture onto the more sophisticated analytical turf are quite content to play in the minor leagues of primitive harping"; "the lingering stench of racism . . ."; "the battle between passion and reason . . ."; "the caldron of ridicule . . ."; and others. However, those metaphors appear in isolation and do not cohere in a rhetorically significant fashion.[65]

Similarly, in his October 17, 1995, address to the Million Man March in Washington, DC, Nation of Islam Minister Louis Farrakhan employed several minor metaphors and an extended metaphor grounded in Biblical allusion when addressing the relationship between black Americans and the major U.S. political parties. Nevertheless, those metaphors were of relatively minor importance in his speech.[66] Thus, despite the fact that metaphors appear in both the speech by Thomas and that by Farrakhan, and the fact that these speeches are important both historically and rhetorically, we do not view metaphor criticism as a productive approach to these texts.

Likewise, George W. Bush's justifications for the U.S. invasion of Iraq in March 2003 are extremely important historically, and they are also interesting rhetorically. However, although close textual analysis of Bush's major speeches reveals various isolated metaphors, once again they do not cohere in a rhetorically significant fashion. Rather, Bush's discourse on Iraq is dominated by mythic images of "Good versus Evil" that provide fertile ground for rhetorical analysis but not for metaphoric criticism.[67] In short, neither the rhetorical sophistication of the text nor its historical significance guarantees that metaphoric criticism will be productive.

METAPHOR CRITICISM TOP PICKS

We believe the following essays are exemplars of metaphor criticism that should be familiar to all beginning rhetorical critics:

Ausmus, William A., "Pragmatic Uses of Metaphor: Models and Metaphor in the Nuclear Winter Scenario," *Communication Monographs* 65 (1998): 67–82. The "nuclear winter" metaphor was a dominant trope in the campaign against atomic weapons in the late twentieth century. Ausmus examines the invention and evolution of the metaphor in two articles by Carl Sagan. Sagan and his coauthors created the metaphor to explain scientific models in *Science*. Sagan then employed the metaphor in *Foreign Affairs* to argue for disarmament.

Black, Edwin, "The Second Persona," *Quarterly Journal of Speech* 56 (1970): 109–119. Black's essay illustrates how rhetors can invite listeners to assume roles or personas—to think of themselves in particular ways—that heighten the persuasiveness of speeches. He illustrates that strategy through analysis of the "Cancer of Communism" metaphor in the Cold War rhetoric of the radical Right in U.S. politics.

Condit, Celeste M., Benjamin R. Bates, et al., "Recipes or Blueprints for Our Genes? How Contexts Selectively Activate the Multiple Meanings of Metaphor." *Quarterly Journal of Speech* 88 (2002): 303–325. The authors evaluate why "recipe" did not successfully replace "blueprint" as the dominant metaphor in 1990s public discourse about genetic research. Drawing from Josef Stern's *Metaphor in Context,* they assess context as a central variable in the construction of multiple meanings in rhetorical transactions.

Daughton, Suzanne M., "Metaphorical Transcendence: Images of the Holy War in Franklin Roosevelt's First Inaugural." *Quarterly Journal of Speech* 79 (1993): 427–446. Roosevelt's ascension to the presidency during the depression yielded unique challenges. He anticipated an audience at once anxious yet unsure of what courses of action to take. FDR combined religious and military "metaphoric clusters." Daughton contends, to create a controlling image of a holy war aimed concurrently to curb public anxieties and to move them to action.

Henry, David, "The Rhetorical Dynamics of Mario Cuomo's 1984 Keynote Address: Situation, Speaker, Metaphor," *Southern Speech Communication Journal* 53 (1988): 105–120. This essay forms a partial basis for our critique of Cuomo's speech that appears earlier in this essay. It is an insightful treatment of the interaction between the speaker's background, the rhetorical situation, and the choice of metaphor as a key persuasive strategy.

Ivie, Robert L., "Metaphor and the Rhetorical Invention of Cold War 'Idealists,' " *Communication Monographs* 54 (1987): 165–182. Ivie's critique, mentioned earlier in this essay, is a compelling analysis of metaphoric depictions of both the United States and the Soviet Union in the rhetoric of the Cold War.

Leff, Michael, "Topical Invention and Metaphoric Interaction," *Southern Speech Communication*

Journal 48 (1983): 214–229. Leff takes issue with conventional treatments of rhetorical precepts, in which argument falls discretely within the province of invention and metaphor within the rubric of style. Grounding his analysis in the teachings of interaction theory, he explores metaphor's inventional potential through a close reading of Loren Eisley's essay, "The Bird and the Machine." His conclusions urge reconsideration of the roles and potentials of metaphor and topics alike.

Osborn, Michael, "Archetypal Metaphor in Rhetoric: The Light-Dark Family," *Quarterly Journal of Speech* 53 (1967): 115–126. In this groundbreaking work, Osborn explores the universal appeal and persuasive potential of archetypal metaphor. He illustrates those characteristics of archetypal metaphor with a discussion of metaphors of light and darkness.

Osborn, Michael, "Rhetorical Depiction," in *Form, Genre, and the Study of Political Discourse* (Herbert W. Simons and Aram A. Aghazarian eds.) (Columbia: University of South Carolina Press, 1986), 79–107. This essay extends Osborn's award winning scholarship on light-dark metaphor. Rather than a replicating of his earlier work, Osborn advances a theory of depiction amenable to the criticism of mediated as well as verbal discourse.

Solomon, Martha, "Covenanted Rights: The Metaphoric Matrix of 'I Have a Dream.'" in *Martin Luther King, Jr., and the Sermonic Power of Public Discourse* (Carolyn Calloway-Thomas and John Luis Lucaites, eds.) (Tuscaloosa: University of Alabama Press, 1993), 66–84. As noted elsewhere in this chapter, a survey of over 100 scholars named King's "I Have a Dream" the greatest speech of the twentieth century. In this critique, Solomon attributes the address's force in part to King's use of metaphor. King depicted black Americans' actions in August 1963, she explains, as a movement to "collect on the debt" owed by white America, a movement that would be complete only when they were able to "cash the check" due.

NOTES

1. The text of King's speech appears in James R. Andrews and David Zarefsky, *Contemporary American Voices: Significant Speeches in American* *History, 1945–Present* (New York: Longman, 1992), 78–81. All quotations from King's speech are from this source. Various online versions of

the text also exist. See for example, http://www.americanrhetoric.com/speeches/Ihavead ream.htm. For an insightful critique of the text, see Martha (Solomon) Watson, "Covenanted Rights: The Metaphoric Matrix in M. L. King's 'I Have a Dream' Speech," unpublished manuscript, University of Nevada, Las Vegas.

2. In 1999, Professors Stephen Lucas (University of Wisconsin, Madison) and Martin J. Medhurst (Texas A&/M University) surveyed academics in the field of speech communication and rhetorical studies, asking them to identify the greatest speeches of the twentieth century. One hundred thirty-seven individuals responded to the survey, ranking speeches based on impact, rhetorical artistry, organization, style, and presentation of arguments. Martin Luther King, Jr.'s "I Have a Dream" was ranked first on the list of the one hundred greatest speeches of the century. The results appeared in *USA Today,* December 30, 1999. For the complete list of the top 100 speeches of the twentieth century and a more detailed discussion of the data collection process employed by Lucas and Medhurst, see http://www.americanrhetoric.com/top100spee chesall.html.

3. Stephen E. Lucas, *The Art of Public Speaking,* 7th ed. (Boston: McGraw-Hill, 2001), 266.

4. Patricia Hayes Andrews, James R. Andrews, and Glen Williams, *Public Speaking: Connecting You and Your Audience,* 2nd ed. (Boston: Houghton-Mifflin, 2002), 293.

5. David Zarefsky, *Public Speaking: Strategies for Success,* 3rd ed. (Boston: Allyn and Bacon, 2002), 276.

6. Zarefsky, 276.

7. Kenneth Burke, *A Grammar of Motives* (Berkeley: University of California Press, 1969), 503.

8. Michael Leff, "Topical Invention and Metaphoric Interaction," *Southern Speech Communication Journal* 48 (1983): 217.

9. Leff, 216–217; J. David Sapir, "The Anatomy of Metaphor," *The Social Uses of Metaphor: Essays on the Anthropology of Rhetoric,* J. David Sapir and J. Christopher Crocker, eds. (Philadelphia: University of Pennsylvania Press, 1977), 7.

10. Marc Peyser, "Paging Dr. Phil," *Newsweek,* September 2, 2002, 55.

11. Burke, 503–504.

12. Malcolm O. Sillars and Bruce E. Gronbeck, *Communication Criticism,* 2nd ed. (Prospect Heights, IL: Waveland Press, 2001), 102.

13. Martha Cooper, *Analyzing Public Discourse* (Prospect Heights, IL: Waveland Press, 1989),

111. Following Aristotle, an enthymeme is an argument comprised of two premises and a conclusion. The speaker omits one of the three elements, leaving it for the audience to complete the argument. We emphasize here Cooper's description of metaphor as functioning *like* an enthymeme rather than fulfilling all of the elements of an enthymeme. See too, Lloyd L. Bitzer, "Aristotle's Enthymeme Revisited," *Quarterly Journal of Speech, 45* (1959): 399–408.

14. Sapir, 9.

15. Burke, 503.

16. Leff, 217.

17. Leff, 219.

18. Leff, 219.

19. Seth Thompson, "Politics Without Metaphors is Like a Fish Without Water," *Metaphor: Implications and Applications,* Jeffery Scott Mio and Albert N. Katz, eds. (Mahwah, NJ: Lawrence Erlbaum, 1996), 191.

20. Seth Thompson, 189.

21. Jeffery Scott Mio, "Metaphor, Politics, and Persuasion," *Metaphor: Implications and Applications,* Jeffery Scott Mio and Albert N. Katz, eds. (Mahwah, NJ: Lawrence Erlbaum, 1996), 130.

22. Seth Thompson, 187.

23. Seth Thompson, 190.

24. Seth Thompson, 193.

25. Seth Thompson, 191.

26. For a parallel study in which a president's choice of metaphors established unrealistic public expectations in policy, see David Zarefsky, *President Johnson's War on Poverty: Rhetoric and History* (Tuscaloosa and London: University of Alabama Press, 1986), especially 21–37.

27. Seth Thompson, 192.

28. William Safire makes a similar point in "The Hitler Analogy," *The Gulf War Reader: History Documents Opinions,* Micah L. Sifry and Christopher Cerf, eds. (New York: Times Books, 1991), 210–212. Sifry and Cerf provide an excellent orientation to Operation Desert Shield and Operation Desert Storm in the introduction to this work.

29. Robert L. Ivie, "Cold War Motives and the Rhetorical Metaphor: A Framework of Criticism," *Cold War Rhetoric: Strategy, Metaphor, and Ideology,* Martin J. Medhurst, Robert L. Ivie, Philip Wander, and Robert L. Scott, eds. (East Lansing: Michigan State University Press, 1997), 72.

30. Ivie, 71, 72.

31. Ivie, 71.

32. Edwin Black, "The Second Persona," *Quarterly Journal of Speech,* 56 (1970), 114–117.

33. Steven Perry, "Rhetorical Functions of the Infestation Metaphor in Hitler's Rhetoric," *Central States Speech Journal,* 34 (1983), 232.

34. For a full explanation and illustration of the critical process, see Karlyn Kohrs Campbell and Thomas R. Burkholder, *Critiques of Contemporary Rhetoric,* 2nd ed. (Belmont, CA: Wadsworth, 1997) especially Chapters 1–5.

35. Campbell and Burkholder, 17–20.

36. The text of King's speech appears in James R. Andrews and David Zarefsky, *Contemporary American Voices: Significant Speeches in American History, 1945–Present* (New York: Longman, 1992), 78–81. All quotations from the speech are from that source.

37. The same survey by Lucas and Medhurst that ranked Martin Luther King, Jr.'s "I Have a Dream" speech first (see note 2 above) also ranked Cuomo's speech eleventh on the list of the top 100 speeches of the twentieth century.

38. Portions of this analysis appeared in David Henry, "The Rhetorical Dynamics of Mario Cuomo's 1984 Keynote Address: Situation, Speaker, Metaphor" *Southern Speech Communication Journal* 53 (1988): 105–120, and are used by permission of the Southern States Communication Association. Other portions appeared in Thomas R. Burkholder, "Irony Through Metaphor: Burkean Master Tropes in Mario Cuomo's Keynote Address to the 1984 Democratic National Convention," paper presented to the Speech Communication Association Convention, San Diego, CA, November 1996.

39. Quoted in Lou Cannon and Helen Dewar, "Gov. Cuomo Rouses Dispirited Delegates," *Washington Post,* July 17, 1984, A1.

40. Quoted in Cannon and Dewar, A8.

41. Hedrick Smith, "Cuomo Would Attack Record, Not Reagan," *New York Times,* July 17, 1984, A1.

42. Smith, A15.

43. Howell Raines, "Democrat Calls on Party to Unify and Seek Out 'Family of America,'" *New York Times,* July 17, 1984, A1.

44. Cannon and Dewar, A8.

45. Mario Cuomo, "Keynote Address," delivered to the Democratic National Convention, July 16, 1984, Associated Press transcript reprinted in *Congressional Quarterly Weekly Report* 42 (July 21, 1984), 1781–1785. All quotations from Cuomo's speech are from that source. The text of Cuomo's speech is also available online at http://www.americanrhetoric.com/speeches/cuomo1984dnc.htm.

46. Wayne N. Thompson, "Barbara Jordan's Keynote Address: Fulfilling Dual and Conflicting Purposes," *Central States Speech Journal* 30 (Fall 1979): 272.

47. Aristotle, *Rhetoric and Poetics,* W. Rhys Roberts and Ingram Bywater, trans. (New York: The Modern Library, 1954), 1358a33–1358b10.

48. Edwin A. Miles, "The Keynote Speech at National Nominating Conventions," *Quarterly Journal of Speech* 46 (February 1960): 26.

49. Miles, 26. See also: Craig R. Smith, "The Republican Keynote Address of 1968: Adaptive Rhetoric for Multiple Audiences," *Western Speech* 39 (1975): 32–39.

50. Wayne N. Thompson, "Purposes," 272.

51. Wayne N. Thompson, "Barbara Jordan's Keynote Address: The Juxtaposition of Contradictory Values," *Southern Communication Journal* 44 (Spring 1979): 224.

52. Jack W. Germond and Jules Witcover, *Wake Us When It's Over: Presidential Politics of 1984* (New York: Macmillan, 1985), 380.

53. Germond and Witcover, 380.

54. Quoted in Smith, A15.

55. *Los Angeles Times,* July 17, 1984, I7.

56. Michael C. Leff, "Topical Invention and Metaphoric Interaction," *Southern Speech Communication Journal* 48 (1983): 218, 223. Also instructive are: Michael Osborn, "Archetypal Metaphor in Rhetoric: The Light-Dark Family," *Quarterly Journal of Speech* 53 (1967): 115–126; Michael Osborn, "The Evolution of the Archetypal Sea in Rhetoric and Poetic," *Quarterly Journal of Speech* 63 (1977): 347–363; and William Jordan, "Toward a Psychological Theory of Metaphor," *Western Speech* 35 (1971): 169–175; Pradeep Sopory and James Price Dillard, "The Persuasive Effects of Metaphor: A Meta-Analysis," *Human Communication Research* 28 (2002): 382–419; Celeste Condit, et al., "Recipes or Blueprints for Our Genes? How Contexts Selectively Activate the Multiple Meanings of Metaphors," *Quarterly Journal of Speech* 88 (2002): 303–325; and Josef Stern, *Metaphor in Context* (Cambridge, MA: The MIT Press, 2000).

57. George Lakoff and Mark Johnson, *Metaphors We Live By* (Chicago: University of Chicago Press, 1980), 153, 156, 157.

58. Paul Ricoeur, *The Rule of Metaphor,* Robert Czerny, trans. (Toronto: University of Toronto Press, 1977), 22.

59. Lakoff and Johnson, 154.

60. William F. Lewis makes passing reference to the wisdom of Cuomo's tack in his assessment

of Ronald Reagan's reliance on, and success with, the narrative form in his presidential discourse. In effect, the analysis of metaphor in Cuomo's keynote reinforces Lewis's thesis as it pertains to how Reagan's rhetoric has redefined the nature of political "debate." See: "Telling America's Story: Narrative Form and the Reagan Presidency," *Quarterly Journal of Speech* 73 (1987): 280–302.

61. Germond and Witcover, 537.

62. Burke, 503.

63. See Thomas R. Burkholder, "Irony Through Metaphor: Burkean Master Tropes in Mario Cuomo's Keynote Address to the 1984 Democratic National Convention," paper presented to the Speech Communication Association Convention, San Diego, CA, November 1996.

64. For a discussion of generic criticism and the genre of political convention keynote addresses see John M. Murphy and Thomas R. Burkholder, "The Life of the Party: The Contemporary Keynote Address," *New Approaches to Rhetoric,* Patricia A. Sullivan and Steven R. Goldswig, eds. (Thousand Oaks, CA: Sage, 2004), 129–148.

65. Clarence Thomas, "I Am a Man, a Black Man, an American," July 29, 1998, available online at http://douglassarchives.org/thom_b30.htm.

66. Louis Farrakhan, "Minister Farrakhan Challenges Black Men," October 17, 1995. Available online at: http://www-cgi.cnn.com/US/9510/megamarch/10-16/transcript/.

67. See, for example, George W. Bush, "Address to the Nation on Iraq from Cincinnati, Ohio," October 7, 2002, *Weekly Compilation of Presidential Documents,* Administration of George W. Bush, October 14, 2002, Vol. 38, No. 41 (Washington, DC: U.S. Government Printing Office, 2002), 1716–1720. Available online at http://www.access.gpo.gov/nara/v38no41.html; "Address to the Nation on Iraq," March 17, 2003, *Weekly Compilation of Presidential Documents,* Administration of George W. Bush, March 24, 2003, Vol. 39, No. 12 (Washington, DC: U.S. Government Printing Office, 2003), 338–341. Available online at http://www.gpoaccess.gov/wcomp/v39no12.html; "Address to the Nation on Iraq," March 19, 2003, *Weekly Compilation of Presidential Documents,* Administration of George W. Bush, March 24, 2003, Vol. 39, No. 12 (Washington, DC: U.S. Government Printing Office, 2003), 342–343. Available online at http://www.gpoaccess.gov/wcomp/v39no12.html; "Remarks to the Community at Camp Lejeune, North Carolina," April 3, 2002, *Weekly Compilation of Presidential Documents,* Administration of George W. Bush, April 7, 2003, Vol. 39, No. 14 (Washington, DC: U.S. Government Printing Office, 2003), 404–407. Available online at http://www.gpoaccess.gov/wcomp/v39no14.html; "Videotape Remarks to the Iraqi People," April 10, 2003, *Weekly Compilation of Presidential Documents,* Administration of George W. Bush, April 14, 2003, Vol. 39, No. 15 (Washington, DC: U.S. Government Printing Office, 2003), 424. Available online at http://www.gpoaccess.gov/wcomp/v39no15.html; "Address to the Nation on Iraq from the *USS Abraham Lincoln,* May 1, 2003, *Weekly Compilation of Presidential Documents,* Administration of George W. Bush, May 5, 2003, Vol. 39, No. 18 (Washington, DC: U.S. Government Printing Office, 2003), 516–518. Available online at http://www.gpoaccess.gov/wcomp/v39no18.html.

CHAPTER EIGHT

THE NARRATIVE PERSPECTIVE

ROBERT ROWLAND

In the summer of 2002, public attention focused on bookkeeping scandals in major corporations such as Enron, Worldcom, and the accounting firm Arthur Andersen. The public also was fascinated and horrified by a series of incidents in which children were kidnapped from their homes, and by the heroic (and successful) efforts of a team of coal miners and others to rescue nine miners who were caught underground for more than two days.[1] At the same time, the public was not focused on other issues that would seem to be at least as important; global warming and the growing federal budget deficit are two examples of issues that were very important, but generated little interest. Nor is the summer of 2002 unique. The single subject that received the most public attention the previous summer was the case of the missing Washington intern Chandra Levy. What explains public fascination with Enron, the kidnappings, the rescue of the miners, the case of Chandra Levy, and so forth, while the public is less interested in equally or more important issues such as global warming? The obvious answer is that Enron, the kidnappings, and the other events that generate public attention are easily understood and interpreted as stories with compelling characters and an interesting plot, but global warming and the budget deficit lack those characteristics.

It is widely recognized that narrative is a human universal found in all cultures and at all times in human history.[2] There is strong evidence in cave paintings and other artifacts that humans have told stories for tens of thousands of years. Whereas ancient humans told stories around the fire and in the caves where they lived, modern humans use all forms of human communication to tell stories. The popularity of narrative easily can be demonstrated by looking at the daily television guide, a listing of movies at the local theater, or a glance at the best seller list. Television is dominated by shows such as the *West Wing*, *Law and Order*, and *C.S.I.* that tell stories. It has always been that way. Forty years ago the shows might have been *Gunsmoke*, *Leave it to Beaver*, and *I Love Lucy*, but narrative always has dominated the medium. And even on programs that at first glance seem to be news or issue oriented, narrative is very common. *Sixty Minutes* is a news show, but the focus of each episode is on using narratives about real people to explore an issue or topic. That same point could be made about many nonfiction programs.

Films and books are also dominated by narrative, both fictional and biographical. So is much popular music. From Cole Porter, to the Beatles, to the present day, great songs often have told stories. A number of authors in a variety of disciplines have noted that narrative is common not only in popular entertainment, but also as a means for explaining phenomena on the most esoteric subjects. From the law, to economics, to even the hard sciences, these scholars have recognized the importance of narrative. For example, Wallace Martin observed that "interest in theories of narrative" is part of a " 'paradigm change'—in the humanities" and that those theories of narrative "inhabit the very center" of disciplines such as biology, anthropology, and sociology.[3] Scholars in rhetoric and communication also have recognized the significance of narrative. No scholar, however, has done more to reveal the importance of narrative than Walter Fisher.[4]

What makes narrative so important? The short answer is that we all like stories, and we find them a useful tool for understanding the world. In the remainder of this chapter, I lay out in more detail why we like stories so much and how they work to explain our world. I begin by describing narrative form and explaining the functions that narrative fulfills for the consumer of the narrative—the audience. I also describe a number of approaches that have been taken to analyze narratives in rhetoric, and I describe in some detail Fisher's "narrative paradigm." After describing current perspectives on narrative, I present a critical essay in which I develop a system for interpreting narratives. I analyze a story concerning American children abducted to and detained in Saudi Arabia to illustrate how a rhetorical analyst can break down the form and function of a social narrative. I conclude this chapter by evaluating the strengths and weaknesses of the narrative approach and citing recommended essays for further reading.

DESCRIBING NARRATIVE FORM AND FUNCTION

What is a narrative and how is it different from other rhetoric? The most basic answer to this question is that narratives are stories, and stories function differently than purely descriptive or argumentative rhetoric. It is one thing to make a strong argument for invading Iraq. It is quite another to tell a story about oppression in Iraq in which real or hypothetical people are treated brutally in order to support an implicit claim that the United States should preemptively attack Iraq.

Narrative Form

What are the component parts of any story? Any story contains characters, a setting, a plot, and a theme. Stories are not about statistics. They are about the actions of characters (mostly people, but sometimes animals and other beings) in relation to other characters and the environment. The main action of a story centers on one or more protagonists. We sometimes call the protagonist the hero or heroine. If there is a protagonist, there must also be an antagonist (or villain) whose narrative function is to create conflict in order to carry the story forward. Oftentimes the antagonist will be a person who fights against the protagonist, although in some cases the antagonist may be the natural environment or even some weakness inside the hero. From Old Testament narratives such as the story of David and Goliath to the present day in great popular film series such as *Star Wars* and *Indiana Jones*, the focus of the narrative is on the conflict between the protagonist and the antagonist.

The examples of the stories of David and Goliath, *Star Wars*, and *Indiana Jones* illustrate the most fundamental principle concerning the relationship between the protagonist and antagonist. The protagonist and the antagonist must be of approximately equal power in a credible and compelling narrative. *Star Wars* would not have been a good film if Darth Vader had been opposed by one of the robots. But when Luke Skywalker and Han Solo joined forces, the battle was more equal and George Lucas was able to tell a series of compelling stories. The point is that if the difference in power between the protagonist and the antagonist is too great, the plot of the narrative will not be interesting because the ultimate outcome will be a foregone conclusion. *Jaws* would have been a much less successful film and novel if the killer fish had been a crazed sturgeon, rather than a giant shark.

The point that effective stories revolve around the conflict between protagonist and antagonist and that this relationship must be based on near parity also illustrates the difference between effective and true stories. In the real world, people often fight against insurmountable odds and have essentially no chance to succeed. Or a person may face an antagonist so weak that there is no question about his or her ultimate success. The point is that what makes a story true and what makes it compelling for the audience are related, but very different concepts.

An almost limitless set of characters and character types can serve as the protagonist (or antagonist) in narrative. Sometimes the protagonist will be a great hero, even an angel or god. In others cases, the protagonist will be an ordinary person who does great deeds. In still other narratives, the protagonist may be one of us or even inferior to us in ability or intellect.[5] In some stories there may be multiple protagonists and antagonists. The plot will move back and forth among each of their stories and the overall message of the story will be woven together out of the different narratives. It would seem that anyone can be a protagonist in a given narrative. There even was a quite short-lived TV series in which the "hero" was a college professor.

Although it might seem that there are so many possible types of protagonists that there is no means of cataloguing them, in fact, from a rhetorical perspective, protagonists fall into two basic types. The protagonist can be one of us and serve the rhetorical function of creating a sense of commonality with the audience or the protagonist can be greater than us and serve as a model for action. When the hero is one of us, his or her rhetorical function is to create what the great critic and theorist Kenneth Burke called a sense of identification or consubstantiality.[6] This type of protagonist is a regular Joe or Jane who shows us what it is like to live his or her life. The character played by Tom Hanks in the film *Philadelphia* was this type of protagonist. He was an ordinary guy, who also happened to be gay and have AIDS. His story served the rhetorical function of breaking down what I believe to be homophobic attitudes by showing the audience that fundamentally he was just like them.

In other stories, the protagonist is not one of us, but instead a hero who serves as a model for action. Throughout American history, the founding fathers have served this kind of rhetorical function. They provided models for how citizens ought to act in a democratic society. We continue to tell stories about them in a radically different time (after all, Jefferson didn't have much to say about global warming), because they serve as heroic models and we still need such models.

The contrast between protagonists who create identification with the audience and protagonists who serve as models to be imitated points to one other conclusion about the way that the protagonist functions in rhetorical narratives. As a general rule, narratives that are designed to produce understanding or sympathy will have protagonists who are ordinary people like us. But if the function of the narrative is to motivate great action, the protagonist generally will be a hero.

Stories rarely involve just a hero and a villain. There often are a host of other characters, including friends, acquaintances, bystanders, and so forth. Although there are so many different types of characters in narrative rhetoric that it would be impossible to catalogue all of them, it is possible to identify several narrative functions that they often fulfill. Supporting characters assist the protagonist or serve as obstacles to be overcome. In that way they function to support the primary conflict between the protagonist and antagonist. Supporting characters also may be used to illustrate narrative themes or create sympathy in the audience. In a film about World War II, a supporting character may be killed or wounded early in the narrative to illustrate for the audience the inhumanity of the Nazi soldiers. Finally, supporting characters may comment on the action, either to create comic relief or to critique the actions of the protagonist and antagonist.

The second basic component that defines any story is setting. The story takes place somewhere. That place and time can be literally anywhere and anytime. In fact, there are some science fiction and fantasy stories that take place in a universe very different from our own. The point is that narrative can take us anywhere that the storyteller can imagine and describe.

The important rhetorical point about setting in narrative is that stories can transport us out of our here and now and put us in places very different from our own world. As I write this chapter, I am sitting in Lawrence, Kansas, a progressive (for Kansas) college town in the American Midwest. But through narrative, a skillful rhetor could transport me to Auschwitz, the battle of Gettysburg, or any other place or time in or out of human history. As a consequence, narrative can be used to break down barriers to human understanding. It is difficult for early twenty-first-century Americans to understand the horrors of the Holocaust. But through narrative, Elie Wiesel and others have taken us to Auschwitz and made us see the horrors of the death camps.[7]

The third component of narrative form is plot. Plot can be defined as the action of the story. Although literary theorists have built any number of theories about plot types in fiction, and historians have developed theories for explaining historical narrative, from a rhetorical perspective there are two important points to be made about plot. First, the function of the plot is to keep the attention of the audience and reinforce the theme or message in the story. In order to keep the attention of the audience, plots generally build to a climax and include multiple points of conflict. The plot generally builds to a climax that resolves the conflict between hero and villain, because the story would not be very interesting if the biggest obstacle were overcome in the first few minutes of the film or the first few pages of the novel. Similarly, the plot must be varied enough and include enough action to keep audience focused on the story. Obviously, the action required to keep audience attention will vary with the audience. For example, if summer movies are any guide, a considerable number of large explosions are needed to keep the attention of adolescents.

The second point in relation to plot in rhetorical narratives is to note that what makes a good plot and what makes a true story are sometimes different things. As Lewis O. Mink notes, "Everyone knows that what makes a story good is different from what, if anything, makes it true."[8] In a gripping mystery novel, for instance, every detail may be a crucial clue. It may be enormously meaningful that the trash truck arrives in the first scene early on Wednesday morning. In real life, in contrast, the only meaning may be that Wednesday is trash day. Nor do real-life conflicts always move in a gradual pattern of escalating conflict to a final climax that resolves the conflict. In the real world, the greatest point of conflict may occur at the beginning of the plot not the end. Thus, rhetorical critics need to recognize that narrative form may be more easily adapted to present certain messages, rather than others, and that some "true" stories are unlikely to be interesting stories for an audience.

The final component of narrative form is theme—the message of the narrative. In some narratives, the theme may be quite explicit. Earlier I mentioned the film *Philadelphia*, which contained a very clear theme opposing discrimination against gay people and advocating tolerance and AIDS research. In other instances, the theme may be implied but not explicitly stated. On the surface, George Orwell's classic novel *Animal Farm* is a fantasy story about animals taking over an English farm. Underneath the surface, the novel is usually treated as an allegorical attack on communism and the Soviet Union. The animal characters and the plot concerning them are meant to reflect Orwell's view that the Russian revolution quickly led to tyranny and oppression of the Soviet people by Stalin and others. The larger point is that some narratives require more understanding of context and rhetorical type in order to identify the theme than do other narratives. The rhetorical analyst needs to keep in mind that in stories where the theme is not explicitly stated there may be considerable variation in audience interpretation of that theme.

The discussion of theme in rhetorical narratives is also important because it points to a difference between narrative in literature and narrative in rhetoric. Although much literature is rhetorical in the sense that it supports a persuasive message, and some narrative rhetoric is also literature in the sense that it may possess great aesthetic power, what makes a good theme in the two related contexts is somewhat different. The theme of a literary narrative may be literally anything—the nature of love, the meaning of beauty, what it means to be left-handed. In great novels or films, the theme may be quite complex and very subtle. The theme may point to the conflicts that human beings feel about love or honor or family or any other subject. In contrast, rhetorical critics are primarily interested in narratives that attempt to persuade an audience to believe a conclusion or reinforce an audience that already has a given perspective. This persuasive function of rhetorical narrative in turn usually requires a theme that is either explicit or clearly implied. If the theme is subtle or overly complex, the audience may miss it.

Consequently, great literature often fails as rhetoric because the theme is too complex for the mass audience. On the other hand, great rhetorical narratives often are inferior literature. Harriet Beecher Stowe's novel about the horrors of slavery, *Uncle Tom's Cabin*, is generally not considered to be great literature. The characters are based on simple stereotypes and show little subtlety. But there is no question that Stowe's novel had an immense rhetorical impact on popular attitudes about slavery in the North in the years leading up to the Civil War.[9] Similarly, Upton Sinclair's attack on the meat packing industry, *The Jungle*, may not be thought of as one of the greatest American novels, but the very lack of subtlety that a literary critic might decry, helped it influence Congress to regulate the industry.[10]

In summary, the four primary components of narrative form are characters, setting, plot, and theme. The first three components define what narrative form is and together they create the theme, which is what the narrative means. To this point, I have focused on narrative rhetoric that tells a complete story in order to make a point. *The Jungle* and *Philadelphia* are good illustrations of that type of narrative. In some cases, however, the rhetor may not retell a complete narrative, but only give the audience a scene from that narrative or tap into a narrative that is well-known to the audience. In these variants of narrative form, the rhetor relies upon the capacity of the audience to fill in the meaning of the narrative from the scene that is presented or to pull out of the well-known narrative the appropriate meaning.

After considering the formal components that define narrative rhetoric, it is appropriate to consider the rhetorical functions that narrative fulfills. If the components of narrative form describe what narrative is and means, the components of narrative function describe what rhetorical narrative does to an audience.

Narrative Functions

There are two related but somewhat different sets of functions fulfilled by narrative form: epistemic and persuasive. Epistemology is the study of how we come to know. Clearly, narrative is one such means. We often use narrative to understand the world. Mink refers to narrative as a "primary cognitive instrument" for comprehending the world.[11] Thus, we make sense of the demand for U.S. intervention in Iraq by translating the situation into a story. One dominant story line is that

Saddam Hussein is a brutal dictator, a modern day Hitler, who oppresses his own people and is seeking weapons of mass destruction in order to threaten the world. In this narrative, President Bush and others who support military action against Iraq are treated as heroes who are willing to fight in order to rid the world of this terrible dictator. Others see the situation through a very different narrative lens. They agree that Hussein is a bad leader, but put much of the blame for the present situation on failed U.S. policy in the past. In this view, U.S. support during the Iran–Iraq war propped up Hussein, and we are now reaping the terrible harvest of that decision. In this narrative, the United States is not heroic, but an arrogant and selfish bully that is trying to control the world. An invasion of Iraq would not be an act of heroism, but a foolish attempt to enforce American domination over another nation.

The point that I am making with the discussion of the two possible narratives concerning Iraq is that people use narrative as a way to understand the world. The narrative acts as a lens that helps the individual to identify the heroes and villains of the story, to determine their motivations, and so forth. Walter Fisher has written extensively about how narrative functions as an epistemic worldview.

Although people use narrative to understand the world, they also sometimes create narratives in order to persuade others to accept a narrative worldview. This rhetorical function is fulfilled by stories in several different ways. In addition to the epistemic functions of narrative, stories serve several important rhetorical functions. Narrative form is well adapted to keeping the attention of an audience, creating a sense of identity between the rhetor and the audience, breaking down barriers to understanding by transporting us out of our humdrum existence to a different here and now, and tapping into basic values and needs in order to create an emotional response. The first function of narrative is to keep the attention of the audience. I made the point earlier that popular culture is chock full of narrative. The reason that there is so much narrative on television, at the movies, in books, and elsewhere is that humans like stories. You would have to look long and hard in the television guide to find a show on a topic such as "Harvard experts talk statistics." But virtually every channel runs fictional or nonfictional stories about people and their lives.

Popular reaction to the events of 9/11 illustrates the power of narrative to energize an audience. Previous to September 2001, experts on terrorism were well aware that there was a serious risk that terrorists might use weapons of mass destruction on U.S. targets. While the risk was known, there was little public attention to it because the testimony of the experts did not fit into what the public found to be a credible narrative. Airplanes flying into tall buildings was perceived to be the stuff of summer adventure movies, not real life. After September 11th, however, there was a powerful narrative to go with the warnings of the experts. That narrative energized the audience and support for action to deal with the terrorist threat increased dramatically.

Thus, narratives that the audience perceives to be credible are a powerful means of getting and keeping the attention of an audience. It is important to note, however, that the key issue in terms of persuasiveness is not the truth of the narrative, but their credibility. Prior to September 11th, a narrative about terrorists using weapons of mass destruction against the United States was not perceived to be credible, no matter how many experts supported it. On the other hand, a narrative may be perceived to be credible when there is little support for it. It is widely believed, for instance, that the nuclear power accident at Three Mile Island was a major disaster. In fact, the best data suggests that there was very little radiation released and that many of the safety systems worked effectively.[12] However, the strong data I have mentioned in no way undercuts the powerful social narrative describing Three Mile Island as a nuclear disaster. In summary, narrative is a compelling means of getting and keeping the attention of an audience. To serve this function, the narrative need not be true, but it must be perceived to be credible.

The second rhetorical function of narrative is to create a sense of identification between the audience and the narrator or characters in the narrative. Great novels such as Harper Lee's *To Kill a Mockingbird* played a role in the civil rights movement because they helped create a sense of identification between white and black Americans. Lee's novel and many other stories showed the audience that the black characters in the books were people just like them. Similarly, narrative can allow us to see the world through the eyes of a Palestinian terrorist and understand what might drive him or her to terrorist acts. One of the most powerful functions of narrative is to generate in the reader/viewer/listener the understanding that "I'm like him or her."

The third rhetorical function of narrative is to break down barriers to understanding by transporting us to another place or time. This function is similar to the identity-related function, but deals with place, time, and culture, rather than personal identity. People understand the world based on their own experiences and culture. That means that they often find it difficult to understand a radically different culture or time. Narrative works better than other forms of rhetoric for ripping us out of our time and culture and placing us in another culture. For example, contemporary Americans may have great difficulty understanding the strict social regulation of women's role in the mid-nineteenth century. While history can describe women's roles in that period, narrative is a much more powerful vehicle for bringing home the restrictions women then faced. By placing us in the time and culture of nineteenth-century American life, the story can show us the barriers that women faced at that time.

The final persuasive function of narrative is to serve as a rhetorical means of tapping into values and needs in order to create a strong emotional reaction. A story about the death of an innocent child or the horrors of the Holocaust can tap into our emotional nature in a way that statistical data and other forms of argument cannot do. A statistical study proving that several hundred children die each year because of improperly installed car seats, for example, lacks the emotional punch of a narrative about the death of a single baby because of such improper installation. The narrative produces this emotional reaction because the story links directly to a basic value, such as life, or a basic need, such as the need for security.

The story in effect enacts the value or need in the context of a particular set of characters.

After identifying the form and function of narrative rhetoric, it is important to consider approaches that rhetorical critics have taken to the study of narrative. In the next section, I summarize various approaches to narrative, paying special attention to Walter Fisher's seminal analysis of the "narrative paradigm."

APPROACHES TO NARRATIVE RHETORICAL CRITICISM

Until relatively recently, rhetorical critics focused their attention on rhetoric that built a clear case for a position. With the rebirth of the study of rhetoric early in the twentieth century, rhetorical critics tended to follow the example of Aristotle in building their theories of rhetoric and methods for analyzing it. Critics who were influenced by Aristotle, often called neo-Aristotelian or traditional critics, usually focused on the three modes of proof identified by Aristotle, logos, ethos, and pathos, that broadly speaking defined rational argument, appeals to credibility, and rhetoric that produced an emotional reaction. In this system, there was little room for the analysis of narrative and neo-Aristotelian critics tended to focus on rational forms of persuasion.[13]

Thus, as recently as twenty years ago, there was not a sizable literature identifying narrative approaches to rhetorical analysis. Walter R. Fisher and Richard A. Filloy were getting at this point in a 1982 essay on "Argument in Drama and Literature: An Exploration," where they noted that "Argument has been conceived traditionally in terms of clear-cut inferential structures, a judgment that limited the study of narrative forms of persuasion."[14] They went on to argue that many works of narrative, including novels such as *The Great Gatsby* and plays such as *Death of a Salesman*, make arguments. While Fisher and Filloy cited a number of modern critics, including Kenneth Burke and Wayne Booth, who had focused on narrative forms of rhetoric, their main point was that critics had not recognized the importance of narrative or the capacity to build narrative arguments.[15] In retrospect, it is astonishing that critics had not recognized the importance of narrative as a means of persuasion and as a method for understanding the world.

In this crucial essay, Fisher and Filloy saw a need for a method to test "one's interpretation of a dramatic or literary work."[16] They outlined a four step process in which the critic first determines "the message, the overall conclusions fostered by the work." At a second step, the critic tests the message by evaluating the "reliability " of the narrator, the words and actions of the other characters and the descriptions of the scenes in the story. At a third step, the analyst considers the outcomes of the story as a means of asking "whether the story rings true as a story in itself." Finally, the critic should test "(a) whether the message accurately portrays the world we live in and (b) whether it provides a reliable guide to our beliefs, attitudes, values, and/or actions."[17] Fisher and Filloy applied their method to critique the implicit argument in both *The Great Gatsby* and *Death of a Salesman*.

The Narrative Paradigm and Rhetorical Criticism

Although Fisher and Filloy provided a method for analyzing argument in narrative, they did not focus on larger issues concerning the way that narrative functions persuasively. In fact, their approach remained quite close to traditions in the discipline that emphasized rational communication. The final step in their narrative methodology essentially called upon the critic to do an argumentative analysis of the claim in a given story. Under this approach, the narrative essentially was transformed into an argument and then tested by the standards appropriate for rational argumentation. Fisher, however, had realized that narrative was more than just a type of argument. It also was a basic form of human communication, what he would call "paradigm" for understanding all communication.

In a series of essays and an important book, Fisher laid out the characteristics of the narrative paradigm. Fisher developed the paradigm as an alternative to traditional rationality, which he believed provided little guidance for citizens concerned with issues of public moral conflict. He argued that traditional rationality privileged the perspectives of experts and created a situation in which ordinary citizens felt disempowered.[18] His solution was to argue that human beings were essentially storytellers, what he called "homo narrans."[19] He based this judgment on the fact that narrative is a human universal found in all cultures, concluding that all communication "whether social, political, legal or otherwise, involves narrative."[20] He later argued that "There is no genre, including technical communication that is not an episode in the story of life."[21] In his book on the narrative paradigm, he made the claim quite strongly that all communication is narrative, stating "All forms of human communication need to be seen fundamentally as stories."[22]

Instead of traditional rationality, Fisher argued for the value of narrative rationality. He argued that narrative rationality is a human universal since everyone knows what makes a good story, and that as a consequence standards of narrative rationality provided a way around the elitism inherent in what he called the "rational world paradigm."[23] Fisher embraced two principles for testing narrative reason: narrative probability and narrative fidelity. He defined narrative probability as a standard for testing "what constitutes a coherent story."[24] He later explained that narrative probability involved three related tests of coherence: structural coherence, which involves testing the internal consistency of the narrative; material coherence, which involves "comparing and contrasting stories told in other discourses"; and characterological coherence, which tests the consistency of action by the characters.[25] In addition to narrative probability, Fisher argued that the critic should apply the standard of narrative fidelity, which tests "whether the stories they experience ring true with the stories they know to be true in their lives."[26] He later added that standards of formal or informal logic also could be applied at this point *when relevant*.[27]

According to Fisher, the narrative paradigm was superior to other approaches to understanding human communication for two reasons. First, he based this view on the claim that narrative is a universal form of communication. As I noted earlier, he argued that all communication is a narrative of one type or another. Second, he argued that the standards of narrative rationality provided a way around elite domination by experts and a method of choosing between empowering and disempowering stories. He went on to argue that the standards of narrative rationality provided the critic with a means of identifying stories that recognize "the truths humanity shares in regard to reason, justice, veracity, and peaceful ways to resolve social–political differences." He cited stories by Lao-tse, Buddha, Zoroaster, Christ, Mohammed, as well as works by political leaders such as Lincoln, Gandhi, and Churchill as meeting these standards.[28]

The narrative paradigm drew a great deal of critical attention. Many critics and theorists praised Fisher and the paradigm for illuminating the way that narrative functions in human communication. Others argued that the narrative paradigm was unclear or overly broad. Barbara Warnick and I both argued that the parameters of the paradigm were unclear, that the standards of narrative rationality were not adequately specified, and that there was a difference between a credible and a true story.[29] I also claimed that narrative was better understood as a mode of discourse as opposed to a paradigm and that it was important to distinguish between works that actually told stories and works that described a topic or made arguments.[30] I also argued that Fisher's criticism of traditional rationality was overstated and that the standards of narrative rationality could not be applied to works of fantasy or science fiction, because those genres were judged by criteria different from realistic fiction.[31]

Although there was considerable debate about the value of the narrative paradigm and how expansive a definition of narrative form should be applied, there was no disagreement about the importance of studying narrative. Fisher's various essays had highlighted the importance of narrative as a form of human communication.

Applications of the Narrative Paradigm

Fisher's work on narrative awakened rhetorical critics to the crucial importance of narrative. The result was a huge increase in narrative criticism, much of it clearly inspired by Fisher's approach. The narrative criticism that was produced fell into two main categories. A number of critics borrowed from Fisher's terminology, especially the standards of narrative rationality, as the primary method of their critique. Other critics used an inductive approach to narrative analysis to discover the specific narrative pattern at the heart of a given story.

An example of the first category of narrative criticism is Ronald H. Carpenter's analysis of "Admiral Mahan, 'Narrative Fidelity,' and the Japanese Attack on

Pearl Harbor."[32] Carpenter uses Fisher's terminology to critique the narrative power of works of Alfred Thayer Mahan on naval power. Mahan was a U.S. Navy officer who wrote extensively on naval history and strategy. According to Carpenter, the Japanese government was influenced by Mahan's work because it possessed strong narrative fidelity that made his story " 'ring true' for the Japanese prior to the attack on Pearl Harbor."[33] Another example of a critique that drew heavily on Fisher's terminology was the analysis by Thomas A. Hollihan and Patricia Riley of "The Rhetorical Power of a Compelling Story: A Critique of a 'Toughlove' Parental Support Group."[34] In this essay, Hollihan and Riley analyzed the narratives found in a "toughlove" support group that advocated parents taking extremely strong stands against adolescent children who behaved badly. They concluded that the "toughlove" narrative "met the needs" of group members and "fulfilled the requirements for a good story" including both narrative fidelity and probability. Hollihan and Riley went on to argue that the "toughlove" story was a dangerous one because it could encourage parents "to get a quick-fix to their problems by ejecting their children from the house when far less drastic actions would be more appropriate."[35]

Numerous other examples of works utilizing terminology drawn from Fisher's analysis of the narrative paradigm could be cited. In general, these essays used a two-step critical process, first breaking down the narrative into coherent themes and then applying the standards of narrative rationality in order to assess those themes. It is important to recognize that Carpenter, Hollihan, and Riley, and other critics tended to use Fisher's terminology for a purpose quite different than that originally proposed by Fisher. Fisher touted the narrative paradigm and the standards of narrative rationality as an alternative to traditional rationality. Critics such as Carpenter, Hollihan, and Riley, used the standards of narrative rationality as a way of explaining why a particular audience found a given narrative to be persuasive. It also should be apparent that the narrative paradigm did not provide critics with a complete road map for how to identify the themes and strategies in a given narrative. This led a number of rhetorical critics to develop inductive approaches to narrative analysis.

Under the inductive approach, the critic does not apply a preexisting theory of narrative, but instead discovers the implicit narrative pattern in a given story. Many examples of scholars taking this approach could be cited. Thomas Rosteck analyzed narrative form in Martin Luther King's final speech. Martha Solomon and Wayne J. McMullen argued that the film *Places in the Heart* was an "open text" that possessed a number of conflicting ideological themes. James Jasinksi identified the narrative argument found in the film *The Big Chill*. Sally J. Perkins discovered the narrative structure found in two feminist plays about the sixteenth-century feminist Queen Christina of Sweden. Robert Strain and I argued that Spike Lee's film *Do the Right Thing* possessed an underlying narrative form similar to Greek tragedy.[36]

William F. Lewis's essay, "Telling America's Story: Narrative Form and the Reagan Presidency,"[37] is a typical example of the inductive approach. In the essay, Lewis argues that much of Reagan's political and rhetorical persuasiveness can be traced to his success as a storyteller. Lewis identifies two different kinds of stories that are found in Reagan's rhetoric: anecdotes and myths. Anecdotes are small stories that Reagan used to keep the interest of his audience. In contrast, myth "informs all of Reagan's rhetoric."[38] Lewis shows how Reagan used both kinds of stories to generate support for his programs and explains why the American people found Reagan's narratives to be so compelling, even though according to Lewis they often were inaccurate.

Lewis's analysis of the narratives at the heart of Reagan's rhetoric brilliantly illuminate much of the reason for Reagan's popularity. At the same time, Lewis's analysis also illustrates the difficulty with the inductive approach to narrative analysis. Although Lewis and the other inductive narrative critics have discovered the narrative patterns present in a number of important speeches, films, and so forth, their approach provides little guidance to how the critic should approach the next narrative analysis. Inductive critics do a detailed analysis of the narrative and pull out of that analysis the narrative theory that applies to the particular work of rhetoric. In effect, they build a new theory of how to approach narrative in every essay. This doesn't provide much guidance for the critic. Thus, there is need for a general approach to narrative analysis that provides the critic with tools for discovering the narrative pattern in any given story. In the following section, I develop such an approach.

NARRATIVE ANALYSIS—A SYSTEMATIC PERSPECTIVE

The narrative critic needs a perspective that is clear and that also allows him or her to explore the complexity present in any given narrative. In other words, the critic needs something that is both systematic and flexible. The best means of achieving both these ends is to apply a critical approach that moves in a three step process from the *form* of the narrative, to the *functions* fulfilled by the particular story, to an *evaluation* of how persuasive the narrative is with a given audience.

The first step in this process is to identify the four formal elements that define all stories: characters, setting, plot, and theme. In relation to characters, it is important to think not only about who the characters are but also about what they represent and their function in the story. For example, both James Stewart and John Wayne made a number of films about the American West. However, their characters tended to represent different messages. Stewart often played an "everyman." He was an average American caught in a difficult conflict doing his very best. In playing such a role, Stewart sent the message that any American could be a hero in the right circumstance. Wayne, in contrast, played a more traditional hero. He was the tough as nails lawman or cavalry officer who personified strength and courage. Both Wayne and Stewart played heroes, but different types of heroes.

After identifying the protagonist(s), it is important to identify the antagonist and supporting players and to consider their roles in the story. The antagonist may be a person or persons, but it also may be something in nature. Discovering the fundamental conflict between the protagonist and the antagonist will provide the critic with a major clue concerning the plot structure as well as the theme of the narrative. Similarly, it is important to consider the roles played by supporting characters in the story and how they are depicted. Role identification of supporting characters can help the critic identify the underlying message in the story.

After identifying the main characters and their roles in the narrative, the critic should focus on the setting of the story. In many cases the setting will be both a particular place and also, by implication, other places of relevance to the audience. So, a film such as *Erin Brockovich* is set in a particular place, but in another sense the setting is anywhere there is a problem caused by corporate misconduct. In narratives in which the plot functions to break down barriers to understanding a different culture or time, the setting will be specific to that culture or time. In that situation, the narrative works not so much to say it could happen here, but to rub the nose of the audience that it "did happen" there.

The next step is to identify the plot. The plot of the narrative often moves in a pattern of rising action in which more and more difficult problems occur, leading to the final crisis in which the issue is resolved. The critic should list the main events in the story and consider what those events and the order in which they happened reveal about the message of the story. The primary function of the plot is to keep the attention of the audience, but careful analysis of the plot may reveal the underlying message of the narrative.

Finally, based on the analysis of characters, setting, and plot, the critic should be able to identify the theme or themes in the story. Here, it is important to recognize that narratives often work by implication and that explicit calls for specific action are rare in narrative rhetoric. In fact, there are many stories in which the underlying narrative form supports a different theme than that enunciated by the narrator. For example, a liberal activist might preface a story about the ballot count in Florida in the 2000 presidential election by saying that his or her goal was to provide information on what went wrong and not to cast blame at a particular person or party. But the story this person told might clearly blame the Bush campaign for manipulating the system. It is important to remember that the theme in the story is in all aspects of the narrative and not just explicit conclusions drawn by the narrator.

In summary, the first step in narrative analysis is to identify the characters and the roles they play, the setting in which the action occurs and any more general implied settings, the plot pattern present in the narrative and what that plot pattern implies about how the audience should react. From this information, the critic should be able to identify the themes in the story and the actions requested of the audience.

In the second step, the critic tests the degree to which the narrative fulfills the four rhetorical functions I identified earlier. Initially, this means considering whether and how the narrative energizes the attention of the audience. Is the story compelling for the audience? The critic also should consider whether the narrative is designed to create a sense of identification between the audience and characters (or the narrator) in the story. Questions to consider include: Who does the author want us to like or admire? Does the author create a sense of identity between the reader/viewer/listener and the protagonist or other characters?

Next, the critic should consider whether the story is designed to bring the message home by placing the audience in a setting very different from their own lives. If the story is set in Des Moines, the answer is probably no. But if the story is set in a sweat shop in Malaysia, the story may well be designed to show ordinary Americans what life is like in a developing nation.

Finally, the critic should consider whether the narrative taps into basic values or needs in order to produce an emotional reaction in the audience. In testing this function of narrative, it is important to remember that the story does not directly tug on the heart strings of the audience. Instead, it uses the incidents in the story to tap into values and needs shared by audience members in order to produce the emotional response.

The final step in narrative analysis is to take the findings of the first two steps and make a coherent argument about the functioning of the particular story. Here, the critic links together the formal and the functional analysis to make an argument about how the story functions (or why it fails to function) for a given audience. At this stage, the critic should ask three final questions. First, the critic should consider whether the formal elements of the narrative are compelling. Is the plot interesting? Are the characters appealing (or, in the case of the antagonist, revolting)? Does the author transport us to the setting of the story? Second, the critic should summarize the degree to which the story fulfills the four functions of narrative. If the story fulfills all four, that is a sign that it is a powerful and coherent narrative. If it fails to fulfill any of the functions, that suggests strongly that it failed as a story. If, on the other hand, it fulfills some of the functions but not all, the critic must consider the importance in the particular context of the functions that were fulfilled.

Finally, the critic should consider the credibility of the story for the audience. I mentioned earlier that the truth and credibility of a story are very different things. The early rock and roll song, "Wake Up Little Susie" by the Everly Brothers, illustrates this point. In the song, little Susie and her date fell asleep in the movie theater and woke up at four in the morning. While that was in fact what happened (at least in the song), they knew that no one would find that story credible. They would be "in trouble deep" with their parents and their friends would say "ooh-la-la" because both the parents and the friends would assume that little Susie and her boyfriend had been having a sexual encounter. While they in fact had just fallen asleep in the theater (it must not have been much of a date or a film), no one would believe that story. As this example illustrates, it is important to consider whether the narrative is a credible one for a given audience.

Earlier, I noted problems with the standards of narrative rationality (narrative probability and narrative fidelity) developed by Walter Fisher in his discussion of the narrative paradigm. Although those standards may have limited value for evaluating the accuracy or truth of a narrative, they are immensely useful for making judgments about the credibility or believability of a narrative. The standards of narrative probability and fidelity get at two aspects of narrative credibility. Humans tend to believe stories that are coherent and stories that are consistent with personal experience. Thus, we expect people to behave in a consistent fashion, and we interpret events through the lens of our own experience in the society. In the song about little Susie, for example, the story that the couple had fallen asleep was not coherent; it did not fit with our understanding about how people behave on dates. And the contrary story that little Susie and her date were off at a lover's lane was quite consistent with experience in the society of the 1950s. That is why their friends said "ooh-la-la." Standards of narrative fidelity and probability can be used by the critic to make a strong case for whether the story had credibility for a given audience or to explain why it lacked that credibility.

At the end of the third step, the critic should be able to make a coherent argument about the rhetorical effectiveness of the narrative for a given audience. It is important to note that this judgment is always in relation to a particular audience. What seems coherent to an early twenty-first century American audience might seem ludicrous to an audience in China or elsewhere. An example may make this point clear: It has been widely reported that many in the Arab world believe that Israel organized the 9/11 attacks and that several thousand American Jews did not show up for work at the World Trade Center on September 11th. In fact, there is exactly no data supporting this story. However, a significant portion of the Arab world apparently finds it to be credible. This audience has been exposed to extremely harsh anti-Israeli rhetoric for many years in the context of the Israeli–Palestinian conflict. In this context, what would seem obviously absurd to almost any American, apparently seems quite credible.

Summary of a Systematic Perspective on Narrative Analysis

1. Form Identification
   a. Identify characters, character types, and what they represent.
   b. Identify the place in which the narrative is set and what it represents.
   c. Sketch the plot pattern and identify points of conflict.
   d. Reason from the characters, setting, and plot to the stated or implied theme.
2. Functional Analysis
   a. Does the narrative energize the audience?
   b. Does the narrative create a sense of identification between characters or the narrator and the audience?
   c. Does the narrative transport the audience to a place or time different from contemporary life?
   d. Does the narrative tap into basic values or needs of the audience?
3. Linking Formal and Functional Analysis
   a. Are the formal elements and the plot compelling?
   b. Does the narrative effectively fulfill narrative functions?
   c. Is the narrative credible for a particular audience?

In the last few pages, I have explained an approach to narrative analysis that can be applied systematically to any narrative. It also can be used to critique speeches and essays that tap into societal narratives. However, I have not provided an approach to testing the epistemic function of narrative. How can the critic apply rhetorical standards in order to test the accuracy of a given narrative? The short answer is that rhetorical standards are of very limited value in making such a judgment. The story of little Susie again illustrates this point. The ultimate question concerning Susie and her date is whether they in fact fell asleep in the theater. This is a factual question and not one where standards of rhetorical coherence are especially useful. Like little Susie's friends and parents, I find it unlikely that two teenagers out on a date would fall asleep in the theater. I find the competing story that they went someplace and had sex to be much more coherent. But coherent and true are not the same thing, and sometimes people behave in inconsistent ways. A story about a popular president risking his presidency and his legacy by having sex with a young White House intern would have to be viewed as incoherent. So would a story about hanging chads and butterfly ballots deciding a presidential election. But these incoherent stories did occur. The point is that rhetorical critics are in a good position to judge the persuasiveness and credibility of a narrative, but the tools of the critic are not well designed for judging the accuracy of the story.

CRITICAL ESSAY

In this section, I illustrate the systematic perspective on narrative criticism by analyzing a narrative concerning children abducted to and held in Saudi Arabia. In a number of instances, Saudi men have married American women and, after the marriage failed, abducted their children to Saudi Arabia, where the children have been held against their will. A recent Congressional hearing told the stories of several mothers who have had their children taken from them and of their efforts to get them back.

Critical Essay: A Narrative Analysis of Stories of Children Abducted to Saudi Arabia

On June 12, 2002, Representative Dan Burton, the chairman of the House Government Reform Committee, held a hearing on "U.S. Citizens Held in Saudi Arabia."[39] In the first minutes of that hearing Representative Burton made the following statement:

> Managing our relationships in the Middle East is one of the most difficult challenges faced by every administration. It's been a problem for every president and every secretary of State since World War II. With all of these massive strategic interests hanging in the balance, it's no wonder that sometimes the problems of average, everyday people get swept aside.

Humphrey Bogart said—and I usually don't quote movies in this hearing, but it's one of my favorite movies, *Casablanca*—Humphrey Bogart once said, "The problems of two little people don't amount to a hill of beans in this world." Great statement. Sometimes that's just the way it is and there's nothing you can do about it.

But there are also times when we have to set aside all those big global issues and do the right thing by the people we're elected to serve. There are times when someone has to say, "Timeout. Let's stop and take a good, hard look at what we're doing." And that's the purpose of this hearing. We need to take a timeout and take a hard look, a good, hard look at our relationship with Saudi Arabia.

The specific problem that I'm talking about is that Saudi men who kidnap their American children and take them away to Saudi Arabia must be taken to task. We've seen cases where these men have violated court orders, taken their children away against their will, and kept them away from their mothers for years, if not decades.

Despite the fact that arrest warrants have been issued for some kidnappings, the Saudi government has refused to lift a finger to help resolve these cases. In fact, the Saudi government has created a safe haven for these child abductors in a country where women and children are treated like property.

Maybe the saddest thing of all is that our government, our State Department, has done very little to help bring these children home. In one of the cases we're going to talk about today, a mother went to the U.S. embassy in Riyadh after her two children. She was trying to rescue them from her abusive father—from their abusive father—and the embassy kicked them out. And after she was kicked out, she was arrested and put into prison in Saudi Arabia. I don't understand that.

One of the reasons I decided to hold this hearing is that I was so appalled at the lack of effort we've made to take the Saudis to task for letting these things happen. We have a lot at stake with Saudi Arabia. We need their cooperation. But at what price? If we're not willing to stand up and fight for American citizens whose children have been kidnapped, then what kind of priorities do we have?

Today we're going to hear the stories of three mothers who had their children snatched away from them. Three things stand out in each of these stories: One, the brutal treatment of women in Saudi Arabia; the incredible courage of these women who did everything they could to rescue their children; and finally, the total lack of effort by our State Department to challenge the Saudi government.

These stories are all so powerful that I'd like to talk about each one of them in detail. But I'm not going to do that, because I can't tell their stories nearly as well as they can. But I do want to mention a few key facts.

Pat Roush has been living this nightmare for 16 years. In those 16 years, she has seen her two daughters one time for two hours. Her ex-husband came to the United States in 1986, kidnapped their two young daughters in violation of a court custody order, and took them to Saudi Arabia. An arrest warrant was issued here in the U.S., but the Saudi government did absolutely nothing.

The year before that, when Pat went to Saudi Arabia to try to salvage their marriage, her husband beat her so badly that two of her ribs were broken and the Saudi police didn't do anything then either.

Over the last 16 years, U.S. ambassadors have come and gone in Riyadh. Some have tried to help and some have not. But it's clear that the Saudis were never told by senior officials that this was a problem that was going to affect the relationship between our two countries.

In 1986, the U.S. ambassador was told by his boss that he had to maintain impartiality in the Roush case. Why? Pat Roush's husband broke the law. An arrest warrant was issued. Why should we maintain impartiality? To me, that attitude goes right to the heart of this problem. Ambassador Ray Mabus deserves special credit in this case. In 1996, he started a new policy: No one from this man's family was allowed to get a visa to come to the United States, it caused a big problem for them.

Unfortunately, after a year, Ambassador Mabus returned to the United States and his policy was discontinued. If this policy had been kept in place, it might very well have put the pressure on them to return these children to their mother. I'm very disappointed that that didn't happen.

We were told just this week that Pat's youngest daughter, Aisha, who is now 19, was recently forced into a marriage with a Saudi man. Pat's older daughter, Alia, was forced to marry one of her cousins a year ago.

Now let me say a few words about Monica Stowers. In 1985, she went to Saudi Arabia with her husband and two young children. When she arrived, she realized for the first time that her husband had a second wife and another child. She didn't know about that. Their marriage fell apart after six months. Her husband divorced her and had her deported without her children.

In 1990, Monica heard that her ex-husband was abusing her children. She went back to Saudi Arabia. She took her children and went to the U.S. embassy to ask for help. Did they put her on the next plane to America? No. At the end of the day, they told Monica that she had to leave the embassy. She pleaded with them not to kick her out. She told them that she would be arrested for overstaying her visa. But the counsel general had the Marine guards carry them out. Sure enough, she was arrested. That actually happened.

Can you imagine that? An American citizen is in a crisis, a mother and her young children, and the embassy staff tell the Marines to drag them out of the embassy so they could be arrested. That actually happened.

Monica is not here today. For most of the last 12 years she has stayed in Saudi Arabia to protect her children. She can leave any time she wants, but her husband refuses to allow their daughters to go. Her ex-husband tried to force her daughter into a marriage when she was only 12 years old. And Monica will not abandon her. While Monica can't be here to testify, her mother, Ethyl Stowers, is here to speak on her behalf, and we're very glad to have her here.

The third story we're going to hear about today is about Miriam Hernandez-Davis and her daughter Dria. They're both here to testify today. The reason they can both be here today is not because anybody in the United States government came to their rescue. The reason that Miriam's daughter is here today is that Miriam was able to scrape together $180,000 to pay two men to smuggle Dria out of Saudi Arabia.

Even though Miriam's husband kidnapped their daughter in 1997, and even though the FBI issued an international warrant for his arrest, she got almost no help from the State Department or our embassy.

The courage of these women, Pat Roush, Monica Stowers, and Miriam Hernandez, and their kids, is just incredible to me. You've all endured terrible pain as a result of what's happened, and it's a real honor to have all of you here today.

These are not isolated incidents. These are three examples of a much bigger problem. The State Department has a list of 46 recent cases involving as many as 92 U.S. citizens who have been held against their will in Saudi Arabia.

The root cause of this problem is the Saudi government. They have refused to respect U.S. law and U.S. arrest warrants. The law in Saudi Arabia lets Saudi men keep American women and children in Saudi Arabia even when they're in violation of court orders, even when arrest warrants have been issued, and even when they've abused their wives and their children. And that's just wrong.

We can't let this go on. Our relationship with Saudi Arabia is important, but this just can't be allowed to continue. The only way we're going to resolve this problem and get these kids home again is by elevating this issue, letting the American people and the people throughout the world know about it. This has to be raised with the Saudis at the highest levels. The Saudis have to be made to understand that if they let this go on, their relationship with us is going to suffer. And I don't think that's happened yet.

I'm preparing a letter to the president. I'm going to ask all of my colleagues on the committee to sign it. We're going to ask the president to raise this issue with Crown Prince Abdullah to try to get it resolved. Just a couple of month ago, President Bush raised the case of Laurie Berenson with the president of Peru. Laurie Berenson was twice convicted of terrorist activities in that country. Surely the Roush family and the Stowers family deserve at least as much.

We in Congress have to do our part as well. We've got to continue to hold hearings like this and write letters and do whatever we can to keep the pressure on. My colleague, Mr. Lantos, who I'm sure will be here in a few moments, held hearings and had Pat Roush testify way back in 1987—15 years ago. He deserves a lot of credit for constantly pushing human rights issues, and we all need to keep doing it.

Approaching Burton's Statement from a Narrative Perspective.   At first glance, Representative Burton's statement does not look much like the narratives that dominate popular culture in film, fiction, and television. Underneath the surface, however, Burton skillfully uses narrative to support a political agenda in regard to U.S. policy toward Saudi Arabia. The stories that he tells clearly are at the core of that agenda in two ways. They reflect his anger at both the Saudis and U.S. officials who fail to confront them, and they also reflect his attempt to pressure the government to change its policies. The aim for the rhetorical critic in looking at this statement is, therefore, to find a way to pull apart Burton's remarks in order to explain the various ways in which it works.

My starting point for approaching Burton's story is a comment by Walter Fisher: "What makes one story better than another" can be explained based on two "features" of the story—"formal and substantive."[40] Fisher is getting at two fundamental goals of narrative analysis, to identify how the story works on an audience and the characteristics of narrative form and content that allow it to produce that impact. Narrative critics have identified a number of functions that can be fulfilled by stories. Fisher focused his attention on the way that stories can be used to serve an epistemological or knowledge generation function in educating an audience. He referred to the capacity of stories to "give order to human experience and to induce others to dwell in them."[41] There are other purposes served by narrative as well, including the capacities to create a sense of shared identification and to tap into shared values.[42] Most narrative critics have focused their analysis on the function fulfilled by a particular narrative or set of narratives and, consequently, have not laid out a complete list of possible functions. However, the previous treatments of narrative can be placed into four main functional categories:

1. Narrative may function to attract the attention of the audience.
2. Narrative may be used to help the audience come to understand a position and therefore create new social knowledge.
3. Narrative can create a sense of shared identity between the audience and people described in the story.
4. Narrative can produce strong emotional responses by tapping into the values and needs of the audience.

In approaching Burton's statement, it is important to identify the rhetorical functions served by the narrative he tells.

How can those functions be identified? The answer to this question at first may seem paradoxical; the critic should begin with narrative form, rather than narrative function. Before the critic can discover the functions served by the narrative, he or she must first uncover the defining characteristics of the story itself. Just as a cook begins with a list of ingredients, the narrative analyst must pull out of the story, the defining ingredients of the narrative. Where should the critic start in this effort? Since Fisher and Filloy focused on how drama and literature often serve an argumentative function, critics have recognized that narrative themes come out of the interaction of characters (including the narrator), the setting, and the plot.[43] Thus, the narrative analyst should begin by identifying the rhetorical forms (characters, setting, plot, and theme) that define the story and move from there to a consideration of rhetorical function. At that point, the critic can turn from "what" the narrative form was, to an analysis of "how" the form of the narrative influenced its capacity to achieve one or more of the possible narrative functions.

The fundamental concern here is to identify the linkage between rhetorical form and function—to figure out how the characters, plot, setting, and theme engage the audience (or fail to do so). In order to achieve that aim, it is important to move in a systematic way from the particulars of rhetorical form (characters and character types, setting, plot characteristics, and implied theme) to a consideration of how (or whether) those particulars fulfilled one or more rhetorical functions. In general, narratives engage an audience in ways that are tied to the form of narrative. An interesting plot may grab the attention of the audience. The characters of the narrative may provide role models to emulate or, alternatively, the protagonist in the story may be an ordinary person with whom the audience will identify. In that case, the audience members may be influenced by the story because they can imagine it happening to them or someone close to them. The setting of a narrative may transport the audience to a reality very different from the one in which they live. And finally, the combination of plot, characters, and setting may produce a narrative theme that in turn taps into the fundamental values or basic human needs of the audience and consequently produces an emotional response.

After the linkage between narrative form and function has been identified, the rhetorical critic can assess the persuasive value of the narrative. Here, the key goal is to consider whether the narrative will be perceived as a "coherent story" that will "ring true" for the audience.[44] Three rules are particularly useful in that regard. In general, persuasive narratives will contain formal characteristics (plot, setting, characters, and theme) that the particular audience will find interesting. (This is the principle that explains why so many television shows focus on emergency room doctors, homicide cops, or high-profile prosecutors and so few on college professors). A second rule is that narratives that effectively fulfill the four functions I have described are more likely to influence an audience than narratives that do not fulfill those functions. Finally, narratives that possess "formal coherence,"[45] or credibility for a particular audience because they draw on aspects of that audience's world, are more likely to have persuasive impact than those that do not. Thus, by moving from form, to function, and then to how the form influenced the function, the critic can explain what was in the narrative, how it worked (or failed to work) on an audience, and draw an overall conclusion about the impact of the story. In the following section, I apply this approach to narrative criticism to the statement of Representative Burton.

Narrative Form and Function in Burton's Statement.   Representative Burton's statement combines narrative with appeals to basic American values and rational argument. In the conclusion, he builds the argument that "The root cause of this problem is the Saudi government." He also appeals to values of justice and to concern for the innocent when he attacks the Saudi government for failing to "respect U.S. law." Burton's ultimate claim is that the Congress should call on the President to pressure the Saudi government to release the abducted children. Implicitly, Burton assumes that a threat from the President to Saudi leaders that failure to release the children could cause "their relationship with us . . . to suffer" would be sufficient to motivate the Saudis to act.

Although Burton relies upon an appeal to basic values and rational argument in the conclusion of his statement, the dominant strategy is clearly narrative. Burton uses the stories of three American women—Pat Roush, Monica Stowers, and Miriam Hernandez-Davis—to build the case that the U.S. government has failed its citizens and must take remedial action. In Burton's narrative (or three related mini-narratives) the protagonist in each case is the American mother. All three women are depicted as strong and loving mothers who have sacrificed mightily for their children and have suffered greatly. Pat Roush tried to salvage her marriage and suffered broken ribs as a consequence. She has worked for sixteen years to protect her children. Monica Stowers stayed in Saudi Arabia for "most of the last 12 years . . . to protect her children." And Miriam Hernandez-Davis "scrape[d] together" $180,000 of her own money in order to save her daughter Dria. These three women are in a sense "everywoman." They each married a man who turned out to be someone other than the person they thought they were marrying. But they refused to give in and instead fought and sacrificed for their children.

There are three different, but related, antagonists in Burton's narrative. At one level, the role of antagonist is played by the husbands who took the children, abused them by forcing them into marriage or other acts, and prevented them from leaving Saudi Arabia. In Burton's narrative, the husbands and their abuse are not described in any detail. They figure far more prominently in the testimony of the women later in the hearing. At a second level, the antagonist is the Saudi government that Burton so strongly attacks in the conclusion. In his brief retelling of Roush's story, Burton states that in response to both the kidnapping of Roush's children and physical abuse that broke "two of her ribs" "the Saudi police didn't do anything."

Although Burton clearly views Saudi government as tyrannical and Saudi society as uncivilized, the focus of his fury is on the U.S. government itself. The most important antagonist facing Roush, Stowers, and Hernandez-Davis is a U.S. government apparently more concerned with trouble-free relations than with the rights of American citizens. In relating Roush's story, Burton cites an American ambassador who "was told by his boss that he had to maintain impartiality in the Roush case." Burton then asks "Why? Pat Roush's husband broke the law. An arrest warrant was issued. Why should we maintain impartiality?" Later, he tells about how when Monica Stowers and her children sought help in the American embassy, "the counsel general had the Marine guards carry them out." Burton clearly finds this action to have been a shocking violation of American value. At the end of his retelling of it, he adds "That actually happened."

In Burton's narrative, the primary antagonist is the United States government itself. Burton describes a government that has lost its values, a government that is more concerned with placating the Saudis than with taking care of its own citizens. In Burton's narrative, the government has become utterly spineless. The one government official who wasn't gutless in Burton's story was Ambassador Ray Mabus who tried to pressure the Saudis into releasing Pat Roush's children. In Burton's narrative, Mabus plays a heroic role, but in another sense, his personal story supports the larger point that American policy has become quite weak. Although Mabus's policy "might very well have put the pressure on them to return those children [of Pat Roush] to their mother," after he returned to the United States, "his policy was discontinued."

The only other characters in Burton's narrative are the children who have been abducted. Burton does not discuss them in any detail. Their role is simply that of innocent victim. These innocent children have suffered not only from being taken from their mothers, but also from being abused by their fathers. Both daughters of Pat Roush were forced into arranged marriages. The children of Monica Stowers also were abused. The only child who has been saved is Dria, the daughter of Hernandez-Davis. And Dria is safe not because of the action of the United States, which provided Ms. Hernandez-Davis with "almost no help," but because Hernadez-Davis spent her own money to get her child back.

The primary setting of Burton's narrative is of course in Saudi Arabia. Saudi government and society are described as uncivilized. They do not respect law.

Worse, they do not protect innocent women and children from abusive husbands. It is a society in which the child of Monica Stowers can be forced into a marriage at the age of 12. While the primary setting of the story is in Saudi Arabia, there is a sense in which the story is set in a soulless bureaucracy that no longer understands the difference between policy and principle. In Burton's narrative only the mothers and Mabus understand that the lives of innocent children must be protected at all cost. Burton implies that the bureaucrats in the Department of State and elsewhere in the government have lost track of both the power of the United States and of fundamental American values.

The primary plot devices in Burton's narrative are betrayal and commitment. The women and their children are betrayed first by their husbands, but in a more fundamental sense they are betrayed by their own country. In Burton's narrative the husbands are almost faceless. He describes their actions as terrible, but as typical of their society. His real fury is reserved for the U.S. government, which has failed its citizens by kowtowing to the Saudis. In sharp contrast to the government, the three mothers have acted with courage and commitment. At the end of telling their stories, Burton's feeling about them comes through quite clearly: "The courage of these women, Pat Roush, Monica Stowers and Miriam Hernandez, and their kids, is just incredible to me. You've all endured terrible pain as a result of what's happened, and it's a real honor to have all of you here today." There clearly is a relationship between the two plot devices. Burton's narrative is based on the premise that if the government had not betrayed the women and their children, but had acted with anything like the commitment shown by the mothers, the kids would have been saved.

There are two primary themes in Burton's narrative. One theme simply concerns the women and their children. In Burton's narrative these innocent people have been abused because of their betrayal by their husbands (and fathers) and also by their own country. The other theme in Burton's narrative is implicit. Although Burton explicitly attacks the State Department for failing to fight for the abducted children, by implication, he argues that while weakness and betrayal go together so too do courage and commitment. If we just have the courage to stick by our principles as the mothers have done and Ray Mabus did, we will be able to force the Saudis to let the kids go.

The analysis of the forms in Burton's narrative makes it quite clear that the story fulfills all four functions of narrative. First, the narrative is well designed to grab the attention of the audience. At the end of the statement, Burton notes that the three stories "are not isolated incidents." He adds that "The State Department has a list of 46 recent cases involving as many as 92 U.S. citizens who have been held against their will in Saudi Arabia." The statistic that Burton cites is not nearly as compelling as the three narratives. It would be easy to ignore the statistic and reason that given the crucial importance of Saudi Arabia in the world oil market, we really are doing all that we can do. Later in the hearing Deputy Assistant Secretary of State for Near Eastern Affairs Ryan C. Crocker testified that,

> We [the State Department] have no higher priority than the safety and security of our citizens. I believe our record shows a consistent and sustained engagement on

child custody cases in line with this priority. But as noted above, we operate in accordance with the laws of our two governments, laws that do not mesh well on civil and social issues.[46]

After hearing the stories of Roush, Stowers, and Hernandez-Davis, Crocker's statement comes across as mere rationalization. The stories of the three women send the message that when the welfare of small children who are American citizens is at stake the government of the United States of America, the strongest nation by far on the planet, could act strongly.

Burton's story also fulfills the second and third functions of narrative rhetoric. Burton uses the three stories to create identity between the audience and the three mothers and their children. Implicitly, he tells us that this could happen to your sister or your daughter or granddaughter. He also draws on the power of narrative to transport us to a different place or time. This function is most clearly fulfilled in his description of how Monica Stowers fled with her children to the American embassy and then was kicked out by American marines on the order of the counsel general. Although Burton's description is brief, one image comes through quite strongly—an American bureaucrat ordering Marine guards to escort a mother and small children out of the Embassy to be arrested by the Saudi police. Here, Burton takes us to two uncivilized places—Saudi Arabia that does not respect the law or the rights of women and children and an American embassy that no longer fights for American citizens.

Burton's narrative also clearly taps into basic American values such as justice, freedom, and honor and also basic human needs concerning family and children. The narrative produces two strong emotional reactions, anger and guilt. It produces anger at the government for selling out our own citizens and guilt that we haven't done more over the years to help the women and their families. There is just a hint of that guilt in one of Burton's final remarks, "We've got to continue to hold hearings like this and write letters and do whatever we can to help keep the pressure on. My colleague, Mr. Lantos . . . held hearings and had Pat Roush testify way back in 1987—15 years ago." Burton seems to be implying that 15 years is an awfully long gap between hearings and that Congress needs to do more.

Although Burton's retelling of the stories of the three women and their children is brief, it is also quite powerful. In the preceding sections, I made the point that his narrative brings life to what otherwise might seem like one more complex foreign policy dispute. The setting, characters, and plot produce a powerful theme that transforms a foreign policy dispute into a call for justice. Burton also effectively fulfills the functions of narrative, especially in relation to shared identity. Clearly, he creates a sense of identification between the women and their children on the one hand and other Americans on the other. He also uses the power of narrative scene to take us out of our here and now to force us to see that similar actions could happen to members of each of our families.

Burton's story also has great narrative credibility. The story possesses internal coherence and also rings true with what we know about treatment of women and children by Islamic fundamentalists. The story is coherent in two senses. First, the Saudi husbands and their government consistently act to deny the women and their children any rights. The three narratives hang together perfectly in that regard. Second, the story is coherent in its depiction of an American State Department more interested in geo-politics than protecting the rights of American citizens. Finally, the story clearly rings true. In the aftermath of September 11, 2001, it was discovered that fifteen of the nineteen hijackers were Saudis. Consequently, this story fits common attitudes about how Islamic fundamentalism threatens American freedom and security. It is important to note that for many Americans the story would have had considerably less narrative fidelity if the hearing had been conducted prior to September 11th, at a time when the dominant perception was that Saudi Arabia was a crucial ally that also helped keep the world oil market stable.

In summary, Burton's narrative powerfully sets forth the case that the United States should use all of our power and moral authority to pressure the Saudi government to release children of American mothers and Saudi fathers to the custody of the American mothers and allow them to leave the country. The previous analysis does not, however, tell us if such a policy in fact would be a good idea. Burton's narrative is by its very nature one sided. We have no rhetorical means of testing whether the stories he tells are accurate. Nor do we know whether U.S. pressure would be effective in gaining release of the children. Burton's powerful narrative avoids questions about culture and consequences of action. Citizens of the United States would be outraged if a foreign government pressured this nation to act because it perceived our culture to be immoral in some way. Surely the Saudis are no different. It is quite possible that pressuring the Saudis might be counterproductive.

It is also possible that larger issues involving oil supplies and stability in the Persian Gulf simply require that the United States look the other way on this issue. I find that position distasteful and immoral, but the effect of U.S. pressure on the stability of the Saudi regime is certainly a relevant question. The key point is that although the standards of narrative criticism are quite useful in revealing how Burton's narrative effectively presents a particular perspective, they do not provide much guidance in determining whether that narrative is either factual or would be the basis of good public policy. Those questions are at their base not rhetorical in nature.

PERSONAL COMMENTS ON THIS ESSAY

The key decision that I made in approaching the Burton story was to let the rhetorical analysis emerge from the form and function of the narrative. One of the perils of rhetorical analysis is the danger that the critic will use a rhetorical method as a set of blinders, rather than as a kind of powerful critical magnifying glass, to explain how the rhetoric functions. Thus, an argumentation critic might always find rhetoric to be dominated by argument. Any rhetorical theory and the terminology associated with it can be turned into a similar set of blinders that essentially shapes the critical process. At the same time, all good criticism is based on the application of rhetorical theories to illuminate the underlying structure and function of a work of rhetoric.

To avoid the danger that critical (rhetorical) terminology can become a set of blinders, but still produce theory-based criticism, my approach is always to begin by identifying the defining formal characteristics of the rhetoric in question, to move from that analysis of form to a consideration of rhetorical function, and then to consider how rhetorical theory illuminates the linkage between rhetorical form and function. The three-step methodology developed in the essay is designed to achieve that aim and, in the process, to apply a kind of theoretical glass cleaner to the critical lenses that I used.

In actuality, there was a key step in the analysis of the essay that came before the three steps I identified. The step that came first was the identification of narrative form in Burton's testimony. If his testimony had been driven by a kind of legalistic case, then an argumentative, rather than a narrative analysis, would have been more appropriate. Alternatively, Burton, who is among the most conservative members of Congress, might have presented a statement shaped by his ideology. In such an instance, ideological analysis would have been the order of the day. In this case, however, Burton's statement was shaped by the stories of the three women. Once I recognized the narrative elements dominating the statement, the appropriate analytical steps became clear.

In sum, rhetorical critics need a wide-ranging knowledge of rhetorical theory and methodology; along with that knowledge, however, they need a healthy skepticism about those theories as well. That skepticism helps critics avoid a situation in which a theory no longer illuminates rhetorical action, but becomes a set of blinders.

POTENTIALS AND PITFALLS OF NARRATIVE CRITICISM

The analysis of a variety of approaches to narrative analysis and the presentation of a systematic method of narrative criticism suggests several potentials and pitfalls associated with the rhetorical analysis of narrative. The most significant potential is the importance of revealing the power of narrative in our society. There is no question that narrative is an extremely powerful rhetorical form. If the battle is between strong statistics on one side and a compelling narrative on the other, there is little doubt that at least in the short run, the narrative will be more influential. Humans love stories and stories are powerful means of making connections with others and tapping into basic values and needs. The immense power of narrative makes it especially important that critics uncover how narratives function in particular instances. Although a number of theorists (myself included) have critiqued the narrative paradigm, the field of rhetorical criticism owes an enormous debt to Walter Fisher for pointing out so forcefully the importance of narrative.

Although narrative criticism can be quite useful, it is not without pitfalls, three of which are particularly important. First, narrative criticism is most easily and appropriately applied to rhetoric that is clearly a story. However, much rhetoric draws on stories that are in some sense out there in society. A speaker or writer might refer to a story about the founding fathers or a story about Chandra Levy or Monica Lewinsky and assume that the audience would fill in the details. The problem is that it is difficult for the critic to know how the audience fills in those details or exactly what gets filled in. There is also a fine line between an example included as support material in a speech or essay and a developed narrative. Although the line between these two types of rhetoric is a fine one, the line is also important. There is a difference between a member of Congress citing the example of Pat Roush and the more developed story told by Burton. Narrative criticism is much more applicable to the developed story, as opposed to the implied reference or short example. The critic can distinguish between these two rhetorical types by considering whether the story in any rhetoric is developed in such a way that it fulfills any or all of the persuasive functions of narrative that I identified earlier. If it does fulfill those functions, the story usefully can be treated as narrative. If it fails to fulfill those functions, it may be more appropriate to consider it an extended example.

A second pitfall of narrative criticism relates to the variability in how human beings interpret stories. Narrative critics need to recognize that different people prefer very different types of narratives. A glance at the best seller list for fiction supports this judgment. Some of us love fantastic novels about space or romantic stories about dashing men and ravishing women. Others like murder mysteries or historical novels. Personally, I prefer the intellectual (often balding) hero, with a subtle sarcastic wit, but that may just be me. My point is that human beings seem to prefer very different types of stories. If that is true in relation to fiction, it probably is true about other types of narratives as well. I made this point earlier when I noted that many in the Arab world found the story that Israeli intelligence had orchestrated the September 11th attacks to be quite credible, when nearly all Americans found that story to be absurd. Consequently, rhetorical critics need to ground their analysis of a narrative in the attitudes of a given audience and recognize that stories that they find to be credible may not be credible to others.

The final pitfall of narrative analysis relates to variation in narrative type. Narrative criticism works best on stories that support a clear theme and that are grounded in the real world as we know it. Narrative analysis of works of fantasy, science fiction, or allegory is more difficult because the critic must not only discover the underlying narrative pattern, but also translate the message out of the category of science fiction or fantasy into the category of realistic narrative.[47] An example may make this point clear: Janice Hocker Rushing has interpreted the first two *Alien* films from a psychological perspective, concluding that in the films "the patriarchy has induced the feminine to fight itself" creating a situation in which "the feminine is actually subverted."[48] My own reading of the films would focus on how the protagonist (Ripley) is both feminine and powerful and also how the films send a strong message that power and money often produce corrupt decision making.

However, I think it would be very difficult to determine one "correct" interpretation of these films because they are works of science fiction set in a time and place quite far from our reality. There inevitably will be much more variation in the interpretation of works of science fiction, fantasy, and allegory than of realistic narratives, such as that of Burton. This point is easily illustrated in relation to allegory, a type of narrative in which the author uses a story set in a place very different from the contemporary world to imply a judgment about our world. Even when a work of allegory has a very clear theme, such as George Orwell's attack on communism in *Animal Farm,* interpretation is more difficult than in realistic narratives. Allegorical interpretation requires a translation process in which the critic translates the allegory into a realistic narrative prior to analyzing it. This translation stage adds complexity to the interpretive process. Thus, the third pitfall of narrative criticism is that the perspective works most effectively on realistic narratives that lay out a clear conclusion. If the narrative genre is not realistic or if the message is complex and confused, narrative critics may be forced to lay out a series of alternative interpretations of the story.

Storytelling is one of the hallmarks of human culture. From the time that humans developed the capacity to use symbols, we have told stories. And stories are among the most powerful forms of persuasion. Yet, until relatively recently, rhetorical critics shied away from analyzing narratives and focused instead on rational argumentation and other rhetorical forms. Although argument is clearly important, narrative plays a crucial role in every human culture. Rhetorical critics need a systematic way of explaining how narratives work to persuade audiences. The approach developed in this chapter is a starting point that the critic can use to break down both the forms present in a given narrative and how those forms function in relation to an audience.

NARRATIVE ANALYSIS TOP PICKS

Fisher, Walter R., "Narration as a Human Communication Paradigm: The Case of Public Moral Argument." *Communication Monographs* 51 (1984): 1–22. This essay is the original statement of the narrative paradigm and the most influential article about narrative published to date in a communication journal.

Fisher, Walter R., *Human Communication as Narration* (Columbia, SC: University of South Carolina Press, 1987). In his book, Fisher fleshes out all aspects of the narrative paradigm.

Hollihan, Thomas A., and Patricia Riley, "The Rhetorical Power of a Compelling Story: A Critique of a 'Toughlove' Parental Support Group." *Communication Quarterly* 35 (1987): 13–

25. Hollihan and Riley provide one of the clearest applications of principles of narrative rationality to a real world story.

Lewis, William F., "Telling America's Story: Narrative Form and the Reagan Presidency." *Quarterly Journal of Speech* 73 (1987): 280–302. Lewis's essay is among the best examples of the inductive approach to narrative analysis. It is accessible and clearly argued.

Rowland, Robert C., and Robert Strain, "Social Function, Polysemy and Narrative-Dramatic Form: A Case Study of *Do the Right Thing,*" *Communication Quarterly* 42 (1994): 213–228. Rowland and Strain illustrate the advantages of the inductive approach, but also the difficulty with the approach as a method of criticism. They discovered that Lee's film possesses a narrative pattern similar to Greek tragedy and explained how that form helped the film send conflicting messages about the appropriateness of violence as a response to racism. At the same time, the essay exposes the need for a systematic approach to narrative criticism since the inductive method requires the critic to sift through all possible narrative forms in order to construct a given critique.

NOTES

1. For example, Jacqueline Jones noted that the story of the rescue of the miners "riveted the attention of a nation at war with terrorism." See Jacqueline Jones, "Solidarity Helps Ensure Security," *New York Times* August 2, 2002: A23.

2. Hayden White notes that "narrative is a metacode, a human universal." See Hayden White, "The Value of Narrativity in the Representation of Reality," *Critical Inquiry* 7 (1980): 6.

3. Wallace Martin, *Recent Theories of Narrative* (Ithaca, NY: Cornell University Press, 1986), 7.

4. In a number of essays and an important book, Fisher explored what he called the "narrative paradigm," for human communication. See especially Walter R. Fisher, "Narration as a Human Communication Paradigm: The Case of Public Moral Argument," *Communication Monographs* 51 (1984): 1–22; Walter R. Fisher, *Human Communication as Narration* (Columbia, SC: University of South Carolina Press, 1987).

5. Northrop Frye has built an entire theory of narrative around the level of heroic power present in the protagonist. See Northrop Frye, *Anatomy of Criticism: Four Essays* (Princeton, NJ: Princeton University Press, 1957).

6. See Kenneth Burke, *A Rhetoric of Motives* (Berkeley: University of California Press, 1969).

7. See Elie Wiesel, *Night*, Stella Rodway (trans.) (New York: Avon Books, 1958).

8. Lewis O. Mink, "Narrative Form as a Cognitive Instrument," *The Writing of History: Literary Form and Historical Understanding*, Robert H. Canary and Henry Kozuchi (eds.) (Madison: University of Wisconsin Press, 1978), 129–130.

9. John Anthony Scott notes that Stowe's novel "helped millions of her fellow citizens to become aware of the shame of slavery and to take their place, side by side with black people in the struggle to end it." See John Anthony Scott, *Woman Against Slavery: The Story of Harriet Beecher Stowe* (New York: Thomas Y. Crowell, 1978), xi–xii.

10. In a biography of Sinclair, Jon Yoder cites a headline in the *New York Times* labeling the Senate passage of a meat inspection act as "a Direct Consequence of the Disclosures Made in Upton Sinclair's Novel." See Jon A. Yoder, *Upton Sinclair* (New York: Frederrick Ungar, 1975), 43–44.

11. Mink, 131.

12. See *Report of the President's Commission on the Accident at Three Mile Island: The Need For Change: The Legacy of TMI* (Washington, D.C.: Government Printing Office, 1979); Robert C. Rowland, "A Reanalysis of the Argumentation at Three Mile Island," in *Argument in Controversy: Proceedings of the 7th SCA–AFA Conference on Argumentation*, Donn Parson (ed.) (Annandale, VA: SCA, 1991), 277–283.

13. One sign of how little emphasis narrative received through most of this century can be found the text *Speech Criticism*, which systematized the neo-Aristotelian approach. The index to that work lists one reference to narration (p. 479) and no references to narrative. See Lester Thonssen, A. Craig Baird, and Waldo W. Braden, *Speech Criticism*, 2nd ed. (New York: The Ronald Press Company, 1970).

14. Walter R. Fisher and Richard A. Filloy, "Argument in Drama and Literature: An Exploration," *Advances in Argumentation Theory and Research*, J. Robert Cox and Charles A. Willard (eds.) (Carbondale, IL: Southern Illinois University Press, 1982), 343.

15. Fisher and Filloy, 345–346.

16. Fisher and Filloy, 360.

17. Fisher and Filloy, 360.

18. Fisher, "Narration as a Human Communication Paradigm," 4–9, Fisher, *Human Communication as Narration*, 67.

19. Fisher, "Narration as a Human Communication Paradigm," 6.

20. Fisher, "Narration as a Human Communication Paradigm," 7.

21. Walter R. Fisher, "The Narrative Paradigm: An Elaboration," *Communication Monographs* 52 (1985): 347.

22. Fisher, *Human Communication as Narration*, xi.

23. Fisher, *Human Communication as Narration*, 75; Fisher, "Narrative as a Human Communication Paradigm," 8–9.

24. Fisher, "Narration as a Human Communication Paradigm," 8.

25. Fisher, *Human Communication as Narration*, 47.

26. Fisher, "Narration as a Human Communication Paradigm," 8.

27. Fisher, "The Narrative Paradigm: An Elaboration," 350.

28. Fisher, "Narration as a Human Communication Paradigm," 16.

29. See Barbara Warnick, "The Narrative Paradigm: Another Story," *Quarterly Journal of Speech* 73 (1987): 172–182; Robert C. Rowland, "Narrative: Mode of Discourse or Paradigm," *Communication Monographs* 54 (1987): 264–275.

30. In addition to "Narrative: Mode of Discourse or Paradigm?" see "On Limiting the Narrative Paradigm: Three Case Studies," *Communication Monographs* 56 (1989): 39–53.

31. See "On Limiting the Narrative Paradigm," and Robert C. Rowland, "The Value of the Rational World and Narrative Paradigms," *Central States Speech Journal* 39 (1988): 204–217.

32. Ronald H. Carpenter, "Admiral Mahan, 'Narrative Fidelity,' and the Japanese Attack on Pearl Harbor," *Quarterly Journal of Speech* 72 (1986): 290–305.

33. Carpenter, 291.

34. Thomas A Hollihan and Patricia Riley, "The Rhetorical Power of a Compelling Story: A Critique of a 'Toughlove' Parental Support Group," *Communication Quarterly* 35 (1987): 13–25.

35. Hollihan and Riley, 23, 24.

36. See Thomas Rosteck, "Narrative in Martin Luther King's *I've Been to the Mountaintop*," *Southern Communication Journal* 58 (1992): 22–32; Martha Solomon and Wayne J. McMullen, "*Places in the Heart*: The Rhetorical Force of an Open Text," *Western Journal of Speech Communication* 55 (1991): 339–353; James

Jasinski, "(Re)Constituting Community Through Narrative Argument: *Eros* and *Philia* in *The Big Chill*," *Quarterly Journal of Speech* 79 (1993): 467–486; Sally J. Perkins, "The Dilemma of Identity: Theatrical Portrayals of a 16th Century Feminist," *Southern Communication Journal* 59 (1994): 205–214; Robert C. Rowland and Robert Strain, "Social Function, Polysemy and Narrative–Dramatic Form: A Case Study of *Do the Right Thing*," *Communication Quarterly* 42 (1994): 213–228.

37. William F. Lewis, "Telling America's Story: Narrative Form and the Reagan Presidency," *Quarterly Journal of Speech* 73 (1987): 280–302.

38. Lewis, 282.

39. *U.S. Citizens Held in Saudi Arabia*, Hearing of the House Government Reform Committee, June 12, 2002. Available On-Line, Congressional Universe, Lexis-Nexis.

40. Fisher, "Narration as a Human Communication Paradigm," 16.

41. Fisher, "Narration as a Human Communication Paradigm," 6.

42. In relation to the creation of shared identity, see Fisher, "Narration as a Human Communication Paradigm," 14–15. In relation to the capacity of narrative to produce a strong emotional response see Lewis.

43. See Fisher and Filloy, 360.

44. Fisher, "Narration as a Human Communication Paradigm," 8.

45. Fisher, "Narration as a Human Communication Paradigm," 16.

46. Ryan C. Crocker, "Statement of Ryan C. Crocker, Deputy Assistant Secretary for Near Eastern Affairs," *U.S. Citizens Held in Saudi Arabia*, Hearing of the House Government Reform Committee, June 12, 2002. Available Online, Congressional Universe, Lexis-Nexis.

47. See Rowland, "On Limiting the Narrative Paradigm: Three Case Studies."

48. Janice Hocker Rushing, "Evolution of 'The New Frontier' in *Alien* and *Aliens*: Patriarchal Co-optation of the Feminine Archetype," *Quarterly Journal of Speech* 75 (1989): 10.

CHAPTER NINE

KENNETH BURKE'S DRAMATIC FORM CRITICISM

FLOYD DOUGLAS ANDERSON

ANDREW KING

KEVIN R. MCCLURE

Messenger: Unwounded of his enemies he fell

Manoa: Wearied with slaughter, then, or how? Explain.

Messenger: By his own hands

Manoa: Self violence! What cause Brought him so soon at variance with himself Among his foes?

Messenger: Inevitable cause–At once both to destroy and be destroyed.

John Milton, *Samson Agonistes*

THE MASTER OF FORM: THE IMPORTANCE OF BEING BURKE

Kenneth Burke (1897–1994) was the leading American rhetorical theorist of the twentieth century. Scholar, editor, poet, novelist, critic, and essayist, Burke's career spanned seven decades. He left behind a school of critics and theorists, and an academic society dedicated to the development and extension of his ideas. In addition, Burke produced a huge body of books, scholarly treatises, and critical essays that are still eagerly read. In a very real sense Burke is still a living presence. His methods are being used by hundreds of scholars: and his ideas evoke lively debate among students of literature, the social sciences, and rhetoric.

Unlike so many of the fashionable scholars of the modern academy, Burke is not a European intellectual or a French expatriate. Born in Pittsburgh, Burke was a college dropout who spent much of his adult life on his small farm. Always on the margins of university life, he wandered from school to school as a visiting lecturer. He was part of Greenwich Village bohemian artistic life during the 1920s, a freelance radical intellectual during the Great Depression of the 1930s, and a failed poet and sometime literary critic during World War II. His greatest period of productivity, from 1945 to 1950, established him as a brilliant critic whose works were thought to be rich in intellectual insight, but often demanding and occasionally impenetrable.

During the 1960s Burke was "discovered" by academic departments in major research universities. As a result of this fame, Burke was constantly in demand, speaking on hundreds of campuses, large and small, from 1960 to 1980. Just before the close of this peripatetic or wandering time, the National Kenneth Burke Society was established in 1978. By the time of his death in 1994, Burke had become an institution. Graduate seminars and undergraduate honors courses on Burke and Burkeanism were given throughout the nation's colleges. New interpretations of his work were constantly being published and signed copies of his books became coveted objects for professors and students. A few persons even began to refer to him as "the master" and other Burkeians began to debunk his reputation as a cult figure and "wise man" on the grounds that hero worship would discourage the reading of his works and stop the future development of his ideas. A decade after his death, Burke is still considered the most creative and influential rhetorician of our time.

Burke's Wonderful Life

Burke had a wonderful life. He grew up in a leafy residential area of Pittsburgh. His turn-of-the century youth was spent in a home with large leisurely rooms full of books, pictures, and magic lanterns. Pittsburgh had not yet become the sprawling metropolis it is today, and Burke and his childhood friends roamed the woods and the fields. The countryside was still close to the city's edge in those prosperous and optimist years before World War I. He was a member of his high school literary group at a time when American high schools routinely had large literary societies. He matriculated at Ohio State and quarreled with the soon to be great James Thurber. Bored with undergraduate life he went on to New York City and attempted (sometimes successfully) to sit in on graduate seminars at Columbia University. During the 1920s, he was in the seething heart of Greenwich Village: he was first the assistant editor and then briefly chief editor of *The Dial*, perhaps the most famous literary magazine of its time. Early in the decade of the 1920s, he bought a farm in New Jersey and his summers were spent truck farming; during the winter he and his growing family remained in Greenwich Village where he pursued a literary career. Burke labored as an editor and produced a steady stream of critical essays, poems, and reviews. He placed his hopes in a collection of poems, *The White Oxen*, and a novel, *Toward a Better Life*.[1] They were labored introspective works, arid, intellectually rigorous, and muscular. But they lacked pace, wit, movement, and poetic imagery. By 1930, it was evident that Burke would make his mark as a critic and not as an imaginative writer.

During the Great Depression (1930–1941), Burke began to be an outsider in American intellectual circles. He criticized his fellow American intellectuals, so many of whom affectionately called Vladimir Lenin "The Little Father" and Joseph Stalin our "Uncle Joe." Burke pointed out that "the Little Father" and "Uncle Joe" had put to death millions of *kulaks,* small entrepreneurs, and former Czarist minor officials. In 1938 he wrote "The Rhetoric of Hitler's Battle," an article exposing Hitler's philosophy and plans at a time when some isolationists and German American Bundists were hopeful that Hitler would mellow in office. Others assured us that we had nothing to fear from a community as highly civilized and prosperous as the German Reich.[2] Burke feared neither Right, Left, or Center. From his small Jersey farm, he gave notice that he would not suffer fools gladly no matter what their pedigree or ideology.

During the 1940s and 1950s Burke was able to secure a series of temporary university posts. During that time, he wrote some of his most famous works: *Grammar of Motives* in 1945, *Rhetoric of Motives* in 1950, and *The Rhetoric of Religion* in 1960. These three works are the heart of the Burke corpus. They contain his matured theory and his two major analytical methods, Dramatism and Logography. During the 1960s, Burke was hailed as an original thinker and a major critic of literature, political discourse, and popular culture. By 1978 a cadre of his followers had formed the Kenneth Burke Society. By the 1990s there were Burkean literary critics, media critics, sociologists, and of course Burkean rhetoricians. There were even a few Burkean economists. When the news came of his death in the late autumn of 1994, my graduate students felt as if they had lost a good friend. Only two had ever seen him or spoken with him, but they all had heard his tapes, read his books, and discussed his ideas. Most of all they had been impressed with his mission. Although he had no academic degrees, Kenneth Burke was more a professor than most of us who teach in colleges and universities today. He had a mission and he professed something.[3]

Burke's Big Ideas

Burke had two or three very big ideas. They gave his life meaning and purpose. One of Burke's earliest big ideas was that of *Symbolic Action.* We do not directly engage our environment. We act on it symbolically. Through language, mathematics, art, and other symbol systems we interpret the world, harness the environment and even reconfigure nature. Because of symbol systems (particularly language) we can preserve the past, accumulate culture, build human knowledge, and plan for the future. Symbols make our societies into "learning societies," and these knowledge communities are the source of all of our power over the world.

Yet symbols also have a dark side. Because we have language we have the unique ability to say "no" to the world as we find it. We can change nature to satisfy human desires, often without even a feeble idea of the consequences of our actions. In large areas of the world, we have interfered in the plant cycle and brought about record yields. In some of these same areas, we have unwittingly let half of our top soil blow away, and we have poisoned the groundwater. We have hurled the skyscrapers into the heavens in a celebration of our dominance over the planet and in the United States alone, we have paved over 50,000 square miles of fertile land, removing it from food production forever. We often know the short-term gains of our actions but are surprised by the unexpectedly horrific consequences of the long term. We are also goaded by symbols, victimized by our myths, and seduced by our own stories. Burke reminds us that symbols are shortcuts to realms of experience; they arouse emotion and desire, and that is why artists use them. And because they arouse us so powerfully, hustlers, dictators, mass advertisers, political figures, preachers, and salesmen also employ symbols. We are constantly being urged by these practitioners of symbolic actions to join something, vote for someone, purchase something, embrace new ideas, change our beliefs and practices, and transform our lives and ourselves in small and large ways.

The second major contribution to which we draw attention is *Perspective by Incongruity.* This was Burke's major method of the 1930s. Burke used this method to bring new and fresh insight to the analysis of conventional problems. He did so by juxtaposing unfamiliar or even opposed terms, metaphors, or images. Burke's image of radicals who were "violent in the pursuit of peace" is an example. Burke's most famous example is the one he took from Thorstein Veblen, the idea of "trained incapacity" by which Burke noted that special insight in one area might end up blinding one to insight in another area. Burke's idea of insight by breaking familiar patterns and increasing inventional power through a kind of self-induced intellectual vertigo is one that is found throughout his work. The term "symbolic action" is itself an example of perspective by incongruity.

The third contribution is simply called *Dramatism.* Burke was fascinated by action. He wanted to know how language was used to get things done. He was less interested in the "truth or accuracy of a statement than in its strategic power." One of the most common ways in which humans made sense of the world was through the language and form of drama. He believed that people viewed their political contests, their sports activities, and their marriages much as they viewed a theatrical production. Burke argued that ordinary humans naturally processed their worlds through dramatic categories. Life was drama. Theatre was a secondary product distilled from the dramatic experiences of life.

Dramatism was the way in which people interacted with their language. Burke did not analyze language as a means of conveying information or truth, but as a vehicle of action. Every human action exhibited the dramatic elements of a who (agent), a where (a scene), a why (purpose), a how (agency—means or strategies or instruments) and a what (acts). In any particular drama one or more terms were dominant. This may be seen by a quick review of paired terms. Thus a drama might be characterized by scene–act ("Given these circumstances, what else could I do?") or agency–act ("technology determines my actions") or agent–act ("Given a person like Stalin, what could we expect but acts of oppression?") or purpose–act ("Because I strove to help others, I became a physician") or act–act ("He hit me, so I hit him").

Burke saw drama everywhere. It is true that new presidential administrations try to get a good drama going as quickly as possible. Sporting teams thrive on conflict between players. Businesses advertise their "story." Corporate leaders are in search of a good script. Ordinary people look for "defining moments" in their lives as if they were living out a scenario, and clergy tell their followers about dramatic reversals of fortune and about finding appropriate "roles" and new "voices." Our lives are saturated with the language of the drama.

CRITICAL ESSAY

This essay demonstrates the power of Burke's method of dramatism by analyzing a segment of the political career of Senator Edward Kennedy of Massachusetts. If politics is drama, the Kennedy family seems especially dramatic and its fortunes correspond to the rise and fall of a Greek Tragic House. Teddy Kennedy's *rise* to heir apparent to his brother's shattered presidency, his tragic *fall* with the death of Mary Jo Kopeckne at Chappaquiddick, his *mortification* during the 1980 presidential campaign, and his *redemption* through suffering enact the ancient communal drama of the scapegoat. Kennedy's campaign reaffirmed the high political ideals of the community even as it brutally crushed his personal aspirations for the nation's highest office. Burke notes that we often see our public leaders within the classic form of the myth of the "Questing Hero." One of our basic dramatic "forms" is that of the hero who rises to greatness, suffers a terrible fall, experiences suffering and ostracism, and as a result of his trials "dies" to his old character, and emerges as a purified redeemer of the community. This journey of fall, guilt, suffering, death (either physical or spiritual), rebirth, and return to serve the community, lifts a public figure out of mundane politics and imparts a transcendent quality. Even a partial fulfillment of the dramatic form gives iconographic power to an otherwise ordinary individual. Since ancient times communities in troubled times have sought out a scapegoat. Unable to blame themselves for bad times, mistakes, or poor decisions, they have blamed a scapegoat and either killed or driven out the victim in order to purify themselves. According to Burke, this pattern is repeated over and over as troubled communities seek to purge themselves of guilt and restore their social health and sense of worth.

Mindful that politics is above all, drama and wishing to make the dramatistic analysis as emphatic as possible, our analysis is presented in three acts, corresponding to the conventional format of a staged play. *Act One* reviews Kennedy's glory days, his fall from grace during the Chappaquiddick incident, and his early 1980 primary election defeats. *Act Two* recounts his efforts to achieve personal and political redemption through the processes of mortification and self-immolation by waging a losing campaign for political principle. *Act Three* explains how he used the occasion of his speech at the 1980 Democratic National Convention to effect catharsis and to dramatically symbolize his new rebirth and identity. Senator Kennedy died as a career candidate and was reborn as an empty vessel, an instrument to serve the community's idealism. Let the play begin!

Act One: From Camelot to Chappaquiddick—Paradise Found and Lost

"The drama of the self in quest," writes William H. Rueckert, "is an extraordinarily complex life-long ritual of death and rebirth, rejection and acceptance, purification and change, disintegration and reintegration; essentially, it is the drama of moral choice."[4] Edward Moore Kennedy's "drama of the self in quest" began with his birth in Boston, Massachusetts, in 1932. The fourth son and youngest of nine children of a wealthy and socially prominent Catholic family, he enjoyed in his childhood all the advantages and opportunities that wealth and influence provide. After graduating from Milton Academy in 1950, he entered Harvard, but dropped out for two years while serving in the U.S. Army. He then returned to Harvard and graduated in 1956. In 1959 he earned a law degree at the University of Virginia. While in law school, he met, courted, and married Joan Bennett, the debutante daughter of a wealthy and socially prominent Catholic family. Following the election of his brother John to the presidency, Edward, 30 and fresh out of law school, succeeded him as United States Senator from Massachusetts. During John F. Kennedy's presidency and throughout the 1960s, Edward (Ted), along with the entire Kennedy family, enjoyed the spotlight of an enamored media and American public. This short-lived period of triumph was later called Camelot after the contemporaneous highly popular Broadway musical of that name (co-starring Richard Burton and Julie Andrews), which had popularized the Arthurian legend in American public consciousness. Unfortunately, this brief triumphal period was followed by two tragic assassinations, John F. Kennedy in 1963 and Robert F. Kennedy in 1968. Moreover, Teddy Kennedy's later actions eventuated in his own fall from grace both in the media and with the American public.

"If the sixties had been a decade of triumph and disaster for the Kennedy's," John Davis writes, "the seventies would witness a steady erosion of the family's image as one by one certain disturbing allegations out of the family's immediate past would come to light."[5] These "disturbing allegations," sometimes about his deceased brothers John or Robert (both, for example, were rumored to have had affairs with actress Marilyn Monroe), were all too often about Teddy; rumors of excessive drinking, fast and reckless driving, compulsive womanizing, habitual adultery, and wild sexual orgies.[6] Early in his senatorial career Teddy Kennedy earned the reputation "as a 'man of the Senate'—hard-working, dedicated, competent (or at least presiding over a staff with such qualities, though choosing talent wisely is in itself a talent)."[7] His image "as the 'Good Senator' in public life" now increasingly came to be contrasted with "the image of the 'swinger' and 'playboy' in private life." In fact, he was likened by Lewis Lapham to a minotaur. Teddy, he thought, seemed to represent "the worst as well as the best that could be found in a man."[8] Lapham himself acknowledged that many of the rumors about Teddy's personal life, like rumors generally, probably had little or nothing to do with his actual behavior or character. That they were widely reported in the press and other media, however, suggests that many people took them to be truthful accounts of his behavior and character. Teddy Kennedy's "drama of the self in quest," at least in many people's eyes, had become the drama of a man making wrong moral choices. Camelot, whatever its shining moments, apparently also had a darker side.

Teddy fell prey to what Burke called "diminished identity" or "identity deficit." Burke has noted that identity is symbolically constructed. It is conferred upon us by others and like image or reputation it can be strengthened or weakened, gained or lost. Thus retired persons often experience a loss of status when they no longer perform prestigious jobs, or former office holders may resent the loss of power and complain that they no longer feel like themselves. Novelists whose books are no longer bought, athletes who hit a long slump, or television evangelists who fall from grace all experience a status dilemma or an identity deficit. Teddy had experienced a similar loss of identity. In 1980 Ted Kennedy's candidacy no longer seemed to invite people to join Camelot. The younger brother of the martyred president reminded people of a hero who had been marred or spoiled, of someone who might have achieved greatness, but had somehow missed the heroic measure.

As Kenneth Burke reminds us, in the Judeo–Christian religion all people are born into a fallen state, burdened by "original sin." The linguistically created social order, the dramatistic equivalent of the "Covenant" in the Judeo–Christian tradition, prescribes what people would be and how they should act; it provides them with their ideals (social, sexual, familial, intellectual, political, and economic) and with a variety of alternative selves from which to chose; it offers a complete set of values in terms of which people can find themselves and measure success and failure, or good and evil. Built into this pre-existing hierarchical Covenant are hundreds of "thou-shall-nots"[9] and "thousands of moral, social, familial, economic, and religious negatives."[10] But people are incapable of keeping all the commandments, and of obeying all the "thou shalts" and "thou shalt nots," of the Covenant and in some way they will fail or disobey. The "linguistic commandments," as C. Allen Carter points out, "set unattainable standards. The result is broken laws, concomitant guilt, and a need for purgation."[11]

The earliest publicity known occasion of Teddy's failure to abide by an institutional "thou-shall-not" was his having used a stand-in on a Spanish examination at Harvard in 1951, which resulted in his temporary suspension.[12] While in law school at the University of Virginia he had at least four encounters with the Charlottesville police because of his reckless driving.[13] In one of the encounters he attempted to avoid a speeding ticket by outdistancing a police car, but was discovered by the officer parked on a side road with the lights out and "doubled up and hiding in the darkness behind the steering wheel.[14] These are regrettable "sins," but surely no one of these acts was of such magnitude as to demand great personal atonement through sacrifice and suffering.[15]

Growing up in the patriarch Joseph Kennedy's home, Teddy must have internalized at a very early age the family's "macho role model," in which "the male dominance principle and the double standard were the ruling modes."[16] These modes seem to have been most attractively personified for Teddy in the figure of his older brother, Jack, who became Teddy's sexual role model. Both Jack and Teddy "had difficulty in relating with any emotional depth to a woman, or seeing her as other than a sex object or a field for conquest."[17] Emulating his older brother, Teddy, too, became "cool" about sex and began a lifelong pattern of pursuing women as sexual conquests. He had "no pretenses about romantic love or emotional involvement [and made] his sexual approaches to attractive girls with a matter-of-fact directness and absence of personal commitment that sometimes startled them." Long after the women's movement had ushered in a new awareness on sexual matters, one in which predatory, "chauvinistic womanizing" was no longer seen as "cool," Teddy not only continued to pursue women as conquests, but to do so in a very public way.[18] According to Max Lerner, the description of the lifestyle of the test pilots in Tom Wolfe's *The Right Stuff* as "hard drinking, hard driving," and engaged in "the private pursuit of manliness" fit Teddy Kennedy's lifestyle perfectly.[19]

Teddy's behavior during the 1969 Chappaquiddick incident–when he drove a car off Dyke Bridge on tiny Chappaquiddick Island, was unable to rescue his passenger, Mary Jo Kopechne, and then waited ten hours before contacting the authorities—raised significant lasting public questions about his character.[20] Although he later spoke to the nation in a carefully crafted television address in which he portrayed himself as a helpless victim of circumstances beyond his control, a spin that enabled him to evade personal responsibility for his behavior,[21] doubts about his character and conduct lingered in public consciousness. From Chappaquiddick on he was viewed by many not only as a reckless driver, a heavy drinker, and compulsive womanizer, but also as someone unable to take responsibility for his actions and as a cowardly person who panics and runs away from problems. These lingering negative perceptions prevented him from being a presidential candidate in 1972 and 1976.[22] Perhaps, when he entered the presidential race in fall 1979, he believed that Chappaquiddick was no longer an issue.

But after a decade, Chappaquiddick refused to go away. It "was lying there," in the words of Tom Wicker, "not so much like a time bomb but as a cancer on his candidacy."[23] President Carter in a veiled reference to the incident during a "town meeting" in New York City was the first to make Chappaquiddick a campaign issue. "He himself," Carter observed, "had never 'panicked' during moments of crisis." The next day Carter sent Kennedy a handwritten note assuring him that he had been discussing "high moments of state," that his remarks were not meant as a personal attack on Kennedy, and that he had not, perish the thought, uttered the dreaded "C" word. "But fairly or unfairly, the black cat of Chappaquiddick was out of the bag.[24] A media feeding frenzy set in immediately. "It seems as though any newspaper that wants to be considered credible," Charles B. Seib wrote, "feels obliged to undertake still another rehashing of Chappaquiddick." In Washington, Seib pointed out, both the *Post* and the *Star* published their versions of the scandal.[25] Columnists and editorial writers, too, seemed compelled to weigh in on Chappaquiddick. At the *New York Times,* for example, three different columnists— William Safire[26] (representing the right) and also Tom Wicker[27] and Anthony Lewis[28] (with center–left perspectives)—expressed their concerns about Chappaquiddick, or as Safire preferred to call it "Waterquiddick."[29] *Reader's Digest,* in the February 1980b issue, printed the most widely read Chappaquiddick expose, an exhaustive and damning rehash of what was already well known by John Barron titled "Chappaquiddick: The Still Unanswered Questions."[30] Television news anchors got in on the act as well. "The tough Kennedy [television] interview," Seib observed, had become "the thing."[31] First Tom Jarriel on ABC and then Roger Mudd on CBS questioned Kennedy not only about Chappaquiddick but also about other aspects of his personal as well as his political life. Because it was well known that Mudd was a personal friend of Teddy and other Kennedy family members, the critical and somewhat skeptical nature of his questions and commentary surprised and shocked many viewers and seemed to surprise Kennedy himself. In response to Mudd's questions about Chappaquiddick, Teddy did accept a limited degree of responsibility.

> I've been impacted by a number of tragedies in my life. . . . Those circumstances which I didn't have control. I could feel the sense of regret and the sense of sadness and the sense of loss. But this was a circumstance in which I did have a responsibility, and that—in that sense it was quite difference from other life's experiences.[32]

For many, however, Kennedy's limited acceptance of responsibility for the death of Kopechne was too little and much too late to be seen as possible atonement or redemption. Conservative writer Richard Brookhiser was no doubt speaking for many people of diverse ideological persuasions when he wrote: "Chappaquiddick raises a host of other issues—panic, cowardice, calculation, perjury, obstruction of justice, manslaughter."[33] Even writers on the left, who were generally sympathetic with Kennedy's positions on the issues, seemed compelled to bring up Chappaquiddick. For example, Alexander Cockburn and James Ridgeway praised Kennedy's as "the decent program" but still wondered which of the two Democratic candidates for president was worse: "[I]s it the man who did not go to the police for ten hours worse than the man who played politics with the hostages for over two hundred days?"[34] If Kennedy really had believed that, after a decade, Chappaquiddick had been forgotten he was greatly mistaken.

Damaging as Chappaquiddick was to Teddy's public image, the so-called "Joan factor" was equally harmful. The "Joan factor" was the notion developed by the news media and widely believed by the public that her husband's conspicuous womanizing and simultaneous neglect of wife and family had driven Joan Kennedy to alcoholism.[35] Asked about the state of his marriage during his television interview with Roger Mudd, Kennedy's response was so feeble and fumbling that he actually reinforced and fueled the widespread negative perception:

> **Senator Kennedy:**   Well, I think it's a—we've had some difficult times, but I think we've—have—we've I think been able to make some very good progress, and its—I would say that it's-it's-it's-I'm delighted that we're able to—to share the time and the relationship that we—that we do share.

Mudd: Are—are you separated, or are you just—what—how do you describe the—the situation?

Senator Kennedy: Well, I don't know whether there is a single—a single word that should—have for a description of it. Joan's involved in a continuing program to deal with the problem of—of alcoholism, and—and she's doing magnificently well, and I'm immensely proud of . . . the progress that she's made. . . . It's the type of disease that one has to continue to—to work on, and she continues to work on, and the program that's been devised is—is in Boston.[36]

Many were unimpressed with Kennedy's proclaimed pride in his wife's progress in overcoming alcoholism. Gail Sheehy, for example, expressed skepticism in a *New York Times* column: "Teddy Kennedy props up a wife who suffers from alcoholism to endorse him in public, though the strain on her delicate balance must be great."[37] Ellen Goodman reported seeing a like-minded bumper sticker in Cambridge, Massachusetts: "Vote for Jimmy Carter, Free Joan Kennedy."

The Kennedy campaign had its credibility undermined by fresh revelations in *Time* and elsewhere about Teddy's continued philandering. "When his marriage began to turn bad," *Time* reported, "there were reports of dalliances with New York socialite Amanda Burden, skier Suzy Chaffee, Washington socialite Lee Huftly, and Margaret Trudeau, among others."[38] Despite the Kennedy campaign's efforts at damage control, the "Joan factor" remained a serious and continuing problem.

In addition to Teddy's publicity perceived "guilt" stemming from character factors, he may also have felt some personal "familial guilt" arising from his unfulfilled political ambitions for the presidency as inculcated by his father and brothers, and by virtue of his having inherited the "head of the family" mantle. The guilt occasioned by surviving his brothers and the challenge of having to measure up to martyrs suggests the strong possibility of additional categorical guilt within Teddy—perhaps a deep sense of guilt for failing to live up to inherited expectations coupled in some way perhaps with sibling rivalry. Steven Robert speculated that Teddy was running against his brothers—against the Kennedy legend—and the legend seems to be beating him: "Could he have . . . some deep, internal doubts about himself? Is there not . . . even a possibility of a suicidal impulse? Is there some deep-seated fear that [he] cannot measure up to John or Robert, or to the office they sought or, ultimately, to the public's notion of what he is, or should be? The wild driving, the womanizing—could they all be an elaborate, unconscious way of saying: Let this cup pass from me."[39]

Entering the 1980 presidential primary campaign, Teddy Kennedy was perceived by many—probably a majority—of the American public to be a "polluted" and "guilty" man, a man who was unwilling, perhaps unable, to control his own unruly impulses—unwilling to slay his own "vile beasts within"—and to obey the commandments set forth in the Social Covenant. He was clearly much in need of the expiation made possible by purgative–redemptive symbolic action and a corresponding rhetoric of rebirth.

Burke notes that the basic religious form is the journey from selfish personal ambition to unselfish love of others and service to the community. The individual must "die" to self in order to be redeemed. This powerful form is not only played out in religious life. Other areas such as the art, sports, science, the military, business, and especially politics have borrowed this form. American business is full of saviors, science is full of charismatic geniuses, art is full of god-like creators. Burke finds it especially important in politics, an activity that he calls "secular piety" or a form of "secular prayer." Politics uses religious forms because it is about joining like minded interests to build community and to oppose all those interests they consider threatening. Political leaders constantly stress unity, and the practice of politics frames personal and communal identity in ways that are both material and spiritual. Political leaders constantly use religious language; speak of great crusades; pronounce personal vows; embark on missions; see visions of the future: and, like the prophets of old, foretell utopian dreams.

Burke often noted that even the most secular and material things become invested by a divinity. Thus, a simple business audit may be expressed as a vindication of our integrity, a sporting event is called a test of moral character, a military victory is called the "will of God," and a particular model of car is advertised as an instrument of human freedom. Likewise a university education is said to confer social mobility and human dignity on its constituents. Religious expressions, attitudes, and symbols have migrated to the secular world. In the section that follows, we will constantly remind the reader that even as drama came out of early religion, much contemporary political drama may be seen as religious ceremony with secular vestments.

Curtain: End of Act One

Act Two: Teddy's Redemption—Slaying the Vile Beasts Within

When Teddy Kennedy began his campaign in fall 1979, he and practically everyone else believed that he would have little trouble taking the nomination away from the sitting president whose poll ratings, hovering near 20 percent, were "as low as any incumbent's have ever been."[40] The American hostages were still in Iran, the economy was in a deepening recession with unemployment approaching 8 percent,[41] inflation was soaring, and several of the most influential constituent groups of the Democratic Party were alienated from President Carter and disagreed with his policies.[42] In fact, a majority of the American people seemed to blame Carter for many of the nation's most serious problems. An NBC/AP telephone opinion survey, for example, found that 66 percent of the people nationwide considered Carter a weak leader. The poll also found that "most Americans blamed [him] for every aspect of the country's worsening economic condition." For example, 78 percent of the people thought he "was at least 'partly to blame' for continued inflation; 68 percent said he was 'partly to blame' for higher prices on energy; and 61 percent faulted him for gasoline shortages."[43] The left wing of the Democratic Party, in particular, was unhappy with Carter's "centrist" ideals and policies and tended to regard him as a "conservative infidel,"[44] a deserter of the party's liberal principles, and a betrayer of its traditions. With the polls registering Carter's growing unpopularity and with his public approval rating hovering close to an all time low of 20 percent,[45] several major figures, representing the diverse constituent groups of the Democratic Party, fearing a debacle in the 1980 election, began urging Teddy to seek the Democratic presidential nomination. Teddy was "the last Prince of Camelot,"[46] a fact that seemed to make it inevitable that he make a run for the presidency. "The press, the polls, other politicians, and most of the people," Morton Kondracke reported, "have come to believe that some irresistible force, some historical or genetic inevitability, was operating to make Kennedy a candidate for president."[47]

With President Carter being made the scapegoat for virtually all the nation's problems by press, media, and public alike, presidential hopefuls in both political parties also began to scapegoat him. Ronald Reagan and the other Republican presidential candidates scapegoated Carter and his policies as the root causes of the nation's diverse problems. Teddy Kennedy, on the other hand, despite his strong record of support for Carter's policies in the Senate, scapegoated the President from the left. Carter's abandonment of traditional Democratic principles and policies, he maintained, were responsible for the nation's diverse problems. "The high-unemployment, high-interest economic policy didn't work for William McKinley," Teddy repeatedly told audiences, "it didn't work for Hebert Hoover, and it won't work for Jimmy Carter. . . . It's time to put a real Democrat in the White House." Throughout the primary Teddy described Carter as "a pale carbon copy of Ronald Reagan" and as a "clone" of Reagan.[48] After it became clear that Reagan would win the Republican presidential nomination, he began telling audiences that, "Mr. Carter has created Ronald Reagan."[49] "His explanation: [B]y bemoaning the limitations of the presidency as he sees it, Carter encouraged Americans to look for someone who proposes simplistic solutions to problems."[50]

Conventional wisdom maintained that Carter was "hopelessly weak" and had little to no chance of winning re-election, whereas Kennedy "couldn't be beat."[51] Public opinion polls bolstered this viewpoint. In late summer 1979, a Gallup poll showed Carter's support among Democrats at 21 percent compared to 54 percent for Kennedy.[52] The same poll showed Carter behind both potential Republican challengers, while Kennedy was far ahead of both Reagan and Ford.[53] Other polls seemed to suggest "that Chappaquiddick was fading as a factor in people's minds."[54] And a poll conducted by Lewis Harris revealed that 71 percent of the American people doubted that President Carter had the competence to be president, whereas 67 percent thought Teddy Kennedy had the right leadership traits for the job.[55] If conventional wisdom and the polls were right, things looked good for the "last Prince of Camelot" in his "historically inevitable" quest for the presidential nomination.

Both the assumption that Carter couldn't win and the assumption that Kennedy couldn't lose proved to be entirely wrong. There were several reasons. The first reason was President Carter's ability to take advantage of his incumbency, as well as his ability to exploit the Iranian situation (and later the

Afghanistan situation) and the plight of the hostages to further himself politically. His inability to secure the release of the hostages was initially one of his greatest political liabilities: nevertheless, by the late fall 1979, his handling of the crisis had actually strengthened his standing in the polls. "A rally-round-the-president-in-a-foreign-crisis syndrome came into effect as Carter scored an unprecedented rise of more than 30 points in his Gallup approval rating."[56] Both Gallup and Harris polls showed "a dramatic reversal" in the Carter–Kennedy race, with Carter leading Kennedy by 8 points (48–40) in the Gallup poll.[57]

A second reason why the conventional wisdom that Teddy could not lose turned out to be wrong was his own weakness as a political campaigner, particularly his ineffectiveness as a political stump speaker. "From virtually the moment that his presidential campaign seemed certain last fall," wrote Thomas Oliphant, "he has been measured against standards—most involving myths about his late brothers—and found by some to be a stumbling, inarticulate bumbler."[58] In the past Oliphant pointed out, "on the few occasions he had been on national television—usually reading carefully drafted speeches—there has never been a problem. The myth of yet another 'Kennedy' was always reinforced."[59] Reading aloud a carefully written manuscript was one thing. Delivering off-the-cuff remarks on the stump was another matter altogether. Morton Kondracke also found Teddy's extemporaneous speaking ineffective: "He couldn't get his syntax straight or make eye contact. . . . He seemed to lack fire and made . . . his listeners doubt whether he really wanted to be president."[60] In one campaign appearance after another he "sometimes seemed to lose his concentration" halfway through his speech and simply wandered through the rest of it, uttering mechanical, "rambling, almost incoherent sentences."[61] Not only did Teddy lack facilty in extemporaneous speaking but many of the speaking techniques that he did employ—shouting and pounding his fists on the lectern, for example—came across poorly on television.

No doubt the most important reason why the conventional wisdom that Kennedy was unbeatable turned out to be false was the lingering public doubt—constantly played up by the news media—about his personal character: about his alleged fast-driving, hard-drinking, swinging, playboy lifestyle: about Chappaquiddick and the "Joan factor." Nor were attacks on Kennedy's character written only by conservative writers and published only in conservative journals of opinion; even some progressive, left-of-center writers and publications questioned Teddy's motives and character. In slightly more than a month after he had formally announced his candidacy, Kennedy had plunged in the opinion polls and, far from being unbeatable, his campaign was generally considered hopeless—a view that was verified soon after by his lopsided defeats in all of the early primaries.[62] His candidacy had been destroyed by what *Time* called "the smoldering resentment against his personal excesses in earlier years."[63] Tom Pettit, on an NBC *Nightly News Report,* had a similar view. "Kennedy has gone nowhere," he stated, "a victim of anti-Kennedy sentiment which cannot be exorcized."[64] "The prince of American politics [had] become a frog."[65] Until his crushing two-to-one defeat by President Carter in the January 21 Iowa primary, Teddy had never lost an election.

The rhetorical situation that Kennedy confronted following his early primary defeats, and given the widespread public perceptions of him as a "guilty" and "polluted" person, was one that called for a rhetoric of redemption. But the drama of redemption requires victimage, a scapegoat, and a kill. For Kennedy, this meant offering himself as the sacrificial scapegoat and enduring the resulting public humiliation and mortification associated with conducting a losing campaign. Only through public humiliation and suffering, as well as through the "slaying" of the "vile beasts within," could Kennedy create the cathartic responses necessary for effecting his public, and perhaps also his private, redemption. Hence, Kennedy's redemptive campaign was the only appropriate or "fitting response" to his rhetorical situation.[66]

In one primary election or caucus after another Teddy shrugged off defeat "with enough humor and grace to win the admiration of political opponents."[67] But his humiliation was not limited to electoral defeats. He encountered the Chappaquiddick issue everywhere he went: and he frequently faced hostile demonstrators, many of them carrying placards calling him a "killer."[68] He appeared at a rally with Mayor Jane Byrne in Chicago, a city that "used to revere his brother John," and was jeered by a sizable minority of the audience. He later confided to a friend that this "had left an ugly scar."[69] It must have also left a scar, especially in light of his strong record on women's issues, when Iris Mitgang, Chair of the National Women's Political Caucus, called him a "known womanizer" whose private life raised serious questions about his fitness for the presidency.[70] Having his marital problems and his personal sexual behavior constantly, openly, and widely discussed and condemned in the media must have left a deep scar indeed. This aspect of his campaign resembled, according to George Will, "a public penance and a stoning. All campaigns involve mortification of the flesh, but Kennedy's has involved spiritual mortification too."[71] Another humiliation came when his campaign began to falter and he found "that professed 'old friends' in the Senate and the nation's statehouses would not even return his phone calls." This "shocked him into the realization of just how lonely it was to be a loser."[72]

By carrying on in the face of one humiliating defeat after another, by remaining good humored in defeat, and by taking the political opprobrium heaped on him and still keeping his dignity, Teddy not only refuted many of the lingering doubts about his character but even won the respect and admiration of many people. On some basic level he understood the power of the dramatic form. "He knew that to gain a new political identity, he would have to play the drama all the way to the end. He could not be drawn into a single harsh word about the friends who had pleaded with him to enter the race and then, scared, did nothing to help him: John Culver of Iowa, for example, or Birch Bayh of Indiana."[73] Even one of the advisors to Ronald Reagan was quoted as saying of Kennedy's behavior in defeat: "You have to admire him for it. He is not a whiner."[74]

At the time, the results of Teddy's redemptive campaign were essentially positive, enabling him to gain at least some measure of public redemption and possibly some measure of private redemption as well. He won five of his last eight primary contests,[75] and a total of ten primaries overall, including the delegate-rich New York primary. These wins suggest that the humiliation and mortification he experienced during the fall campaign and during his early primary election defeats had afforded him a sufficient measure of public redemption to permit him to prevail in the later primary contests. Kennedy's comeback enabled him to win a total of 1,235 convention delegates, but Carter's total of 1,982 was 316 more votes than were required to win the presidential nomination. Kennedy had lost the nomination, but he had "effectively divided the party."

Newsweek's political writers theorized that his loss of the presidential campaign was "the moral equivalent of victory." Although Teddy had been forced to endure "a string of early humiliations" he did so "with little bitterness, he has remained true to his social goals and his dignity in the face of adversity has begun to persuade some people that [he] is more than a playboy politician who once drove off a bridge."[76] In suffering a self-imposed political death by conducting a losing campaign for principle, Kennedy was perceived to be saying no to his own "vile beasts within." The atonement afforded by his symbolic death, however, opened the possibility of rebirth. The electorate, too, was caught up in the drama. By participating in the form they now "saw" Kennedy in a new role. His old public identity as shallow playboy was dead. In dying to his old identity, he began to be reborn as the selfless guardian of the embattled Democratic liberal heritage.

Curtain: end of Act Two

Act Three: Teddy's Rebirth—Paradise Regained

"All year," *Time* commented, "the irony has been that the further Kennedy seemed from the nomination, the better he performed and was received by the voters. There seemed to be some form of liberation in losing."[77] This irony also seemed to be true in the case of Teddy's speech before the Democratic National Convention, August 12, 1980, at Madison Square Gardens. His presentation of this speech—which represents the cathartic climax, the final purgative-redemptive moment of his campaign—was masterful a "purification ritual" and a "ritual of rebirth."[78] Teddy portrayed himself as "cleansed" and reborn man.

Teddy began on an appropriately self-deprecating note (an opening tactic often employed by public speakers, but especially suitable for a vanquished and defeated political candidate). His purpose, he avowed, was "not to argue for a candidacy but to affirm a cause . . . the cause for which the Democratic Party has stood in its finest hours . . . since the days of Thomas Jefferson, the cause of the common man—and the common woman."[79] It was the cause of Woodrow Wilson and the "New Freedom," of Franklin Delano Roosevelt and the "New Deal," and of John F. Kennedy and the "New Frontier," and to "fair and lasting prosperity" that had been the motivation behind his own presidential campaign, Teddy told his listeners. But that historic "cause and commitment" now seemed endangered by the increasingly conservative mood of the country. There was even some in his own party (he did not name President Carter, but his listeners understood his meaning) who shared this conservative mood, who had strayed from the party's historic purposes, and who had sought "refuge in reaction." "We cannot," Teddy pleaded, "let the great purposes of the Democratic Party become the bygone passages of history."[80]

But before developing his theme further, Teddy launched an attack on the Republicans, especially their presidential nominee, Ronald Reagan, who probably more than anyone else personified the growing conservative mood of the county. In his attack, Teddy symbolically eviscerated Reagan. In what was described as "a lyrical sequence of scorn,"[81] Teddy quoted past statements made by Reagan to support the charge that he was "no friend" of labor ("Unemployment insurance is a prepaid vacation plan for freeloaders"); "no friend" of the cities ("I have included in my morning and evening prayers every day the prayer that the Federal Government does not bail out New York"); "no friend" of the elderly ("Social Security should be made voluntary"); nor was he "a friend" of the environment ("Eighty percent of air pollution comes from plants and trees").[82] Attacking Reagan enabled Kennedy to unite, at least temporarily, the diverse factions—his own delegates as well as Carter's—of the deeply divided Democratic Party around their common opposition to a dreaded foe. "During a national election," Burke points out, "the situation places great stress upon a division between the citizens. But often such divisiveness . . . can be healed when the warring factions join the common cause against an alien enemy (the division elsewhere thus serving to reestablish the principle of continuity at home)."[83]

Teddy now got back to his theme, "a trumpet for the liberalism that was being derogated by many in his own party."[84] He depicted his campaign as a crusade to resist the growing conservative tide and to defend traditional liberal principles against those, both inside and outside his party, who would derogate them. To amplify the enduring quality of Democratic values in opposition to changing political "fashions," Teddy employed an extended fashion metaphor. "The commitment we seek is not to outworn values but to old values that will never wear out. Programs may sometimes become obsolete but the idea of fairness always endures."[85] Unlike fashions that come into style and go out of style, human wants and needs endure. "The poor," for example, "may be out of political fashion, but they are not without human needs. The middle class may be angry, but they have not lost the dream that all Americans can advance together."[86] Despite changing political fashions, Teddy assured his listeners, his presidential quest had championed the enduring "old values": economic justice, fairness, hope—"new hope"— for a better life. "And someday, long after this convention, long after the signs come down, and the crowds stop cheering, and the bands stop playing," Teddy wished to be remembered as the defender of enduring, traditional Democratic principles and values. "We kept the faith," he assured the faithful, "but the work goes on, the cause endures, the hope still lives, the dream shall never die."[87] His presentation of these lines—which Devlin has described as representing "not only the essence of the speech . . . but also what the . . . campaign was supposed to be about"[88]—brought cheering and applause as well as tears to many eyes. He had achieved a moment of transcendence. Burke posits that after suffering symbolic death, one may be born anew. And in the drama of political salvation, one becomes the perfect emblem of the community, a purified vessel of its aspiration, hopes, and vision.

As he concluded, Teddy sought to dramatically symbolize his rebirth and new identity. He did so by quoting lines from Tennyson's *Ulysses,* lines he said his "brothers quoted and loved—and that have special meaning to me now":

> *I am part of all that I have met . . .*
> *Tho much is taken, much abides . . .*
> *That which we are, we are—*
> *One equal temper of heroic hearts . . . strong in will*
> *To strive, to seek, to find, and not to yield.*[89]

In identifying his own redemptive journey with that of Ulysses, Teddy suggested to his listeners the nature of his new identity. Just as the aging wanderer Ulysses returned from his years of journey and struggle a chastened but a wiser man, Kennedy had returned with a sense of new hope and renewed faith, ready "to strive, to seek, to find, and not to yield."[90]

As Teddy spoke "nearly each of the text's 150 well paced sentences drew shouts, laughter, or applause."[91] He was interrupted a total of fifty-one times by applause, and on five occasions there was sustained applause and prolonged chanting of the "We want Kennedy."[92] Tears filled the eyes of most convention delegates. Many of Teddy's supporters wept throughout his presentation. "Often we sailed against the wind," Teddy intoned, "but we always kept our rudder true. There were so many of you who stayed the course and shared our hope. You gave your help, but even more you gave your hearts. . . . When I think of you. . . I recall the poet's words, and I say: "What golden friends I had."[93] This intonation brought sustained applause but also profuse weeping. "Both pitiful weeping and mirthful laughter," Burke writes, are "akin to love," but "they are not identical with it."[94] In fact, "tragic catharsis through fear and pity operates as a *substitute* for catharsis through love."[95] "One's state of identification or communion with the object of one's pity is nearly like the kind of identification or communion one feels for a love object." What Burke calls "perfect catharsis" arises from "a sense of universal love"[96] and, like other forms of perfection, it is humanly unattainable. "Insofar as such a condition is not attained," Burke says, "the next best thing is a sense of radical pity that lies on the slope of tearful release."[97] The catharsis effected by Teddy's speech, then, was not "perfect catharsis," it did not engender feelings of "universal love," but if not "perfect" it was "the next best thing." Kennedy and his audience (both the convention delegates and the much larger television audience), who pitied him and wept for him, were "cleansed by a bath of pitiful tears, a benign orgastic downpour."[98]

The dramas enacted during political campaigns also afford audience members with opportunities to take pleasure in "sympathetic mediations" on the varied misfortunes and sufferings of political figures. For example, in pitying

Kennedy, less exalted (and less fortunate) Americans could be "to that extent exalted"; identifying with Kennedy in his fallen state enabled them to be "overtly charitable" while simultaneously feeling "covertly superior." For Kennedy's supporters, those who loved him and shared his ideology, feeling consubstantial with him was easy. His political opponents, both inside and outside the Democratic Party, had greater difficulty identifying with him. But, Burke points out, "pity solves this problem too. For Aristotle observes that we pity undeserved suffering, and thus we could in imagination pity even our worst enemy, if we imagined him undergoing heavier punishment then even we would wish on him."[99] When Kennedy's campaign had faltered and he began to suffer public humiliation, many of his political opponents took "unseemly glee" in his "difficulties, something akin to the pleasure children sometimes take pulling the wings off flies."[100] At this point pity took over. As Kennedy's "punishment" seemed to be even greater than they "would wish on him," his opponents were enabled to pity him—George Will, William Safire, and some of Ronald Reagan's advisors were among those who did so[101]—for they could at once be openly and broadly generous toward Kennedy while covertly feeling themselves to be his moral better. This, too provides a kind of "cleansing." In identifying with Kennedy in his fallen state, both his supporters and his opponents were taking pleasure in "sympathetic mediations" on his suffering. In granting him expatiation and forgiveness for his "sins" they were simultaneously gaining vicarious purging, cleansing, and expiation from their own "sins." They were alienating "from themselves to [Kennedy] their own uncleanliness."[102]

At the conclusion of her husband's speech, Joan Kennedy appeared on the stage and embraced him, suggesting to many that their marriage too had been renewed.[103] As Teddy hugged his wife, the convention's most tumultuous demonstration erupted. Ignoring repeated calls to order by Chairman Thomas "Tip" O'Neill, Teddy's supporters danced, sang, and chanted: "We want Teddy!" O'Neill gave up as the convention band began playing "medleys of *For He's a Jolly Good Fellow, McNamara's Band* and *Happy Days Are Here Again.*"[104] On the convention floor many delegates talked enthusiastically about how much Teddy's speech had moved them. *Time,* for example, quoted Gary Brandt, a six-foot-two-inch, 230-lb. welder from Ohio. Wiping tears from his eyes, Brandt said of Teddy, "He could have turned the damned country around. If he'd talked that way during the campaign, this would have been his convention."[105] Morton Kondracke wrote that "Kennedy had a brilliant day in the sun, delivering what may be one of the best political speeches of our time, one that served as a catharsis for his sullen supporters and may get the bulk of them working for the Democratic ticket in the fall."[106] L. Patrick Devlin, expressing the view of many academic critics, wrote: "Here was a candidate—the champion of rejected ideas and rejected himself—able to resurrect the Kennedy legacy in the impressive instance of the convention speech."[107] Perhaps Teddy's friend and college roommate, former California Senator John Tunney, best described the nature of the 1980 Kennedy campaign. It was, according to Tunney, "a campaign of atonement."[108] He added: "That campaign and that speech spell the end of the Chappaquiddick era. It was something that had to be done."[109]

Curtain: End of Act Three

Epilogue

Our analysis demonstrates that Teddy Kennedy achieved some degree of public redemption by suffering the mortification and symbolic self-immolation associated with waging a losing campaign for political principles. As a drama of political purification it involved scapegoating, self-atonement, and purification. Kennedy's 1980 presidential primary campaign was selected to serve as our representative dramatic form because it is widely considered an exemplar of the rhetoric of self-atonement. Burke teaches us that such a rhetoric is eventuated by a fall from grace and is characterized by sacrifice, suffering, humiliation, mortification, and purgation, all designed to slay the "vile beasts within." But symbolic self-slaying also leads to transcendence and rebirth. As Milton's Samson was able to slay his enemies through his own self-destruction, so Kennedy's symbolic death enabled him to slay the doubts, charges, and accusations hurled against him by his enemies. By offering himself as a victim and suffering the resulting mortification with good cheer, Kennedy gained some measure of public expatiation for his publicly perceived shortcomings. His self-victimage resulted, at least for the moment, in rhetorical transformation and symbolic rebirth.

Several conclusions follow from our drama. First, the selection of Kennedy's 1980 presidential primary campaign as our typical political drama as a rhetoric of self-victimage was shown to be an efficacious choice. Second, a redemptive rhetoric of public mortification was found to be the only appropriate—or "fitting"—response to the rhetorical situation with which Kennedy found himself confronted following his early primary defeats. Waging a losing campaign for political principles enabled him to achieve some degree of public redemption. Third, it was dramatic form that drew its spectators into the play. As Burke would say, we became collaborators inside the form. Kennedy's story became our story.

We have illustrated the utility of Burke's major analytical tools through the study of a single political campaign. Following Burke, we treated the campaign as a drama that began with guilt and a dream of salvation. It is a drama of ritual death and dying, but it is also a drama of ritual transcendence and rebirth. And it is a drama that ends with the attainment and maintenance of a state of redemption, of a new identity, and of a strengthened sense of community. Our analysis was also a reminder of the power of form. Burke's genius was to see that these common forms are repeated endlessly in human events and that dramatic form allows us to participate in the larger events of our communities. Form gives shape and meaning to what might otherwise appear to be a shapeless mass of sequential events. And it allows students of form a special insight into the power and the limits of the various life scripts in which we are caught up as players. Our last admonition is to go and read Burke. His ideas provide insight into the constant rhetorical struggle that characterizes everyday life.

PERSONAL COMMENTS ON THE ESSAY

Writing an essay illustrating Kenneth Burke's methods is a daunting task. First of all, Burke has so many methods that we were afraid the article might turn into a catalog of examples. Thus we chose to use a few of his major ideas with the assumption that students would benefit from methods with fewer working parts and broader applications. We wanted the reader to understand that Burke believes that drama is not a metaphor for life but the stuff of life itself. We frame our world in dramatic terms with plot, scene, character, dialogue, climax, and resolution. The categories of drama come out of the structure of our mind and are part of our sense making apparatus.

We chose Ted Kennedy because the Kennedy family appears to be a modern variant of a Greek Tragic House. They exhibit the flawed greatness that we have always associated with tragedy. Once we had explicated the terms of Burke's drama, the case study of Teddy Kennedy's misfortune almost wrote itself. Our problem was to know how much to include, and we wound up cutting nearly thirty pages from the original chapter.

We found it hard to gain a balance. The first article merely outlined the dramatic terms, and the bulk of the article was critical application. Our editor wisely suggested there was too little theory, too little Burke, and too much exposition. Our second draft expanded theory and method and cut half of the application. This time our editor suggested the piece was too theoretical. It seemed to have embraced method for the sake of method rather than finding insights into the language of politics in contemporary America. Finally, we attempted to balance theory and application by condensing our explanation of the method and making our application to the case study more pointed and direct. We believe we were successful in reaching this balance in our third and final draft.

Burke was a great theorist, but he had contempt for mere method unless it had a strong practical application. He wanted his methods to give people the tools that would allow them to understand the world around them and to make decisions on the basis of that understanding.

We also wanted the reader to understand Burke's method in the context of his life and moral outlook. We believe we have been able to do so. We hope that this chapter will create greater interest in the life and work of Kenneth Burke. Finally, we are deeply grateful to the editor who gave us the opportunity to write this piece.

POTENTIALS AND PITFALLS

Kenneth Burke warned us that we were surrounded by politicians and advertisers who were trying to manipulate us. He provided us many rhetorical tools that we could use for our defense. Some critics think he gave us too many. I must also admit that some of Burke's books and articles are hard to read and that occasionally his ideas are dense and complex. He tends to analyze persuaders with exhausting thoroughness. He seems to have a hidden agenda and he uses examples from Goethe, Shakespeare, Coleridge, the New Testament, Matthew Arnold, and from ancient philosophy, examples that assume his readers are quite well read.

But if Burke demands a bit of work from the reader he gives us much more in return. Using only three terms (Division, Identification, and Hierarchy), Burke teaches us to analyze social movements. Using a simple set of dramatic ratios (the Pentad), he gives us the tools to understand and critique a speech, a campaign, a social movement, a piece of literature, or a revolution. Further, Burke was a reformer whose entire life was dedicated to making the world a better place, and his method is infused with the idea of moral choice. Burke's methods are particularly good at unmasking hidden meanings and coded phrases. In short, although Burke demands our full attention, he provides us with powerful and insightful strategies for dealing with the world.

DRAMATIC FORM CRITICISM TOP PICKS

Burke, Kenneth, "Dramatism," *International Encyclopedia of the Social Sciences*, vol. VIII., David L. Sills (ed.) (New York. Macmillan and Free Press, 1968), 445–452. Here in Burke's own words is the best description of dramatism ever penned. It defines the key words and illustrates basic concepts. The article is one of the most lucid pieces of criticism ever written, and it is one of the best short articles Burke wrote in his seventy-year career. We recommend it to anyone who wants to use an off-the-shelf version of Dramatistic theory.

Burke, Kenneth, *"Anthony on Behalf of a Play," Philosophy of Literary Form,* 3rd ed., (Berkeley: University of California Press, 1974), 329–343. This article uses the famous speech of Mark Antony from Shakespeare's *Julius Ceasar* to illustrate the explanatory power of dramatism. Burke's analysis gives the reader a much deeper appreciation of Shakespeare's profound understanding of the dynamics of human communication. Burke uses the device of having Antony reveal his tactics in composing and delivering the speech in a series of brilliant "asides" to the reader. The reader is given a blow by blow account of one of the most successful pieces of persuasion ever written.

Burke, Kenneth, "The Rhetoric of Hitler's Battle" in *The Philosophy of Literary Form, 3rd ed.,* (Berkeley: University of California Press, 1974), 164–190. Three years before Hitler declared war on Europe, Burke wrote this profound article warning us about the kind of horrors the Nazi dictator had in store for the world. This article makes use of the scapegoat and prefigures Burke's expansion of his method from Dramatism to Logography. It has long been considered the most brilliant short example of Burke's critical method at work. Thus, it is often assigned to students as an introduction to Burke.

Cathcart, Robert S., "Instruments of His Own Making: Burke and Media," *Extensions of the Burkean System*, James Chesebro (ed.) (Tuscaloosa: Alabama University Press, 1993), 287–308. Robert Cathcart's article shows extensions of Burke from traditional rhetorical analysis to media settings. Cathcart uses the insights of various theorists to apply Burke to film, television, advertising, and computers.

Crable, Bryan, "Burke's Perspective on Perspectives: Grounding Dramatism in the Representative Anecdote," *The Quarterly Journal of Speech* 86 (2000): 318–333. Bryan Crable's article shows the wide uses that can be made of Dramatism. It adds one of Burke's most potent concepts, the Representative Anecdote, and applies the method in a great variety of situations. Crable is one of the best young Burke scholars in the nation, and he has a very vivid way of putting things.

Griffin, Leland M., "A Dramatistic Theory of Social Movements," *Landmark Essays in Kenneth Burke,* Barry Brummett (ed.) (Davis, CA: Hermagoras Press 1993). Griffin, the inventor of movement studies in discourse, writes about his excitement at having found Burke's Dramatism. Griffin had spent thirteen years searching for a method that would be comprehensive enough to deal with a large number of messages produced by a large number of people in a big, loosely organized movement. Although this is an early example of the uses of dramatism, it is one of the most interesting and imaginative.

NOTES

1. Kenneth Burke, *Toward a Better Life* (University of California Press, 1966).
2. Kenneth Burke, "The Rhetoric of Hitler's Battle," in The Philosophy of Literary Form (University of California Press Berkeley, 1969, 1945).
3. William Rueckert, "A Field Guide to Kenneth Burke—1990," in *Extensions of the Burkeian System,* James W. Chesebro (ed.) (University of Alabama Press, 1993), 13.
4. William H. Rueckert, *Kenneth Burke and the Drama of Human Relations* (Minneapolis: University of Minnesota Press, 1963), 45.
5. John H. Davis, *The Kennedy's: Dynasty and Disaster, 1848–1983* (New York: McGraw-Hill, 1984), 609.
6. Max Lerner, *Ted and the Kennedy Legend: A Study in Character and Destiny,* (New York: St. Martin's Press, 1980), 145–153; and Dugger, 744–746.
7. Richard Brookhiser, "The Last Kennedy," *National Review,* March 21, 1980, 340.
8. Lapham, 38.
9. Rueckert, 131.
10. Rueckert, 132.
11. C. Allen Carter, *Kenneth Burke and the Scapegoating Process* (November: University of Oklahoma Press, 1996).
12. Lerner, 43.
13. Lerner, 48; also see William Safire, "Prelude to the Bridge," *New York Times."*
14. Lerner, 48.
15. For a description of the factual basis of Kennedy's "swinger" image see Lerner.
16. Ronnie Dugger, "The Trashing of Teddy," *The Nation,* June 21, 1980, 746.
17. Lerner, 150.
18. For discussions of Teddy Kennedy's sexual attitudes and behavior, see especially Lerner, 145–153; also see Hirsch, 111, 203; and Dugger, 744–746. For a feminist perspective on Teddy's womanizing and extramarital relationships see Suzannah Lessard, "Kennedy's Woman Problem—Women's Kennedy Problem," *Washington Monthly,* December 1979, 10–14.
19. The irony was that, despite his image as a "swinger" and "chauvinistic womanizer," Kennedy had one of the strongest voting records in the Senate on women's issues. Dugger (744) gives the following description of his record:

    He has supported federal programs for prenatal care and counseling for pregnant teenagers, local rape crisis centers, training displaced homemakers, increasing women's opportunities for scientific careers, insuring equal credit and support for woman-owned businesses, prohibiting discrimination on the basis of pregnancy for victims of spouse abuse, expanded daycare and closing the male–female wage gap in federal employment. In the criminal code he inserted a provision to abolish the requirement of corroboration of the victim's testimony in rape cases. He's for Medicaid funding for abortions for poor women when there are serious health consequences.
20. See John Barron, "Chappaquidick: The Still Unanswered Questions," *Readers Digest,* February 1980, 66–72, 219–242.
21. Edward Kennedy, "Speech of July 25, 1969," *New York Times,* July 26, 1969, A10. For a useful pentadic analysis of Kennedy's Chappaquiddick address see David A. Ling, "A Pentadic Analysis of Senator Edward Kennedy's Address to the People of Massachusetts July 25, 1969," *Central States Speech Journal* 21 (1970):81–86.
22. Davis, 575–601.
23. Tom Wicker, "Reprieved by 'Jaws,' " *New York Times,* November 9, 1979, A35.
24. "Jimmy Strikes Back," *Newsweek,* October 8, 1979, 26.
25. Charles B. Seib, "Enough of Chappaquiddick," *Washington Post,* November 16, 1979, A21.
26. William Safire, "Waterquiddick," *New York Times,* November 12, 1979, A21.
27. Tom Wicker, "Reprieved by 'Jaws,' " A35.
28. Anthony Lewis, "Lower the Gate," *New York Times,* November 15, 1979, A31.

29. Safire, "Waterquiddick," A21.

30. Hersh, 66–72, 219–242.

31. Seib, "Enough of Chappaquiddick," A21.

32. "Teddy." Correspondent Roger Mudd. *CBS Reports*, CBS. November 4, 1979.

33. Brookhiser, "The Last Kennedy," 341.

34. Quoted in Dugger, 744.

35. For a fuller discussion of the "Joan Factor," see Marcia Chellis, *Living with the Kennedys: The Joan Kennedy Story* (New York: Simon and Schuster, 1985), 143–147. Another helpful work is Lester David, *Joan: The Reluctant Kennedy* (New York: Warner, 1975); also see "The Vulnerable Soul of Joan," *Time*, November 5, 1979, 19.

36. "Teddy," 4, 5.

37. Quoted in Ellen Goodman, "Joan: Nobody's Victim Anymore," *Boston Globe*, February 21, 1980, 17.

38. "The Kennedy Challenge," *Time*, November 5, 1979, 20; also see Carl Rowan, "Kennedy Candidacy Masochistic Move," *Fort Wayne Journal Gazette*, November 2, 1979, 2A; Rowan professes dismay that *Time* would print the names of the women with whom Kennedy had been involved, but he then proceeded to pass along *Time's* list to the thousands of readers of his syndicated column.

39. Steven Roberts, "Ted Kennedy: Haunted by the Past," *New York Times Magazine*, February 3, 1980, 74, 55.

40. Morton Kondracke, "Superman Crashes," *New Republic*, December 21, 1979, 7.

41. "Teddy's Long-Shot Scenario," *Newsweek*, May 12, 1980, 54.

42. Kondracke, 7.

43. Thomas E. Cronin, "Looking for Leadership 1980," *Public Opinion*, February/March 1980, 15.

44. William Safire, *Lend Me Your Ears, Great Speeches in History* (New York: W.W. Norton, 1997; revised and expanded edition), 933.

45. "Teddy's Long-Shot Scenario," 54.

46. Kondracke, 7.

47. Dugger, 742.

48. Kondracke, 7.

49. Alexander Cockburn and James Ridgeway, "Into the Abyss," *Village Voice*, August 13–19, 1980, 10; "Ted Knew His Chances Were Slim," *Chicago Tribune*, August 17, 1980, sec 3:11; "What Makes Teddy Run? Liberal Convictions, and a Refusal to Admit Defeat," 22.

50. "Vowing Defiance to the End" *Time*, July 21, 1980, 21.

51. "Vowing Defiance to the End," 21.

52. Kondracke, 7.

53. Kondracke, 7.

54. Kondracke, 7.

55. Kondracke, 7.

56. Kondracke, 7.

57. Cronin, 17.

58. Thomas Oliphant, "Why Is that Man on Television Always Shouting," *The Boston Globe*, May 2, 1980, 2.

59. Oliphant, 2.

60. Safire, "Lend Me Your Ears," 933.

61. Kondracke, 8.

62. "What Makes Teddy Run? Liberal Convictions, and A Refusal to Admit Defeat," 21; also see Kondracke, 8.

63. "Kennedy Goes Out In Style—And Looks Ahead," *Time*, August 25, 1980, 25.

64. *NBC Nightly News*, February 26, 1980.

65. Will, "Kennedy May be Wrong but He's No Amateur," C7.

66. We borrow the phrase "fitting response" from Lloyd Bitzer, "The Rhetorical Situation," *Philosophy and Rhetoric 1* (1968): 1–14. Although we do not employ Bitzer's situational method, we believe an analysis based on it would draw the same conclusion we have, namely that Kennedy's redemptive campaign represented the only appropriate response.

67. "Kennedy Goes Out In Style," 25.

68. Rowan, 2A.

69. "Kennedy Goes Out In Style," 25.

70. "Kennedy Private Life Questioned; He is Called 'Known Womanizer,' " *New York Times*, September 22, 1979, 7.

71. Will, "Kennedy May be Wrong But He's No Amateur," C7.

72. "Kennedy Goes Out In Style," 25.

73. Lewis, A23.

74. "What Makes Teddy Run? Liberal Convictions, and A Refusal to Admit Defeat," 21.

75. "Teddy's Long-Shot Scenario," 54.

76. "Teddy's Long-Shot Scenario," 54.

77. "Kennedy Goes Out In Style," 25.

78. Burke, *Attitudes Toward History*, 317, 318.

79. Edward M. Kennedy, "Principles of Democratic Party: Common Hopes for the Future,"*Vital Speeches of the Day*, August 12, 1980, 714. In 1999, Stephen Lucas and Martin J. Medhurst surveyed a sample of public address scholars, asking them to identify the greatest speeches of the twentieth century. One hundred thirty-seven individuals responded to the survey, ranking speeches based on impact, rhetorical

artistry, organization, style, and presentation of arguments. Teddy Kennedy's DNC speech was ranked seventy-sixth on the list of the 100 greatest speeches of the century. The results appeared in *USA Today*, December 30, 1999. For the complete list of the top 100 speeches of the twentieth century, see http://www.americanrhetoric.com/top100spe echesall.html.

80. Kennedy, 714.
81. "Madison Square Garden of Briars," 16.
82. Kennedy, 716.
83. Kenneth Burke, *Language as Symbolic Action, Essays on Life Literature and Method,* (Berkeley and Los Angeles; University of California Press, 1968), 51.
84. Safire, "Lend Me Your Ears," 933.
85. Kennedy, 714.
86. Kennedy, 714.
87. Kennedy, 714.
88. Devlin, L. Patrick Devlin, "An Analysis of Kennedy's Communication in the 1980 Campaign," *Quarterly Journal of Speech* 68 (1982): 417.
89. Kennedy 716. Also see Alfred Lord Tennyson, "Ulysses," *Works,* (London: Macmillian, 1891), lines 65–70. In Kennedy's quotation of *Ulysses* he left out some telling passages in which the aging wanderer Ulysses admits his weakness and lost strength to his followers.

Apparently Kennedy did not wish his audience to think he had been weakened or had lost strength by his campaign struggles.

90. Kennedy, 716. Also see Tennyson, "Ulysses," lines 65–70.
91. "Madison Square Garden of Briars," 16.
92. Devlin, 416.
93. Kennedy, 716.
94. Kenneth Burke, "Catharsis Second-View," *The Centennial Review* 5 (1961):108.
95. Burke, "Catharsis Second-View," 108.
96. Burke "Catharsis Second-View," 109.
97. Burke "Catharsis Second-View," 109.
98. Burke, "On Catharsis or Resolution," 344, 345.
99. Burke, "Catharsis Second-View," 109.
100. Will, "Kennedy May be Wrong. . .," C7
101. Will, C7; Seib, A21; and "What Makes Teddy Run?" 21.
102. Burke, *A Grammar of Motives,* 406.
103. Ironically, however, they were divorced shortly after this.
104. "Madison Square Garden of Briars," 16.
105. "Madison Square Garden of Briars," 16.
106. Morton Kondracke, "The Dream is Dead," *The New Republic,* August 23, 1980, 6.
107. Devlin, 416.
108. "Kennedy Goes Out In Style," 25.
109. "Kennedy Goes Out In Style," 25.

CHAPTER TEN

FRAMING ANALYSIS

JIM A. KUYPERS

If you have ever had a picture framed, you know that the frame you chose emphasized some elements of the picture at the expense of others. Similarly, if you were to reframe the picture, you would notice that the very elements previously emphasized—colors, patterns, composition—would subsequently be deemphasized by the new frame. Instead, a different combination of elements would be highlighted. Similar to pictures, ideas and events—facts—are also framed. When we frame in a particular way, we encourage others to see these facts in a particular way. Framing in this sense can be understood as taking some aspects of our reality and making them more accessible than other aspects.

The tremendous power of frames to shape the manner in which we interpret certain issues and situations is readily discernable in a study by Paul M. Sniderman, Richard A. Brody, and Philip E. Tetlock. These researchers used mandatory testing for HIV (human immunodeficiency virus) as the issue for their study. They found that the effect "of framing is to prime values differentially, establishing the salience of the one or the other. [A] majority of the public supports the rights of persons with AIDS [acquired immunodeficiency syndrome] when the issue is framed to accentuate civil liberties considerations—and supports . . . mandatory testing when the issue is framed to accentuate public health considerations."[1] Another powerful example of frames is provided by Thomas Nelson and colleagues. Using a local news story about a Ku Klux Klan march as their issue, these researchers presented audiences with either one of two stories: "One framed the rally as a free speech issue, and the other framed it as a disruption of public order. Participants who viewed the free speech story expressed more tolerance for the Klan than those participants who watched the public order story."[2]

Frames are so powerful because they induce us to filter our perceptions of the world in particular ways, essentially making some aspects of our multidimensional reality more noticeable than other aspects. They operate by making some information more salient than other information; therefore, they "highlight some features of reality while omitting others."[3] We rarely notice this process, especially the omission of information, because our public attention is highly selective. Our judgments about the world are in part due to what standards come to our minds, but also are related to information that is easily accessible.

William Gamson asserted that a "frame is a central organizing idea for making sense of relevant events and suggesting what is at issue."[4] In noting that facts remain neutral until framed, Gamson argued that they "take on their meaning by being embedded in a frame or story line that organizes them and gives them coherence, selecting certain ones to emphasize while ignoring others."[5] Framing, then, is the process whereby communicators act—consciously or not—to construct a particular point of view that encourages the facts of a given situation to be viewed in a particular manner, with some facts made more or less noticeable (even ignored) than others.

When highlighting some aspect of reality over other aspects, frames act to define problems, diagnose causes, make moral judgments, and suggest remedies. They are located in the communicator, the text, the receiver, and the culture at large. Frames are central organizing ideas within a narrative account of an issue or event; they provide the interpretive cues for otherwise neutral facts. Framing is, however, a normal part of the communication process. We need ways to negotiate the massive amounts of information that comes to us everyday. Large and complex ideas and events figuratively cry out for framing since they have so many elements demanding attention. Because of this, framing analysis is a particularly useful way to understand the impact of rhetoric. Although framing analysis can be used to better understand any rhetorical artifact, it is particularly suited for understanding the effects of mediated communication. Considering that we receive the vast majority of news about our world from the news media, I intend to focus the remainder of this discussion on framing analysis and the mass media.

FRAMING AND THE MEDIA

Although framing analysis may fruitfully be used to analyze a large variety of rhetorical artifacts, I wish to focus on one particular area that I feel is ripe with potential for framing analysis: the news media. To do this, we first need to locate framing analysis within the family of methods used to study the news media. Specifically, we will look at how the media set an agenda by focusing the attention of the public on some issues and not others: agenda-setting. After this we will look at how the media induces its audiences to interpret the news in a particular manner: agenda-extension.

The Agenda-Setting Function of the Press

The agenda-setting function of the press has received enormous attention from scholars during the past quarter century. Part of the strength of agenda-setting theory is that it affirms that the media "do have a great deal of influence" upon political decision making; moreover, it clearly demonstrates that the media are especially influential in telling the general population what to think about.[6] For example, Maxwell E. McCombs and Donald L. Shaw found that voters learn about an issue "in direct proportion" to the attention given that issue by the press.[7] They asked if the key issues in a political campaign, as reported by the general public, correlated with actual media content. They found that the mass media provided voters with the "major primary sources of national political information"; more importantly, however, they found that voters tended to share what the media defined as important.[8]

Other studies have confirmed these results; for example, Sheldon Gilberg et al. found that the press could set our government's agenda, even to the point of influencing the content of a State of the Union address.[9] The influence of the press in this regard is highlighted by McCombs and Shaw: "[T]he press is an independent force whose dialogue with other elements of society produces the agenda of issues considered by political elites and voters. Witness the major role of the elite press as a source of information among major decision makers. Through its winnowing of the day's happenings to find the major events, concerns, and issues, the press inadvertently plays an agenda-setting influence role."[10]

Following the logic of agenda-setting theory, we can say that the mass media shape what the public "perceives" as "political reality." Moreover, the mass media also shapes how political elites understand what voters and opinion leaders are thinking about. In a sense, a relationship develops between the press, its sources, and the public audience that determines "what is *accepted* as the public agenda."[11] Unfortunately, research data suggests that this relationship is unidirectional—press content affects public concern, but public concern does not affect that which the news focuses upon.[12] Press influence of public knowledge takes on more importance when we consider the degree to which we rely upon the press for information about our local communities, our country, and the world. The further information is removed from our day to day experiences the more we must rely on the news media to provide us with the information we desire. Because of this, the "news media exercise a near monopoly as sources of information and orientation."[13]

From Agenda-Setting to Agenda-Extension

Communication researchers Judith F. Trent and Robert V. Friedenberg wrote that "the media set public priorities just by paying attention to some issues while ignoring others. They determine what issues are important and in this way play an important role in structuring our social reality."[14] This structuring of our perceptions of the important news we receive is well known to those who study mass communication; early in the 1980s researchers interested in this area began to discover an evaluative component to media news. These researchers postulated that news media provide contextual cues "by which to evaluate the subject matter" under consideration.[15] Although the press must provide a proper context in which to understand the news, reporting the news so a *press-supported context* will be produced moves beyond agenda-setting and involves the influencing of public opinion. I call this extra dimension of press reporting agenda-extension.[16]

Agenda-setting can be described as the role the media play in focusing the public's attention on a particular event or issue over another, primarily by how much attention the media gives to that event or issue. Since the mid-1990s, however, some scholars using agenda-setting theory have begun to focus on the persuasive aspects of news coverage. This new area of endeavor is called second level agenda-setting, and it posits that the media can focus pubic attention on particular attributes within an event or issue.[17] This notion of second level effects allows us to see how the media would be elevating one attribute over another in the mind of the public. Since a particular attribute of an issue would be foremost in the public eye, it seems likely that the public would use that particular attribute to evaluate a politician's actions. The public becomes primed to evaluate the president, for example, by how well he handles the particular issue covered by the press. The more the press covers an issue, the more the public will evaluate the president's success or failure in relation to the content of media coverage.

Anne Johnston, surveying work in agenda-setting research, shed light upon the agenda-extension process.[18] She stated that news stories not only provide their audiences with the important topics to think about, but they also provided "contextual cues or frames in which to evaluate those subjects."[19] One of the earlier examples of this is provided by Gladys Engel Lang and Kurt Lang, who argued that this type of agenda-extension was operating during the Watergate hearings.[20] They found that agenda-extension begins when media gatekeepers decide to publish a particular story because issues are often framed by station managers, producers, or editors by *how they decide to tell a particular story.* Although deciding what story to tell is the first step in all news reporting, the press takes a second step when determining how much attention to give to the story. As pointed out by Doris Graber, it is at this "point where ordinary agenda-setting activities can most readily turn into deliberate agenda-building [agenda-extension]."[21]

By continually focusing on an issue, the media thrusts it into the forefront of national thought; the media generated context, at this point, becomes crucially important. In the Watergate example, Lang and Lang noted that coverage was first framed in terms of the election campaign. The nation became obsessed, however, as soon as the media switched frames, moving from the framework of the 1972 presidential campaign to the framework of continual Washington corruption. Shanto Iyengar and Adam Simon also show how framing can induce audience members to interpret events in a particular manner. Sharing the results of their study on the first Gulf War, these researchers found that "content data (showing that network news coverage was preoccupied with military affairs and highly event oriented) and survey data are coupled to show that respondents reporting higher rates of exposure to television news expressed greater support for a military as opposed to a diplomatic response to the crisis, because the news media framed the events in the Gulf episodically as a series of military actions."[22]

It is at this point that the notion of agenda-extension moves beyond second-level agenda-setting in that it posits that the media not only focuses attention on particular attributes of an issue, making some portions more salient than others, it does so in such a manner that a particular political agenda is advanced. More to the point, second level agenda-setting examines *what* attributes are stressed, agenda-extension—as will be seen below—allows us to see *how* those attributes are stressed to influence audience reaction.[23]

Neutral Role of the Press

Providing contextual cues for proper interpretation is an important part of media responsibility. A problem occurs, however, when the media place their partisan context over a neutral one needed by the people or government. In America we generally think of the media as being objective sources for the news we need to make informed decisions. We also generally believe that the press should be fair in its treatment of all sides of an issue. Journalism ethics researcher Louis A. Day suggested that reporters must "clearly distinguish between fact and opinion."[24] When writing for the public, journalists must place news stories into "perspective" by providing "relevant background."[25] This involves being objective, fair, and truthful. According to Mitchell Stephens, objectivity involves both impartiality and the reflection of the "world as it is, without bias or distortion of any sort."[26] In short, the news as a true image of the world. A laudable goal but difficult to put into practice.

The notion of agenda-extension allows researchers to determine if something other than the above idealized norms operate within press stories. By framing an issue, the media have a decision to make: They can frame it to reflect their view of the world; they can frame it to reflect what they think their audiences wish to hear; or they can, as accurately as possible, frame it to impart the meaning of those speaking/writing on it. The last of these choices seems to adhere best to the requirements of a fair and responsible press. According to Day, media practitioners should "strive to keep their personal preferences and opinions out of news stories. . . . [They should be] concerned with facts and impartiality in the presentation of those facts."[27] Framing analysis can help us determine if journalists are living up to these standards.

Framing Analysis as Rhetorical Criticism

So far this chapter has provided a brief overview of relevant agenda-setting and agenda-extension theory. I think it safe to say that the power of the media to establish the relevance of some issues and events over others and thus control the content and direction of public discussion is great. In particular we discussed agenda-extension, which includes the concept of framing: the central organizing principle of continued news coverage. In short, framing involves how the press organizes the context through which the public will view news. At its heart this is a rhetorical process, thus I now turn to demonstrating how framing analysis can fruitfully be used for rhetorical criticism.

Recall that some facts are emphasized by certain frames and others are not; it is this presence or absence of certain facts that may reveal the implicit aspects of the news coverage. Perhaps the easiest way to detect frames is by comparative analysis. Robert M. Entman provides a good example of how to conduct such a study when he comparatively analyzed the narratives within news stories about the KAL 007 and Iran Air 655 shootdowns.[28] Recall that in 1983 Soviet Migs shot down a Korean jumbo jet that had flown into Soviet airspace, and in 1988 the *U.S.S. Vincennes,* while operating in the Persian Gulf, shot down an Iranian airbus. All aboard both planes perished. Because of their similar nature, these incidents could have been reported on in a similar fashion. Entman thought that because of this, any differences in the information that comprised the frames would be easier to detect. According to Entman, "frames reside in the specific properties of the news narrative that encourage those perceiving and thinking about events to develop particular understandings of them."[29] Specifically, the above properties of which Entman speaks reside in the press narrative accounts of events; they are composed of key words, metaphors, concepts, symbols, and visual images. These elements will consistently appear within a narrative and "convey thematically consonant meanings across . . . time."[30] Thus, framing makes some ideas more salient than others, while making some ideas virtually invisible to an audience. However, to detect this, one must examine more than a single news story.

Once the framing process is initiated, often by the interaction of sources and journalists, the established frame guides both audience and journalist thinking. Entman called this type of frame an "event-specific schema," since it was a frame generated in response to a specific event. Once in place, an event-specific schema— a frame—encourages journalists to "perceive, process, and report all further information about the event in ways supporting the basic interpretation encoded in the schema."[31]

How was this accomplished? In terms of agenda-setting, the mere occurrence of reporting should be taken into account. Entman used news items appearing in *Time, Newsweek, CBS Evening News,* the *Washington Post,* and the *New York Times.* During the two-week period following the KAL 007 shootdown, the *New York Times* printed 286 stories, and the *Washington Post* printed 169 stories. During the two-week period following the shootdown of Iran Air 655 the *New York Times* printed 102 stories and the *Washington Post* printed 82 stories. Thus, the actual coverage helped to determine the importance of the event. So, the importance of the issues has been established, but what frame was generated? He found that the destruction of KAL 007 was framed as a moral outrage, whereas the destruction Iran Air 655 was framed as a technical problem.

These and other findings reported by Entman demonstrated how frames impose a specific interpretation onto events. They often obscure contrary information that may be presented in a particular case. Entman found that "for those stories in which a single frame thoroughly pervades the text, stray contrary opinions . . . are likely to possess such low salience as to be of little practical use to most audience members."[32] In terms of the two shootdowns, this meant that although it was perfectly acceptable for political elites to describe the KAL shootdown as a brutal attack, it was far less likely for them to describe it in terms of a tragedy; the frame had been set: the Soviets were evil and at fault. To think of the shootdown in terms of tragedy runs against the frame and would mitigate the culpability of the Soviets. In contradistinction, the Iran Air 655 shootdown was framed as a technical problem. To call it other than an accident or tragedy, or to suggest American Gulf policy was at fault, would run counter to the established frame.

In *Presidential Crisis Rhetoric and the Press in a Post-Cold War World*, I performed a comparative analysis of the rival frames used by the Clinton administration and the printed press when discussing crisis situations in North Korea, Bosnia, and Haiti.[33] Specifically, I combined framing analysis, agenda-setting theory, and rhetorical criticism to discover how the Clinton administration framed the situations and how the press framed the situations as a response to the administration's statements. I examined the *Washington Post* and the *New York Times* during a ten-day period following each of President Clinton's public statements concerning the above crises.

In order to discover frames, I began by analyzing the administration's statements for narratives. Next, I specifically looked for the various framing devices that may have been used by the Clinton administration: key words, metaphors, and concepts. Having accomplished this, I repeated the analysis on news stories and editorials contained in the *New York Times and the Washington Post*. Three questions guided my investigation: (1) How did the Clinton administration frame the crisis situations in Haiti, North Korea, and Bosnia? (2) When responding to the Clinton administration, how did the press frame the respective situations? (3) Did the frames of the president and the press ever coalesce to present an unified contextual whole?

I reasoned that unless the reader had firsthand access to transcripts of the Clinton administration's utterances, all public knowledge about the crises were filtered through the frame of the press. However, I also found that although the *content* of presidential messages was being reported, the *context* in which the message was originally uttered often was not conveyed. In this manner the administration was not treated as a news source, providing informative utterances about the situation, but rather it was forced into an oppositional role to that of the press.

For example, during the North Korean situation, the press framed the crisis in a manner that highlighted the potential drama of the North Koreans' withdrawal from the nuclear nonproliferation treaty. The Clinton administration framed the crisis in a manner that stressed calm negotiation and the budding reconciliation of North and South Korea. For another example, in 1995 President Clinton declared he would send 20,000 U.S. troops to Bosnia for peacekeeping missions. The press was predisposed to accept his decision to send troops.[34] Because of this, perhaps the most important frame the administration advanced—that the mission was acceptable to the American people and relatively risk free—was actually adopted in whole by both papers examined. Such was not the case in other areas. For instance, I found that the press framed the issue of Congressional support for the mission differently than the Clinton administration framed it. According to the press, the Republican-controlled Congress was openly hostile and partisan in its deliberations. This frame was so well structured that it made contrary opinions, such as the president's, irrelevant. At a time when calm deliberation and consensus were extremely important for the U.S. government to project, the press was advancing a contradictory impression of the continuing discussion between Congress and the White House over U.S. involvement in Bosnia. In this manner, then, *the press was intentionally miscommunicating the direct assertions of the president of the United States.*

As yet another example of oppositional framing, consider that when President Clinton took office in 1993 the country was threatened with a flood of Haitian refugees. Eventually, this turned into a year-long crisis for the Clinton administration. I found that the press framed the situation as a domestic issue, and the administration framed it as a foreign policy issue. The Clinton administration stressed a foreign policy that had as its focus the return of democracy to Haiti and the aversion of a massive humanitarian tragedy. The press frame stressed a domestic focus that highlighted its perception of an "inhumane" administrative policy of returning all Haitian boat people to Haiti. Although the press did report what the administration said, the context surrounding these statements by the administration was modified by the frame of the press. The domestic, legal issue of the administration's policy became the focus rather than the restoration of democracy. In such a setting the administration was presented, not as a source of news but as one side of a partisan battle with the press.

In another project, I charted the potential effects the press have upon the messages of political and social leaders who discuss controversial issues.[35] Specifically, I was looking for examples of press bias being injected into news coverage of the speeches of five political actors: Senator Charles Davidson, President William J. Clinton (two speeches examined), minister Louis Farrakhan, Senator Trent Lott, and minister Reggie White. I thought the best way to begin looking for press bias was to examine the original utterances of these political actors and then compare that to the press coverage during a two-week period following the speeches. In all, over 700 press reports in 116 different newspapers were examined. I did not differentiate between new stories, news analysis, editorials, and opinion pieces since I sought to determine if editorial position correlated with the content of news stories and news analysis stories. In each chapter, the following general questions were answered: How did the speakers frame the issue? How did the press, responding to the speakers, frame the issue? And at what time, if at all, did the frames converge to present a unified contextual whole?

The findings of this study are striking. More often than not, the press advanced its own interpretation of events over that of the speaker, if that speaker's comments went against press supported positions. I also discovered that press supported positions corresponded to a narrow range of liberal political beliefs. Non-mainstream left positions were ignored or dismissed; moderate and right-leaning positions were denigrated and actively argued against. I found that the press would actively help certain politicians and social leaders on the left who espoused the same point of view adopted by the press. However, those who stepped beyond this narrow range of liberal reporting, moving to the right, or even further to the left, were denigrated or ignored.

I argued that this process occurs through four distinct reportorial practices: sandwiching (the placement of pro-press position statements on either side of non–press-supported statements); lopsided use of sources (pro-press sources used at a rate of two to one or higher over quotations from those who disagree with the press, often making a minority point of view seem to be a majority point of view); labeling (calling those who disagree with press-supported positions denigrating names); and the omission of alternate facts (leaving out information that would contradict with what press asserts is the correct point of view).

One other important aspect of framing involves how the press uses labels or names. Zhongdang Pan and Gerald M. Kosicki suggested that the words chosen by a news reporter reveal the way that reporter categorizes what he or she is reporting upon.[36] For Pan and Kosicki, word choice often "signifies the presence of a particular frame."[37] They cited the descriptions of Saddam Hussein given by American reporters during the Gulf War. Hussein was described as the "Iraqi dictator," a description that placed him in the same category, in the minds of Americans, as Hitler, Mao, Stalin, and other loathsome totalitarians. Contrast this with describing him as the "Iraqi leader," "Iraqi president," or the "Iraqi commander in chief." From this example, we can see that the lexical choices made within the various framing devices (names used to describe an individual) act to frame the news story in such a manner that a dominant reading is suggested.

For another example, consider the U.S. press descriptions of Yugoslavian President Slobodan Milosevic given during the NATO bombing of Serbia. He was described as an "evil dictator," "a cruel and determined enemy," and "a brutal dictator" to name only three. Frequent comparisons were made with Adolf Hitler as well: "Adolf Hitler had a 'final solution.' Slobodan Milosevic has 'ethnic cleansing.' Each leader's term gives a brilliant, if not positive, spin to his massacres."[38] If the press described Milosevic as the "Yugoslavian leader," "Yugoslavian president," or the "Yugoslavian commander in chief," considerations about Milosevic's legitimacy would be quite different.[39]

Naming works for leaders at the national level as well. For instance, family psychologist and president of Focus on the Family James Dobson has been given various pejorative labels by the mainstream professional press: "dingbat," "zealot," "crazy," "intolerant," "Ayatollah," "and the "'Godzilla of the Right,' who is similar to David Duke of the Ku Klux Klan."[40] Former Senate Majority Leader Trent Lott has been referred to as "hater," "homophobe," "narrow-minded," "extremist," "prejudiced," and "right-wing radical."[41] Contrast these label with those given to President Clinton following his speech "One America": "passionate," "congenial," and "up there with President Abraham Lincoln and Martin Luther King Jr."[42] As can be seen from these examples, the labels the press uses to describe a politician or social leader will help to establish a frame from which to understand remarks from that politician.

Although it may seem ironic, labeling can also work by lack of labels. The manner in which the U.S. media reported the 2001 scandal involving Democratic Congressman Gary Condit demonstrates that frames can in part be defined by what information is left out. Condit received enormous press attention because of his numerous alleged affairs, including one with Chandra Levy. Standard reportorial practice is to identify members of Congress with their party affiliation. However, between May and July 2001 the major networks (ABC, CBS, and NBC) reported 179 stories on Condit, but mentioned his party affiliation only fourteen times: only 8 percent of the stories labeled Condit as a Democrat. In the majority of those fourteen stories, Condit was labeled as a "conservative" Democrat linked to the "right-wing" of the party. However, Condit's voting record placed him, after "12 years in Congress [with] a 48% rating from the American Conservative Union and a 52% score from the liberal Americans for Democratic Action."[43]

CRITICAL ESSAY

For my critical essay I have written about minister Louis Farrakhan's speech at the Million Man March. I am interested in Farrakhan's rhetoric because he delivers a message pointedly different from other black leaders. The Million Man March garnered tremendous media coverage as well, so I thought his speech would have generated a good deal of press coverage. In the simplest terms, I thought I would conduct a framing analysis of Farrakhan's speech, and then look for all mainstream press articles about the speech printed during the two weeks following the speech. I would then examine those articles for frames, eventually comparing the frames generated by Farrakhan and those generated by the press.

Rarely does a newspaper article provide the entire text of a speech, so by comparatively analyzing the speech and subsequent news coverage we can more easily detect any differences in frames. By looking at all the press coverage we can make generalizations at the national level. This will also allow us to see if the press presents a cohesive frame of the speech or if it instead allows for multiple interpretations.

Critical Essay: Press Framing of Minister Louis Farrakhan's Million Man March Speech

On October 16, 1995 Minister Louis Farrakhan[44] spoke to approximately 600,000 Americans—primarily black men—gathered in front of our nation's Capitol.[45] The subject of his speech was atonement and reconciliation. The speech was the culminating moment of the march and was delivered over the course of approximately two and one-half hours.[46] The Cable News Network reported that over 2.2 million households tuned in to watch parts of the speech. Commentators have put forth numerous reasons for the march, but the basic reason, according to the man who called it into being, Louis Farrakhan, was for atonement and reconciliation.

In this essay I examine Louis Farrakhan's speech and the subsequent press coverage using a rhetorical version of framing analysis. In doing this, I proceed in two main sections: a discussion of framing analysis and the analysis of Farakhan's speech and the press coverage it generated.

Theoretical Considerations: Questions of Agenda-Setting, Agenda-Extension, and Framing Analysis

In 1963 Bernard C. Cohen made a then arresting observation: The press "may not be very successful in telling its readers what to think, but it is stunningly successful in telling its readers what to think about."[47] This is the gist of agenda-setting theory. In its simplest form, this theory affirms that the media "do have a great deal of influence" upon political decision making and that the media are especially influential in telling the general population what to think about.[48] Maxwell E. McCombs and Donald L. Shaw stated that, "Through its winnowing of the day's happenings to find the major events, concerns, and issues, the press inadvertently plays an agenda-setting influence role."[49] Agenda-setting confirms that there is a direct correlation between the amount of press coverage and the public's perception of the importance of certain issues. As Judith F. Trent and Robert V. Friedenberg state: "[T]he media set public priorities just by paying attention to some issues while ignoring others. They determine what issues are important and in this way play an important role in structuring our social reality."[50]

Many researchers have since moved beyond Cohen's understanding. The media still tell us *what* to think about; however, they also tell us *how* to think about it. Doris Graber stated that this is the "process whereby news stories influence how people perceive and evaluate issues and policies."[51] The media often "frame" an issue intentionally or not, so that it will be interpreted in a specific manner. I have called this agenda-extension: "[I]t posits that the media not only focus attention on particular attributes of an issue, making some portions more salient than others, it does so in such a manner that a particular political agenda is advanced. Simply put . . . agenda-extension allows us to see how those attributes are stressed to influence audience reaction."[52]

Obviously, this moves beyond agenda-setting since it involves the influencing of public opinion. Framing analysis provides one way of seeing how this occurs. A frame is, according to William Gamson "a central organizing idea for making sense of relevant events and suggesting what is at issue."[53] Although facts remain neutral until framed, they "take on their meaning by being embedded in *a frame or story line* that organizes them and gives them coherence, selecting certain ones to emphasize while ignoring others."[54] An example of how this works is found in the results of a study by Gladys Lang and Kurt Lang about the Watergate hearings. In their analysis, Lang and Lang discovered that news coverage of the Watergate break-in was initially framed as part of the 1972 election campaign; this led the public to associate it with partisan politics. However, once the press switched frames, moving from the campaign to a new frame of continual Washington corruption, the nation became obsessed—and a presidency tumbled.[55] Frames can possess such power because they alter how we interpret the reality around us. As Entman stated, to frame is to take "some aspects of a perceived reality and make them more salient in a communicating text, in such a way as to promote a particular problem definition, causal interpretation, moral evaluation, and/or treatment recommendation for the item described."[56]

Thus frames define problems, diagnose causes, make moral judgments, and suggest remedies. They operate by making some information more salient than other information; therefore, they "highlight some features of reality while omitting others."[57] For example, Thomas E. Nelson, Rosalee A. Clawson, and Zoe M. Oxley conducted a study that used a local news story about a Ku Klux Klan march as the controlled frame. They presented audiences with either one of two videotaped stories. The first story stressed a free speech frame. Viewers were presented with a theme that stressed both Klan members and protesters wanting to share their respective messages. Quotes shared in the taped stories included a protester showing a sign reading: "No free speech for racists." Another quote came from a Klan supporter who said: "I came down here to hear what they have to say and I think I should be able to listen if I want to. . . ." Images shown included the chanting of protesters and a Klan leader speaking into a microphone. Finally, four interviews were presented, three of which were Klan supporters wishing to hear the Klan message. The second story stressed a disruption of public order frame. Viewers were presented with a theme that stressed that Klan marches tend to be disorderly and potentially violent. Quotes given included an observer saying: "Here you have a potential for some real sparks in the crowd." Another quote came from a reporter who said: "The tension between Klan protesters and supporters came within seconds of violence." Images shown included police officers in front of Klan members protecting them from the crowd. Finally, three interviews were presented, each of which mentioned the violence and disruption of public order. The results of the study are instructive: "Participants who viewed the free speech story expressed more tolerance for the Klan than those participants who watched the public order story."[58] This study demonstrates that the power of frames to sway opinion is great, even with such an emotion provoking subject.

Robert M. Entman provides another example of the power of framing. He comparatively analyzed the narratives within news stories about the 1983 KAL 007 and the 1988 Iran Air 655 shootdowns.[59] The first involved the Soviet Union shooting down an Korean jumbo jet that had flown over Soviet airspace; all 269 persons on board perished. The second incident involved the *U.S.S. Vincennes* shooting down an Iranian Airbus over the Persian Gulf; all 290 persons perished. Entman felt that the incidents could have been reported upon in a similar fashion by the American press. He also felt that any differences in information that comprised the frames used by the press would be easy to detect given the similarities of the incidents. He examined reports from a variety of media: *Time, Newsweek, CBS Evening News, the Washington Post,* and the *New York Times.*

In order to detect frames, Entman looked for key words, metaphors, concepts, symbols, and visual images. He argued that frames are fashioned by particular words and phrases that consistently appear within a narrative and "convey thematically consonant meanings across . . . time."[60] He found that the KAL shootdown was framed as a moral outrage, whereas the Iran Air shootdown was framed as a technical problem. Although the differences in the frames were striking, Entman stressed the implications of the frames used: "for those stories in which a single frame thoroughly pervades the text, stray contrary opinions . . . are likely to possess such low salience as to be of little practical use to most audience members."[61] So although it was perfectly acceptable for political elites to describe the KAL shootdown as a brutal attack, it was far less likely for them to describe it in terms of a tragedy; the frame had been set: The Soviets were evil and at fault. To think of the shootdown in terms of tragedy runs against the frame and would mitigate the culpability of the Soviets.

For the remainder of this critical essay, I will perform a framing analysis on Louis Farrakhan's speech delivered at the Million Man March. First, I examine Farrakhan's speech for frames. The basic question answered is "How did Louis Farrakhan frame the issue?" After answering this question, I look for frames residing within all mainstream printed press news coverage in a two-week period following the speech. The basic question answered is "How did the press, responding to Louis Farrakhan, frame the issue?"[62] Finally, I detail how the frames produced by Farrakhan and the press failed to produce a unified contextual whole.

How Did Louis Farrakhan Frame the Issue?   Farrakhan's speech presents his audience with a complex blending of religion and politics. Early in his speech he asserted that there is a "hostility now in the great divide between the people. Socially the fabric of America is being torn apart and it's black against black, black against white, white against white, white against black, yellow against brown, brown against yellow. We are being torn apart."[63] He had seen the divisions between blacks and whites in America. He sees the place to begin to heal the divisions between the races is within black communities across the country. His speech is framed in such a manner that the major problem is depicted as the racial division brought on by a lingering white supremacy. Both blacks and whites must work to eliminate this.

The divisions can be overcome in part by blacks and whites accepting responsibility for their share in black America's problems. At the personal level, blacks must follow God and stop hurting each other. Farrakhan implores black men to "accept the responsibility that God has put upon us, not only to be good husbands and fathers and builders of our community, but God is now calling upon the despised and the rejected to become the cornerstone and the builders of a new world."[64] White supremacy harms both blacks *and* whites. Blacks have become fractured and put down; whites have "whitened" history and religion, producing a "sick" world view. Both races must evolve out of white supremacy as part of the movement toward the more perfect American union. Never does Farrakhan imply that the races cannot live together, rather he suggests that they each have their work to do before coming together to form the more perfect union he envisions.

In constructing his notion of white responsibility, Farrakhan brings up the Willie Lynch speech.[65] Farrakhan shares this story to help explain the divisions black Americans must overcome. The story also grounds his later arguments about white America's responsibility for the black condition. Farrakhan recites the 1712 speech of Willie Lynch, allegedly a white slaveholder who is said to have delivered this address on how to control black slaves. In its essence, Lynch advises slave owners to sow discord and distrust among their slaves as a method of control. Light-skinned slaves were to be pitted against dark-skinned slaves. House servants were to be pitted against field hands. Young were to be pitted against old, and so on and so forth.

Importantly, Farrakhan does not use the speech to say that all whites are racists; neither does he say that all black problems result from white supremacy. He instead offers listeners the opportunity to incorporate his conceptualization into their process of atonement: "The real evil in America is not white flesh, or black flesh. The real evil in America is the idea that undergirds the set up of the western world. And that idea is called white supremacy."[66] Farrakhan makes it clear that every black man in America must accept a personal portion of responsibility for the condition of black America today: "Who is it that has to atone? [Audience]: Me. Who went wrong? [Audience]: Me. Who got to fix it? [Audience]: Me. Who should we look to? [Audience]: Me."

Throughout the speech runs a theme of movement toward a more perfect American union. This ultimate social union comes first from a union of the differences within the black communities across the nation. On this matter Farrakhan stated: "There's a new Black man in America today. A new Black woman in America today. [F]rom this day forward, we can never again see ourselves through the narrow eyes of the limitation of the boundaries of our own fraternal, civic, political, religious, street organization or professional organization." Before black healing can occur, however, the government (white) must atone for its past wrongs, namely, white supremacy. This is the unfinished business facing whites. Whites must look to the past of slavery and atone. Once this happens, however, blacks must accept this, forgive, and move on. While waiting for the government to atone, black Americans must also atone.

Farrakhan frames the march as part of a larger process of atonement. He outlines eight specific stages of growth: point out the fault, acknowledge the fault, confess the fault, repent, make amends, forgiveness, reconciliation, and perfect union. During this process black Americans must look to themselves as a source of strength; they must not look to whites or the government for help until this process is completed. However, the process of which Farrakhan speaks involves more than only atonement: Blacks must accept blame for their troubled communities. Both whites *and* blacks must accept blame for white supremacy. Blacks must also join organizations that promote black unity. As a people they must organize to help themselves. This involves spiritual renewal: Join a church, synagogue, temple, and take the pledge.

The pledge is the cornerstone of Farrakhan's envisioned change. The men in the audience are led by Farrakhan in a pledge to renounce violence of any kind except in self-defense; to go home and build up their communities; to stop the use of illegal drugs; and to support black owned and operated businesses. Ultimately, however, blacks must come together first, and then the government must ask for forgiveness. To overcome the remnants of white supremacy, Farrakhan suggests that blacks "don't have to bash white people," rather all they have to "do is go back home and turn our communities into productive places. All we gotta do is go back home and make our communities a decent and safe place to live. And if we start dotting the Black community with businesses, opening up factories, challenging ourselves to be better than we are, white folk, instead of driving by, using the "N" word, they'll say, look, look at them. Oh, my God. They're marvelous. They're wonderful. We can't, we can't say they're inferior any more."[67]

How Did the Press, Responding to Louis Farrakhan, Frame the Issue?
Overwhelmingly, the press coverage focused on the character of Farrakhan. The press framed coverage of Farrakhan's speech as a critique of his character. The press prejudged Farrakhan, and used this judgment to define his character during the march. Two other frames of note were discovered: Farrakhan's message and comparisons between Martin Luther King, Jr., and Farrakhan.

Farrakhan's Character.   Simply put, the press framed Minister Farrakhan as a racist, sexist, bigoted, Jew-hating "homophobe." However, these allegations were not based upon Farrakhan's speech at the Million Man March. Instead, reporters and columnists shared their prior opinions of Farrakhan. In this sense, the reporters were reporting not what Farrakhan said, but rather on their own preconceptions. For example, *The Boston Globe* stated that "the Black Muslim minister, who has often made remarks denounced as racist, sexist and anti-Semitic. . . ."[68] *The New York Daily News* stated that "Farrakhan's past slurs against Jews recently expanded to add Arabs, Vietnamese and Koreans to the list of 'bloodsuckers' of the black community. . . ."[69]

Whereas news stories tended strongly to suggest that Farrakhan is a racist, sexist, and so on, editorials and opinion essays came right out and stated this was the case. For instance, columnist Tom Teepen wrote: "All honor to the many black leaders who refused on principle to participate because Farrakhan is a career bigot—racist, anti-Semitic, homophobic and woman-baiting [sic]."[70] *The New York Daily News* editorially stated that Farrakhan's "hateful history" and "vile anti-white, anti-Semitic bent" are everything, and that it was this "context" through which readers should view his speech.[71] *The Chattanooga Free Press* editorially asserted that although Farrakhan "toned down his racism" for his speech, he was a "vicious hater and power seeker. . . ."[72] Columnist Dan Schnur personalized the accusations when he wrote that "Like [Mark] Fuhrman and David Duke, Farrakhan is a racist. He is a bigot. His own demons, his own hatred, will drive him back into the shadows of public discourse."[73] Lars-Erik Nelson wrote that "It's all too easy to denounce Farrakhan's bigotry. His remarks about Jews are vicious and uncivilized. And he surrounds himself with black-shirt, Gestapo Wanna-be bodyguards and thugs. . . ."[74]

These judgments were based solely on the press's prior opinion of Louis Farrakhan, and not on what he actually said during the March. Because Farrakhan was framed as so vile a man, the press had to ask if one could separate the message from the messenger because, in the eyes of the press, Farrakhan was obviously a "flawed messenger for racial unity."

The Message of the March versus Farrakhan's Message. The press actually reported on two messages. One was the message from the March and the other was what the press said Farrakhan's message to the marchers was. The message of the March was of unity and brotherhood. Farrakhan's message, which the marchers were to have separated from the messenger, was racist. The message the March sent is well expressed by The Tampa Tribune: "The message of self-reliance, family values and community uplift could have come from a Christian Coalition flier or a Pat Buchanan speech. But it didn't. It came from Monday's Million Man March for black men. . . ."[75] Editorially speaking the *Daily News* stated that the men came "for a day of atonement and reconciliation" but that they "and the millions who share their quest for a better life deserve better than Farrakhan's self-aggrandizement."[76] *The New York Times* stated that the black men who attended the rally heeded a "call for personal atonement and racial solidarity" but then went on to report that Farrakhan's speech compounded "the controversy that led up to the rally over whether the message of uplift could be heard effectively beyond Mr. Farrakhan's own record as an aggressive black separatist leader."[77] Ignoring Farrakhan's stress on the eight steps to atonement, *The Washington Post* stated that although "Farrakhan called the Million Man March a day of atonement for black men, his address often focused on the historic sins of white America."[78]

Farrakhan's message to the marchers was framed oppositionally to that of the march itself. The press focused on two main areas: white supremacy and Farrakhan's separatism. For example, the *Chicago Sun-Times* wrote that Farrakhan "urged blacks to unify while railing against what he said was an American society that is oppressive, dominated by whites and intolerant of anyone of color. '(The) idea of white supremacy is you should rule because you're white,' Farrakhan said. . . . 'That makes you sick, and you produce a sick society and a sick world.'"[79] The *Asheville Citizen-Times,* implying that Farrakhan was addressing white America only, stated: "'White supremacy,' he said, is the root of America's suffering. 'That makes you sick,' Farrakhan said, 'and you produce a sick society and a sick world.'"[80] Many examples contained even less detail. *The Boston Herald,* for example, simply stated, "Farrakhan denounced 'white supremacy' as 'the real evil in America.'"[81]

Concerning the issue of separatism the press depicted Farrakhan as wishing for the racial segregation of black and whites, and for being a "divisive" leader: Black and white America are to simply to "go and do their own thing," according to press interpretations of Farrakhan. For instance, *The New York Times* provided a common example of this when it wrote that Farrakhan sounded an "aggressive and divisive note, calling for African–American leadership in building 'a more perfect union' but also attacking Lincoln, the Founding Fathers, President Clinton and 'the power and arrogance of white America.' [The] appeal was by blacks to blacks and, if not explicitly separatist, spelled out no clear role for white people."[82] Along similar lines, columnist Jane Ely stated that "Minister Farrakhan and his appeal for racial separatism have contributed way too much to the chasm of bile and distrust that has widened understanding among races and, especially in recent days, threatened to heat to a boil that could ever scar the base that is America. Worse, through his stern refusal to even soften his dangerous rhetoric of hate and dissention, Farrakhan clearly has shown his intent to pursue his relentless way as far as he can in separating the races and fomenting their distrust of one another."[83]

The Tampa Tribune asserted that the crowd would be "unlikely to accept the separatist, anti-Semitic philosophy of . . . Farrakhan. . . ."[84] The *Los Angeles Times* stated that despite "the many issues that divide him from most Americans—including his racist comments, advocacy of black separatism and his nationalist hybrid of Islamic scripture—Farrakhan's message of self-reliance and independence from white America strikes a responsive chord that many find lacking in other black leaders."[85] Columnist Thomas Eagleton echoed the separatist framing of his fellow journalists when he wrote, "When [Farrakhan] talks about black men taking responsibility for their own well-being, accepting responsibility and caring for their families, he's as conservative as Clarence Thomas. When he talks about God sending the idea of the march to and through him, he is off on a flight of egotistical fancy. When he attacks the founding Fathers, Abraham Lincoln and the 'power and arrogance of white Americans,' he puts on his separatist, nationalist hat."[86]

Little was mentioned of Farrakhan's sophisticated explanation of atonement. Although atonement was often given as the reason for the March, Farrakhan had been separated from the March. Because of this, he had been separated from the message of atonement.

Farrakhan versus King.   Finally, the press forced comparisons between Minister Farrakhan and Reverend Martin Luther King, Jr. Framing here was concise: King's speech was short and inclusive; Farrakhan's was long and exclusive. King focused on unity; Farrakhan focused on a separatist black nationalism. King was good; Farrakhan was bad.

For example, editorially speaking, the *Daily News* stated: "At his best, Farrakhan led the assembled in a pledge to care for their families and their communities. . . . But even then, his goal seemed to be his own inauguration as the leader of black America. Contrast that with the greatest moment in civil rights history—the 1963 March on Washington. There the Rev. Martin Luther King Jr. spoke briefly but left the nation with an enduring dream. For it to be realized, there must be a healing of the races. Despite repeating his call for dialogue with Jews, Farrakhan's vile anti-white, anti-Semitic bent disqualifies him."[87] The *Chicago Sun-Times* boldly summed up the Million Man March this way: "Oh, that the message from Minister Louis Farrakhan . . . had risen to the occasion. Unfortunately, he failed. Would that he had taken a lead from the 'I Have a Dream' speech of Dr. Martin Luther King Jr. and raised his voice in an uplifting tone. Farrakhan spoke 150 minutes . . . of divisiveness, contrasted with the 19 minutes of 'bring us together' oratory of Dr. King. By all measurements, less was better."[88] The *Plain Dealer* expressed brief but similar sentiments: "Farrakhan's long speech . . . was almost anticlimactic. It was not the emotional equivalent of Dr. Martin Luther King Jr.'s 'I Have a Dream' speech 32 years ago."[89]

The *St. Louis Post-Dispatch* summed the framing of the press well when it wrote, "America has left behind the hallowed memory of Martin Luther King when blacks and whites assembled to share King's vision of all races walking hand in hand. King's 'I Have a Dream' speech would have sounded out of place at the Million Man March. Farrakhan is not the new Dr. King."[90]

Did the Frames Converge to Present a Unified Contextual Whole? From the above examples I think it safe to say that at no time did the frames of the press accurately match those presented by Farrakhan. Moreover, the press took an extraordinary negative view of Farrakhan. Of forty opinion essays, only two were positive concerning *the event;* eight took a more or less objective view of the event; however, a full thirty were negative, focusing exclusively upon *Farrakhan's character.* Editorials were similarly written. Five of the seven were distinctly negative *toward Farrakhan,* with two taking a more objective view of *the event.* So while Farrakhan garnered the lion's share of attention from the March, his character was assassinated.

Recall frames act to define problems, diagnose causes, make moral judgments, and suggest remedies. Both Farrakhan and the press presented frames that contained these elements. Farrakhan spoke at length to the divisions between and within black communities across the nation. He relayed the Willie Lynch story to highlight the importance of overcoming these divisions for black healing and unity. He would have blacks and whites in America walk separate paths on the road to forgiveness and unity. Whereas Farrakhan saw lingering white supremacy and problems in black communities as preventing better socioeconomic progress for blacks, the press saw only white racism as the continuing cause of black problems. According to Farrakhan, blacks must look first to themselves, atone, and then forgive. Whites must do the same, with blacks accepting white atonement. The press ignored this story, and instead cast Farrakhan as pushing for black separatism, even though he did not advocate this in his speech.

Farrakhan saw that the healing of black hurts must come from two main sources. First, blacks must atone for their own sins, and then walk away from the actions that have hurt black communities across the nation. Second, they must also accept the government and white atonement for white supremacy. Only when these actions are taken can healing occur. The press mentioned atonement, but separated it from its spiritual dimensions and from the notion of a white supremacy that hurts both blacks and whites. When white supremacy is mentioned, it is used to impugn Farrakhan's character, casting him as a demagogue trying to call white America names.

The press brought with it judgments made prior to Farrakhan's speech. The framing of Farrakhan's character—"Farrakhan the bigot"—was so strong that it prevented the press from covering his speech any other way. Thus the press relayed its prejudgments as news about the March. Whereas Farrakhan's March message was a complex blend of spiritual and secular action, the press only relayed that message through a secular interpretation. This interpretation was tainted by the press's own prejudgment of Farrakhan, the press's own vision for racial unity, exemplified through a mythic portrayal of Martin Luther King, Jr.

Implications of Press Framing.   Following World War II the Commission on Freedom of the Press issued a report titled *A Free and Responsible Press.* The basic premise of the report was that "the power and near monopoly position of the media impose on them an obligation to be socially responsible."[91] This idea of social responsibility is summed by Theodore Peterson: "Freedom carries concomitant obligations; and the press, which enjoys a privileged position under our government, is obliged to be responsible to society for carrying out certain essential functions of mass communication in contemporary society."[92] Among the standards listed by the commission were five that bear particular note:

1. The press must provide "a truthful, comprehensive, and intelligent account of the day's events in a context which gives them meaning."[93]
2. The press must serve as a "forum for the exchange of comment and criticism."[94]
3. The press must project "a representative picture of the constituent groups in society."[95]
4. The press must assume responsibility for "the presentation and clarification of the goals and values of the society" in which it operates.[96]
5. The press must provide "full access to the day's intelligence."[97]

The overwhelming majority of mainstream papers in America assert that they subscribe to the sentiments expressed by the Commission on Freedom of the Press; this is seen in their own statements of principle and codes of ethical conduct. For example, *The Washington Post* asserts it still adheres to the 1935 principles penned by then publisher Eugene Meyer. Four of Meyer's principles have special relevance to this study: "The first mission of a newspaper is to tell the truth as nearly as the truth can be ascertained. The newspaper shall tell ALL the truth so far as it can learn it, concerning the important affairs of America and the World. The newspaper's duty is to its readers and to the public at large, and not to the private interests of its owners. The newspaper shall not be the ally of any special interest, but shall be fair and free and wholesome in its outlook on public affairs and public men."[98]

The American Society of Newspaper Editors' statement of principles has been in existence since 1922. Articles 1 and 4 are particularly relevant to this study:

ARTICLE I: The primary purpose of gathering and distributing news and opinion is to serve the general welfare by informing the people and enabling them to make judgments on the issues of the time.

ARTICLE IV: Every effort must be made to assure that the news content is accurate, free from bias and in context, and that all sides are presented fairly. Editorials, analytical articles and commentary should be held to the same standards of accuracy with respect to facts as news reports. Significant errors of fact, as well as errors of omission, should be corrected promptly and prominently.[99]

The Society of Professional Journalists hold similar views: "Members of the Society of Professional Journalists believe that public enlightenment is the forerunner of justice and the foundation of democracy. The duty of the journalist is to further those ends by seeking truth and providing a fair and comprehensive account of events and issues. [Moreover, journalists must examine] their own cultural values and avoid imposing those values on others."[100] The Associated Press Managing Editors' Code of Ethics states in part that, "The good newspaper is fair, accurate, honest, responsible, independent and decent. The newspaper should strive for impartial treatment of issues and dispassionate handling of controversial subjects."[101]

These codes of conduct express clear norms. As I have stated in a different venue, "The press *voluntarily* commits to providing the American public with the *full details* of important issues within an *unbiased context.* In short, the press says it acts to serve *all Americans* regardless of political position."[102] The papers in this study represent the mainstream media; they subscribe to the codes of conduct cited above; they offer themselves as unbiased and objective sources of news. However, this study has shown that the mainstream press injected its favored political ideology into the very information it gave to the public as objective news. As Gary C. Woodward stated, "Political journalism is—against its own high standards—a flawed enterprise," because it cannot live up to its stated goal of objectivity.[103]

In this sense then, the mainstream press failed miserably in carrying out its own stated goals of objectivity. In the present case, it violated numerous tenets of its own norms of reportorial practice. Some of the more egregious examples of these violations included failure to provide "a truthful, comprehensive, and intelligent account of the day's events in a context which gives them meaning." More specifically, the press failed to accurately portray the March and the content of Farrakhan's speech. The press also failed to "assure that the news content is accurate, free from bias and in context, and that all sides are presented fairly." Farrakhan's words were not relayed accurately, nor in a context free from bias. Instead, the press imposed its own system of preheld values upon Farrakhan and reported that as news. In short, the press "imposed" its "own cultural values . . . on others." Finally, the press utterly failed to "strive for impartial treatment of issues and dispassionate handling of controversial subjects."

PERSONAL COMMENTS ON THE ESSAY

This above critical essay could have taken many different turns. That is the nature of criticism. Specifically, I could have included more discussion of theory. I made a decision to limit the number of studies cited in a general manner and instead focused on detailing several studies I thought of particular interest. I could also have spent more time discussing agenda-setting theory. I decided against that, however. The purpose of that material was to provide an introduction to agenda-extension studies, and not to focus on agenda-setting. Ultimately, my goal was to streamline the theoretical material and focus on the actual analysis. Thus the theory section was acting to function as an orientation for my readers; it was not a full literature review. Rather, it acted to highlight and provide examples of the major ideas necessary to *support the analysis of this essay.*

In terms of the actual analysis, other decisions could have been made. For example, at one point I thought it might be of interest to omit the section analyzing Minister Farrakhan's speech and instead comparatively analyze the mainstream press and the black American press coverage of the speech. I thought of that after reading this statement by the American Society of Newspaper Editors: "The typical newspaper journalist is still a liberal, college-educated, white-male baby boomer."[104] Such a comparison might have brought up interesting contrasts between black and mainstream journalists. Ultimately, though, I felt that contrasting the original utterances of Farrakhan with the mainstream press coverage would present results in which different frames would be most easily detected. Additionally, this study could also have focused upon broadcast coverage. How did the major news networks—NBC, ABC, and CBS—frame the speech? How did the two major cable news channels—FOX and CNN—frame the speech? One could also have included weekly news magazines such as *Time, Newsweek,* and *U.S. News and World Reports.* Regardless, each of these changes would have wrought a different essay.

One decision researchers must frequently make concerns what results to share from the actual analysis. Often decisions must be made about relevance; also, one can become so bogged down in details that the overall picture is lost. For example, during this analysis I identified several minor frames I did not include in the actual essay. I reported in the essay, "Two other frames of note were discovered: Farrakhan's message and comparisons between Martin Luther King, Jr., and Minister Farrakhan." What I did not report was that I also had identified a subframe in which an exchange between Minister Farrakhan and President Clinton was reported. One reason for not including this information was simply space; including that information would take several pages. Also, it was redundant in terms of the final evaluation I would make. I felt I already had enough information in the essay to justify my conclusions. Finally, it was not as interesting to me as the material on Farrakhan and King.

In terms of the evaluation section of the essay, I thought that using press generated norms of conduct to evaluate their reportorial practice (as revealed through the framing analysis) would be interesting and fair. I did not wish to complicate the essay by developing a theoretical explanation of press ethics, rather I wished to advance a standard of practice from which to then judge press conduct. By including the actual press norms, I was also providing an explicit example of the norms of judgment I was using in order to evaluate the press. Criticism should offer evaluations, but they should flow from the analysis and also be readily available for your readers to see.

POTENTIALS AND PITFALLS

Framing analysis is especially well suited for comparative analyses. Those using this approach to criticism will find that comparing and contrasting frames will produce clear results. It is also an approach to criticism that is particularly well suited for determining the world views of those producing the discourse being studied.

Careless critics often find what they set out to find. Framing analysis might well exacerbate this tendency if a critic is not careful in its application. It is very easy to "discover" a frame and then impose it upon the remainder of the rhetorical artifact. Critics must be especially careful to examine the entire rhetorical artifact before determining what frames are operating. That is to say, do not assume a particular frame is operating and then go look for it. The best framing analyses allow the rhetorical artifacts to speak for themselves.

FRAMING ANALYSIS TOP PICKS

Entman, Robert M., "Framing U.S. Coverage of International News: Contrasts in Narratives of the KAL and Iran Air Incidents," *Journal of Communication* 41.4 (1991): 6–27. An outstanding study that shows well the possibilites of comparative framing analysis. Although from a social scientific perspective, this study demonstrates well the enormous power of frames; additionally, it suggests possiblities for more rhetorically oriented studies.

Entman, Robert M., "Framing: Toward Clarification of a Fractured Paradigm," *Journal of Communication* 43 (1993): 55. Another well written introduction to the concept of framing. Entman is particularly effective at bringing together disparate nuances of framing to facilitate a more cohesive understanding of the concept.

Gamson, William A., "News as Framing: Comments on Graber," *American Behavioral Scientist* 33 (1989): 157. This essay provides a brief and extremely well written definition of the concept of framing. It is a must read for any student serious about using framing analysis.

Kuypers, Jim A., *Presidential Crisis Rhetoric and the Press in the Post-Cold War World* (Westport, CT:

Praeger, 1997). This book provides a detailed conception of framing analysis for rhetorical studies. It also shows how the nature of frames change over time by looking at three different events spaning three different time periods: two weeks, six months, and one year.

Kuypers, Jim A., *Press Bias and Politics: How the Media Frame Controversial Issues* (Westport, CT: Praeger, 2002). The first chapter of this book provides, from a rhetorical perspective, a detailed introduction to the concept of framing. Since the heart of this book consists of six chapters that apply framing analysis, readers will be exposed to numerous examples of how one uses framing analysis as rhetorical criticism.

Nelson, Thomas E., Rosalee A. Clawson, and Zoe M. Oxley, "Media Framing of Civil Liberties Conflict and Its Effects on Tolerance," *American Political Science Review* 91.3 (1997): 567. This well conducted study provides detailed examples of the contruction of frames used for social scientific research. In so doing, this study also helps guide rhetorical scholars in discerning differences among frames residing in rhetorical artifacts.

NOTES

1. Paul M. Sniderman, Richard A. Brody, and Philip E. Tetlock, *Reasoning and Choice: Explorations in Political Psychology* (Cambridge, England: Cambridge University Press, 1991), 52.

2. Thomas E. Nelson, Rosalee A. Clawson, and Zoe M. Oxley, "Media Framing of Civil Liberties Conflict and Its Effects on Tolerance," *American Political Science Review* 91.3 (1997): 567.

3. Robert M. Entman, "Framing Toward Clarification of a Fractured Paradigm," *Journal of Communication* 43 (1993): 53.

4. William A. Gamson, "News as Framing: Comments on Graber," *American Behavioral Scientist* 33 (1989): 157.

5. Gamson, 157.

6. Judith S. Trent and Robert V. Friedenberg, *Political Campaign Communication: Principles and Practices,* 2nd ed. (New York: Praeger, 1991), 107.

7. Maxwell E. McCombs and Donald L. Shaw, "The Agenda-Setting Functions of the Mass Media," *Public Opinion Quarterly* 36 (1972): 177.

8. McCombs and Shaw, 185.

9. Sheldon Gilberg, Chaim Eyal, Maxwell E. McCombs, and D. Nichols, "The State of the Union Address and the Press Agenda," *Journalism Quarterly* 57 (1980): 584–588.

10. Maxwell E. McCombs and Donald L. Shaw, "Agenda-Setting and the Political Process," *The Emergence of American Political Issues: The Agenda-Setting Function of the Press,* Donald L. Shaw and Maxwell E. McCombs (eds.) (St. Paul, MN: West Publishing, 1977), 151.

11. McCombs and Shaw, "Agenda-Setting and the Political Process," 152.

12. For instance, see Roy L. Behr and Shanto Iyenger, "Television News, Real-World Cues, and Changes in the Public Agenda," *Public Opinion Quarterly* 49 (1985): 38–57.

13. Maxwell E. McCombs and Sheldon Gilberg, "News Influence on Our Pictures of the World," *Perspectives on Media Effects,* Jennings Bryant and Dolf Zillman (eds.) (Hillsdale, NJ: Lawrence Erlbaum, 1986), 11.

14. Trent and Friedenberg, 108.

15. Trent and Friedenberg, 109.

16. I first used this term in 1997. See Jim A. Kuypers, *Presidential Crisis Rhetoric and the Press in the Post-Cold War World,* (Westport, CT: Praeger, 1997).

17. For five recent studies exploring the second level effect of agenda-setting see Maxwell McCombs, Donald L. Shaw, and David Weaver, *Communication and Democracy: Exploring the Intellectual Frontiers in Agenda-Setting Theory* (Mahwah, New Jersey: Lawrence Erlbaum, 1997); Esteban Lopez-Escobar, Juan Pablo Llamas, Maxwell McCombs, and Federico Rey Lennon, "Two Levels of Agenda-Setting among Advertising and News in the 1995 Spanish Elections," *Political Communication* 15

(1998): 225–238; Spiro Kiousis, Philemon Bantimaroudis, and Hyun Ban, "Candidate Image Attributes: Experiments on the Substantive Dimension of Second-Level Agenda-Setting," *Communication Research* 26.4 (1999): 414–428; Maxwell McCombs, Esteban Lopez-Escobar, and Juan Pablo Llamas, "Setting the Agenda of Attributes in the 1996 Spanish General Election," *Journal of Communication* 50.2 (2000): 77–92; Sei-Hill Kim, Dietram Scheufele, and James Shanahan, "Think About It This Way: Attribute Agenda-Setting Function of the Press and the Public's Evaluation of a Local Issue," *Journalism & Mass Communication Quarterly* 79 (2002).

18. Anne Johnston, "Trends in Political Communication: *A Selective Review of Research in the 1980s," New Directions in Political Communication: A Resource Book,* David L. Swanson and Dan Nimmo (eds.) (Newbury Park, CA: Sage, 1990), 329–362.

19. Johnston, 337.

20. Gladys Engel Lang and Kurt Lang, "The Media and Watergate," *Media Power in Politics,* Doris A. Graber (eds.) (Washington, D.C.: Congressional Quarterly Press, 1984), 202–209.

21. Doris A. Graber, *Mass Media and American Politics,* 3rd ed. (Washington, DC: Congressional Quarterly Press, 1989), 288.

22. Shanto Iyengar and Adam Simon, "News Coverage of the Gulf Crisis and Public Opinion: A Study of Agenda-Setting, Priming, and Framing," *Communication Research* 20.3 (1993): 365. Italicized in original.

23. Agenda-setting generally allows for the examination of the type of issues reported on and their frequency of occurrence in articles. Agenda-extension allows for the discovery of any differences in the framing of the same issue. Because of this, using an agenda-extension perspective allows the researcher to comparatively analyze news content for bias. For example, in the 2000 elections, were Bush's themes positively or negatively framed when compared to the themes expressed by Gore? For a good example of using agenda-setting to determine coverage of candidates issues see, Russell J. Dalton, Paul Allen Beck, Robert Huckfeldt, and William Koetzle, "A Test of Media-Centered Agenda-Setting: Newspaper Content and Public Interests in a Presidential Election," *Political Communication* 15 (1998): 463–481. Of note is that these researchers

found that no bias was seen in the papers covered simply because the papers covered the issues brought up by the candidates. This type of logic is a limitation of agenda-setting research. Using an agenda-extension perspective, one moves beyond frequency of reporting to examine the manner in which the papers reported the issues—thus one may look for bias.

24. Louis A. Day, *Ethics in Media Communication* (Belmont, CA: Wadsworth, 1991), 35.

25. Day, 35.

26. Mitchell Stephens, *A History of News: From the Drum to the Satellite* (New York: Viking Penguin, 1988), 264.

27. Day, 32.

28. Robert M. Entman, "Framing U.S. Coverage of International News: Contrasts in Narratives of the KAL and Iran Air Incidents," *Journal of Communication* 41.4 (1991): 6–27.

29. Entman, "Framing U.S. Coverage," 7.

30. Entman, "Framing U.S. Coverage," 7.

31. Entman, "Framing U.S. Coverage," 7.

32. Entman, "Framing U.S. Coverage," 21.

33. Kuypers, *Presidential Crisis Rhetoric and the Press in the Post-Cold War World.*

34. For example, *The New York Times* stated editorially: "If all sides conclude that the United States and its allies are prepared to apply military force to support a serious diplomatic initiative, the prospects for peace may improve. No one pretends that the latest American plan is a triumph of principle. But it is a workable compromise" ("Force and Diplomacy in Bosnia," August 31, 1995: A24). "Having come this far in brokering a Balkan peace, the United States is obliged to take on a significant share of the peacekeeping operation" (Peace and Peacekeeping in Bosnia," October 6, 1995: A30). "America's leading diplomatic role in bringing about a Bosnian peace agreement, as well as its claims to NATO leadership, create a strong obligation to contribute significant forces to peacekeeping" ("Congress Must Vote on Bosnia," October 20, 1995: A34). The *Washington Post* echoed this support: "FINALLY, AFTER 3 [and] 1/2 years of war, NATO planes and U.N. ground troops have replied with heavy and suitable force to a deadly attack seen as coming from the Bosnian Serbs. [I]t sets a standard for allied performance anew" ("Answering the Bosnian Serbs," August 31, 1995: A22). "It would be grotesque, having so far left ground duty to its

allies for fear of American casualties, if the United States still did not join the allies after a peace agreement had cut the risk way back" ("A Bosnia Peace Force," September 24, 1995: C6).

35. Jim A. Kuypers, *Press Bias and Politics: How the Media Frame Controversial Issues.* (Westport, CT: Praeger, 2002).

36. Zhongdang Pan and Gerald M. Kosicki, "Framing Analysis: An Approach to News Discourse," *Political Communication* 10.1 (1993): 55–75.

37. Pan and Kosicki, 62.

38. Ben Kauffman, "As You Were Saying . . . Evil Euphemisms Must Not Pass Our Lips Unexamined," *Boston Herald* (May 2, 1999): A28.

39. In all fairness to the press, a majority of the papers examined did use these terms. However, enough pejorative examples of naming exist to color the otherwise neutral descriptions.

40. "Dingbat," Judy Mann, "Clinton Surrounded in Dirt, But Where's the GOP?" *Washington Post* (April 26, 1998): C23; "Ayatollah" and "Zealot," Editorial, "GOP Trap: Squeezed by Zealots," *Charleston (WV) Gazette* (May 6, 1998): A4; "Crazy," Cokie Roberts and Steve Roberts, "Ideological Purity: Republicans Could be Headed for Trouble with Moderates and Economic Conservatives," *Dallas Morning News* (May 24, 1998): J5; "Intolerant," Howard Park, "The Chief Character Defect of the Religious Right Is Intolerance," *Paradise (CA) Post* (May 21, 1998). "Godzilla of the Right," Frank Rich, "Godzilla of the Right," *New York Times* (May 20, 1998): A23, found in Dobson, Letter to Focus on the Family constituents, July 1998.

41. Kuypers, *Press Bias,* 147–167.

42. Kuypers, *Press Bias,* 53–88.

43. Found in Media Research Center, "Avoiding Gary Condit's Democratic ID," (July 12, 2001). http://www.mrc.org/news/reality/2001/Fax20010712.html. This report focuses exclusively on broadcast, not print reporting.

44. Minister Louis Farrakhan is the national representative of the Honorable Elijah Muhammad and the Nation of Islam. For additional information on Minister Farrakhan and the Nation of Islam, see the Nation of Islam web site (http://www.noi.org) and the *Final Call* (http://www.finalcall.com/).

45. This number is contested. March organizers suggest over 1 million and U.S. Park Service

representatives suggest less than 600,000 attended.

46. Louis Farrakhan, "Million Man March Speech." Transcript from Minister Louis Farrakhan's remarks at the Million Man March. http://www-cgi.cnn.com/US/9510/megamarch/10-16/transcript/index.html. Since there were no page numbers in this document, I have included none in citations. All Farrakhan quotes come from this speech.

47. Bernard C. Cohen, *The Press and Foreign Policy* (Princeton: Princeton University Press, 1963), 13. For a background reader on the function of agenda-setting see, James W. Dearing and Everett M. Rogers, *Agenda-Setting* (Thousand Oaks, CA: Sage, 1996).

48. Judith S. Trent and Robert V. Friedenberg, *Political Campaign Communication: Principles and Practices,* 2nd ed. (New York: Praeger, 1991), 107.

49. Maxwell E. McCombs and Donald L. Shaw, "Agenda-Setting and the Political Process," *The Emergence of American Political Issues: The Agenda-Setting Function of the Press,* Donald L. Shaw and Maxwell E. McCombs (eds.) (St. Paul, MN: West Publishing, 1977), 151.

50. Trent and Friedenberg, 108.

51. Graber, *Mass Media,* 287.

52. Kuypers, *Press Bias,* 10.

53. William A. Gamson, "News as Framing: Comments on Graber," *American Behavioral Scientist* 33 (1989): 157.

54. Gamson, 157.

55. Gladys Engel Lang and Kurt Lang, "The Media and Watergate," *Media Power in Politics,* Doris A. Graber (ed.) (Washington, DC: Congressional Quarterly Press, 1984), 202–209.

56. Entman, "Framing: Toward Clarification," 52. Italicized in original.

57. Entman, "Framing: Toward Clarification," 53.

58. Thomas E. Nelson, Rosalee A. Clawson, and Zoe M. Oxley, "Media Framing of Civil Liberties Conflict and Its Effects on Tolerance," *American Political Science Review* 91.3 (1997): 567.

59. Entman, "Framing U.S. Coverage," 6–27.

60. Entman, "Framing U.S. Coverage," 7.

61. Entman, "Framing U.S. Coverage," 21.

62. All papers contained in the Lexus/Nexus database were included for this portion of the study. I examined editorials, opinion essays, and news articles. In all, there were 107 articles: 60 were news articles, 40 were opinion pieces, and 7 were editorials.

63. Farrakhan.

64. Farrakhan.

65. The authenticity of the Willie Lynch speech is dubious at best. For information on the speech see the website on this topic provided by the University of Missouri–St. Louis, Thomas Jefferson Library Reference Department: http://www.umsl.edu/services/library/blackstudies/lynch.htm. The library states that the provenance "of the following text is unclear. This speech was purportedly given by a slave owner, William Lynch, on the bank of the James River in 1712. Analysis now suggests that the document was written in the mid to late twentieth century." See http://www.umsl.edu/services/library/blackstudies/narrate.htm for an analysis of the speech.

66. Farrakhan.

67. Farrakhan.

68. Zachary R. Dowdy, "Black Men Hear Appeal to Action," *The Boston Globe* (October 17, 1995): A1.

69. William Goldschlag, Dave Eisenstadt, and Raphael Sugarman, "Farrakhan Foes Quick to React Minister Should Atone, They Say," *Daily News* (October 17, 1995): 23.

70. Tom Teepen, "Separating Message From Messenger at the Million Man March," *Star Tribune* (October 21, 1995): A18.

71. Editorial, "Minister Me Holds Court," *Daily News* (October 17, 1995): 32.

72. "The Washington March," *Chattanooga Free Press* (October 17, 1995).

73. Dan Schnur, "The March Wasn't Really Necessary," *The San Fransico Chronicle* (October 18, 1995): A23.

74. Lars-Eric Nelson, "Farrakhan Preached A Positive Message," *Daily News* (October 18, 1995): 31.

75. William March, "March Meaning: Enormous Turnout Raises Questions about Political Direction of Blacks," *The Tampa Tribune* (October 19, 1995): Nation/World 1.

76. Editorial, "Minister Me Holds Court," *Daily News* (October 17, 1995): 32.

77. Francis X. Clines, "The March On Washington: Overview," *The New York Times* (October 17, 1995): A1.

78. David Maraniss, "A Clear Day, A Cloud of Contradictions; At Event Designated for Reconciliation, Its Organizer Stresses White America's Sins," *The Washington Post* (October 17, 1995): A19.

79. Charles Pereira, Doug Mills, Mark Wilson, and Brian Jackson, "'We Are One' 400,000 Black Men Join Show of Atonement, Unity," *Chicago Sun-Times* (October 17, 1995): A1.

80. "Million Man March Largest Black American Gathering Since 1963," *Asheville (NC) Citizen-Times* (October 17, 1995): A1.

81. Andrew Miga, "On the March!: Black Unity Rally Draws Thousands to Nation's Capital," *The Boston Herald* (October 17, 1995): A1.

82. R. W. Apple Jr., "The March on Washington: News Analysis: Ardor and Ambiguity," *The New York Times* (October 17, 1995): A1.

83. Jane Ely, "Clinton Had a Powerful Message, Too," *The Houston Chronicle* (October 18, 1995): 22. Both sentences are the original text.

84. William March, "March Meaning; Enormous Turnout Raises Questions about Political Direction of Blacks," *The Tampa Tribune* (October 19, 1995): Nation/World 1.

85. Sam Fulwood, III, "Blacks Ponder Next Steps after Historic Rally," *Los Angeles Times* (October 18, 1995): A1.

86. Thomas Eagleton, "The March Others Could Not Produce," *St. Louis Post-Dispatch* (October 22, 1995): B3.

87. Editorial, "Minister Me Holds Court," *Daily News* (October 17, 1995): 32.

88. "Kup's Column," *Chicago Sun-Times* (October 18, 1995): 64.

89. Jonathan Tilove, "March Seems a Holiday after Summer of Tension," *The Plain Dealer* (October 17, 1995): A1.

90. Thomas Eagleton, "The March Others Could Not Produce," *St. Louis Post-Dispatch* (October 22, 1995): B3.

91. See Fred S. Siebert, Theodore Peterson, and Wilbur Schramm, *Four Theories of the Press* (Urbana: University of Illinois Press, 1956), 5.

92. Siebert, Peterson, and Schramm, 74.

93. Siebert, Peterson, and Schramm, 87.

94. Siebert, Peterson, and Schramm, 89.

95. Siebert, Peterson, and Schramm, 91.

96. Siebert, Peterson, and Schramm, 91.

97. Siebert, Peterson, and Schramm, 91.

98. "Eugene Meyer's Principles for The Washington Post," *The Washington Post.* http://www.washpost.com/gen_info/principles/.

99. American Society of Newspaper Editors' Statement of Principles. "ASNE's Statement of Principles was originally adopted in 1922 as the 'Canons of Journalism.' The document was revised and renamed 'Statement of Principles' in 1975." The full document can be obtained at http://www.asne.org/kiosk/archive/principl.htm.

100. Code of Ethics, Society for Professional Journalists. http://spj.org/ethics_code.asp.

101. For the complete listing of the Associated Press's code of ethics, see http://www.asne.org/ideas/codes/apme.htm.

102. Kuypers, *Press Bias*, 202.

103. Gary C. Woodward, "Narrative Form and the Deceptions of Modern Journalism," in *Political Communication Ethics: An Oxymoron?* Robert E. Denton, Jr. (ed.) (Westport, CT: Praeger, 2000), 127.

104. "The Newspaper Journalists of the '90s," A Survey Report of the American Society of Newspaper Editors, April 1997, p. 5. (Convention copy) Restin, VA.

    Final report available at:
    <http://www.asne.org/kiosk/reports/97reports/journalists90s/coverpage.html>

CHAPTER ELEVEN

FANTASY-THEME ANALYSIS

THOMAS J. ST. ANTOINE

MATTHEW T. ALTHOUSE

MOYA A. BALL

In the final game of a tied series, the Marauders and the Blue Sox struggle in an epic battle for the championship. With the score tied in the bottom of the ninth, there are two outs and a base runner is on second. A designated hitter for the Marauders, Spikes O'Reily, steps to the plate, taps the soil from his cleats with his bat, and loosens his swing. The pitcher, ace reliever Cannonball Braden, makes eye contact with the catcher. The two Blue Sox players exchange nods, and Braden launches the ball from the mound. Before the streaking fastball can pass over the plate and into the catcher's glove, O'Reily manages to swing his bat into the ball's path. The ball is struck, races past the first baseman's glove, and rolls into right field. As the fielder stops the ball, the base runner at second, Pokey Howard, rounds third and sprints toward home. Howard begins the slide. Simultaneously, the catcher stretches for the ball, which is rocketing from right field. From within the cloud of blinding dust produced by Howard's slide, the umpire makes the close call: "Safe!" Of course, fans of the winning Marauders from the City of Champions are jubilant. They praise the speed of the base runner, the timely batting of Spikes O'Reily, and—of course—the perceptiveness of the umpire. The fans of the losing team from Baseballville, however, are livid and decry the umpire's call. Given the importance of the championship game, they cannot believe that an official's incompetence cost the Blue Sox their rightful claim to the title.

FANTASY-THEME ANALYSIS: AN INTRODUCTION

If you can imagine how fans might tell interpretive stories about this hypothetical scenario, you can appreciate the scope and the goals of Ernest Bormann's fantasy-theme analysis. This method is used to look at how a group dramatizes an event and at how that dramatization creates a special kind of myth that influences a group's thinking and behaviors. In this context, the word "fantasy" does not refer to a fiction created by a group. Instead, a fantasy is a technical term that is the key to understanding the social reality of a group. Bormann explains that the word "fantasy" can be traced back to its Greek root "*phantastikos,* which means to be able to present or show to the mind, to make visible."[1] For instance, fans of the losing Blue Sox from Baseballville may have at the core of their stories the fact that their team failed to win. However, explanations of the loss will be shaded by the way they manipulate stories about the event. Consequently, in the process of talking about the loss, their discussions may lead to a number of colorful speculations. "The ump was a bum," "The ump was partial to the other team," or "The ump was paid off." Possibly, these reflections may not be accurate, but they "make visible" a shared social reality for the fans. What is more, these imaginings are narrative manifestations that provide a rhetorical critic with a special perspective on the beliefs and values of a given group of people.

The purpose of this chapter is to provide a guide for using and appreciating fantasy-theme analysis, which illuminates the worldview shared by a rhetorical community. In Ball's words, fantasy-theme analysis can be used to address questions like, "How does communication function to divide individual from individual, group from group, and community from community? How does communication function to create a sense of community, integrating individuals and groups into large, cooperative units? How does communication function to interpret reality for symbol using beings?"[2] During the past several decades, scholars have used Bormann's fantasy-theme analysis to examine a myriad of topics, including group decision making, corporate communication, and political cartoons, to name a few. Regardless of the subject matter, these studies share some basic assumptions that are outlined in this chapter. In particular, the first part of this chapter surveys fundamental concepts associated with fantasy-theme analysis and with symbolic-convergence theory, which provides the theoretical chassis on which Bormann's method rests. The second part of the chapter provides a case study. In this section, we examine fantasy themes that have guided perceptions of higher education in the United States during the twentieth century.

Fundamental Concepts

To conduct a fantasy-theme analysis, a critic must understand at least four basic terms: *fantasy theme, chaining, fantasy type,* and *rhetorical vision.* Arranged here from the most basic unit to the most intricate, these concepts help us understand how imaginings shared in interpersonal and small-group contexts may evolve into ways of thinking at a cultural level.

Fantasy Theme.   The term *fantasy theme* refers to a narrative construal that reflects a group's experience and that helps a group understand that experience. Sonja K. Foss states that a fantasy theme is "a word, phrase, or statement that interprets events in the past, envisions events in the future, or depicts current events that are removed in time and/or space from the actual activities from the group."[3] Although a fantasy theme can incorporate verifiable facts, it is a dramatization, which means it is creative and imaginative. As Bormann explains, "When people dramatize an event, they must select certain characters to be the focus of the story and present them in a favorable light while selecting others to be portrayed in a more negative fashion."[4] Therefore, it follows that individual groups may form unique perspectives on a single event in the past and create distinctive prognostications about their respective futures.

In light of such thinking, it is not surprising that fans from the City of Champions and from Baseballville create dissimilar fantasy themes about the championship game. Reflecting back on the event, fans of the Marauders praise the heavy hitter who produced the final run batted in: "Spikes O'Reily is the best player on the face of the planet! Without question, he's destined for the Hall of Fame!" To make these assessments, the fans may not be objective by comparing the batter's statistics with those of other active players or with those of anyone enshrined in the Hall. However, their approximations do provide a socially-constructed and accepted perspective for their community. Simultaneously, fans of the losing Baseballville Blue Sox call Spikes O'Reily "the luckiest man alive," an estimation that may not be entirely true. The batter may be, in fact, highly skilled. Yet, the rhetorical assertion that he is "lucky" fosters a shared sense of veracity for the disappointed community of Baseballville.

Chaining.   When fantasy themes are shared and are elaborated, group fantasy chains may occur. Chaining happens when dramatizations that resonate with a community "catch on." Put differently, fashionable fantasy themes created by small groups may propagate through media including, but not limited to, public speeches, interpersonal interaction, and television. In face-to-face exchanges, evidence of chaining becomes manifest when people in a group become excited about discussing the theme, and they elaborate it. Further, as Bormann, Knutson, and Mulsof note, "The members respond in an emotionally appropriate way. That is, they express emotions such as happiness, sadness, anger, and pleasure in a way that fits into the initial mood of the dramatization."[5] In mediated communication, evidence of chaining may become manifest when creators of texts borrow, adapt, and disseminate frequently used dramatized images and ideas.[6] Of course, not all fantasy themes find acceptance and thus chain out; indeed, some face disinterest and rejection. Yet, when they do stir attention, successful fantasy themes cause emotional responses reminiscent of the ones evoked by previous stories. Consequently, because of the sharing of fantasy themes, the initial dramatizations of a few people may lead to a shared symbolic reality for many.

For instance, media in Baseballville may discuss vigorously the unfairness of their team's loss. The debate is broached by talk-radio personalities and leads to editorializing on local TV sports shows. Phrases such as "constant bias" and "injustice for the underdogs" are used. Consequently, when hearing these broadcasts, people familiar with the Blue Sox may become irked by the game's outcome and may contribute to dramatizing conversations, even though they might not be avid fans who actually watched the game. That is, casual fans and other interested parties for whom the dramatizations resonate may get caught up in fantasizing about the matter of "their team" getting bested because of "bias" and "injustice." What is more, common perceptions that result from chaining foster a group's sense of togetherness. In a rhetorical community, shared fantasy themes make available motives that impel people to beliefs and to actions that are grounded in a "social reality filled with heroes, villains, emotions, and attitudes."[7]

Fantasy Type. Simply put, a fantasy type is an umbrella term for a cluster of recurring, related fantasy themes. According to Bormann, a fantasy type is a "stock scenario repeated again and again by the same characters or by similar characters."[8] This kind of scenario can include recognizable plot lines, scenes, situations, and representations of people. To illustrate the concept, William Benoit et al. compare a fantasy type to "a saga, which is also called a myth, [which] is another form of often repeated expressions that carries special meanings to the group members for whom they are intended."[9] Also, Foss illustrates the concept with the example of Watergate, which has led to the creation of terms like "Billygate to describe Jimmy Carter's brother's Middle-Eastern affairs, Irangate to describe the Iran-Contra affair during Ronald Reagan's administration, and Whitewater to describe Bill Clinton's involvement in a failed real-estate venture. . . ."[10] Once established, fantasy types enable the use of shorthand allusions to a community's shared stories. Consequently, the utilization of fantasy types provides the critic with evidence of shared fantasy themes.

In Baseballville, fans expect their Blue Sox to be defeated, although they wish this situation would change. More specifically, the squad has a long-standing reputation for losing in close games. So, when they were bested by the Marauders from the City of Champions, fans from Baseballville exclaimed, "It figures! The umpire strikes again!" On the surface, this may seem like a benign comment. However, if the phrase "The umpire strikes again" has recurred over the years, it may represent a fantasy type that brings to mind a number of related fantasy themes. When fans hear the phrase uttered, they might recall a story about an umpire's peculiar expanding and contracting strike zone in the 1983 series. Also, they might recollect the tale about a fair ball called foul that resulted in a lost, pivotal game in the 1994 season. Moreover, because fans are conditioned to see close games lost, the fantasy type provides a serviceable frame of reference for explaining the Blue Sox defeat against the Marauders.

Rhetorical Vision. A rhetorical vision refers to a composite drama that is made up of related fantasy themes that have been clustered into specific fantasy types. When linked together into a rhetorical vision, confederate fantasy themes reveal a coherent, unified, and holistic picture of a community's shared beliefs. Moreover, rhetorical visions feature recognizable characters and plots that, when alluded to in a variety of contexts and discussions, can trigger responses similar to those observed in the original interaction that spawned it.[11] Bormann claims that within a rhetorical vision a critic may be able to detect a "master analogy" that "pulls the various elements together into a more or less elegant and meaningful whole. Usually, a rhetorical vision is indexed by a key word or slogan [such as] The New Deal, The New Frontier, Black Power, The Cold War, The New Left, The Silent Majority, and The Moral Majority."[12] Bormann claims that words such as these call forth recollections of stories that resonate with specific communities.

For instance, Thomas G. Endres examines narratives of young, unmarried mothers, who must deal with the disadvantages and social stigmas of their situation. In their stories, he discerns rhetorical visions concerning being "down and out" (e.g., the mothers feel negatively about themselves and victimized by close friends, acquaintances, and family members), trying to "make the best" of their circumstances (e.g., the mothers learn to ignore social stigmas associated with having a child outside of a marriage and learn to visualize a positive future), and attempting to become a "young, upwardly mobile mother" (e.g., the mothers replace feelings of victimage with feelings of empowerment).[13] Based on the results in Endres's study, one might speculate that if some details of these visions were introduced to a group of young, unmarried mothers, they would identify with and respond emotionally to the ideas presented.

In the case of the Marauders, the words "Iron Dynasty," a master analogy for a rhetorical vision, may evoke affective reactions from people in the City of Champions. They might immediately be reminded of certain fantasy types that elucidate their team's championships during the 1970s. Further, those fantasy types illuminate the team's recent, successful run for the championship against the Blue Sox. One such fantasy type might include "clutch heroes," like Pokey Howard. In fans' minds, this player's deft base running exemplifies how the Marauders always perform their best at critical moments. Another fantasy type evoked by mention of "Iron Dynasty" might be "dramatic finishes," a category of fantasy themes about compelling climaxes in important games. In the present case, fans from the City of Champions are reminded of how the Sox gained an early lead. However, the story ended spectacularly because of Spikes O'Reily's timely run batted in. In all, remembrances of stories like these support a coherent rhetorical vision, "a unified putting-together of the various scripts that gives participants a broader view of things."[14]

How to Conduct Fantasy-Theme Analysis

With an understanding of its basic concepts, one can address the business of conducting fantasy-theme analysis. Put simply, to do a fantasy-theme analysis, one needs to examine discourse for fantasy themes, chaining, rhetorical visions, and fantasy types. Yet, to accomplish these tasks, a critic should proceed with caution, being aware of an important point associated with examining rhetoric for dramatizations: It matters how audiences communicate. With many frequently used methods of rhetorical criticism, the goals of analyses are to apprehend key characteristics of a message or to discern the appeal of a message's source. However, fantasy-theme analysis places emphasis on the audience—not on the message or on the message's source—and their reactions to and utilizations of dramatizing messages. With this thought in mind, a critic is ready to conduct a fantasy-theme analysis by finding evidence of dramatized messages, by categorizing those messages, and by constructing rhetorical visions.

Finding Evidence. To find evidence of dramatized messages, or fantasy themes, a critic must first find an appropriate topic for analysis. Ball recommends considering communicative events such as "a decision-making group, a rhetorical controversy, a social group, a support group, a rhetorical community, a policy-making unit, a political campaign, a social movement, or the like that is intellectually intriguing, about which there are questions to be answered." Certainly, a critic may select virtually any topic for analysis. However, a critic must be ready to argue (1) for the topic's social significance and (2) for its role in some kind of persuasive process. Once a topic is selected, rhetorical texts concerning the topic must be found. Therefore, a critic may gather videotapes of meetings, transcripts of speeches, interviews, and similar artifacts that may reveal dramatizations. Within these artifacts, a critic searches for "evidence of shared narratives, dramatic communication, imagery, figures of speech, and the like,"[15] while remembering the definition of a fantasy theme: It is an imaginative and dramatic message used to interpret an audience's past, present, or future, as revealed by the given texts. Bormann reminds us that for a message to be dramatic, "The action is set in a time and place other than the here-and-now of the group."[16]

For instance, in transcripts of conversations, a critic might look for words that trigger a chaining event. At a recent meeting of the Baseballville Booster Club, one person says, "I sure hope we have a better season next year." To this, another person replies, "Yes, we do not want a repeat of 'The Game.'" With mention of "The Game," other group members enthusiastically add interpretive recollections of the less-than-satisfactory results of the lost championship game: "Our lousy manager, Sparky Croft, should have brought in our all-star reliever, Cannonball Braden, sooner." "We could never win at the Marauder's Indian Rivers Stadium! We can be a horrible road team." Or, "I still can't believe that rotten call the umpire made!" Again, because of individuals' emotional responses to a remembrance of "The Game," critics might speculate that they have found evidence of fantasy themes.

Categorizing Messages. Once critics find evidence of dramatizations in a group's discourse, they must categorize and count the themes to make determinations about a group's attitudes and values. This requires a careful look at a text's characteristics. For visual media, like a film, a critic may need to examine it scene by scene. For speeches, each sentence in a transcript may need to be scrutinized. Formulating categories requires hard work; however, many scholars agree that the themes found may be categorized according to settings, to characters, and to actions. For instance, Karen Foss and Stephen Littlejohn found data that fit into these three categories in the 1983, made-for-TV movie called *The Day After*. The film deals with the pressing, Cold-War concern of nuclear holocaust, which prompted approximately 100 million Americans to watch the event on ABC. In their study, Foss and Littlejohn demonstrate that themes relating to characters were few. Instead, scenic elements and plotlines dominate the film. In the shattered remains of American civilization, characters appear helpless as they labor to cope with prominent themes, including attempting to survive deadly radiation and pollution (scenic elements) and endeavoring to find limited service and resources (plotline). With this reading of the film, Foss and Littlejohn do more than the important work of finding and counting themes revealed in the discourse. With this reading, the authors of the study establish the "manner in which the film addressed various thematic components"—a critical accomplishment that illuminates America's mood in the early 1980s concerning the threat of nuclear war.[17]

In the process of categorization, a critic may also search for fantasy types. Like fantasy themes, fantasy types can be difficult to identify, especially for outsiders to a group who have not participated in a community's creation of meaning through dramatization. Nevertheless, through careful study, special "scripts" in a culture become evident, exhibiting recurrences of "particular fantasies with similar plot lines, scenes, characters, or situations."[18] For instance, a critic examining the discourse of talk radio in the City of Champions hears "Babe Ruth" and "Spikes O'Reily" uttered in the same sportscaster's breath. In this case, Ruth represents an archetypal fantasy with which O'Reily is now associated. That is, Ruth's legend is well known by many baseball fans. Because a clear comparison is being made, commentators are suggesting, for instance, that O'Reily swings a bat with the same ferocity as Ruth. Consequently, the fantasy type used provides people with a way to interpret the actions of and to set expectations for the Marauder's heavy hitter. Although not all fantasy-theme analyses search for and identify fantasy types, their discovery can substantially reinforce a critic's study.

Constructing Rhetorical Visions.   After categorizing fantasy themes and types found in discourse, a critic searches for a rhetorical vision. There is no easy, formulaic way to accomplish this task, as the complexities of a vision may be many. Additionally, more than one rhetorical vision may be functioning within a given community at one time. However, Ball provides some hints concerning thoughts a critic might consider when reaching this step of a critical study. In a rhetorical vision, there will be "heroes and villains, key personae, characterizations, attitudes about work, praising and blaming, valorization of some emotions and not others, behavior that is praised and behavior that is censured, insiders and outsiders, and a multitude of beliefs and values that, ultimately, become warrants for argument and action."[19]

Although finding rhetorical visions in discourse may appear daunting, there are some precedents that may prove useful. As noted previously, a critic may find a master analogy (e.g., "New Deal") embedded in the dramatized discourse. Additionally, prior fantasy-theme analyses suggest that many rhetorical visions correspond to three genres—the pragmatic, the social, and the righteous. As Bormann, Knutson, and Mulsof explain, a pragmatic rhetorical vision "is shared by people who seek practical and utilitarian views." In a pragmatic rhetorical community, people extol the virtues of science, of effectiveness, and of common sense. Pragmatic people value goals and accomplishments. The social rhetorical vision "celebrates interpersonal relationships and the development of good families at the concrete level as well as in the utopian envisioning of the future achievement of the family of humankind's residing at peace on the spaceship earth." Not surprisingly, these visions feature idealistic notions of harmony and freedom, as relationships are paramount concerns. Finally, righteous rhetorical visions may be shared by those "who take part in a consciousness that is dedicated to some overarching cause or position."[20] For instance, in a certain community, soldiers killed in battle might be eulogized as brave men who wanted to "do the right thing" for their country, despite individual consequences: a "higher calling" guided the soldiers' gallantry.

In Baseballville, an examination of newspaper articles and radio talk-show transcripts reveal two complementary visions about the city's team: the Blue Sox as "hard-luck losers" and as "lovable losers." About the first vision noted here, a critic finds that the team is subject to numerous scenic impediments. Unfortunate injuries to key players, poor managerial decisions, mystical curses conjured by the trading of star players—excuses like these have kept the home team from "winning the big one," although they have experienced some moderate successes. About the second vision, a critic finds evidence of character-based fantasy themes that suggest the exceptional personal attributes of players in the team's history. Generally, players are represented as altruistic, heroic, and charismatic. Because of these characteristics, Baseballville takes great pride in the team and believes they embody the persona of the city. Consequently, in their narratives about the Blue Sox, residents of Baseballville expect the team should win a championship eventually, as "good things happen to good people." Both visions appear to be social in nature, as they relate to community and to feelings of interpersonal connection. In all, by identifying rhetorical visions such as these, a critic can speculate about the values and behaviors of the rhetorical community that cheers for the Blue Sox.

About Symbolic-Convergence Theory

At this point, it is valuable to pose this question: Why is fantasy-theme analysis an important, critical tool? Simply put, it helps us see how stories shape reality and, therefore, how people may act in relation to that socially constructed reality. Yet, a more complete answer to this question rests with an understanding of symbolic-convergence theory. Although fantasy-theme analysis is the tool for rhetorical criticism associated with Bormann's work, symbolic-convergence theory is the theoretical mold in which that tool is forged. The theory underscores the human tendency to share dramatized narratives, which leads to the potential for persuasion. According to Bormann, rhetoric does not always occur through rational means. Argument, evidence, refutation—these are all parts of a traditional perspective on rhetoric. However, Bormann argues that through the sharing of fantasies, "private symbolic worlds incline toward one another" and "come more closely together, or even overlap."[21] It is this overlap created by shared dramatizations that results in a "convergence" that makes shared attitudes, values, and actions possible.

To illustrate symbolic convergence, let us consider yet another hypothetical, but not unlikely, story about baseball. In the City of Champions, a decision must be made about its sports venue, Indian Rivers Stadium. Should it be demolished to make way for a new, state-of-the-art facility for the Marauders, or should it be restored to its former glory? In favor of a new stadium is the owner of the Marauders, Briefcase Michaels, who is generally perceived as a well-meaning and likable fellow. Yet, as an astute capitalist, he is motivated by financial gain. Therefore, with a corporate backer, he generates a profitable plan for a new facility that features luxury boxes and a four-star restaurant that overlooks the playing field. Michaels's conceptualization of "SuitCorp Park" is thoughtful and financially sound. Despite this resounding logic of his plan, some fans view it skeptically, as they venerate tradition and the sense of continuity embodied by Indian Rivers. The stadium is situated in an old, established neighborhood in the city. So, the park is a landmark for the community, which is more important to many nearby residents than the conveniences of a new stadium. Therefore, as Bormann might speculate, fans are, to some degree, predisposed to consider the SuitCorp Park proposal in relation to symbolic resources created by dramatized stories of Indian Rivers. Consequently, to make a decision about the present, fans might rely more on fantasies about the past than on rationality. In the following sections, this example concerning the future of Indian Rivers Stadium will be revisited to illustrate three characteristics of symbolic-convergence theory.

It Is a General Theory.   Broadly speaking, a general theory deals with tendencies of humans that are readily recognized by actual participants in communicative events. Put differently, a general theory makes sense to "ordinary people." In the case of symbolic-convergence theory, it is general because of its emphasis on our propensities for sharing narratives. Who could deny that dramatized story telling is an important part of phenomena such as interpersonal relationships, cultural cohesion, and public speeches? Because of its versatility and applicability, Bormann labels symbolic-convergence theory general, as it is "transhistorical and transcultural" and as it is able to "account for broad classes of events."[22]

If symbolic-convergence theory suggests the universality and persuasive potential of sharing dramatized stories, what might the citizens of the City of Champions say about the situation concerning Indian Rivers Stadium? To save their stadium from the economic interests of SuitCorp, fans of the Marauders may tell dramatized stories about Indian Rivers' past. The venue, which is located east of the Mississippi River, has served as the site of late-inning comebacks, of heart-pounding playoff games, and of legendary championship victories. Although the structure is nearly a century old and in need of repair, critics of plans for SuitCorp Park argue that the advantages of luxury boxes and elegant restaurants cannot replace feelings of nostalgia. Certainly, in other cities, this kind of thinking may not spare an old sports stadium from destruction, as newness, progress, and luxury tend to be valued. Yet, in the City of Champions, many residents say the stadium should remain to preserve the past and to provide inspiration for the team's future. The point here is that symbolic-convergence theory does not hold that all communities share the same fantasy themes. Instead, it simply posits that people do share fantasies, and those fantasies may create a common consciousness that provides the premises upon which collective decisions are made.

Moreover, because it is a general theory, symbolic-convergence theory is valuable because it suggests a "plausible pattern of communication."[23] That is, from a rhetorical perspective, the theory proposes a broad means by which meaningful change in a community can occur and be studied. Bormann believes that a successful persuasive campaign may hinge on dramatic stories; the use of alluring, resonating fantasy themes can entice "converts."[24] These themes encourage people to participate in a shared consciousness that fosters a sense of inclusiveness. Thus, before a referendum for renovations to Indian Rivers Stadium is due for a vote, proponents may (perhaps unknowingly) utilize principles of symbolic-convergence theory. They may assume that the stadium embodies traditions that people in the City of Champions revere, traditions that belong to "everyone" in the metropolis. Therefore, to encourage citizens to participate in the preservation of the stadium, proponents may borrow phrases from an old, local folksong about baseball called "Swingin' Shaun Austin." Consequently, the slogan, "What would Swingin' Shaun say?" is born and becomes popular because it resonates with residents' sense of shared narratives.

It Is a Grounded Theory.   To understand symbolic-convergence theory as a grounded theory, one should know that it is an empirically based undertaking that relies on both humanistic and social-scientific investigations. In a manner of speaking, all criticism is empirically based insofar as it relies on the presentation of evidence such as excerpts from speeches and transcripts of meetings. However, many forms of rhetorical criticism emphasize the insights of the critic to produce the conclusions of studies. Symbolic-convergence theory, on the other hand, emphasizes audience responses to generate the results of studies. Thus researchers often employ social–scientific methods for theory development. Bormann explains the grounded nature of symbolic-convergence theory by writing, "Thus, we begin with humanistic rhetorical qualitative analysis to analyze messages, shift to the social science methods for the study of audience response, and then return to humanistic critical analysis to explain in depth the way rhetoric functions in terms of response."[25] By saying that social–scientific methods are important to his thinking, Bormann is not claiming that every fantasy-theme analysis requires the use of surveys or experimental observations. Rather, he is claiming that social–science research enhances the critical power of symbolic-convergence theory and, consequently, of fantasy-theme analysis.

Social science plays an important role in Bormann's thinking because he bases symbolic-convergence theory on research conducted in the quantitative realm of small-group communication. In fact, Bormann's work is influenced significantly by the research of Robert Bales. In his book titled *Personality and Interpersonal Behavior*, Bales asserts that groups create fantasy chains for two reasons. First, communicators in small groups may harbor common psychodynamic issues. Consequently, when topics of interest are raised, the potential for sharing fantasies emerges. Second, dramatizing messages may occur when a group works on a common project that produces problems. If these problems result in tension between group members, they may employ imaginative language to soothe matters. In both cases presented here, Bales's conclusions are based on observations of participants in actual interactions.[26] What is more, because of the assumptions of social–scientific methodology, the results produced by Bales's research purport (1) to lead to some degree of predictability of human behavior: and (2) to allow for replication, meaning that the conclusions of one study can be reproduced in others.

Bormann took Bales's thinking about sharing group consciousness and applied it to rhetoric. Of course, to make this leap, Bormann needed to avoid the temptation to merely "relabel" the phenomenon of public discourse with terminology about small-group interaction. Therefore, over decades, scholars have conducted numerous studies about symbolic-convergence theory to strengthen the link between dramatizations and public discourse, including hundreds of studies conducted and supervised by Bormann at the University of Minnesota. Based on these efforts, he concluded that the phenomenon of group fantasizing affects and is applicable to persuasive events on a public scale.[27]

It Is an Epistemic Theory.   If a theory of communication is epistemic, simply stated, it suggests that discourse creates reality. Of course, this statement does not imply that the use of the words "pink elephant" conjures a physical one out of thin air. Instead, it implies that words can change the way people relate to the world and to one another. Words can, according to an epistemic approach to communication, create beliefs, affect perceptions, and motivate actions, especially in the absence of certainty. As Pierre Thevenez elucidates, "Man acts and speaks before he knows. Or, better, it is by acting and in action that he is enabled to know."[28] If this statement is meritorious, then human knowledge is not final, as people continue to act and to speak. Hence, knowledge evolves over time through the processes of human interaction. In the case of symbolic-convergence theory, Bormann takes the notion of rhetoric as epistemic and relates it to the public sharing of fantasies. Thus, he claims the sharing of dramatized communication can socially construct the reality of a community.

One might argue that the myth of Indian Rivers Stadium as "the greatest venue in baseball" is an epistemic construct, created by participants in a rhetorical community that chains fantasy themes. Fans of the Marauders are fond of saying, "Indian Rivers is the toughest place in which an opposing team can play. It's loud. It's crazy. It's intimidating. No one wins an important game against us at the Rivers!" Indeed, the Marauders have won pivotal games and have made spectacular plays on their home field. However, according to statistics, it is not truly the toughest place to play. The team that boasts the most wins at home is the Green Wave of Coastal City, and the team with the best winning percentage at home is the Red Streaks of Central City. In both categories, the Marauders rank second and third respectively. Nevertheless, because of fantasies perpetuated by people in the City of Champions and by sports commentators, Indian Rivers boasts a special ethos that impels fans to cheer loudly and to heckle opposing players mercilessly. That is, the myth has created the "reality" that encourages fans to be loud. What is more, because of the stadium's myth, people are mounting a very "real" campaign to curtail SuitCorp Park and to preserve Indian Rivers.

CRITICAL ESSAY

Although we must now leave Baseballville and the City of Champions behind, we take with us our appreciation of fantasy-theme analysis to explore rhetorical visions of higher education in America. Many students attend college thinking that it is the "smart thing to do" or the "best preparation for the future and for a career."[29] The nation's leaders often propose that enabling more people to attend college will solve many social problems, including economic inequality or a lack of responsible citizenship. Moreover, throughout the twentieth century until today, higher education has been promoted as a democratic institution that provides opportunities for individuals from all social classes. Americans agree that higher learning is critically important, yet there is ambiguity about the nature and purpose of a college education. Many Americans emphasize the professional and practical benefits of higher education. Other Americans, however, emphasize more abstract benefits of an education including the duty that college graduates have to their communities.

In the critical essay that follows, we examine such differences and related dramatizations of higher education in public discourse. We address questions such as, "What do we expect from our universities?" and "Why do we go to college?" In considering these questions, we find that two different views, or what Bormann calls rhetorical visions, of higher education emerge. One rhetorical vision, which we call the communal idealist vision, depicts a college education as an intellectual enterprise that values service to others and learning for the sake of learning. The competing vision, called the individual utilitarian vision, interprets higher education as a practical experience that prepares students for worldly success. Public discourse about higher learning is important because it shapes expectations for colleges and universities. Moreover, those expectations are influential in determining, to name just a few considerations, whether students attend college, how schools are evaluated, and what kind of public and private resources are made available to educational institutions.

Critical Essay: Institutions of Higher Learning and Fantasy Themes

Fantasy-theme analysis is based on the phenomenon of group fantasizing. Groups often talk about "characters, real or fictitious, playing out a dramatic situation in a setting removed in time and space from the here-and-now transactions of the group."[30] These messages are fantasy themes, and they often carry over into public discourse. As Ernest G. Bormann notes, "the dramatizations which catch on and chain out in small groups are worked into public speeches and into the mass media and, in turn, spread out across larger publics, serve to sustain the members' sense of community, to impel them strongly to action."[31] In other words, public messages often help listeners to assign meanings to the events and ideas that shape their everyday lives. Similar fantasy themes can be sorted into categories of related themes, clusters called fantasy types. Once a critic accomplishes the work of identifying fantasy themes and types, he or she can assemble them into a coherent rhetorical vision. A rhetorical vision is "a unified putting-together of the various shared scripts that gives the participants a broader view of things."[32] That is, people who share a group of fantasies and fantasy types may also share a unified perception of social reality.[33]

To create and live in a unified social reality, people participate in dramatizations that chain out in a rhetorical community, allowing participants to assign meaning to and make sense out of important experiences, characters, and ideas in the life of that community. Thus, fantasy theme analysis is "a form of rhetorical criticism that highlights the way groups construct shared symbolic realities."[34] Essentially, this process of dramatizing sanctions groups of people to work together in understanding their world. Moreover, group fantasizing allows layers of meaning to build, one on top of another. Imagine, for example, the deposits of calcium that form around a grain of sand as a pearl is formed in an oyster. Similarly, fantasies layer meaning around an event or a concept that allows the perceptions of a rhetorical community to expand.

Fantasy-theme analysis can help us to understand organizations, including schools, businesses, and governments. If a rhetorical vision contains a group's view of symbolic reality, it will then provide members of an organization with emotions, values and attitudes, heroes and villains, and hence, their motives for action. Bormann explains, "when a person appropriates a rhetorical vision he gains with the supporting dramas constraining forces which impel him to adopt a life style and to take certain action."[35] The influence of the rhetorical vision on organizations is best understood from the perspective of institutional theory. According to this theory, for an organization to be legitimated, its structures and practices must be seen as consistent with the values of the society within which the organization exists.[36] Organizational structures and actions, whether rational or not, are often constructed symbolically to show that the organization meets the demands of public opinion. W. Richard Scott summarizes the environment's influence on organizations by stating, "Cultural controls can substitute for structural controls. When beliefs are widely shared in categories and procedures taken for granted, it is less essential that they be formally encoded into the organizational structure."[37]

Through the chaining of fantasies, rhetoric can influence and reaffirm the values held by an audience, and those values will influence organizations. For example, an organization's methods of guaranteeing legitimacy are often used as criteria to judge the organization.[38] Thus, opinions about higher education establish expectations and criteria for evaluating those institutions, and fantasy-theme analysis of public discourse about higher education provides the critic with evidence that the audience has dramatized those opinions. Accordingly, if the public views a college education as career preparation, schools will not be seen as successful unless graduates obtain well-paying jobs. Likewise, the individualistic views of higher education and communal views of higher education can be connected to conditions with which contemporary colleges and universities must deal.

To consider the role of public discourse in creating expectations for higher education, the critic should identify evidence of fantasy themes chaining out and clustering into fantasy types. The fantasy-theme analysis should then consider the implications of these fantasy types and their formation of a rhetorical vision of higher education. A rhetorical vision will suggest what the purposes of education ought to be. As a result, the vision will reflect the community's ideas on issues such as what students should learn in college, what majors ought to be offered, or what a graduate can expect to do after college.

To accomplish the tasks listed in the above paragraph, we assembled a cross section of twentieth and early twenty-first century discourse about higher education. The rhetorical artifacts examined here were chosen to provide a diversity of positions about the purposes of higher education and to represent the thinking of a variety of rhetors, including educators, politicians, and business leaders. We began by reviewing the indices of the periodical *Vital Speeches of the Day* and identifying speeches about higher education. We also included edited anthologies of speeches and essays on higher education and books that elaborate on the attitudes toward higher education that were seen in *Vital Speeches of the Day*. Finally, we unearthed a few surveys and empirical studies that verified the fantasies found in the discourse were embraced by the general public. In all, the rhetoric examined provided us with evidence that the individual utilitarian and communal idealist visions of higher education had, indeed, chained out.

The Individual Utilitarians in Higher Education.   Twentieth- and early twenty-first-century discourse on higher education contains evidence of two very different sets of fantasy types chaining out to create opposing visions. We explore first the individual utilitarian vision, which favors an experiential education encouraging immersion in society. This vision emphasizes the discovery of useful knowledge, practical education, and the economic benefits of learning. Unlike the idealist vision, utilitarians see education as a means of achieving some other end outside the academic realm. The individual utilitarians speak positively about the development of public land grant institutions and the access to higher education provided by programs such as the G.I. Bill, which provided funding for college to military veterans. These developments are celebrated for making college a possibility for most citizens, regardless of economic class, for the first time in human history. On the other hand, they eschew the elitism that surrounded the founding of America's first colleges. Not surprisingly, their heroes are the "self-made individuals" who, despite disadvantages in life, used a college education to achieve wealth and success. The villains of this fantasy are elitist, esoteric thinkers who seem to "waste" resources pursuing impractical academic ends. The following subsections present fantasy types that construct an individual utilitarian perspective of college learning.

The Self-Reliant Fantasy Type.   The notion that a student goes to college to become self-reliant was the most common fantasy type supporting the individual utilitarian vision. Throughout the last century, proponents of this vision claimed that college graduates should attain independence by endeavoring for financial self-sufficiency and by having a successful career. Recently, a number of political leaders articulated the relationship between a college degree and the ability to make a living, thus, avoiding dependence on others. President Clinton, for example, remarked, "to make the American dream achievable for all, we must make college affordable to all."[39] President George W. Bush also perpetuated this fantasy in his 2002 State of the Union when he said, "Good jobs begin with good schools."[40]

Before Presidents Clinton and Bush, the idea that an education makes one a self-reliant individual was offered by leaders such as Allen Crow of the Detroit Economic Club. In 1944, he stated that "Higher education . . . must include among its primary functions, the instruction of folks in how to acquire what they need and what they want, by taking care of themselves."[41]

Interestingly, contemporary critics of education argued that the self-reliant fantasy type became dominant in the second half of the twentieth century. Educator and author Alan Bloom, who is opposed to the individualistic perspective, observed that students primarily embrace individualism in their college lives.[42] That is, most people, he claimed, attended college for self-gain and self-improvement. Despite the motivation underpinning the fantasy type at hand, American egalitarianism embedded in the utilitarians' vision dictated that opportunities for education must be available to all of the nation's citizens.

The Equal Opportunity Fantasy Type.   In the twentieth century, the prospect of attending college represented a democratic equalizer meant to erase lines of social class and privilege. Secretary of Education Richard Riley celebrated the fact that "American education has become more open, more diverse, and more inclusive."[43] Politicians such as President Clinton also used the equal opportunity fantasy type to appeal to voters, speaking of college as a privilege to which all citizens are entitled. In a speech given in 1998, Clinton said,

> I have something to say to every family listening to us tonight: Your children can go on to college. If you know a child from a poor family, tell her not to give up—she can go on to college. If you know a young couple struggling with bills, worried they won't be able to send their children to college, tell them not to give up—their children can go on to college . . . we can make college as universal in the 21st century as high school is today.[44]

Along with politicians, business leaders and educators identified with America's universal access to higher education. The unprecedented access that Americans have to higher education was often seen as cause for commemoration. In

1953, the Chair of Standard Oil, Robert Wilson, represented this mode of thinking: "One of the noteworthy things about higher education in America is that there is so much of it. . . . Nowhere else has it been possible to offer the advantages of higher education to so many."[45] From this perspective, equality of opportunity translated to economic terms and emphasized the right of all individuals to make a good living and thereby transcend economic and social class distinctions. In 1916, philosopher John Dewey explained, "A society which is mobile . . . must see to it that its members are educated."[46] Indeed, this fantasy type demonstrated that the cherished ideal of all Americans having an opportunity to prosper was linked to the notion of universal access to higher education.

Contemporary educators also recognized that students primarily go to college to improve their professional opportunities. Robert Spaeth of St. John's University commented, "We can do little to influence what sort of students will enroll in our colleges; they will be individualists, and they will expect their individualism to be encouraged by the college they choose."[47] Institutions often indulge this individualism by promising students that a degree will lead to high paying jobs and desirable careers. Professors Robert Solomon and Jon Solomon, authors of a book on their observations and criticism of contemporary education, contended "social mobility in the United States is very largely determined by education. Education is the gateway to the professions and, these days, to managerial jobs in business and other organizations."[48]

Higher education has thus been legitimated as a valuable institution because it provides opportunities for all. From this perspective, it is believed that we diminish class distinctions by providing educational opportunities to anyone who wants to go to college. We now turn to the final component of the individualistic vision, the idea that college develops in students a work ethic and a character suited for personal success.

The Practical Mind Fantasy Type. From an individualistic perspective, a college education was expected to motivate a student to succeed in life, to encourage ambition, and to help a student become the type of person who can fulfill that ambition. In a 1987 commencement address, Robert Spaeth stated, "Students . . . determine for themselves what they 'want to get out of' their college experience."[49] In short, along with the acquisition of specific professional skills, the most successful students were expected to be diligent and practical. Along similar lines, Du Pont executive Chaplin Tyler, in a 1938 speech at Virginia Military Institute, observed that an overall "working philosophy" is far more important than any specific course of study. Such a philosophy includes things like logic and "unswerving faith in cold facts."[50]

The ability to persevere in the face of hardship was also cited as an important characteristic for individual success. The collegiate experience presented students with challenges and exposed them to uncertain experiences, and this strengthened the will to succeed. Some who labeled perseverance as the most important asset for a career saw higher learning as an inferior method of training. In a 1937 speech to a convention of college deans, corporate attorney Robert H. Jackson, asked why we value a college education. He valued the formative years a young person spends in college and wondered if those years should be spent gaining real-world experience. He spoke from personal experience and claimed he learned much when he was "tossed into the strife to sink or swim," and students learned less because they were "removed from the struggle of life."[51] Whether they are successful or not, colleges are expected to transform students, and many individualistic thinkers have called for practical, hard working, and ambitious graduates.

Assembling the Individual Utilitarian Rhetorical Vision.   A coherent rhetorical vision of higher education emerges when one assembles the fantasy types we have discussed. This rhetorical vision, called individual utilitarianism, emphasizes the practical benefits a degree gives to individual students. Twentieth- and early twenty-first-century discourse provides evidence that fantasy types emphasizing self-reliance, equal opportunities, and practical mindedness have chained through rhetorical communities and shaped what we expect from our colleges and universities. A variety of empirical studies also verify that this fantasy has chained out in the American public. For example, survey data gathered by researchers at the Lumina Foundation for Education showed strong support for expanded access to higher education, and the research group, Public Agenda, documented the belief that college should be attainable for all economic classes.[52] Researchers at the Ford Foundation and at UCLA's Higher Education Research Institute (HERI) provided evidence that most students expected that their education would provide them with basic skills, career preparation, and better earning power.[53] Annual studies by HERI also showed that faculty embraced such a pragmatic view.[54]

As we have seen, the heroes of this vision are the graduates who use their degrees to become independent and successful. These people are revered for their determination, and an education further empowers them to survive in a competitive world. Robert Jackson honored such rugged individualists: "The world has an overabundance of those who paddle pretty well in still water. The world cries for men who can navigate 'white water.' I see plenty of it ahead."[55] Additionally, educators are honored for attempting to provide expanded access to higher learning, and elitists are the villains of the individualist vision. University president James Rosser criticized colleges for "educating the sons and daughters of the already elite, or the already able to aspire."[56] Although educators who provide practical training are granted heroic status, the vision condemns professors who are disconnected from the real world or who pursue studies that do not have tangible, material benefits. Robert Lutz of the Chrysler Corporation complained that students often get a "dumb" education "from silly classes based on trendy theory and from curricula that look like they were designed by a TV game-show programmer."[57]

Public narrative construals provide additional evidence of the utilitarian vision. This vision regards the establishment of America's earliest colleges, the private colleges of the colonial era, as an attempt to provide an education only to the most elite students and to offer an impractical classical curriculum. Therefore, one of the most significant narratives in the history of higher education has been the establishment of large public universities. The establishment of these land grant universities was celebrated by utilitarians because, unlike the elite colleges, they provided expanded access to higher education and provided research and instruction in practical subjects such as business, industry, and agriculture. University of Texas President Homer Rainey, like many others, identified this as a landmark story in higher education: "In the thirty years between 1830 and 1860 there was waged in this country the battle for free public schools." According to Rainey the result was "the finest system of public education that any society has ever known."[58] Likewise, the founding of Cornell University, which pioneered the elective system, was a story often heralded as a victory for practical education. Cornell claimed to offer instruction to any student in any subject and was seen as a landmark in the struggle to develop curriculum based less on the classical liberal arts and more on the basic needs of contemporary society. Finally, the G.I. Bill was a popular narrative for individual utilitarians. This federal program was credited with making higher education available to the masses. When President Clinton proposed increasing educational funding for working families, he called it the "G.I. Bill for American workers."[59]

The core values of this vision embrace learning as the acquisition of skills for survival; they eschew any intellectual experiences that cannot be shown to make students more employable or independent. For example, graduates are expected to find employment related to their degrees. Faculty research is expected to discover useful information. Accordingly, a college's primary focus must be on serving the needs of undergraduates. The vision would also privilege academic disciplines and curricula that can be clearly linked to practical benefits. One would obviously expect students who hold the individualist view to prefer classes that are linked to their careers and to dismiss classes that do not seem to provide such skills. Additionally, schools should offer a large variety of majors to accommodate students who choose diverse professions. A final core value of the vision mandates that a college's constituency be composed of students from all socioeconomic backgrounds who are pursuing the opportunities offered by the institution.

The Communal Idealists in Higher Education.   Having examined the individual utilitarian vision, we now turn to the opposing rhetorical vision of higher education. Many twentieth century rhetors emphasized the community in legitimating higher education. It was often assumed that the good of an entire society is promoted by an educated citizenry. From this perspective, speakers depicted higher education as a means of encouraging students to appreciate their communities and to place service to others before self-gain. Put differently, communal idealism views college as a place to retreat from society and to exercise the intellect. This vision expects colleges to prepare graduates for leadership roles in the community. Also, communal idealists view learning as an end in itself and value learning for learning's sake. In this vision, heroes are those contemplative students and professors who seek to develop the intellect for the purpose of creating a more perfect and democratic society. Its villains include those people who selfishly use higher education for material gain.

The Servant–Leader Fantasy Type.   The communal idealistic vision of higher educa-tion is based on a clearly articulated model of leadership. Rather than encourag-ing individualistic ends, college teaches students to lead by sharing their talents in service to others. In this servant–leader fantasy type, graduates are seen as a select minority of people who must fill leadership roles for the greater community, and ideal leadership comes in the form of service to the community. In other words, college is thought to take the finest young people and inculcate in them a sense of responsibility to others.

Contemporary statements by leading educators articulated the value of the leader who is committed to service. John Howard of the Rockford Institute sug-gested that, "although you make a living by what you get, you make a life by what you give."[60] In the language of other recent educational advocates, servant–lead-ers were very necessary, and they claimed the desire and ability to serve others should be nurtured in college. In an essay published in 1992, history professor Ralph Ketcham defended civic education as a way of training students to partici-pate in democracy: "Human beings do have the capacity to rise above the narrow and self-serving states of mind, and this capacity can be nourished."[61] To encour-age service to others, Harvard president Derek Bok argued in 1992 that educators must teach students to "deepen their concern for those who need help, to build within them a strong sense of ethical responsibility, to help them acknowledge that exceptional talent carries with it exceptional responsibility for the welfare of others."[62]

The servant–leader fantasy type has a long history that was seen throughout the early twentieth century. Princeton President Harold Dodds told his graduates in 1949 that they belonged to an elite group of educated leaders. He said, "you are under, and will be under all the days of your life, the heavy responsibility of being qualified for membership in that creative minority which . . . decides the great is-sues of life."[63] Dodds also argued that members of this elite minority can not hon-orably escape the role as leaders and that it would be disgraceful for an educated person to shirk his or her responsibility to lead. He was concerned that educated citizens were often "guilty of the sins of civic indolence, private self-interest and slavery to party spirit. These concerns added up to gross neglect of civic duty."[64]

In sum, colleges have long been expected to teach students a sense of social and civic responsibility, and those who serve the community are those who are most suited to lead. Next, we explore higher education's role as critic in the community.

The Watchdog Fantasy Type.   An additional communal function of higher educa-tion is the role of the independent watchdog. As this fantasy type chained out, col-leges were expected to be critics in the community by checking the power of government and challenging the accepted truths of culture. Essentially, the watch-dog fantasy type called on schools to act as an authority that monitors the gov-ernment, industry, and other powerful institutions.

Fantasy themes envisioning the academy as a watchdog were elaborated throughout the twentieth century, but they were especially powerful during the crises leading up to World War II. President of the University of Wisconsin, Glenn Frank, argued that education provides a democracy with corrective criticism: "To Jefferson the freedom of scholars to examine and the freedom of journalists to express were liberties without which neither the political nor the economic liberty of the people could conceivably be secure."[65] That is, this fantasy type used by Frank suggested that academics should use their insight and influence to keep other powerful groups in check.

Part of higher education's watchdog role also allowed for an independent community of thinkers given time to contemplate freely. In a 1935 speech, Robert M. Hutchins advocated theoretical training and a separation of the academy from every day affairs. For Hutchins, the key to fighting controversial ideas was to debate rather than ignore them: "[T]he American people must decide whether they will . . . tolerate the search for truth. If they will, the universities will endure and give light and leading to the nation."[66] In response to the depression and the rise of fascism in Europe, Glenn Frank also emphasized the value of a system of higher education that was allowed free inquiry and used the results of that inquiry to inform other institutions, such as government. As part of the watchdog role, comes the expectation that university research provides the world with knowledge and wisdom. The discovery and preservation of information has long been recognized as a benefit to the community. "Great universities," Frank claimed, "can prosecute and publish fearlessly objective researches into the living issues of state and nation."[67]

Rhetors in the later decades of the century also observed that education teaches students to think insightfully and to avoid seeing the world uncritically. Recently, in 2002, author and professor John Rodden argued that "such concerns are especially compelling today in light of 9/11" because education allows students to "assess the value of data we consume every day."[68] Bloom further cautioned that people not properly educated lack critical abilities: "Lack of education simply results in students seeking for enlightenment wherever it is readily available, without being able to distinguish between the sublime and trash, insight and propaganda."[69] As revealed in the next section of this essay, the communal idealists expected colleges to provide students with a miniature community that prepares them to function and interact within a larger community.

The University as Microcosm Fantasy Type.   A final communal view of higher education embraced the value of schools as small communities, within which students learn to function in larger communities. When he was president of Princeton, Woodrow Wilson emphasized the need for a campus to be a community of scholars who motivate one another. As an administrator on campus, Wilson worked to shape the environment within his school, and he tried to convince students to embrace the academic community. Wilson said, "A college body represents a passion. . . . [A] passion not so much individual as social, a passion for the things which live, for the things which enlighten, for the things which bind men together in unselfish companies."[70] Living in this community provided the student with practical lessons in how to serve his fellow citizens and, more importantly, how to selflessly serve an institution larger than oneself. Wilson elaborated: "A college is a brotherhood in which every man is expected to do for the sake of the college the thing which alone can make the college a distinguished and abiding force in the history of men . . . men shall be ashamed to look their fellows in the face if it is known that they have great faculties and do not use them for the glory of their alma mater."[71]

The notion of a miniature community was recently articulated by philosophy professor Robert Solomon and professor of classics Jon Solomon in a book that examined the current state of higher education. They asserted, "The university should be a model for democracy as well as a training ground for democracy."[72] Through activities such as student government and campus media, including student run newspapers, television, and radio stations, students learned to assess, shape, and interact with public opinion. Learning to respond to the public discussion and attitudes that invariably exist on a campus will prepare students to function in the public sphere after graduation. This persisted as a key role for colleges and universities.

Assembling the Communal Idealist Rhetorical Vision.   The communal idealist vision of higher education emphasizes the servant–leader, the watchdog, and the miniature community. The discourse honors those who approach higher education as a community of scholars left to contemplate freely and to teach students to lead. Robert Hutchins argued that "The greatest university is that in which the largest proportion of . . . scholars are the most competent in their chosen fields."[73] The vision despises the selfish individuals who are interested only in self-gain. Harold Dodds remarked, "All history teaches that struggle for power and influence divorced from unselfish ends is self-destructive and in the end unsatisfying."[74] More recently, Willard Butcher of the Chase Manhattan Corporation contended that "A total commitment to personal gain—'meism'—at the expense of society's overall well-being, even if it gets you to the top, will ensure you are *not* a leader."[75]

While the communal idealist fantasy can be seen chaining out in public discourse, empirical data provides further evidence of its popularity. Annual HERI surveys indicated support for increased interaction between students and faculty to establish a more robust academic community, and data gathered by Pew Charitable Trust showed a preference for the traditional classroom experience over nontraditional online classes.[76] Studies by HERI have shown that faculty believed a college education ought to help a student develop moral character, commitment to community service, and responsible citizenship.[77] Likewise, students hoped their schooling would help to develop leadership skills.[78] In sum, communal visions have chained through the public, and, although they are not as popular as individualistic visions, research documents their persistence at the grassroots level.

Central to the communal vision are many of the same narratives that the utilitarians dramatized. Yet those narratives take on a decidedly different form. The communal idealists edified the founding of the colonial colleges. This was seen as a story in which the success of the American revolution and the establishment of a democratic government was due to the availability of leaders who were trained in American colleges.[79] In 1938 Harvard President James Conant recognized the ongoing role of those early colleges in preparing the elite to be leaders: "Thomas Jefferson in the early days of the last century spoke of the necessity of 'culling the natural aristocracy of talent and virtue from every condition of the people, and educating it at the public expense for the care of the public concern.' In the great wave of enthusiasm for universal schooling, this principal of Jefferson's has tended to become submerged."[80] Because it values the establishment of the colonial colleges, this vision is highly suspicious of the establishment of the land grant universities and the G.I. Bill. These events represented a move away from the style of education that best prepared the finest students to lead and a loss of community which was found in smaller, less bureaucratic institutions. In a 1984 commencement address, Harold Logan of W.R. Grace and Company questioned the contribution made by large state universities: "I submit that one of the things we have gotten is a weakening of the private-education system in this country by the rapid growth of our State-subsidized university which has grown to such a size as to lose all personal touch."[81]

The vision's core values downplay the practical benefits of learning and emphasize the intellectual and spiritual benefits. The ideal college prepares its students for responsible participation in the community. Its mission includes forming an educated citizenry, inculcating a sense of citizenship, and nurturing the moral character of students. The curriculum of this college is not based on practical value but on intellectual merit, and the student body is composed of an academically elite group of students who will provide leadership after graduation. Unlike the individual vision, which could accommodate nontraditional learning, the communal idealist vision would prefer the traditional experience of a residential college. Finally, faculty research would include not just the discovery of practical data. Research would promote the contemplation of the values that shape the community. Having described opposing visions of higher education, the next section examines their consequences.

Implications for Educational Institutions: Striking a Balance

The goal of this study is to use fantasy-theme analysis to identify the purposes of higher education, as they are expressed in twentieth- and early twenty-first-century American rhetoric. Fantasy-theme analyses "illuminate how individuals talk with one another about their here-and-now concerns until they come to share a common consciousness and create a sense of identity and community."[82] The public discourse we examined suggests that this symbolic convergence process has occurred among audiences with an interest in higher education. Americans have assembled fantasies into two competing rhetorical visions, and, as a result, there is not clear consensus on its purpose. Derek Bok explained, "the bonds of understanding between our universities and the nation have not grown stronger. . . . [N]either educators nor community leaders share a clear, compelling view of what universities can do for the society."[83]

As demonstrated in this study, rhetorical visions shape public expectations for and sentiments about organizations. To maintain legitimacy, then, higher education must be sensitive to both the individual utilitarian and communal idealist visions, as they characterize beliefs exhibited by Americans. The key to success for higher education may lie in accommodating both visions. Too often, colleges help students develop utilitarian skills while downplaying the importance of the community. The communal fantasy themes identified in this study, however, can provide a foundation for restoring the communal idealistic vision.

The ability to participate in a vital community has diminished in the twentieth century, and this breakdown in community has led to severe problems. Many educators lament the belief that the individualistic model dominates contemporary higher education. Robert Spaeth of St. John's remarked:

> Individualism is so rampant in American higher education today that it goes unnamed and often unnoticed. It is, I believe, our way of life . . . it has produced the very failures that critics are constantly bringing to our attention. Individualism has infected both student bodies and faculties, and the two groups encourage it in one another. Students by and large come to college today to major in a field that will lead to a career—their own career—by means of which they hope to become successful and at least materially comfortable.[84]

Examples from other spheres of public discourse also reflect concern for a lack of community. Robert A. Nisbet, in his book *The Quest for Community*, observed that "Despite the influence and power of the contemporary State there is a true sense in which the present age is more individualistic than any other."[85] Likewise, the themes identified as characteristic of the institutional environments surrounding higher education in the twentieth century seem to be individualistic. Nisbet argued that the release from the contexts of community have not led to freedom and rights but "intolerable aloneness and subjection."[86] Furthermore, he saw individualism as the defining characteristic of twentieth century thought: "[I]t is by no means unlikely that for our own age it is alienated or maladjusted man who will appear to later historians as the key figure of twentieth century thought."[87]

To truly serve contemporary culture, higher education should provide communal experiences that help students to overcome the individualism of the current age. A balanced rhetorical vision will not only present higher education as an enterprise for equipping students for individual success, but it will also demonstrate that higher education is an enterprise for equipping students to selflessly serve the community. Assuming that the American public craves community, colleges and universities must protect the communal idealist vision or risk becoming ineffectual. Too often, educators fail to demonstrate this to the public. Harvard President Derek Bok argued, "Today, universities need new ways to serve the public. . . . [W]e must associate ourselves prominently once again with efforts to solve problems that really concern the people of this country."[88] Put simply, if the communal idealistic vision is to continue to resonate with the public, advocates must make it appealing.

To conclude, fantasy theme analysis has helped us to recognize the meaning that rhetorical communities have given to a college education. Schools have very specific expectations that must be met for them to survive and maintain legitimacy. Over the years, fantasies have chained out in the public and have crystallized into vivid rhetorical visions. Understanding those visions will help explain why so many people feel obligated to attend college, why colleges behave as strangely as they do, what a student can expect from his or her degree, and why colleges should be preserved, revolutionized, or both. In short, we better understand our institutions and what it will take to succeed within them.

PERSONAL COMMENTS ON THE ESSAY

We chose to write our critical essay on higher education because of the natural link between fantasy themes and institutional theory, which suggests that public opinion influences life inside organizations. As we tried to show in our theoretical considerations section, fantasy-theme analysis helps us better appreciate organizations such as school, work, church, and government.

Furthermore, the purpose of a college degree is an especially relevant topic. We hope that the questions raised in this essay are questions that you have already thought about. At some point, you might have talked with parents, classmates, or professional colleagues about what you expect to get from your college years. Perhaps this essay will help you to deal with these questions in a new way. Effective rhetorical criticism will often raise questions and provide solutions to problems in our everyday lives. Criticism should provide useful insights that help us to better understand and interact with our world.

The next step in this line of study might be to compare and contrast different approaches associated with different types of rhetors. For example, we might have looked at the difference between educators and those outside of education. It would also be useful to conduct studies on various campuses to determine the extent to which these fantasies have chained out. A close examination of conditions on our campuses might help to determine the ways that students, faculty, and administrators apply the two rhetorical visions. Although the study originally consisted of more observations on public discourse about higher education, we limited the essay to the most common and influential fantasy types.

POTENTIALS AND PITFALLS

Although fantasy-theme analysis is a serviceable, as well as fashionable, critical tool, it is not without its detractors. Prominent protests may be found in essays written by G. P. Mohrmann. In these works, he strikes two significant blows against Bormann's method. First, Mohrmann claims that fantasy-theme analysis is not an appropriate extension of Bales's work on small-group interaction. In this context, fantasies can be used as mere jokes or as manifestations of individuals' needs to enhance their "self-picture, to feel more attractive and powerful, to discharge aggression, or dispel anxiety."[89] Put simply, fantasies may be used as a buffer against reality, not as a creation of it. If this is the case, one possible pitfall of fantasy-theme analysis may include a critic's inability to discern "meaningful" fantasies that do, in fact, chain out in the public realm. Second, because Bormann allegedly misconstrues Bales' work, Mohrmann claims fantasy-theme analysis does not show us much about human interaction. That is, he asserts Bormann's technique is simply a process of naming, with terms such as fantasy themes and fantasy types, revealing "the presence of agile minds" of critics, but tellling "us little about communication, little about the human condition."[90] In short, in some cases, fantasy-theme analysis might be little more than a labeling device.

Nevertheless, used adeptly, fantasy-theme analysis boasts noteworthy potentials. For instance, Bormann claims discursive logic and fantasy themes are interrelated, despite Mohrmann's protestations to the contrary. That is, people in public settings do, indeed, make choices based on attitudes formed by the sharing of dramatizations. Bormann writes that "Discursive argument requires a common set of assumptions about the nature of reality and proof."[91] Without rhetorical visions that are produced by the sharing of fantasy themes, a community would have no common set of assumptions upon which to base the premises of their arguments. Put differently, some rationalists may posit that fantasies are not verifiable and, therefore, not remarkably influential. However, for those who subscribe to a narrative perspective, fantasies may be central to understanding human communication.

Another potential of fantasy-theme analysis it that it assumes a multistep flow of information, rather than a conventional two-step flow. Benoit et al. explain the difference between the two: "Instead of moving simply from the media to opinion leaders and to the public, information flows in all directions between all agents creating a web of interaction and making possible a unified rhetorical vision."[92] Therefore, students who hope to attend college may not get all of their information about higher education solely from newspapers or from literature produced by colleges. Rather, students may also construct their impressions of college from a variety of informal sources, including friends and coworkers. If this instance is representative of the way people formulate beliefs, then fantasy-theme analysis accounts well for the means by which messages spread from small groups to larger publics and back.

FANTASY-THEME ANALYSIS TOP PICKS[93]

Ball, Moya A., *Vietnam-On-The-Potomac.* (New York: Praeger, 1992). To examine the escalation of the Vietnam War, Ball investigates the role of small-group communication in President Kennedy's and Johnson's administrations. Ball scrutinizes declassified documents and interviews with Presidential advisors utilizing Bormann's critical method.

Bormann, Ernest G., "Fantasy and Rhetorical Vision: Ten Years Later." *Quarterly Journal of Speech* 68 (1982): 288–305. Here, Bormann responds to his critics, including G. P. Mohrmann and Rod Hart, who question the theoretical foundation of fantasy-theme analysis. In his response, Bormann refines the method's technical terms and discusses its growing body of literature.

Bormann, Ernest G., "The Symbolic Convergence Theory of Communication and the Creation, Raising, and Sustaining of Public Consciousness," *The Jensen Lectures: Contemporary Communication Studies,* John I. Sisco (ed.) (Tampa: The University of South Florida Press, 1983), 71–90. As the title of this essay indicates, Bormann focuses on how usage of fantasy themes develops public consciousness. Moreover, Bormann provides a remarkably lucid and concise account of the principles that underpin fantasy-theme analysis.

Bormann, Ernest G., *The Force of Fantasy: Restoring the American Dream.* (Carbondale: Southern Illinois Press, 1985). This is the acme of Bormann's work. Using fantasy-theme analysis, he traces changes in American political discourse from colonial Puritanism to Abraham Lincoln's "romantic pragmatism." More than that, Bormann spells out the basics of his method and provides rich examples.

Bormann, Ernest G., John F. Cragan, and Donald C. Shields, "In Defense of Symbolic Convergence Theory: A Look at the Theory and Its Criticisms after Two Decades." *Communication Theory* 4 (1994): 259–294. "Two Decades" provides readers an with elaborate response to critics of symbolic convergence theory. Also, the essay provides an extensive literature review of studies utilizing symbolic convergence theory and fantasy-theme analysis.

Bormann, Ernest G., John F. Cragan, and Donald C. Shields, "An expansion if the Rhetorical Vision Component of the Symbolic Convergence Theory: The Cold War Paradigm Case." *Communication Monographs* 63 (1996): 1–28. The authors explain the "life" of a rhetorical vision. More specifically, they claim the life cycle of a rhetorical vision is shaped by three kinds of communication including consciousness raising, raising, and sustaining, and by three rhetorical

principles including novelty, explanatory power, and imitation.

Bormann, Ernest G., Roxann L. Knutson, and Karen Mulsof, "Why do People Share Fantasies? An Empirical Investigation of the Symbolic Communication Theory." *Communication Studies* 48 (1997): 254–276. To address the question posed in the essay's title, the authors explore characteristics of dramatized narratives. Along the way, they provide clear explanations of kinds of rhetorical visions (i.e., pragmatic, social, and righteous) and of dimensions of dramatized messages (i.e., reality, time, moral, and emotional).

Cragan, John F., and Donald C. Shields, "The Use of Symbolic Convergence Theory in Corporate Strategic Planning: A Case Study." *Journal of Applied Communication Research* 20 (1992): 199–218. This essay boasts two enticing features. First, it provides clear explanations for terms associated with fantasy-theme analysis. Second, it provides a case study that demonstrates how Bormann's theory guided the reconstruction of a company's shattered identity.

Endres, Thomas G., "Rhetorical Visions of Unmarried Mothers." *Communication Quarterly* 37 (1989): 134–150. In this essay, Endres investigates unmarried mothers, an infrequently studied group, with both fantasy-theme analysis and Q-methodology. Q-methodology, a kind of factor analysis, allows rhetorical criticism to be fortified with social–scientific inquiry.

Rarick, David L., Mary B Duncan, and Laurinda W. Porter, "The Carter Persona: An Empirical Analysis of the Rhetorical Visions of Campaign '76." *Quarterly Journal of Speech* 63 (1977): 258–273. The authors of this essay explore audience perceptions of Jimmy Carter's personality during his campaign for the White House. In their investigation, they reinforce the notion that fantasy-theme analysis is an audience-centered method.

NOTES

1. Ernest G. Bormann, "The Symbolic Convergence Theory of Communication and the Creation, Raising, and Sustaining of Public Consciousness," *The Jensen Lectures: Contemporary Communication Studies,* John I. Sisco (ed.) (Tampa: University of South Florida Press, 1983), 74.

2. Moya A. Ball, "Ernest G. Bormann: Roots, Revelations, and Results of Symbolic Convergence Theory," *Twentieth-Century Roots of Rhetorical Studies,* Jim A. Kuypers and Andrew King (eds.) (Westport, CT: Praeger, 2001), 221.

3. Sonja K. Foss, *Rhetorical Criticism: Exploration and Practice* (Prospect Heights, IL: Waveland Press, 1996), 123.

4. Ernest G. Bormann, *The Force of Fantasy: Restoring the American Dream* (Carbondale, IL: Southern Illinois University Press, 1985), 9.

5. Ernest G. Bormann, Roxann L. Knutson, and Karen Mulsof, "Why do People Share Fantasies? An Empirical Investigation of the Symbolic Communication Theory." *Communication Studies* 48 (1997): 255.

6. See, for example, William L. Benoit, Andrew A. Kluykovski, John P. McHale, and David Airne, "A Fantasy-Theme Analysis of Political Cartoons on the Clinton-Lewinsky-Starr Affair," *Critical Studies in Media Communication* 18 (2001): 377–394.

7. Ernest G. Bormann, "Fantasy and Rhetorical Vision: The Rhetorical Criticism of Social Reality, *Quarterly Journal of Speech* 58 (1972): 398.

8. Bormann, *The Force of Fantasy*, 7.

9. Benoit et al., 380.

10. Foss, 125.

11. Bormann, "Fantasy and Rhetorical Vision," 398.

12. Bormann, *The Force of Fantasy*, 8.

13. Thomas G. Endres, "Rhetorical Visions or Unmarried Mothers," *Quarterly Journal of Speech* 37 (1989): 139–141.

14. Ernest G. Bormann, "Symbolic Convergence Theory: A Communication Formulation, *Journal of Communication* 35 (1985): 133.

15. Ball, 222.

16. Bormann, "The Symbolic Convergence Theory of Communication and the Creation, Raising, and Sustaining of Public Consciousness," 72.

17. Karen A. Foss and Stephen W. Littlejohn, "*The Day After:* Rhetorical Vision in an Ironic Frame," *Critical Studies in Mass Communication* 3 (1986): 320.

18. Bormann, "Symbolic Convergence Theory: A Communication Formulation," 132.

19. Ball, 222.

20. Bormann, Knutson, and Mulsolf, 257.

21. Ernest G. Bormann, "Fantasy and Rhetorical Vision: Ten Years Later." *Quarterly Journal of Speech* 68 (1982): 134.

22. Bormann, "Symbolic Convergence Theory: A Communication Formulation," 132.

23. Ball, 221.

24. Bormann, "The Symbolic Convergence Theory of Communication and the Creation, Raising, and Sustaining of Public Consciousness," 129.

25. Bormann, "Fantasy and Rhetorical Vision: Ten Years Later," 305.

26. Robert F. Bales, *Personality and Interpersonal Behavior* (New York: Holt, Rinehart, and Winston, 1970).

27. Bormann, "Fantasy and Rhetorical Vision: Ten Years Later," 292.

28. Quoted in Robert L. Scott, "On Viewing Rhetoric as Epistemic," *Central States Speech Journal* 18 (1967): 15.

29. A recent *Chronicle of Higher Education* survey shows that Americans have extremely high confidence in higher education, ranking it with institutions such as the military and local police forces. However, this high ranking comes with criticism of tenure, affirmative action, big-time athletics, and ambiguity on the purpose of education. Americans seem to agree on the importance of general education and leadership training in colleges, while they place less value on the research role of higher education. Findings are presented in Jeffrey Selingo, "What Americans Think About Higher Education." *Chronicle of Higher Education* 49.34 (2003): A10.

30. Ernest G. Bormann, "Fantasy and Rhetorical Vision: The Rhetorical Criticism of Social Reality," 397.

31. Bormann, 398.

32. Bormann, *The Force of Fantasy*, 8.

33. Ernest G. Bormann, "Fantasy Theme Analysis and Rhetorical Theory," *The Rhetoric of Western Thought*, 5th ed., James L. Golden, Goodwin F. Berquist, and William E. Coleman (eds.) (Dubuque, IA: Kendall Hunt, 1993), 368.

34. Linda L. Putnam and George Cheney, "Organizational Communication: Historical Development and Future Directions," *Speech Communication in the 20th Century* T.W. Benson (ed.) (Carbondale, IL: Southern Illinois University Press, 1985): 146.

35. Bormann, "Fantasy and Rhetorical Vision," 406.

36. W. Richard Scott, *Institutions and Organizations* (Thousand Oaks, CA: Sage, 1995), 41.

37. W. Richard Scott, "Unpacking Institutional Arguments," *The New Institionalism in Organizational Analysis*, Walter W. Powell and Paul J. DiMaggio (eds.) (Chicago: University of Chicago Press, 1991), 181.

38. Robert A. Francesconi, "James Hunt, The Wilmington 10, and Institutional Legitimacy," *Quarterly Journal of Speech* 69 (1982): 50.

39. Bill Clinton, "2000 State of the Union," *Vital Speeches of the Day* 66 (2000): 260.

40. George W. Bush "2002 State of the Union" *Vital Speeches of the Day* 68 (2002): 260.

41. Allen B. Crow, "Higher and H-I-R-E Education," *Vital Speeches of the Day* 11 (1944): 379.

42. Allan Bloom, *The Closing of the American Mind* (New York: Simon and Schuster, 1987), 91.

43. Richard Riley, "The State of American Education," *Vital Speeches of the Day* 66 (2000): 323.

44. Bill Clinton, "1998 State of the Union," *Vital Speeches of the Day* 64 (1998): 259.

45. Robert E. Wilson, "A Businessman Looks at Higher Education," *Vital Speeches of the Day* 20 (1954): 213.

46. John Dewey, *Democracy and Education* (New York: Macmillan, 1916): 103.

47. Robert L. Spaeth, "Individualism vs. Liberal Arts Education," *Vital Speeches of the Day* 54 (1987): 24.

48. Robert Solomon and Jon Solomon, *Up the University* (Reading, MA: Addison and Wesley, 1993), 61.

49. Spaeth, 24.

50. Chaplin Tyler, "Industry and You: The Field for College Graduates," *Modern Speeches on Basic Issues* Lew Sarrett and William Trufant Foster (eds.) (Boston: Riverside Houghton Mifflin, 1939), 401.

51. Robert H. Jackson, "Why a College Education?" *Modern Speeches on Basic Issues* Lew Sarrett and William Trufant Foster, (eds.) (Boston: Riverside Houghton Mifflin, 1939), 401.

52. A study conducted by the Lumina Foundation for Education ranked schools by how selective and affordable they are for average students from low income families. The study concluded that nearly all private and most four year public institutions are "too selective" or "too costly." Such a conclusion reveals a general belief that college ought to be widely accessible and affordable. For a discussion of the study see Stephen Burd, "Report on College Access Angers Private Institutions." *Chronicle of Higher Education* 48.19 (2002): A27. See also Sara Hebel, "Poll Shows Value Americans Place on a College Education," *Chronicle of Higher Education* 46.36 (2000): A38. This article presents a public opinion survey prepared by Public Agenda which finds that "Most Americans now believe that there cannot be too many people going to college" (A38).

53. The Higher Education Research Institute at UCLA conducts annual nationwide surveys of the attitudes and aspirations of incoming freshmen. In the Fall of 2000, for example, this well known study found that 70 percent of freshmen identified the ability to make more money as a reason for going to college, and 71 percent identified training for a career as a reason for attending college. Results were published in Thomas Bartlett, "Freshmen Pay, Mentally and Physically, as They Adjust to Life in College." *Chronicle of Higher Education* 48.21 (2002): A35–A37. In a national poll on diversity in higher education by the Ford Foundation, 85 percent of voters felt that it was very important for education to provide basic skills and 72 percent felt that career training was very important. Results are available at www.pbs.org/als/race/media/poll.

54. The Higher Education Research Institute at UCLA also conducts a national survey of faculty attitudes. In their 1998–1999 findings, 70 percent of faculty saw the purpose of higher education as preparation for employment and 99 percent thought it was important for students to learn to think clearly. Results are published in Denise K Maguer, "The Graying Professoriate" *Chronicle of Higher Education* 46.2 (1999): A18–A21.

55. Jackson, 59

56. James M. Rosser, "Universal Access and Entrance and Exit Requirements," *Vital Speeches of the Day* 47 (1981): 368.

57. Robert A. Lutz, "The Higher Education System," *Vital Speeches of the Day* 62 (1996): 651.

58. Homer Rainey, "Are Too Many Youth Going to High School and College?" *Vital Speeches of the Day* 5 (1939): 461.

59. Bill Clinton, "A Bridge to the Future," *Vital Speeches of the Day* 62 (1996): 707.

60. John A. Howard, "Ennobling Obligations," *Vital Speeches of the Day* 54 (1987): 317.

61. Ralph Ketcham, "A Rationale for Civic Education," *Current* (November 1992): 12.

62. Derek Bok, "The Social Responsibilities of American Universities," *Representative American Speeches* 64.6 (1992): 114.

63. Harold Willis Dodds, "The Cultivation of Individual Excellence," *Vital Speeches of the Day* 15 (1949): 555

64. Dodds, 555.

65. Glenn Frank, "The Critical Function in Democracy," *Modern Eloquence*, Vol. 7 Ashley H. Thorndike (ed.) (New York: PF Collier and Son, 1936), 199.

66. Robert M. Hutchins, "What is a University," *Modern Speeches on Basic Issues*, Lew Sarrett and William Trufant Foster (eds.) (Boston: Riverside Houghton Mifflin, 1939), 56.

67. Frank, 202.

68. John Rodden, "But Professor, What are the Humanities For?" *Vital Speeches of the Day* 68 (2002): 346.

69. Bloom, 64.

70. Woodrow Wilson, "The American College," *Modern Short Speeches,* James Milton O'Neill (ed.) (New York: Century, 1923), 203.

71. Wilson, 204.

72. Solomon and Solomon, 89.

73. Hutchins, 51

74. Harold Willis Dodds, "The Art of Living," *Modern Eloquence,* Vol. 7, Ashley H. Thorndike (ed.) (New York: PF Collier and Son, 1936), 137.

75. Willard C. Butcher, "Applied Humanities," *Vital Speeches of the Day* 56 (1990): 623.

76. Annual surveys of faculty by the Higher Education Research Institute at UCLA indicate that more interaction between students and faculty outside the classroom is a rising priority. The HERI has observed a steady increase in this desire for community since its inception. Findings of the survey are discussed in Robin Wilson, "A Kinder, Less Ambitious Professoriate," *Chronicle of Higher Education* 49.11 (2002): A10–A11. See also "Students Embrace the Internet, but Not as a Replacement to Classrooms, Study Finds," *Chronicle of Higher Education* 49.5 (2002): A47, which discusses a survey sponsored by Pew Charitable Trusts' Pew Internet and American Life Project. In the study, 79 percent of the respondents said the internet had a positive impact on their classes, but most did not see it as a replacement for traditional classes.

77. Although a much higher number of faculty in the Higher Education Research Institute's annual surveys link higher education with career preparation, a significant number in 1998–1999 recognized that higher education could be important for character development (57.5 percent), building commitment to community service (36.2 percent), and preparation for responsible citizenship (60 percent). And, only 26.7 percent agreed that the chief benefit of college is to increase earning power. Results for 1998–1999 are presented in Denise K Maguer, "The Graying Professoriate," *Chronicle of Higher Education* 46.2 (1999): A 18–A21.

78. Freshmen in the Higher Education Research Institute's studies have also indicated recognition of communal utilitarianism. In the fall of 2000, for example, 32 percent identified becoming a community leader as a reason for attending college, and 42 percent wanted to become cul-

tured. Results are presented in Thomas Bartlett, "Freshmen Pay, Mentally and Physically, as they Adjust to Life in College," *Chronicle of Higher Education* 48.21 (2002): A35–A37. The findings of the 2001 HERI freshman study indicated that students may not be interested in politics, but they do wish to make a difference in their local communities. Findings are presented in Alex P. Kellogg, "Looking Inward, Freshmen Care Less About Politics and More about Money," *Chronicle of Higher Education* 47.20 (2001): A47, A50. Again, although overshadowed by career training, 56 percent of voters in the Ford Foundation's survey on diversity in higher education felt that preparing for effective civic participation and leadership was very important for colleges. Results are available at http://www.pbs.org/als/race/media/poll.

79. John F. Roche, *The Colonial Colleges in the War for American Independence* (New York: Associated Faculty Press, 1986), 73.

80. James B. Conant, "Education For American Democracy," *Vital Speeches of the Day* 4 (1938): 420.

81. Harold R. Logan "A Case for Preserving Higher Education," *Vital Speeches of the Day* 50 (1984): 287.

82. Bormann, *The Force of Fantasy,* 3.

83. Bok, "The Social Responsibilities of American Universities," 109–110.

84. Spaeth, 24.

85. Robert A. Nisbet, *The Quest for Community* (New York: Oxford University Press, 1971), 9.

86. Nisbet, 25.

87. Nisbet, 10.

88. Derek Bok, "Reclaiming the Public Trust," *Current* (November 1992): 7.

89. G. P. Mohrmann, "An Essay on Fantasy Theme Criticism, *Quarterly Journal of Speech* 68 (1982): 111.

90. Mohrmann, 131.

91. Ernest G. Bormann, "Fantasy and Rhetorical Vision: Ten Years Later," *Quarterly Journal of Speech* 68 (1982): 292.

92. Benoit et al., 379.

93. The authors of this chapter are ultimately responsible for compiling this list. However, we are grateful to Dr. Bormann himself for providing his suggestions.

CHAPTER TWELVE

THE MYTHIC PERSPECTIVE

JANICE HOCKER RUSHING

THOMAS S. FRENTZ

If you are like most people, you probably already have lots of experience with myths. Perhaps a parent read you fairy tales when you were young; maybe you found the war stories from the *Iliad* and the *Odyssey* exciting when you were older; or possibly you were enchanted by the film *The Princess Bride,* or even by television series such as *Hercules, Xena: Warrior Princess,* or *Buffy the Vampire Slayer.* But experiencing myths is one thing, writing *mythic criticism* is another.

Basically, mythic criticism means using myths, as well as theories about them, to understand communicative events. If you have read published essays of mythic criticism, you may think this is a formidable set of skills to acquire. We think, however, that anyone with the motivation and resolve to give it a try can learn to do mythic criticism. We also think it helps if you are "called," like Luke Skywalker was when Obi Wan Kenobi first appeared to him. If you accept this call, you will embark upon a journey complete with challenging quests, potentials and pitfalls, ritual tutors and, if you're lucky, some personal insights.

We thought it might be interesting to speak about mythic criticism as if you have been called to such a journey. Now if we get real here, your "call" may simply be an assignment to write a mythic criticism; and if you want to complete the course successfully, you'll have to accept it. Whatever! One way to hear this call is to put yourself in the shoes of "Jane," our mythical heroine, who, like many such heroes, is what Kris Kristofferson once called "a walking contradiction, partly truth and partly fiction."[1] That is, as storytellers we take some liberties in developing her character, but she's based on a real person, and she goes through many of the trials our students have gone through on this path called "mythic criticism." We are her tutors, like Merlin for King Arthur, Kyle Reese for Sarah Conner, or Karl Rove for George W. Bush. That doesn't mean that we know all there is to know about being mythic critics, it just means that we've been down this road before. We tell this story in the voice of Tom, who tends more toward the dramatic in public than does Janice, although she often sets up his best lines, like Paul Schafer does for David Letterman.

At any rate, we develop ourselves and Jane as characters on a journey, because all myths have such characters. And we divide the quest, or the plot, into three phases—"Departure," "Initiation," and "Return"—mimicking those that mythologist Joseph Campbell finds present in myths about the hero. This way, you can see myths in action—not only in the critical essay we offer on *The Matrix*, but also in this chapter as a whole.

So let's get started, and see where this Yellow Brick Road leads.

DEPARTURE

I am just spreading the paper napkins for our microwaved lunch when Janice walks in from her Rhetorical Criticism class.

"So Janice. Have you analyzed your last fantasy theme?"

"We certainly did," she answers with a tired smile. "We just 'chained out' all over *Blade Runner*."

"That's a weird choice! What could fantasy-theme analysis possibly have to say about that?"

"Well, they had a lot of fun with the 'character' fantasy type—especially the obsession with *eyes*."

"Oh, I get it," I start to perk up. "'Eyes, I just do *eyes*.' 'Not an easy man to *see* . . . I guess.' 'I've *seen* things you people wouldn't believe. Attack ships on fire off the shoulder of Orion. I've watched C-beams. . . .'"

"Get a new movie," Janice cuts me off before I get fully revved. Since this film came out, a lot of my conversation is replicant speak. And the movie debuted in 1982.

"So what's next?" I ask, conceding to her preference for human talk.

"Our stuff," she answers. "I begin 'myths to critique by' next week."

"And that must mean that Jane's coming in for spring training."

"You got it. But since this is a form of criticism that you supposedly know something about, why don't you hang around and help for a change?" Janice says, trapping me with a turkey sandwich.

Jane is an honors student with a double major in English and Communication. Like most honors students, she has this irritating habit of actually wanting *to learn* what is being taught in her classes. Before Janice begins any new unit in criticism, Jane makes an appointment for an "overview." What she really wants is extended time to ask all those annoying questions that garner her evil looks from students who just want to get on with it. Because Jane is quirky, bright, and possessed of a wonderful set of critical sensibilities, Janice indulges her. And now, apparently, so will I.

I hear an insistent knock on Janice's door and, sure enough, there's Jane—right on time.

"Come on in," Janice says, "you remember Tom from the film course you took two semesters ago?"

"Yeah, sure," she says, shooting me an 'I'm-not-sure-why-you're-here' glance as she grabs a fistful of our WOW potato chips.

Jane's a piece of work. There's an odd symmetry to her. The right side of her hair is a hot pink buzz cut, while the left sports a wild mass of lime green curls. She balances the Medusa side with three thin, silver rings through her right eyebrow. This creates a sort of diagonal line down her face, as my eye travels from the lime green to the three silver things and back again. "I think she's trying to make a statement here," I catch myself thinking, as I silently hum the line in the song from the old musical, *Bye-Bye Birdie:* "Kids these days. Why can't they be like we were, perfect in every way, oh what's the matter with kids, today?" But in most ways, there's nothing at all the matter with Jane, today or any other day. She's just being, well, just being Jane.

"So Dr. Jan, what's up next?"

"Mythic criticism."

"What's that?"

"That's where we'll try to generate some nonobvious insights into a text by using myths as our interpretive framework. You know—we've tried to do this with situations, classical modes of rhetorical proofs, narratives, the strange and wonderful world of Kenneth Burke, genres, and just today through fantasy themes. Myths just give us another way to unlock the communicative secrets of texts," Janice leads off.

"So—what do you mean by 'myths'?" Jane prods. "You mean, like Zeus and Venus and all that?"

Time for me to earn my keep. "Sure. Myths are just big stories," I say, knowing that's not going to satisfy her.

"Sorry Dr. Tom, but we've already done big stories. They're called narratives. Are we simply splitting semantic hairs here?" she asks, with a bit of an edge.

"No," Janice replies, trying to repair my *Sesame Street* opening. "All myths are narratives, but not all narratives are myths. If you say to me, 'today I got up at 6:30, brushed my teeth, took a shower, ate breakfast, read the paper, and came to school,' that's a brief narration of your first few hours. But that's not a myth. See, myths are long-enduring stories, often anonymously created, that dramatize a culture's deepest beliefs and dilemmas. They tell of origins and destinies, are filled with heroes and villains, and educate the young into the society's values. So when Tom says, 'myths are just big stories,' that's probably what he had in mind," she concludes.

Jane still looks unconvinced, so Janice presses on a bit. "Remember Tom's film class?"

"Vaguely."

"Do you recall watching *Meshes of the Afternoon,* the great American *avant garde* film by Maya Deren?"

"That bizarre movie with lots of keys and big flowers? Are you saying *that* was a myth?" Jane looks puzzled, but intrigued.

"Not exactly," Janice cautions, "although it certainly has mythic elements in its dreamlike form and evocative symbols. The reason I brought it up is that Deren once defined myth for her close friend, Joseph Campbell, as 'facts of the mind made manifest in a fiction of matter.'[2] This suggests that although myths are at least partially fictional, they also tell us something 'factual' about the state of our minds. In fact, Campbell goes on to say that we misunderstand the communicative functions of myth when we expect them to tell us 'truths' about the objective world in which we live. Myths can tell us 'truths' all right, but they're truths about our psyches, our interior minds, not about our historical conditions."

"OK—I got it." A light bulb seems to go off over Jane's head. "That's why people are always writing things like, 'Four Myths of Mental Health Care,' or 'Five Myths of the Perfect Marriage.' When we think that narratives should accurately represent the outside world, and then discover that they don't, we call them 'myths,' by which we mean 'falsities' or 'lies.' Right?"

"Absolutely," we say in unison. "And that's why myths are so often placed in opposition to science, which *is* supposed to represent accurately the outside world," Janice adds.

"So that's the reason people dump on myths? Because they don't accurately represent external reality?"

Janice and I look at each other, knowing it's time to introduce "the big one"—the aspect of myth that really sets academics off.

"Yes, but there's a little more to it than that," I begin slowly. "Some people believe that myths are oppressive because they legitimate existing power structures or privilege one group at the expense of another. Although the American frontier myth is, on the one hand, an inspiring story of American optimism and adventure, it has, on the other hand, justified the genocide of countless Native American peoples. It celebrates freedom and rugged individualism, but it also is still used to defend bully-ish foreign policies and irresponsible management of natural resources."

"And myths can gloss over important differences in social class, gender, and race, implying that 'one story fits all,'" Janice interjects. "To take another example, the 'self-made man' myth teaches that in America, you can 'pull yourself up by your bootstraps' and get rich if you just work hard enough and have a few breaks. But the reality is, those 'breaks' are much more likely to come your way if you're a white male from a 'good family' who puts you in 'good schools' than if you're an African American female born into poverty. The 'self-made man' usually has quite a bit of help from his friends."

"And just to make things even more complicated," I add, "myths are sometimes self-effacing."

"What on earth do you mean by that?" Jane demands, showing no tendencies whatsoever toward self-effacement herself.

"He means that they hide the fact that they're 'myths' and not 'reality,'" Janice explains. "Check out some of Roland Barthes's fascinating little essays on myths in 1950s French culture. He writes about everyday activities, like wrestling and travel, and texts, like advertisements for soap and margarine, as 'mythic' because they present things that have a cultural *history* as if they were timeless and 'natural'—'just the way things are.' Like, who's to say that the only landscapes that are 'scenic' are ones with lots of vertical variations? How come plains are not interesting and don't get good press? It's travel guidebooks that do this, he suggests, and that notion is all tied up with mountains having come over time to signify religious experience. But mountaintops aren't just 'naturally' spiritual. It's their mythic history—how they're *represented* in language—that associates them with God."[3]

"So whenever you discover people talking about what's 'natural' or 'essential', like when we say, 'women are naturally more nurturing than men,' you might want to ask if there are myths that support that belief and also erase the fact that they are myths," I summarize with a flourish.

"Geez," Jane says, "are myths good for *anything?*"

"Well, many people think they are," I say. "Mythologists like Joseph Campbell and depth psychologists such as C. G. Jung think that myths can give us important information about the cultural psyche, information that's easy to miss if we don't believe that cultures have any inner life, or if we discount myths because they don't do what science does or because they can be oppressive. We have found this analogy between myths and dreams to be useful: *Dreams are to the personal unconscious what myths are to the cultural unconscious.* Dreams and myths—often depreciated as trivial—can tell us something valuable about ourselves. Of course, the authors of a mythic text, such as a speech or a film, get the chance to shape it more than you do your dreams, so the analogy between dreams and myths isn't perfect. There is a conscious element to many mythic expressions that you don't find in dreams."[4]

"Well, going back to that analogy, do you mean that myths, like dreams, bring up all that Freudian sex and aggression stuff?" Jane asks.

"Sure, they can," Janice explains. "Critics can use a Freudian or Lacanian perspective to show how a text reveals something about the unconscious at the same time as it conceals it. That is, its symbols express a wish for sexual or aggressive gratification—that's the 'Id' talking—but they also distort this wish so that our conscious minds won't recognize it. Check out some of film critic Vivian Sobchack's work, like this great piece called "The Virginity of Astronauts," where she argues that although it seems like sex is missing from most science fiction films, it's there if you 'read between the lines,' so to speak. It's just that it's projected onto the aliens and into space."[5]

"Really?" Jane's getting interested. "I'm not sure I buy that." I noticed she was taking down the reference in her notebook.

"But mythic texts can also bring up more than the Id," I pick up the thread. "If Campbell and Jung are right that some myths have universal or 'archetypal' symbols, then they express meanings that originate in the collective unconscious as psychic potentials, not merely those that are repressed because they are socially taboo. Such myths can point the way to cultural growth and individual self-actualization because these psychic potentials represent moral possibilities for a culture. However, that can only happen if they are interpreted carefully and acted upon consciously."

"Whoaaa, that's pretty heavy. I'm not sure I follow you. Can you put this in English?" Jane asks.

"Well," Janice hesitates, and I can tell she's scrolling through the countless bibliographic references on her mental hard drive. "Did you ever see Stanley Kubrick's film *The Shining?* Way back in the 1980s, Robert Davies, James Farrell, and Steven Matthews did an overlooked piece of criticism on it that really opened it up for me. They argued from a Jungian perspective that the Overlook Hotel was Jack Torrance's psyche, and that he represented the typical Western tendency to work real hard (remember the 'self-made man myth'), to concentrate only on his conscious self, and to ignore everything that was going on in his unconscious."[6]

"Which was considerable," I throw in. "Remember Danny Torrance's friend Tony?" I crook my index finger and croak, "Redrum, redrum!"

"Yeah!" Jane says, "and that horrible woman in that hotel room. . ."

"Room 237," Janice recalls with a shudder. "She was Jack's *anima,* or unrecognized 'feminine side.' Anyway, these critics think the movie made a compelling case that our culture needs to balance its one-sided focus on *progress* with attention to our unconscious, or we'll end up like Jack at the end."

"Heeerrree's *Johnny!!!*" I grin in my best demonic Jack Nicholson imitation.

"OK, I think I get you," Jane says, her light bulb glowing. "Myths or mythic texts can actually help us to face things we need to face in order to be more, more . . ."

"Whole," Janice fills in. She likes that word, perhaps a tad too much.

"That seems important. But it also seems important to be suspicious of myths because they can lie or oppress people. I'm confused," Jane complains.

"Well, you aren't alone," Janice says. "Many mythic theorists and critics tend toward one 'camp' or the other—they *either* think we should ruthlessly unmask myths because they distort, lie, and oppress, or they think of myths as psychological or spiritual revelations from 'the other side' that are crucial for living a meaningful life."

Jane mulls that one over a bit, polishes off the last of our WOWs, and then ventures somewhat cautiously, "It sounds to me like some myths are tied up with religion somehow."

"Well, all myths have a 'religious' or 'sacred' dimension, in the sense that they provide meaning for those who believe them," I clarify.

"But the question for a critic is whether this meaning provided by the myth is oppressive or liberating," Janice pushes the ambiguity a bit further.

"Well, which is it?" Jane demands. She always seems to want the bottom line on complex questions before she opens up to multiple perspectives.

"Both," Janice says with finality.

"So is there at least a list somewhere of Important Myths Rhetorical Critics Should Know? I mean, I don't know all that many myths. Give me a handout," Jane taunts.

"Well, I don't exactly have a handout," Janice looks pained; she is prone to "Bad Teacher" dreams, and I figure I'd better rescue her quick.

"There isn't any great list in the sky," I say. "But there are some helpful places to turn.[7] A great reference book is Mark Morford and Robert Lenardon's

Classical Mythology if you want to know all about the Greeks and Romans. Or if you want to know specifically about *hero* myths, Campbell says that most myths about a hero . . ."

"Which would be most myths," Janice says, relieved.

"Yeah, most myths about heroes conform to the same general structure, which he calls a *monomyth*. This structure—a plot line really—unfolds in three phases: *Departure,* in which the hero-to-be is 'called' to a quest and leaves home; *Initiation,* in which the hero endures trials, dangers, and often captivity as a prelude to acquiring wisdom; and *Return,* when the hero comes back to share his or her newfound wisdom or 'boon' with the family, tribe, or culture."[8]

"Now there are endless spin-offs on this general structure," I continue, going for the Gold. "In her helpful book, *The Hero and the Perennial Journey Home in American Film,* Susan Mackey-Kallis identifies three variations. *Creation/recreation myths* tell of origins—of the cosmos, of our earth, and of people and creatures. Mackey-Kallis sees films like *2001: A Space Odyssey, The Lion King,* and *Contact* as falling within this pattern. She also speaks of *coming-of-age myths,* which chart different kinds of human initiation—from child to adolescent, adolescent to adult, adult to elder, and even elder to ashes. Films like *The Natural, Bull Durham, Thelma & Louise,* and *The Piano* are cast in this vein. Finally, she identifies *the grail myth,* which tells of redemption from evil, sin, or death. The King Arthur legends epitomize this variant, as do aspects of Christ's journey and, somewhat transparently, films like *Indiana Jones and the Last Crusade.*"[9]

While I take a deep breath, Janice continues our musing on good myths to know.

"Now many myths fit nicely under Mackey-Kallis's three variations of the monomyth, but we can identify at least three more that seem particularly relevant to American culture. First, there are the myths of romantic love that chart the agonies and ecstasies of erotic intimacy. These include classic love stories like 'Eros and Psyche,' 'Tristan and Isolde,' 'Romeo and Juliet,' updated film versions like *West Side Story,* and all the variations found in daytime soap operas. We even examined James Cameron's *Titanic* in terms of how the romantic love myth clashed with its myth of technological progress."[10]

"Then there's the American frontier myth," Janice perseveres. "We've already spoken of the potential of this tale to legitimate environmental irresponsibility and American colonization, but there are many variations as the myth evolves. In 1983, I argued that, during the 'Urban Cowboy' era, the western hero was forced into artificiality when his scene got transposed from the open range to the city. Later I traced how, once the land-based frontier has been settled and civilized, the myth simply continues in space, especially in films like *Star Wars* and the *Alien* series. Even though the infinity of space seems more conducive to spiritual wisdom than environmental exploitation, the frontier myth often prefers 'search and destroy' to 'search,' and simply continues to colonize and exploit planets and moons in outer space."[11]

"Hey," I chime in, "I'm feeling left out here. Let's turn to *our* stuff for a moment. For us, a mythic motif that is especially relevant to today's world involves technological progress, what has been called 'The Frankenstein Myth.' This story tells of the gradual separation of humans from their tools up to and even beyond the point where the tools become free from human control. Born in the ancient myth of Prometheus, who stole fire (the root of technology) from the gods, through Mary Shelley's *Frankenstein*, and up through countless films, like *The Terminator* trilogy, *The Matrix* trilogy, and *A.I.*, this story continues to evolve in our cultural psyche."[12]

"We think this myth is important because it expresses our ambivalence about all the technology we think we can't do without," Janice elaborates. "On the one hand, we love it—think of all those cool gadgets James Bond uses, like a cigarette that knocks out his enemy with a puff of gas. But we're also really scared of it."

"I'll be back," I say in my best Arnold Schwarzenneger impression.

Jane is writing furiously now, looking a bit like a cyborg herself.

"Now," I continue, "Robert Jewett and John Shelton Lawrence offer an intriguing twist on Campbell's monomythic structure. They note that in the American version of the monomyth, the hero starts out *separated* from family, tribe, or community; *comes into these groups* to save them from some peril; but then *leaves again* to be on his own (it is usually a 'his' here). Although this structure is not at all limited to the western genre, countless American westerns do honor it. Think of *Shane, High Noon, The Magnificent Seven,* and *High Plains Drifter,* just to name a few. Apparently, the American monomyth prefers its heroes to be iconoclastic individuals rather than civic-minded community leaders. Lawrence and Jewett expose how the American monomyth forsakes democracy and prefers a superhero who'll get the job done *for* us."[13]

"Almost all of your examples come from film. So is mythic criticism limited to movies?" Jane asks reasonably.

"Absolutely not," Janice jumps back in. "Like Mackey-Kallis, we happen to be interested in films, but other forms of public address can clearly be interpreted mythically. Take Martin Luther King's 'I Have a Dream' speech, for example. Almost everybody can recognize how he brilliantly tries to expand the myth of the American Dream to include his race. Or look at what Walter Fisher does with the American Dream in political elections, or John Arthos does with Louis Farrakhan's use of the shaman–trickster myth in the Million Man March, or what Randall Lake does with notions of mythic time in Native American Protest Rhetoric. Or you can analyze magazine articles mythically, as Farrel Corcoran does with news magazine stories about Soviet funerals, or . . ."[14]

"OK, I think I've got a vague inkling of what myth is, but I've got a paper to write. *What's mythic criticism?*" she demands, cutting us no slack, even though the lunch "hour" has come and gone forty minutes ago.

This has been invigorating, but Jane is younger than Janice or me and the old folks are wilting here. Somebody's got to end this deal.

"How about we take a breather," I say, instituting what I hope to be the rhetoric of goodbye. "Why don't you go to Janice's class next week, read the examples on the syllabus and then come back if you want, and we'll take up that question."

INITIATION

Exactly one week later, I'm unpacking Janice's battered, but still functioning, NFL lunchbox. A colleague of ours gave that to her back in 1984 as consolation for all the football talk she had to endure when the departmental rhetoricians gathered for lunch. Janice knows absolutely nothing about the NFL, but she inexplicably regards this lunchbox as a priceless treasure.

"Don't nuke the lunches just yet," she cautions. "Jane's on her way up the stairs and she's carrying a big brown paper sack."

"And that can only mean we're about to begin 'Round 2' on mythic criticism?"

Jane walks in without knocking, sporting an ensemble that blends at least three contradictory life styles. "Lunch!" she announces triumphantly, ripping open the bag, passing out giant Snickers bars to me and a bag of baby carrots to Janice. "OK now, listen up. I've got to write this mythic criticism paper, and I'm lost."

"Didn't you pay attention in class?" I chide her.

"Probably as much as you ever did," Jane says.

"Well," Janice begins, "how does a piece of criticism usually start?"

"With some mystery or anomaly in a text that my review of the literature can't make go away," Jane answers dutifully.

"Guess there's a reason why you're an honors student," I say.

"Yeah, well, sure, I've got plenty of questions about movies and politics and rock music, and so forth, but how do I know when some *mythic* approach will help to unscramble my intrigue?"

"That's a great question," Janice says. Always begin with positive reinforcement, she maintains, but somehow I've never gotten the hang of it. "Sometimes the text makes overt references to a myth. If a movie's name is *Excalibur* or *Merlin*, it's pretty obvious we're dealing with mythic material here. Or, as in one of my favorites—*The Princess Bride*—the title tells you up front it's going to be a fairy tale."

"'My name ees Imigo Montoya. You keelled my father, prepare to die,'" I say, rolling my Rs quite impressively, if I must say so myself.

"Later," Janice replies, refusing to get distracted. "The question is, are the mythic elements so up-front as to present no problem for you to explore, in which case you probably don't have a criticism, or is there something puzzling that a criticism will help you work out? With this movie, does it make any difference that the fairy tale is book-ended by the old man reading the story to his grandson? Or that the usual themes of romance and adventure are presented comically?"

"Or you may just have a fragment that gets you started," I offer, "an allusion to a myth but not the whole thing. Like when George W. Bush said of Osama bin Laden that he wanted him, 'Dead or Alive.' You could ask yourself whether the Bush administration reacted to September 11th in other ways that recall the mentality of the Old West—act decisively, shoot straight, and take 'em out."

"'A man's gotta do what a man's gotta do'?" Jane gets into the act.

"Precisely," Janice replies. "Or you could be dealing with a text that is another episode in a myth that is still evolving, so you want to show what this latest installment says about where the culture is now. Take a look at how Karen Rasmussen and Sharon Downey analyze Vietnam War films such as *Platoon* and *Full Metal Jacket.* They deal with a long history of war mythology in America, but show how it gets subverted in films about this war. Or, consider what Constance Penley has to say about *The Terminator* and *La Jetée*—she thinks both films use the time-travel theme of science fiction to develop that technology myth we mentioned earlier; these films comment on how our dependence on technology could bring about an apocalyptic future."[15]

"Maybe you sense that one of those large mythic themes we talked about last week is present, and you want to see how this text acts it out," I add. "Perhaps you think *Fight Club* is a coming-of-age myth, and you want to explore what kind of lessons it teaches about what it means to be a 'man' in a super-materialistic society."

"Hmm," Jane muses. "You mean, like, what did it mean that that Edward Norton character was so interested in buying all the perfect things and then his apartment building got blown up?"

"Yeah," I say, getting excited. "That might have something to do with the materialistic aspect of the American Dream myth."

"You might have two myths going here," I add. "The American Dream and coming-of-age."

"And the Brad Pitt character . . . ."

"Tyler Durden!" Janice shouts.

"Yeah, Tyler Durden is the other guy's 'tutor' in initiating him into manhood," Jane enthuses. "I wonder what it means that he does his mentoring with his fists."

"*Voila!*" I cheer, giving Jane a thumbs-up. "You better sit right down at your PC and get started on this one."

Janice now provides the summing-up I usually do. "Any or all of these approaches might get you started. The point is that you want to show how myth functions in a text or a set of them to tell us something important we didn't know. Your purpose could be to show how the myth helps make this text persuasive. Or you could show how the text employs myth to make a statement about the condition of the cultural psyche—remember, this is how the myth functions as a collective dream. Or you might want to show how the existing power structure is reaffirmed or undermined in the text. Or maybe you do all of those things, and . . ."

"Wait, slow down, I can't write that fast," Jane implores. "Say that again—slowly."

"I thought you were an honors student," I rebuke her.

Jane smiles, forgetting her semi-alienated, counterculture pose for a moment. "This doesn't sound all that hard."

Potentials and Pitfalls

"It's actually quite fun," Janice enthuses. "Myths are inherently entertaining. They catch people up emotionally, not just intellectually—and that includes us when we act as critics, as well as when we're the audience."

"And that can be a plus or a minus," I add.

"Yeah," Jane says, "because people may get behind some horrible social policy because it's cast in mythic terms, and it's our job to point that out."

"It's very important to do that—as well as to point out how myths can enrich our lives by symbolizing possibilities we hadn't thought of," Janice says.

"Of course, there *are* pitfalls," I throw in, not wanting this to be *too* easy. "Like confusing renaming and/or retelling with interpretation."

"'Just when you thought it was safe to go back in the water,'" Jane replies wearily. "Go figure."

"That's where you just rename the characters with mythic terms and retell the text's story using mythic language, and think you've done a mythic interpretation," I expound. "For example, let's say you decide to do a mythic analysis of the film *The Empire Strikes Back.* So you say something like: 'Well, Luke Skywalker is the hero-to-be, Princess Leia is the heroine, Yoda is the spiritual mentor, and Darth Vader is the enemy. This film is a heroic initiation myth where to become a full-fledged hero, Luke must leave his friends, learn how to use the Force from Yoda, get captured and suffer, break free and defeat Darth Vader, and finally save his friends.' Can you see how this 'mythic analysis' doesn't really do much more than rename the characters and retell the story in mythic language?"

"Yeah I can see that," Jane nods, "but how can I be sure I'm not just doing this renaming, retelling thing?"

"The best way," Janice cuts back in, "is to talk through your idea with someone before you write. You'd be amazed what can occur to you in the midst of a good conversation."

"Or, as a second choice, have someone read what you've written," I say. "If you've just reworked the characters and story using mythic terms, your reader, if she or he is being honest with you, might say something like, 'Yeah, so? What's the point?' Take those kinds of reactions as signs that you've done more categorizing than analyzing."

"If, on the other hand," Janice continues, "your reader says something like, 'Really? Huh, I never thought of that,' this should tell you that you've teased your reader with something that s/he didn't see, and that what you've said is intriguing enough to check what you've said against the text. If you get that kind of response, hand the paper in."

"Just a sec," Jane says. "Are there some texts that simply resist a mythic interpretation—no matter how intriguing I find them?"

"Sure," I reply. "Some texts are just better analyzed using another perspective; maybe there aren't any discernible references to myth."

"And it would be challenging, if not impossible, to use myth to analyze a text that is trying to undermine conventional narrative structure," Janice amplifies. What could you do with *Pulp Fiction,* for example, or the film *Momento,* which both try to tear down the way we normally think stories unfold?"

"Or disco music," I contribute, "which imitates the beat of techno-culture, but doesn't have a story line?"

"So what do you do then?" Jane asks.

"Nothing," I laugh. "Turn those over to critics whose specialty is interpreting anti-structure."

"Unless you want to show how these texts work to *undermine* myth. But that's probably too complicated."

"Fair enough," Jane answers, grabbing her backpack. "Can you guys give me an example or two of mythic criticism that I can use as a model of what I should be trying to do? Anything come to mind?"

Janice and I look at each other. Jane seems initiated enough into her journey into the heart of mythic criticism for something a bit challenging. Janice rummages on her bookshelves and pulls out a reprint of a recent essay we wrote.

"Here," she says, "see what you can make of this. It's from *Critical Studies in Media Communication*, on the 1999 film *The Matrix*."[16]

"Good choice," I say. "It should illustrate some of the things we've been talking about—it relies somewhat on Campbell's monomyth, it's an episode in the still-evolving myth of technology, and it deals with both the psychological and the ideological aspects of that myth."

"You may have to enter the 'belly of the whale,' as Campbell says, but you'll fight your way out," Janice cautions.

"Geez, thanks," Jane says, "that was a cool film."

"'Guns . . . lots of guns,'" I drone in my best Keanu Reeves zombified monotone.

"Can we talk about this next week?" Jane asks, ignoring me.

"Why not?" Janice and I say.

"But let's bring our own lunches," I add, feeling suddenly a little queasy about my next class.

The next week at lunchtime, I'm expecting Jane to pop in, and I'm secretly looking forward to it.

"Something's up," Janice says. "Jane was quiet and sullen in class today, and that's not her style."

As if cued to prove Janice right, Jane slouches in, tosses the reprint on Janice's desk, and slumps down in her chair. "All right. You guys win. If you gave me this article to put me on a 'road of trials,' it worked. I thought I left here last week with a pretty decent grasp of what mythic criticism was all about, but this thing is damn near incomprehensible! Myths I've never heard of, theories about male gazes, mothers as mathematical grid systems, something called *puers* and *puellas* . . . I'm sorry, but this example has put me back to ground zero," she concludes in defeat.

Janice and I just sit there. Big mistake. At the end of last week's session, we were both tired and, with too little thought, gave her something that was written for academic professionals, not beginning students of rhetorical criticism. Now it looks as if our own insensitivity has undone all our good deeds.

"Don't you have something simpler?" she asks a bit more softly. "I'm sorry I said those things about your work, but I was just so frustrated."

"Look," Janice soothes, "it's our fault, not yours. Sometimes professors just lose sight of how tedious their published stuff can be—even when it's on 'fun' texts like *The Matrix*. We'll rework this piece so that you can understand it, and maybe even use it as a model for your own piece of mythic criticism. Is that fair?"

"So how long do you figure it will take you to dumb this one down?" Jane asks, still not sure there isn't a professorial conspiracy against hard-working students like herself.

"We don't need to 'dumb anything down' for you," Janice insists. "We'll just streamline the analysis a bit so that you can see how this perspective works, OK?"

"Two weeks?"

"Two weeks," Janice promises.

As Jane leaves, I turn to Janice. "What could you possibly have been thinking? How are you going to have time to rewrite that article!?"

"I'm not," Janice smiles. "You are. I'll do the second draft, of course, but if I'm teaching the class, the least you can do is supply the examples. Besides, this article needs your 'essential self.'"

"And that would be?" I ask.

"Total transparency."

"Be afraid, be *very* afraid." But I exit with the reprint clutched tightly in hand, knowing 'a man's gotta do what a man's gotta do.'

Two weeks later, here's what we give Jane:

CRITICAL ESSAY: MYTH AND SPECTACLE IN *THE MATRIX*

When would-be hero Neo finally meets his mentor Morpheus in 1999's heavily hyped film, *The Matrix*, Morpheus offers him the choice of a blue pill or a red one. If he takes the blue, he will wake up the next morning having conveniently forgotten they ever met. If he downs the red, his familiar reality will be shattered forever as he enters a totally alien world. Although as critics we like to regard ourselves as open-minded, we now think we saw the film initially through the comforting haze of the "blue pill." As many know, the story line tells of a computer-generated reality that programs people's minds to live out a virtual, pacified existence while their bodies lie captive, hidden from awareness, reduced to battery cells that recharge the computers. We must have replicated this internal plot in our viewings. Just as the sleeping people within the Matrix see only their virtual existence while remaining blind to their embodied slavery, we too, sitting captivated in our snug theatre seats, were initially so benumbed by the visual style of this film that we failed to appreciate an important mythic advocacy amidst the surface glitter.

Apparently, we weren't alone. Many critics deride *The Matrix* as an overwrought spectacle. Like us, they may share the guilty pleasures of an exhilarating ride, but are incensed that the film's innovative ideas get ground into narrative dust by the visual pyrotechnics of its special effects. "Part of me wants to dismiss *The Matrix* as a loud and empty spectacle, 1999's apex of dazzling technological style over substance," Andrew O'Hehir complains. "It lacks anything like adult emotion, and its themes and images arrive at a dizzying, stupefying pace, as if vomited up by some voracious creature that ate the last 20 years of sci-fi and action-movie history and only partially digested them."[17] Lisa Schwarzbaum isn't much of a fan either. "[T]he real soullessness here is built into the production . . . and groundbreaking special effects . . . *The Matrix* sells itself as a gaudy chop-socky concoction with expensive Hollywood action details—a blast of Holly-Kong glitz that never approaches the stylistic cohesiveness of, say, John Woo's *Face/Off* or the charisma of the propulsive star John Travolta."[18] And Bob Graham seems to speak for many when he says, "It's astonishing that so much money, talent, technical expertise and visual imagination can be put in the service of something so stupid. . . . So this is what more than 100 years of cinematic history has come to: special effects with no movie."[19]

But at least some see past this movie's exhibitionism toward a tale worth telling. Roger Ebert glimpses its worth despite his irritation: "It's kind of a letdown when a movie begins by redefining the nature of reality, and ends with a shoot-out. We want a leap of the imagination, not one of those obligatory climaxes with automatic weapons fire."[20] Stuart Klawans detests the excess precisely because there is substance to squander: "Like a guest at a potlatch, laughing to see his host's worldly goods go up in flames, I roared at *The Matrix*—roared and at the same time was humbled, knowing that Warner Brothers had such magnificence to burn."[21] Anthony Farrante is actually intrigued by the fractured narrative that typically draws guffaws for its retrofitted "second coming" theme: "[T]he pleasure of THE MATRIX is how complex the story really is. Once you think you've got it all figured out, it throws another surprise into your face."[22] Even O'Hehir, so disdainful of the film's brandishments, still admits to some intrigue over the plot: "[I]n a limited and profoundly geeky sense, this might be an important and generous film."[23] Perhaps there is more here, such comments suggest, than meets the eye.

Forced back to the theatre several times by honors students outraged at our dismissal of what was fast becoming a canonical text for the post-*Blade Runner* generation, we began to see a few of the geeky ways in which *The Matrix* might be profound. Eventually, we recognized that this film was extending, in some culturally significant ways, a technological myth that we and others have called the "Frankenstein complex."[24] A still-evolving tale, this myth warns of our enslavement to technology; as in Mary Shelley's original *Frankenstein*, the tools of our own making become "monstrous" and come to haunt us.[25] But in film, this same technology, materialized as spectacular visual effects, often hides the very warning implicit in the myth.[26] Our critical task is thus identical to the initiation ritual of the hero—namely, to break free from our addiction to technology and "wake up" to how dependent we have become on its devices. What Neo must do within *The Matrix* is thus a microcosm of what we must all do in everyday life to prevent becoming totally controlled by our own artifice.

Like Neo at the outset of *The Matrix*, we are already pretty well caged within our technology-defined cells. Lots of people find life on the internet much more fulfilling and exciting than anything in the clunky old world of material reality. Cell phones, once a curious novelty for the yuppie technophile, are fast evolving into pacemakers for the psyche. Look around anywhere—in supermarkets, on street corners, in the aisles of airplanes, at tables in expensive restaurants, in college classrooms, even in public restrooms. It's hard to find anybody nowadays either *not* talking on a cell phone or with one, like some handgun from the old West, strapped to his or her belt waiting for the next "beep" to trigger a quick draw. We are so intent on multitasking that we drive a car, talk on a cell phone, and listen (presumably in the other ear) to a CD. The boundaries of technological activities are blurring as well. Where once we could speak confidently of watching television or surfing the web, these two activities have now merged so that we can do either on our television set and/or our home computer. The myth of technology is not an archaic story about knights in armor, damsels in distress, and fire-breathing dragons, but rather something that impacts our daily lives in important ways.

If *The Matrix* extends the technology myth through its fragmented but innovative plot line, while at the same time it retards it through its spectacular visual effects, then it seems reasonable to place ourselves within this myth/spectacle tension and look a little more closely at what is going on. Because the myth in this movie follows quite closely the three general phases of Joseph Campbell's monomyth,[27] we use his general framework as an organizing schema. However, because the visual effects and action sequences of *The Matrix* often work against this very framework, we pause, from time to time, to examine how the cinematic technology subverts the myth of technological evolution.

Departure

The first time we see the young protagonist—"Thomas Anderson" in his day job at a computer software firm and "Neo" the notorious hacker at night—he is asleep in the depressing urban pod he calls home. The numbing ads that scroll down his computer screen suddenly give way to these stark words:

> Wake up Neo . . .
> The Matrix has you . . .
> Follow the white rabbit.

While he struggles to comprehend this strange command from nowhere, his monitor spells out, "Knock, knock, Neo," just as there is a rapping at his door. It is a be-metaled set of poster children for postmodernism enlisting his nocturnal services. Though he still struggles to shake off sleep, this doubting Thomas must already suspect something is wrong with his life picture; he retrieves a disk from a fake book entitled *Simulacra and Simulation,* as if he conceals his piracy beneath a darkly skeptical Baudrillardian cover. Warned not to get caught, Troy, the bored leader of this brat pack, hints obliviously at Neo's condition: "Yeah, I know, you don't exist." As if picking up the clue, Neo muses, "You ever have that feeling where you're not sure if you're awake or still dreaming?" Attributing it to "mescaline; it's the only way to fly," Troy persists in his *idiot savant* vein, "Hey, it just sounds to me like you may need to unplug, man. You know, get some R & R?"[28]

At first refusing an invitation to do just that, Neo reconsiders when he sees the white rabbit tattooed on the left shoulder of the woman who is draped over Troy. At this film's revision of *The Terminator*'s (1984) "Tech Noir" nightclub, a slicked-back woman-in-black confronts Neo with, "I know why you're here." Introducing herself as "Trinity," she alerts Neo that the legendary hacker whose fame he well recognizes is female. "I just thought, um . . . you were a . . . guy," he confesses, too self-contained to see past his own nose. "Most guys do," Trinity retorts. There will be many more surprises, but Neo suggests he may be up to them when he answers her query with another. Trinity whispers in his ear: "It's the question that drives us, Neo. It's the question that brought you here. You know the question, just as I did." Like the riddle put to mythic heroes such as Parsifal in his search for the Grail ("Whom does the Grail serve?"), it is only asking the right question—not having the right answer—that indicates a frame of mind receptive enough to see an alternative reality. "What is the Matrix?" he replies. "The answer is out there, Neo. It's looking for you, and it will find you—if you want it to," she responds, and with this acceptance of his "call," Neo joins the long narrative history of heroic attempts to lift the veil of technology from their eyes.

Though Neo wants to answer his own question, he will have to awake to the fact that his everyday life is only a mental construct detached from his body—a rather tall order for someone who has heretofore had little reason to question that his physical sensations were real and his analytical talents were effective. However, the senses, this film repeatedly implies, deceive and pacify. Cypher, the Judas in this tale and in digital terms the "0" to Neo's "1," knows that the taste of a juicy steak he is eating while inside the Matrix is supplied by his virtual programming, but he relishes it anyway because he decides, as many of us would, to trade in the blight of authenticity for the euphoria of illusion. Dark glasses, worn here by the freedom fighters and the mechanized agents, do more than quote *The Terminator* or *Men In Black* (1997); they shield the eyes from the mirage of the Matrix. As Thomas Anderson, Neo is upbraided by his boss for not taking his job seriously enough. This isn't really the problem, and a window washer hangs outside, cleaning Neo's view.[29] He is not yet ready to see clearly, though, and when he receives a cell phone via Fed Ex and the occult Morpheus warns him that he is in danger and must escape by leaping off his skyscraper onto a scaffold, he exclaims to himself in disbelief, "No way! No way—this is crazy!"

But, of course, it's not crazy. For when Neo finally meets Morpheus, he is told, "You have the look of a man who accepts what he sees because he's expecting to wake up." Ironically, this is not far from the truth. Neo is veiled from the truth, Morpheus explains, because he is enthralled by his own projected image which, unknown to him at this point, is merely a mental construct and not the complete self he believes it to be. "Unfortunately, no one can be told what the Matrix is," Morpheus continues, "you have to see it for yourself." "But what *is* the

Matrix?" Neo insists, and Morpheus replies, "It's the world that has been pulled over your eyes to blind you from the truth." It is Neo's initiatory task to pull that veil from his eyes.

Initiation

Meeting the Mother. Neo has no clue that his body is wrapped in a techno-placenta in a dark underworld baby ward—umbilical tentacles attaching him to what must be both his source of sustenance and theirs. Webster's locates the origins of "matrix" in the Latin *ma* for "womb," and the French *matr-* or *mater* for "mother."[30] Chad Eby notes that William Gibson uses "matrix," a synonym for cyberspace, as "mother" or "womb" in *Neuromancer,* and that "this analogy evokes a spatial feminine structure that is complete in itself—the turned on by itself parthenogenic womb . . . as the pre-oedipal 'archaic mother' . . ."[31] Similarly, James Beard says that Gibson's characters *"embrace* it erotically (after all, technophilia means 'love' of technology), even *oedipally,"* and that the main character, Case, "penetrates ('jacks in' is Gibson's pun) the 'mother'."[32]

Although it is usually coded masculine, as opposed to nature as feminine, technology as mother is not foreign to science fiction, particularly when it emphasizes humans' extreme dependence on the machine. The astronauts in *2001: A Space Odyssey* (1968), *Alien* (1979), and *Aliens* (1986) are pictured sleeping like infants in the uterine spaceship, and in *Alien* they refer to the ship's computer as "Mother." The Matrix is indeed a false mother who, as *Psycho*'s Norman Bates might say, "isn't quite herself today." As machine-made, she can't be, and she is monstrously alien because she results from the reduction of the mother's plenitude to the electronic world of "0s" and "1s".

Throughout the technology myth, the typically male hero must relate not only to his mother, but to a feminine "love interest." Everything not artificially woman is generally repressed in this myth, so it often falls to a feminine "other" to help the masculine hero to wake him up to his overdependence on technology, whether or not that technology is teamed up with a dominating "mother." That is, whatever the hero has *not* seen clearly is in the best position to help him to see now.[33] Although Trinity occupies this role of the female romantic partner, we do not think their relationship ever catches fire. If we wonder what has happened to the erotic feminine in this film, however, we need look no further than the mother Matrix herself. As the scenic backdrop for everything that isn't, this is where the action is. By contrast, what occurs in "reality" aboard the Nebuchadnezzar, unless produced by a program simulating the Matrix, is dull and bleak. The John Woo-style cadences of Neo, Trinity, Morpheus, and Agent Smith—a seamless stitchery of high technology and balletic Kung Fu—are airborne courting rituals in which the characters gaze at and repeatedly penetrate each other with bullets.[34] Myth and spectacle, often at odds in this film, merge here in a technologized mother upon which we as spectators can gaze for a visual feast of displaced erotic desire.

Descending to the Body.   At a mythic level, Neo's most urgent task is to get his body back. After self-assuredly popping the red pill Morpheus offers him, he immediately spirals down an *Alice in Wonderland* rabbit hole to Hell. Morpheus explains that it will disorient Neo's simulated programming so that the rebels can locate his body among the fields of indistinguishable pods where all bodies are encased for the keeping. As Cypher warns, "buckle your seat belt, Dorothy, 'cause Kansas is goin' bye-bye." But just before his mythic descent begins, our attention shifts to a remarkable special effect. As Neo waits for whatever is going to happen, he catches sight of himself in a cracked mirror and, fascinated by his own image, reaches out to touch it. The mirror liquefies and begins to coat him with its substance. "It's going into replication," cautions Trinity, who is monitoring Neo's vital signs; "we've got a fibrillation!" Neo's reflection seems bent on destroying its source, which is itself a simulation of the "real" Neo.[35] In like manner, we are captivated by this oozing mercurial takeover of Neo's body, a stand-in for our own, as this spectacle evokes the typical "how do they *do* that?" awe. Thus, while Neo's plight warns of humanity's technological co-optation, the technological pleasures of spectacle themselves screen us from the prophecy.

Not a moment too soon, Tank gets a connection and Neo drops out of his virtual world where people program computers into its "real" negation where computers program humans. Whereas once humans planted, raised, and harvested crops for their sustenance, in a cannibalistic inversion of the food chain, computers now puree the dead to feed newborn babies, who in turn fuel the computers. In his chilling metaphor of evolution, Agent Smith later turns the humans' "safety valve" argument—that overpopulation and ruin of one frontier justifies expansion into the next—against Morpheus. By colonizing and destroying their own environment, humans act more like viruses than like the mammals they take themselves to be. Thus humans must be supplanted by the agents' higher life form. "You are the disease . . .," he articulates with measured finality, "we are the cure."

The scene of Neo in his pod with feeding lines protruding obscenely from his spine all the way up to the back of his neck is undeniably horrific. Bolting upright in his mechanical womb, hairless and covered with natal slime, Neo takes his first look at "the real world." What he sees, and what we see, are thousands of "pod cribs" housing indistinguishable bodies that provide the computers with an endless supply of energy. Filmed with extreme long shots, from high angles, and through red-tinted filters, this is an impressively gooey technological Hell. Flashes of electricity dance among the pods, perhaps to animate the inert bodies to perform their nutritional function. A high-tech nursemaid, no doubt sensing a waking body, buzzes in, hovers over Neo, rips this problem child from his life-support lines, and flushes him down a "toilet" into a sewer far below. This is one of those scenes people remember for its high "yuck factor," like the Terminator cutting out his eyeball with an exacto knife. More than likely, we will tell our friends about this gore rather than assimilate the narrative importance of Neo's captivity. Once again, the film's spectacle competes with its mythic message. Morpheus and his crew quickly rescue Neo and land him on their ship.

Mythically, however, this scene is crucial. Neo has to get his body back if he is going to grow out of his non-seeing house of mirrors. This task reiterates the task of the traditional mythic hero, who must endure being swallowed into the "belly of the whale" or other symbols of the Devouring Mother's womb, where his former self is consumed.[36] In the Frankenstein myth, the hero's plunge is often into captivity, where he must recognize and identify with the "other"—such as an "inferior" race or gender—that he has oppressed.[37] The oppressed "other" in this part of the story is his own split-off biological, unreflected body, and he must, quite literally, get himself together.

Spiritual Mentoring. Initiation rituals correct excessive individual pride, when the elders take the novice back to the deepest level of mother-child identity, forcing a symbolic death through temporary dismemberment or dissolution, and then ceremonially rescue him. In these moments, the group acts as a kind of "second parent" at his rebirth.[38] Once back in the good mother ship, a much-atrophied Neo lies prone on a surgical gurney, every square morsel of his body pierced with needles. Although these are apparently acupuncture tools needed to summon his fragile unity back to strength, the impression is one of woundedness. He has lost his hair, mythic symbol of masculine strength, he is punctured by lesions that once bound him to the mother Matrix, and he is completely dependent upon his adoptive tribe for nourishment.

In most hero myths, the initiate undergoes prolonged and often grueling instruction from those who already possess the wisdom and skills he must acquire to accomplish the task at hand.[39] Because that task will demand inner resolve as well as outer resources, his central guides may be supernatural, or if human, they must be acquainted with the interior life of the spirit. In the Frankenstein myth, the spiritual realm is also a part of what the hero has repressed in order to progress technologically, for he has been playing God himself. Thus, his spiritual tutor commonly appears in the form of an "other," often a woman or a person of color.[40] Here, the spiritual elder is a rebellious black man whose name means, paradoxically, son of sleep and god of dreams. His name also suggests his ability to morph between two worlds, and recalls the historical Orpheus, who descends to Hell and back on his own "road of trials." Morpheus's spiritual guide in turn is an earthy, yet mystical black woman.[41] It is Morpheus's job to lift the dreamy veil of illusion from Neo's eyes.

Neo must learn how to deploy his considerable physical talents in a virtualized form. At first, Neo is completely ineffective in the sparring program Morpheus has created to mimic the Matrix because he is still relying on the Matrix's temporal and spatial *a prioris* which, as we have found, are deceptive—mother as the mythical Maya, or veil of illusion. Mid-battle, Morpheus mocks, "Come on! Stop trying to hit me and *hit* me!" With this, Neo kicks into Kung Fu warp speed, presumably by projecting all of his physical skills into his residual self-image, and by ceasing to think the way he has been programmed to think in his false reality. He freezes his fist an inch from Morpheus's face. Back at the control monitors, an awestruck Mouse whispers, "I don't believe it."

Once again, this scene in which Morpheus teaches Neo to fight with his entire being and not just his mind is central to understanding Neo's mythic quest. But once again, visual effects blunt the mythic point, for the scene unfolds as one of the film's most impressive action spectaculars. Shot in slow motion, Morpheus's and Neo's martial arts savagery is magically transformed into something resembling an underwater ballet. As they walk up walls and beams, doing flips and somersaults in flight, the training lesson comes across more as a romanticized dance than a rehearsal for combat. As in so much of this film, the sexual tension is displaced into the spectacular effects rather than located in the relationship between the hero and the feminine "other."

Even with his impressive new skills, becoming one in mind and body is not the same as becoming "the One." If Morpheus's martial arts instruction leads Neo to the door, the Oracle shows him how to walk through it. It is significant that the Oracle embodies two kinds of "otherness"—she is black and female. The scene with Neo and the Oracle is unsettling because the extraordinary unfolds within the ordinary—as often occurs in myth—and because the Oracle's lessons come cloaked in koan-like paradoxes, themselves embedded in chit-chat about baking cookies and breaking vases. But Neo encounters the Oracle within the Matrix, and so it is not surprising that even here, in the den of "Truth," spectacle leaves its traces, as the visual effects of the monk-like child bending a spoon with his or her mind linger longer than the intricacies of spoken dialogue.

In fact, both Trinity and the Oracle hold the keys to Neo's Oneness, even more than Morpheus, who prepares him to meet them. As conductor of the pre-Christian Orphic tradition that not only stresses death and descent into the underworld as a prelude to resurrection, but worships the Goddess TriVia, Morpheus places the Oracle's truth ahead of his own. As far back as the Stone Age, the Great Goddess was a trinity, venerated in her three forms as a young woman, a birth-giving matron, and a wise old woman, and serving as the prototype for countless threefold goddesses.[42] Trinity as Virgin-Mother-Crone seems far more apropos to this film than the too-easy allusion to Father-Son-Holy Spirit, a trio that, though it does emphasize embodiment and transformation, is a patriarchal takeover that represses its feminine roots, a crucial source of redemption for a technological hero. Trinity herself clues us into the right mythic framework when she aborts Neo's masculine presumption in the nightclub. By herself, Trinity may appear primarily as a sleek-and-chic virginal love object who, by the way, kicks butt, but in the context of the whole myth, "the Trinity" is also Mother—as in the second mother of the Nebachudnezzar crew, and Crone—as in the Oracle who taunts Neo with his destiny.

Oracle: So—what do you think? Do you think you are "the One?"

Neo: Honestly, I don't know.

Oracle: You know what that means [pointing to a plaque over her door]? Latin. Means "Know thyself." I'm gonna let you in on a little secret. Being the One is just like being in love. No one can tell you you're in love. You just know it, through and through, balls to bones.

With this declaration, the Oracle invalidates all instruction, including her own. If and when Neo comes to know that he is the One, he will learn it through bodily intuition, from an impassioned commitment of the heart, not a rational decision of the mind.

Reintegrating the Feminine.   Whereas Neo is insufficiently aware of Trinity throughout most of the story, as Cypher notes, she watches him right from the beginning scene. Later, although Trinity in her strapless outfit at the nightclub may invite the gaze of others, it is she who again looks at Neo, not the other way around.

When Agent Smith "kills" Neo, which in the rules of the Matrix does away with his body as well, Trinity leans over Neo's limp form inside the rebels' ship, insisting with quiet desperation:

> Neo? I'm not afraid any more. The Oracle told me that I would fall in love, and that that man, the man that I loved, would be the One. So you see—you can't be dead—you can't be—because I love you. You hear me? I love you.

She kisses Neo, he stirs, and she commands, nearly pilfering Sarah Connor's line to Kyle Reese in *The Terminator,* "Now get up!" In this moment, Trinity's love bequeaths *empathy* to Neo, the singular relational quality that no amount of spectacular action can impart. The virtual Neo who rises from the dead is not the same construct Agent Smith ostensibly blew away.

Although she is a compelling visual icon and goes through the required motions to awaken Neo, something seems peculiarly off-center with the Trinity-and-Neo duo. This kiss has no sizzle. Their relationship, in fact, never approaches the complexity of Molly and Case in *Neuromancer* or the sexual intensity of, say, Kyle Reese and Sarah Connor or Rick Deckard and Rachael Tyrell in *Blade Runner.* Instead, when Trinity emerges from watching Neo from off to the side, she fights with him side by side. Trinity relates to Neo as his buddy or sibling, a fairly conventional way, according to Sobchack, to contain female sexuality in science fiction films.[43]

In their fight scenes, Neo and Trinity reflect one another in their sleek black leather, their measured, in-your-face attitudes, and their karate-kicking *machismo.* When the two of them step into the lobby of the building where Morpheus is imprisoned, we see them in full frontal assault mode, Neo on the right, Trinity on the left. They sport the same dark glasses, the same slick hairdos, and nearly the same clothes. As a Matrix security guard yells, "Freeze!", the two turn to gaze at each other, forming a near-perfect mirror image that moves in sync as they spring to opposite sides of the frame. In the precisely choreographed mayhem that follows, quick cuts back and forth between Trinity and Neo catch each in hang-time gymnastics, their black coats floating incongruously amidst a barrage of bullets. One might be the other—it doesn't seem to matter—as they step tranquilly onto the elevator, the door closing over the dyad, now Neo on the left and Trinity on the right.

Throughout *The Matrix*, as we have noted, Trinity's eroticism is displaced onto the special effects. Desire is directed not to her body, but literally "up there" on the screen. Whereas she helps Neo get his body back, in a way that is as disquieting as it is grand, she loses her own in the bargain. It is difficult, however, to recognize this loss because we're so captivated by the rain of bullets, the shattering of (styrofoam) pillars, and the carnage of killing, which, we can quickly rationalize, is not "really" killing because those being blown away are, after all, just mental contructs generated by the Matrix. Here, as elsewhere in this film, extreme violence becomes indistinguishable from the innocent mayhem committed in computer games all over America.

Claiming Insight.   To gain the boon of insight in the myth of technology, the hero must trade in his ego for a larger sense of himself in relation to others.[44] The final struggle between Neo and the agents is, in fact, two battles, the first dominated by sight before Neo's "death," the second permeated by insight after his "resurrection." It does not end in a gun battle, even though it starts with one, and even though the multitudes of spent shell casings drifting languidly through the air with the actors invite us to read it that way. Initially, Neo comes armed with nothing more than his preprogrammed martial arts training plus weapons. "So what do you need besides a miracle?" Tank asks when Neo announces he is reentering the Matrix to free Morpheus. "Guns," Neo answers decisively, "lots of guns," as an awesome rack of weaponry sure to quicken the pulse of NRA members everywhere slides before him. He must still believe that he can defeat the agents from the outside in, by shooting or karate-kicking them into virtual oblivion. But as long as Neo relies exclusively on his physical skills and Luddist weapons, he lacks the Oracle's in-the-marrow consciousness that would complete his initiation and set him apart from his virtual antagonists. Every time Neo or Trinity blasts one away, the agent simply rematerializes in another virtual human and takes up the fight again. Reiterating the lesson of Frankenstein's bride that technological cures for technological problems merely make those problems worse,[45] this film asserts, at least on the narrative level, that guns can't kill machines.

When Neo arises after Trinity's kiss, though he is still projecting his mind into the Matrix, he does so with full consciousness. He is shot cinematically so that he dominates the space that used to dominate him, and an intensified natural coloring contrasts his new image from the Matrix and its agents, which are always seen through a green filter.[46] When an incredulous Agent Smith attacks with renewed fury, Neo slowly turns away and fends him off with one arm as calmly as an adult might bemusedly repel the flailing of a petulant child. Then, in a blur, Neo boots Smith at least thirty feet away. Trinity has enabled Neo to see the inner reality of the Matrix, to move in and out of its virtual constructs, knowing that the entire thing is a complex mirror of himself, as all of technology-as-menace is a projection of our human "shadows" (a feared extension of our senses that we have "auto-amputated" from awareness).[47] This knowledge is prefigured by the mystical child in the Oracle's foyer who shows Neo that it is not the spoon s/he is playing with that bends, it is one's self.

Thus, when in the second phase of the battle all three agents empty their weapons at him, Neo realizes Morpheus' earlier prognosis that when he's ready, he will not have to dodge bullets. He simply raises his hand and transforms the virtual slugs back into their digital forms as 0s and 1s; as displacements of himself, they are not really all that terrifying. Finally, when a visibly shaken Smith stands up to a charging Neo, Neo digitalizes his self-construct, passes into Smith's circuitry, and incarnates within him—fracturing him back into disconnected electrical impulses. But as so often happens in this film, even this mythic denouement is overshadowed by the computer generated effects of Neo entering and "moving" through Agent Smith's destabilized personage.

The Return

The film's ending completes the circle of its beginning: As the frame fills with fluid green digits, a phone rings, and we hear but do not see a voice—Neo this time instead of Trinity. Having vanquished their best agents, Neo is calling the computers. The screen warns of danger—the call is an anomaly—but Neo speaks with confidence:

> I know you're out there. I can feel you now. I know that you're afraid. You're afraid of us, you're afraid of change. I don't know the future. I didn't come here to tell you how it's going to end. I came here to tell you how it's going to begin. I'm going to hang up this phone, and then I'm going to show these people what you don't want them to see. I'm going to show them a world without you, a world without rules and controls, without borders and boundaries. A world where anything is possible. Where we go from there is a choice I leave up to you.

The last scene thus begins not with spectacular display, but with embodied speech. It is not Luddist, as were Neo's actions before his death, but revelatory, promising to see and to show. We might well ask what kind of sight he advocates. Neo's "world without rules and controls, without borders and boundaries . . . where anything is possible," sounds suspiciously reminiscent of the limitless technological frontierism of which Agent Smith accuses the humans.

But given what he has learned, and especially his empathy with the machines' fears—which directly reverse our fears about them—it seems more likely that his descent into Hell and back has taught him to identify with the "other," whether that be his captive body or the technological extensions of himself. If he does indeed "show these people what you don't want them to see"—undoubtedly that their bodies are enslaved—the machines' "choice" is whether to sever them from their life supports, which would kill not only the people but the machines that feed on them, or to realize their ultimate interdependence. Such connection is what Neo has learned from the Oracle and from Trinity. The "other" is in fact him. Neo must be looking inward to his self rather than outward to his image, then, speaking from insight, not sight. With this hard won perspective he is able to stand up to the false Mother as no mere boy can.

Neo's voiceover concluded, the phrase "System Failure," superimposed over the numbers, grows until it fills the frame. The digital array implodes through a dissolve to Neo hanging up the phone, and he flies off over the Matrix's illusion of a cityscape. Soaring literally upward, once more he might evoke the uninitiated hero's hope for limitless flight as an escape from his duty to return to his people.[48] But given the way the story has evolved, we read Neo's ascendance as cutting the umbilical chord to mother Matrix, as he apparently no longer needs material telephone lines to transport himself between worlds. Perhaps as "the One," he has gotten the fragments of his self together.

Conclusion

Neither an array of spectacular effects nor a seamless extension of the myth of technology, *The Matrix* seems to occupy an uneasy middle ground between the two. By entering that contested center, we have tried to reconstruct this mythic tale by stitching its fragments together, all the while noting how the film's state-of-the-art technology tries to break them back apart. But perhaps there is a subtle inevitability at work here, for movies without spectacular effects, particularly when they are *about* technology, are unlikely to snag our attention. Yet this attention is also prone to disembody us. It may well be that any significant cultural statement about our technological predicament must entail an irony of myth and spectacle, for an omission of spectacle defies at least one reality and a compromise with awareness defiles another. If so, then perhaps seeing what there is to see in such films requires, as Morpheus teaches Neo, that we "free our minds" so as to feel our way simultaneously through worlds that are paradoxical.

RETURN: PERSONAL COMMENTS ON THE ESSAY

"Sheee's baaackkk," I whisper, as Jane strolls confidently into Janice's office the next week.

"Yessss!!!" she proclaims. "I couldn't do that thing you gave me originally, but I can do this. Well, more realistically, I can do something like this," she says, emitting a miraculous memory trace of the modesty expected of a student.

"Well, let's see what you got," I say, cutting her no slack. "What do you take to be our central critical point?"

"That *The Matrix* is an important film because it extends the myth of Frankenstein narratively, but the special effects and action sequences deflect our attention away from that contribution," she answers, with the sort of memorized self-assurance that comes from guessing your professors would ask something like this.

"You go girl!" Janice applauds.

"See, we're not effete snobs after all," I say.

"Well, it's not like it's perfect," she adds, showing the edge we've come to consider charming. "I do have a few questions."

"Why doesn't that surprise me?" I ask.

"Like, for one thing, I remember you saying a couple of weeks ago that a common error in mythic criticism is to retell the story using mythic language, instead of using a myth to come up with some nonobvious insights into the text, right?"

"That's right," Janice agrees, and I can see that "Bad Teacher" sign reappear on her forehead.

"But it seems to me that your initial section, the one you call 'Departure,' is pretty much plot summary in mythic terms. You don't do that much with the tension between myth and spectacle there."

"You're right," Janice admits, trying not to sound defensive, "but that's because we took out the theoretical perspective of . . ."

"Naa, come on, you can't pull that number, Janice," I interrupt. "But there is more going on there than just plot summary. Remember that in this particular film, the mythic story is pretty fragmented from the get-go. Many of the critics we cite complain about that very thing. And so part of what we're trying to do in that first section is to reconstruct the narrative coherence to the overall story line, so that when, in the next section, we alert you to how the effects often undermine the myth, you'll have a feel for what's being undercut."

"So retelling a story in mythic terms is all right if it furthers your overall critical objective?" she asks.

"Sure," Janice says, "as long as that's not *all* you do. Do you see how we use the reactions of other film critics?"

"I think so," Jane responds. "You use them to set up what you intend to do. One set of critics is hung up on the special effects, while the other is all torqued out because the story, which might be important, doesn't make much sense. But neither group examines the effects *and* the story together—that's where you two come in. Right?"

"Right as rain," I say. "That's one way to *use* literature as part of an argument justifying what you intend to do in your critique. I've always found that using literature argumentatively, to justify your own critical posture, is hard for students to grasp. I'm not sure why, but part of the difficulty may be the connotation of the phrase, 'review of literature.' That suggests a *summary* more than an *argument*."

"One thing bothers me, though," Jane says, ignoring my mini-lesson in research methods, as Janice is getting that concerned look again. "You guys cite so many sources that I don't know. Everything from some science fiction novel called *Neuromancer,* to lots of mythic sources I've never even heard of, to tons of old science fiction movies I've never seen. If I have to know all that to do this, I'm back to square one again!"

"Don't worry about that," I say. "We know all that stuff because we're old and we don't have lives. . . ."

"Speak for yourself, geezer guy," Janice cuts me off.

"You do need to do some reading, of course. But to do your version of what we've done here," I plow ahead, "all you really need, in addition to the reviews, is two central texts: Joseph Campbell's *The Hero with a Thousand Faces* and a video or DVD of *The Matrix*. Now, you would need to have read Campbell thoroughly, and you would need to have watched the film until you begin to use its dialogue in your everyday conversations, so it's not a piece of cake."

"I'll go with that, but I think she also needs some sources on the technology myth, so she'd know what's been said already about how this myth has evolved," Janice suggests.

"Yeah, do that in your spare time," I agree.

"Whew! Thanks, guys, this really eases my mind," Jane says, as she heads toward the door.

"So have you picked a text to write about?" Janice asks.

"*Fight Club*. I'm going to knock your socks off."

"I have no doubts. You can borrow my copy and watch it tonight," I say magnanimously.

"I'll take you up on that, but not tonight. Some of us from the class are getting together."

"To pop a few brews?" I query.

"They want me to talk about what I've been doing in here the last three weeks," she answers sheepishly. She's now at the head of the stairs, and she shouts back, "go read Campbell on 'The Ultimate Boon'—I'll expect a report tomorrow."

"She's like the Terminator," I whisper to Janice. "She'll be back."

"I know," Janice smiles. "Some kids these days are like we were. They just *are* 'perfect in every way'."

Just as I'm heading off to class, Jane returns to stick her head in the door. "What kind of criticism do we do next?"

"Don't even *think* about it!" I say, catching her grin as we gently close the door behind her.

MYTHIC CRITICISM TOP PICKS

Barthes, Roland, *Mythologies*, A. Lavers (trans.) (New York: Wang and Hill, 1957). One of the most influential books on mythology for cultural studies, this book is a brilliant collection of short essays on myth in French life of the 1950s. It is one of "the" works that illustrates how myth works ideologically in everyday life. The long concluding essay, "Myth Today," lays out Barthes's semiological method of analysis, and is as difficult as it is important. But the short essays are fascinating and can be read by a novice.

Campbell, Joseph, *The Hero with a Thousand Faces* (Princeton: Princeton University Press/Bollingen Series 17, 1949/1972). Referred to throughout this chapter, this book is one of the most-used and best-known sources on the hero myth.

Freud, Sigmund, *A General Introduction to Psychoanalysis* (New York: Pocket Books, 1920/1952). Reissued as *Introductory Lectures on Psycho-analysis*, James Strachey (trans. and ed.), Peter Gay (intro.) (New York: W. W. Norton 1989). A comprehensive overview of Freud's theories of the unconscious, including his ways of thinking about errors ("Freudian slips"), individual pathologies, dreams, folklore, art, and myth.

Jung, Carl G., Marie-Louise von Franz, Joseph L. Henderson, Jolande Jacobs, and Aniela Jaffe (eds.) *Man and his Symbols*, Garden City, NY: Doubleday, 1964). A good introduction to

Jung's "archetypes" and how they occur in art and myth. This is a "coffee table book," beautifully illustrated and written for the lay person rather than the theorist. It includes chapters by Jung and several of his followers.

Lawrence, John Shelton, and Robert Jewett, *The Myth of the American Superhero*, (Grand Rapids, MI: Wm. B. Eerdmans 2002). Extends their first book, *The American Monomyth*, into popular culture in the current era, arguing that the most typical American hero myth differs from Campbell's monomyth in significant ways.

Mackey-Kallis, Susan, *The Hero and the Perennial Journey Home in American Film* (Philadelphia: University of Pennsylvania Press, 2001). Adapts Perennial Philosophy and mythic frameworks such as Joseph Campbell's to the analysis of many American films.

McGee, Michael C., "In Search of 'The People': A Rhetorical Alternative," *Quarterly Journal of Speech* 61 (1975): 235–249. This article, along with several of McGee's essays, helped push the field of Communication into thinking about rhetoric in a Marxist vein. Here, McGee considers how myths form, decay, and compete with one another through rhetorical processes.

Morford, Mark P. O., and Robert J. Lenardon, *Classical Mythology*. 7th ed., (Oxford: Oxford University Press, 2003). A great reference for classic Greek and Roman mythology. It includes the stories themselves, plus interpretations, as well as a comprehensive review of mythology in literature, art, music, dance, and film. For classical mythology, this is that "list in the sky" referred to in the chapter.

Murdock, Maureen, *The Heroine's Journey: Woman's Quest for Wholeness* (Boston: Shambhala, 1990). An important companion piece to Joseph Campbell's *The Hero with a Thousand Faces*, because Murdock argues that Campbell's monomyth does not generalize well to women. She builds an alternative mythic framework for heroines by adapting and changing crucial aspects of Campbell's monomyth.

Rushing, Janice Hocker, and Thomas S. Frentz, *Projecting the Shadow: The Cyborg Hero in American Film* (Chicago: University of Chicago Press, 1995). This book integrates archetypal and ideological aspects of myth so as to examine the Frankenstein myth of technology in popular films. The analysis of *The Matrix* in this chapter depends upon the framework developed in this book.

NOTES

1. Kris Kristofferson, "The Pilgrim: Chapter 33," Perf. Kris Kristofferson. *The Austin Sessions* (Atlantic Recording Corporation, 1999).

2. Joseph Campbell, *Myths to Live By* (New York: Bantam Books, 1972), 10.

3. Rowland Barthes, *Mythologies*, A. Lavers (trans.) (New York: Wang and Hill, 1957).

4. Campbell, *Myths to Live By;* Anthony Storr, *The Essential Jung* (Princeton: Princeton University Press, 1983).

5. Vivian Sobchack, "The Virginity of Astronauts: Sex and the Science Fiction Film," *Alien Zone: Cultural Theory and Contemporary Science Fiction Cinema*, Annette Kuhn, (ed.) (New York/London: Verso, 1990), 103–115. See also Constance Penley, "Time Travel, Primal Scene, and the Critical Dystopia," *The Future of an Illusion: Film, Feminism. and Psychoanalysis* (Minneapolis: Univ. of Minnesota Press, 1989), 121–139; Sonia Livingstone and Tamar Liebes, "Where Have All the Mothers Gone? Soap Opera's Re-playing of the Oedipal Story," *Critical Studies in Mass Communication* 12 (1995): 155–175.

6. Robert A. Davies, James M. Farrell, and Steven S. Matthews, "The Dream World of Film: A Jungian Perspective on Cinematic Communication," *Western Journal of Speech Communication* 46 (1982): 326–343.

7. Mark P. O. Morford and Robert J. Lenardon, *Classical Mythology*, 7th ed. (Oxford: Oxford University Press, 2003).

8. Joseph Campbell, *The Hero with a Thousand Faces* (Princeton: Princeton University Press/Bollingen Series 17, 1949/1972).

9. Susan Mackey-Kallis, *The Hero and the Perennial Journey Home in American Film* (Philadelphia: University of Pennsylvania Press, 2001), 27–33.

10. Janice Hocker Rushing and Thomas S. Frentz, "Singing Over the Bones: James Cameron's *Titanic*," *Critical Studies in Mass Communication* 17 (2000): 1–27.

11. Janice Hocker Rushing, "The Rhetoric of the American Western Myth," *Communication Monographs* 50 (1983): 14–32; Janice Hocker Rushing, "Evolution of 'The New Frontier' in *Alien* and *Aliens:* Patriarchal Co-optation of the Feminine Archetype," *Quarterly Journal of Speech* 75 (1989): 1–24; Janice Hocker Rushing, "Mythic Evolution of 'The New Frontier' in Mass Mediated Rhetoric," *Critical Studies in Mass Communication* 3 (1986): 265–296.

12. Mary Shelley, *Frankenstein* (New York: Bantam, 1818/1991); Janice Hocker Rushing and Thomas S. Frentz, "The Frankenstein Myth in Contemporary Cinema," *Critical Studies in Mass Communication* 6 (1989): 61–80; Janice Hocker Rushing and Thomas S. Frentz, *Projecting the Shadow: The Cyborg Hero in American Film* (Chicago: University of Chicago Press, 1995).

13. Robert Jewett and John Shelton Lawrence, *The American Monomyth* (Garden City, NY: Anchor/Doubleday, 1977); John Shelton Lawrence and Robert Jewett, *The Myth of the American Superhero* (Grand Rapids, MI: Wm. B. Eerdmans 2002).

14. Walter R Fisher, "Reaffirmation and Subversion of the American Dream," *Quarterly Journal of Speech* 59 (1973): 160–167; John Arthos Jr. "The Shaman-Trickster's Art of Misdirection: The Rhetoric of Farrakhan and the Million Men," *Quarterly Journal of Speech* 87 (2001): 25–40; Randall A. Lake, "Between Myth and History: Enacting Time in Native American Protest Rhetoric," *Quarterly Journal of Speech* 77 (1991): 123–151; Farrel Corcoran, "The Bear in the Back Yard: Myth, Ideology, and Victimage Ritual in Soviet Funerals," *Communication Monographs* 50 (1983): 305–320.

15. Karen Rasmussen and Sharon D. Downey, "Dialectical Disorientation in Vietnam War Films: Subversion of the Mythology of War," *Quarterly Journal of Speech* 77 (1991): 176–195; Penley.

16. Thomas S. Frentz and Janice Hocker Rushing, "'Mother Isn't Quite Herself Today': Myth and Spectacle in *The Matrix*," *Critical Studies in Media Communication* 19 (2002): 64–86.

17. Andrew O'Hehir, "Short Attention Spawn," *Salon*, April 2, 1999, n. pag. (On-line magazine). Retrieved April 6, 1999, from http://www.salon.com/ent/movies/reviews/1999/04/02reviewa.html.

18. Lisa Schwarzbaum, "The Matrix," *EW Online*, April 2, 1999, n. pag. (On-line magazine). Retrieved April 8, 1999, from http://www.ew.com/ew/review/movie/0,1683,563,matrix.html.

19. Bob Graham, "Lost in the 'Matrix'," *San Francisco Chronicle*, March 31, 1999, E-1. (On-line newspaper). Retrieved April 29, 1999, from http://www.sfgate.com/cgi/bin/article.cgi?file=/chronicle/archive/1999/3/31DD49124.DTL.

20. Roger Ebert, "The Matrix," *The Chicago Sun Times*, March 3, 1999, n. pag. (On-line newspaper). Retrieved March 10, 1999, from http://www.suntimes.com/ebert_reviews/1999/03/033101.html.

21. Stuart Klawans, "The End of Humanism," *The Nation*, April 26, 1999, n. pag. (On-line magazine). Retrieved April 30, 1999, from http://www.thenation.com/issue/990426/0426klawans.shtml.

22. Anthony Ferrante, "The Matrix," *Eonline*, April 2, 1999, n. pag. (On-line magazine). Retrieved April 28, 1999, from http://www.eonline.com/Review/Facts/Movies/Reviews/0,1052,71731,00.html.

23. O'Hehir, n. pag.

24. Issac Asimov, "The Myth of the Machine," *Asimov on Science Fiction* (Garden City, NY: Doubleday, 1981), 160–162; Rushing and Frentz, "The Frankenstein Myth in Contemporary Cinema"; Rushing and Frentz, *Projecting the Shadow*, 67; Langdon Winner, *Autonomous Technology: Technics-out-of-control as a Theme in Political Thought* (Cambridge, MA: The MIT Press, 1977), 280.

25. Shelley.

26. Rushing and Frentz, *Projecting the Shadow*.

27. Campbell, *The Hero with a Thousand Faces*.

28. Thanks to Roberto Loar for calling our attention to the importance of this dialogue.

29. We are indebted to Tai Estopy for this insight.

30. *Merriam-Webster's New Collegiate Dictionary*, 7th ed. (Springfield, MA: Merriam-Webster, 1967), 522.

31. Chad Eby, *Hacking the Body: The Puer Aeternus in Cyberspace* (Unpublished master's thesis, University of Arkansas, Fayetteville, 1997), 26–27.

32. James S. Beard, *Rhetorical Mapping of Technological Psychosis: A Burkean Reading of William Gibson's Neuromancer* (Unpublished doctoral dissertation, Northwestern University, Evanston, IL, 1999), 98.

33. Rushing and Frentz, *Projecting the Shadow*; see also Campbell, *The Hero with a Thousand Faces*, 109–120.

34. Roger Horrocks sees this as a common auto-erotic theme in westerns. *Male Myths and Icons: Masculinity in Popular Culture* (New York: St. Martin's 1995), 54.

35. We are indebted again to Roberto Loar for his careful reading of this scene.

36. Campbell, *The Hero with a Thousand Faces*, 90–95.

37. Rushing and Frentz, *Projecting the Shadow*, 213.

38. Joseph L. Henderson, "Ancient Myths and Modern Man," *Man and His Symbols*, Carl G. Jung, Marie-Louise von Franz, Joseph L. Henderson, Jolande Jacobi, and Aniela Jaffe (eds.) (Garden City, NY: Doubleday, 1964), 130.

39. Campbell, *The Hero with a Thousand Faces*, 69–77.

40. Rushing and Frentz, *Projecting the Shadow*, 25–27.

41. According to O'Hehir, in Hollywood, "blackness is the universally understood symbol for superior wisdom," n. pag.

42. Ralph Abraham, *Chaos, Gaia, Eros: A Chaos Pioneer Uncovers the Three Great Streams of History* (New York: HarperSanFrancisco, 1994), 84–85; Barbara Walker, *The Woman's Encyclopedia of Myths and Secrets* (San Francisco: Harper & Row, 1983), 1018.

43. Sobchack, 106.

44. Campbell, *The Hero with a Thousand Faces*, 172–192.

45. Rushing and Frentz, *Projecting the Shadow*, 74–75.

46. We are indebted to Grant Florer for this observation.

47. Rushing and Frentz, *Projecting the Shadow;* Marshall McLuhan, *Understanding Media: The Extensions of Man* (New York: McGraw-Hill, 1965). 41–47.

48. Campbell, *The Hero with a Thousand Faces*, 196–207.

CHAPTER THIRTEEN

FEMINIST ANALYSIS

DONNA M. NUDD

KRISTINA L. SCHRIVER

WHY FEMINISM?

Susan Faludi once said, "[A]ll women are born feminists, but most get it knocked out of them."[1] In fact, on most high school and college campuses professors chronicle the "I'm not a feminist but" phenomenon that suggests Faludi is right. In other words, although most women will not self-identify as a feminist, many will profess agreement with the ideals comprising a feminist agenda. So, we have many women (and men) saying, "I'm not a feminist, but I believe in equal opportunity" or "I'm not a feminist, but I believe women should be treated with dignity and respect." This trend lead bell hooks (who chooses not to capitalize her name) to conclude that a more profitable way to offer feminism is to say "I advocate feminism" rather than "I am a feminist." The first phrase "discourages a focus on stereotyped perspectives of feminism . . . and prompts the question 'What is feminism?' "[2]

Although many stereotypes surround feminists, focusing on and articulating what feminism advocates is far more important to our understanding of feminist rhetorical criticism. However, describing feminism is a daunting and complex task since feminism has many different veins of thought. These varying perspectives make talking about feminism, in general, quite difficult. Despite its difficulty, communication scholars Cheris Kramarae and Paula Treichler explain their version of feminism as "the radical notion that women are people."[3] Although Kramarae and Treichler's definition does not capture the theoretical disagreements that exist in feminism, it does express the common spirit of most strands of feminism. *Feminism is a pluralistic movement interested in altering the political and social landscape so that all people, regardless of their identity categories, can experience freedom and safety, complexity and subjectivity, and economic and political parity—experiences associated with being fully human.*

Feminist advocates argue for the necessity and profitability of their activism and critical inquiry by evidencing the *patriarchal* systems most civilizations have been operating under for several thousand years. Although some critics, even feminist critics, argue that we are now living in a post-patriarchal world,[4] the majority of feminist critics believe that patriarchy is still entrenched in our political and value systems. For example, Allan G. Johnson writes in *The Gender Knot* that three principles encompass the still present patriarchal system: male domination, male identification, and male centeredness. According to Johnson, *male domination* refers to the simple fact that men have populated most positions of authority in major societies. Men head large corporations, nation–states, churches, colleges and universities, and most other positions of social importance. Although a few women have temporarily taken these seats of prestige, the exceptions have done little to dismantle male domination. In sum, the exceptions are too infrequent and account for only a small fraction of power positions. Johnson outlines the consequences of male domination by writing, "[Male domination] means that men can shape culture in ways that reflect and serve men's collective interest." Additionally, he adds, "male domination promotes the idea that men are superior to women."[5]

Johnson believes that a critique of patriarchy is incomplete if it simply notes degrees of male domination. He argues that we must also note instances of *male identification*. Male identification locates our cultural values in maleness and masculinity. According to Johnson, in a male-identified society the activities of men underscore what it preferred, normal, and desirable. The qualities commonly associated with masculinity, such as competition, individualism, invulnerability, rationality, and physical strength, are honored. The qualities commonly associated with femininity, such as cooperation, nurturing, emotionality, and care, are undervalued or trivialized.[6] Besides being undervalued, feminine identified people in our masculine-identified society are measured by a rigged yardstick. What is deemed desirable is always out of reach. Though competition is valued in our society, being a woman carries expectations of acting feminine; hence, acting aggressively and competitively will often be met with disapproval, if not hostility. However, a woman never exercising qualities associated with masculinity has little chance for advancement, since those are the qualities our society rewards. These basic assertions about male identification are not categorically true. Some women appear to successfully pair feminine traits with a masculine sensibility. A handful of critics point to the rash of recent films and television shows that feature conventional feminine beauty with highly physical and aggressive feats (*Alias, Charlie's Angels, Dark Angel, Tomb Raider*) as evidence that male and female identification are becoming intertwined. However, Mary Spicuzza notes that even these shows deserve our critical attention. She writes, "plenty of butt kicking women on screen are ultimately concerned with being sexy, finding a man to complete their lives, and settling down." Spicuzza, quoting many communication scholars, adds, "Women heroines are less concerned with achieving female liberation than satisfying male fantasy."[7] Regardless of where one stands on this media issue, it is clear that matters surrounding gender identification are complicated, fluctuating, and ripe territory for the rhetorical critic.

Finally, Johnson advocates a focus on our society's *male centeredness*, meaning that our cultural attention is mainly focused on males. "Pick up any newspaper or go to any movie theater and you'll find stories primarily about men and what they've done or haven't done or what they have to say about either."[8] Sporting activities represent one of many culturally significant areas where men seek and receive acclaim. Large populations of men and women watch men's sporting events. Millions watch the Super Bowl, *Monday Night Football,* the World Series, and the NBA Championship series.[9] Advertisers spend copious amounts of money to market products during these events knowing the viewing audience is large. Although women play sports, they do not attract an equivalent viewing audience. The rise of the WNBA provides evidence for a male-centered, as well as a male-identified, society. Naming the organization the *Women's* National Basketball Association highlights that men play a "normal" game of basketball. If one were to say, "I'm going to watch a basketball game," in most cases the assumption would be that a men's game was about to be viewed. A feminist critic would likely argue that the male centeredness is so seemingly natural in our society it remains unspoken. However, if one were watching a basketball game featuring female players, chances are the sex of the players would be spotlighted: "I'm watching a *women's* basketball game," thus underscoring it's a deviation from the norm.

If we turn our attention to the criticism of the WNBA style of play, feminists see demonstrated how a male-centered society and a male-identified society are mutually reinforcing ideas. WNBA players do not always play the game in the same style as the men. The fact that a slam-dunk has only been executed in one WNBA game produced criticism that the league's play lacked excitement. Since men play with a showboating style, that type of athletic execution is preferred. Additionally, women excelling at professional basketball face overt problems with male identification. Cynthia Cooper of the Houston Comets writes, "In the league's second year, people began putting labels on me. The media began comparing everything about me to my male counterpart. I was labeled the "Michael Jordan of women's basketball' and the Comets the 'Chicago Bulls of the WNBA.' I'm not complaining about being compared to one of the greatest male players basketball players ever, but I want people to remember my athletic abilities under my name—not his."[10]

Feminists argue that the mixture of male centeredness and male identification create enormous disparities in our society. With one sex, and the corresponding gendered system attached to biology, at society's center a systematic disparity is maintained. Females and/or femininity are rendered invisible or marginalized under the patriarchal rubric. Carol Tavris notes the invisibility of women in our patriarchal history: "In history, the implicit use of men as the norm pervades much of what school children learn about American and Western civilization. Was Greece the cradle of democracy? It was no democracy for women and slaves. Was the Renaissance a time of intellectual and artistic rebirth? There was no renaissance for women."[11] Tavris maintains that the stories told in our society about our history, our struggles, our values, are wrapped up in masculine precepts. As such, the experiences following the culturally constructed ideas of femininity receive little attention and thus are given little value. Many feminists argue that this occurs because we have bound biological sex with a narrow set of socially constructed ideas about how that sex operates—those constructed ideas are called *gender*. For this reason, patriarchal principles are extremely harmful to homosexuals who push the boundaries of gender scripts.

However important it is to point out the features of patriarchy, sexist oppression is not the only oppression of interest to feminism. Late twentieth-century feminism concerned itself with interlocking systems of oppression, noting that most systems of discrimination share common characteristics and must be seen together if liberation struggles are to gain ground. For these reasons feminist scholars such as bell hooks, mentioned above, reference the dominant framework as a *white supremacist capitalist patriarchy*.[12] This term underscores that we not only live in a sexist society but a society that discriminates based on economic circumstances and race. A thorough feminist critique will not fail to interrogate how all these ideological systems work together to marginalize discrete groups of people.

So, we will summarize by answering the question that heads this section: Why Feminism? Most feminists believe that we live in a complex social structure guided by patriarchy. They believe this patriarchal system must change. Moreover, the understanding of patriarchy cannot be a simple calculation. Engaged human beings are likely to identify egregious cases of sexism; however, most feminists believe that much of the sexism of the patriarchal framework remains unchallenged. Feminists therefore are motivated to expose the fundamental ways, the often subtle, taken for granted ways, in which societal members undervalue and diminish women. That done, feminists propose new ideas, assumptions, and viewpoints allowing for humans to realize a wide range of possibilities and promise. But, as stated before, not all feminists are alike; therefore, different feminists have different priorities and solutions. In the next section, we will explore these differences and their relationship to rhetorical criticism.

AN INTRODUCTION TO FEMINIST RHETORICAL CRITICISM

Feminist thought has always been quite diverse in its theories and practices. One of the main theoretical differences among various feminists surrounds disagreements over gender differences. This disagreement is referred to in feminist writings as the "minimalist/maximalist debate." A feminist *minimalist* believes that men and women are more alike than different; therefore, the policies and social organizations privileging men can easily adapt to women if they are just granted access. *Maximalists*, as you might imagine, believe that women and men are more different than alike. With that premise in mind, feminist maximalists argue that women will never achieve success and comfort in social institutions created by men for men, which describes most of our current arrangements. Men and women are too different, they argue, to make such a fit agreeable. In other words, our social and political landscape must be altered or transformed to accommodate the distinctions between men and women.

From this theoretical debate, many categories of feminism have emerged. Jill Dolan notes that we can generally see American feminism separated into liberal, cultural, and materialist segments.[13] Liberal feminist approaches locate the oppression of women in the systematic failure to include women in dominant structures and cultural production. A liberal feminist rhetorical critique would be interested in the exclusion of women from systems of representation. Are women given a voice in the political system? Can you find women in recent films you've seen, stories read? If so, how many women were featured in comparison to men? Did the stories showcase the women as competent, able to solve problems, lead others, and champion a cause? Liberal rhetorical feminist critics are diligently employing language strategies within the current structures to increase the stature and number of women in places of political and social power. Liberal feminists are also minimalists.

Cultural feminists, on the other hand, are maximalists. They argue that women's nature, primarily shaped by the ability to give birth, is decidedly different from men's. "Because they can give birth, women are viewed as instinctually more natural, more closely related to life cycles mirrored in nature."[14] Cultural feminists argue that women have a unique and valuable perspective that is not adequately reflected in today's society. This deficit of perspective creates a world of domination and violence. Moreover, some cultural feminists have situated themselves within another subcategory of feminist thought, ecofeminism. Ecofeminists believe that if society adopted the nondominating feminine perspective, the likelihood of continuing ecological devastation would diminish. But this is just one of many cultural feminist perspectives. A rhetorical critic adopting a cultural feminist perspective is likely to critique current rhetorical practices for their sexist domination as well as suggest ways in which a feminine perspective could rehabilitate the rhetorical situation. Does a given communication artifact convey the largely feminine characteristics of caring, nurturing, cooperation, and intuition? Does it glorify aggression, competition, and individualism to the exclusion of other perspectives? How do the messages around us "normalize" a distinctly masculine perspective? How could we infuse and balance our public discourse by including a feminine perspective? These are some of the many questions guiding the explorations of a rhetorical critic that is also a cultural feminist.

Finally, materialist feminists believe that symbol-using humans are historical subjects that are largely socially constructed, not biologically driven. A materialist feminist is interested in analyzing social conditions, such as the influence of race, sexual orientation, and class that work together to define women and men as categories and seemingly erase the possibility of other categories being established (for example, intersexed and transgendered). As such, this strand of feminism is also interested in unearthing the symbolic systems of gender that oppress all people, not just women. Materialist feminists may study the way masculinity has been constructed in such a way that men, too, have little freedom and dimension in society. So, although liberal feminists are primarily interested in social representation, materialist feminists reveal how people "have been oppressed by gender categories."[15] A materialist feminist might approach a rhetorical artifact by noting the ways in which a particular rhetorical artifact situates masculinity and femininity as stale categories, instead of giving the concept room for growth and movement. Do movies, or other culturally significant discourse, outfit men and women with retrograde notions of masculinity and femininity? How so? Can we point to messages around us that transform the somewhat rigid categories of gender in positive ways? These and similar questions would be of interest to the rhetorical critic with a materialist feminist perspective.

Positioning materialist feminism along the minimalist/maximalist continuum demands some attention. Since materialists underscore the social construction of gender, they very rarely look for "real" differences and similarities. Instead, materialists question the constructed categories of gender and offer the concepts dimension and redefinition if it aids the attainment of freedom, safety, complexity, subjectivity, and equality—the goals of feminism.

Although these categories represent large sects of feminist thought, other feminists strands not covered in this chapter apply a feminist lens to a Marxist perspective, psychoanalytical thought, and global issues; there are even feminists operating from libertarian and conservative political perspectives.[16] Feminists in different academic fields have established a literature base specific to their field of inquiry. Therefore, one is likely to see feminist legal studies, feminist international relations, and feminist medicine as well as feminist literary criticism. Women of color, who have traditionally had a complicated relationship with feminism, are interested in the way their ethnic and racial identities intersect with feminism. So, if one delves into the literature about feminism, one is likely to see discussions about Chicana feminism, black feminism, Asian feminism, and Native American feminism to name a few.[17] These discussions have greatly added to the understanding of liberation struggles for, as it was mentioned before, feminist thought has become keenly aware that analyzing gender is just one important piece of the puzzle.

When engaging in feminist rhetorical criticism, consideration should be given to how the critic positions an argument on the map of feminism so that those reading the criticism know the assumptions about gender infused in the analysis. In this next section we will first briefly outline the history of feminist criticism within the rhetorical tradition. Next, an explanation of the methods or approaches feminist rhetorical critics utilize to analyze our symbolic systems will follow. Alongside with these general explanations, numerous specific examples from feminist rhetorical critics will be provided.

FEMINIST CRITICISM AND THE CHALLENGE TO RHETORIC

Feminist thought is a useful line of critical inquiry when studying rhetorical strategies. The need for such inquiry has been well documented.[18] The *rhetorical tradition* tethers itself to a long history of oral argument and public oratory. This tradition also has an equally long history of excluding female rhetors or feminine ways of speaking. Sometimes this was done either by making public address unavailable to women through systematic discrimination or by refusing to recognize the many women who did take the podium. When feminist thought merges with rhetorical criticism, it is usually an attempt to foreground how gender is operating or being sculpted in particular ways by language choices. Feminists are also interested in discovering new symbolic strategies, or making visible little known language systems, in an effort to dismantle current gender hierarchies. So, another important part of feminist rhetorical criticism is suggesting that alternative, yet equally valid forms of producing symbolic meaning exist.[19] Although we do know that many women enlisted public address as a vehicle for their ideas, we also know that women's position in society relegated message making to other terrain. Feminist rhetorical criticism reclaims this forgotten rhetorical past. All of these concerns have meant that feminist rhetorical scholars have developed somewhat unique approaches to analyzing rhetorical artifacts.

Since feminists are interested in changing the mainstream value system in which we live, one avenue of feminist rhetorical criticism involves using the techniques of rhetorical criticism (many covered in this book), applying a feminist lens or agenda, and analyzing the text. It should not be surprising, given the activist approach of feminist rhetorical scholars, that many use these techniques to study their own feminist history. For example, Susan Schultz Huxman studied the rhetorical vision of Elizabeth Cady Stanton, Anna Howard Shaw, and Carrie Chapman Catt, feminist leaders in the late nineteenth- and early twentieth-centuries. From analyzing the most notable speeches of each revolutionary, Schultz explains that even though the women had disagreements and conflict, when viewed as a rhetorical package the womens' views worked well together and strengthened the larger women's rights movement.[20] Knowing how rhetoric functioned in the past gives today's feminists an important body of knowledge from which to work for change.

Feminists working for contemporary social change, using modern technology and sensibilities, also receive ample attention from feminist rhetorical critics. For example, Anne Teresa Demo explored the visual rhetoric of the Guerrilla Girls, a New York activist group that challenges the sexism of the art world. Guerrilla Girls, formed in the mid-1980s and still active today, use posters, billboards, flyers, and press conferences to draw attention to the grotesque underrepresentation of female artists in galleries, museums, and art history reviews. Guerrilla Girls never reveal their identity; instead, they appear on literature and at press conferences clothed in black garb and gorilla masks. Demo analyzes the group's rhetoric, largely visual in nature, and argues that their techniques of *humorous mimicry* (they mimic traditional femininity by using the color pink, calling themselves "girls," and writing in ultra polite, feminine tones), *historical revision* (they published their own art history book and take on the persona of overlooked artists in press conferences), and *strategic comparison* (they use quotes given by conservatives to support their progressive agenda) are persuasive because they highlight the tension and incongruity in our social order.

Although analyzing speeches and texts particular to the feminist agenda remains essential, today feminist rhetorical scholars analyze a vast array of cultural communication for its relation to gender concepts. Not surprisingly, feminist rhetorical critics tend to focus on mediated communication, as television, film, newspapers, music, music videos, and so forth, transmit messages about gender widely and quickly.

Brenda Cooper, for example, examines the narrative structure of the film *Thelma & Louise.* By examining the way the movie was filmed and the point of view privileged by the movie's plot packaging and camera angles, Cooper argues that *Thelma & Louise* turns the idea of a "male gaze" on its head and, in turn, constructs a "female gaze." Put differently, the film is framed in such a way that it makes a mockery of violent masculinity and blatant sexism—activities glorified in many other Hollywood films. Cooper provides many examples in which the audience sees "female characters actively challenging patriarchal conventions rarely available in mainstream media."[21]

In the last half of this chapter you will read an essay about the 2001 film *Shallow Hal.* The directors of *Shallow Hal,* Bobby and Peter Farrelly, also directed the wildly successful comedy *Something about Mary.* Feminist rhetorical scholars Kristin J. Anderson and Christina Accomando analyze the 1998 box office smash for the way the film normalizes stalking, a crime that disproportionately affects women, and blames the victim, in this case, Mary. They do not, however, end their analysis with the film itself. They also look at the way movie reviews serve to translate the misogynist messages of *Something about Mary.* To support their conclusions, Anderson and Accomando analyze the use of a modern Greek chorus in the film. When another stalker is revealed in the film, the chorus returns to sing, "'There's something about Mary that [those who don't know her] don't know.' That is there's something about Mary that actually causes men to stalk her."[22] Turning their attention to reviews, Anderson and Accomando analyze the description of stalking in major newspapers for the authoritative framing of the criminal behavior. They write, "How is the film described if it isn't described as a woman stalked by five men? Reviews construct the film as, at least in part, a sweet and innocent love story." By constantly referring to the stalking as romantic behavior, the theorist note, "That half the reviews examined here reinterpret illegal surveillance techniques, false identities, and violence . . . to mean courtship."

These films are just a few of the modern mediated message examples feminist rhetorical scholars find socially significant. As noted above, feminist rhetorical critics have analyzed paintings, songs, videos, editorials, advertisements, web pages, and television, as sites in which gender and power are communicated.

The section that follows concretely outlines some of the more common methods of feminist criticism used by rhetorical scholars. It is not meant to be an exhaustive list, but you should be able to see that many of the approaches discussed in the following section were used in the examples of feminist rhetorical criticism described above.

APPROACHES TO USING FEMINIST CRITICISM

Feminist rhetorical scholars are important to feminism because they see patriarchy as being maintained by a symbolic system, a language that defines gender in narrow and specific ways. Through our communication practices and language choices we have both a poverty and power when it comes to gender. The poverty comes when language use sculpts masculinity and femininity in ways that are not complex, resulting in disparity and domination. Another poverty of thinking occurs when language and communication practices are used so that masculinity and femininity are seen as the only two gendered choices. In many cultures, Native American cultures for example, more than two genders exist.[23] Many feminists are interested in opening up our symbolic system so that many genders flourish and those wanting to express themselves outside of our current gender codes feel the freedom to do so. Herein lays the power of language. By systematically analyzing our language choices and communication practices, one can in part effectively undermine the patriarchal logic of gender. This is the work of feminist rhetorical critics.

There are perhaps countless ways one could go about analyzing rhetorical artifacts for the meaning produced about gender. However, if one looks over the history of feminist rhetorical criticism, four prominent critical techniques emerge.[24] (1) Feminists are interested in *redefining* gendered ideals and gendered behavior. (2) Feminist rhetorical scholars are *recovering* communication practices that have been forgotten or considered unimportant. (3) Feminist rhetorical criticism is interested in *recording* the cultural production of the rhetorical artifacts we consume so as to uncover the ways in which gender is created (as well as arguing that gender is created, not natural). (4) Feminist rhetorical theorists create new theories of rhetoric that champion feminist ideals. They engaged in a *revisioning* of rhetorical theory. As mentioned earlier, depending on the type of feminism to which one subscribes, some of the choices will be more or less appealing. For example, liberal feminists are interested in women's representation in the current social world. Therefore, a liberal feminist might be more interested in the second and third critical approach. Liberal feminists' particular theoretical interests make showcasing forgotten female rhetors and demonstrating how women are excluded from the communication process a priority. Materialist and cultural feminists, interested in reordering our values and institutions, might favor techniques one and four, as both suggest new ways of thinking. That being said, it is possible that all feminist theoretical perspectives could use any number of these approaches to further knowledge about their feminist argument. A feminist rhetorical criticism may use one of these approaches or combine several together.

Redefining

While attempting to redefine what it means to be a gendered human being, feminist rhetorical critics generally undertake one of several tasks. First, feminist rhetorical critics note the way language is used to describe gendered ideals in stereotypical ways. Second, they try to create new language that will give nonpatriarchal dimension to people's lives or a language to effectively demystify patriarchy. Third, feminist critics reclaim words used to straightjacket masculinity and femininity and thereby infuse them with new meaning.

Prominent rhetorical scholars have long held the premise that patriarchy is largely maintained by language. Put differently, male domination, male identification, and male centeredness are stable ideas because the words we use in everyday speech acts keep them anchored. Dale Spender argues that language is man-made.[25] Men "invented" the words we now use to convey meaning. For much of our rhetorical history, men held center stage; the words they used to generate ideas were disseminated and popularized. Women's words were silence. Man-made words became further entrenched when societies created dictionaries that discerned what a *real* word is. Dictionaries quickly became the definitive authority for what was excluded and included in our language. However, the sources used by dictionary makers were overwhelmingly male authored. The words coined by women to describe their experiences and social situations fell off the map. Kramarae writes, "The dictionary is not designed by women or for women's exercise of imagination. . . . It's not only a hostile system for women, but it is constantly referred to as the only system. It does not encourage ideas or new connections and relationships, or imagination about how we could write and talk our past and future."[26] Every year new words are added to standard dictionaries, but the initial deficit of language, it is argued, still haunts women today. Thus, it is important to note the way language is often used to paint a biased picture of gender. The words we choose often unknowingly privilege a patriarchal perspective. As such, feminists are interested in making visible the current, and inadequate, language systems in our culture. Also, women strive to symbolically represent, and thus legitimate, experiences they could not previously explain. For example, words such as sexual harassment did not exist until the second wave of feminism took root in the 1970s.[27] Julia T. Wood notes, "Our language gave victims no socially recognized way to label what happened to them as wrong or unacceptable. Since the term was coined, people who suffer unwelcome sexual conduct have a way to name their experiences and demand institutional and legal redress."[28]

Another example of this sort of redefinition can be found when exploring the intersections of oppression. Black American women, and often men, were subjected to a color caste system. Black Americans with lighter skin and European facial features consciously and subconsciously gained more privilege and were considered more attractive in both white and black communities. Today, and this is especially true for black women, some of the most prominently featured sport straight hair, Anglo facial features, and lighter skin shades.[29] This subtextual belief was difficult to talk about until it was given a name: Colorism. Colorism describes the discrimination that many blacks experience, a discrimination that is certainly racist, but also can be a very complicated mixture of racism and sexism. While some prominent athletes that do not fit the Anglo mold have gained the cultural spotlight, here one can see some examples of colorism's influence. *Ebony,* a magazine targeting an African American audience, featured tennis great Serena

Williams on the cover of its October 2000 issue. Although Serena, and her sister Venus, stormed and transformed the largely Caucasian tennis world with their muscular bodies and beaded hair, *Ebony*'s cover showed Serena with long, blond, and straight hair. It is difficult to draw complete conclusions from this example. Serena may have considered the implications of the look and chosen it anyway. Feminists of course believe in personal choice. What this demonstrates is words such as colorism and sexual harassment can be controversial, because it is not always clear when it is appropriate to use new language. Yet, many feminists believe that a healthy dialogue about such issues will not only legitimate the definitions but also clarify their boundaries.

Some feminists have created definitions that express empowering ideals. The word *womanist* was coined by black women to describe the richness women of color experience when they unite and the fullness such perspective could bring to feminism, if included. Accordingly, Alice Walker writes, "Feminist is to Womanist as lavender is to purple."[30]

The second definitional technique used by feminists involves taking words that were once used to diminish femininity and reclaiming them for feminist purposes. Mary Daly notes that under patriarchy, the term *spinster* is a sexist category used to label unmarried women as unfulfilled and useless. No such derogatory word exists for men choosing not to wed. Daly turns the notion of spinster on its head by repeatedly using the term to mean "one who spins." She adds, "A woman whose occupation is to spin participates in the whirling movement of creation."[31]

Riot Grrrls, started by punk rockers in Washington, DC, also use nondeferential language in their own publications (called "zines," as in short, self-published magazines) to reshape and redefine femininity. "Riot grrrls see zine writing and publishing as a basic method of empowerment; zine production is self-motivated, political activism that a girl can do entirely independently. Zines subvert standard patriarchal mainstream media by critiquing society and the media without being censored."[32] The language play involved with naming the group Riot Grrrls should not escape notice. Changing the spelling of "girl" to "grrrl" visually as well as semantically alters the passivity of the word. The term girl is often used to describe grown women, unconsciously relegating women to a protected and less competent category. When a growl is added to the word, it is given force and stature.

Many feminist critics have taken to writing their own dictionary definitions or altogether rewriting the dictionary.[33] Although inventing new language is often considered "against the rules," many feminists argue the language rules are rigged and need to be reorganized and reinvigorated. Feminist rhetorical criticism utilizing redefinition (1) explains and names how language functions to regulate femininity and masculinity and/or (2) creates or reinvents language that expands the possibilities of gender.

Recovering

Throughout this chapter, you will hear that women and feminine ways of speaking have been systematically excluded from the public realm for much of the rhetorical tradition. However, this exclusion was not complete. For periods of time, generally around social reform platforms such as suffrage and abolition, women produced rhetorical texts. Some even raucously overtook the podium in defiance of established norms. However, in most anthologies of public discourse you will find few women. In noted compilations of public speeches, women account for a small percentage of speakers. Although the historical exclusion of female rhetors is partly responsible for the disparity, it does not always explain their absence. Regardless of the dearth, the notable absence of women "confirms that men continue to serve as standard for communication performance and that women are peripheral in terms of significant discourse."[34]

Karlyn Kohrs Campbell's anthology *Man Cannot Speak for Her* uses the approach of recovering rhetors lost in a male-centered society. Also, Kohrs Campbell's work recovers the rhetorical options surreptitiously proposed by women facing enormous prohibitions. Despite being discouraged from taking the podium, women such as Christine de Pizan, a fourteenth-century French feminist, wrote books for women that clearly serve as rhetorical theory. Christine de Pizan's books *The Book of the City of Ladies* and *The Treasure of the City of Ladies* provide discursive theory that differs from the dominant traditions of time, but is no less valuable. Kohrs Campell takes issue with many rhetorical scholars that argue "no woman has added to rhetorical theory during this time."[35] According to Kohrs Campbell, the "practices in *The Book of the City of Ladies* add an important dimension to understanding the power of conversation as performance and, in that sense, embodied discourse."[36]

Not all feminist recovering involves archival investigations of classical texts. In contemporary artifacts, our patriarchal society often pushes women to the margins. Elizabeth Dole, for example, was criticized for stepping down from her office at the Department of Transportation when her husband ran for president in 1996. However, a feminist rhetorical analysis demonstrates that Dole's rhetorical significance should not be overlooked. Gutgold notes that Dole was a groundbreaking rhetor at the Republican National Convention in 1996. Her rhetorical style, infused with stories, personal pronouns, and nonverbal intimacy, had never been seen at a political convention. Although Gutgold ultimately argues that Dole was unsuccessful in transitioning to a Presidential candidate, "Dole's long and varied career makes for an ideal exploration into how a woman modifies her speech with her changing roles."[37] As more women enter the public arena, feminist analysis grows increasingly necessary.

Feminist rhetorical critics approaching a rhetorical artifact by recovering are (1) acknowledging rhetors that patriarchy has erased and/or (2) recovering the lost significance of a visible female rhetor.

Recording

Another analytical approach used by feminists is to record cultural production. This means that the techniques used to create an artifact are scrutinized. An important part of this approach is the understanding that an artifact does not stand apart from the processes that make it. By analyzing these *systems of production* one can understand quite thoroughly how messages about gender are created and sometimes understand why a message is packaged a particular way. In sum, this approach analyzes how the rhetorical artifact was put together, not just the end result.

Communication scholar Sut Jhally's criticism of MTV music videos is a form of feminist criticism utilizing this approach. Jhally's highly regarded video *Dreamworlds II* records the processes comprising sexist music videos. His research reveals that men direct 90 percent of music videos. Additionally, he documents the roles, clothing, and behavior of the men and women performing in the videos to demonstrate that music videos overwhelmingly tell a story about male sexual fantasy. Jhally's analysis also notes the camera angles that place men at the center and women at the periphery. When the camera does focus on women it usually only focuses on one part of her, generally the buttocks, legs, or breasts. These production techniques serve to visually dismember women—making women objects, and even more disturbingly, only one part of an object. These are just a few examples of the way that the production of the rhetorical artifact is analyzed.

Jean Kilbourne's work in advertising also functions as a rhetorical criticism that analyzes the production of advertisements. Her analysis of advertising parallels that of Jhally's work in music videos. Kilbourne analyzed advertisements for the way women's bodies were arranged in the ads to convey a message of demure femininity or sexualized objectification; how the print or voice copy accompanying the ads reinforce these gendered messages; as well as how the images were produced to flawlessness through airbrushing, thus equating femininity with physical perfection. In sum, the conscious choices of the artifact's production are detailed for the meaning they convey.

A feminist approach to analyzing cultural production (1) uncovers who is behind the rhetorical artifact and (2) closely analyzes how the rhetorical artifact is put together.

Revisioning

Finally, an important part of feminist criticism is creating new theories about rhetoric. This approach analyzes a specific rhetorical artifact or artifacts as part of a larger project that revisions what it means to engage in rhetoric. As mentioned before, the definition of rhetoric was once solely used to describe the written and spoken word used to persuade. Feminist theoretical thought worked hard to expand that definition. This was important feminist work since women, as historical subjects, would be significantly excluded from the rhetorical history if defined so narrowly. The work of Karen Foss and Sonja Foss in this area extrapolates new theories about what constitutes *significant* rhetoric. In their book *Women Speak*, significant rhetoric emanates from ordinary individuals not noted for their historical accomplishments. Females or even groups of females in private as well as public domains create significant rhetoric; significant rhetorical works include ongoing rhetorical dialogues that are dramatically different from speechmaking. This is an important theoretical departure, because as Deirdre Johnson notes, much of the work women do is ritualistic and impermanent[38]; hence, feminist rhetoric should include symbolic activities that are less concrete and finished. Revisioning these theoretical ideas, then, it is possible to see much of what women do as historically significant rhetoric. These activities include baking, children's parties, gardening, letter writing, herbology, and needlework, among others. These activities produce meaning, but have had their significance diminished in the patriarchal world.

Likewise, rhetorical theorists such a Sally Miller Gearhart theoretically question some of the fundamental ideas about the way we disseminate ideas. As a society we have for years believed that trying to persuade somebody through discourse was a rational alternative to violence. However, Gearhart notes that common rhetorical techniques have an ability to produce a personal violation as "real" as violence. Instead of trying to change someone through rhetorical message making, a feminist rhetorician opposing domination would create a rhetorical situation that makes change possible, but doesn't insist on change. Using both the feminist rhetorical approach of revisioning and redefining, Gearhart brings new language into the realm of rhetoric. For example, she uses the word *enfoldment* to describe a rhetorical process whereby you offer, make yourself available, surround, listen, and create an opening with your rhetoric, rather than "penetrating the mind" of those you engage.[39] Influenced by Gearhart, other theorists have built on this premise. Foss and Griffin, for example, have outlined a theory of *invitational rhetoric*. This theory suggests a rubric for actualizing rhetoric of nondomination that invites participants to a point of view, but does not create a rhetorical imposition. "The stance taken by invitational rhetors toward their audience obviously is different from that assumed by traditional rhetors. Invitational rhetors do not believe they have the right to claim that their experiences or perspectives are superior to those of their audience members and refuse to impose their perspective on them."[40]

A feminist rhetorical criticism using the approach of revisioning (1) questions the assumptions underlying desirable rhetoric and (2) offers new rhetorical insights and possibilities as well as frameworks to analyze such rhetoric.

CRITICAL ESSAY: A FEMINIST RHETORICAL ANALYSIS OF *SHALLOW HAL*

In the fall of 2001, Twentieth Century Fox released a film, *Shallow Hal*, directed by Bobby and Peter Farrelly, the brothers whose previous films include *Dumb and Dumber* (1994), *Something about Mary* (1998), and *Me, Myself and Irene* (2000). The director's fourth major film, *Shallow Hal*, was lauded by a prominent American critic as one of the ten best of 2001.[41] *Shallow Hal's* major moral, one we would expect many feminists to embrace wholeheartedly, is that for women, *interior* beauty, not exterior beauty, is what truly counts. A feminist rhetorical analysis of the DVD of *Shallow Hal* allows us to investigate more deeply in what ways the film's proposed moral is both underscored and undermined.

We proceed with two main sections. First, we provide a brief discussion of feminist rhetorical criticism as related to film and television. Feminist criticism is especially interested in the representations of gender in these two mediums because the messages are distributed quickly and widely. As bell hooks notes, "Television and film also are critical texts. . . . because they are the primary tools used to socialize oppressed peoples to internalize the thoughts and values of white supremacist capitalist patriarchy."[42] Thus, it is important to understand the ways that feminist rhetorical critics unpack films for their content—how they strive to be critical cultural consumers. Second, we analyze more specifically how this particular film, *Shallow Hal,* was put together and the rhetorical choices made in its production. Doing so allows us to better discern the inherently contradictory messages in this popular Farrelly brothers' film about what constitutes "a beautiful woman" in our society.

Feminist Rhetorical Approaches to Film and Television Artifacts

We believe patriarchy is maintained by a symbolic system, a language that defines gender in narrow and specific ways. By systematically analyzing our language choices and communication practices, we can, in part, effectively undermine the patriarchal logic of gender. There are numerous ways one could go about analyzing rhetorical artifacts for the meaning produced about gender. However, if one looks over the history of feminist rhetorical criticism as it particularly relates to television and film, three prominent critical techniques emerge: recording, recovering, and revisioning. Feminist scholars *recover* communicators or communication practices that have been forgotten or considered unimportant. Feminists *record* the cultural production of the rhetorical artifacts we consume so as to uncover the ways in which gender is created. Finally, by developing new theories of rhetoric that champion feminist ideals, feminists *revision* rhetorical theory.[43]

Recovering.   Many feminist scholars are committed to recovering and documenting the contributions women have made in various fields. In the national and international film and television industries, the Women's Film Pioneers Project, spearheaded by Jane Gaines at Duke University, epitomizes this type of archival work.

> The Pioneers project began as a collaborative effort to advance research on the accomplishments and history of women filmmakers from the early years of cinema through to the coming of sound. The original emphasis was on directors, writers, and producers. Recently, the project has expanded to include editors, exhibitors, publicists, and others working in the early years. The interest in directors, writers, and producers has been linked to a large archival project inspired by the need to discover, restore, preserve, exhibit, and distribute extant 35mm films. However, this emphasis does not exclude the parallel interest in women audiences in the silent period.[44]

Rediscovering the work of early women in the film and television industries and female spectators is not the only type of "recovery" work that interests feminist scholars, however.

That the film and television industry is *still* male dominated there can be no doubt. A recent study by Martha M. Lauren reveals that women comprised only "17 percent of all executive producers, producers, directors, writers, cinematographers, and editors working on the top 250 grossing films of 2002."[45] If 17 percent seems like a low percentage, it's disheartening to discover that in particular fields, such as directing, the percentage is even lower; indeed, only one in ten directors in Hollywood is a woman[46] and one in ten directors of American television shows is a woman.[47] Because women still seem to be rather systematically excluded from powerful positions in the industry, feminist scholars also seek to make the work of *current* women in the industry more visible. For example, in her book, *Women Filmmakers of African and Asian Diaspora,* Gwendolyn Foster analyzes selected films by six contemporary filmmakers of African and Asian decent—Julie Dash, Zeinabu Irene Davis, Mira Nair, Nogzi Onwurah, Pratibha Parmar, and Trinh T. Minhha.[48]

Beyond recovering and illuminating early and contemporary women filmmakers and their contributions, feminist scholars also at times take a second look at women's genres within the film and television industry that the dominant culture has dismissed as trivial. A prime example here is Tania Modleski's book *Loving with a Vengeance: Mass-Produced Fantasies for Women.*[49] Modleski's sophisticated analysis of women and their complicated relationship to soap operas pioneered the way for feminists to ask questions about other genres such as women's films, which our culture has often dismissed as "chick flicks" or "weepies."[50]

Recording.   Feminists interested in studying film and television texts also are interested in recording the cultural production of the rhetorical artifacts we consume and, in doing so, shedding light on the complex ways in which gender is created. In this analytical approach, techniques used to create the artifact are intensely analyzed. Most importantly, the artifact does not stand apart from the processes that make it. By analyzing these systems of production, we can better understand how messages about gender are created and packaged. In sum, this approach analyzes how the rhetorical artifact was put together, not just the end result.

Exemplifying this approach is the book *From Mouse to Mermaid: The Politics of Film, Gender, and Culture.* In their introduction to this collection, the editors underscore that they view "Disney" in multiple ways.

> **First, Disney is Walt:** the seventeen-year-old who practiced his signature and subsequently wrote it on the title frame of each film his company created; the kindly "Uncle Walt" who addressed us on Sunday evenings as host of *The Wonderful World of Color;* the FBI informant who gave J. Edgar Hoover access to film scripts; the man who died on December 15, 1966, in St. Joseph's Hospital across the street from his Burbank studio; the cryogenically frozen body of urban legend that sleeps somewhere deep in the bowels of Disneyland. **Second, Disney is a Studio:** a pro-

duction facility that grew from one camera in Disney's Uncle Bob's garage in 1923 to its 1990s multiple incarnations as Walt Disney Pictures, Touchstone, Hollywood, Caravan, the many subsidiaries of Buena Vista Television and the Disney Channel, as well as the recent studio acquisitions Miramax and Merchant/Ivory. **Third, Disney is a canon of popular film.** Between 1939 and 1992, the feature-length productions alone number 245, only seventy-seven of which were produced while Walt was alive. **Fourth, Disney is a multinational corporation:** in 1940, public stock in the Disney Company sold for $5 a share and today Disney is an entertainment and media conglomerate worth an estimated $4.7 billion. **And fifth, Disney is an ideology:** a sign whose mythology and cultural capital is dependent on and imbricated in all the above manifestations of the name "Disney." (Bold Font ours.)[51]

Collectively, the essayists in *From Mouse to Mermaid* encourage readers of "Disney" to be cultural critics, pushing us to ask difficult questions about our own pleasures in watching or experiencing "Disney." Thus, these feminist communication scholars ask us to not just examine a cultural artifact from a particular feminist perspective—for example, documenting sexist stereotypes in a particular Disney film—but rather to consider Disney film as cultural capital, to think of it in terms of its production, its languages, its audiences, its ideologies.

Revisioning.   Perhaps the most important contribution feminists have made to the study of film and television is in their revisioning of cinematic theory. The most referenced work in the history of feminist film theory is undeniably Laura Mulvey's "Visual Pleasure and Narrative Cinema."[52] In her essay, Mulvey reasons that because most filmmakers in Hollywood are male, the voyeuristic gaze of the camera is male; moreover, the male characters on the screen make women characters the object of their gaze. Consequently, the spectator's gaze ends up reflecting the voyeuristic male gaze of the camera and the male characters. In essence, Mulvey theorizes that the dominant male gaze in mainstream American films reflects and satisfies the male unconscious.

Mulvey's revisioning of psychoanalytical film theory in terms of gender construction profoundly influenced the way feminist scholars and others thought about film and television texts. For many feminist media scholars, Mulvey's main thesis rang true, for it appeared that in classic films, such as Hitchcock's, women were consistently made into passive objects of male voyeurism who primarily existed to fulfill the desires and express the anxieties of male spectators.

Mulvey's pivotal 1975 concept of the "male gaze" has been revisited these last twenty-nine years by many other feminist communication scholars who have amended or revised or critiqued it in significant ways. For example, some scholars have argued that women spectators may reject the male gaze and instead identify or construct a "female gaze" in reading mainstream television shows, such as *Cagney and Lacey,* or mainstream movies, such as *Thelma & Louise.*[53] Scholars in queer studies, have noted that Mulvey's articulation is problematic because the "male gaze" is premised on heterosexuality. These scholars have reconceptualized the way the gaze works in order to shed light on the ways homosexual as well as heterosexual audiences might be processing various mainstream films, such as *The Fight Club* or *Boys Don't Cry*.[54] Mulvey's theoretical concept of the "male gaze" has also been critiqued by scholars who see the need for the gaze to be both *materially* as well as *psychoanalytically* constructed.[55] hooks, for example, reminds us that the politics of slavery denied the slave the right to look, so much so that a "critical or oppositional gaze" has long been a strategy of resistance and assertion of agency for black Americans in the face of domination. This gaze complicates the viewing experience in American cinemas in different ways for female and male black American spectators.[56]

A Feminist Rhetorical Reading of *Shallow Hal*

Shallow Hal is a film that reached and continues to reach a large, young viewing audience. In this essay, we scrutinize the rhetorical choices made by the directors of the film and the producers of the DVD regarding *Shallow Hal's* representations of women, beauty, and sexuality. As feminist rhetorical critics, we approach this task in the spirit of "recording," as we are most interested in analyzing how the film was put together and the rhetorical choices made in its DVD production. We also approach the film and its DVD, however, in the sprit of "recovery" as we seek to recover some of the lost rhetors of the film.

Specifically, this essay proceeds by summarizing the plot of the film, and then analyzing the film's sight gags (overt visual comedy), its portrayal of "inner beauty," and its marketing strategies. We argue that the film *Shallow Hal* ultimately reinforces the discrimination women feel under current definitions of beauty in our society. Second, we examine the extra text in the *Shallow Hal* DVD. After analyzing the brothers' offhand remarks about women in the film as compared to their male counterparts, we conclude that many women's contributions in this film are marginalized and that the rhetorical positioning of the Farrelly brothers suggests that this marginalization will continue in future films. Finally, after analyzing the director's, special effects creator's, and Gwyneth Paltow's take on the "fat suit," we make connections between Hollywood's fascination with the fat suit and other forms of discrimination now deemed unacceptable.

The Plot and Proposed Moral of Shallow Hal. The plot of the Farrelly brothers' fourth major film, *Shallow Hal*,[57] cowritten with Sean Moynihan is rather simple.[58] Before the opening credits, the audience sees a 9-year-old Hal at the bedside of his dying father, a reverend. High on morphine, his father advises the 9-year-old Hal that he should find himself "a classic beauty, with a perfect can and great toddies" because "hot young tail's what it's all about."[59] The film then opens with images of the adult Hal (Jack Black) and his closest male buddy, Mauricio (Jason Alexander) at a dance bar. Here, these two rather dumpy-looking men try pathetically, desperately, and unsuccessfully to pick up only the most gorgeous, sexy women. Similar scenes follow that continue to underscore Hal's shallowness until his chance encounter with Tony Robbins in a stuck elevator. The television guru hypnotizes Hal so that, from then on, he will only see the "inner beauty" of people he encounters. Soon following the hypnosis, Hal and Mauricio return to the dance club. Hal, from his point of view, is seen dancing with three model-perfect women: while from friend, Mauricio's point of view, Hal is seen dancing with a trio of women whom Mauricio describes as a "pack of stampeding buffalo."[60] The next day, Hal meets the woman of his dreams, Rosemary (played by Gywneth Paltrow and, alternately, by Ivy Snitzer). Even though there are a few moments in which the audience is privy to the "real" 300-pound Rosemary, for the most part throughout the courtship, the audience vicariously sees Rosemary through Hal's eyes, which means seeing Rosemary as the movie-star thin, Gywneth Paltrow.[61] Rosemary is a volunteer at both the hospital burn unit and a member of the Peace Corps; she also, fortuitously, happens to be the daughter of Hal's boss. Hal's dating of Rosemary and Hal's novel insights for Rosemary's father's corporation, lead to an inevitable and immediate rise in Hal's career. Meanwhile, Hal's friend Mauricio mourns the loss of his immature friend and consequently secures the magic words, from Tony Robbins, to dehypnotize Hal to his old shallow ways of seeing. The ending of this romantic comedy is rather predictable in that Hal's original, real-world vision is restored; yet Hal *chooses* to see beyond Rosemary's physical characteristics to love Rosemary for who she truly is. He appreciates her humor, her altruistic worldview, and her inner beauty. He is in love, and he genuinely sees her as beautiful.

Shallow Hal's repeatedly underscored moral—*that one should not judge people, in particular women, by their physical appearances*—appears to be a rather revolutionary one for Hollywood and one we would expect feminists to truly embrace. For the Farrelly brothers' film strives to argue, as Tony Robbins in the film itself testifies, that everything we "know about beauty is programmed: television, magazines, movies"; media images are all falsely telling us what is beautiful and what is not.[62] And indeed, evidence for this thesis occurs early in the film when the unenlightened Hal explains that he is seeking a woman with the "face" of Paulina in a *Sports Illustrated* layout, the "beams" and "teeth" of Heidi Klum, the "knockers" and "ass" of Britney Spears, the "grille" of Michelle Phifer, and the "smile" of Rebecca Romijn-Stamos.[63] So from one angle, it would appear that feminists would rejoice in Hal's transformation in this film from an unenlightened, immature, shallow, middle-aged adolescent to a more complicated man who is genuinely in love with Rosemary, a good-natured, funny, altruistic, plus-size woman.

But what's fascinating to us, as materialist feminists, is the way the Farrelly brothers' movie and the supplementary material on the DVD continuously undermine its intended revolutionary message. In this criticism, we will look closely at the film's rhetorical choices, analyzing the comic gags and its construction of "inner beauty." Then we'll analyze the production of the film by reviewing select material from the DVD, including the cover jacket images, the Farrelly brothers' voice over commentary about the making of the film, and the rhetorical implications of Hollywood's latest craze—the fat suit.

Shallow Hal's Sight Gags and Construction of "Inner Beauty"

The Farrelly brothers had a reputation for over-the-top humor prior to *Shallow Hal*. Their lowbrow films testify that no topic or groups of people are immune to the Farrelly brothers' mockery. Anyone who had seen any of their previous movies would probably find the humor in *Shallow Hal* rather tame in comparison. Yet, if, by the standards previously established in the other Farrelly brothers' films, the crude, visual humor was *underplayed* in *Shallow Hal*, then why did the film's sight gags come under such close scrutiny by reviewers.[64] We believe that what is the most "off" and therefore the most notable about the sight gags in *Shallow Hal* is that they consistently undermine, rather than reinforce the film's intended thesis.

Consider that before Hal met Tony Robbins, Hal would never have given the real Rosemary a second glance since he was a shallow man who was always proverbially judging a book by its cover, a man who would never give a 300 pound woman a second glance. Undeniably, the film's overall message is to prove how shallow and wrong Hal's perspective is. Yet virtually all of the sight gags in the film are clichéd jokes that primarily work by reinforcing society's stereotypical, often mean-spirited assumptions about overweight people. The film's visual jokes encourage audiences to judge overweight people by the effects of their weight. Hence, the audience is prompted to laugh when they see Rosemary inhale a huge milkshake she was supposed to be sharing with Hal. Or when we see Rosemary do a cannonball that displaces such a large volume of water in the neighborhood pool that it quenches a barbeque and literally propels a child to the top of a tree. Or when we see a perplexed, "caught-in-a-practical-joke" Hal unfurl Rosemary's sexy, lavender g-string that is literally a yard wide. Or when we see Rosemary's weight anchor a canoe such that our hero, Hal, is literally paddling mid-air.

One could counter argue that the humor lies in the audience NOT seeing the obese Rosemary in each of these instances, but rather seeing, as Hal does, the svelte Gywneth Paltrow. For example, audience members who empathize with Hal can vicariously smile at the incongruity of seeing a model-thin woman having the freedom to consume a double burger rather than peck at a salad. Or slurp down that jumbo shake for two rather than sip a Perrier.

We do not deny that humor is undeniably complex, but we believe it is important to acknowledge that in general, the sight gags only work because as audience members, we see the *reality* that Hal is not privy to. Sometimes, we are given glimpses of the very large Rosemary by the filmmakers. For example, we see glimpses in the film of stand-in Ivy Snitzer or see the slim Paltrow casting a huge reflection in a store window. Thus, the filmmakers continually prompt viewers to see the 300-pound Rosemary, so that we imagine her even when she is not literally in the scene. Hence, when a scene features only Gywneth Paltrow, the viewer projects the large Rosemary into the scene and thus, the visual gag becomes no fundamentally different than the tried and true "fat jokes" so pervasive in American culture. There really is no laughing "with" Rosemary, only a laughing "at." In general the humor is sophomoric in both its sexism and weightism.

If the humor in the film is problematic, so is its point of view and its construction of "inner beauty." Like most films, the point of view in *Shallow Hal* allows the audience to have full knowledge. As audience members we see many scenes that Hal is not privy to (for example, the meeting between Tony Robbins and Hal's friend, Mauricio). But a film can privilege a particular character's perspective and *Shallow Hal* privileges Hal's. Thus, for the vast majority of the film, the audience sees what Hal sees; that is, Gwyneth Paltrow in all her physical, film star perfection. Indeed, from the time Rosemary is introduced, we visually see Paltrow for most of the film; and we very rarely see the 300-pound Rosemary. On the DVD, one of the Farrelly brothers explains why Gywneth Paltrow was cast to represent *inner* beauty:

> A few . . . critics have problems with the movie, saying, ultimately why is our idea of beautiful women . . . ah . . . Gywneth Paltrow's character. And our defense to that is "well, it's not *our* idea, it's [*Hal's*] idea and that was because of what his father tells him—to go out and look for the perfect girl, with the perfect butt, great toddies, good-looking. . . . He's describing, basically Gwyneth. Not that we don't think Gwyneth is the ideal beauty, but that's not what we were proclaiming. We set up this [first] scene specifically to not have to answer those questions, which of course we had to anyway."[65]

But, of course, the main reason the Farrelly brothers were repeatedly asked to answer this question is because their defense of their choice to cast Gywneth Paltrow as *inner* beauty, is lame. Everyone knows Gywneth Paltrow was not only cast but also featured, primarily for her *outer* beauty.

Paradoxically, the filmmakers give us a film whose "revolutionary" moral is for society *not* to judge large people by their appearances *within* a film that is undeniably Hollywood-traditional in starring the ultra-thin Gwyneth Paltrow, rather than a genuine plus-size actress like Rosie O'Donnell, Kathy Bates, Carmryn Manheim, or Queen Latifah. And perhaps an even greater irony lies in the fact that even Paltrow's body was not-quite-perfect-enough by Hollywood standards, for in the film's bedroom scene, where the audience sees a full-body shot of the backside of Paltrow as she removes her sexy negligee and bikini underwear is, if we are to take the Farrelly brothers at their word, actually NOT Gywneth Paltrow, but a "butt double."[66]

Shallow Hal fits neatly into Laura Mulvey's theory that most films are primarily designed to provide pleasure to the male spectator. There are numerous scenes in this film in which women are seen as the objects, not the subjects of the gaze, a gaze in which women's bodies are inevitably eroticized. Hal eroticizes only sexy women before his Robbins-induced hypnosis and, after his Robbins-induced hypnosis, he eroticizes all inherently "good" women, even unattractive ones. Perhaps if our hero discovered the erotic in a relationship with the 300-pound Rosemary, the film might have broken new ground. But Hal's bedroom scene is not shared with Gwyneth Paltrow in her fat suit, it is a conventional bedroom scene with a not-so-attractive male hero and a stunningly attractive Gywneth Paltrow.

Thus, Hal is typical of the film hero whom theorist Laura Mulvey discusses in her book *Visual and Other Pleasures*. Hal is the active hero who advances the narrative, controlling the events, the women, and the erotic gaze.[67] Gywneth Paltrow functions primarily as erotic spectacle. In spite of their noble intentions, the Farrelly brothers offer no new language of desire.

Shallow Hal—the DVD

DVDs are enormously beneficial to rhetorical scholars. Not only do they allow critics to replay scenes easily with close-captioned dialogue, but DVDs also provide supplementary materials regarding various systems of production, such as marketing, advertising, costuming, filming, or editing. Hence, a DVD differs from a VHS copy of a film; for a DVD is not just a repackaging of a film for distribution, but rather it is, as Brookley and Westerfelhaus note, "a synergistic package comprised of product and promotion."[68] As such, it deserves a close, critical reading. In this section, we will again consider the film's intended moral—*to not judge people by their appearances*—as we review the rhetorical packaging of images on the cover jacket of the DVD, the Farrelly brothers' own rhetoric in the DVD commentary, as well as the technical wizardry and the rhetorical implications of the fat suit.

Visual Images from the DVD. Marketing of DVDs relies in part on the selection of key images that try to capture the essence of the film and strike a chord with the audience (in the case of DVDs, the renter or buyer). Similarly, filmmakers choose a very select amount of photos or jpgs from the actual film to send out in their press packets, photos that ideally capture the essence of the film while simultaneously sparking the imaginations of writers and reviewers in the print media.

The front cover of the *Shallow Hal* DVD, features a curvaceous Gwyneth Paltrow, wearing a very tightly fitted, bright pink t-shirt and small-checkered, pink and white skirt. Her body is positioned mostly profile, so that her what-can-only-be-digitally-manipulated breasts perk out quite nicely. She is holding both hands, in a rather schoolgirl way, with Jack Black. Jack Black is wearing a loosely fitting spotted yellow shirt with oversize brown trousers. The calves of Paltrow's naked legs in her slim, heeled sandals contrast with Black's workman-like boots. Paltrow's two-inch heels also make her appear slightly taller than Black. The couple is not looking at each other; rather both appear to be looking directly at the potential purchasers of the DVD—Paltrow with a teasing, lovely smile and the wide-eyed Jack with a smirk that suggests he can't believe he's lucky enough to be holding hands with this leggy blond. Behind the couple is a blue brick wall with the couple's shadows: a slight, realistic shadow of Black and a more-defined shadow behind Paltrow that is not realistically hers, but rather that of a 300-or-more-pound woman. Above the title, *Shallow Hal,* is the film's slogan in smaller print, "True Love Is Worth the Weight!"

The DVD's cover jacket, which is also used on the VHS version, epitomizes the same paradox we have been discussing in this essay. The slogan's pun, "True

Love Is Worth the Weight" alludes to this being a story of a hero's lengthy quest for romance, as well as underscoring his true love of a large or weighty woman. But the main "feel" of the front cover belies the latter reading of the slogan, for the images of the two stars is nothing more than yet another photographic reiteration of a male's pleasure and a female positioned-as-erotic spectacle. Paltrow's sexual come-on positioning is so strong on the cover jacket, so brightly and digitally enhanced, that the shadows behind the stars seem to just blend into the background. The oversize shadow of Paltrow, like the large Rosemary in the film, is seen in only a negligible way and only to the most conscientious viewer.

That the Farrelly brothers are intent on selling the film as both a stereotypical romance and as an original comedy is also shown in the selection of photos that their marketing department distributed to the press. Consider the three most reoccurring photos accompanying the reviews: the slim Paltrow as Rosemary, sweetly and jointly sipping the jumbo shake with Hal (Jack Black); the slim Rosemary and Hal paddling a canoe, with Rosemary "anchoring" one end and Hal up in the air on the other; or Hal, looking perplexed as he stretches out sexy, lavender-laced, bikini underpants that are literally a yard wide. Similarly, in the two-minute theatrical trailer for *Shallow Hal* which establishes the slim Rosemary and Hal's courtship, no less then nine sight gags are featured; including a scene not in the film, of the slender Gywneth Paltrow leading/pulling an exhausted horse with a severely bowed back. In another section of the DVD, "Deleted Scenes," there is a scene from the bedroom, in which the bed itself collapses under Paltrow's "weight." In essence, most of the press photos, the theatrical trailer, and the deleted film clip function in much the same vein as the sight gags analyzed earlier in this essay. These images are thinly disguised fat jokes embedded in a stereotypical romance, images that are consistently at odds with the film's intended thesis.

Farrelly Brothers' Commentary from the DVD.   Robert Alan Brookey and Robert Westerfelhaus have examined how the "extra text" in DVDs function rhetorically. They note that "extra text offers consumers access to commentary by those involved with making the film, and it positions this commentary as authoritative."[69] In doing so, the extra text in DVDs *direct* viewers experience of the film. In this section, we'll look closely at the "authoritative" words of the directors of *Shallow Hal* in the DVD's extra text called "Commentary by the Farrelly Brothers." In the next section, we'll look closely at the "authoritative" words of the creator of the fat suit, Tony Gardner. In both cases, we'll place the "authoritative" voices of the directors and visual effects creator in a larger cultural context.

In the DVD's "Commentary by the Farrelly Brothers," there are four reoccurring topics of discussion. In the voice over (which accompanies the silent reshowing of the film), the brothers make candid observations about working with the film's major actors, offer brief introductions of many performers who played minor characters, comment about filming in Charlotte, North Carolina, and endorse the film's musicians who did the various songs that were included in the film's score.

In listening to their commentary the first time, we were struck perhaps most profoundly by the major differences between the way the actors playing male minor characters were introduced as compared to the actresses who were playing the female minor characters. To check the accuracy of our initial impressions, we watched "Commentary by the Farrelly Brothers" two more times. We tallied whether the actors, male and female, were introduced by full names, whether their professional credentials were cited, whether they were noted for having worked previously on Farrelly brothers films or were recently discovered. We did not analyze the brothers' introductions to musicians, crewmembers, or actors playing major characters.[70] The 107 minor characters that were introduced range from those with a few speaking lines, such as Hal's co-workers, to local extras in the background. The length of the Farrelly brothers' improvised commentary is, of course, restrained by the length of time each of the minor characters appear in the film (since the brothers are just conversing as the film runs with no sound.) Table 13.1 displays the results.

These tallies served to confirm our initial, more subjective impressions. In the Farrelly brothers' commentary, male actors playing minor roles are more likely, as compared to their female counterparts, to be referred to by their full names, to be identified by their professional credits, and to be reemployed by the brothers.[71]

Our analysis of the Farrelly brothers' commentary strongly suggests the proverbial "good ol' boy' network" at work. The Farrelly brothers, unconsciously or consciously, seem to rehire more male actors to play minor roles, than actresses. In securing many of the actresses for *Shallow Hal,* the brothers, instead, seemed to rely heavily on Charlie Weston who auditioned "a hundred women" in New York.[72] Indeed, at one point in the commentary, one of the brothers refers to these women who were "discovered" by Charlie Weston as "Charlie's Angels."[73]

"The Farrelly Brothers Commentary" strongly suggests that the makers of *Shallow Hal* do not uphold the same principles when it comes to the male and fe-

TABLE 13.1   Directors' Introductions of the Minor Characters in "Commentary by the Farrelly Brothers"' on *Shallow Hal* DVD

	FEMALE	MALE	TOTAL
Total references to actors playing minor characters	54	55	109
Actor pointed out, but actor's name not recalled or specifically referenced or actor only referred to by first name	18	3	21
Actor identified by first and last name	36	52	88
Actor's professional credentials referenced	10	24	34
Actor worked on previous films with the Farrelly Brothers	2	13	15
Actor "discovered"	9	2	11

male actors. With regard to women, the directors simply do not practice what they preach. *Shallow Hal* contends that we should appreciate people for what they do, for who they inherently are, and not judge them by their outward appearances. *Shallow Hal* seeks to teach its audience to value people who have altruistic occupations, those who take care of a sick grandmother, volunteer at the city's hospital or join the Peace Corp. In "The Farrelly Brothers' Commentary" the directors occasionally underscore a minor male actor's altruism—the male friend who snuck into their apartment and cleaned it up; another male friend, a doctor, who treats their friends without insurance.[74] That the Farrelly brothers value men's talent as well as their altruistic acts is shown in the way the directors continually cite male actors' major professional achievements. There is a strong sense, upon listening to the commentary, of the Farrelly brothers' immense loyalty to male actors and their appreciation of their career successes. On the rare occasion that the brothers mention an actress' previous professional credits, most often it is invariably about her appearing in a *Playboy* or *Baywatch* or having a career as "a model."[75] Male actors playing minor roles are more likely to be introduced by what they have accomplished; whereas for the actresses, on the rare occasion in which they are introduced by their accomplishments, the Farrelly brothers more often than not highlight a previous occupation that inevitably employs only conventionally attractive women.

But it was not just beautiful women who had to be cast according to the demands of the screenplay, unattractive people also had to be either cast or supplemented by the makeup and special effects department. So let us now briefly examine the Farrelly brothers' commentary on some of those performers who played "unattractive" female characters.

Let us begin with Ivy Snitzer, a very large actress who on some occasions serves as a stand-in for the 300-pound Rosemary in *Shallow Hal.* The audience never sees Snitzer's face in the film, though we see her back, her calves, and so forth. On the occasions that she does appear in the film and in "The Farrelly Brothers' Commentary," the directors either do not comment on her or they offer unintentionally, yet somewhat problematic comments. Without a doubt, Ivy's longest scene in the film occurs when Hal is avoiding her, after having learned from Mauricio that the hypnosis that made him believe "really ugly girls" were "supermodels" was broken. In Snitzer's longest scene in the film, the audience sees her from the back, seated at the hospital, talking to Hal on the telephone. The voice over in "The Farrelly Brothers Commentary" in this scene is not about Snitzer, rather it centers on the brothers' admiration of the male writer of the detective novel that Hal was reading in the last scene in the film.[76] Like Hal, who in this part of the film is avoiding seeing the large Rosemary, the Farrelly brothers in this scene in "The Farrelly Brothers Commentary" avoid talking about Snitzer. But in all fairness to the directors, they do discuss Snitzer's contribution at an earlier point in the commentary, and their comments are revealing. Snitzer is commended for her "abundance of inner beauty" and for being the "heart and soul of the crew."[77] That Snitzer is seen as part of the *crew,* not a member of the cast is particularly interesting, for it displaces her as an actress and repositions her as another technician, a crew member who has mastery over an "effect." Though Snitzer, of course, holds no mastery of light, sound, camera angles, or props; the effect Snitzer then must be contributing to the film is that of her "fat."

In "The Farrelly Brothers' Commentary" and on other sections of the DVD, Ivy Snitzer is characterized, in general, as a good egg, a gal who helped Paltrow understand her part, a trouper who endorsed the film and its message, a woman whom everyone liked. And we do not mean to imply here that the Farrelly brothers and others were wrong in these assertions. What we are arguing is that regardless of her own and the directors' noble intentions, she was still somewhat exploited in the making of this film. In an interview, Ivy Snitzer noted how proud her family is about her appearance in *Shallow Hal:* "I think my mother's whole Girl Scout troop is going to opening night!."[78] Yet, sadly, in *Shallow Hal's* listed credits, Ivy Snitzer is not credited at all, not as part of the cast, not as part of the crew, not as a stand-in or body-double, not even as a consultant.[79]

To best describe the way that we believe Ivy Snitzer was used in the process of making this film, we might turn momentarily to feminist bell hooks. In *Teaching to Transgress,* bell hooks notes that in those of our classrooms that are still predominantly white, a "spirit of tokenism" may prevail. Often if there is one lone person of color in the classroom he or she is objectified by others and forced to assume the role of *native informant.*[80] As an example, hooks provides a classroom setting in which the students have been assigned a novel by a Korean American author. White students turn to the sole Korean student in the classroom to explain what they do not understand. According to hooks, this practice places an unfair responsibility on the Korean student and assumes that "experience" makes him or her an expert. In the making of *Shallow Hal,* the filmmakers often put Ivy Snitzer in the position of the "native informant" as they conveniently assume that Snitzer represents all plus-size people. This is not only evident in "The Farrelly Brothers' Commentary" but it is also evident in interviews with Gywneth Paltrow: "[M]y double, Ivy Snitzer, was really supportive. I was nervous and she was so supportive of it, she said, 'I think it's so great.' She loves it when I'm in the fat suit, and that made me feel good. The only concern I had with wearing the suit was about offending people who are overweight. I was concerned about that, but actually it has been fine. . . ."[81] Thus, the Farrelly brothers and Gywneth Paltrow rely on Snitzer to be their "native informant." The implication is that if Ivy Snitzer embraces the film, its jokes, and Paltrow's impersonation of a large person, than all overweight American audience members will embrace *Shallow Hal.*

In general, "The Farrelly Brothers Commentary" in the DVD is most fascinating to us for what the Farrelly Brothers improvised language unintentionally reveals. Male actors playing minor characters, no matter what they physically look like, are more likely to benefit from the good old Farrelly boy network. In contrast, women, particularly attractive ones, are less likely to be cited by their complete names and are more likely to have been recently "discovered" by the Farrelly brothers or Charlie Weston. And on the rare occasion that an actress' professional credits are referenced, it's typically in reference to an industry tied to the beauty culture.

The Fat Suit.   Another noteworthy section of the DVD is a mini-documentary, called "Seeing through the Layers," that shows viewers the wizardry behind the creation of very unattractive characters for *Shallow Hal*. "Seeing through the Layers" features a series of brief interviews with the makeup effects designers, the Farrelly brothers, actresses, and an actor who were made unattractive for their particular parts in *Shallow Hal*. The thirteen-minute documentary primarily focuses on the make up artist's skill in transforming very *attractive* actresses into unattractive ones.[82] The documentary is fascinating in that the person mainly responsible, Tony Gardner, is both articulate and thoughtful as he describes the various technical challenges this particular film set forth and how he tried to meet them.

The viewer learns that there was quite a "learning curve" for the makeup artists in designing the fat suit for Gywneth Paltrow, the major challenge being that they had to design a fat suit that was "comfortable" (multiple, lightweight pieces for the actress to wear in accordance with what was needed for a camera shot); a fat suit that appeared "realistic" and "not too cartoonish" and was "lighthearted" enough to work in a romantic comedy.[83] Moreover, the makeup artists had to create a prosthetically enhanced "fat" face that would allow enough of Paltrow's facial attributes to be clearly "recognizable" to an audience, while simultaneously being "elastic" enough for her acting to come through.[84] In the documentary, Tony Gardner traces the evolution of the fat suit, and Paltrow describes the demands on the performer *prior* to its construction (full body cast so that the make up artists could construct a fat suit to perfectly fit her frame) as well as *after* its construction (the time-consuming demands to literally put on the fat suit costume and the extensive prosthetics and make up to create the fat Rosemary's face). The documentary testifies that makeup artists, such as Gardner, can effectively create realistic fat suits that actors enjoy wearing and performing in, fat suits that meet the directors' and producers' expectations, fat suits that audience members find relatively convincing.

Gardner's fat suits for Gywneth Paltrow and the actress that played Rosemary's mother are of course among the many recently created in Hollywood. Beyond those featured in *Shallow Hal*, consider some of these examples—Robin Williams in *Mrs. Doubtfire*, Goldie Hawn in *Death Becomes Her*, Martin Lawrence in *Big Momma's House*, Mike Myers in the Austin Powers movies, Eddie Murphy in *Nutty Professor* movies, Martin Short in *Primetime Glick*, flashback or dream sequences of Julia Roberts in *America's Sweethearts*, Courteney Cox Arquette in *Friends*, and Damon Wayans and others in *My Wife and Kids*.

The DVD documentary, "Seeing through the Layers" and the recent proliferation of fat suits prompts us to pose an ethical question: Does the fact that makeup artists have the talent and technical know how to create fat suits ultimately justify their use in film and television?

A number of reviewers and activists have responded to the use of fat suits in *Shallow Hal* and other films with a resounding "no." In an excellent essay on this subject, Marisa Meltzer discusses how humor aimed at minority groups has changed through the years.

Over the past several decades, comedy has gradually become less broad and more sensitive to overt racism. . . . We've come a long way since Peter Sellers was cast as bucktoothed Chinese sleuth Sidney Wang in *Murder by Death*. By now, the cardinal rule of humor—you can only make fun of a group if you're part of it—is familiar enough to be a punch line itself. (Remember Jerry Seinfield's outrage over his Catholic dentist's Jewish jokes?) But fat people are the last remaining exception.[85]

To Meltzer's dismay, "Fat people are now America's favorite punch lines." Meltzer, like many others, contends that fat suits are the moral equivalent of blackface.

In calling for a boycott of *Shallow Hal*, the National Association to Advance Fat Acceptance (NAAFA) makes the same claim. The executive administrator, Maryanne Bodolay, explains:

Putting thin performers in fat suits is no different than putting white performers in blackface. . . . To have these actors become "fat" and then film them gorging on food and breaking chairs is an insult to the 55 percent of Americans who are deemed "overweight." . . . These movies are giving people permission to make fun of fat people. . . . Hollywood is intent upon perpetuating the myth that fat people are miserable and unattractive, and that the path to happiness is through losing weight. In reality, beauty comes in all sizes, and people can find happiness at whatever size they are.[86]

Diane Bliss, the founder and chair of the recently formed Screen Actors Guild's Plus-Size Task Force (PSTF)[87] cites an academic study that documents NAAFA's claim about the media's stereotypical representations.

Michigan State University did a study of the representations of plus-size people in TV and film and statistically proved what our common sense tells us: people of size are more likely to be portrayed as stupid, lazy, unemployed, a member of an ethnic group, and the target of the joke. Older plus-size women are fairly frequently portrayed in a positive, non-stereotypical light as nurturing mothers, but we're seldom portrayed as desirable love interests or leading ladies.[88]

Some of the members of the Plus-Size Task Force have expressed in various interviews why they are fighting Hollywood's current depictions of large people. What emerges from these sources first is that the plus-size actresses resent the limited roles available to them. For example, Diane Bliss says, "When I moved to L.A. four-and-a-half years ago, most of the auditions were for the 'fat chick.' Nearly every time someone was described as a plus-size woman, there was always a negative adjective attached."[89] Rebekah Derrick adds, "The main problem is that the roles we're offered have nothing to do with anything but weight."[90] The plus-size activists also resent the industry's double standard for male and female actors of size: "Why is the chunky and average-looking Jim Belushi considered "leading man material" a star of his own sitcom," Diane Bliss asks, "while his wife is played by the gorgeous Courtney Thorne-Smith, size 2?"[91] In speculating as to why plus-size characters are often caricatures, Sarah Sachs notes "All races, all personalities are overweight; it's always something to be picked on because it's universal—there's someone in each category that could be overweight. That's why it's an easy target."[92] Actress Lisa Brounstein believes it has more to do with capitalism, "Our society says that overweight, plus-size or fat people need to diet to fix themselves. There is a billion-dollar diet industry that's telling us that we need to fix ourselves. I think that's how Hollywood gets away with making fun of us."[93]

With its paucity of interesting roles, its double standard regarding acceptable size for actors and actresses, and its "diet industry" marketing incentives, Hollywood is an industry that clearly discriminates against plus-size actresses. One can easily understand why plus-size actresses, with limited opportunities available, would be taken aback when two roles for large women in *Shallow Hal*—Rosemary and her mother—are earmarked for thin actresses. A number of reviewers concur with the plus-size actresses' observations. For example, a reviewer for the *New Daily News* writes, "Casting a heavy actress in a lead romantic role is still as impossible to imagine as it once was to think of women having the vote or serving in the military. . . . It's good that U.S. movies are giving lip service to the idea that big is beautiful, but it's time they cast those movies from real life and not from the bins of the special effects department."[94]

Essay's Conclusion

All in all, there can be no denying that the moral of *Shallow Hal*—*that one should not judge people, in particular women, by their physical appearances*—is constantly undermined in both the film and in the DVD supplements. The film's sight gags, its clichéd idea of "inner beauty," and its predominantly adolescent male point of view, when considered in conjunction with *Shallow Hal's* iconic marketing images, the rather sexist "Farrelly Brothers' Commentary," and the political perception that Hollywood's fascination with "fat suits" echoes their previous fascination with "blackface," we are hoping that readers of this essay will agree that *Shallow Hal* undermines its intended revolutionary message. Or as, Peter Travers, a reviewer for *Rolling Stone* articulated his experience with *Shallow Hal*:

> There is something condescending, not to mention hypocritical, about asking an audience to laugh uproariously at the spectacle of a fat person being sneered at and dissed as "rhino," or "hippo" or "holy cow," and then to justify those laughs by saying it's society's fault and tacking on a happy ending that allegedly teaches us a moral lesson. It won't wash.[95]

PERSONAL COMMENTS ON THE ESSAY

Writing the essay on *Shallow Hal* was for us as researchers an exercise in finding the limits or boundaries of feminist criticism. Although the feminist critique has opened up dramatically over the last couple of decades, a researcher employing feminist criticism still has to ask: Are the issues salient to gender? Here are some of the things we considered, yet abandoned.

First, we considered looking at the genre of "fat-suit" films altogether, rather than just one film. As mentioned, many recent films feature notable performers wearing fat suits in romantic comedies. We noticed that male performers (those donning fat suits) outnumbered female performers in this genre. Moreover, the women wearing the fat suits played the "straight" roles while the men played over-the-top comic characters like Fat Bastard in the *Austin Powers* films. Yet even more interesting is the number of African American performers that have built a franchise out of the fat-suit film, most notably Eddie Murphy. Although Murphy plays many characters in the *Klumps* films, both he and Martin Lawrence played large African American women in their respective films. As you can see, the construction of gender in the films is interesting and would likely produce an important piece of critical work in the area of feminist rhetoric. Upon reflection, though, our interests produced some initial analysis that revealed the central issues at work were not clearly about gender. They were a collection of social, political, and historical issues regarding African American performers that are probably more accurately placed in the area of cultural criticism.

We eventually settled on an investigation of the DVD *Shallow Hal* and its supplementary material. This idea won out over the others because seeing how the movie was put together, how the directors and actors theorized about the film, and the overall marketing of *Shallow Hal,* noticably altered our perceptions of the film. Indeed our opinions of the film were shaped, reshaped, and reordered as this material was viewed. Given the proliferation of DVDs, as well as entertainment television shows and other specials focusing on the "making of" most Hollywood films, we liked our angle and thought it an important avenue of investigation. It is clear that the process of making the film is becoming increasingly transparent and an important component of any film's marketing. Finally, we noticed that our perceptions were most potently altered by the supplementary material related to gender. They revolved around the way femininity was marketed, women were hired (or rehired), and the positioning of female beauty throughout the film and in contrast to the DVD commentary.

POTENTIALS AND PITFALLS

Feminist rhetorical analysis is well suited for many communication artifacts that exist in our cultural world. Given that gender is one of the primary ways we determine social behavior, very few artifacts are devoid of gendered implications. It must be stressed again, though, that gender is only one of the many identities that complex humans use to interact with the world. While looking for the gendered implications of a rhetorical artifact, one must be vigilant not to undermine or dismiss the other identities at work in the communication processes and fail to understand their impact as well.

Additionally, we believe that critical work requires equal part critique and equal part solution. It is often easy to point out what is oppressive about a communication artifact and then fail to offer any solutions. Many critics of feminist theory suggest that by pointing out all the ways communication oppresses women, one runs the risk of largely positioning women as victims. A potential pitfall of feminist analysis is failing to offer concrete alternatives to patriarchal order. For example, although the above essay primarily combined the feminist approach of recovering and recording to critically analyze the film, other approaches could be utilized as well. Although one part of the feminist project is to critique existing rhetorical practices for their patriarchal logic, the other two approaches offered in this chapter center on feminist solutions. In sum, feminist rhetorical critics should offer new solutions, new ways of thinking. Therefore, as an alternative or supplement, the essay above could have focused more on creating new definitions for beauty and attractiveness, instead of critiquing the rhetorical contradictions of the directors. Also, the essay alludes to the need for new language and new theories of cinematic representation that transcend existing formulas and standards. This too could have been the focus of the paper or should be the focus of other researchers that build on this analysis. With that in mind, a feminist rhetorical critic might take a film such as *Shallow Hal* and compare it to *My Big Fat Greek Wedding*, another romantic comedy featuring a larger lead actress. By comparing the two films, one could argue that *My Big Fat Greek Wedding* achieves where *Shallow Hal* fails. The paper could detail the specific ways in which *My Big Fat Greek Wedding* provided a positive, transformative character, a character decidedly more interesting than Paltrow's. Additionally, *My Big Fat Greek Wedding* provides a point of analysis about ethnicity. The film *Shallow Hal* deals with definitions of beauty, but the definitions are largely Caucasian in their orientation. Other ethnicities and subcultures have different standards of attractiveness and a wider acceptance of different body types. One has to be careful not to entrench assumptions that undermine a critique of race, class, heterosexism, and so forth, while striving to analyze gender.

In sum, a feminist critic puts together the analytical rubric that works best to elucidate all the strategies of domination made rigid by language and may also suggest new rhetorical paths to take—paths that achieve freedom, safety, complexity, subjectivity, and equality.

FEMINIST ANALYSIS TOP PICKS

Campbell, Karlyn Kohrs, *Man Cannot Speak for Her: A Critical Study of Early Feminist Rhetoric, Vol. 1* (New York: Greenwood Press, 1989). This book simultaneously investigates feminist rhetoric and offers news ways of thinking about the rhetorical process. One of the most important works in feminist rhetorical scholarship.

Campbell, Karlyn Kohrs, "Rhetorical Feminism," *Rhetoric Review* 20 (2001): 9–12. A concise essay that provides a survey of the work done by feminist scholars in the field of communication.

Beginning critics will find this history very helpful.

Condit, Celeste M., "In Praise of Eloquent Diversity: Gender and Rhetoric as Public Persuasion," *Women's Studies in Communication* 20 (2) (1997): 91–116. Condit's article is an excellent example of feminist revisioning. She provides a through rationale for new ways of communicating gender. The article also will further a student's understanding of the different positions on gender that rhetorical scholars take.

Dow, Bonnie J., and Mari Boor Tonn, " 'Feminine Style' and Political Judgment in the Rhetoric of Ann Richards," *Quarterly Journal of Speech* 79 (3) (1993): 286–302. An excellent case study of the rhetoric of former Texas Governor Ann Richards. Dow and Tonn expand upon the notion of a feminine style of speaking while analyzing Richard's public address.

Hamlet, Janice D., "Assessing Womanist Thought: The Rhetoric of Susan L. Taylor," Communication Quarterly 48.4 (2000): 420–437. This essay provides an interesting rhetorical analysis of the former editor of *Essence* magazine. The study is an excellent example of feminist scholarship and furthers understanding of Womanist scholarship.

Hanke, Robert, "The 'Mock-Macho' Situation Comedy: Hegemonic Masculinity and Its Reiteration," *Western Journal of Communication* 62.1 (Winter 1998), 74–93. Well done and easy to understand analysis of the television shows "Home Improvement" and "Coach." This essay allows the student to see the ways in which portrayals of masculinity are critiqued in feminist analysis.

Lotz, Amanda D., "Communicating Third Wave Feminism and New Social Movements: Challenges for the Next Century of Feminist Endeavor," *Women and Language* XXVI (2003): 1–9. This essay provides students with an overview of feminist thought from the perspective of the communication field. This article is helpful for students seeking to understand the complex and contradictory messages about feminism in the media and elsewhere.

Sellnow, Deanna, "Music as Persuasion: Refuting Hegemonic Masculinity in 'He Thinks He'll Keep Her,'" *Women's Studies in Communication* 22 (1999): 66–85. This essay is an excellent example of how feminist rhetorical scholars analyze different texts. Sellnow analyzes both the lyrics and musical form in a song for its feminist implications.

Shugart, Helene, "She Shoots, She Scores: Mediated Constructions of Contemporary Female Athletes in Coverage of the 1999 US Women's Soccer Team," *Western Journal of Communication* 67 (1) (Winter 2003), 1–31. Shugarts analysis of famous female athletes unearths the patriarchal strategies used to subordinate these successful and empowered women. Shugart provides theoretical language for understanding these strategies.

NOTES

1. Susan Faludi, "Whose Backlash Is It Anyway?: The Women's Movement and Angry White Men," FSU Student Government Summer Lecture Series, Florida State University, Tallahassee, June, 25 1997.

2. Karen A. Foss, Sonja J. Foss, and Cindy Griffin, *Feminist Rhetorical Theories* (Thousand Oaks, CA: Sage, 1999), 79.

3. This definition appears in Kramarae and Treichler's *A Feminist Dictionary* (London: Pandora Press, 1985) as well as on many bumperstickers.

4. See Christine Hoff Sommers' *Who Stole Feminism* (Simon & Schuster; reprint edition, 1995).

5. Allan G. Johnson, *The Gender Knot* (Philadelphia: Temple University Press, 1997), 5.

6. Johnson, 6.

7. Mary Spicuzza, "Bad Heroines," *MetroActive* [On-line]. Available at htpp://www.metroactive.com/papers/metro/03.15.01/cover/woman-film-0111.html.

8. Johnson, 8.

9. For example, http://www.superbowl.com notes that an estimated 131 million viewers watched Super Bowl XXXV and marketing departments spent 2.5 million for each 30-second advertising spot.

10. Cynthia Cooper, "Do you Know Who I am?" *American Society of Newspapers Editors* [Online]. Available at htpp://www.asne.org/kiosk/editor/00.jan-feb/cooper1.html. 2000, para. 22.

11. Carol Tavris, *The Mis-Measure of Woman* (New York, Simon & Schuster, 1992) 18.

12. For a more thorough explanation of the use of this term, view *bell hooks: Cultural Criticism and Transformation*, Sut Jhally (dir.), Media Education Foundation, 1997.

13. Jill Dolan, *Feminist Spectator as Critic* (Ann Arbor: University of Michigan Press, 1988), 3–16.

14. Dolan, 7.

15. Dolan, 10.

16. For examples of groups that fall into these categories see http://www.ifeminists.net/> and <http://www.iwf.org/.

17. For a more thorough listing of the categories of feminism, see Julia T. Wood's Chapter 3 of *Gendered Lives.* (Belmont, CA: Wadsworth, 2003).

18. Karlyn Kohrs Campbell, *Man Cannot Speak for Her, Vol. 1* (New York: Greenwood Press, 1989).

19. For example, see Karlyn Kohrs Campbell, "Three Tall Women: Radical Challenges to Criticism, Pedagogy, and Theory." *The Carroll C. Arnold Distinguished Lecture* (Boston: Allyn and Bacon, 2003), 4.

20. Susan Schultz Huxman, "Perfecting the Rhetorical Vision of Woman's Rights: Elizabeth Cady Stanton, Anna Howard Shaw, and Carrie Chapman Catt, *Women's Studies in Communication* 23 (2000): 307–336.

21. Brenda Cooper, "'Chick Flicks' as Feminist Texts: The Appropriation of the Male Gaze in Thelma & Louise," *Women's Studies in Communication* 23 (2000): 277–306.

22. Kristin J. Anderson and Christina Accomando, "Madcap Misogyny and Romanticized Victim-Blaming: Discourses of Stalking in *There's Something About Mary," Women & Language* 22 (1999): 27.

23. *Gender: The Enduring Paradox,* videorecording. Smithsonian 1990.

24. See Krista Ratcliffe, *Anglo-American Challenges to the Rhetorical Tradition* (Carbondale, IL: Southern Illinois University Press, 1995). Ratcliffe's work on feminist rhetorical strategies has been adopted for this section. We have expanded her analysis beyond the Anglo-American tradition and added the examination of cultural production as an option in lieu of rereading traditional rhetorical texts.

25. Dale Spender, *Man Made Language* (Boston: Routledge & Kegan Paul, 1985).

26. Cheris Kramarae, "Punctuating the Dictionary," *International Journal of Society and Language* 94 (1992): 137–138.

27. Sue Wise and Liz Stanley, *Georgie Porgie: Sexual Harassment in Everyday Life* (New York: Pandora, 1987).

28. Wood, 306.

29. Teri Kwal Gamble and Michael Gamble, *The Gender Connection.* (New York: Houghton Mifflin, 2002), 354.

30. Alice Walker, *In Search of My Mother's Garden: Womanist Prose* (New York: Harcourt Brace Jovanovich, 1983), xii.

31. Mary Daly, *Gyn/Ecology: The Metaphysics of Radical Feminism* (Boston: Beacon, 1978), 3.

32. Jessica Rosenberg and Gitana Garofalo, "Riot Grrrls: Revolution from Within," *Signs: Journal of Women in Culture & Society* 23 (1998): 810.

33. Besides Kramarae and Treichler's work, previously footnoted, see also Mary Daly's *Websters' First New Intergalactic Wickedary of the English Language* (Boston: Beacon, 1987).

34. Karen A. Foss and Sonja K. Foss, *Women Speak: The Eloquence of Women's Lives* (Prospect Heights, IL: Waveland Press, 1991), 10.

35. See James A. Herrick's quote of George Kennedy in *The History and Theory of Rhetoric: An Introduction,* 2nd ed. (Boston: Allyn and Bacon, 2001) 152.

36. Kohrs Campbell, *Three,* 6.

37. Nichola Gutgold, "Managing Rhetorical Roles: Elizabeth Hanford Dole from Spouse to Candidate 1996–1999," *Women & Language* (1) Spring 2001:

38. *Monuments are for Men; Waffles are for Women: Exploring Gender Permanence & Impermanence,* videorecording, University of California Extension Center for Media and Independent Learning, 2000.

39. Sally Miller Gearhart, "Womanpower: Energy Re-Sourcement," *The Politics of Women's Spirituality: Essays on the Rise of Spiritual Power within the Feminist Movement,* Charlene Spretnak (ed.) (Garden City, NY: Doubleday, 1982), 143.

40. Sonja K. Foss and Cindy Griffin, "Exploring Rhetoric Beyond Persuasion: A Proposal for an Invitational Rhetoric," *Communication Monographs* 62 (1995): 6.

41. A list of Richard Roeper's (of Ebert and Roeper) ten best films of 2001 can be found at http://www.reel.com/reel.asp?node=features/awards/awards01/critics.

42. Foss, Foss, and Griffin, 89.

43. See footnote xx.

44. http://www.duke.edu/web/film/pioneers/ (Accessed August 24, 2002.)

45. Martha M. Lauzen, "The Celluloid Ceiling: Behind-the-Scenes and On-Screen Employment of Women in the Top 250 Films of 2002," Executive Summary (August 23, 2003) [On-line] Available at http://www.5050summit.com/stats2003.html.

46. Sarah Ebner, "Culture, Television & Radio: Breaking the Celluloid Ceiling; There are Fewer Women Film Directors Than Ever Before." *Birmingham Post* (June 24, 2003): 12.

47. Elizabeth Guider, "Little Progress in TV." *Daily Variety* (June 27, 2003).

48. Foster, Gwendolyn Audrey, *Women Filmmakers of the African and Asian Diaspora: Decolonizing the Gaze, Locating Subjectivity* (Carbondale, IL: Southern Illinois University Press, 1997).

49. Tania Modleski. *Loving with a Vengeance: Mass-Produced Fantasies for Women* (New York: Routledge, 1984).

50. Leibowitz, Flo, "Apt Feelings, or Why 'Women's Films' Aren't Trivial," pp. 219–29. Bordwell, David (ed.); and Carroll, Noël (ed.). *Post-Theory: Reconstructing Film Studies* (Madison: University of Wisconsin Press, 1996.)

51. Bell, Elizabeth, and Laura Sells, *Mouse to Mermaid: The Politics of Film, Gender, and Culture* (Bloomington and Indianapolis: Indiana University Press, 1995).

52. Laura Mulvey, "Visual Pleasure and Narrative Cinema," *Screen* (16.3) (Autumn 1975): 6–18.

53. See for example, Lorraine Gamman, "Watching the Detectives: The Enigma of the Female Gaze," L. Gamman and M. Marshment (eds.), *The Female Gaze: Women as Viewers of Popular Culture* (Seattle: Real Comet Press, 1989): 8–26. Also Brenda Cooper, "'Chick Flicks' as Feminist Texts: The Appropriation of the Male Gaze in *Thelma and Louise*," *Women's Studies in Communication* 23 (2000): 277–306.

54. See Robert Alan Brookey and Robert Westerfelhaus, "Hiding Homoeroticism in Plain View: *The Fight Club* DVD as Digital Closet," *Critical Studies in Mass Communication*, 19.1 (2002): 21–43. Also see Brenda Cooper, "*Boys Don't Cry* and Female Masculinity: Reclaiming a Life & Dismantling the Politics of Normative Heterosexuality," *Critical Studies in Mass Communication* 19.1 (2002): 44–63.

55. See Jane Gaines, "White Privilege and Looking Relations: Race and Gender in Feminist Film Theory" *Screen* 29 (1988): 4.

56. Sue Thorman, "Feminism and Film," In *The Routledge Companion to Feminism and Postfeminism*, Sarah Gamble (ed.) (New York: Routledge, 1998), 102.

57. *Shallow Hal*, Bobby Farrelly and Peter Farrelly (Dir.). Gwyneth Paltrow and Jack Black (Perf.). 2001. DVD. Twentieth Century Fox, 2002.

58. Throughout this section of the essay, we will be citing from the Twentieth Century Fox DVD version of *Shallow Hal*. When citing from the actual film on the DVD, we will note the specific chapter number; for example, (*Shallow*, Chapter 3). When citing from the "Commentary by the Farrelly Brothers," we will indicate as such, for example, ("Commentary," Chapter 19).

59. *Shallow*, Chapter 1.

60. *Shallow*, Chapter 8.

61. In this description and subsequent analysis of the film, we need to distinguish between Gwyneth Paltrow, in her own body, playing the Rosemary character, and the 300-pound Rosemary (played by Paltrow in a fat suit or by Ivy Snitzer). The language available to us to describe these two different bodies of Rosemary is charged. Our cultural construction of beauty in twentieth-century America gives us a multitude of ways to describe Paltrow's body (model-thin, perfect, svelte, normal, beautiful) all of which have positive connotations. Although we try to avoid pejorative adjectives (obese, overweight, fat) to describe the second body type of Rosemary, the adjectives available to us (very large, plus-size, 300-pound) all seem woefully insufficient, in that they do not allow us to provide a laden-free or inherently positive description.

62. *Shallow*, Chapter 20.

63. *Shallow*, Chapter 6.

64. For easy access to over thirty reviews of *Shallow Hal*, proceed to the following website: http://www. metacritic.com.

65. "Commentary," Chapter 1.

66. "Commentary," Chapter 16.

67. Laura Mulvey, *Visual and Other Pleasures* (Basingstoke, England: Macmillan, 1989).

68. Brookey and Westerfelhaus, p. 25.

69. Brookey and Westerfelhaus, p. 24.

70. Comments about the actors who played major characters were not included in the analysis for our table; these include Rosemary, Hal, Hal's friends—Mauricio and Walt, Hal's neighbor—Jill, and the TV guru—Robbins.

71. Again, these claims are made only based on the brothers' improvised comments, they do not account for the actors and actresses as cited in the actual film credits for *Shallow Hal*, nor do they represent the Farrellys' actual hiring practices.

72. "Commentary," Chapter 11.

73. "Commentary," Chapter 8.

74. "Commentary," Chapter 13 and 9.

75. "Commentary," Chapter 18, 7, and 8).

76. "Commentary" Chapter 23.

77. "Commentary," Chapter 9.

78. "Gwyneth's Double Breaks Her Silence." Interview with Ivy Snitzer. *Entertainment Tonight*

Online (November 9, 2001). Retrieved on October 7, 2002, from http://www.etonline.com/celebrity/a7536.htm.

79. *Shallow,* Chapter 28.

80. bell hooks, *Teaching to Transgress* (New York: Routledge, 1994), 43.

81. "Gwyneth Gets Heavy!" Interview with Gwyneth Paltrow. *Entertainment Tonight Online* (November 9, 2001). Retrieved on October 7, 2002, from http://www.etonline.com/celebrity/a3291.htm.

82. Although there is a brief section on Ivy Snitzer, the three, we presume, conventionally unattractive actresses who were made even more unattractive for their scenes in the dance bar—Bonnie Aarons, Lisa Brounstein, and Fawn Irish—are *not* interviewed in this 13-minute documentary. Nor is Nan Martin who played Nurse Tanya Peeler.

83. "Seeing Through the Layers." *Shallow Hal.*

84. "Seeing Through the Layers." *Shallow Hal.*

85. Marissa Meltzer, "Hollywood's Big New Minstrel Show." *Bitch.* Winter 2001. Retrieved on November 6, 2002, from http://www.bitchmagazine.com.

86. "Fat Rights Organization Boycotts 'Shallow Hal,'" Press Release. NAAFA (November 7, 2001). Retrieved on October 8, 2002, from http://www.nafaa.org/news/shallow.html.

87. "The mission of the Plus-Size Task Force of the Screen Actors Guild is to achieve realistic portrayals of plus-size women in television and film. Our goals are to educate, inform, and lobby the industry from within; encourage those who positively portray plus-size women by publicly recognizing them; acknowledge and educate those perpetuating insensitive representations; produce measurable results; and empower SAG members." (Interview).

88. Interview with Diane Bliss. *Big Fat Blog.* n.d. Retrieved on October 8, 2002, from http://bigfatblog.com/interviews/bliss.php.

89. "ET's Exclusive—Plus-Size Panel." Interview with Lisa Bounstein, Susanne Wright, Tess Borden, Rebekah Derrick, Sharon Sachs, Megan Cavanagh, Diane Bliss, and Alex Alexander. *Entertainment Tonight Online* (November 27, 2001). Retrieved on October 8, 2002, from http://www.etonline.com/celebrity/a7755.htm.

90. "ET Exclusive—Plus Size Panel."

91. A reviewer for the *Philadelphia Inquirer* echoes these women's concerns: "We live in a culture where such guys as John Goodman, John Candy and Al Roker are embraced as jolly and lovable. But the full-figured gals such as Camryn, Rose and Oprah are held at arm's length, the inevitable talk of their weight frequently coming between them and their audience. Where men are concerned, a few extra pounds are no object. Where women are concerned it becomes the subject." Carrie Richey, "'Shallow Hal' tries to have it both ways." Review of *Shallow Hal. Philadelphia Inquirer* (November 9, 2001). Retrieved on October 7, 2002, from http://ae.philly.com/entertainment/ui/philly/movie.html?id=49495&reviewId=5945.

92. "ET Exclusive—Plus-Size Panel."

93. Lisa Brounstein is the actress who played one of the "ugly" women dancing at the bar in *Shallow Hal.* She is a "staunch defender" of *Shallow Hal.* She is also an active member of the Screen Actors Guild's Plus-Size Task Force. "Et Exclusive—Plus-Size Panel."

94. Bernard, Jami, "Thin on Respect." Review of *Shallow Hal. New York Daily News* (November 11, 2001). Retrieved on October 8, 2002, from http://nydailynews.com.

95. Travers, Peter, Review of *Shallow Hal.* Rolling Stone December 6, 2001). Retrieved on October 8, 2002, from http://www.rollingstone.com/reviews/movie/printer friendly.asp?mid=2043294.

CHAPTER FOURTEEN

IDEOGRAPHIC CRITICISM

RONALD LEE

For most students, communication is a pragmatic discipline. It provides methods of analysis, a storehouse of strategies, and tried-and-true techniques for aiding an advocate in effectively advancing a cause. Whether in public speaking, argumentation, public relations, or persuasion, the paradigm of an advocate moving a specific audience toward a predetermined end dominates undergraduate communication pedagogy. When students first approach rhetorical criticism, they typically bring this orientation with them.

For several years, I was assigned to teach COMM 201. This course had a daunting title, *Introduction to Research Methods in Communication Studies*. Given the makeup of my department, the other faculty members expected me to prepare sophomores for upper-division courses in both the social–science and humanist traditions. So, I set out to cover experimental, survey, ethnographic, and *critical* methods. How precisely was I supposed to provide a useful introduction to rhetorical criticism in two-and-a-half weeks (five 75-minute class periods)? Moreover, how was I supposed to prepare students to fulfill an assignment to write their first critical paper? Well, I did what I suspect almost every communication professor does. I presented a highly pragmatic approach of criticism. This is a critical methodology that I rarely use in my own scholarly work.

By presenting such a model, however, I introduced students to a clear point of departure for much of contemporary rhetorical criticism. Understanding the commitments of the pragmatic model, along with its limitations, provides a vocabulary of concepts which other approaches to criticism radically recharacterize. Of particular note is the so-called "ideological turn" in rhetorical criticism. Although the phrase "ideological turn" captures a particular attitude toward criticism, it includes under its umbrella a constellation of different perspectives and methods.

This chapter focuses on Michael Calvin McGee's *rhetorical materialism* (theoretical perspective) and *ideographic criticism* (critical methodology). Beginning in the 1970s, McGee wrote a series of essays that changed the way a generation of critics think about, talk about, and do criticism. Even those who reject his program have been obliged to enter an ongoing conversation with his vision of rhetoric and the critical methodology he has promulgated.

McGee taught at the University of Memphis, the University of Wisconsin-Madison, and for the twenty years before his death at the University of Iowa. Beyond his own writing, he influenced a generation of Iowa graduate students, a number of whom now rank among the most influential rhetorical theorists and critics in the field.

In what follows, I outline, as a point of departure, a pragmatic approach to criticism. Second, I explain the ideological turn in criticism by contrasting it to this pragmatic approach. Third, I detail the particular commitments of McGee's rhetorical materialism. Fourth, I explain how this rhetorical materialism is expressed in the doing of ideographic criticism. Finally, for my critical essay, I illustrate the use of ideographic criticism in an analysis of Senator Edward Kennedy's "Truth and Tolerance in America" speech delivered at Liberty Baptist College on October 3, 1983.

POINT OF DEPARTURE

In 1968, Lloyd Bitzer wrote a very widely read essay entitled, "The Rhetorical Situation." This article served as the perspective for my COMM 201 class. It is the classic presentation of an approach that focuses on understanding the strategic way an advocate may overcome obstacles to success. All of its component parts are defined in terms that point the critic toward an instrumental effect. By instrumental effect, I mean the persuasive influence that messages, deliberately employed, have on a targeted audience.

As Bitzer approaches a text for critical analysis, his attention is drawn to the situation that called forth the discourse. In adopting this focus, he views a work of rhetoric as "pragmatic," because it "functions ultimately to produce action or change in the world." "The rhetor," Bitzer writes, "alters reality by bringing into existence a discourse of such a character that the audience, in thought and action, is so engaged that it becomes a mediator of change."[1]

Bitzer's view presupposes a particular epistemology. It takes for granted that objective conditions in the external world call forth discourses. "Nor should we assume," he argues, "that a rhetorical address gives existence to a situation; on the contrary, *it is the situation which calls the discourse into existence* (my emphasis)."[2] There is a brute presence to situations; these situations present exigencies (problematic circumstances); and these exigencies can be "completely or partially removed if discourse, introduced into the situation, can so constrain human decision or action as to bring about the significant modification of the exigence."[3]

Assume for a moment that you are taking a class in corporate advocacy. During the semester, the instructor presents you with a series of case studies. In these cases, you are reading about organizations that have run into trouble. One of these cases involves the 1992 charges brought against Sears Auto Centers. Sears was accused of systematically pressuring customers into buying parts and services they did not need. Customers from across the country complained of having paid hundreds of dollars for unnecessary repair work. Former Sears' employees revealed to government investigators that intense pressure to boost revenue, due to a commission pay system and unrealistic sales goals, forced them to oversell. Various states brought suit against the corporation. The story sparked a firestorm of highly negative publicity and, ultimately, threatened the health of one of Sears' most important retail sectors.

In addition, you are given materials that describe Sears' public relations response to this crisis. You are asked by the instructor to evaluate Sears' public messages based on what you have been told about the situation. You follow Bitzer's approach to criticism. First, you identify the exigencies (loss of business and profit, civil and criminal prosecution). Second, you locate the audiences that can be mediators of change and thus ameliorate the exigencies (Sears' customers, relevant law enforcement agencies). Third, you examine the constraints that limit the range of possible rhetorical responses (for instance, offering every regular, automotive center customer a free set of tires would be financially infeasible). Finally, you evaluate the rhetorical strategies that Sears did enact and make judgments about their wisdom. Evaluating the "wisdom" of these choices will almost certainly be preoccupied with judgments of their effectiveness.

IDEOLOGICAL TURN IN CRITICISM

Notice how narrow the range of judgment is in this pragmatic model of criticism. The critic is limited to assessing advocates' skills in meeting their predetermined ends.[4] Other questions, especially those concerning competing values or the veracity of the discourse, are left aside. As a result of not posing such questions, criticism takes on a decidedly establishment bias. The danger is that conventional wisdom and tradition, typically determined in concert with entrenched interests and institutions, become equated with truth. In the present case, our student critics may feel restricted to looking at the world through the eyes of Sears' corporate officials. "We can clarify this issue," Philip Wander, himself an important figure in the ideological turn, has remarked, "by asking ourselves what in everyday language we would call the person . . . who examines or rewrites drafts of . . . statements so that their impact on specific audiences can be ascertained or improved; for whom policy, audience, and situation are a given and the overriding question is how to assess the effectiveness of the speech?" His answer is "not . . . a critic." "We would," Wander concludes, "be more inclined to call him or her a 'public relations consultant.'"[5] Once critics begin to ask, "Whose interests are served by these messages that construct this particular version of the truth?" they are dealing with ideology. So, before we can continue, we must come to some workable understanding of this troublesome concept.

Ideology in the most general sense is "any system of ideas . . . directing political and social action."[6] The questions swirling around ideology ask: To what extent are these ideas true or false? What forces perpetuate these particular ideas? What groups benefit from and what groups are disadvantaged by these ideas?

The underlying assumption is that ideology "usually does not mirror the social world. . . . [B]ut exhibits some transformation of it."[7] We generate concepts, myths, images, and stories about the nature of our world. These ideas are used to interpret social reality. These interpretations may create falsehood and distortion. Importantly, these distortions are not neutral in their effect for they work to the advantage of some groups and to the disadvantage of others.

For example, there are two broad perspectives on poverty in America.[8] One perspective focuses on poor people as the cause of their own condition. They lack education; they have an inadequate work ethic; they form unstable families often headed by unwed mothers; they frequently have criminal records and are part of the illegal drug culture; and they fail to manage their money wisely. A second perspective focuses on poverty as the consequence of an economic and political system. On this view, capitalism has created an economic system that requires surplus workers to assure an abundance of cheap labor. The social effects of this system are viewed as having fostered racism, urban ghettoes, and a dramatic and unfair skewing of the distribution of material resources.

Each perspective warrants very different political actions. The first justifies programs to help the poor improve themselves. These efforts typically include job training, education, counseling, and strict law enforcement. The second view justifies structural changes in the system that will lead to the redistribution of resources. These efforts might include a steep progressive tax structure, generous government spending on housing and medical care, and the federal regulation of business to assure fair and equal treatment of employees. In addition, these perspectives are advocated with quite different discourses. The first uses messages that talk of "markets," "merit," "competition," and "opportunity." The second talks of "equal treatment," "compassion," "exploitation," and "profiteering."

The example of poverty brings us to the heart of the matter. At its root, ideology concerns the relationship among discourse, power, and truth. If we spend a few moments with each term, we should arrive at a workable understanding of ideology.

Discourse

The term *discourse* refers to "language in use, or more broadly, the interactive production of meaning."[9] This definition highlights a distinction between contextual and abstract uses of language. For the sake of illustration, consider the phrases *moral language* and *moral discourse.* As I turn around in my chair to look at my bookshelves, I see several works of moral philosophy. These include A. J. Ayer's *Language, Truth and Logic,* R. M. Hare's *The Language of Morals,* and Charles Stevenson's *Ethics and Language.* These authors chose to feature the word *language* in their titles because they are interested in the linguistic properties of ethical propositions. Each of these scholars provides a unique account of the meaning of the word *good* in the statement "X is good." Their treatment of this statement is apart from any consideration of any actual utterances of the word *good.* They do not examine any particular speakers, audiences, or contexts. They are not interested in whether any specific object, person, or state of affairs is in fact good. Instead, their interest is wholly theoretical (or what moral philosophers call meta-ethical).

I also have on my bookshelves books and journals that contain treatments of moral discourse. The authors of these works explore the moral utterances of actual speakers—Abraham Lincoln, Adolf Hitler, Martin Luther King, Jr., Nelson Mandela, and many others—in order to understand the meaning of their moral talk in historical context. These scholars do examine particular speakers, audiences, and contexts. Although their interest is in part theoretical, it is a theoretical interest grounded in a concern for the influence of specific moral messages in the world of practical affairs.[10]

Power

Once the term *discourse* is substituted for *language,* the relevance of power should become more obvious. Actual advocates are trying to influence the course of events in a manner that promotes their interests. Some advocates have more resources (money, access, technology, networks of influential friends) than others. Some advocates are pressing a case on behalf of established institutions and traditional ways of doing things, and others are working for groups with little social or economic standing who find their interests at odds with the status quo. These disparities in position and resources make a huge difference in the ability to influence audiences.

Let us begin working from the most everyday of examples to grander illustrations of national political life. When I was an undergraduate, I was a participant in a perpetual pinochle game in the student lounge. If a player had to attend class, another student would take the vacated seat. As we started each new game and assigned various responsibilities, someone would always say to the person assigned to tally the points, "It is a poor scorekeeper who cannot win for her team." This aphorism captures one face of power—the illicit power exercised by those in positions of authority. So, in place of the card-game scorekeeper, we might just as well speak about Jeffrey Skilling, the former president of Enron, and David Duncan, the Arthur Andersen partner who oversaw the auditing of the Enron Corporation books. They are accused of profiting mightily from the creation of false reports documenting Enron profitability. They had the power to manufacture an allegedly misleading discourse that persuaded thousands of investors to put money into their enterprise.

Power, of course, is often exercised without any tinge of corruption. The President describes the crisis of terrorism, uses his authority as commander-in-chief to mobilize the armed forces, and urges the nation's citizens to sacrifice for the common good. Like the previous cases, this is an example of a powerful individual making an explicit decision that alters some state of affairs. And also like the other cases, it is done largely through the use of discourse. The President characterizes a situation as a "crisis," calls forth the historic precedents for the use of military force, and exhorts the citizenry to unite behind his leadership.

In the examples we have used thus far, a person or group who possesses power makes an explicit decision to exercise that power to bring about a particular result. Yet, many of the most interesting discursive expressions of power are far more subtle and commonplace. Such cases are not the result of a single decision, but rather the product of power that is exercised by a way of talking that constitutes social and political culture. These forms of power go under a number of different names depending on the particular theorist and circumstance, including socialization, legitimation, domination, and hegemony. Each term suggests that belief systems are perpetuated by powerful political, social, and economic interests. Yet, it would be impossible to locate a set of decision makers that consciously decide on such matters. In advanced industrial societies, the apparatus of indoctrination is hidden and often denies its own existence.

For instance, Americans do not think of their children's education as an exercise in political propaganda. Instead, the schools are viewed as quintessentially democratic institutions governed by local communities.[11] Education is seen as the critical and objective study of the world. Yet, upon reflection, it is obvious that stable societies must have an efficient way to pass on values and customs to each new generation. The fact that we interpret this process as education rather than indoctrination exemplifies the masking of power.

When I teach political communication, I title the second day of class discussion, "All I Really Needed to Know about Politics I Learned in Kindergarten"[12] My purpose is to draw my students' attention to the subtle ways in which Americans are socialized into a particular view of the political world. There are some obvious patriotic lessons passed on in the early years of elementary schooling, such as reciting the Pledge of Allegiance and singing "My County 'Tis of Thee," but there are also a host of subtle, supposedly nonpolitical, and yet critically important beliefs inculcated in children during these formative years. For instance, children learn that they are required to go to school and that school officials have power over them. Importantly, this power appears sweetly benign as personified by kindergarten teachers. This benevolent image of power is reinforced in the stories of the Founding Fathers, children's paternal conception of the President, and classroom visits by Officer Friendly. Students also learn the importance of order, the value placed on finishing work in a timely matter, and the rewards that are passed out to the best and most obedient students. These are beginning lessons about the merit system in a capitalist economy.[13] As these pupils continue on in their education, they come to understand the country through the positive meanings associated with liberty, freedom, equality, tolerance, and democracy. These concepts are then organized into larger stories such as the American Dream.[14]

The school is not the only institution socializing the citizenry. The media present powerful representations of national life. Advertising, for example, bombards viewers with the values of consumerism. Industrialization and urbanization weakened the traditional sources of socialization—church, family, and ethnic community. Commercial messages filled this void by switching their focus from the features of goods (product-based advertising) to selling consumers a lifestyle that they may purchase by selecting particular products.[15] Now, advertising rather than religion and tradition has become the dominant source of individual identity. Notice, we do not think of beer and automobile advertising as political. Yet, thousands and thousands of commercial messages construct for us a particular view of the country. It is a place where men and women are beautiful; it is a place where everyone is affluent; and it is a place where consumption makes people happy.

To put this point about power in yet another way, I would remind you of what instructors tell all students of argumentation and persuasion. Those who have the power to define the terms of the controversy have a tremendous rhetorical advantage. For instance, if I am an opponent of preferential systems of college admission, I can shape the terms of discussion if I get to define affirmative action as an attack on the impartial and objective standard of merit. After all, if John has a higher SAT score than Jose, then John should be admitted and Jose should be turned away. What could be fairer than to make a decision on the color-blind criteria of merit? On the other hand, if I am a supporter of affirmative action, I generally prevail if the evidence of merit, especially standardized test scores, is defined as the byproducts of privilege. Of course Jose, whose parents are first-generation, working-class immigrants, is not going to have the same kind of elaborated vocabulary as John, whose professional parents both had the advantage of advanced graduate educations. From this point of view, the accident of birth explains John's 95th percentile verbal score on the SAT far better than some concept of merit. In fact, Jose's very respectable 85th percentile score, given his social and economic position, may be the more "meritorious" achievement.

On a larger scale, this is what examining the relationship between discourse and power makes evident. Powerful interests, through the communication apparatuses of an advanced society, define the very terms of discussion. Yet, if you have a vision of some cabal sitting in a room pulling the strings that determine what the public will believe, then you have a terribly oversimplified view of power. The United States is a democratic republic, it has an advanced capitalist economy, and it is a predominantly Christian nation. These traditions and institutions together create a set of belief systems that shape our view of the world. They are perpetuated by political, economic, and social interests. Their domination of our thinking is virtually invisible because it is not imposed by some identifiable thought police. Rather, it merely appears as the American way of life.

Truth

From what I have already said about power, I suspect that it is obvious that "truth" is dependent upon standpoint or perspective. There are often various versions of the truth. Each version may be sponsored by those who represent a different set of interests.

In an earlier life, I spent a summer attending law school. One of my courses was *Torts*. Tort law concerns civil action taken by a plaintiff in order to receive compensation for the wrongful act of a defendant. This is the form of the law that is derisively characterized as "ambulance chasing." If you were to slip, fall, and break your leg on a patch of ice in front of a retail store, then you might bring a civil action in order to receive compensation for your injury. You would argue that the proprietors had been negligent because they failed to clear the ice away from the store entrance.

My law professor was especially good at disabusing students of any simple positivist view of the law. As naïve outsiders, we may think of the application of the law as a relatively straightforward and rational procedure. First, the facts are discovered. Second, the relevant law is found. Third, an objective decision is made about the match between the facts and the law. The law, based on this view, either applies to these facts or it does not. Supposedly, it is this predictable, rational procedure that assures justice.

As my law professor told us, the lawyer's job is to *characterize* the facts and the law in ways that are to the advantage of our client. The law is a rhetorical enterprise which pits opposing interpretations of the facts and of the law against one another. The more persuasive version of the "truth" wins the verdict. Neither the law nor the facts are settled matters, but rather objects that may be differently constructed in discourse.[16]

In our slip-and-fall case, the facts may be complicated. Perhaps at the time you came to the store an ice storm was in progress. The defendant's lawyer argues that it was impossible for anyone clearing sidewalks to keep up with the rate of ice formation. Moreover, you were inappropriately dressed in high-heeled shoes. No reasonable person would venture out in these conditions wearing that type of shoe. So, the plaintiff was the one who was negligent and the defendant did everything a reasonable person could expect. Both the facts and the law may be persuasively characterized.

What I have said about the law is equally true of nearly any enterprise concerned with the construction of social reality. For example, many histories are written of the same event. Even when the relevant facts are generally agreed upon, the placement and characterization of those facts within a larger narrative may radically change the meaning of events.[17] So, taken together, discourse and power may create persuasive versions of the truth. These versions may be widely accepted and serve as the basis for decisions in the world of practical affairs.

I fear that the work we have done so far creates too inclusive a domain for ideology. If we define ideology "as any discourse bound up with specific social interests," then it becomes hard to think of any discourse, at least in some remote sense, that does not fall under its umbrella.[18] There is no simple way out of this problem. We might try to distinguish "social interests" from all possible human interests, but this exercise does not get us very far. Eating is a human interest (a bodily need), but certainly the production, selling, marketing, and meaning of food is tied up with serious economic and political interests. If we can say that the social interest is better organized and more powerful and that its relationship to dominant cultural discourses is more obvious, we can be more confident in calling such affected discourses ideological. Conversely, if the social interest appears disorganized and lacking in influence, and its relationship to dominant cultural discourses is unclear or weak, we may view these discourses as relatively non-ideological.

Remember that discourses that meet these criteria may resist the label "ideology." Americans do not typically refer to the public school curricula, advertising, or the law as examples of ideological discourse. Yet, these discourses are paradigm cases of ideology. This quality of ideology denying itself is a central characteristic of the concept. In summary, on this view, ideological discourse is a "discourse bound up with specific social interests." It produces a version of the truth and perpetuates belief systems on behalf of powerful interests. This account has set aside many thorny theoretical issues, but for our purposes it is enough to recognize that discourse, power, and truth are bound up in the concept of ideology.

RHETORICAL MATERIALISM

Michael Calvin McGee's participation in the ideological turn is based on his construction of a particular theoretical perspective on rhetoric that underwrites a method of critical analysis. I will begin with an explanation of McGee's theory, rhetorical materialism, and then proceed to his method, ideographic criticism.

McGee identifies himself as a "rhetorical materialist." He uses this self-identifier to distinguish his program from traditional critical–theoretical approaches that had largely dominated the field into the 1970s. This is an important point to grasp. McGee was not theorizing in a vacuum; he was instead providing a perspective that stood in opposition to what was then the prevailing disciplinary paradigm.

McGee was reacting against a regime of rhetorical theory built on the authority of revered figures and texts. At that time, communication scholars largely thought about rhetoric through the ideas and theoretical prescriptions of such great thinkers as Aristotle, Isocrates, Cicero, Quintilian, St. Augustine, Francis Bacon, George Campbell, and Richard Whately. The result of this approach was "a 'rhetoric' which is on its face uninformed by historical or immediate contact with actual practice." "The theory and technique of rhetoric," McGee writes, "come less from human experience than from the metaphysical creativity and inspiration of particular writers." "What has been called 'rhetorical theory,'" McGee contends, "through much of our tradition is not theory at all, but a set of technical, prescriptive principles which inform the practitioner while, paradoxically, remaining largely innocent of practice."[19]

Under this old regime, accounts of rhetoric come down as commandments from on high. They were frequently divorced from any actual discussion of how people do, in fact, engage in the practice of public persuasion. A speech was determined as eloquent and effective based on the application of classical theories. So, if the speaker was found to follow the advice of Aristotle, then the speech must have been both worthy and successful. Not surprisingly, the discourse surrounding contemporary social upheavals, especially the antiwar, civil rights, and women's movements, did not resemble the speeches given by the ancients. I suspect it is obvious that the mediated age of celebrity and 15-second ads operates on different principles than addresses to the Athenian Assembly, the Roman Senate, or the British Parliament.

By contrast with this earlier tradition, McGee is committed to the exploration of actual rhetorical encounters. McGee's sense of materialism is captured in the definition he offers of rhetoric. "Rhetoric," he writes, "is a natural social phenomenon in the context of which symbolic claims are made on the behavior and/or belief of one or more persons, allegedly in the interest of such individuals, and with the strong presumption that such claims will cause meaningful change."[20] From this definition, we may proceed to unpack the dimensions of rhetorical materialism.

First, the "natural social phenomenon" is the recurring human experience of the relationships among "speaker/speech/audience/occasion/change." You cannot live in the social world without being impacted by these relationships. Each time you are addressed as an audience—for instance, as the reader of this chapter, as a student in a class, or as a citizen of the republic—you enter into this confluence of relationships. You cannot avoid it. It is not simply an idea but an unavoidable part of living in the social world.

Second, the phrase *in the context of which* features for McGee the problematic relationship between *discourse* and *rhetoric*. Rhetoric represents the entire experience of the complex social relationships among speaker/speech/audience/occasion/change. Discourse is residue that is left behind. It is the copy of the "speech" which has been saved. McGee uses an analogy to explain the rhetoric–discourse distinction. "We can construct," he writes, "the nature, scope, and consequence of a nuclear explosion by analyzing its residue when the raw matter and even the energy inherent in its occurrence have dissipated. Thus it is possible to reconstruct the nature, scope, and consequence of rhetoric by analyzing 'speech' even when 'speaker,' 'audience,' 'occasion,' and 'change' dissipate into half-remembered history." So, from a particular discourse we have the tracings that will permit a "reconstruction *of the whole phenomenon* . . . for it is the *whole* of 'speaker/speech/audience/occasion/change' which impinges on us."[21]

Third, the phrase "symbolic claims" suggests, for McGee, that "*every* interactivity of society contains or comprises a claim on some human being's belief and/or behavior."[22] Unlike conventional accounts of rhetoric, McGee does not distinguish rhetoric from coercion. He understands rhetoric as a species of coercion. It is, he writes, a "coercive agency," but certainly one that is preferable to other physical forms of coercion. He suggests that it is preferable in two different senses. First, when an audience acquiesces to rhetoric, it does so feeling that some more personal account was given for imposing the speaker's will. Second, the symbolic is preferable because it sublimates the "pain" of more violent forms of coercion. So, rhetoric may be thought as a preferable, more ethical form of coercion, but it is a form of coercion nonetheless.

Fourth, the phrase *behavior and/or belief* should draw the reader's attention to the complexities of moving from a change in belief to altering behavior. The scholarship in persuasion and social psychology is filled with the difficulties inherent in the process of changing beliefs to influence attitudes in order to ultimately create new behaviors. This process is complex even in the simplest of direct transactions (speaker—message—target audience), but considerably more difficult to account for in the intricate communication environment of contemporary society. Beliefs and attitudes are shaped by ideology and other diffuse discourses that influence the tenor of an entire society.

Fifth, the phrase *allegedly in the interest of the audience,* McGee explains, "calls to attention the relationship between 'speaker' and 'audience' as 'leader' to 'follower.'"[23] The relationship between leader/follower and speaker/audience is a continuing theme in McGee's work. "Every 'audience,'" he writes, "comes together with an interest and the expectation that the 'speaker' will aid in procuring that interest. And every 'speaker' comes to 'audience' with the desire to accomplish an otherwise impossible task by mobilizing a collective force."[24] As you can imagine, the tension of interests between leader and follower, speaker and audience is at the center of any ideological criticism. For the rhetorical creation of a sense of collectivity among audience members requires the invention of messages that appear to harmonize the interests of the leader and the people.

Finally, the phrase "the strong presumption that such claims will result in meaningful change" draws our attention to the issue of rhetorical effects. Few social-science models of any stripe have much success at predicting cause–effect relationships. Certainly, any retrospective claim of a direct effect between a particular feature of a message and a specific historical outcome is foolhardy. The message variable is at best one among a bundle of other forces (economic, demographic, political, cultural, and so forth) and to try to draw specific causal connections is impossible. Yet, in the everyday world we "conduct a continual deliberation based on our ability to model the environment and to predict the consequences of changing it."[25] Even though we can neither explain nor control all the factors that influence change, our public discourse is filled with such talk. We do speak as if speech is a powerful agency to control the environment. This talk creates a sense of the collective and then speaks as if the collective will can shape meaningful social change. In these rhetorical transactions, we create a discourse that reveals the world in which we live. It is powerfully shaped by the ideological commitments that we share. As these commitments are modified, the messages reflect these changes. We can map the ideological shifts in our society by paying attention to these messages.

Up to this point, I have introduced you to ideology and materialism. I suspect many of you have recognized the influence of Karl Marx on the ideological turn in criticism. Marxism certainly creates the intellectual background against which many ideological critics work.[26] Yet, at the same time, the last twenty years have witnessed the collapse of communism and, at least in some respects, the repudiation of Marxism. So, one might naturally be led to wonder if ideological criticism itself is not a spent intellectual enterprise. This is why Michael McGee is such an interesting and important intellectual figure in rhetorical studies. Although admittedly influenced by Marxism, his commitments to this tradition have always been tempered.

McGee describes himself as a *Marxissant* and his politics as planted firmly in the tradition of Anglo-American liberalism.[27] "A *Marxissant,*" McGee explains, "is one who accepts the fundamental categories and logic and maybe even methods of Marxist analysis, but is not a party member and is not committed to the social state or the dictatorship of the proletariat." "A *Marxissant*," he continues, "believes that theory is alive, not frozen or sterile or orthodox, and it needs to be developed and moved forward. But most fundamentally . . . *Marxissants* are more nationalistic, in that they tend to deny the international aspects of Marxist theory."[28] These sentiments have introduced a number of commitments that may at first appear confusing. Upon reflection, however, I actually think you will find them quite straightforward.

First, McGee finds the intellectual approach of Marxism useful for understanding society, but he does not ascribe to its political program. Second, McGee does not accept Marxist theory (or any theory) as orthodoxy. So, the fact that Marx made a claim in the nineteenth century pertaining to the British Empire does not mean that it should be taken as holy writ by twenty-first-century theorists trying to understand liberal democracies and advanced capitalism. Instead, Marxism is an interesting point of departure for thinking about society. Third, McGee does not accept the universalistic aspects of Marxism. In saying that he is a nationalist, he means that he believes that national culture is a critically important element in explaining society. "Marxist theory holds," he observes, "that if you are a worker living in Cleveland, you have more in common with a worker in Gorki than you do with a banker in Columbus. And this is not true."[29]

What does it mean to say that McGee is a liberal in the Anglo-American tradition? It means that McGee's work is focused on the tradition and language of the English and American political experience. "If we're going to have a true politics of the left in Anglo-America," McGee argues, "it must be liberal politics. There's no choice, because liberal politics is all that will fly here. If we cannot talk about what we want to accomplish in the terms of liberalism, then we are condemning ourselves to a life of marginality."[30] So, a commitment to liberal/progressive, conservative, or even radical politics must be articulated in the language of Anglo-American liberalism. To use any other political vocabulary, for instance the terminology of Marxism or Fascism, dooms the advocate to irrelevancy. Only liberal discourse can form a collectivity that can make a significant difference. The important social movements in American history have made their way by appeals to the core commitments of liberalism—liberty, equality, property, rule of law, and so forth.

Given the commitments of rhetorical materialism, how does McGee proceed as a rhetorical critic? What critical apparatus does he mobilize to glean the ideological commitments that are present in a text? The answers to these questions revolve around the concept of the "ideograph."

IDEOGRAPHIC CRITICISM

Critics need a way to move between discourse and ideology; they need a rhetorical window on the exercise of power and the accompanying promulgation of truth. In Dana Cloud's words, critics require a methodology that provides "an analytical link between rhetoric—understood as situated, pragmatic, instrumental, and strategic discourse—on one hand, and ideology—the structures or systems of ideas within which individual pragmatic speech acts take place and by which they are constrained—on the other."[31]

Michael McGee's concept of the "ideograph" provides just this link between rhetoric and ideology. The definition of "ideograph" is surprisingly complex, given its very ordinary and everyday nature. So, let us begin with a list of ideographs and then move to their formal characteristics. In the American context, the following words and slogans are examples of ideographs: <equality>, <freedom>, <freedom of speech>, <law and order>, <liberty>, <national security>, <privacy>, <property>, <rule of law>, and <separation of church and state>.[32]

McGee lists the "characteristics" (in italics) that would constitute a "formal definition of 'ideograph.'"[33] I have commented on each of these seven characteristics below:

1. *"An ideograph is an ordinary language term found in political discourse."*[34] Ideographs are not technical terms or words used by experts or privileged insiders; rather they are terms that appear regularly in ordinary public talk. These are words that you will encounter on the news, hear on talk radio programs, find in the texts of political speeches, encounter in grade-school classrooms, and use in everyday conversation.

2. *"It is a high-order abstraction representing collective commitment to a particular but equivocal and ill-defined normative goal."*[35] On the highest level of abstraction, ideographs are ambiguous, although they have a high emotional affect. For instance, the words <liberty>, <freedom>, and <equality> are emotionally evocative, but they have little cognitive meaning unless tied to specific situations. They are general enough in their meaning that they may be used in a wide variety of contexts. The ideograph <liberty> might be employed by either side in the abortion debate or it might be evoked by either side in the controversy over the meaning of separation of church and state. Ideographs are "normative" because they are value terms that are used to make judgments. Ideographs are "goals" because they represent something to be obtained or a path to follow. So, political candidates might urge their audiences to pursue the path of <freedom>.

3. *"It warrants the use of power, excuses behavior and belief which might otherwise be perceived as eccentric or antisocial, and guides behavior and belief into channels easily recognized as acceptable and laudable. Ideographs such as 'slavery' and 'tyranny,' however, may guide behavior and belief negatively by branding unacceptable behavior."*[36] The essential function of an ideograph is to warrant the exercise of power. Taking or not taking action is justified in the name of ideographs. Some ideographs are positive (<liberty>, <freedom>, <equality>), and behaviors that can be justified by positive ideographs are regarded as socially acceptable. Some ideographs are negative (<tyranny>, <socialism>, <censorship>), and behaviors that further these values are branded as unacceptable.

4. *"And many ideographs ('liberty,' for example) have a non-ideographic usage, as in the sentence, 'Since I resigned my position, I am at liberty to accept your offer.' "*[37] Ideographs "signify and 'contain' a unique ideological commitment."[38] They are the public vocabulary of ideology. So, when terms such as "liberty" and "freedom" are used in nonideological contexts, they do not function as ideographs.

5. *"Ideographs are culture-bound, though some terms are used in different signification across cultures."*[39] Ideographs are universal because they exist in all societies. Specific ideographs are culture bound. The Anglo-American liberal tradition features a defining set of ideographs—the focus on <liberty>, for instance— that would not appear, or at least not appear with the same significance, in other cultures.

6. *"Each member of the community is socialized, conditioned, to the vocabulary of ideographs as a prerequisite for 'belonging' to the society."*[40] Becoming a member of a culture requires understanding the society's ideographs. As part of being socialized as an American, every school child learns to respect <property>, to love <liberty>, and to guard <freedom>.

7. *"A degree of tolerance is usual, but people are expected to understand ideographs within a range of usage thought to be acceptable: The society will inflict penalties on those who use ideographs in heretical ways and on those who refuse to respond appropriately to claims on their behavior warranted through the agency of ideographs."*[41] These penalties may range in severity. Speaking in ways that use ideographs inappropriately may result in political marginalization. Absent the appropriate language, advocates will simply fail to find an audience. Rhetorical sanctions may be imposed as deviant rhetors are labeled "traitors," "demagogues," or "extremists." This may result in public scorn and rhetorical exile. Finally, legal and economic sanctions may be inflicted on those who are determined to be guilty of "subversion" or "treason." This can result in prosecution or loss of employment. During the Red Scare of the 1950s, Joseph McCarthy employed many of these terms to punish the American Left. Likewise, since the rise of the Christian Right in the late 1970s, religious conservatives have been charged with possessing an insufficient commitment to <tolerance> and <pluralism>. Critics on the Left have punished them with accusations of "racism," "homophobia," and "sexism."

Ideographs are especially important for understanding the relationship between leaders and citizens. They are the storehouse of words and phrases from which leaders select appeals to warrant exercises of power. These are the terms that are used when leaders claim to be acting in the name of <the people>.[42] "Ideographs represent in condensed form," Condit and Lucaites explain, "the normative, collective commitments of the members of a public, and they typically appear in public argumentation as the necessary motivations or justifications for action performed in the name of the public."[43]

Remember ideographs are abstract terms that take on more specific meaning as they are placed in given contexts. Like other terms of value, ideographs are often in tension with one another. "An ideograph," McGee writes, "is always understood in its relation to another."[44] So, <freedom> is always understood in relationship to <order>, <responsibility>, and the <rule of law>. In any given circumstance, advocates may argue that one ideological commitment is more important than another. For instance, in the civil rights struggles of the 1950s and 1960s, segregationists and integrationists battled over the preeminence of particular sets of ideographs. Segregationists held that <property> rights permitted proprietors of restaurants, motels, retail stores, and other <private> businesses to decide who they would serve. If owners of apartment buildings did not want to rent to black families, they should have that prerogative as controllers of private property. Integrationists held that the ideological commitment to <equality> demanded that businesses who served the <public> had an obligation to treat each customer alike. The resulting public accommodation and open housing legislation put into law regulations that elevated, in this context, <equality> over <property>.

In brief, this example depicts the synchronic and diachronic dimensions of ideographic analysis. The *synchronic dimension* explores the tension among ideographs at a particular time. In the civil rights illustration, there were advocates posing differing ideological constructions of segregation in an effort to influence passage of specific legislation. The *diachronic dimension* explores a society's changing ideological commitments through time. In America, <equality> has become an ever more important ideological commitment and its prominence has come at the expense of other ideographs, including <property>.[45]

I want to return for a few moments to the "point of departure" at the beginning of the chapter. Recall that I contrasted a pragmatic model of criticism (Bitzer's rhetorical situation) with ideological criticism. With the introduction to McGee's ideographic criticism, I want to spend a little time contrasting the two approaches. I draw your attention to three specific differences: the nature of effects, the concept of audience, and assumptions about reality.

Effects

In the pragmatic model, the critic is interested in evaluating the instrumental impact of a particular speaker's message on a target audience. The effects are quite narrow in conception. Did the message have the particular effect that the speaker desired? For instance, did the Sears' public relations campaign bring customers back to its Auto Service Centers?

In ideographic analysis, the critic is interested in examining the discourse as a symptom of changes in ideology and, thus, public consciousness. Put differently, the discourse itself is understood as the effect rather than the cause. When ideographs change, for instance <equality> displaces <property>, this reflects a change in ideology. The society has begun to justify political actions in new ways and warrant the exercise of power in different ideological terms.

What caused these changes in ideology? This is a very difficult question and is beyond the scope of rhetorical analysis. Typically, such changes are the result of economics, demographics, conflict, or some other social malady. The result of such forces change social reality—the way Americans think about race has changed dramatically over the last century—and these changes are then reflected in the society's rhetoric. These rhetorical changes are marked by new relationships among the culture's ideographs.

Audience

In the pragmatic model, the audience is often assumed to be a fixed target. The audience pre-exists the message. Thus, the advocate adapts the message to a set of audience predispositions and behaviors. The critic's work is to assess the choices that the rhetor made.[46]

In ideographic analysis, the audience itself is taken to be rhetorically constructed. Power is exercised and political actions are justified in the name of <The People>.[47] The audience does not pre-exist the message, but is actually constituted by it. Adolf Hitler constructed the German people as a superior Aryan race. Martin Luther King, Jr., constructed a people who were judged by the "content of their character" rather than the "color of their skin." Ronald Reagan characterized ordinary Americans as "heroic." In each case, these definitions of <The People> become ideological premises upon which to justify taking particular forms of political action. Understanding the changing ideological construction of <The People> is at the center of doing ideographic criticism.

Reality

In the pragmatic model of criticism, there is an implicit assumption that an objective situation (circumstances, audiences, constraints) is present that may be instrumentally altered by the strategic use of discourse. The situation pre-exists the discourse. In ideological criticism, there is an explicit assumption that rhetoric constitutes reality. As I mentioned earlier, ideological criticism concerns the relationship among discourse, power, and truth. The constellation and relationship among ideographs maps the shape of this rhetorically constituted reality.

FINAL THOUGHTS

All criticism involves making arguments on behalf of judgments. "When a . . . critic," Wayne Brockriede writes, "states clearly the criteria he has used in arriving at his judgment, together with the philosophic or theoretic foundations on which they rest, and when he has offered some data to show that the rhetorical experience meets or fails to meet these criteria, then he has argued." Confronted with this form of critical argument "a reader has several kinds of choices: he can accept or reject the data, accept or reject the criteria, accept or reject the philosophic or theoretic basis for the criteria, and accept or reject the inferential leap that joins data and criteria."[48]

Using Brockriede's notion of criticism as a template, let us think through how a critic may use ideographic criticism to form an argument on behalf of a judgment. First, ideographs are a kind of *data*. They direct the critic to look for the presence of ideographs in a text. The critic looks both for the tension among ideographs at a single point in time and for changing patterns of ideographic tensions over time. These patterns are the critic's data.

Second, the *theoretical foundation* of ideographic analysis is rhetorical materialism. It is the commitments of rhetorical materialism that underwrite the relationship among rhetoric, discourse, and ideology. It is only when rhetoric and ideology are understood in particular ways that ideographic criticism becomes compelling. The data provided by ideographs represent patterns of public consciousness. These patterns are maps of changing ideological commitments. As a result, the critic reveals the changing patterns by which power is justified.

Third, ideographic criticism does not present any single set of *criteria for evaluation*. Rather, the results of ideographic criticism provide data that underwrite several different forms of evaluation.

a. An ideographic criticism documents progressive or regressive ideological–rhetorical trends. Celeste Condit and John Lucaites, in their book *Crafting Equality,* have documented the increasingly important role <equality> has played in American public consciousness. By and large, they tell an affirming story of an improving and more just America. The ascendancy of <equality>, they argue, has had positive consequences on the moral quality of our national discourse. Used in this way, the reader is asked to judge the positive and negative quality of the ideographic trend.

b. Ideographic criticism believes ideology is false consciousness. For these critics, public rhetoric often rationalizes political acts that help the powerful and disadvantage the powerless. The acceptance of these explanations accounts for why the people who have the least complain the least. The poor, for instance, have been led to believe that the cause of their deprived circumstances is their own failings.[49] Dana Cloud, in her ideographic analysis of family-values discourse, draws precisely this type of conclusion. "<Family values> talk," she writes, "functioned during the [1992 Presidential election campaign] to scapegoat Black men and poor Americans for social problems." She continues, "Ultimately, in constructing the family as the site of all responsibility and change, the rhetoric of <family values> privatizes social responsibility for ending poverty and racism."[50] Employed in this matter, readers are asked to accept or reject the discourse as a distortion promulgated for the purpose of established interests.

c. Ideographic criticism reveals political irony. Irony lies in the incongruity between the actual result and the normal or expected result. Kenneth Burke's general formula—"what goes forth as *A* returns as non-*A*"—captures this sense of this trope.[51] A particularly good illustration of irony is the famous postulate by the nineteenth-century economist Thomas Malthus. He reasoned that "population, when unchecked . . . tends to increase up to the limits of 'the means of subsistence.'"[52] Given this premise, one could then reason that helping the poor (*A*) actually hurts the poor (non-*A*). The compassionate (*A*) are really those who appear to lack compassion (non-*A*). "It did not hurt the Malthusian theory," Mark Blaug argues, "that it justified resistance of the upper classes to all efforts to reform social and political institutions: for if poverty had its roots in the unequal race between population and subsistence, only the working class itself, by practicing prudential restraint could improve its own conditions."[53]

Irony is not limited to the discourses of poverty and welfare. For example, Celeste Condit and Ann Selzer explored the newspaper coverage of a Kansas murder trial. They found, ironically, that the journalistic standards of <objectivity> lead "to a prosecution bias in the reporting of criminal trials."[54] Objectivity (*A*) led to bias (non-*A*). In the critical essay that accompanies this chapter, I explore the ironic function of <tolerance> in Senator Edward Kennedy's "Tolerance and Truth in America" address. I argue that the force of <tolerance> is to limit rather than enlarge the acceptable means of political expression. Tolerance (*A*) leads to intolerance (non-*A*).

Irony is a complex form of evaluation. By exposing inconsistencies of ideological warrants, it opens up semantic space for resistance. These terms begin to lose some of their positive emotive force and, ultimately, these justifications for the exercise of power become less compelling. This form of ideographic criticism suggests lines of counter argument and alternative political narratives. The reader is left to judge the merits of these new ways of looking at the world.

CRITICAL ESSAY

For my critical essay, I have written an analysis of Senator Edward Kennedy's 1983 "Tolerance and Truth in America" speech, which was delivered to an audience of faculty members and students at Liberty Baptist College. Senator Kennedy's discussion of religion, politics, and public discourse demonstrates the ironic consequences that an ideological commitment to <tolerance> entails. In promoting civility in the public square, a society may often silence the citizenry's most cherished moral beliefs.

You may wonder why I chose a twenty-one-year-old speech for analysis. My selection had motivations beyond the text's usefulness as a classroom illustration. In the aftermath of September 11th, the tension between religious conviction and public speech has produced tears in the fabric of American civil society. It did so in two related ways. First, Osama bin Laden issued a *fatwah* on February 23, 1998, calling on Muslims to "kill the Americans and plunder their money wherever and whenever they find it."[55] His justification, in large part, rested on the depiction of the United States as a "pagan" nation. Americans are "pagan" because they have formed a society in which the place of religion is proscribed in national life. The commitment to religious pluralism has no place in the ideal theocratic state envisioned by followers of al-Qaeda.

Second, within the United States, September 11th lead to acts and statements of religious intolerance. Some American Muslims suffered through frequent and often severe episodes of harassment. Incidents ranged from ethnic profiling to verbal and physical assault. During the twelve months following attacks, the American-Arab Anti-Discrimination Committee documented over 700 violent incidents targeting Arab Americans, including several murders; over 80 cases of illegal and discriminatory removal of passengers from aircraft; a 400 percent increase in employment discrimination; and numerous instances of denial of service.[56]

Beyond individual acts of bigotry, American public discourse was littered with intemperate remarks by prominent religious and political leaders. For instance, the Reverend Franklin Graham, son of evangelist Billy Graham, said during a November 16, 2001, interview on the NBC *Nightly News* that Islam was "a very evil and wicked religion." "It wasn't Methodists flying into those buildings, it wasn't Lutherans," Graham told NBC. "It was an attack on this country by people of the Islamic faith." In a recently published book, entitled *The Name*, Graham writes, "The God of Islam is not the God of the Christian faith. The two are different as lightness and darkness." "Much is said and published today about how peace-oriented Islam is," he continues. "A little scrutiny reveals quite the opposite."[57]

In another example, Dr. Jerry Vines, former President of the Southern Baptist Convention, said in a widely reported public speech that "Christianity was founded by the virgin-born Lord Jesus Christ. Islam was founded by Muhammad, a demon-possessed pedophile who had 12 wives, and his last one was a 9-year-old girl." "Allah," he continued, "is not Jehovah. Jehovah is not going to turn you into a terrorist that'll try to bomb people and take the lives of thousands and thousands of people." In saying this, he drew the lesson that the contemporary American commitment to religious pluralism had gone too far. "Today, people are saying all religions are the same. They would have us believe Islam is just as good as Christianity. But I'm here to tell you . . . that Islam is not as good as Christianity."[58]

In a last troubling example, Cal Thomas, a widely syndicated political columnist, wrote on May 21, 2003, that the United States was threatened by the presence of Muslim citizens within its borders. He argued that "when Muslims gain political power, the historical and contemporary record is not encouraging for people who hold democratic values and are of the 'Judeo-Christian' persuasion."[59]

Beyond the stresses of September 11th, the mingling of the religious and the political have been prominent in a whole host of recent controversial issues. These would include debates over the morality of stem cell research and the prospects of legalizing homosexual civil unions. Over and over again in contemporary national life the country struggles with the proper relationship between faith and politics.

Edward Kennedy's 1983 speech at Liberty Baptist College is a very good text with which to think. You will find in reading the analysis that I am quite critical of this vision of religious tolerance. Yet, I find Kennedy's presentation of the essential issues a vivid portrait of what is at stake.

Critical Essay: Reflections on <Tolerance>: An Ideographic Analysis of Edward Kennedy's Speech at Liberty Baptist College

American elected officials fill their discourses with phrases emphasizing their subordinate relationship to the public. They call themselves "public servants" and in meeting regularly with constituents, standing for election, and in countless other acts of deference they recognize their "public accountability." In defending any legislative or executive act, the democratic script requires our political leaders to offer justifications in terms of the "public good."

Though this word "public" appears everywhere in the discourse of American national life, its meaning is far from a settled matter. Like all important political symbols, it has high affect and low cognitive specificity.[60] Put differently, the citizenry reacts emotionally to the term, as it does to "liberty," "freedom," "equality," and other important American symbols but its meaning is ambiguous and subject to considerable change as it moves among differing contexts. Michael McGee has called such terms "ideographs." "An ideograph," he writes, "is an ordinary language term found in political discourse. It is a high-order abstraction representing collective commitment to a particular but equivocal and ill-defined normative goal." Ideographs function to "warrant the use of power."[61]

As with all ideographs, the changes in the meaning of "public" are marked by altered relationships with other ideographs. <Public> and <private> are in a dialectical tension that shifts with context and history. In the segregated world of the Old South, the prerogatives of <private property> permitted landlords, innkeepers, and business owners to turn away patrons on the basis of race. With the passage of Title II of the Civil Rights Act of 1964, discrimination in places of public accommodation because of race, color, religion, or national origin was prohibited. As a result, the sphere and privileges of <private property> were diminished by the demands of <equality>. The <public>, in this context, became more important than the <private> in the hierarchy of American values.

By mapping such discursive shifts, the critic may illuminate important changes in ideology and the concomitant alterations in public consciousness. With the passage and eventual general acceptance of the premises of the 1964 Civil Rights Act, the acceptable rhetorical choices open to speakers changed. To invoke now the rights of <private property> to justify turning away a customer of color is to announce oneself a racist. Three generations ago, such an argument would fit comfortably inside a particular political tradition. Today, this tradition has no respectable members.

Beginning in the 1970s, a series of events led to another deep division over the proper relationship between <public> and <private>. The grounds of this controversy were very different, but once again the fundamental character of the <public> was at issue. This time it was not a matter of which groups in America were entitled to full citizenship (the issue of civil rights), but rather which <private> beliefs could be responsibly brought to bear in discussions of <public> issues. Where <equality> mediated the dispute between <public> and <private property>

in the case of segregation, the ideograph <tolerance> was at the center of this dispute.

In the 1970s and 1980s members of conservative religious congregations began to organize politically and through this organization sought to influence the outcome of elections, the appointment of federal judges, the passage of legislation, and the general ideological direction of American politics. This emerging coalition of religious conservatives went under a number of names and organizational titles. Generally, it was known as the New Christian Right. Although initially, the name of the Reverend Jerry Falwell's political organization—the Moral Majority—was widely used to identify the movement.

Beyond the traditional liberal/conservative disagreements over policy issues, these religious conservatives hoped to reverse the trend toward what they saw as an increasingly coarse and debased culture. This divide was called by some commentators a "culture war"—a war that drew battle lines along an orthodox–progressive rift. "Orthodoxy," James Hunter explains, "is the commitment on the part of adherents to an external, definable, and transcendent authority." "Progressivism," on the other hand, holds that "moral authority tends to be defined by the spirit of the modern age, a spirit of rationalism and subjectivism."[62] Those holding orthodox religious views pressed a social–conservative agenda into the center of the American political dialogue. Over a period of years and in many different contexts, vigorous debates sprung up over family values, regulation of pornography, the wisdom of overturning *Roe v. Wade*, government funding of the arts, the provision of gay rights, the distasteful language and images in popular media, and a host of other cultural issues. Although religious conservatives also tended to favor fiscal constraint, low taxes, market economics, and a large military, they often did so for cultural reasons. For instance, representatives of the New Christian Right have frequently argued that high taxes and inflation force both parents to work. A fiscally disciplined government, they believe, would create a tax policy that would permit mothers to stay at home with their young children.

The progressive/orthodox cultural divide was in an important sense about the theory of democratic public communication itself. Very different views of moral authority guide the inventional choices that advocates on each side of the cultural divide have made. These divergent moral commitments create two different rhetorical styles. Their differing systems of belief demand a certain form of expression and the forms of expression themselves have become elements of controversy. The certainty of religious faith may lead to the articulation of political principles grounded in moral absolutism. Such an approach clashes with a deliberative legislative style built on the virtues of political bargaining. It is one thing to disagree with the utility of a particular policy, but it is quite another to argue that those on the other side are immoral, blasphemous, or un-Christian.

At the pitched height of this "culture war," Senator Edward Kennedy of Massachusetts, the living embodiment of the Democratic liberal tradition in contemporary U.S. politics, accepted an invitation to deliver an address at Liberty Baptist College.[63] The Reverend Jerry Falwell, pastor of Thomas Rhodes Baptist

Church and Chancellor of the college, was the personification of the New Christian Right. He had founded the Moral Majority, and he had articulated the argument justifying the entrance of Christian evangelicals into the secular world of national politics.[64] Senator Kennedy had often been the target of the Moral Majority's attacks. No two individuals in 1983 were better representatives of the progressive and orthodox voices in the U.S. "culture war."

The Senator's speech is particularly interesting because it is so self-reflexive. The very fact of the event itself—Kennedy speaking to the students and faculty at Liberty Baptist College—is the subject of the talk. There is something utterly American about offering an invitation to a speaker with whom you strenuously disagree and then for the speaker to accept an invitation to speak before a group that is so hostile to his ideological orientation. It is a ritual embodying American political <pluralism> and <tolerance>. Such rhetorical moments run deep in American democratic mythology, for they recall the unfettered exchange of ideas in the New England town meeting and the American commitment to protect the voice of minority opinion against the power of the majority.

Moreover, this is a self-reflexive religious occasion. It recalls the 1960 election in which John Kennedy's Catholicism was an overriding issue. In JFK's famous address to the Houston ministers, he provided the most memorable contemporary statement on religious toleration. The tension here is even more complex. In 1960, Protestants feared the influence of the papacy on a Catholic president. John Kennedy had to convince the Protestant majority that his membership in the Roman Catholic Church was consistent with American pluralism. In 1983, it is not the influence of Church hierarchy that threatens pluralism, but religious orthodoxy. Interestingly, many conservative Catholics were quite sympathetic with the Moral Majority. Edward Kennedy, although well known as a Catholic, was hardly in good standing with the Church. His pro-choice position on abortion, for instance, made him an anathema to many faithful Catholics. This tension between church teachings and the politics of Catholic politicians was a constant refrain during this period. These clashes were particularly memorable for Governor Mario Cuomo of New York and Vice Presidential candidate Geraldine Ferraro.

If we think of this address as the second part of the Kennedy discourse on religious tolerance—John Kennedy's Houston ministers address as the first—then the younger brother got the more difficult assignment. This assertion requires some elaboration. John Kennedy's challenge was more difficult politically and certainly the stakes were higher, but Edward Kennedy's task is more difficult rhetorically and philosophically. John Kennedy had to do two things: First, he had to dispel unfounded Protestant fears by making known the real position of the American Catholic Church, and second, he had to explain that anti-Catholic bigotry had no place in the American creed.[65] Put differently, this was essentially a speech about civil rights. American Catholics had a right to be full-fledged citizens in the United States. He asked Americans to write Catholics fully into a broad and inclusive sense of <The People>.

By contrast, Edward Kennedy was not coming to ask for religious inclusion, but rather requesting restraint on religious expression. From the perspective of the

Moral Majority, this circumstance was filled with irony. At least in one sense, Kennedy's mission may be interpreted as an attempt to exclude evangelical, fundamentalist Christian participation in electoral politics. This exclusion is based on the uncomfortable moral message brought as a critique to Kennedy's own progressive politics.

All of this points to the complexity of <tolerance>. Certainly, as John Kennedy maintained in 1960, <tolerance> does not permit a religious litmus test for public office. But what requirements does <tolerance> place on the style of religious expression when it enters the political arena? One would assume that a commitment to <tolerance> would stop short of reducing moral argument to mere pronouncements of taste or preference. American <pluralism> is not supposed to result in a "naked public square" in which citizens cannot bring serious moral/religious argument to bear on the important issues in national life.[66]

This is not the first time that this address has been the subject of an academic rhetorical analysis. Robert Branham and Barnett Pearce were also struck by the use of "tolerance" as a means of negotiating between, what they called, the "incommensurability [of] worldviews."[67] Their interest was quite different than mine. Branham and Pearce went about explaining Kennedy's negotiation among competing audiences and how this negotiation was to the benefit of both the Senator and Reverend Falwell. "Kennedy offered Falwell," they contended, "legitimacy and respect as a rhetor in the public arena, and Falwell offered Kennedy arenas in which he could revise his image and defuse what had to be anticipated as his most strident opposition. The means of accomplishing this was 'civility,' that elusive melody best sung in duet."[68] Branham and Barnett explained Kennedy's address and Falwell's participation in the occasion in terms of effectively managing a set of situational exigencies.[69]

By contrast, I have an ideological interest that drives my analysis of the speech. Kennedy's rhetorical characterization of important ideographs—<public>, <private>, <tolerance>—warrants a particular use of power. It dismisses certain forms of political expression as unreasonable and unwelcome in the public square, while commending other utterances as reasonable arguments that elevate public debate. These forms of political expression, at least by implication, are tied to particular groups. Although billed as a "nonpolitical" speech, the language of the address has the profoundest consequences for empowering some parties and viewpoints and silencing others. Although I do not carry out a thoroughgoing diachronic analysis, I am yet interested in documenting how significantly this discourse departs from the rhetoric of civil rights. Many of its references—slavery and abolition, anti-Semitism and anti-Catholicism, Pope John XXIII and Martin Luther King, Jr.—recall earlier appeals for inclusion based on <equality>, but this address instead uses <tolerance> as a means of exclusion. Unpacking this ideological complexity is the purpose of this critical analysis.

In what follows, I provide an overview of the themes in Senator Kennedy's address, "Tolerance and Truth in America." Second, I examine the speech's construction of the public, private, and technical spheres. Third, I explore how the tension between Kennedy's construction of <public> and <private> shapes the meaning of <tolerance>. Finally, I argue that there is an erupting irony of exclusion in Kennedy's treatment of religion that is symptomatic of democratic liberalism.

The Themes in "Truth and Tolerance in America".   The speech "Truth and Tolerance in America" is a sophisticated rhetorical effort. As such, it does not fall conveniently into discrete parts, for sections of the speech perform multiple tasks. Nonetheless, for simplicity's sake, I have divided the text's forty-four paragraphs into six functional sections.

Section 1: Civility Ritual.   The immediate events leading up to the speech and the opening of the speech itself were exercises in the American ritual of civility. Both Reverend Falwell and Senator Kennedy, although political opponents, paid homage to the nation's commitment to listen respectfully to others' ideas and then engage in spirited debate. For instance, Reverend Falwell hosted a dinner for the Kennedy family before the address.[70]

At the beginning of the speech, Senator Kennedy thanked Reverend Falwell for his "generous introduction." He joked with the students, "In honor of our meeting, I have asked Dr. Falwell, as your chancellor, to permit all students an extra hour next Saturday night before curfew. In return, I have promised to watch 'The Old Time Gospel Hour' next Sunday."[71]

I refer to this opening as ritualistic because it is a common, oft-repeated rhetorical gesture that is underwritten by the American culture.[72] The host warmly welcomes the speaker and thanks him for coming. The speaker thanks the host for his hospitality and for the invitation to speak. Even if the two parties have serious disagreements, they engage in a rhetorical dance that highlights the civil and respectful nature of their disagreement. In this particular speech, this commonplace takes on added importance because it is itself central to the topic of the address.

Section 2: Characterization of Topic and Construction of the Audience.   Kennedy tells the audience that he has come to Liberty Baptist College to "discuss my beliefs about faith and country, tolerance and truth in America." He says, "We cannot turn and should not turn aside from a deeper, more pressing question—which is whether and how religion should influence government."[73]

He defines his address as a "nonpolitical speech."[74] In this context, "nonpolitical" means nonpartisan. "Since I am not a candidate for president," Kennedy says, "it certainly would be inappropriate to ask for your support in this election—and probably inaccurate to thank you for it in the last one."[75] Kennedy implies that the topic of this "nonpolitical speech" should not divide the audience along party lines, because he is going to speak to the basic ideological commitments that unite Americans.

The immediate audience for this address was made up of "students, faculty, administrators, and residents of Lynchburg."[76] However, the mediated audience was a good deal larger. This speech was widely covered by the national press.[77]

In the speech itself, Kennedy constructs the students of Liberty Baptist College as representatives of an American religious people. They embody a conservative political view with which he disagrees, but they are a people who listen carefully to argument and accept the American pluralist tradition of respecting differences. "I know," he tells the audience, that "we begin with certain disagreements . . . But I also hope that tonight and in the months and years ahead, we will always respect the right of others to differ—that we will view ourselves with a sense of perspective and a sense of humor."[78]

Section 3: History of Religious Intolerance and the Separation of Church and State.   In this section of the address, Kennedy provides examples of religious intolerance in America. These include the exile of Roger Williams and his followers from Massachusetts, the anti-Catholic laws in colonial Maryland and Pennsylvania, the discrimination faced by Jews in all thirteen colonies, and the harassment of Baptists in Virginia.

Kennedy provides an interesting example of religious intolerance within the coalition of believers that make up the Moral Majority. "[B]ecause the Moral Majority has worked with members of different denominations," Senator Kennedy explains, "one fundamentalist group has denounced Dr. Falwell for hastening the ecumenical church and for 'yoking together with Roman Catholics, Mormons, and others.' "[79] Kennedy argues that on "this issue, [Falwell] himself has become the target of narrow prejudice."[80]

With this background of religious discrimination, Kennedy enters into a short history of the American commitment to religious freedom and the separation of church and state. During the revolution, he tells the audience, "Catholics, Jews and nonconformists all rallied to the cause and fought valiantly for the American commonwealth—for John Winthrop's 'city upon a hill.' " After the war, "when the Constitution was ratified and amended, the framers gave freedom for all religion—and from any established religion—the very first place in the Bill of Rights."[81] He refers to Thomas Jefferson's pronouncement that "his proudest achievement was . . . drafting the Virginia Statute of Religious Freedom."[82] Kennedy lists the various religious traditions that could be found among the founders.

Then, Senator Kennedy moves to a key section of the address. Here he introduces the value of <pluralism>. As a prelude to offering a definition of this pivotal concept, he says, "In 1789 their fear was of factional strife among dozens of denominations. Today there are hundreds—and perhaps thousands—of faiths and millions of Americans who are outside any fold."[83] "Pluralism," Kennedy continues, "does not and cannot mean that all of them are right; but it does mean that there are areas where government cannot and should not decide what is wrong to believe, to think, to read, and to do."[84]

Kennedy recognizes that the "separation of church and state can sometimes be frustrating for women and men of deep religious faith." "They may," he explains, "be tempted to misuse government in order to impose a value which they cannot persuade others to accept." This is the "temptation," which can start us down a "slippery slope where everyone's freedom is at risk." "Let us never forget," he warns, "today's Moral Majority could become tomorrow's persecuted minority."[85]

Section 4: Public and Private.   A meaningful <pluralism> demands a workable boundary between <public> and <private>. "The real transgression," Kennedy argues, "occurs when religion wants government to tell citizens how to live uniquely personal parts of their lives." "Some questions," he continues, "may be inherently individual ones or people may be sharply divided about whether they are. In such cases—cases like Prohibition and abortion—the proper role of religion is to appeal to the conscience of the individual, not the coercive power of the state."[86]

There are other circumstances that may be deemed <public>. The <public>, for Kennedy, is determined by questions "which we must decide together as a nation, and where religion and religious values can and should speak to our common conscience."[87] Kennedy uses the "issue of nuclear war" as a "compelling example." "It is," he says, "a moral issue; it will be decided by government, not by each individual; and to give any effect to the moral values of their creed, people of faith must speak directly about public policy."[88] For instance, "the Catholic bishops and the Reverend Billy Graham have every right to stand for the nuclear freeze—and Dr. Falwell has every right to stand against it."[89]

Section 5: Imposed Will and Essential Witness.   The terms of the entire argument are now stated. On the one hand, "no religious body should seek to impose its will"; and, on the other hand, religious leaders should "state their views and give their commitments when public debate" involves "ethical issues."[90] Kennedy describes this distinction as "drawing the line between imposed will and essential witness."[91] In different language, Kennedy tells the audience, "we keep church and state separate—and at the same time, we recognize that the city of God should speak to the civic duties of men and women."[92]

Senator Kennedy proposes four tests "which draw the line and define the difference" between imposed will and essential witness. He spends the next 17 paragraphs elaborating on these tests. The first test is that "we must respect the integrity of religion itself."[93] We should remember that religion has often been wrongly invoked to "sanction prejudice and even slavery, to condemn labor unions and public spending for the poor."[94] "God," Kennedy argues, "has taken no position on the Department of Education—and that a balanced budget amendment is a matter for economic analysis, not heavenly appeals."[95] In short, "religious values cannot be excluded from every public issue—but not every public issue involves religious values."[96]

The second test holds that "we must respect the independent judgments of conscience."[97] People of good will often disagree on matters of public policy. "Those who proclaim moral and religious values can offer counsel," Kennedy argues, "but they should not casually treat a position on a public issue as a test of fealty to faith."[98] When we do "apply moral values to public life, let all of us avoid the temptation to be self-righteous and absolutely certain of ourselves."[99] The "respect of conscience" implies a willingness to respect the moral disagreements of others as sincere and well-intentioned. The application of religious teachings to the practical world of politics is hardly a certain matter without room for differences.

The third test commands that "in applying religious values, we must respect the integrity of public debate." "Faith," Kennedy says, "is not substitute for facts."[100] Even if privately one's faith makes him certain of the correct position on a public issue, this private certainty does not excuse this person from engaging in public debate. Religious-based conviction cannot permit the use of unreasonable means of advocacy. There is a temptation, when so sure of one's position, to use whatever rhetorical means necessary to succeed. This kind of demagoguery undermines serious public debate, which is at the center of a pluralist democracy.

The fourth and final test demands that "we must respect the motives of those who exercise their right to disagree."[101] "The more our feelings diverge," Kennedy advises, "the more deeply felt they are, the greater is our obligation to grant the sincerity and essential decency of our fellow citizens on the other side."[102] As an example, Kennedy argues that those "who favor E.R.A. are not 'antifamily' or 'blasphemers' and their purpose is not 'an attack on the Bible.'"[103]

Section 6: Conclusion. Kennedy concludes the speech with an appeal for peace. "For as the apostle Paul wrote long ago in Romans, 'If it be possible, as much as it lieth in you, live peaceably with all men.'"[104]

Public, Private, and Technical Spheres

This speech has a remarkably pleasing quality. We could all get along if we observed the rituals of civility, the conventions of fair debate, and the rules of sweet reason. All this trouble started when some among the religious sought either to "impose their will" on areas of purely personal concern or to bring their harsh judgmental language to bear on public policy matters. To use Roderick Hart's terminology, Senator Kennedy is arguing that some religious leaders have violated the rhetorical provisions of the "church–state contract."[105] They did so by straying out of their own sphere of influence—spiritual matters related to the church and public matters related to ethics—and straying into the world of politics. If we could just keep everything in its rightful place—follow the dictates of civic decorum and say the right thing at the right time—the nation would be a more peaceful place.

Recall that Senator Kennedy framed this event as "nonpolitical." He acknowledged a disagreement with his audience on partisan matters of policy and sought common ground on the American commitment to "tolerance" and "pluralism." After all, freedom of religion and the nation's subsequent religious diversity are matters of first importance to the faithful. I think it is fair to assume that Kennedy hoped this speech would be received as a philosophical statement of common national values.

Among the most valuable lessons one can learn about ideology is that it often comes wrapped in discourses that deny its very existence. When someone tells you that a message is "nonpolitical," you should be on guard for the implicit introduction of ideological warrants. In this case, the boundary between Kennedy's "imposed will" and "essential witness" is hardly a matter that can be understood apart from ideology, for it demands attention to two of the central ideographs in the liberal democratic tradition—<public> and <private>. As I noted earlier, in the civil rights struggle these two terms mediated the tension between <equality> and <property>. By limiting the domain of the <private> in such areas as housing, employment, and customer service, the commitment to <equality> became more central to American society.

In this text, <private> and <public> are reified into three apparently separate spheres of activity—private, public, and technical. These distinctions are drawn from the history of liberal thought. The changing boundaries among these spheres, what Jurgen Habermas has called "colonization,"[106] have received a good deal of scholarly attention in the last fifteen years.[107] Kennedy has vested interests in maintaining a particular set of boundary lines and these interests have real consequences.

Rhetorical Construction of the Private Sphere.　To begin, let us catalogue, as best we can, those things that appear to fall within the private sphere in Kennedy's address. This cataloguing is rather tricky, for each item does not imply the private in the same way nor does it get placed in this sphere on the same grounds. Some items were labeled private because they were personal, others are subjective, and still others are said to have limited force in civic discussion. The Senator's speech mentions nine items that appear to belong inside the private domain:

- *Conscience:* "[W]e must respect the independent judgments of conscience. Those who proclaim moral and religious values can offer counsel, but they should not casually treat a position on a public issue as a test of fealty to faith."[108]
- *Motive:* "We sorely test our ability to live together if we too readily question each other's integrity. . . . [T]he more our feelings diverge, the more deeply felt they are, the greater is our obligation to grant the sincerity and essential decency of our fellow citizens on the other side."[109]
- *Nonmajority values:* "[W]omen and men of deep religious faith . . . may be tempted to misuse government in order to impose a value which they cannot persuade others to accept."[110] "Some questions may be inherently individual ones or people may be sharply divided about whether they are."[111]
- *Personal lives:* "The real transgression occurs when religion wants government to tell citizens how to live uniquely personal parts of their lives. The failure of Prohibition proves the futility of such an attempt when a majority or even a substantial minority happens to disagree."[112]
- *Prohibition and abortion:* "In such cases—cases like Prohibition and abortion— the proper role of religion is to appeal to the conscience of the individual, not the coercive power of the state."[113]

- *Religion:* "When people agree on public policy, they ought to work together, even while they worship in diverse ways."[114]
- *Truth:* "I believe there surely is such a thing as truth, but who among us can claim a monopoly on it?"[115]
- *Voting:* "John Kennedy said at that time, 'I believe in an America where there is no (religious) bloc voting of any kind."[116]

In this collection of words and phrases, at least three different senses of <private> emerge. They certainly overlap in their use, but for our task they may be separated for purposes of analysis.

Private as Independent or Nonconsensus Judgment or Choice. Any individually held view, which is apart from a national consensus, is in the domain of the private. The term "conscience" designates the source of independent judgment. Such independent judgments deserve respect, meaning the speaker should not be criticized for offering them in an open forum, but there public force is to be severely circumscribed. Decision makers should listen respectfully to such appeals but should not be bound by them. As a rule of decorum, advocates should refrain from questioning the private motives of those who speak in the public sphere. Instead, they should presume the decent intentions of their opponents.

Private as Personal Conduct. There are certain parts of life and forms of conduct that are understood as "personal." In the context of this address, religious devotion, the drinking of alcoholic beverages (Prohibition), and the decision to terminate a pregnancy (abortion) would all fall under the rubric of the <private>. Voting is a special case of personal conduct. Organizing others into a voting blocs, based on beliefs rightly assigned to the personal sphere (such as religious devotion), is a violation of the liberal–democratic boundary between <public> and <private>.

Private as an Unverifiable Claim. The dimensions of private captured in (1) and (2) all point to a largely subjective view of truth. Kennedy believes that "there surely is such a thing as truth," but no one "among us can claim a monopoly on it."[117] Many claims to truth, especially those based on the transcendent, may exist above and apart from the person, but they cannot be established through any agreed upon public methods of verification. This explains the distinction in the address between "facts" (publicly verifiable) and "truth" (not publicly verifiable). As a result, when religious truth is brought to the public square, it must come as a private moral commitment and not as a claim that binds public decision makers.

Rhetorical Construction of the Public Sphere. Following a parallel procedure, I have identified six items that appear to fall within the public domain in Kennedy's address. Again, the Senator's discourse is more suggestive than explicit. It is the evident tension between <public> and <private> that permits me to make these judgments with some confidence.

- *Debate:* "In applying religious values, we must respect the integrity of public debate."[118]
- *Facts:* "In [public] debate, faith is no substitute for facts."[119]
- *Government office:* "Respect for conscience is most in jeopardy—and the harmony of our diverse society is most at risk—when we reestablish, directly or indirectly, a religious test for public office."[120]
- *Issues requiring collective action (for example the Nuclear Freeze proposal):* "[T]here are other questions which are inherently public in nature, which we must decide as a nation. . . . the issue of nuclear war is a compelling example." Kennedy elaborates, "It is a moral issue; it will be decided by government, not by each individual."[121]
- *Peace:* "As fellow citizens, let us live peaceably with each other; as fellow human beings, let us strive to live peaceably with men and women everywhere."[122]
- *Standards of civility:* "I hope for an America where we can all contend freely and vigorously, but where we will treasure and guard those standards of civility which alone make this nation safe for both democracy and diversity."[123]

In this collection of words and phrases, different senses of <public> emerge. I have identified three dimensions of <public> life.

Public as Collective Action to Regulate Other-Regarding Actions.   There is a distinction between issues that require collective action—<public>—and issues that require individual moral suasion—<private>. So, for example, only the will of the collective <public>, as expressed in government action, can adopt policies that will lessen the likelihood of a nuclear war. By contrast, through moral suasion, one could influence a pregnant woman to forego an abortion or induce an alcoholic to stop drinking. Less obvious, but I believe lurking in the intellectual background, is an appeal to John Stuart Mill's distinction between "self-regarding" and "other-regarding" actions. "But neither one person, nor any number of persons," Mill wrote, "is warranted in saying to another human creature of ripe years that he shall not do with his life for his own benefit what he chooses to do with it."[124] However, "[a]s soon as any part of a person's conduct affects prejudicially the interests of others, society has jurisdiction over it."[125] Kennedy appears to believe that there is a distinction between those activities that primarily impact the individual who decides to engage in them and those activities that threaten the interests of others. The self-regarding actions should be considered a matter of private choice and the other-regarding actions as a matter of public jurisdiction and regulation.

Public as Official Office and Action.   Officials who hold government office must be evaluated in terms of <public> rather than <private> standards. So, no candidate for elected office or nominee for appointed office should be disqualified on the basis of religion. Kennedy does not make clear how other criteria may fall out across this boundary. On occasion, distinctions have been drawn between <public> and <private> conduct. So, for instance, an official may be a poor family member (for example, adulterer or neglectful parent) and, yet, carry out official duties in an exemplary manner (for example, eschew interest-group contributions or stand up for the poor).[126]

Public as Civic Debate.   The notion of public debate appears to be equated by Kennedy with civic discussion. In this sense, public has quite a narrower meaning than merely speaking in front of an audience. Churches, for instance, are public places and ministers speak from the pulpit to large audiences. Yet, this occasion would only become public, in the sense Kennedy appears to imply, if the minister's homily took up civic matters. Religion, after all, is conceived by the Senator as private. Moreover, there are rules of <public> conduct which differ from rules of <private> behavior. In this speech, the rules of <public> conduct focus on the code of "civility" and the requirements of "public debate." The implication is that one might conduct a <private> discussion in quite a different way from a <public> one. In speaking with my wife about an issue of national importance, I certainly may call into question the other side's motives. In discussing who we might vote for, we certainly may entertain issues that have to do with the candidate's <private> conduct. However, if we were invited to take part in a <public> debate about these matters, the demands of civility would preclude raising such issues in front of a wider audience.

Rhetorical Construction of the Technical Sphere.   Lurking behind the grand liberal clash between <private> and <public> is a more prosaic sphere—the technical realm. In the twentieth century, government has become more and more complex and with that complexity has evolved an ever growing reliance on specialized expertise. Areas of decision that were once the object of public debate and legislative deliberation have increasingly been relegated to regulatory agencies or other technical offices for determination.[127] Expertise has two related appeals: Professional judgment is supposed to examine issues objectively without the undue influence of politics; and experts are supposedly able to unwind the complexities of issues and thus reach more rationally considered judgments.[128]

The technical emerges from the tension between <public> and <private>, although here these terms take on somewhat different meanings. The tension is between the general public and its representatives and the expertise of specialists. Public comes to mean something close to "lay public." The public's representatives are thought to be involved in partisan politics. So, in this sense, the technical is an oasis of expertise and objective judgment. Yet, the technical is hardly private. Judgments are not made based on individual or subjective consideration. Judgments are made following standardized procedures promulgated by a professional community. There is, as a result, a form of accountability that extends beyond the consequences of private decisions.

In Kennedy's speech there are only hints of items that may fall within the technical sphere. When I mention them, they may well appear to the reader as merely another part of the public debate. Yet, I am confident that there is here another strain in the <public>/<private> tension.

- *Law:* "As Professor Laurence Tribe, one of the nation's leading constitutional scholars has written, 'Law in a nontheocratic state cannot measure religious truth'—nor can the state impose it."[129]
- *Economic analysis.* "[A] balanced budget constitutional amendment is a matter for economic analysis, not heavenly appeals."[130]

In these brief examples, two different dimensions of the technical emerge.

The Technical as Governmental Institutions Shielded from Politics.   In this sense of technical, the courts are the preeminent institution in the technical sphere. In the paragraph following the quotation from Laurence Tribe, Senator Kennedy identifies abortion as a private issue. Of course, the abortion question was settled by the Supreme Court. The point of clash between left and right on questions of reproductive freedom has to do with the proper site of decision. Liberals argue that the availability of abortion is tied to a woman's right to privacy. This right was promulgated by the Court in *Roe v. Wade.* Conservatives argue that the issue of abortion should be correctly left to the legislature, for it is the representatives of the people that ought to make such moral choices. In this context, the Court is a technical sphere because it brings learned judgment to the reading of the Constitution and because it is sheltered by the structure of the judicial branch from the influence of partisan politics.

The Technical as Objective Policy Analysis.   In distinguishing "economic analysis" from "heavenly appeals," Kennedy is making an observation about objectivity. The findings of economic analysis are credible because they must meet the standards of professional practice. When policy makers make appeals based on economic analysis, they are calling on a disciplinary ethos to underwrite their claim.[131] The findings of the Court and the conclusions of professional economists are certainly used in public debate, but much of their authority comes from their gestation in the technical sphere.

The Meaning of <Tolerance>

For Senator Kennedy, the commitment to <tolerance>, properly understood, serves as a regiment of border guards around the perimeter of the <public>. The terms of entry are found in the eight dimensions I have listed in the analysis of the three spheres. These dimensions in turn become, for Kennedy, the operational meaning of <tolerance> in a liberal democratic society.

Ironically, given the ordinary meaning of "tolerance"—the sense of allowing something or of indulging beliefs or practices differing from one's own—<tolerance> as a border guard tolerates very little. Crossing this boundary requires a quite extensive list of documents—it is hardly an easy crossing.

What does Kennedy's <public> look like? It appears to have two dominant features. First, this <public> has limited the agenda of items that may be subject to open discussion and debate. Second, this <public> has restricted the list of *topoi* (topics) that may serve as resources for the invention of argument. Let me take up each in turn.

The <public> agenda is restricted to civic debate about other-regarding actions that require collective deliberation in order to regulate. Conversely, any self-regarding action, which may be influenced by individual moral suasion, is a <private> rather than <public> matter. Even if a consensus on this principle existed, which it may, the constitutive terms of this axiom are so ambiguous that their meaning will certainly change with each advocate's application of the criteria.

We know from the illustrations in Senator Kennedy's address that abortion is a paradigm case of a "personal" and thus self-regarding action. We also know that nuclear war, racism, and poverty are paradigm cases of public and thus other-regarding action. Notice how Kennedy labels abortion as outside the public sphere by definition. Whether abortion is a self- and other-regarding action is the essential question at issue. This is precisely the point at which people of faith want to introduce religious–moral argument.

Interestingly, there are those who have characterized racism as essentially a personal issue. The argument that the rights of <private property> permitted landlords, motel operators, store owners, and restaurateurs to make personal decisions about serving African Americans was a viable argument in America less than forty years ago. Likewise, the same argument that what was necessary was the moral suasion of individual consciences rather than collective public action was offered. So, Southern segregationists could talk about how they felt or their personal moral outlook or their independent judgment of conscience.[132]

My point is that the invoking of <tolerance> always comes with serious ideological consequences because there is no objective standpoint from which to draw the <public>/<private> line. What stands inside the public sphere, as other-regarding action, and what stands outside, as self-regarding action, is always based on a process of persuasive definition. These definitions have everything to do with the exercise of power. Senator Kennedy wants to use his political power to assure the legal provision of abortions; forty years before George Wallace and Bull Connor wanted to exercise their political power to maintain American apartheid.

The second feature of Senator Kennedy's <public> is even more troubling. The first feature restricted what could be talked about in public, but the second restricts how citizens may argue and deliberate over issues of civic importance. Only an argument warranted by *consensus values* and supported by *verifiable evidence* is permitted into the public realm.

In listening to Senator Kennedy, he appears as someone who is merely calling for more civility in the cause of producing a dignified and serious public dialogue. Think for a moment about how ideologically loaded such calls to civility inevitably are. Those with power—those who enjoy the presumption of the settled present—have always chastised the subordinate class for its failure of decorum.[133] There is an enormous rhetorical advantage if your opponent must speak on your terms and follow your rules.

Kennedy's restriction on the *topoi* of public debate goes to the very heart of the function of the <public>. Ideally, the public stands between the intimate sphere and the official sphere. It is a place where people bring moral views, gestated in the intimate sphere of the family, to bear on public issues. The resulting debate and discussion becomes a recognizable public opinion. This public opinion then asserts influence on government officials and makes a difference in the exercise of state power. Notice, on this view, the public is the place of mediation between private values and state action.[134]

If the public does not convert private values into public opinion, then what is the meaning of democracy? What would the will of the people comprise if not the amalgam of private morality? The answer, I suppose, and the one apparently offered by Senator Kennedy is that public values and private values are different in kind. The values of the public are not grounded in the life histories of private citizens, but rather they are of a wholly different type that does not require that choices be made among competing private values. The liberal fear is that if you begin to make such choices, the peaceful civic order will be disturbed.

So, if private values are set aside, what language of value can be used in public discourse? I see only two rhetorical choices: appeals to rights and appeals to utility. Interestingly, rights and utility are largely the discursive domain of the technical. Courts settle matters of rights and the appropriate subject-matter experts calculate the costs and benefits, in other words the utility, of various policy options.

Rights talk is the rhetoric of drawing lines in the sand. Over this line you shall not cross.[135] So, for example, *Roe v. Wade* posited a right to privacy and said that the state may not interfere with the privacy of a woman's body and, therefore, may not prevent her from terminating a pregnancy. The concept of separation of church and state draws a line—for instance, prayer in the public schools—over which the state may not step. Notice the rhetorical similarity between the language of rights and Kennedy's boundary drawing around the public sphere. In each case, the force of the discourse is to draw a line and post a guard. Notice that rights do not make substantive moral claims. To say that a woman has a right to choose is far different than saying that abortion is a moral good.

To speak of utility is to talk pragmatically about the respective effectiveness of various alternatives. Utility is the calling card of the technical sphere; experts can calculate the respective costs and benefits of various alternatives. As Senator Kennedy put it, "a balanced budget constitutional amendment is a matter for economic analysis."[136] Notice, too, how explicitly the speech favors "facts" over "faith." It is only the objective, observable, and verifiable material of the sciences that should influence public opinion and official action.

Religious discourse is essentially about human purpose. What is our purpose and given that purpose how should we live? This is the moral tradition of virtue not of rights and utility. "The virtues," Alasdair MacIntyre writes, "are precisely those qualities the possession of which will enable an individual to achieve *eudaimonia* and the lack of which will frustrate his movement toward the *telos*." By *eudaimonia,* Aristotle meant a state "of a man's being well-favored himself and in relation to the divine."[137] The God who said, "Only the man who says goodbye to all his possessions can be my disciple" (Luke 14:33), is no utilitarian. The apostles who left the upper room to convert the world largely by their own martyrdom hardly engaged in an objective cost-benefit analysis.

I draw your attention to these implications not for the purpose of advocating a religious morality, but rather to illustrate how deeply <tolerance> is implicated in the American cultural divide. In the way it is evoked here, an entire moral tradition is denied its voice. This situation has been characterized by Richard Neuhaus as the "democratic paradox": "We insist that we are a democratic society, yet we have in recent decades systematically excluded from policy consideration the operative values of the American people, values that are overwhelmingly grounded in religious belief."[138]

The ultimate irony is that <tolerance> is the most effective ally of intolerance.

PERSONAL COMMENTS ON THIS ESSAY

My own background influences my views on the place of religion in the public square and affected the shape of this essay. Like most other critics working in the tradition of the "ideological turn," I readily acknowledge that my construction of the truth is a product of my standpoint. To do otherwise would be hypocritical. Having said this, I still have a responsibility to make arguments that my readers will find convincing. I am not merely asserting this as my unsupported opinion.

I am a practicing Roman Catholic, and I do not believe that there is any easy distinction between private piety and public advocacy. The notion of citizen is only meaningful when individuals can bring their private morality to bear on public issues. Yet, as a Catholic, I am well aware of the long record of American discrimination against those of my faith. I am familiar with much of the grubby history of Catholic bigotry that polluted the nation's public discourse. To put this differently, I believe that <tolerance> is a two-edged sword. There is no easy set of rules for assuring simultaneously both the robustness and the civility of the public dialogue.

I took as my task the explication of these complications. Tolerance begets intolerance. Anglo-American liberal discourse is fraught with irony. We are left to muddle our way through as best we can. Another critic, with a different background and other ideological commitments, would have made other choices. My essay was driven by theorizing on the relationship among the public, private, and technical spheres. Another critic, calling on different theoretical literature, would have approached <tolerance> quite differently. The ideological predispositions of the critic will always influence the nature of the criticism.

POTENTIALS AND PITFALLS

Ideographic criticism is especially powerful when applied to discourses which celebrate particular values. This is so for three reasons: (1) Ideographic criticism links the celebration of particular values to the justification of power. (2) Ideographic criticism demonstrates the ways in which a particular celebrated value subordinates and organizes competing values. (3) Ideographic analysis can map alterations in value orientation over time and thus show the changes in a society's public discourse, which reflect changes in citizenry's public consciousness.

The critic must be careful in generalizing from ideographic analysis. A single speech or a small set of messages may not represent anything particularly important about the public. In fact, official pronouncements from government leaders may be resisted by the citizenry. One lesson we should learn from the fall of the Soviet Union and the communist regimes of Eastern Europe is that a regime's justifications for power are often not accepted by the populace. Kept in line by the brute force of the state, the citizens apparently never bought into the government's propaganda. When given an opportunity, they quickly seized the chance to topple their countries' leaders.

In my short essay on Edward Kennedy's "Truth and Tolerance" speech, I tried to demonstrate that he articulates an influential strain in liberal thinking. His speech is important because it represents a significant segment of the U.S. political culture. If it is merely an idiosyncratic expression of <tolerance> by one lone Senator, then it is of little consequence.

IDEOGRAPHIC ANALYSIS TOP PICKS

Cloud, Dana, "The Rhetoric of <Family Values>: Scapegoating, Utopia, and the Privatization of Social Responsibility," *Western Journal of Communication,* 62 (1998): 387–419. This essay explores the phrase <family values> as an ideograph. It examines the ideological force of this ideograph and concludes that it works to victimize the poor. It has the force of blaming the poor for their own circumstances. It also works to absolve the fortunate of any responsibility for society's disadvantaged.

Condit, Celeste, and John Lucaites, *Crafting Equality: America's Anglo-African Word* (Chicago: University of Chicago Press, 1993). This prize-winning book is an excellent example of a diachronic analysis of ideographs. The authors trace the development of <equality> through American history.

Condit, Celeste, and J. Ann Selzer, "The Rhetoric of Objectivity in the Newspaper Coverage of a Murder Trial," *Critical Studies in Mass Communication* 2 (1985): 197–216. This essay explores the ideological commitment of journalism to the ideograph <objectivity>. In exploring the coverage of a Kansas murder trial, they demonstrate the ironic effect of <objectivity>. The commitment to <objectivity> leads to reporting that is biased toward the prosecution.

Martin, Martha, "Ideologues, Ideographs, and 'The Best Men': From Carter to Reagan," *Southern Speech Communication Journal* 49 (1983): 12–25. This essay argues that the aftermath of the Watergate scandal provided Jimmy Carter with an opportunity to create a presidential image of "good moral character," "intelligence," and "competency"—an ideographic cluster that mirrored the nineteenth century's definition of "best men."

McGee, Michael Calvin, "An Essay on the Flip Side of Privacy." *Argument in Transition: Proceedings of the Third Summer Conference on Argumentation,* David Zarefsky (ed.) (Annandale, VA: Speech Communication Association, 1983), 105–115. This essay illustrates the ideological complexity of the abortion debate. McGee demonstrates that the abortion debate implicates a series of underlying ideographic tensions. These are tensions among <public>, <private property>, <liberty>, and <equality>.

For a theoretical grounding in ideographical analysis read in the following essays:

McGee, Michael Calvin, "The 'Ideograph,' A Link between Rhetoric and Ideology," *Quarterly Journal of Speech* 66 (1980): 1–16.

McGee, Michael Calvin, "In Search of the 'People': A Rhetorical Alternative," *Quarterly Journal of Speech* 61 (1975): 235–249.

McGee, Michael Calvin, "A Materialist's Conception of Rhetoric." *Explorations in Rhetoric: Studies in Honor of Douglas Ehninger,* Ray E. McKerrow (ed.) (Glenview, IL: Scott, Foresman, 1982), 23–48.

NOTES

1. Lloyd F. Bitzer, "The Rhetorical Situation," *Philosophy and Rhetoric* 1 (1968): 3, 4.
2. Bitzer, 2.
3. Bitzer, 6.
4. Philip Wander makes this same point in commenting on the alledged sterility of neo-Aristotelian (Traditional) criticism, which shares many of the same commitments as Bitzer's situational approach. In making his remarks, Wander refers to Forbes Hill's essay on President Richard Nixon's speech of November 3, 1969. See Philip P. Wander, "The ideological turn in modern criticism," Central States Speech Journal 34 (1983): 1–18; and Forbes I. Hill, "Conventional wisdom—traditional form: The President's message of November 3, 1969," *Quarterly Journal of Speech* 58 (1972): 373–386.
5. Wander, 9.
6. Antony Flew, "Ideology," *A Dictionary of Philosophy* (New York: St. Martin's Press, 1979), 150.
7. Edward B. Reeves, "Ideology," *Encyclopedia of Religion and Society* (Walnut Creek, CA: Altamira Press, 1998), 234.
8. This example is laid out in great detail in Murray Edelman, *Political Language: Words that Succeed and Policies that Fail* (New York: Academic Press, 1977).
9. Robert T. Craig, "Communication," *Encyclopedia of Rhetoric* (New York: Oxford University Press, 2001), 135.
10. Michael McGee draws much the same contrast in his discussion of "instantiation." See Carol Corbin (ed.) *Rhetoric in Postmodern America: Conversations with Michael Calvin McGee* (New York: Guilford Press, 1998), 144–151.
11. See Ronald Lee and Karen K. Lee, "Multicultural Education in the Little Red Schoolhouse: A Rhetorical Exploration of Ideological Justification and Mythic Repair," *Communication Studies* 49 (1998): 1–17.
12. My lecture title is a take off on the best-seller by Robert Fulghum, *All I Really Needed to Know I Learned in Kindergarten: Uncommon Thoughts on Common Things* (New York: Villard, 1988).
13. See David Easton and Jack Dennis, *Children in the Political System: Origins of Political Legitimacy* (New York: McGraw-Hill, 1969); and Fred I. Greenstein, *Children and Politics* (New York: Yale University Press, 1965). [Editor's note: they are also the same lessons used about merit systems in communist countries.]
14. See H. Mark Roelofs, *Ideology and Myth in American Politics: A Critique of a National Political Mind* (Boston: Little, Brown, 1976); and John K. White, *The New Politics of Old Values,* 2nd ed. (Hanover, NH: University Press of New England, 1990).
15. See Stuart Ewen, *Captains of Consciousness: Advertising and the Social Roots of Consumer Culture,* 25th anniversary ed. (New York: Basic Books, 2001); and William Leiss, Stephen Kline, and Sut Jhally, *Social Communication in Advertising: Persons, Products and Images of Well-being,* 2nd ed. (London: Routledge, 1997).
16. This may explain why so many theorists have been preoccupied with the law as a paradigm for understanding rhetoric more generally. See, for example, Chaim Perelman and L. Olbrechects-Tyteca, *The New Rhetoric: A Treatise on Argumentation* (Notre Dame, IN: University of Notre Dame Press, 1969); Stephen E. Toulmin, *The Uses of Argument* (Cambridge, England: Cambridge University Press, 1958); and James Boyd White, *Heracles' Bow: Essays on the Rhetoric and Poetics of Law* (Madison: University of Wisconsin Press, 1985).
17. See Hayden White, *Metahistory: The Historical Imagination in Nineteenth-Century Europe* (Baltimore: Johns Hopkins University Press, 1973), 1–42.
18. Terry Eagleton, *Ideology: An Introduction* (London: Verso, 1991), 9.
19. Michael Calvin McGee, "A Materialist's Conception of Rhetoric," *Explorations in Rhetoric: Studies in Honor of Douglas Ehninger,* Ray E.

McKerrow (ed.) (Glenview, IL: Scott, Foresman, 1982), 24.

20. McGee, "A Materialist's Conception of Rhetoric," 38.
21. McGee, "A Materialist's Conception of Rhetoric," 39.
22. McGee, "A Materialist's Conception of Rhetoric," 39.
23. McGee, "A Materialist's Conception of Rhetoric," 41.
24. McGee, "A Materialist's Conception of Rhetoric," 41.
25. McGee, "A Materialist's Conception of Rhetoric," 43.
26. See James A. Aune, *Rhetoric and Marxism* (Boulder, CO: Westview, 1994).
27. Carol Corbin (ed.) *Rhetoric in Postmodern America: Conversations with Michael Calvin McGee* (New York: Guilford Press, 1998), 94–100.
28. Corbin, 95.
29. Corbin, 95.
30. Corbin, 94.
31. Dana L. Cloud, "The Rhetoric of <Family Values>: Scapegoating, Utopia, and the Privatization of Social Responsibility," *Western Journal of Communication* 62 (1998): 389.
32. Placing a term or slogan inside angle brackets, <liberty>, has become the conventional way of identifying an ideograph within the communication literature.
33. Michael Calvin McGee, "The 'Ideograph': A Link between Rhetoric and Ideology," *Quarterly Journal of Speech* 66 (1980): 15.
34. McGee, "The 'Ideograph'," 15.
35. McGee, "The 'Ideograph'," 15.
36. McGee, "The 'Ideograph'," 15.
37. McGee, "The 'Ideograph'," 15.
38. McGee, "The 'Ideograph'," 7.
39. McGee, "The 'Ideograph'," 15.
40. McGee, "The 'Ideograph'," 15.
41. McGee, "The 'Ideograph'," 15, 16.
42. See Michael Calvin McGee, "In Search of the 'People': A Rhetorical Alternative," *Quarterly Journal of Speech* 61 (1975): 235–249.
43. Celeste M. Condit and John L Lucaites, *Crafting Equality: America's Anglo-African Word* (Chicago: University of Chicago Press, 1993), xii–xiii.
44. McGee, "The 'Ideograph,'" 14.
45. See, Condit and Lucaites.
46. Other rhetorical scholars have critiqued Bitzer's objective view of the rhetorical situation. They have suggested that situations do not pre-exist discourse, but instead are largely constituted by it. See, for example, Richard Vatz, "The Myth of

the Rhetorical Situation," *Philosophy and Rhetoric* 6 (1973): 154–161; and Robert J. Branham and W. Barnett Pearce, "Between text and context: Toward a Rhetoric of Contextual Reconstruction," *Quarterly Journal of Speech* 71 (1985): 19–36. For an overview of Situation Theory see, Marilyn J. Young, "Lloyd F. Bitzer: Rhetorical Situation, Public Knowledge, and Audience Dynamics," *Twentieth-Century Roots of Rhetorical Studies*, Jim A. Kuypers and Andrew King (eds.) (Westport, CT: Praeger, 2001), 275–302.
47. See Maurice Charland, "Constitutive Rhetoric: The Case of the *Peuple Québécois*," *Quarterly Journal of Speech* 73 (1987): 133–150.; and Michael Calvin McGee, "In Search of the 'People': A Rhetorical Alternative," *Quarterly Journal of Speech* 61 (1975): 235–249.
48. Wayne Brockriede, "Rhetorical Criticism as Argument," *Quarterly Journal of Speech* 60 (1974): 167.
49. See Edelman.
50. Cloud, 387.
51. Kenneth Burke, *A Grammar of Motives* (Berkeley: University of California Press, 1969), 517.
52. Mark Blaug, *Economic Theory in Retrospect*, 4th ed. (Cambridge, England: University of Cambridge Press, 1985), 550.
53. Blaug, 551.
54. Celeste Condit and J. Ann Selzer, "The Rhetoric of Objectivity in the Newspaper Coverage of a Murder Trial," *Critical Studies in Mass Communication* 2 (1985): 197.
55. "Jihad Against Jews and Crusaders: World Islamic Front Statement" (February 23, 1998), 2. Retrieved from http://www.efreedomnews.com/News%20Archive/Terrorists/Fatwah2_BinLaden.htm.
56. ADC Research Institute, "Executive Summary," *Report on Hate Crimes and Discrimination Against Arab Americans: The Post-September 11 Backlash* (2003). Retrieved from http://www.adc.org/hilal/web/executive.htm.
57. Michael Wilson, "Evangelist Says Muslims Haven't Adequately Apologized for Sept. 11 Attacks," *New York Times*, (August 15, 2002): A14; Fred Jackson, Jim Duke, and Jody Brown, "Evangelist Graham in Presidential Hot Water over Comments: White House Hosts Ramadan Gathering," *Agape Press* (November 20, 2001). Retrieved from http://www.familypolicy.net/nf/franklin-11-20-01.shtml; Hanna Rosin, "Younger Graham Diverges from Father's Image," *Washington Post* (September 2, 2002): A3.

58. Jim Jones, "Baptist Calls Islam Founder "Pedophile"; Church Leaders Agree, Muslims Outraged," *Pittsburgh Post-Gazette* (June 13, 2002): A5.

59. Cal Thomas, "It's Time to Confront the Threat from Within," *Baltimore Sun* (May 21, 2003): 19A.

60. See Roger W. Cobb and Charles D. Elder, "The Political uses of Symbolism," *American Politics Quarterly* 1 (1973): 305–338; Murray Edelman, "Symbols and Political Quiescence," *American Political Science Review* 54 (1960): 695–704; and Richard M. Merelman, "Learning and Legitimacy," *American Political Science Review* 60 (1966): 548–561.

61. McGee, "The 'Ideograph,"' 15.

62. James Davison Hunter, *Culture Wars: The Struggle to Define America* (New York: Basic Books, 1991), 44.

63. The college has since been renamed Liberty Baptist University.

64. See Jerry Falwell, *Listen, America!* (Garden City, NY: Doubleday, 1980).

65. See Harold Barrett, "John F. Kennedy before the Greater Houston Ministerial Association," *Central States Speech Journal* 15 (1964): 259–266; Beryl F. McClerren, "Southern Baptists and the Religious Issue during the Presidential Campaigns of 1928 and 1960," *Central States Speech Journal* 18 (1967): 104–112; and John M. Murphy, "Comic Strategies and the American Covenant," *Communication Studies* 40 (1989): 266–279.

66. The phrase "naked public sphere" was coined by Neuhaus. See Richard John Neuhaus, *The Naked Public Square: Religion and Democracy in America* (Grand Rapids, MI: Eerdmans, 1984).

67. Robert J. Branham and W. Barnett Pearce, "A Contract for Civility: Edward Kennedy's Lynchburg Address," *Quarterly Journal of Speech* 73 (1987): 428.

68. Branham and Pearce, 440.

69. For a discussion of the situational perspective on criticism, see Bitzer. Also, see Robert J. Branham and W. Barnett Pearce, "Between Text and Context: Toward a Rhetoric of Contextual Reconstruction," *Quarterly Journal of Speech* 71 (1985): 19–36.

70. Owen Peterson (ed.) *Representative American Speeches* 1983–1984 (New York: H. W. Wilson, 1984), 53.

71. Edward M. Kennedy, "Tolerance and Truth in America," *Representative American Speeches 1983–1984*, Owen Peterson (ed.) (New York: H.

W. Wilson, 1984), 55. "The Old Time Gospel Hour" was the name of Reverend Falwell's nationally syndicated radio broadcast.

72. See Eric W. Rothenbuhler, *Ritual Communication: From Everyday Conversation to Mediated Ceremony* (Thousand Oaks, CA: Sage, 1998).

73. Kennedy, 56.

74. Kennedy, 55.

75. Kennedy, 55.

76. Peterson, 53.

77. For example, stories about the speech appeared in the following major newspapers: C. Bohlen, "Kennedy Visits the Falwell Empire," *The Washington Post* (October 4, 1983): A1, A4; J. Margolis, "Teddy Goes to Moral Majority Country to Praise and Condemn," *The Chicago Tribune* (October 4, 1983): sec. 1, 14; and E. Randolph, "Kennedy Warns Falwell on Perils of Religious Zealotry," *The Los Angeles Times* (October 4, 1983): part 1, 6.

78. Kennedy, 55.

79. Kennedy, 55.

80. Kennedy, 55.

81. Kennedy, 56, 57.

82. Kennedy, 57.

83. Kennedy, 57.

84. Kennedy, 57.

85. Kennedy, 57.

86. Kennedy, 58.

87. Kennedy, 58.

88. Kennedy, 58.

89. Kennedy, 58.

90. Kennedy, 58, 59.

91. Kennedy, 59.

92. Kennedy, 59.

93. Kennedy, 59.

94. Kennedy, 59.

95. Kennedy, 59.

96. Kennedy, 59.

97. Kennedy, 59.

98. Kennedy, 59.

99. Kennedy, 60.

100. Kennedy, 60.

101. Kennedy, 61.

102. Kennedy, 61.

103. Kennedy, 62.

104. Kennedy, 63.

105. Hart argues that the implied contract states that the United States government's "rhetoric will refrain from being overly religious and [organized religion's] rhetoric will refrain from being overly political." Roderick P. Hart, *The Political Pulpit* (West Lafayette, IN: Purdue University Press, 1977), 44.

106. See Jurgen Habermas, *The Theory of Communicative Action,* vol. 2 (Boston: Beacon, 1987).

107. See, for example, Craig Calhoun (ed.) *Habermas and the Public Sphere* (Cambridge, MA: The MIT Press, 1992); Frank Fischer, *Technocracy and the Politics of Expertise* (Newbury Park, CA: Sage, 1990); G. Thomas Goodnight, "The Personal, Technical, and Public Spheres of Argument: A Speculative Inquiry into the Art of Deliberation," *Journal of the American Forensic Association* 18 (1982): 214–227; Ronald Lee and Shawn J. Spano, "Technical Discourse in Defense of Public Virtue: Ronald Reagan's Explanation of the Iran/Contra Affair," *Political Communication* 13 (1996): 115–129; Robert Patterson and Ronald Lee, "The Environmental Rhetoric of 'Balance': A Case Study of Regulatory Discourse and the Colonization of the Public," *Technical Communication Quarterly* 6 (1997): 25–40; and Charles A. Willard, *Liberalism and the Problem of Knowledge: A New Rhetoric for Modern Democracy* (Chicago: University of Chicago Press, 1996).

108. Kennedy, 59.

109. Kennedy, 61.

110. Kennedy, 57.

111. Kennedy, 58.

112. Kennedy, 58.

113. Kennedy, 58.

114. Kennedy, 55, 56.

115. Kennedy, 55.

116. Kennedy, 56.

117. Kennedy, 55.

118. Kennedy, 60.

119. Kennedy, 60.

120. Kennedy, 60.

121. Kennedy, 58.

122. Kennedy, 63.

123. Kennedy, 62.

124. John Stuart Mill, *On Liberty* (Indianapolis: Bobbs-Merrill, 1956), 93.

125. Mill, 92.

126. This distinction between an exemplary public life and a checkered private one has been applied to Senator Kennedy himself. Likewise, his brother John Kennedy was a notorious womanizer, but yet arguably one of America's ablest presidents.

127. See Habermas, *The Theory of Communicative Action;* Theodore Lowi, *The End of Liberalism: The Second Republic of the United states,* 2nd ed. (New York: Norton, 1979); and Patterson and Lee.

128. See Walter Lippmann, *Public Opinion* (New York: Free Press); and Willard.

129. Kennedy, 57.

130. Kennedy, 59.

131. In rhetorical studies, Stephen Toulmin has grounded an informal logic on the appeal to argument fields and Charles Willard has developed what he calls a "rhetoric for modern democracy" based on technical argument within and between disciplines. These projects are much in the same spirit as Kennedy's appeal to the expertise of the judiciary and to the objectivity of economic analysis. See Stephen E. Toulmin, *The Uses of Argument* (Cambridge, England: Cambridge University Press, 1958); and Willard.

132. See James J. Kilpatrick, *The Sovereign States: Notes of a Citizen of Virginia* (Chicago: Henry Regnery, 1957); and James J. Kilpatrick, *The Southern Case for School Segregation* (New York: Crowell-Collier, 1962).

133. See Ronald Lee, "Language and Political Power: A Perspective on Radical/Revolutionary Rhetoric," *Current Continental Research* 3 (1981): 155–164.

134. See Jurgen Habermas, *The Structural Transformation of the Public Sphere: An Inquiry into a Category of Bourgeois Society,* Thomas Burger and Frederick Lawrence (trans.) (Cambridge, MA: The MIT Press, 1989).

135. See Ronald Beiner, *What's the Matter with Liberalism?* (Berkeley: University of California Press, 1992).

136. Kennedy, 59.

137. Alasdair MacIntyre, *After Virtue: A Study in Moral Theory* (Notre Dame, IN: University of Notre Dame Press, 1984), 148.

138. Neuhaus, 37.

CHAPTER FIFTEEN

CRITICAL RHETORIC AND CONTINUAL CRITIQUE

RAYMIE E. McKERROW

JEFFREY ST. JOHN

What is meant by "critical rhetoric" and what does it mean to use it as a way to understand or analyze rhetorical practice? If critique is "continual" does that mean that one never can decide what one thinks about past rhetoric—as the project of criticism unfolds anew with each moment? What's the point of criticism if judgment is not reached in some sense—so that we know what we think about an event? What, then, does it mean to "continually critique"? As another way of introducing this subject: How should one frame critical rhetorical practice? Is it best conceived as a formalized *method* of rhetorical analysis, as Norman Clark has suggested?[1]

In what follows, we respond to the questions introduced above in underscoring the thesis that critical rhetoric is best viewed as a fluid and flexible *orientation,* not a formal, rule-governed method. Thus, our purpose in this essay is to establish the argument that critical rhetoric has never been intended to serve—either primarily or secondarily—as a conventional rhetorical method. Believing this, we present a reading of critical rhetorical practice *qua* orientation precisely because we are not convinced that the kinds of rhetorical artifacts that the critical rhetoric project engages are best evaluated through method-based means. We hold, rather, that the adoption of an orientation—in all that we conceive that term to embody—toward the analysis of those phenomena is the best way to ensure that critical rhetoric is applied to the fullest of its emancipatory potential. In our view, a method-based critical rhetoric can be neither truly a "critical rhetoric" nor the optimal venue for evaluating rhetorical phenomena in an increasingly fragmented and destabilized social world.

Before taking up these matters in greater detail, we think it is important to revisit the putative "starting point" for the critical rhetoric project. From a traditional perspective, the starting point for criticism focuses on an active *agent* who seeks to effect change in his or her environment through suasive speech, symbolic expression, or other stylized means of broadcasting an idea, creating an event, or taking a public stand. Examples from the last century abound: Picasso's *Guernica;* self-immolating Buddhist monks in the early years of the Vietnam War; the silent candlelight vigils of women and men symbolically protesting domestic abuse. Each of the persons involved in these kinds of protests is, of course, identifiable as a sentient actor, and may certainly be evaluated rhetorically for the words or deeds he or she has said or done at a particular time and place. Picasso painted; morally impassioned monks lit themselves on fire; this much is clear. Criticism that begins with the focus on the agent is a worthwhile endeavor, but is not the only approach that might be useful in answering specific questions. Thus, while acknowledging the value of an agent-centered approach, we wish to stress that there exist other means of achieving answers to questions one might have about events, and that such means are sometimes grounded upon conceptions of public space, power relations, and the nature of public speech and action which are not as accessible to analysis from an agent-centered approach.

The starting point for the critical rhetoric project is not the active agent seeking change, though as noted above, we do not deny the efficacy or reality of agency as an ever-present persuasive force in human affairs. Rather, we simply choose to begin elsewhere. As McKerrow has indicated in an encyclopedia article on critical rhetoric:

> Two forms of critical analysis comprise the critical practice. A critique of domination has as its aim an emancipatory purpose, and can best be styled as a "freedom from" (McKerrow, 1991) that which otherwise limits its potentiality. A critique of freedom has as its aim a reflexivity which grounds its actions in a constant reflection on the contingency of human relations, and can best be styled as a "freedom to" (McKerrow, 1991) move toward new relations with others. In the former instance, the recognition of power in its repressive role is paramount; in the latter, the recognition of power as productive is paramount. In both instances, the assumption is that a critique may move beyond mere criticism (McKerrow, 1991) and incorporate an interrogation of the assumptive ground from which critical analysis arises. . . . Thus, if one is working within the constructs of a democratic state, the assumptions that ground democracy are as open to critique as are the actions that emanate from that state. Whether one is focusing attention on a critique of domination or of freedom, as originally set forth, the "telos" which animates both reflects a commitment to change: "Whether the critique establishes a social judgment about 'what to do' as a result of the analysis, it must nonetheless serve to identify the possibilities of future action available to the participants" (McKerrow, 1989, p. 92). The commitment to recursivity or a constant critique does not imply a dismissal of a commitment to change.[2]

In promoting an analytic perspective that underscores this commitment, our starting point lies in an understanding of *form* in the sense offered by Kenneth Burke. Taking up his injunction that the "symbolic act is the *dancing of an attitude*,"[3] we would claim a similar perspective for critical rhetoric. Following Burke, we would note that form does not necessarily (or even mainly) entail the study of phenomena that are "formal" in the sense of a series of one-to-one epistemic correspondences, though the degree of formality in the discursive formation may surely vary. Rather, form suggests to us something about (1) the relational properties that inhere in a particular event, or, to frame it more expansively, in a particular discursive formation; and (2) the effect(s) that form may have on the rhetorical choices and interventions which it may or may not be possible to achieve in light of form's influence on artifacts, discourses, and contexts. With this much in mind, we would stress that what the individual agent can or cannot do assumes a much different flavor when precise questions of form are brought to bear. In particular, within the critical rhetoric project as we are articulating it, the rhetorical emphasis does not hinge on an agent's ability to perform certain rhetorical acts. Rather, the emphasis is on those seen or unseen relational properties within which the agent—as agent—is contained and with which he or she must contend in the social world.

To use Jim Kuypers's language in his essay in this volume, we might say that the critical rhetoric project reframes a reframing of rhetorical analysis.[4] This is not at all to dismiss other modes of analysis, or other starting points. As we alluded above, different questions require different foci on the influence of the agent-as-agent; we take the validity of that proposition to be self-evident, but worthy of reproduction in this space nonetheless. To argue, for example, that an agent-centered point of departure is *the* premier analytic frame for all analysis of public action is as wrongheaded as arguing that the same distinction in fact belongs to critical rhetoric. Both assertions are or would be fatuous, nondemonstrable, and unhelpful. As we see it, what prompts the adoption of a particular perspective is not the critical frame itself but *the questions one seeks to answer* (and this is just as true under more traditional formulations as it is for the critical orientation advanced here). The chosen rhetorical mode is informed by the phenomenon, not the reverse. For this reason, critical rhetoric is (or should be) as open to embrace or dismissal as any other frame of inquiry.

We have yet to support our initial claim that *orientation* is the preferred frame within which critical rhetoric operates. To establish that claim, we will work to connect our assertion above (about the primacy of the phenomenon—as opposed to rhetorical agent—under investigation) with some claims about social actors and their actions. In what follows, we examine first the relationship among critical rhetoric, social action, and orientation. This is accomplished by using, as a prime illustration of theory's role as a container within which criticism operates, a specific essay that may direct one's understanding of the critical rhetoric project in ways we would not prefer. Consistent with the "inventional" or "fragmentary" nature of the project, as ably outlined by Michael Calvin McGee,[5] we offer several brief analyses or cases in order to show what we think is actually at work within a critical rhetoric orientation. We seek, then, to explain both (1) the ground of our starting point; and (2) our claims about orientation as a modality; in both cases, through a discussion of the relationship among critical rhetoric, social action, and orientation itself. As suggested above, we begin with one scholar's call for an adaptation of critical rhetoric in the promotion of a "critical servant," subjecting it to analysis to illustrate a principal of criticism: if the theoretical frame is cloudy or unclear, the critical act that follows from it will be less useful.

CRITICAL RHETORIC AND SOCIAL ACTION

Norman Clark has linked his framing of the rhetorician as "critical servant"[6] to Raymie McKerrow's original statement of the critical rhetoric project.[7] In so doing, we believe that Clark has (1) tried to turn McKerrow's critical rhetor into a social actor who acts in certain contexts that are not necessarily of his or her own making;[8] and that he has (2) described his own "the critical servant" in a way that does not significantly distinguish that "servant" from McKerrow's "rhetor."

In his essay, Clark first identifies a contrasting pair of options that he claims are available to every citizen in a community. As Clark reads it, a social actor may either (1) freely and usefully serve the public good (the *opheleia*); or (2) work against his or her own will in servitude or subjugation (the *douleia*). Clark understandably embraces the former category and tries to infuse his critical servant with the aims and outcomes of a selfless civic engagement. In Clark's view, a person's decision to serve the public in a spirit of *opheleia* must be accompanied by an enthusiasm for real action. A practical outlook is key here. The philosopher Isocrates' "conception of the role of rhetors in society" was for Isocrates—and is for Clark as well—"inextricably linked to an understanding of practical, useful political service."[9] Clark calls his critical servant's brand of public service an "orientation," not a method, a point we would ask the reader to keep in mind.

Clark's critical servant serves his or her community and its members by doing good; by combining beauty and virtue; and in general by adopting an attitude that becomes a "purposive and artistic act."[10] The critical servant functions as the kind of person whose commitment to serving the public is constantly directed toward doing what is best for the community. His or her service is freely offered, because slavery and forced labor are antithetical to the ideals of *opheleia*. It is, in fact, the very threat of one's slide into *douleia* that provides the social actor with a powerful internal check against the rise of pride and other human failings. Though idealistic in its premises, relying as it does on what would seem to be a rare mix of discipline, selflessness, and dedication, Clark's argument is mainly consistent to this point in its development.[11] Less persuasive, however, are (1) Clark's claims about the relationship between knowledge and community; and (2) his view of the critical servant's role as the source of a community's wellspring of good judgment and good will.

At this stage in his argument, Clark rejects McKerrow's[12] suspicion of universal truth, charging McKerrow with standing in "binary opposition" to Plato; and, Clark accuses both McKerrow and Plato of a critical nearsightedness. Clark then works to show how his critical servant overcomes the problems that he (Clark) has outlined. Clark claims—and the insertion of numbers here is ours, to permit further commentary below—that

> [1] Critical servants situate their knowledge of possible actions within the history of the community. [2] Some of the knowledge found in the history of the community may lay claim to universality. [3] It is not a service to the community to render this knowledge *a priori* inaccessible, as Plato would have it, or *a priori* sus-

pect, as some postmodern theorists would. [4] Instead, critical servants work to ground this knowledge in the present community, as a resource for social critique. [5] Since the knowledge is tied to the community, it retains its persuasive force. [6] However, it is always temporally relative, always situationally contingent, and always subject to further critique and revision.[13]

We argue that Clark's claims here—at the heart of his case—seem difficult to sustain. To be as fair to his position as possible, we will address each of Clark's six sentences above in turn.

We do not object to Clark's first sentence [1], other than to note that the phrase "Critical servants" here could be replaced with no change of meaning by "Aristotelians," "Platonists," "Ramists," "Benthamites," "Southern Agrarians," or "standpoint feminists." In other words, we think that there is almost no group of critical thinkers for whom "knowledge of possible actions within the history of the community" is *not* a crucial element of its understanding of how communities solve their problems. In this respect, the "critical servant" appears to us to be no different than other social actors.

In his second sentence [2], Clark attempts to assign agency to "knowledge," as if "knowledge" were a person capable of thinking and acting. There appears to be no other possible agent in his sentence to whom thought and action might be ascribed. We do not understood how "knowledge" can be understood to act self-consciously on its own behalf and toward its own ends.

In his third sentence [3], Clark clears conceptual space for his critical servant by jettisoning almost all current players from the rhetorical stage. Plato on the one hand and all postmodernist theorists on the other are invited to leave.

In Clark's next two sentences [4, 5], "knowledge," which he had previously depicted as self-aware and self-originating, is now made to stand in the service of the critical servant, who is called to apply it to his or her community in a manner that somehow (we are not told) transforms it into a "resource for social critique." We are not convinced that knowledge can function in this dual role.

It is the sixth and final sentence [6], however, that we take to be the most damaging to Clark's overall argument. Clark has sought to root his position in a set of local knowledge claims whose practical outcomes prove their own value. In other words, he seems to be arguing that a community knows itself best and may therefore govern itself best (with the aid of its critical servants). But he now offers up a postmodernist description of how knowledge itself should be handled—that is, with a healthy suspicion. Knowledge, he asserts, is "always temporally relative, always situationally contingent, and always subject to further critique and revision."[14] What does this claim mean for social action by a critical rhetor?

We worry that Clark seems to be offering his critical servant the best of both worlds, without any of the drawbacks. His servant is allowed to act confidently in clearly "good" ways, but is at the same time permitted to be insightfully skeptical about things that are not so good. We think there is a problem with that arrangement. Clark's ideas about service are based on the ability of the servant to work with(in) the community's values, and to seek change consistent with what that agent sees as being "good for the community." But how does the servant know what is good? Who gets to offer a counterclaim if what the servant says is good really isn't? Clark provides important checks and balances on the agent's sense of self in its refusal to operate from a place of pridefulness or personal aggrandizement, but neither pride nor aggrandizement can be lasting categories if the community is forever "subject to further critique and revision" and if, at the same time, its ethical decision making functions as a kind of independently objective standard of evaluation.

Clark alleges that ensuring that the servant acts appropriately is what "critical rhetoric ought to do: reclaim or re-use the knowledge of the historically-situated community to propose change."[15] This ideal is laudable. But we would question the way in which Clark seeks to get to where we think he is going. Recall that his entire argument for the agent-doing-good-in-the-community is modeled on a framework that Clark argues is explicitly *critical*. Is this the task of a person operating within a critical rhetoric orientation to "propose change" by individual agents? If so, what is the status of the change proposed? How will it be enacted? McKerrow has addressed similar questions in the context of how the rhetorical critic perceives and evaluates *time*. Within what he terms the "postmodern polity," McKerrow argues that,

> The obligation of the critic is to determine how time functions, and then to work from that knowledge to an interpretation of its role in the discursive event. That the interpretation may include a critique of the culture's conception of time as inappropriate to its objectives is one possibility among many that may be enjoined in the performance.[16]

Keep in mind that critical rhetoric does not deny the possibility of an individual acting. But critical rhetoric *does* pursue a reframing of the basis for that action, and it understands action's meaning(s)—in a sphere of social action—very differently than do formulations for rhetorical inquiry grounded in Clark's assumptions.

We contend that the basis for action within a critical rhetoric framework hinges on the relational properties underlying the production of discourse by the agent. We reverse the order of Clark's evaluations of agency, examining the agent (that is, his critical servant) initially not as a cause but as an effect. It is on an agent's agency *understood as an effect* that the critical rhetoric project focuses its primary attention. An agent's becoming a cause, in the sense of his or her doing or saying something, or an agent's taking of a position: neither of these is somehow automatically precluded from critical rhetoric's scope. Far from it, for change—indeed, of the very kind Clark is hoping for—would be almost impossible to consider if one were blinded to either agent or agency. But there remains for us here a crucial caveat. Wouldn't it serve the critic to consider the broader *rhetorical* possibilities for freedom (or limitation) of action that might exist in a given discursive formation—either through its denial or resistance, or through its refashioning into an unfamiliar form—*prior* to essaying a formal evaluation of that action itself? If so, and we think it does, then a different kind of language is needed. What is needed is a set of terms that are not susceptible to being interpreted as the effects of prior social practices or prior social action.

Let us be as clear as possible in our meaning here. We are asking: Can a social actor be an effect and a causal agent at the same time? We believe that she can, but we qualify that claim by noting that *the claim itself* muddies the waters of its own evaluation. McKerrow is careful to establish this point in his first account of critical rhetoric.[17] The evaluation of an agent's influence influences both the agent and the evaluation. To better frame a context for continual critique, the critic must insistently acknowledge that rhetorical power lies in whatever social activities ground the discursive act under investigation.[18] The power to do and say things in or for a community, for example, is not necessarily something the critical rhetor could arbitrarily "share . . . with the audience,"[19] as that sharing presumes that power is both a discrete possession that the speaker controls and one that may be distributed as he or she chooses. Once again, we do not suggest that the power to act is an illusion; but once again: The starting point for critical rhetoric is not with the agent as *rhetor*. It lies with a careful study of the social or communal situation out of which the rhetor acts.

What, if any, are the specific consequences of our concerns for Clark's argument? First, we think that Clark's willingness to embrace "orientation" is itself a type of restraint on potential action, given the intermingling of assumptions about whether or not the critical servant is truly free to act as he or she would like (see our discussion above on this point). Recall that the role of the critical servant is to serve the communal good. On this logic, our objections to Clarke's formulation are basic but, we think, no less potent. We ask: Who is to say that what the community deems the "good" is in fact the good in all or even most instances? What external standard is that good checked against (if any)? How do those who would enact the good monitor their own progress toward that end? To operate within Isocrates' frame (if we may step away for a moment from the specifics of Clark's argument) is not necessarily to argue only for what the community already accepts as prevailing social relations. We have already offered three examples of agents' crafting of powerful symbolic objections to extant cultural or political conditions (Picasso, Monks, and vigils). To develop this point further would detract from our central claims, but we would at least suggest that for Isocrates, understanding the community's values is not the same as faithfully preserving those values in an unaltered form. We do not see how this proportion could be any less true of Clark's critical servant.

From our perspective, then, the question here is not one of protecting a preferred version of the needs (or the good) of the community, but is rather one of being open to the possibility of any and all avenues toward *freedom*, for two reasons. First, a "critical rhetoric" is by definition one that seeks to liberate. As noted earlier, "a [critical rhetor's] critique of freedom . . . has as its aim a reflexivity that grounds its actions in a constant reflection on the contingency of human relations and can best be styled as a 'freedom to' move toward new relations with others."[20] Second, we think that to begin with the presumption that the rhetor knows best, particularly in the absence of even partial knowledge of those formation(s) which may inform, restrain, or enable other options, is short-sighted. What are needed are opportunities for a critical rhetor's engagement with the community that permit the broadest array of choices for action—but with the clear and minimal understanding that whatever action is proposed or undertaken may well make for social or communal relations that are not as good or efficient or desirable as one might have hoped, or that are simply wrong for that society at that time. Commitment to change, even when selfless and well-intended, cannot be enacted in a single-minded way. Improving the social arena requires a comprehension of that arena that we think is unavailable to the "critical servant" as that social actor is presently formulated by Clark.

THE CRITICAL RHETOR: ACTION AND ORIENTATION

Critical rhetoric functions as a form of critique, one committed to the analysis of moments of the integration of power and knowledge.[21] It is informed by a fluid *telos*—purpose, goal, end state—for which the phenomenon observed, in the cultural and power-based conditions in which it occurs, is precisely the field of operation itself; moreover, this is not an independent or putatively fixed *telos*, and not one of a static rhetorical observer. The critique is *telos* driven, but in a way that acknowledges the unseen or unexplored influences of power and knowledge in the equation. It is a critique of "a relativized world" that does not take itself so seriously as to believe that once instantiated, any change in the world is thus "finished" and complete.[22]

Commitment to a critical rhetoric does not preclude the naming of an oppressor or an oppressee, nor of taking a contextualized stance about the truth or falsity of a claim. What one can say is that the oppression thesis (that is, domination within the context of a "freedom from" oppression) allows for a coexistence of oppressor and oppressed within a discursive formation that is not in every sense of their own making. Once identified and altered in some way, the formation that otherwise perpetuates one set of power relations is inescapably immersed in yet another set—and thus a new relation may come into being. The point, patently, is that one does not escape from the conditions or conditioning of culture. The material reality of lived experience may or may not require changes in particular power relations. In part, what critical rhetoric does is examine the impact of particular discursive formations on the lived conditions of a people, and at the same time raises the question of social change. With respect to truth and falsity, one can say what it is that the community believes to be true, as those beliefs are expressed through language and action. To say a discourse is permanently "false" is to presume an independent stance or privileged position of one who speaks from within the truth. To say that a particular discourse does not work to achieve its ends, or that the ends achieved have deleterious consequences, is not to engage the truth or falsity of a discourse per se; it is rather to engage that discourse's meaning at the level of experience and to critique various implications for the possibilities of freedom that it enjoins.

Second, and relatedly, it is not the case that a critical rhetoric, as a transformative practice, removes itself from the recognition of the material force of rhetoric. That force is simply exercised in a contingent realm rather than within a deterministic world. Materiality *is* recognized: Rhetoric itself may have material force; it may invoke change in the lived conditions of a people through its expression. The province of critique, the possibility of taking a position on the expression of materiality, is not lost from within a critical rhetoric position. The meaning and efficacy of that critique, and the position it privileges at the moment of response to the effects of material rhetoric, is transformed from one of perceived permanence—for example, this is the way it is going to be—to one cognizant of and responsive to an otherwise relativized world. That which becomes will remain other than it is.

As McKerrow has observed, "the subject, as citizen and social actor, is capable of acting. . . . While not wholly formed through discourse, it is through that discourse that the subject gives expression"[23] to its being-in-the-world. The fixation on the role of the rhetor as active agent in modernity is transformed, in this perspective, into a concern for the role of a subjectivity which is itself formed through the very discourse to which it gives expression. As speaking subject, it expresses judgment in the form of critique—a position on the world as it exists, leading to a world that it might yet become. What is implicit is that in and through its expression, the becoming world is once again subject to reflexive judgment as to its well-suitedness in the lives of those it engages. As was already suggested above, the work in this formulation is to seek to remain within a more traditional focus on the speaking subject as the source that effects all change. Although that may well be advantageous, the focus of a critical rhetoric is on its rendering the present formation into being, and from that analysis, what the potential avenues for change are that might be further explored.

Orientation versus Method

This analysis brings us to an assessment of the role of "method" in relation to a critical rhetoric project. To select any one artifact as an exemplar of the approach is to increase the potential for reifying that artifact as the "way to do this sort of criticism." The recurring (though inexact) parallel to Burkeian criticism may be instructive. Burkeian criticism takes an orientation toward events and creates a frame of response where none existed. Burke did not write critical essays from stylized headings (for example, Agent, Scene, Agency, Act, Purpose)—much less from the later addition, Motive. Rather, he suggested these critical elements as ways of thinking through the event in question. Conversely, we have used the "orientation" as a "method" in essays that stand as exemplars for future students of discourse. The conceiving of critical rhetoric not as method but as an orientation serves to keep one's options open with respect to more "methodological" approaches. There is no denying that certain critical terms or concepts, such as examining discourse from the perspective of a "scene–act" ratio, or by "perspectives by incongruity," might well add to an understanding of how that discourse came into being at this time rather than at another time, or how it functioned in relation to changes in the social order. We assume that the orientation provided through critical rhetoric does not preclude the adoption of a critical vocabulary, or even a more precise ethnographic approach in unpacking discursive formations, or in seeking answers to specific questions. But conceiving critical rhetoric in terms of a formal "method" robs it of the flexibility it otherwise possesses in being responsive to certain questions. Even more importantly, it potentially robs critical rhetoric of its salience. As McKerrow argues, "[A] critical practice must have [social and cultural] consequences."[24] Such practice also opens up the analytic frame to what McGee has appropriately termed the "inventional" process of doing criticism, in operating from an assessment of "fragments"—in which the goal is to gain an understanding of how certain fragments coalesce around particular themes or values, and what that then means in terms of understanding how one engages "freedom from" domination or "freedom to" become in ways not yet considered or deemed possible.[25]

If the above is not sufficient as an explanation of the choice of orientation as opposed to method, three additional reasons for making this choice may assist in grounding our rationale. First, the critical opportunity invites the possibility of critique rather than mere criticism. In other words, the "opportunity" goes beyond what "method" would normally imply or even entail in seeking to promote questions about the fundamental assumptions on which the current good is grounded. For example, although those who responded to government propaganda in the early "critical thinking" movement were (appropriately enough) highly critical, they did not seek to go beyond their criticism to question the fundamental nature of democracy. Rather, they acted fully within the assumptive framework of what was understood in their time as the appropriate means of engaging the public in a democratic state.[26] This is not to say that one's method might not invoke critique, but rather that the orientation expressly invites such an attitude at the outset of engaging a critical question in a fully fleshed out context of critique.

Second, the "opportunity" is one that is focused on the possibility of a critical inventive act on the critic's part, rather than the shaky assumption that the speaker is the source of invention. The critic's role is best understood through and within and amid what has been constructed by the discourse: the discourse into which the critic enters and the discourse emerging from the critic's engagement with the same. What this means is that the opportunity exists to go beyond any single artifact or expression to "invent" a formation that helps to explain how any one fragment comes into being at a certain moment. We've long understood that prior rhetoric impinges on future possibilities; what the orientation toward invention suggests, contrary to a narrow focus on method, is that there is more than meets the eye in one's appraisal of an artifact, and that the role of the critic is not simply to *reflect* a given reality, but to partake in the *creation* of a reality heretofore unavailable to the mind's eye.

Finally, the inventive act, whether in the context of a critique of domination or a critique of freedom, requires the analytic and political flexibility necessary to ensure that invention is possible. We would argue that this flexibility is not available within the confines of a (formal) prescribed method.

CRITICAL ESSAY: CRITICAL RHETORIC AS ORIENTATION: TWO EXERCISES IN INVENTION

In seeking to parallel other essays in this volume by putting into practice the critical lens we have articulated in the preceding discussion, we have focused our attentions on the inventional nature of the critical act. In so doing, our purpose is not to capture the "essence" of how one practices critical reflection, but rather to suggest one approach to living out what Barbara Warnick (following Burke, as cited above) correctly observes is an *attitude* toward criticism.[27]

In fulfilling the "exercise" we will focus attention on two primary themes in contemporary discourse. First, we will examine the discourse surrounding civility, which is fully ensconced within the democratic judgment that for deliberation to be true to its goals, it must be rational. Second, we examine a rational argument that goes against the grain—that articulated by "race traitor" rhetoric.

Part One: Civility

There are several theories demarcating what it means to be part of a civil society. The common perception is that one participates as a qualified citizen within a society that is at once part of the "state apparatus" (in that one is never far removed from oversight by a central authority) and simultaneously exists apart from the state—or is antithetical to the state.[28] Our formulation will not follow this standard separation, because we believe it to be a convenient fiction masquerading as a natural artifact of the collectivizing impulse. This is not to deny the convenience of maintaining the fiction, especially when the interests of civil society and the state are at odds with one another—but what of the relation when they are in concert? Where is the dividing line between state and society when the two are in league with each other, embracing the same normative values, and with the people complicit (in Gramsci's sense) in creating and maintaining the "rules for conduct" that govern the state-as-society's everyday affairs? As noted elsewhere,[29] the primary problem when both are in league is that "who is invited to the table"—who is determined in advance to be rational and reasonable, or capable of adhering to civility standards—is established in advance by whomever is in control, with the cooperation of those who in theory are part of a separate body inscribed as "civil society." It makes little sense, in this arrangement, to consider these entities as separate and autochthonous, since they subscribe to a discursive formation that undergirds both, and in giving expression to its dictates generally perpetuates the normative guidelines inherent within the formation. The power relationship is acknowledged and accepted as unexceptional in its force with respect to "maintaining the peace"—a goal of the state that the community (civil society) fully endorses.

To consider a counter-force to the above prized "possession," consider the following observations on the nature of civility:

- Civility may well be a virtue. But, it probably is not a virtue that will be of much help in deciding the political questions that ultimately matter.[30]
- When civility becomes a sensitivity that, like indiscriminate tolerance, casts aside regard for the truth, it bears little resemblance to civility understood as liberal learning, manners and morals, behavior appropriate to the discourse of civilized people, or even plain courtesy.[31]
- "More" civil society in the contemporary Middle East could well mean increased symbolic and practical burdens for women.[32]
- [T]he social totality shaping civil society is a sphere of inequality and conflict—and . . . maybe revitalizing civil society requires heightened levels of political struggle over state policy rather than good manners and "civil discourse."[33]
- Nothing is written in stone or is true by definition; a "robust" civil society can serve all sorts of purposes, and the presence or absence of bowling leagues proves nothing by itself.[34]

Taken together, we believe the above sentiments about civility capture two "truths" for the present moment. First, it is surely the case that those voices immersed in the controversy over what constitutes civil society and its essential component, civility, are at least somewhat cognizant that merely "being civil" in contributing to "civil society" may not be sufficient to advance the rights or interests of citizens. Second, as Rabo notes in reference to Middle Eastern societies—and the same could be said as applied to some subcultures within the United States—more "civilness" in society may simply mean that the present normative standards for behavior toward others are strengthened, not reformed.[35]

What these disparate voices also suggest, from the perspective of an "inventional" process, is that discursive power relations must be factored in when the intricate relationship between the state and civil society is under analysis, and moreover, whenever the nature of what in fact constitutes "civil discourse" within a civil society is addressed. If only those who are already deemed "civil" are invited to a conference dedicated to examining the decline of civility in a society, what might one expect in the way of the conferees' contributions and perhaps the meeting's outcome? If the discursive formation that is fashioning who can say what in what circumstance is not challenged by the inclusion of those who might effortlessly violate its strictures through their mere presence (and through their discourse), what chance is there for social change that redresses the balance of "who gets to be civil?" As Ehrenberg argues, the presence of social inequalities within a community makes seeing "civil society" as necessarily "anti-state" problematic.[36] What force more effectively reproduces injustices than a civil society that is already complicit with the dictates of a state that does not have that society's best (or even ancillary) interests at heart? Would it seem inappropriate for those who are in the "lower" social position with respect to inequalities, however measured, to be suspicious of the claims of a civil society that it *does* have their interests at heart? We unfortunately have no confidence that a formal method of analysis could insightfully answer these queries or others like them.

Part Two: Race Traitor

"Treason to whiteness is loyalty to humanity." With this as their constantly repeated slogan, a group of self-proclaimed "race traitors" has sought to redress the privileges that accrue to a dominant race within the United States by seeking to "dissolve the forces that hold whiteness" within that privileged status. As the creators of the magazine that carries their creed, *Race Traitor,* argue, "if it becomes impossible for the upholders of white rules to speak in the name of all who look white, the white race will cease to exist."[37] A primary reason for focusing on this discourse is that those who proclaim that the rest of those who are white (as are the authors) are wrong in the failure to cease an enjoyment of the privileges of whiteness would not be among those whom we might consider "civil" or worthy of a place at the table when discussing race relations. After all, they have essentially "opted out" by virtue (or vice?) of their very discourse, or so it would seem were one to operate from within normative standards for civil talk. And that is precisely the point: There may be times in civil society when saying "no" is critical—and saying so in a manner that alerts other members of society to the existence of wrongs that have been committed in their name. There is an old expression about hitting a mule on the head with a two-by-four to get its attention. Although we abjure the injury this expression implies, we would note that just as there is some truth to the folk wisdom it conveys, there is also some truth to the need for civil society to be hit on the head, if only metaphorically. This does not mean that paradigm-shifting action is inevitably more "right" or "truthful" than the torpor secured by its obverse. But it *does* suggest that a forced compliance with the prevailing norms of civil discourse will preclude the allowance for such shifting—to the potential detriment of the society that precludes conflictual expression.

The strength and limitation of the race traitor "movement" has been well chronicled.[38]

Rather than repeat their keen analyses, we would like to reflect on the primary argument, as it underscores what a critical rhetoric perspective promotes. A key element in their analyses is that marginal discourses like those evinced within the *Race Traitor* movement are not always facile. In fact, in light of our argument, we think the *Race Traitor* phenomenon is a prime example of the very thing it says it seeks to avoid. By making race a fixed ontological determinant, it reifies that which should not be used to target populations as a criterion of significant difference. Race is a social, not a purely biological construct, and as such, may be altered through the kind of "dismissal" argued for by the *Race Traitor* advocates. As Flores and Moon point out, the argument promoted by this group is not particularly helpful because it promotes a binary vision of race—in being a traitor to whiteness, one must extol blackness: "The claim that whiteness is 'evil' is often directly contrasted with the glory of blackness."[39] Other "races" or ethnicities are "folded into" this mix by dint of their participation in varying degrees of "in-betweenness," as persons who are either more or less white or more or less traitors to whiteness through their adoption of a "reverse oreo" mentality. To the contrary: A stance that does not value the individuality of difference brought forward through Asian ethnicity or any other nonwhite/nonblack cultural influence is simply renaming the power relation in the guise of blackness—you are "with us" or "against us" becomes the default polarized position. Whether blackness ought to be valorized and reprivileged over whiteness is not the question here: That any other group would not have the same possibility as would members of the valorized "color" is merely to renew a racist argument from a different vantage point.

It would appear, from the critique above, that not counting by race—whether in terms of population census, the presence or absence of students of color on college campuses, or in other ways—would be a preference. To avoid race by not counting would be a good thing. At least that is another "fragment" that needs to be considered in the context of this discussion. Flores and Moon do indeed raise the question, and their argument is instructive if not compelling. When their argument about "the elimination of racial categories in local, state, and government agencies" is raised, "the racial paradox reminds us that questions of whether or not we 'count' race are not the same as questions of if and how we can eradicate racism."[40] As they later ask, if particular minorities were in need of special services, how would that be known, if not through extant methods of inquiry? "Most vulnerable," they observe, "are traditionally disenfranchised peoples who often depend on targeted monies and social programs."[41] In other words, it is not sufficient simply to stop counting—as if that would by itself render color invisible. What is not as compelling is the impression one is left with that we stop there— that exposing "race traitors" as racist and continuing to support "counting by race" is at all sufficient to end the argument. From a critical rhetoric perspective, what may also be said is that this is an opportunity for critique, not of domination by the state with respect to continuing a dependence on its programs, but rather a critique pointing to a possible freedom to become something other than we are at present. To enhance civil society through a process whereby the *difference* is acknowledged for what it brings to the conversation, as it is relevant to, or important in the consideration of events would seem to be a *telos* toward which we might aim. That "counting" *per se* would no longer be the chief determinant of when *color* matters would allow for the full play of difference, including color. The aim, as McKerrow has argued,[42] is not to make color invisible, but instead to allow for its contribution when and where it does make a difference in the conversation.

How one accomplishes this new set of social relations (and the corresponding critique it would invite) is beyond the scope of this analysis. But the point we wish to make is that discursive and artifactual fragments, as an invitation to invention, lead us to the possibility of wondering what the world would be like if those depending on governmental social programs were no longer dependent; or if the color of their skin were no longer a contributing factor in that dependence (or cultural perceptions thereof). Flores and Moon are correct in their caution: To do away with racial categorization in the present would likely disadvantage those for whom such "counts" count. But to leave it as "this is the way it is" is insufficient; a call for a different future is simultaneously a call for a different "civil society" in which color matters, but not by virtue of its count. It matters for what it brings to the dialogue, wherein difference is respected as a valued commodity or as a resource for resolving society's ills.

CONCLUSION

This chapter has sought to reframe and remind: to reframe critical rhetoric's practice as an *orientation*, and to further the explanatory power of an inventional, critical modality in its engagement of discursive and artifactual fragments in the social world. How one carries the impetus to utilize its perspective forward remains open. There is a danger in citing examples of the kind of criticism we envision, as in citing particular approaches one risks the reification of that approach as the prime exemplar of "how to do critical rhetoric." We are rather content with the more ambiguous, yet potentially more fruitful, charge to our readers: Consider placing yourself inside an orientation that asks questions about the nature of language as it reveals particular formations between and among people, and the productive capability of power in enhancing social action. Opening one's attitude toward events by considering the context whereby the event has come into being will go a long way toward realizing the potential of this critical perspective. Just as Kenneth Burke eschewed using critical markers (for example, the "Pentad") in advancing critical judgment, we would remind readers that critical rhetoric functions as an intellectual backdrop to the critical act—it enjoins asking questions related to how the context forms discourse rather than how discourse affects publics. Recognizing the power accorded the speaker in traditional analyses of public oratory, it also suggests that there is more to the story. By asking questions of the speaker as a product of the discourse that produced him or her, we hope to understand how the discourse came to be at this time rather than another time, and what possibilities for freedom it hinders or makes available. Intervention as a means of remedying social ills demands no less from us than understanding how we come to be in this time and place, with these sets of attitudes toward events, ourselves, and others. Critical rhetoric is but one starting point in the path toward social action.

PERSONAL COMMENTS ON THE ESSAY

Exercising one's voice is about choices, whether responding to another person who has asked a question or writing a scholarly essay. There are, of course, differences in the nature of each response, but the fact remains that one could choose several different ways to "style" one's commentary. That was the situation we faced when asked by the editor to compose a chapter related to Critical Rhetoric. To make it possible to compare different approaches, the editor has had a marked influence on the structural components of each chapter, but has left what is said, and how it is argued, to each author's choice. So, why did we make the choices we made, and what problems did that create for us?

We chose to focus on one particular essay (Clark's) as an object of critique for two reasons. First, because the essay, if interpreted as we have, moves the critical rhetoric project in directions that we see as less profitable or useful in maintaining the focus and hence promise of the perspective. Second, because it gave us an opportunity to provide an illustration of a narrowly focused critical response to particular expressions. In this latter instance, the approach is as important as the argument being advanced: We wanted to show students how critical reflection might work in actual practice. In making this choice, the primary difficulty is in accurately reflecting what the original author intended (as near as we can determine—knowing intention is a problem in itself) prior to subjecting that intention (as we interpret it) to critical commentary. Once that problem is resolved to our satisfaction (and we didn't ask the original author if there was agreement), the second problem is making the case clear to readers who have not participated in the conversation about critical rhetoric. Whether we have been successful in this latter goal is left to the reader's judgment.

We also, for our critical essay, chose two critical case studies as illustrative of what it means to take this perspective seriously and apply the "mind-set" or "attitude" toward particular objects of inquiry. Civility and Race Traitors would seem an odd duo to consider, but their very difference made sense to us in illustrating what it means to take "fragments" of contemporary discourse, and through critical reflection, comment on the nature of the discourse and its influence. Here, the problem is to be clear about the nature of an "orientation" toward the object, as differentiated from a "method" of analysis. The latter, borrowing from science, works "methodically" through a set of criteria or questions in seeking answers. The former is not as "neat and clean," hence is both more problematic (how do we know the "answer" is right?) and more open (possibilities are not foreclosed by methodological constraints). We consider the advantage (openness) to outweigh the disadvantage, in part because we are not sure any "answer" will be right for all time.

POTENTIALS AND PITFALLS

In writing theoretical essays, one hopes to have an influence on the work of other scholars. With respect to what has become known as the "critical rhetoric project," it appears that the initial ideas have had a heuristic impact. As the following "critical bibliography" suggests, several scholars have provided several new perspectives. These have taken form as extensions of the theory, corrections of what are perceived to be shortcomings or critical weaknesses, or the creation of oppositional views in order to illustrate the fundamental flaws in the approach.

If you begin with the recognition that traditional rhetoric has a history of emphasizing the "great man speaking well," decentering the role of the speaker as the origin of thought, words, and action raises significant questions. What becomes of the object of criticism if the focus is not on the person speaking?

When you add to this purported "removal" of the active speaker/rhetor a commitment to a recursive or continual critique, a question about the possibility of criticism itself competes for attention. If critique is never ending, what can we say about any specific instance of communication as to its value in achieving specific goals?

If you then suggest that the nature of critique does not rest in "method" but rather exists as an "orientation" toward an object, the negative reaction becomes even more strident. How can you possibly know what it is you have or can argue, if you cannot rest your argument on the mantle of objective, methodical assessment of an object or event?

In short, these are the kinds of problems or pitfalls that arise when advancing the "critical rhetoric project." There are others, to be sure, but one could argue that they all can be reduced, in essence, to the issues just delineated.

Issue One: The Existence of a Subject

McKerrow attempted to deal with this "flaw" in assessing the possibility of a subject or speaker within a critical rhetoric perspective:

> If the subject is decentered . . . can there be a role for the speaker as agent of social change? I answer this question in the affirmative. Resituating the subject does not necessitate the destruction of the speaker. . . . By giving voice to critique, the subject renews self.[43]

What is implied in this response to the issue is that the speaker, though decentered, is not "dead" to the issues involved. At the same time, it also means that we are already immersed in a set of social practices and rituals that are not of our own making—and that we speak from within a conversation that has already prefigured for us the possibilities of expression as well as the range of interpretations that might be most likely. This does not mean everything is "fixed" and determined ahead of time—but it does mean that the discursive formation is not open-ended and infinite with respect to who can say what to whom with what effect. You can yell "Fire" in a crowded room—but in so doing, you already know the possible impact of giving voice to that expression—if there were no fire, nor a possibility of one, what would happen to you as a consequence of people's believing you and acting on that belief? Kuypers does an eloquent job of considering this issue, arguing in part that the role of critical rhetoric "diminishes" the speaker's contribution.[44] Although we wouldn't use that label, it is the case that critical rhetoric changes the landscape within which speakers act and react. In aiming for the retention of what is termed "prudence" or "practical wisdom," which in turn actively engages ethical conduct or action, Kuypers argues that a critical rhetoric perspective may fail to contain prudence or "prudent action." Ethics is not automatically removed when adopting a critical rhetoric perspective. Rather, the "scene" (to use a term from Burke's pentadic orientation toward criticism) shifts from the speaker to the context in which the speaker acts. Prudence, as reflective of moral conduct or right action, is still possible within the rhetorical moment. The critical concern is not in "not accounting for the agent as the causative force" but rather lies in "accounting for ethical action or its absence in the rhetorical context." Reminding us of the importance of ethical considerations is a valuable contribution to the project; hence, Kuypers's points are well taken—and accommodated within a slight shift from a focus on the speaker as active agent to the speaker as part of a larger context in which rhetorical action is taken.

Issue Two: The Possibility of Criticism

We might start with the observation that criticism and critique are different objects. Criticism is the shallower, narrower term—with a focus on "making things better." Critique, on the other hand, goes deeper and broader—its focus, while on "making things better" is also on the assumptions that ground the very object of critique. As McKerrow has noted, the propaganda critics of the early twentieth century certainly were focused on improving democracy.[45] But, they did not go beyond that to actively suggest that the very assumptions on which democracy was premised were themselves subject to revision. When invoking "critique" as the operative term, we are suggesting that not only do we want to improve our lot, but we want to subject the foundations underlying our social relations to scrutiny. Critique does not mean "everything we find is wrong"—that is, it is not inherently fault finding. We may decide, after examination, that for now at least, specific social practices are fine the way they are. That isn't always likely, but it is at least a logical possibility—and one we need to retain in order not to fall into an irreversible litany of "this is wrong, this is wrong," ad infinitum.

Dana Cloud argues, among other things, that the critical rhetoric project may well rob us of the possibility of critique.[46] If we can never finish, how do we say anything is ever "wrong" or in need of correction? Consider the possibility that rhetoric is a moral and material force: It acts on us at every moment of our lives. If that were not the case, we would not be able to affirm such phrases as, "A child who lives with criticism learns to criticize." Living in a social relationship bound by the continual expression of one's flaws may well have an impact on how one sees oneself. Kent Ono and John Sloop's articulation of a "telos" (purpose/goal) for a "sustained critical rhetoric" adds immeasurably to the power of the theoretical stance to make a difference. What is suggested is simply this: We do act with purpose within discrete historical moments, and we do judge the social worth of our actions at that moment as hopefully positive. What the critical rhetoric orientation suggests is not that we can't decide anything in the moment, but that once decided, once acted on, as we move on we can't just rest on our laurels. We can't just brush the dust off our hands, say the job is done, and assume all is now right with the world. It may be for then, and for always, but we owe it to ourselves to ask: What changes in power relations does this action portend, and how do those changes affect others? Does the correction of one inequity produce another down the road—one that also should be remedied? What the orientation commits us to is not indecision in the moment, but the realization that action is never final. There is no "fini" to the play of human life.

Issue Three: Orientation *Re Deviva*

Revisiting this issue at the end of an essay devoted to suggesting its merits may seem overkill. Hopefully, we have addressed the primary concerns raised with respect to this issue. Consider Burke's dramatism and the role of the pentad—Scene, Act, etc. function as a rough equivalent to "who-what-when-where-how." Just as you do not see a newspaper article with subheads identifying the discussion of "who" or "what" you will not see Burke's own critical works identifying "Scene" as distinguished from a discussion of "Act." (Chapter 9 by Anderson, King, and McClure exemplifies this.) Rather, the terms function as a framing device—serving to give the journalist or the critic a set of tools with which to understand an event. Forgetting to mention "scene" might be dumb or it might be equally irrelevant to the story or event. But forgetting to think about whether it is or not would be foolish. Critical rhetoric is oriented toward questions of power and their influence in framing social actions—what is or is not possible to express or do in specific settings. Forgetting to ask, in the process of examining rhetoric's material force, whether scene or act were somehow implicated would not be wise. Thus, critical rhetoric is not itself a "method" but saying that does not mean one is solely committed to whimsy in reflecting on an event. One can appropriate method in the act of examining a rhetorical context—while mindful of the broader issues that critical rhetoric brings to bear on the examination.

CRITICAL RHETORIC TOP PICKS

The following lists are not exhaustive, but reflect work done in advancing the "critical rhetoric project" in both theoretical and critical terms. We have moved beyond the editor's request and provided three lists. The first contains essays that owe their impetus to the original McKerrow essay in 1989. The second contains our top picks for theoretical contributions and extentions. The third contains our top picks for analyses using a critical rhetoric orientation.

Works on Critical Rhetoric by McKerrow

McKerrow, Raymie E., "Critical Rhetoric: Theory and Praxis," *Communication Monographs 56* (1989): 91–111. Lead Essay. Reprinted in *Cont-*

emporary Rhetorical Theory: A Reader, J. L. Lucaites, C. M. Condit, S. Caudill (eds.) (New York: Guilford Press, 1999); Chinese translation published in *Western Rhetoric: Critical Paradigms and Methods* (China Social Sciences Publishing House, 1999); *Readings in Rhetorical Criticism*, C. Burghardt (ed.) (State College, PA: Strata Publishing, 1995).

McKerrow, Raymie E., "Critical Rhetoric in a Postmodern World," *Quarterly Journal of Speech 77* (1991): 75–78.

McKerrow, Raymie E., "Critical Rhetoric and Propaganda Studies," *Communication Yearbook 14*, J. Anderson (ed.), (Newbury Park, CA: Sage, 1991), 249–255.

McKerrow, Raymie E., "Critical Rhetoric and the Possibility of the Subject," *The Critical Turn: Rhetoric and Philosophy in Postmodern Discourse*, I. Angus & L. Langsdorf (eds.) (Carbondale, IL: Southern Illinois University Press, 1993), 51–67.

McKerrow, Raymie E., "Corporeality and Cultural Rhetoric: A Site for Rhetoric's Future." *Southern Communication Journal 63* (1998): 315–328.

McKerrow, Raymie E., "Space and Time in a Postmodern Polity." *Western Journal of Communication 63* (1999): 271–290.

McKerrow, Raymie E., "Critical Rhetoric," *Encyclopedia of Rhetoric*, T. Sloane (ed.) (New York: Oxford University Press, 2001), 619–622.

McKerrow, Raymie E., "Coloring Outside the Lines." *Southern Communication Journal 67* (2002): 290–294.

Primarily Theoretical Works Related to Critical Rhetoric

Charland, M., "Finding a Horizon and Telos: The Challenge to Critical Rhetoric," *Quarterly Journal of Speech 77* (1991): 71–74. Although finding much to commend in the perspective, it raises concerns about the potential for "continual critique" to turn into an infinite process, with no end in sight. Also raises concerns about the role of the active agent. McKerrow's response to these two pieces is "Critical Rhetoric in a Postmodern World" cited above.

Clark, N., "The Critical Servant: An Isocratean Contribution to Critical Rhetoric," *Quarterly Journal of Speech 82* (1996): 111–124. This essay has been subjected to extensive analysis within the present essay. It alleges that critical rhetoric does not observe or properly credit the relationship between the rhetor and the audience. Drawing on Isocrates, a classical Greek rhetorician, Clark offers a theoretical replacement for the missing pieces of a critical rhetoric perspective in suggesting that Isocrates' approach provides for a "contingent good" serving the interests of the community.

Cloud, D. L., "The Materiality of Discourse as Oxymoron: A Challenge to Critical Rhetoric," *Western Journal of Communication 58* (1994): 141–163. This essay chronicles the shift toward a discussion of discourse as material. In particular, McGee and McKerrow's work is critiqued for its alleged shortcomings in advancing ideological criticism. Cloud proposes an alternative perspective in remedying the problems inher-

ent within McGee's and McKerrow's formulations.

Gaonkar, D. P., "Performing with Fragments: Reflections on Critical Rhetoric," *Argument and the Postmodern Challenge*, R. E. McKerrow (ed.) (Annandale, VA: Speech Communication Association, 1993), 149–155. This essay critiques the alleged absence of reason as a hallmark of deliberative discourse that is a consequence of assuming a critical rhetoric stance.

Greene, R. W., "Another Materialist Rhetoric." *Critical Studies in Mass Communication 15* (1998): 21–40. This study extends beyond Cloud's critical analysis, in arguing for a new understanding of what it means to theorize rhetoric as "material." In the process, it critiques McGee, McKerrow, and Cloud, and offers a rationale for replacing their formulations with a new definition of rhetoric as material that will better account for the use of rhetoric in changing power relations.

Hariman, R., "Critical Rhetoric and Postmodern Theory," *Quarterly Journal of Speech 77* (1991): 67–70. This essay, along with Charland's (see above) is an invited response to the critical rhetoric essay. In part, it suggests that McKerrow's essay is written in a modernist vein, hence does not separate itself as a truly postmodern contribution. The essay also notes the problematic status of the rhetor as active agent affecting a specific audience if one adopts the orientation provided by a critical rhetoric perspective.

Kuypers, J. A., "Doxa and a Critical Rhetoric: Accounting for the Rhetorical Agent through Prudence," *Communication Quarterly 44* (1996): 452–462. As the title suggests, this analysis provides a "correction" to the absence of a central agent enacting change by recasting the sense of doxa and its corollary, "prudence" or "practical wisdom" (for example, doing the right thing). The changes place responsibility for ethical action within an understanding of the community's will to action.

Murphy, John M., "Critical Rhetoric as Political Discourse," *Argumentation and Advocacy 32* (1995): 1–15. This essay interrogates McKerrow's penchant for creating dichotomies (in this case—disassociations between opposites, as in permanence/change or domination/freedom) and critiques the absence of an active subject seeking change through the power of the word. Murphy proposes an alternative to the study of public discourse, based in Mikhail Bakhtin's concepts.

Ono, K. A., and J. M. Sloop, "Commitment to 'Telos'—A Sustained Critical Rhetoric," *Communication Monographs* 59 (1992): 48–60. This essay is sympathetic to the project, and responds directly to the criticism that continual critique makes it impossible to ever "take a stand" for some specific change, as one is always in the mode of critic rather than acting to create change. By crafting the role of "telos" as the purposeful act of an agent, Ono and Sloop advance the theoretical power of critical rhetoric as a means of enacting change in the world.

Primarily Critical Studies

Berkowitz, S. J., "Empathy and the Other: Challenging U.S. Jewish Ideology," *Communication Studies 48* (1997): 1–18.

Flores, L. A., and D. G. Moon, "Rethinking Race, Revealing Dilemmas: Imagining a New Racial Subject in *Race Traitor*," *Western Journal of Communication 66* (2002): 181–207.

Glenn, C. B., "Critical Rhetoric and Pedagogy: (Re)Considering Student-Centered Dialogue," *Radical Pedagogy 4* (2002 Winter) (np). Retrieved from www.radicalpedagogy.com.

Gunn, J., and D. E. Beard, "On the Apocalyptic Sublime," *Southern Communication Journal 65* (2000): 269–286.

Hasian, M., "Legal Argumentation in the Godwin-Malthus Debates." *Argumentation and Advocacy 37* (2000): 184–197.

Hasian, M., and F. Delgado, "The Trials and Tribulations of Racialized Critical Rhetorical Theory: Understanding the Rhetorical Ambiguities of Proposition 187" *Communication Theory 8* (1998): 245–270.

Hasian, M., and T. Parry-Giles, " 'A Stranger to its Laws': Freedom, Civil Rights, and the Legal Ambiguity of Romer v. Evans," *Argumentation and Advocacy 34* (1997): 27–42.

Leffler, M., "Things Made by Words: Reflections on Textual Criticism," *Quarterly Journal of Speech 78* (1992): 223–231.

Owen, S. A., and P. Ehrenhaus, "Animating a Critical Rhetoric: On the Feeding Habits of American Empire," *Western Journal of Communication 57* (1990): 169–177.

Rosteck, Thomas, "Form and Cultural Context in Rhetorical Criticism: Re-reading Wrage," *Quarterly Journal of Speech 84* (1998): 471–490.

Sloop, J. M., " 'The Parent I Never Had': The Contemporary Construction of Alternatives to Incarceration," *Communication Studies 43* (1992): 1–13.

Sloop, John M., "Disciplining the Transgendered: Brandon Teena, Public Representation, and Normativity," *Western Journal of Communication 64* (2000): 165–189.

NOTES

1. Norman Clark, "The Critical Servant: An Isocratean Contribution to Critical Rhetoric," *Quarterly Journal of Speech 82* (1996): 111–124.
2. Raymie E. McKerrow, "Critical Rhetoric," *Encyclopedia of Rhetoric,* T. Sloane (ed.) (New York: Oxford University Press, 2001), 619–622.
3. Kenneth, Burke, *The Philosophy of Literary Form* (Berkeley, CA: University of California Press, 1941/1973), 9 (emphasis his).
4. Jim A. Kuypers, "Framing Analysis," *The Art of Rhetorical Criticism,* Jim A. Kuypers (ed.) (Allyn and Bacon, in press).
5. Michael Calvin McGee, "Text, Context, and the Fragmentation of Contemporary Culture," *Western Journal of Speech Communication 54* (1990): 289.
6. Clark, 114.
7. Raymie E. McKerrow, "Critical Rhetoric: Theory and Praxis." *Communication Monographs 56* (1989): 91–111.
8. Clark, 116.
9. Clark, 113.
10. Clark, 114, 115.
11. Clark, 116–118.
12. See McKerrow, 1989, and McKerrow, Raymie E. I. Angus & L. Langsdorf (eds.) "Critical Rhetoric and the Possibility of the Subject." *The Critical Turn: Rhetoric and Philosophy in Postmodern Discourse,* (Carbondale, IL: Southern Illinois University Press, 1993), 51–67.
13. Clark, 118.
14. Clark, 118.
15. Clark, 122.
16. McKerrow, Raymie E., "Space and Time in the Postmodern Polity," *Western Journal of Communication 63* (1999): 287.

17. McKerrow, 1989.

18. McKerrow, 1989, 98.

19. Clark, 112.

20. McKerrow, "Critical Rhetoric," 2001, 619.

21. McKerrow, 1989, 91.

22. McKerrow, 1989, 91.

23. McKerrow, 1993, 64.

24. McKerrow, 1989, 92.

25. McKerrow, 1990, 279.

26. Raymie E. McKerrow, "Critical Rhetoric and Propaganda Studies," *Communication Yearbook 14* J. Anderson (ed.) Newbury Park, CA: Sage, 1991), 249–255.

27. Barbara Warnick, "The Critical Rhetoric Proposal: Its Context and its Aftermath." Paper presented at the National Communication Association convention, Atlanta, GA, 2002.

28. See Nicanor Pelis, *Shaping Globalization: Civil Society, Cultural Power and Threefolding* (Queson City, Philippines: Center for Alternative Development Initiatives, 1999); and Sam Eisenstadt & Wolfgang Schluchter, "Introduction: Paths to Early Modernities—A Comparative View." *Public Spheres and Collective Identities,* Samuel N. Eisenstadt, Wolfgang Schluchter, & Bjorn Wittrock (eds.). (New Brunswick, NJ: Transaction Publishers, 2001), 1–19.

29. Raymie E. McKerrow, "Coloring Outside the Lines: The Limits of Civility." *Vital Speeches of the Day 67 (February 15, 2001):* 278–281: and Raymie E. McKerrow, and Jeffrey St. John, "Legitimizing Public Discourse: Civility as Gatekeeper," *Proceedings Of The Fifth Conference Of The International Society For The Study Of Argumentation.* Frans H. van Eemeren, J. Anthony Blair, Charles A. Willard, & A. Francisca Snoek-Henkemans (eds.). (Amsterdam: Sic Sat Press, 2002), 747–751.

30. James Schmidt, "Is Civility a Virtue?" *Civility,* Leroy S. Rouner (ed.) (Notre Dame, IN: University of Notre Dame Press, 2000), 37.

31. Edwin J. Delattre, "Civility and the Limits to the Tolerable," *Civility,* Leroy S. Rouner (ed.) (Notre Dame, IN: University Notre Dame Press, 2000), 151–167.

32. Annika Rabo, "Gender, State and Civil Society in Jordan and Syria." *Civil Society: Challenging Western Models,* Chris Hann and Elizabeth Dunn (eds.) (London, Routledge, 1996), 155–177.

33. John Ehrenberg, *Civil Society: The Critical History of an Idea.* New York: NYU Press, 1999), 249.

34. Ehrenberg, 249.

35. Rabo, 174.

36. Ehrenberg, 249.

37. Noel Ignatiev and John Garvey (eds.), *Race Traitor.* (New York: Routledge, 1996), 10, 36.

38. Dreama Moon and Lisa Flores, "Antiracism and the Abolition of Whiteness: Rhetorical Strategies of Domination among 'Race Traitors,'" *Communication Studies* 51 (2000): 97–115: and Lisa A. Flores, and Dreama G. Moon, "Rethinking Race, Revealing Dilemmas: Imagining A New Racial Subject in *Race Traitor,*" *Western Journal of Communication 66* (2002): 181–207.

39. Flores and Moon, 189.

40. Flores and Moon, 200.

41. Flores and Moon, 200.

42. McKerrow, "Coloring Outside the Lines," 2001.

43. McKerrow, "Critical Rhetoric and the Possibility of the Subject," 64.

44. J. A. Kuypers "Doxa and a Critical Rhetoric: Accounting for the Rhetorical Agent through Prudence." *Communication Quarterly 44* (1996): 452–462.

45. McKerrow, "Critical Rhetoric and Propaganda Studies."

46. D. L. Cloud, "The Materiality of Discourse as Oxymoron: A Challenge to Critical Rhetoric." *Western Journal of Communication 58* (1994): 141–163.

BIOGRAPHICAL SKETCHES OF AUTHORS

MATTHEW T. ALTHOUSE is Assistant Professor of Communication at the State University of New York (SUNY) College at Brockport, where he teaches courses in public address, rhetoric and religion, and qualitative research methods. He has published essays in *Communication Quarterly* and in a volume titled *Comics & Ideology.*

FLOYD DOUGLAS ANDERSON is Professor of Communication at the State University of New York College at Brockport. He is the author or coauthor of numerous articles on both historical and contemporary rhetorical theory and/or criticism. He is a Past President of the Eastern Communication Association and was the 2001 recipient of the Donald H. Ecroyd and Caroline Drummond Ecroyd Teaching Excellence Award. His research interests include the history of rhetoric and public address, meta-theory and meta-criticism, dramatistic rhetorical theory and criticism, and political rhetoric.

MOYA A. BALL is recently retired as Associate Professor of Speech Communication and Associate Vice President for Academic Affairs at Trinity University, San Antonio. As well as chapters and articles, she has authored *Vietnam-on-the-Potomac.* Her research focuses on the Vietnam decision-making activities of Presidents Kennedy, Johnson, Nixon, and their advisors.

WILLIAM L. BENOIT is Professor of Communication at the University of Missouri. He has published over 120 journal articles and book chapters, and is the author or editor of eight books including *Accounts, Excuses, and Apologies* and, *The Clinton Scandals and the Politics of Image Restoration.* He was selected as the American Communication Association's Outstanding Teacher at a Doctoral Institution. He is also the recipient of the American Communication Association's Gerald M. Phillips Mentoring Award and also the University of Missouri Gold Chalk Award for graduate mentoring. He has served as the ed-

itor for the *Journal of Communication.* His primary interests are rhetorical theory and criticism, and political communication.

THOMAS R. BURKHOLDER is Associate Professor and Basic Course Director at the Hank Greenspan School of Communication, University of Nevada—Las Vegas. He teaches courses in rhetorical crititicism, rhetorical theory, history of United States public address, and college teaching in communication. He also directs the large, multisection basic course program in public speaking and interpersonal communication. His research interests include nineteenth-century U.S. public address, the rhetoric of woman suffrage, political rhetoric, and presidential rhetoric. His scholarly work has appeared in *Communication Studies, The Southern Communication Journal, The Western Journal of Communication,* and in various book chapters. He is coauthor, with Karlyn Kohrs Campbell, of the second edition of *Critiques of Contemporary Rhetoric,* and is currently coediting, with Martha Watson, a volume on the history of nineteenth-century U.S. protest rhetoric. In addition, he has served as a reviewer for various national and regional journals.

KATHLEEN FARRELL is professor and Chair of the Department of Communication, St. Louis University. She teaches and researches instances of contemporary and historical public argument, argument theory, and argument pedagogy. Her work includes studies of the rhetoric of the American Left, public discourse of the American Cold War era, arguments about the relationship between politics and aesthetics in the 1930s, and the South African Truth and Reconciliation Commission. She frequently presents her work at international, national, and regional conferences, and has published in numerous scholarly journals, edited volumes, and proceedings. She is the author of *Literary Integrity and Political Action.* She has been active in local politics and community advocacy groups.

THOMAS S. FRENTZ is professor of Communication at the University of Arkansas, Fayetteville. He is the coauthor of *Projecting the Shadow: The Cyborg Hero in American Film* and *The Communicative Experience.* Additionally, he has published over two dozen articles and presented numerous convention papers. He received the Golden Anniversary Monograph Award from the National Communication Association and the Michael M. Osborn Teacher–Scholar Award from the Southern States Communication Association. He teaches classes in film, rhetoric, cultural studies, and qualitative methods. His research interests include language use, rhetorical theory, film criticism, and personal narratives.

DAVID HENRY is Professor and Director of the Communication Department at the Univeristy of Nevada. He teaches courses in rhetorical theory and criticism, political communication, persuasion, and argumentation. His scholarship focuses on public advocacy in a variety of contexts, including presidential rhetoric, nuclear politics, social movement studies, and scientists as political advocates. Coauthor with Kurt Ritter of a book on Ronald Reagan's political oratory, he has published articles and reviews in the *Quarterly Journal of Speech, Communication Monographs,* the *Rhetoric Society Quarterly, Communication Education, Communication Studies,* the *Southern Communication Journal,* and in multiple volumes of collected essays. He received the 1998 University Distinguished Teaching Award at Cal Poly State University, San Luis Obispo, and shared with all contributors to *Eisenhower's War of Words: Rhetoric and Leadership* (Michigan State University Press) the 1995 Marie Hockmuth Nichols Award for Outstanding Scholarship in Public Address. Henry was the Editor of the *Western Journal of Communication* in 2000–2002, was the founding book review editor for *Rhetoric & Public Affairs,* and is the Editor-elect for the *Quarterly Journal of Speech,* 2005–2007.

FORBES I. HILL, Emeritus, Queens College of the City University of New York, has published in the field of history of rhetoric and public address. He is the author of "Aristotle's Rhetorical Theory," in James J. Murphy and Richard Katula's volume, *A Synoptic History of Classical Rhetoric.*

ANDREW KING is Professor at the Department of Speech Communication at Louisiana State University. He is the author of *Postmodern Political Communication, Power and Communication,* and coeditor of *Twentieth-Century Roots of Rhetorical Studies.* He is the former editor of the *Quarterly Journal of Speech* and the *Southern Communication Journal.* He was selected as the American Communication Association's Outstanding Teacher at a Doctoral Institution in 1998. Professor King's academic interests lie in the areas of communication and power, and medieval and Renaissance rhetorical theory. He is a past president of the Kenneth Burke Society.

JIM A. KUYPERS is Senior Lecturer and Director of the Office of Speech at Dartmouth College. He is the author of *Presidential Crisis Rhetoric and the Press in a Post-Cold War World, Press Bias and Politics: How the Media Frame Controversial Issues,* and coeditor of *Twentieth-Century Roots of Rhetorical Studies.* He is a former editor for the *American Communication Journal.* He is the recipient of the American Communication Association's Outstanding Contribution to Communication Scholarship Award, the Southern States Communication Association's Early Career Research Award, and Dartmouth College's Distinguished Lecturer Award. His research interests include political communication, meta-criticism, and the moral/poetic use of language.

RONALD LEE is Professor of Communication Studies at the University of Nebraska—Lincoln. He teaches and writes about contemporary rhetoric and political culture. His work has appeared in the *Quarterly Journal of Speech, Political Communication, Western Journal of Communication, Communication Studies, Southern Communication Journal, Argumentation and Advocacy,* and *Technical Communication Quarterly.* He is presently completing a book on the rhetorical negotiation of presidential legacies.

KEVIN R. MCCLURE is Associate Professor of Communication Studies at the University of Rhode Island. His work has appeared in *Communication Quarterly* and the *Western Journal of Communication.* He teaches and writes about rhetorical theory and criticism.

RAYMIE McKERROW is Professor in the School of Communication Studies at Ohio University, Athens, Ohio. He has published in the areas of modern rhetoric, argumentation theory, and critical/cultural approaches to contemporary rhetoric. He is past president of the Eastern Communication Association and the National Communication Association, and received the Charles H. Woolbert Research Award from the National Communication Association.

DONNA M. NUDD is Associate Professor of Communication at Florida State University. Her essays have appeared in *Text and Performance Quarterly, Bronte Society Transactions, Communication Education,* and the *Modern Language Association Series.* As a practitioner in performance, she has served as director and dramaturge for Terry Galloway's one woman shows which were shown in Edinburgh, London, New York, Toronto, Mexico City, and alternative venues throughout the United States. In 2001, Donna Marie Nudd and Terry Galloway, life-long colloborators, won NCA's Irene Coger award for lifetime achievement in Performance. Her major areas of interest include feminist criticism, pedagogy, radical performance and adaptation for film and theatre.

ROBERT C. ROWLAND is Professor and Chair of the Department of Communication Studies at the University of Kansas. He is the author of *Israeli & Palestinian Symbol Use* (with David Frank), *Analyzing Rhetoric, The Rhetoric of Menachem Begin: The Myth of Redemption Through Return,* and more than thirty published essays on rhetorical criticism, argumentation, and narrative. A recent study found that he was one of the thirty most published scholars in the field. Professor Rowland's research interests include critical methodologies, public argument, argumentation theory, and political communication.

JANICE HOCKER RUSHING is Professor in the Department of Communication at the University of Arkansas, Fayetteville. She is the coauthor of *Projecting the Shadow: The Cyborg Hero in American Film,* and of many articles on the rhetorical criticism of the media. She is the recipient of the Michael M. Osborn Teacher–Scholar Award from the Southern States Communication Association. Her writing interests include mythology, gender, and values in contemporary media and in American academia.

KRISTINA SCHRIVER is an Assistant Professor of Communication and Director of Forensics at California State University, Chico. Her work has been published in *Text and Performance Quarterly* and *Women's Studies in Communication,* among others. Her research interests are in the area of performance and feminist studies, with an emphasis on performance and social protest.

THOMAS J. ST. ANTOINE is Assistant Professor of Communication and Director of the Frederick M. Supper Honors Program at Palm Beach Atlantic University. His work has been published in the *Florida Communication Journal* and in *Research on Christian Higher Education.* He has also presented papers at numerous conventions and is a former editorial assistant for the *Quarterly Journal of Speech.* His teaching and research interests include the rhetoric of higher education and organizational rhetoric.

JEFFREY ST. JOHN is Assistant Professor in the School of Communication Studies at Ohio University, Athens, Ohio. He received his doctorate from the University of Washington, has contributed research in argumentation theory at international conferences, and has published in the area of legal rhetoric in *Rhetoric and Public Affairs.* He teaches courses in argument and legal communication and on critical perspectives on the public sphere.

MARILYN J. YOUNG is the Wayne C. Minnick Professor of Communication at The Florida State University. She has authored two books, *Flights of Fancy, Flight of Doom: KAL 007 & Soviet–American Rhetoric* and *Coaching Debate.* Her research interests are in argumentation; rhetorical theory and criticism; and political (particularly international) rhetoric, especially the development of political language and argument in newly emerging democracies.

INDEX